Praise for *America's Queen*

"Extraordinary detail . . . a truly stunning feat. The quintessential rap on the world-famous widow. Bradford successfully punctures the Kennedy myth."
—*The Washington Monthly*

"Bradford's biography of Jackie may hold up as the best until enough time passes for the Kennedy archives to release new material. Bradford tracks down all the rumors, stories, and gossip providing documentation to refute them or evidence of their accuracy." —*Nashville Tennessean*

"Valuable for its clear-eyed attempt to understand Jackie's complex drives and emotions—and the portrait that emerges has more faces than Picasso. You're left feeling both appalled and admiring. Bradford's depiction of her devastating grief—which still surfaced years after JFK's assassination—is heartbreaking." —*Newsweek*

"Authoritative, detailed and fascinating. . . . Seldom has a life been so full of material fortune and tragic misfortune. Bradford has captured its breadth and depth." —*The Memphis Commercial Appeal*

"From sources including sister Lee Radziwill Ross and longtime family friend George Plimpton, Bradford is able to gain insights that help construct a three-dimensional portrait of a woman whom many Americans worshiped for one-dimensional reasons." —*Ft. Worth Star Telegram*

"Penetrating the barriers that Jacqueline Kennedy Onassis placed around herself, Bradford presents us with both the woman we knew and the woman Onassis wouldn't allow us to know." —*The Daily News*

"Bradford has innate integrity. . . . There has not been, nor will there be, a better biography of Jackie." —*Times Literary Supplement*

"Copiously detailed, richly researched . . . even devoted Jackie-philes will learn something new." —*Richmond Times-Dispatch*

"[This] book is probably the definitive one on the subject."
—*The Washington Post*

ABOUT THE AUTHOR

Sarah Bradford is a historian and biographer. She is the best-selling author of several biographies, including *Disraeli*, selected as a *New York Times* Notable Book of the Year; *George VI; Princess Grace;* and *The New York Times* bestseller *Elizabeth*. Married to the Viscount Bangor, she lives in London.

America's Queen

THE LIFE OF

Jacqueline Kennedy Onassis

SARAH BRADFORD

PENGUIN BOOKS

PENGUIN BOOKS
Published by the Penguin Group
Penguin Group (USA) Inc., 375 Hudson Street, New York, New York 10014, U.S.A.
Penguin Group (Canada), 90 Eglinton Avenue East, Suite 700, Toronto,
Ontario, Canada M4P 2Y3 (a division of Pearson Penguin Canada Inc.)
Penguin Books Ltd, 80 Strand, London WC2R 0RL, England
Penguin Ireland, 25 St Stephen's Green, Dublin 2, Ireland (a division of Penguin Books Ltd)
Penguin Group (Australia), 250 Camberwell Road, Camberwell,
Victoria 3124, Australia (a division of Pearson Australia Group Pty Ltd)
Penguin Books India Pvt Ltd, 11 Community Centre, Panchsheel Park,
New Delhi – 110 017, India
Penguin Group (NZ), 67 Apollo Drive, Rosedale, North Shore 0632, New Zealand
(a division of Pearson New Zealand Ltd)
Penguin Books (South Africa) (Pty) Ltd, 24 Sturdee Avenue,
Rosebank, Johannesburg 2196, South Africa

Penguin Books Ltd, Registered Offices: 80 Strand, London WC2R 0RL, England

First published in the United States of America by Viking Penguin,
member of Penguin Putnam Inc., 2000
Published in Penguin Books 2001

9   10

Copyright © Sarah Bradford, 2000
All rights reserved

Acknowledgements for permission to use copyrighted materials
appear on pages 479–480.

THE LIBRARY OF CONGRESS HAS CATALOGED
THE HARDCOVER EDITION AS FOLLOWS:
Bradford, Sarah.
America's queen / by Sarah Bradford.
p.   cm.
ISNBN 0-670-89191-6 (hc.)
ISBN 978-0-14-100220-0 (pbk.)
1. Onassis, Jacqueline Kennedy, 1929–   2. Celebrities—United States—
Biography.   3. Presidents' spouses—United States—Biography.   I. Title.
CT275.O552 B73 2000
973.922'092—dc21
[B]   00-043895

Printed in the United States of America
Set in Weiss
Designed by Nancy Resnick

For Sam Peabody

CONTENTS

Four Days in America:
November 22–25, 1963

~

*It's hard to re-create the impact of the President's funeral and those four days
in America, but that was when Jackie became indelibly inscribed on the mind
of anyone who watched that event. All of her life, I think, people who had seen
that, and those days, never thought of her in any other way.*[1]

—Ambassador William vanden Heuvel

The President's thirty-four-year-old widow was marble behind her heavy black
veil, white marble with the strong features of an ancient statue, noble in her
frozen grief, as if she represented all the heroes' widows down the centuries since
Andromache mourned Hector outside the walls of Troy. On that day she restored
America's pride, exorcising the shame of the killing of the thirty-fifth President
and becoming, in Frank Sinatra's words, America's queen. Deliberately, she created a myth, draping the real personality of her dead husband—the vital, witty,
sexually addicted, supremely intelligent John F. Kennedy—with the dignified funereal trappings of Abraham Lincoln. From that moment, holding the hands of
her two small children as she gazed down on her assassinated husband's coffin,
she became an icon, a legend beyond the scope of ordinary experience, burdened
with the dreams and expectations of millions of strangers, a burden she would
carry to her own grave.

Yet Jacqueline Bouvier Kennedy was a complex woman of many facets, concealed insecurities and intricate defense mechanisms, a strong urge toward the
limelight contrasting with a desire for privacy and concealment. Again, to use a
classical image, she was like a nymph retreating ever further from the human gaze
into the depths of the wood. She used the image herself in one of her rare published pieces, written for her school magazine at the age of sixteen: the story of a
marble nymph in Central Park who comes alive for a day and seduces an ordinary
New Yorker into a day of enchantment before stepping back on to her pedestal.

Behind the mask of beauty and fame lay a shrewd mind, a ruthless judgment of people, antenna finely tuned to any sign of pretentiousness or pomposity, and a wry, even raunchy sense of humor. She was a loyal friend, yet withdrew her friendship at any perceived disloyalty. She craved money and valued fame, yet her tastes were essentially simple and she was at her happiest on the back of a horse in the Virginia countryside. She lived through tragedy and scandal, clinging to her identity until she finally achieved independence and a life of her own.

CHAPTER ONE

Golden Gatsby Years

~

That was in my life, and I think in Jackie's as well, a really happy and far too brief time ... Everything was so simple then. Complication, confusion, wounds, suffering hadn't entered our lives ...

—Jackie's sister, Lee Radziwill, talking of their Long Island childhood[1]

She was born with a sense of theater, of carefully choreographed exits and entrances, an eagerly awaited baby, who arrived an improbable six weeks late in Southampton Hospital, Long Island, on July 28, 1929. The birth had been scheduled to take place in a New York City hospital but Jackie, characteristically, chose to make her first appearance on a hot Sunday at the height of the summer season in the newly fashionable Hamptons. She was the first child of Janet Norton Lee and John Vernou Bouvier III, born just over a year after their wedding in nearby East Hampton, where both her grandparents owned comfortable summer houses in what was virtually Wall-Street-on-Sea. Within months of her birth, the stock market crash of October 1929 had cast its shadow over the Bouvier family fortunes, giving Jackie and her younger sister, Lee, born four years later, a sense of insecurity and fear of poverty that was to last almost all their lives.

From early on Jackie became aware of sexual politics within her family, of power emanating from the dominant male, with women as lesser elements competing for his attention. It was a game she quickly learned to play, extracting the maximum she could from the situation. All her life she would be irresistibly drawn to the most powerful, successful man in a group. (A cousin said of her fondness for a man like her future father-in-law, Joseph P. Kennedy, "If Jackie was at the court of Ivan the Terrible, she'd say, 'Ooh, he's been so misunder*stood* . . .' ")[2]

The two dominant males in Jackie's early life were her paternal grandfather, Major John Vernou Bouvier Jr., and her father. Her grandfather, known as "Grampy Jack" or "Grampy Bouvier" to his ten grandchildren and "the Major" to everyone else, was the center of summer family life at Lasata, the stucco, ivy-clad house on Further Lane. It was strategically situated near the ocean and the Maidstone Club, the heart of East Hampton social life, where the Bouviers had purchased a cabana in 1926. At Lasata, the Major was not only the undisputed head of his household but a personage in the village of East Hampton as well. As a former trial lawyer he was fond of the sound of his own voice and would regularly deliver the speech at the Memorial Day celebrations in East Hampton, which marked the opening of the summer season.

When the Bouviers first arrived in East Hampton as summer visitors in 1912, the place was still a "simple" resort compared with the more sophisticated Southampton, with saltbox houses, a duck pond and a village green sheltered from the ocean by huge sand dunes. Inland, flat potato fields stretched to the horizon. The Bouviers' first house was a three-story, verandaed building called Wildmoor on Appaquogue Road; in 1925 the Major's wife, Maude Sergeant, bought Lasata with her father's money. It was not until 1935 that the Major, having inherited a considerable fortune from his uncle Michel Charles "M. C." Bouvier, took over the house and began to live the expansive life to which he felt entitled, and which ended, at his death, in the financial ruin of the family.

Each May the various Bouvier households would move out of their Park Avenue apartments for the summer to East Hampton, where Maude would transplant her entire household staff to Lasata. Lasata—an Indian name meaning "place of peace," a misnomer as far as the explosive Bouvier family was concerned—stood on a comfortable twelve acres, with a tennis court, Black Jack Bouvier's stables for eight horses, each stall marked with its occupant's name in gilded lettering, tack room, jumping ring and paddock, extensive vegetable gardens, a grape arbor and Maude's "Italian garden," edged with boxwood and dotted with classical statues. Bouvier accounts of Lasata as "built along the lines of an English country manor" exaggerate its size, but the Bouviers, following the Major's example, were given to exaggeration.

The gardener/caretaker, Paul Yuska, was the only year-round employee at Lasata, but the permanent servants from Manhattan were an important part of the Bouvier household, particularly Pauline, former nursemaid, governess and housekeeper to the John Vernou Bouviers in their less prosperous days in Nutley, New Jersey, where they had lived for twenty-two years before moving to Park Avenue, and Esther, who gambled on the stock market and the races and was always a source of ready cash for the family.

John Vernou Bouvier Jr. was a dapper figure given to loud explosions of temper— "God damn it to hell!" Although the Major was proud of his army rank, his war experience was limited. A lawyer by training, a graduate of Columbia Law School, he was commissioned aged fifty-two on July 22, 1918, as Major in the Judge Advocate Section of the Officers Reserve Corps of the U.S. Army and honorably discharged five months later, in December 1918. Subsequently he became a partner in his uncle's Wall Street firm.

Sunday was the day for Bouvier gatherings, either at the Major's apartment, 765 Park Avenue, after Mass, to which he would take his granddaughters, or in summer at Lasata, for a ritual Sunday lunch of roast beef followed by peach ice cream (homemade on the back porch by the French chauffeur) around the huge oak table in the beamed dining room. While Maude remained a gentle figure in the background, organizing the household from her upstairs bedroom or looking after the flowers in the garden and the house, the Major was a dominant—and always audible—presence. Maude's once delicate features and figure had been transformed by dropsy (she wore long, flowing skirts to conceal her swollen legs and ankles), but the Major, aged sixty-five when Jackie was born, preserved an immaculate physique, the result, he claimed, of very hot baths followed by very cold ones; during this routine, his yells of anguish could be heard throughout the house.

He was a snappy dresser: his invariable East Hampton Sunday attire was a brown tweed jacket, white shirt with high, stiff collar, white linen trousers, black socks and white shoes. He was intensely proud of his Hercule Poirot–like mustache, carefully groomed every morning and waxed until the points stood out beyond his cheeks. He owned a red Nash convertible with primitive gearshifts, which he would rev in an earsplitting racket for some five minutes until the vibrating floorboards (he was stone-deaf) told him the engine was ready. Then he would take off in a shower of gravel and hurtle dangerously—he was also shortsighted—through the village lanes to the old Catholic church of St. Philomena. Afterward at Sunday lunch he would turn off both his hearing aids and sit oblivious to the noisy bickering of his family, composing a poem for one of them, to be read out at the end of the meal.

Although the Major's literary style was florid and his verse no more than doggerel, his interest in poetry transmitted itself to Jackie, his favorite grandchild. "He really adored her and I think felt that she had enormous potential in the field that he cared about, which was literary," Lee said. "They had quite a correspondence together and many flowery letters were exchanged. I don't know if *he* got her interested in poetry but she started to love poetry at an exceptionally early age and she gave him great pleasure. It was mutual, and it was very nice to watch them together. When he would come to see her ride in Madison Square Garden I remember he would lose his control completely and start screaming at the horse and jumping up, and it was amusing and touching. I think that if it hadn't been for this exceptional bond she had with my grandfather Bouvier and my father that she never would have gained the particular strength and independence and individuality she had. Because we didn't have a very normal family . . ."[3]

One particular fantasy of the Major's became an important influence on how his family saw themselves. Throughout Jackie's childhood he was engaged on the construction of an elaborate—and mythical—genealogical family treatise, which was privately published in 1940 as *Our Forebears*. The Bouviers were Catholics of southern French descent; the Major took pride in his ancestry and, according to his own account, spoke French, having spent a year at school in France. Being the Major, however, mere French descent was not enough: it had to be aristocratic, and as two French families were involved, doubly so. As recorded in *Our Forebears* the Bouviers were "an ancient house of Fontaine near Grenoble,"[4] but later research revealed that the Bouviers in question were not their ancestors. That honor belonged to a family of artisans and small shopkeepers in the village of Pont-Saint Esprit, near Arles, whose descendants still live there. The American Bouviers were descended from Michel Bouvier, who arrived from France in about 1815 in Philadelphia where he established a successful business as a cabinetmaker (one of his clients being Napoleon's brother, Joseph Bonaparte) and importer of marble and mahogany. He made a solid fortune that his son, Michel Charles Bouvier, vastly increased by successful operations on the stock exchange. The Bouviers were descended from the second French family through Michel's second wife, Louise Vernou, daughter of John Vernou, whose family, according to Jackie's grandfather, "is one of the most illustrious and ancient of the Province of Poitou." However, there is no proof of any connection between the aristocratic Poitevin family and the John Vernou who arrived in Philadelphia, possibly from the French West Indies, in the last decade of the eighteenth century. His signature on his application for citizenship on October 25, 1808, is barely literate, certainly not that of an educated aristocrat.[5]

Our Forebears was treated by the Major's descendants with the reverence accorded the family Bible, and in 1961 Mary Van Rensselaer Thayer's authorized biography of Jackie as First Lady was still peddling the aristocratic family line. However, it was then that the fake was gently unmasked by an American historian.[6] The truth is that the Bouviers were third-generation French immigrants who had made good but felt it necessary to fantasize about their ancestry, converting shopkeepers into nobles. In the class-conscious America of the Bouvier sisters' youth everyone "in Society" knew exactly where everyone else came from and White Anglo-Saxon Protestant families ruled the roost. Even after the Bouviers' unmasking in the sixties, Jackie's eccentric cousin Edie Beale boasted to writer Gail Sheehy in 1972, "We're all descended from fourteenth-century French kings."[7] When Jackie married John F. Kennedy in 1953, newspaper reports trumpeted the alliance of the wealthy Boston Irish senator with the descendant of a family of French aristocrats. "I don't know how Janet [Jackie's mother] got away with this," Gore Vidal said. "Well, it only worked with the press, I mean they were somehow Plantagenets and Tudors—it was just nonsense. They were pretty lowly born . . ."[8] They were Catholics, but not grand Catholics, of Mediterranean descent in a Protestant WASP world. None of this was to matter outwardly to Jackie, as the classy beauty she grew up to be, but it contributed to an inner sense of apartness; as she told society bandleader Peter Duchin in reference to Newport, many years later, "You and I, Peter, both outsiders." It did not make her feel in any way inferior, but the opposite, contributing to her sense of her uniqueness. She never found it necessary to be part of a crowd, and felt an affinity with creative people, artists, oddballs. It is worth noting that of the three important men in her life—John F. Kennedy (Boston Irish Catholic on both sides), Aristotle Onassis (Greek) and Maurice Tempelsman (Jewish)—not one could remotely be called a WASP.

Beyond her love for "Grampy Jack," Jackie adored her father, the glamorous, larger-than-life John Vernou Bouvier III, known as Jack, who resembled his father in looks but in nothing else. Her grandfather, John Vernou Bouvier Jr., was by nature a "joiner" and committeeman: he was on the standing committee of the Columbia Law School Alumni, vice president of the College Alumni and member of the Council of the Delta Kappa Epsilon Fraternity, as he records proudly in *Our Forebears*, member of the Society of the Cincinnati of Maryland (through his great-grandfather Captain James Ewing), president of the Sons of the Revolution in the State of New York (through a great-great-grandfather, John Griffith), General-President of the General Society of the Sons of the Revolution, member of the Military Order of the Loyal Legion of the United States, etc. On the other hand, John Vernou Bouvier III was a free spirit, who seems to have handed down his dislike of committees and pompous organizations to his daughter. Possibly under pressure from his father he joined the New York State Sons of the Revolution, and the Cincinnati of Maryland, but the only organizations in which he showed any active interest were his Yale Senior Society, Book and Snake, and his clubs in New York—the Yale Club and the Racquet and Tennis Club. Jack Bouvier adored his overindulgent mother but clashed frequently with his father, who disapproved of his son's undisciplined, self-indulgent way of life. They had noisy rows during which the Major would roar at him, threatening to disinherit him, a sanction that showed diminishing returns.[9]

Jackie's father was a spectacularly attractive man in a flashy way. His looks were exotic, the very opposite of the all-American boy; his extremely dark complexion, inherited from his Bouvier forebears, had earned him various nicknames: "the Sheik," after Rudolph Valentino, "the Black Orchid" or, more commonly, "Black Jack." He sported a pencil-thin Clark Gable mustache over finely molded sensual lips and was often taken for the star. Indeed, the parting shot of Rhett Butler, played by Gable, in *Gone With the Wind*, "Frankly, my dear, I don't give a damn," might have been his motto. He had thick black hair, always beautifully groomed with an arrow-straight parting, and piercing blue eyes. He was extremely vain (a friend, visiting him for a weekend at the Swordfish Club in Bridgehampton, could not help noticing that Black Jack had hung no fewer than six photographs of himself on the wall) and spent a good deal of time on maintaining his looks. He had a fine, muscular physique and kept himself fit by working out in a private gym in a closet in his apartment or at the Yale Club, and kept up his tan under a sunlamp, or by sunbathing naked at the window of his Park Avenue apartment, or in the men's cabana area of the Maidstone Club. His clothes were always perfectly tailored, his shirts by Brooks Brothers; even at East Hampton in the summer he was always to be seen in gabardine suits. He was a keen, although never superlative, sportsman, and liked attending prizefights, horse races and major football games. He was a gambler, on racing and on the stock exchange, and had been expelled for gambling from his prep school, Phillips Exeter. He was uninterested in intellectual or cultural pursuits and his academic record was abysmal: at Yale he was known principally as a giver of parties attended by bevies of pretty girls. He was a compulsive womanizer and, later, a heavy drinker.

Like his daughter Jackie he knew instinctively how to pose for the camera and, also like her, he had an instinctive sense of theater and of his own image. He was the type of male that many men dislike on sight or regard as a joke, and that women find hard to resist. He had a reputation for treating his women badly, overwhelming them with attention when he was pursuing them, dropping them quickly and without remorse when he had tired of them. Spoiled by his mother, he seemed incapable of establishing a responsible relationship with a woman. Proud though he was of his wife Janet's looks, chic and prowess as a horse-woman, he was essentially a predatory male, a risk-taker, incapable of resisting temptation or self-gratification. He was certainly incapable of providing either his wife or his daughters with the stable husband and father figure they seem to have yearned for. He was more like a lover than a father to his daughters—flaunting, ir-responsible, and fun to be with, intolerant of bores or boredom, loving and de-manding. Some of his less admirable traits rubbed off on his daughters. When walking one day with Jackie and Lee in Central Park, he noticed an elderly lady showing signs of wanting to chat with them. "Go tell her to jump in the lake," he said to Jackie, who later became famously intolerant of bores.

Despite the pain his infidelity caused her mother and the fact that the breakup of their marriage for that reason was demonstrably his fault, Jackie enjoyed his success with women. "She told me about the complicated relationship with her fa-ther, whom she admired and respected because women were crazy about him," John "Demi" Gates, an early admirer of Jackie's, said. "For example, if there was Parents' Day at Farmington, she'd say to him about the mothers of some of her friends, 'What about her?' and he'd say, 'Yes, I've had her,' or he'd say, 'No, but I think that's pretty imminent!' She thought that that was the most wonderful thing. She had all the wrong standards, all the wrong standards, and yet she became something very special in spite of this. Her mother would take the brass off a door knob."[10]

Black Jack's standards were amoral and based on superficial values. The only virtues he recognized were the macho ones of physical courage, athleticism and style; the image was the message. The main game in life was to attract the oppo-site sex using every trick in the book, the implication being that when it comes to sex everyone is easily fooled, all being fair in love and war because—Black Jack's constant refrain, and who should know better than he?—"All men are rats." This last maxim certainly helped his elder daughter get through the more turbulent pe-riods of her life and was amply borne out by her experience.

If Black Jack Bouvier's standards were suspect, Janet's were little better. Most people had been taken by surprise when Black Jack, already aged thirty-seven, married Janet Norton Lee at St. Philomena's Catholic Church in East Hampton on July 7, 1928. The wedding was followed by a grand reception at the Lees' sum-mer home, a handsome house on Lily Pond Lane designed by the architect Harrie Lindberg for Edward Cowcroft in 1905. Janet, a friend of the Bouvier twins, Jack's sisters Maude and Michelle, was sixteen years younger than her bridegroom and—not that Black Jack would have cared—an Episcopalian. The couple were completely unsuited; Janet, chic, petite and pretty, with great charm and a daz-zling smile when she chose to exercise it, was tough, disciplined and inhibited, yet had, under her ladylike exterior, a violent temper. She came from an unhappy home. Her father, James T. Lee, the son of a New York doctor and schools super-intendent, had made a fortune in real estate and banking; a tough-looking charac-ter, with steely eyes and a rattrap mouth, he liked to boast that he had made two million dollars by the time he was thirty, then lost it in the financial crisis of 1907. A remarkable businessman, he subsequently made another large fortune in bank-ing and New York real estate. He won several awards for the designs of his build-ings; it was perhaps from him that Jackie inherited her interest in architecture and the city of New York. It was probably from him also that she inherited the vein of steel in her character, which led John Kennedy's national security adviser, McGeorge Bundy, to joke that she was a woman with a "whim of iron." Lee dis-liked his wife, Margaret Merritt, and never spoke to her; by the time Janet mar-ried, her parents were living separate lives although they never formally divorced.

Unsurprisingly, James Lee detested Black Jack and disapproved of his marrying Janet. As families, the Bouviers and the Lees, despite being neighbors on Park Avenue and at East Hampton, did not get along. The Bouviers, proud as they were of their ancestry, looked down on the Lees as their inferiors. Janet's parents were second-generation Irish immigrants and the Lee fortune was of recent origin. In the Bouviers' eyes, Janet was making a calculated climb up the society ladder in marrying Black Jack. The Lees certainly seem to have been socially insecure. James T. Lee's obituary in the *New York Times* after his death, aged ninety, on Janu-ary 3, 1968, makes no mention of his antecedents or those of his wife. He is de-scribed merely as being "born in New York on Oct. 2, 1877, the son of Dr. James Lee and Mary Norton Lee. His father was once superintendent of the city's public schools."

Despite a rumor that both James and Margaret Lee were the children of Irish immigrants (confirmed by a recent authority on Jackie, who states that both her paternal great-grandparents were immigrants from County Cork at the time of the potato famine),[11] the *National Cyclopedia of Biography* glamorizes their parents with Confederate backgrounds: James Lee's father is described as having been born in Maryland and having fought with the Confederate Army during the Civil War, while Margaret Merritt is listed as the daughter of Thomas Merritt of Savan-nah, Georgia, "a Confederate army veteran and an importer of New York City." The Maryland-Lee connection was later propagated publicly by Janet, among other fantasies and half-truths, in a biographical article written about her in 1962 after Jackie had become First Lady.[12] Indeed, several of her friends described her to the present author as "a Southern belle."

Although James Lee was born and died a Catholic, his daughter Janet attended all the right WASP schools—Miss Spence's in New York City, one year at Sweet Briar College in Virginia, another at Barnard College in New York—and made her debut at Sherry's, describing her religion as Episcopalian. She also told the au-thor of the article that she had had a hankering to be a writer and had taken courses in playwriting and short-story writing at Columbia University, but her literary career did not extend beyond ghostwriting some hunting stories for a magazine.

Given the dislike between the two families and Black Jack's well-documented reputation as a womanizer, the omens for the marriage were inauspicious. Janet later said, as women often do whose marriages fail, that she had married Black Jack to get away from her father, and she certainly did so against James Lee's will. But the evidence is that she was also strongly physically attracted to Black Jack, which might well have been a factor in her extreme bitterness when the marriage broke down. Even on their honeymoon sailing to Europe on the *Aquitania*, Black Jack could not resist a flirtation with the Newport heiress Doris Duke. Or with the gaming tables. When Jackie was in her teens and spending a vacation at the Château de Borda Berri near Biarritz with a crowd of young friends, she told Demi Gates, " 'You know, when my father and mother came here on their honeymoon, to Biarritz, he was a terrible gambler and he gambled away all the money, Mother's, his . . . The night they arrived he went to the casino and came back very depressed because he had lost everything . . .' She said that her mother gathered together whatever money they had and won it all back."[13]

Jackie was christened three days before Christmas 1929 in the church of St. Ignatius Loyola on Park Avenue in New York City. She was given the name Jacqueline Lee, a gesture intended to placate her severe maternal grandfather, who was by far the richest of her immediate relations, and she wore the robe he had worn for his own christening. James T. Lee had been designated her godfather but Black Jack seized the opportunity afforded by the late arrival of his detested father-in-law to substitute his favorite nephew, nine-year-old Miche, in his stead (presaging, in a curious way, the manner in which Hugh D. Auchincloss II, Jackie's stepfather, stood in for him to escort Jackie up the aisle at her wedding to John F. Kennedy).

Two months earlier, in October 1929, two events had occurred that foreshadowed the decline and fall of the Bouvier family. On October 8, Jack's younger brother, William Sergeant "Bud" Bouvier, who had never fully recovered from being severely gassed and wounded in France in the First World War and had since become an alcoholic, died of drink, divorced and alone in California, leaving his young son Miche in the care of his brother Jack. The circumstances of his death, following a public shaming for failing to provide alimony for his ex-wife and their son, had severely dented the Major's family pride and left the family with ineradicable feelings of guilt as well as shame. Eight days later the stock market crashed; Black Jack, sensing a collapse in the market, had sold his shares short and made $100,000 but lost as much a month later when the market plunged still further in November. The Major lost a small fortune with no means of recouping it but continued to live life as comfortably as ever on his dwindling capital.

On the surface, however, the young Bouviers' life seemed sunny and serene. In New York and at East Hampton they were a glamorous couple on the social scene. Many years later, Jackie told Peter Duchin how she remembered her mother's scent and the softness of her fur coat as her parents leaned over her bed to say good night before an evening out listening to Eddie Duchin perform. In New York they lived rent-free in an eleven-room duplex in the prestigious apartment building at 740 Park Avenue, built and owned by Janet's father. Central Park, which for so many years was to be the physical focus of Jackie's life and where Black Jack sweated around the reservoir in a special rubber suit to keep his weight down, lay two blocks to the west. In the summer at East Hampton they rented a charming cottage, Rowdy Hall, on Egypt Lane near the Maidstone Club, where the infant Jackie first made the social columns with her second birthday party and was reported that season showing her Scottie dog Hootchie at the East Hampton Show. Her parents gave lavish parties with a speakeasy atmosphere at the Devon Yacht Club, and for summer baseball games at the Maidstone, Jack invited a visiting team called, naturally, the Wall Street Stars, while Janet captained the women's side.

The family's life revolved around animals: dogs—Hootchie the Scottie; Sister, a white bullterrier; Tally-Ho, a Dalmatian; Caprice, a Bouvier des Flandres; and Great Dane King Phar—and, above all, horses. Janet was a fine, highly competitive horsewoman, winning prizes at horse shows throughout the east and at the annual National Horse Show at Madison Square Garden. She kept four horses including the chestnut Danseuse, Jackie's favorite. Impeccably turned out, she featured regularly in the society press—"She wears the very smartest riding habits at Long Island horse shows . . ."—and in the sports pages, where her courage, skill and determination on a horse were admiringly recorded: "[Her expression was] as determined as tennis champion Helen Wills Moody when clearing difficult jumps and that once over and done, her dazzling smile was worth coming miles to see."[14] Under her mother's guidance, Jackie lived for horses and riding; at age two she was put on a horse, the leading rein held by her mother, and photographed. At five, she and her mother took third prize in the family event at the East Hampton Show; another photograph from that same summer shows her, face set in angry frustration, leading her pony away from defeat at a Smithtown, Long Island, show.

In photographs of the time Jackie appears as a sturdy, dark-haired child, staring directly, even aggressively, at the photographer. She had the Bouvier wide-set eyes, although hers, like her mother's, were brown, in contrast to Black Jack's dazzling blue, and thick, dark, curling hair. Like her mother, she was physically courageous and intensely competitive; when her pony threw her at the East Hampton Show she dusted herself off and climbed on it again.

On March 3, 1933, her sister, Caroline Lee Bouvier, was born. Named after her Bouvier great-grandmother, Caroline Maslin Ewing of Philadelphia, the little girl was always known as Lee. "I was so sorry I'd never been called my Christian name, which was Caroline," Lee said, "but it was to please this rather unpleasant grandfather. It certainly was to no avail at all and I got lumbered with being called Lee, which was, you know, both our middle names."[15] The family nicknames for the two sisters were "Jacks" and "Pekes."

Jackie's relationship with her younger sister was curious from the beginning: a mixture of closeness and intense rivalry, protectiveness and the desire to dominate, jealousy and interdependence. It was a relationship that eventually soured, but was important to both for most of their lives. "Jackie's relationship with Lee was very much S & M," said Gore Vidal, who was connected to the sisters through his mother's previous marriage to Hugh D. Auchincloss II, who subsequently became their stepfather, "with Jackie doing the S and Lee the M."[16] "I think you always have some sibling feelings," Lee said, "but I felt more devotion than anything else. As a small child I think I was probably as annoying as any younger sister. I was knocked out by a croquet mallet for two days—that sort of thing—so we had plenty of those sibling rows and fights."[17] From the beginning it was a rivalry in which Lee, except for brief periods, was always the loser, Jackie the star. Lee felt this most strongly in their relationship with their father: Black Jack adored both his daughters and was proud of their looks and accomplishments, but his passion for Jackie (and hers for him) was overriding and semi-incestuous. "They were so close and then this horse, Danseuse, was the trio in their relationship for a good ten years. My father, the horse and Jackie. I have a book that she did for herself and for me after my father's death with nearly every letter he'd written to each of us—at *least* half of it was about this horse and the next step of what hunt team she could go into, what class she thought she could do next year at the [Madison Square] Garden." Lee could not compete with Jackie in the equestrian field; her father would put her on the piebald pony, Dancestep, which she disliked. "He wanted me to be a rider as well as Jackie and he forced me to have five, six falls in a row with the horse continuously refusing a fence . . ." Asked if she minded her father's obvious preference for Jackie, Lee admitted that she was hurt by it "because I *revered* him and just longed for his love and affection. What I loved the most was being here with him in East Hampton and he would take me out way beyond those breakers and that was my special moment with him." Being four years younger than Jackie obviously made a great difference: "I was too young to be that athletic and to be able to challenge everything. I just couldn't live up to what he wanted at that age."

Janet Bouvier was extremely highly strung, possibly as a result of a tense, unhappy atmosphere in the Lee household. She told her daughters that her own childhood had not been happy. She used to sit at the table with her two sisters and their parents, the mother whom she adored and the father she seems rather to have disliked, who were not even on speaking terms. "Her father would say, 'Would you please tell your mother this . . .' and her mother would say, 'Would you please tell your father that . . .' and so it was very sad. And then they separated, and we were never close, to say the least, to my grandfather Lee. He was a very severe man, a miser and a terribly successful businessman. He didn't have much warmth or charm."[18]

Nor was the Bouvier household serene. A strong strand of individuality bordering on eccentricity ran through the family, and relations between the adult members were often explosive and fueled by sibling rivalry. The Major disapproved of Black Jack, but grandmother Maude spoiled him. Jack was not close to his sisters, the twins Maude and Michelle, who had inherited their mother's delicate features and red-gold hair, or to Edith, who had resented the twins since their birth. Edith was always known as "Big Edie" to distinguish her from her daughter "Little Edie," both of whom had the striking Bouvier looks. Big Edie, married to Phelan Beale, a Philadelphia lawyer, had a great voice, which she liked to make heard, warbling the "Indian Love Call" and "Smoke Gets in Your Eyes," to the intense irritation of her siblings. Little Edie's stunning looks and figure made her the star of the family; she once lost her bathing suit diving into the Maidstone Club pool and was thereafter known as "the Body" for obvious reasons. She had a string of beaux and claimed to have been practically engaged to John F. Kennedy's older brother, Joe Jr. Big Edie's rampant infidelities and bohemian lifestyle lost her her husband; her marriage became another casualty in the Bouvier family.

Jackie's favorite among her cousins was her godfather, Michel "Miche" Bouvier, whom Black Jack treated virtually as his own son and who often stayed with them in New York and at Wildmoor, where they now spent their East Hampton summers. Among her own generation were "Scotty," Henry C. Scott Jr., two years older, a daredevil she admired; his sister, "Shella," Michelle, her exact contemporary; and John H. Davis, also born in 1929, the future family biographer. (When his first book on the family appeared, Jackie, regarding it as a betrayal, froze him out.)

In any case, Black Jack Bouvier was too much of an individual to fit in with any cozy family scene, even had it been provided. He considered himself and his daughters superior to the rest of the Bouviers, with the result that Jackie and Lee, unlike the Kennedys, never regarded themselves as part of a clan. It was fun being a Bouvier on the East Hampton social scene, on the beach or around the pool at the Maidstone, playing with the cousins and taking part in the East Hampton Shows, but Jack Bouvier always wanted his daughters to be the stars. On family occasions and at Sunday lunches he would deliberately stir things up by complimenting one of them: "Lee's going to be a real glamour girl someday. Will you look at those eyes . . . and those sexy lips of hers?" The rest of the family called these effusions "Vitamin P [Praise]." More usually the doses of Vitamin P were for Jackie: "Doesn't Jackie look terrific? Girl's taken all prizes in her class this year . . . and she's the prettiest thing in the ring to boot."[19]

Years later Lee wrote lyrically of her memories of East Hampton summers, of the ocean, which both girls loved (an early poem of Jackie's, written at the age of ten, was entitled "Sea Joy"), evoking the sense of freedom they felt as they escaped from New York at the beginning of June in the four-door navy blue Ford convertible, often pursued by the police (Janet was frequently stopped for speeding), their arrival and the unpacking of summer clothes—four pairs of shorts, red, blue, white and gray, four striped shirts and two pairs of sneakers. For Jackie it meant riding Donny, the family nickname for Danseuse, and going to the station on Friday nights to meet her father on the Cannonball Express from New York, rushing to put pennies on the track before the train arrived. There would be a brief return to East Hampton for Halloween and then it was back to New York until next June.

As Jackie turned seven, her family began to disintegrate. Her parents argued constantly and Janet took out her frustrations and pent-up anger on her children, sometimes slapping them. In the latter half of the thirties the balance of power between the couple shifted in Janet's favor. Black Jack was in the wrong and knew it, although he was unable to give up his pursuit of women. A photograph of the period shows Janet in riding clothes, perched stylishly on a fence, but behind her back her husband is openly holding the hand of a pretty young woman, Virginia Kernochan. It was published in the *New York Daily News* the day after it was taken, with the inevitable insinuations, which were deeply humiliating to Janet. James T. Lee, anxious to get rid of his detested son-in-law, advised his daughter to consult a divorce lawyer but Janet, still unwilling to abandon her marriage, refused. The incorrigible Black Jack, reckless as ever, was not about to change his ways: he used Wildmoor out of season as a rendezvous for parties with stockbroker friends and showgirls and, while his family were safely in East Hampton during the summer, the New York apartment for similar purposes. Asked why her mother had shown such bitterness toward her father, Lee said, "I suppose she'd been incredibly hurt by him in the early days, or years, rather, of their marriage . . . He looked at other women and he liked to flirt. I know thousands of men do that but I guess she just couldn't handle it . . ."[20]

An additional cause of friction was finance. Black Jack's stock-exchange fortune had dipped severely; in 1933 and 1934 he had been forced to apply to his father-in-law for a loan to keep going, and was only too aware that even his Park Avenue home was dependent on James T. Lee's grudging charity. As his sense of failure deepened, his pride was wounded. Although there was a temporary improvement in his stock-exchange fortune in 1936, he was being pressed by the estate of M. C. Bouvier for outstanding debts, including a loan of $25,000 dating from 1930, and by the Internal Revenue Service for a considerable sum in back taxes. For her part, Janet was bitterly resentful of his inability to provide the stability, love and affection that she needed to make up for her chilly relationship with her father. She resented, too, that the children so obviously adored their father, preferring his company to hers. Subconsciously the girls took the part of their fascinating, loving father against their disciplinarian mother. "Both girls hated their mother," said a friend who knew them at Farmington. "Jackie had a very close semi-incestuous relationship with her father who at the same time she was ashamed of. Janet didn't like her daughters, only her Auchincloss children."[21] Janet's violence toward her children continued even when they were adults: "Michael Canfield told me that Janet would strike her [Jackie] in fits of temper," a cousin said. "He said they were very violent, that she'd strike out and she [Jackie] didn't like that at all. I can see that because you could tell with Janet: she had one of those tempers that was like a thunderstorm, you could see it coming."[22] Perhaps it would have been truer to say that the girls resented Janet's constant carping criticism. "She expected so much from each of us," Lee remembered, "that I don't recall exactly but it was never defined in a particular area . . . [just] simply excelling and perfection so there was an awful lot of criticism. But that may have been her unhappiness with herself . . ."[23]

At the end of September 1936 Janet demanded a six-month trial separation; Black Jack moved out of the apartment to a room at the Westbury, almost a home away from home for him since the Polo Bar was one of his favorite rendezvous for assignations. The couple were together again for the following summer in East Hampton but on their return to New York after Labor Day they parted for the last time. According to one of Jackie's biographers, that last summer in East Hampton as a family had been a sad ordeal. In East Hampton everyone knew each other's business and at the riding club, where Jackie spent most of her days, "all the kids knew and some made a point of needling Jackie. But when she didn't want to hear something she didn't listen. She had a lot of grit for a little girl."[24] Another member of the club remembers a wistful Jackie wandering around "like a motherless kitten," talking to the grooms and lavishing attention on the horses. "You somehow sensed she was a thousand miles away, existing in a world of manufactured dreams."[25] With some justification, the Lees blamed Black Jack: "There was no excuse in the world for Black Jack," Janet's younger sister, Winifred d'Olier, said. "He was a terrible guy . . . He was the worst man you could possibly find."[26]

The next summer, 1938, Janet rented a house at Bellport, forty miles from her daughters' beloved East Hampton, to set a distance between herself and Black Jack. The girls spent August with their father, but even at Lasata life was falling apart at the seams and the family were more than ever at each other's throats. The Major had fallen in love with an Englishwoman, Mrs. Mabel Ferguson, who lived and worked in New York. "When Grandmother found out about it," Edie Beale said, "her heart shattered. The affair killed her . . ." Maude died less than two years later, on April 2, 1940.

For Jackie, the heartbreak was private, the humiliation public. On January 26, 1940, the *New York Daily Mirror* broke the news of her parents' separation under the headline "Society Broker Sued for Divorce," and published details—supplied apparently by Janet's lawyer—of Black Jack's women, with dates and photographs. Then the big news services ran the story and it was reprinted in tabloids and newspapers across the country. In public Jackie developed a protective shell of reserve, so none of her school friends or teachers seem to have realized the hurt that lay behind it. "It was, of all the divorces I've heard about and watched, I think probably one of the very worst," Lee recalled, "because there was such *relentless* bitterness on both sides, only myself and Jackie, one felt constantly pulled in the other one's direction, and then they spoke of each other in such very unpleasant ways."

It was now that Jackie developed the capacity to shut out things she didn't want to hear, to block out pain, which stood her in good stead later in life. "Jackie was really fortunate to have or acquire the ability to tune out, which she always kept," Lee said. "It was like for the years from ten to twenty never hearing anything [from your parents] except how awful the other one was. Until it gets like a broken record and you start to ignore it because you know when it's coming . . . I envied her [Jackie] so much being able to press the button and tune out . . ."[27] But even Jackie could not tune out entirely. The bitterness of her parents' divorce and its public nature left her with deep insecurities, repressed anger and a fawnlike shyness of the world beyond a circle of trusted friends. It also enhanced the escapist, romantic side of her nature, her love of poetry and books, a fantasy world in which she could lose herself and hide from unpleasant reality. All her life she preferred to skim the surface, afraid to probe at what might lie beneath. She found physical release from her demons in riding hard over fences, and was a courageous, competitive horsewoman. Black Jack told her future husband, John F. Kennedy, "If you have any trouble with Jackie, put her on a horse."

In 1939, as her East Hampton world was breaking up, Jackie, aged ten, wrote a poem celebrating her love for the ocean, illustrating it with a drawing of herself, head thrown back, hair blown by the wind, standing in front of huge rolling breakers:

> When I go down to the sandy shore
> I can think of nothing I want more
> Than to live by the booming blue sea
> As the seagulls flutter around about me
>
> I can run about when the tide is out
> With the wind and the sea all about
> And the seagulls are swirling and diving for fish
> Oh—to live by the sea is my only wish

Me—1939[28]

CHAPTER TWO

Daddy's Little Girl

~

You know, Peter, we both live and do very well in this world of WASPs and old money and society. It's all supposed to be so safe and continuous. But you and I are not really of it. Maybe because I'm Catholic and because my parents were divorced when I was young—a terribly radical thing at the time—I've always felt an outsider in that world.[1]

—Jackie to Peter Duchin

Janet obtained a Reno divorce from Black Jack in June 1940. After the death of Jackie's grandmother, Maude Bouvier, in April that year, the life she had known at Lasata became virtually a thing of the past. From then on Jackie seems to have adopted the motto of her heroine, Scarlett O'Hara (she read *Gone With the Wind* three times that year): "I won't look back." As East Hampton faded into the past, New York, which remained her home for most of her life, became the focus of her now largely WASP world. After the divorce, Janet and her daughters moved into an apartment at One Gracie Square, near the Chapin School for Girls, which Jackie had attended since September 1935.

According to a contemporary pupil, Miss Chapin's was "still full of misses" when Jackie went there and the atmosphere was predominantly WASP female. The headmistress, Miss Ethel Gray Stringfellow, lived with a Miss Evelyn Scott, who did not work at the school. The Latin teacher lived with the extremely masculine gym teacher, whose training, to the girls, seemed like preparation for war: they were expected to shinny up ropes and to wriggle across the gym floor on their stomachs "as though bullets were whizzing overhead." The school motto, prominently displayed everywhere, was *"Fortiter et Recte"*—"Go bravely and rightly"—while Miss Stringfellow's mantra, "Be conspicuous by being inconspicuous," delivered a confusingly contrasting message. The school uniform Jackie wore in the lower grades consisted of a turquoise linen jumper with a belt worn over a white cotton blouse with a Peter Pan collar and turquoise linen bloomers;

in the upper school she wore a turquoise blouse and dark green serge skirt over dark green serge bloomers.

The school day began when the uniformed girls marched into the Assembly Room for prayers, which consisted of the Episcopalian version of the Lord's Prayer, the recital of memorized Bible verses and a reading by an upper school girl, after which there would be school announcements. They left to a military march thumped out by the piano teacher. "The school in her [Jackie's] day was predominantly Protestant," Minnie Hickman remembered. "One, perhaps two, Catholics per class could creep in. There were very few Jewish girls, certainly none with obvious names . . ."[2] Jackie's Catholic experiences were somewhat limited: "We certainly weren't Catholics like the Kennedys," Lee said, "but we went to church every Sunday in New York with my grandfather Bouvier when we lived there. And we went to this convent called Helpers of the Holy Souls three times a week, so we were meant to be grounded in the Catholic faith."[3]

"The expectation was that we would marry well," Minnie Hickman said. "To train us for marriage we were sent to dancing school at eight or nine years of age. Jackie was sent to the twice-weekly school at the Colony Club run by a Miss Hubbell. This lady carried a silver-headed cane, which she would pound on the floor in time to the music. Our partners were selected from the ranks of Buckley, St. Bernard's and Allen Stevenson schools. They were reluctant to attend dancing school and had to be shepherded out of the men's room by Miss Hubbell and her cane . . ."[4] The boys wore Eton jackets or neat blue suits, the girls party dresses, and both sexes were expected to wear white gloves. Jackie far preferred Miss O'Neill's ballet classes, which sparked a lifelong interest in ballet; although she knew not only that she was too tall to be a professional dancer but that her family would never allow it, she thought, briefly, of designing costumes and began to collect ballet books.

Jackie was already a rebel, unsubdued by the discipline at Miss Chapin's. She was brighter than most of her classmates and would get through her work quickly, then was left with nothing to do but doodle and daydream. All the teachers, interviewed by Mary Van Rensselaer Thayer twenty years later, remembered her for her beauty and, above all, her mischief. "She was the prettiest little girl," recalled a Miss Affleck, "very clever, very artistic, and full of the devil."[5]

Jackie made lifelong friends at Miss Chapin's, notably Nancy Tuckerman, who acted as her Girl Friday, confidante and guardian until her death. Janet Felton, who also worked with Jackie when she became First Lady, remembered her at Miss Chapin's: "She was as naughty as everything, she would disrupt whatever she could, but very talented. We would be taken on these ghastly bird walks to Central Park and we had to tiptoe, and of course Jackie would scream and yell, and she'd be caught drinking out of public fountains—and I mean she'd be sent to the headmistress every second week because she was so naughty! Anyhow, I think she had the best sense of humor and of the ridiculous throughout her life. Behind people's back she would know their number and really either imitate them or do something. Then she would make people do things. With Nancy [Tuckerman], who didn't know anything about horses, she said that to be lucky you had to walk under a horse! She sent Lee off to do her dirty work. I mean she always got others to do her dirty work . . ."[6]

Sally Smith Cross, a classmate at Miss Chapin's, remembered her "irrepressible exuberance" and splendid athleticism. "I can visualize her now," she recorded, "with thick brown braids bouncing, as she ran into the center of 'The Roof' for a game of corner kickball. I can also see her being chastised and sent to Miss Stringfellow's office for having challenged the inexperienced young teacher of Modern Dance . . . She was a very able student and also a ringleader whose stuffed zebra, Flapjack, became our class mascot . . . she could turn cartwheels, something which I never mastered."[7]

Jackie might have been a tomboy at school, but in the strictly disciplined atmosphere of her mother's apartment, she took refuge in reading, like many lonely children. This is how she recalled her New York childhood:

> I lived in New York City until I was thirteen and spent the summers in the country. I hated dolls, loved horses and dogs, and had skinned knees and braces on my teeth for what must have seemed an interminable length of time to my family.
>
> I read a lot when I was little, much of which was too old for me. There were Chekhov and Shaw in the room where I had to take naps and I never slept but sat on the windowsill reading, then scrubbed the soles of my feet so the nurse would not see I had been out of bed. My heroes were Byron, Mowgli, Robin Hood, Little Lord Fauntleroy's grandfather, and Scarlett O'Hara.[8]

Of this rather conventional list, one name stands out as unusual: Lord Fauntleroy's grandfather is an example of Jackie's fixation with older men or, perhaps, a reminder of the grandfather she now rarely saw, Grampy Jack.

⁓

Black Jack's fortunes continued to decline, and in order to economize he moved out of the Westbury into a two-bedroom apartment, with a maid's room, at 125 East 74th Street and gave up two of his automobiles, keeping only the Mercury convertible. He cut down on dining out, but never stinted on his beloved daughters. He paid for Danseuse's keep at Durland's livery stables so that Jackie could ride her in Central Park, and for Jackie's tuition at Miss Chapin's. As the girls grew up, he gave them charge accounts at Saks. Every Sunday he would pick them up from their mother's in the Mercury, tooting a special signal on the horn. They would go for walks in Central Park, taking with them dogs borrowed for the day from pet shops, then lunch at Schrafft's with friends from school, go to a movie and stuff themselves with pistachio ice cream. Or they might watch baseball practice at Baker Field, or racing at Belmont Park, where their father would introduce them to the top jockeys. There were trips downtown to lunch on Wall Street, and once

Black Jack took them to the visitors' gallery at the New York Stock Exchange to look down on the jostling, shouting brokers, who had once been such an important part of his world.

Although he tried not to let his daughters see it, his world was steadily diminishing. He had been deeply shaken by his mother's death and by his divorce from Janet, which left him with a sense of failure. He now went rarely to Lasata and gave up keeping his horses there, although Jackie and Lee still spent August with him at East Hampton. The *Social Spectator* of August 30, 1941, features Jackie looking grown-up and graceful, taking a fence on Danseuse at the East Hampton Horse Show; she won the blue rosette in the Hunter Hacks class and the first prize for horsemanship for children under fourteen.

On June 21, 1942, Janet dealt Black Jack the final blow by marrying a man far richer and, in social terms, better bred than he was, Hugh D. Auchincloss II, or Hughdie as he was always known, heir to a Standard Oil fortune and two magnificent houses, Merrywood in McLean, Virginia, and Hammersmith Farm at Newport, Rhode Island. Jackie and Lee were taken by surprise, partly because their mother had not warned them and partly, according to Lee, because at least two other beaux were on the scene. "I remember being totally surprised," Lee recalled, "because she [Janet] called up and we were at that moment at my grandfather Lee's house. Jackie took the phone first, and Jackie said, 'She's gotten married.' And I said, 'Who to?' And she said, 'Mr. Auchincloss.' I was expecting two other people instead so I was really taken aback. Apparently he had two days' leave because he was in the Navy and so this was her reason as to why we weren't there . . ."[9]

In fact, Jackie and Lee had already met Hughdie and his eldest son by his Russian first wife, Hugh D. Auchincloss III, always known as Yusha, the previous December, ten days after the Japanese bombing of Pearl Harbor. Janet had taken the girls on a sightseeing tour of Washington. Yusha, a shy fourteen-year-old home for the Christmas vacation from Groton School, was particularly attracted by the twelve-year-old Jackie. They shared a passion for history and, at this emotional moment as America entered the Second World War, feelings of patriotism and hero worship. Jackie wondered what would become of France—she had a poodle she called "Gaullie" after General de Gaulle. Mornings of that week before Christmas were spent sightseeing in Washington—Mount Vernon and the Washington Monument, the Capitol, the White House (Jackie had toured it earlier that year with her mother and later recalled how unwelcoming it had seemed). They spent a long time at the Lincoln Memorial, with Jackie reading aloud his inspiring words etched in stone. She particularly loved the National Museum of American History: "One of her special interests was the American Indian," Yusha recalled, "although she was also fascinated by pirates . . . Her father, Jack Bouvier, whom she greatly loved, [she] imagined as a swashbuckling pirate."[10] Poignantly their last sightseeing tour was to Arlington Cemetery and the Lee Mansion, beneath which Jackie would one day be buried beside John F. Kennedy. Looking down over the tomb of the Unknown Soldier from the First World War and the rows of white graves, they wondered how many more there would be now that America was again at war and whether any of their friends might ever be buried on that hillside. "What a peaceful place to be," Jackie mused. On their last afternoon at Merrywood, standing on a rock overlooking the rapids of the Potomac, Jackie invited Yusha to come to New York for the Easter vacation: he could stay with his grandmother at 903 Park Avenue and Jackie would take him sightseeing.

Yusha acted as his father's best man at his marriage to Janet at Merrywood. He welcomed the advent of Jackie and Lee into his family, and for Jackie he was the elder brother she had always longed for. Two days after the wedding Hughdie left for naval service with British intelligence in Jamaica, while Janet, after a formal tour of her new in-laws, returned to Jackie and Lee at her parents' house in East Hampton.[11]

After Hughdie was transferred back to Washington later in the summer of 1942, Janet, Jackie and Lee moved into Merrywood, a house that played an important part in Jackie's life over the next few years. There was something about it that captivated those who lived there. After the marriage of his mother, Nina, Gore Vidal had found himself the reluctant stepson, aged ten, of Hughdie, and wrote about it as the Laurel House in *Washington D.C.*; he recalled it again in his autobiography *Palimpsest*, and the physical sense of Merrywood, amid the trees on the high Potomac palisades, remained with him all his life: "From terraced lawns, there was a steep rocky drop to the river, down which it was dangerous to walk, much less to run, and so, of course, I often ran this hazardous course, leaping from rock to rock. To this day I still dream of making that descent to the swift mud-brown, swirling river . . ."[12]

Jackie's bedroom had been Gore's; when she moved in, she told him, she found some of his old shirts still there with his name on them and used to wear them for riding. It was a small, twin-bedded room with an adjoining bathroom that had a white-tiled floor "unchanged since the thirties" and a large window with a view of the lawn, woods and the river. Later it was the room she shared with Jack Kennedy. The large brick neo-Georgian house with its white pilasters reminded her of Tara in *Gone with the Wind*. Its situation, in fifty acres of woods high above the rushing rapids of the Potomac, appealed to her sense of romance and her love of nature: "I will never know which I love best, Hammersmith [Farm] with its green fields and summer winds or Merrywood in the snow with the river and those great steep hills . . ."[13] she wrote to Yusha. Yusha, with the poetic soul of his Russian forebears, wrote mystically to her of their shared love for Merrywood, which he saw as a guiding spirit: "Merrywood is a sort of heaven where there can be no desires, no fears, no selfish, superficial ambitions except the ambition of love and happiness. Merrywood . . . is a spirit. You can feel her and know her more than anyone else because I want you to. Your true self is in the character of Merrywood and I hope you shall never change and I don't think you ever shall for Merrywood has told you not to . . ."[14]

Jackie first saw Hammersmith Farm, just outside Newport, Rhode Island, in the summer of 1943. Described by Yusha merely as "a spacious shingled 1880s cottage," it has twenty-eight rooms, and could only be regarded as a cottage in comparison with the mansions and Vanderbilt châteaux on Newport's Bellevue

Avenue. Built in 1887 by Yusha's great-uncle, John Auchincloss, it was subsequently taken over by his grandmother Emma Jennings Auchincloss and his grandfather Hugh D. Auchincloss, who died in 1913. Hughdie inherited it, after his marriage to Janet, on the death of his mother in September 1942. Then it was still furnished in heavy Victorian style, especially the "deck room" with dark, musty upholstery, bear-, tiger- and leopard-skin rugs and, hanging from the ceiling (it still does), a stuffed pelican caught by his grandfather around the turn of the century. At the time of Jackie's first visit the large, formal gardens had still not been overtaken by wartime economies; she particularly liked the rock garden and the sunken garden, designed by Frederick Law Olmsted, where she pirouetted, or sat and painted, when she was not down by the boat dock on the bay composing poems or dreaming up romantic stories. The glory of Hammersmith Farm was, and is, its situation on the top of a hill with a spectacular view down over green fields to the waters of Narragansett Bay.

The war was very much on Jackie's mind,[15] as Yusha recalled. The window blinds were lined with black and a careful lights-out regime was maintained in case of enemy attack because of the nearby torpedo station. A submarine net stretched near the Hammersmith boathouse to protect the station on Goat Island. Naval ships were constantly steaming in and out of the bay. On January 8, 1943, just a few months before Jackie arrived at Hammersmith, a young U.S. Navy ensign, twenty-five-year-old John Fitzgerald Kennedy, in command of four motor torpedo boats, had left the Melville Torpedo Boat Training School across the bay for Jacksonville, Florida, ultimately destined for the Pacific and his historic mission on PT 109, when he would show true heroism in rescuing his wounded shipmates after the wreck of their torpedo boat. As he said later, while he was sitting on the deck at Hammersmith Farm sipping a daiquiri and nibbling at the inevitable codfish ball, he had thought then that the view east from his boat to Hammersmith Farm was one of the loveliest he knew.

In Lee Radziwill's recollection, at Hammersmith it was always summer: "Our trip up there was always June first and somewhat of a voyage because it was eight hours on the train and you took absolutely everything you'd want all summer. And, it being a big farm on the bay, there was so much to do—the first animals my stepfather got when he reopened Hammersmith were two Guernsey cows that were named after us, Jacqueline and Caroline!"[16] The house stood in ninety acres of green fields, a paradise for Jackie and her horses, dogs and cattle. The farm superintendent, Bob Burgess, from Guernsey, was in charge of setting up the farm to provide food supplies for the Navy; Yusha and Jackie both had their chores: Yusha helped milk the Guernseys and Jackie collected the eggs from the Rhode Island Red hens.

Jackie had a new, ready-made family and two large new homes in what realtors would call desirable locations. Her stepfather, "Uncle Hugh" or simply "Unk" to her and Lee, was seriously rich: his mother, Emma Jennings Auchincloss, a Standard Oil heiress, had left him enough money to found a brokerage house, Auchincloss, Parker & Redpath. A large, kindly, stammering man, Hughdie was proud of his ancestry and kept a copy of his family tree in his bathroom at Hammersmith.

The original Auchincloss had been a Scot from Paisley; his maternal bloodline included the distinguished Burr family, and his mother's sister had married a Rockefeller. "He was a kind man and he was a gentle man but he was a man who stayed in the nineteenth century in many ways," Jamie Auchincloss, Hughdie's son by Janet, said. "And the circle of his friends—he had a great many good friends but they assuredly were all white and all Protestant and all wealthy, all members of clubs [living] a very comfortable existence."[17] A friend of Jackie's described Hughdie as "awfully stuffy." He prided himself on being, and was, a gentleman. Like many very rich men, he was somewhat penny-pinching: in order to save electricity in winter, the carcasses of deer for the table would be left on the back porch rather than occupying space in the freezer.[18]

December 1942 was Jackie's first Auchincloss family Christmas. Jackie and Lee always put on a Christmas Eve Nativity play for their mother; now they had a Joseph in Yusha and a wise man in Hughdie. Jackie was Mary and Lee, who had a lovely voice, played an angel and sang carols; the rest of the cast remained silent. The part of Jesus was taken, somewhat blasphemously, by one of Janet's small dogs. This idyllic scene, however, was not necessarily typical of life in the complicated Auchincloss family.

Hughdie had been married twice before, first to a woman of Russian descent, Maria Chaprovitsky, daughter of a Russian naval officer and Yusha's mother. Jackie liked to refer to Yusha's "noble blood lines": one of his ancestors on his mother's side had been Catherine the Great's private secretary, an intellectual who wrote the Empress's letters to Voltaire, while on his father's side an Alexander de Chaprovitsky had, it was rumored, married an illegitimate daughter of Peter the Great. Yusha's maternal grandfather, Count Nicholas de Chaprovitsky, had been killed in the Russo-Japanese War at the battle of Tsushima when his battleship, the *Alexander III*, had been blown up with the loss of all on board. Yusha's mother, Maria, had been born in the same year as the ill-fated Grand Duchess Anastasia and had played with her as a child during summers in the Crimea. After Yusha's birth, Maria fell in love with another man and Hughdie divorced her. He then married Nina Gore Vidal, daughter of the blind Oklahoma senator, T. P. Gore, and mother of Gore Vidal, and fathered a daughter, also called Nina but known as Nini, and a son, Tommy. Asked by his mother whether he would like Hughdie as a stepfather, the ten-year-old Gore's answer was an emphatic no—"largely on aesthetic grounds. After my father [the handsome athlete and aviator Eugene Vidal], the large, cumbersome, stammering Hughdie was simply neither plausible nor decorative."[19] Gore's portrayal of Hughdie and his sexual problems in *Palimpsest* is wickedly funny. Hughdie kept a collection of pornography, most of which Nina forced him to throw into the Potomac; he was incapable of having an erection and, according to Gore's mother, who was an alcoholic and therefore not entirely reliable, the conception of her two children by Hughdie took place with the aid of a spoon. (Jackie, Gore said, knew exactly what this meant.) Not surprisingly, Nina left Hughdie in 1940 to marry her lover, General Robert Olds. Gore's dislike of his stepfather was keenly reciprocated. "The story that amused the family," a cousin said, "was that Yusha was supposed to have once had a fight with Gore and Gore sort of played dead and fell down on the floor and Yusha was terrified and ran to his father and said, 'I've just killed Gore,' and Hughdie's supposed to have said, 'Good.' "[20] Although fond of Hughdie, Jackie found him as boring as did his acerbic stepson, who wrote, "My lifelong passion for bores began with Hughdie." He and Jackie used gleefully to recall Hughdie's sayings: "All good cooks are fat. The ultimate test of a cook is, Can she make codfish cakes?"[21]

Gore detested Janet—"inadvertently a laugh a minute"—but there was no doubt as to who was the dominant influence in the Auchincloss household. Hughdie used to say wryly to his son Jamie, "To speak to your mother is to interrupt her." "So," Jamie recalled, "I didn't hear my father say much in the twenty-nine years I knew him and he was always deferring to my mother's wishes and desires. Sometimes when there was a family argument I wish not only that he'd stuck up for himself but that he'd stuck up for one of us . . . But he had been married twice, really badly, disastrous marriages before he married my mother, and he was looking from 'I cannot afford another argument, let alone another divorce, and if I did divorce I would be left alone.' And my mother was ultimately devoted to him and didn't want a divorce herself but she could withdraw, if he didn't immediately come in on her side, no matter how ludicrous it might be, of any argument big or small. And there were some tiny arguments that got awfully big, and some big arguments that should have been probably taken all the way to the Supreme Court and not just left within the family."[22] Another family friend, "Oatsie" Leiter, who adored Janet and found her charming, admitted that she had "a violent temper which exploded and went away—she was very volatile. Hughdie would just sit with the newspaper in front of his face."[23]

Life in the Auchincloss households was, therefore, not entirely serene. John F. Kennedy once took up Vidal on an article he wrote for *Look* in which he described the "golden ambience" of Merrywood: "What's this golden season shit you're telling, Gore? It was *The Little Foxes*."[24] An Auchincloss cousin described a visit once as "Nothing but the sound of slamming doors, great feet thundering up and down the stairs, slapping across faces, vile oaths, with Hughdie sitting sort of slumped in the middle of it."

The key to this explosive family atmosphere was Janet, variously described as "a monster" and "utterly charming." To be fair to Janet, life had not been easy for her, with a cold, estranged father, a rampantly unfaithful husband, a divorce in her early thirties leaving her with two daughters to bring up and no alternative but to marry for money. She chain-smoked and bit her nails. There were also social insecurities in Janet, which accounted for some of the tension: "She was not, she didn't belong to the class to which she aspired and in a sense joined by marrying Hughdie," Gore Vidal said. "And I think that made her very nervous . . ." There were also rumors, inevitable in the prejudiced atmosphere of the time, that she was either Jewish, having been born Levi, not Lee, or an Irish Catholic, neither of which would have been acceptable in Auchincloss circles. When Nini Gore Auchincloss, aged ten, repeated her mother's comment, "I wonder what will happen when Hughdie finds out that Janet's father was Mr. Levi," Janet became utterly hysterical instead of denying it.[25]

"I guess she was a bit suspicious of people," an English friend said. "Hughdie was wonderful with her. He was a darling sort of teddy bear and calmed her down because she was so highly strung, but she was a very kind woman and had a good sense of humor."[26] She had two large households to run in wartime when the shortage of help had begun to affect even the grandest families. "Janet brimmed with energy," her New York interior decorator, Elisabeth Draper, said. "She was a perfectionist, very selective, very meticulous in everything she did, from the way she sat to the way she wiped her lips after a meal."[27] Both Merrywood and Hammersmith were always full of people, even during the war years, with dinner parties, cocktail parties, lunches. One of Jackie's contemporaries remembered children's parties at Merrywood and Hughdie as "a very nice gentleman of the old school, he was always nice to young people . . . Janet was apparently a tough lady but I never saw that part of her. What I saw was a very charming pretty woman. I heard she was very ambitious for her girls but I never saw any tough side of her at all . . . I went to a birthday party [for 'Little' Janet Auchincloss] and they brought a pony into the living room and the pony 'went to the bathroom' on the Aubusson carpet. Janet didn't turn a hair."[28]

"I don't care what any of the writers have said," an observer of the Washington scene recalled. "They've all been down on her. They've all said Janet Lee is a social-climbing whatever, but I thought she was class. She just had this dignity about the way she held herself. She had these marvelously understated tweedy clothes and she always looked terrific and she behaved herself in a very elegant way."[29]

Gore Vidal, hardly an unbiased witness, described what he called the "poison-ivied" view at Merrywood when his former stepmother Janet presided at the wedding of his half sister Nini to Newton Steers in 1957: "Janet Auchincloss was a small woman, with a large pouter-pigeon bust that neatly balanced large low-slung buttocks set atop sandpiper legs. The sallow face was all great curved nose-beak set between small fierce dark eyes. With me, she was her usual rude self . . ."[30] The social and physical strains on Janet increased with her two pregnancies by Hughdie, and the births of Janet Jennings Auchincloss in 1945 and James Lee, always known as Jamie, in 1947. "My mother," Lee Radziwill said, "tried to do her best [but] she just took too much on and couldn't handle it. I mean, couldn't handle dealing with so many children. She ran both houses beautifully but I think the children suffered from it." Asked whether Jackie had insecurities as a result of her mother's tension, Lee replied, "Oh, I'm sure she did because with our somewhat critical mother it would be totally unnatural not to have had any insecurities."[31]

Jackie's attitude toward her mother in those years was ambivalent. On the one hand, she was too intelligent not to appreciate what her mother was trying to do for her and Lee. "She was the most assiduous of mothers," Gore Vidal admitted. "Nini said that everything those girls became was due to their mother. She arranged these marriages, she pushed them and did everything for them, saw to it that they had these glamorous coming-out parties—constantly pushing them, pushing them, pushing them . . . Jackie quite appreciated what her mother did. Jackie was no fool—I think she found her as tiresome as everybody else did."[32] Part of Jackie went along with her mother's program because it fitted in with her idea of her own future, which was, as was most women's at that time, a brilliant marriage. Part of her, the self that was unaffected by the worldly and often unadmirable standards of her parents, revolted against it. When she was still a girl she shocked one of her mother's friends with an outburst against her mother, saying "how awful it was that she was so pushy and so social and that she only cared about social things, the white glove life, and it was all so phony . . ."[33] Jackie could be provocative and quietly defiant toward her mother, tuning out at the evening ritual, what Lee termed "this *painful* hour before dinner at Hammersmith called the cocktail hour, when for some extraordinary reason not even drinking Coca-Cola we had to be sitting there, just the two of us. I don't know where my steps and halves were—it was just the two of us. And she [Jackie] would bring down a pile of magazines to look at during this session and then my mother would just scream and say, you know, 'I'm talking to you!' which she really wasn't, she was talking to my stepfather. 'Put that magazine down!' And the minute she started talking again she [Jackie] would start to read the magazine.

"I don't think Jackie ever disliked my mother as you've heard," Lee said. "I think that she was always grateful to her because she felt that she had intentionally enlarged her world—our world—for our sake as much if not more than for her own sake. I think she was always far more grateful than I was for that . . . She appreciated it so much."

Her mother's marriage into the WASP establishment and the entrée into every social set at the highest level had a momentous effect on Jackie's life, opening up to her new avenues of possibility beyond One Gracie Square and August in East Hampton. As an intelligent twelve-year-old she was well aware of the potential this new life might hold for her. "She was absolutely ready to move on to a bigger screen and more scope, and excited about it and curious," Lee said. Lee, though, was confused and apprehensive: "I was, I'd say, fearful, sorry to leave here [East Hampton] really for good because I loved my life here, and I suppose it was the happiest time and certainly the time I felt the safest." Jackie, Lee said, was always less attached to East Hampton than she was. For Lee, Janet's marriage "meant more or less a permanent split from the way things had been with my father and my grandfather and Lasata . . . because from then on we only came every summer for six weeks to spend with my father and that would start getting discussed months before . . . 'He can't have you then,' etc. . . ."

All her life, Jackie would have this ability to move on without looking back, making a definitive break from a previous existence. She turned her back on the Bouviers, with the exception of Black Jack, and embraced a new family, the Auchinclosses, particularly Yusha: "We *loved* having a brother at long last," Lee remembered. "It was very exciting when he would come back for vacations and Jackie was hoping he would introduce her to some of his devastating friends. He's a terribly nice person and was so sweet to us both."[34]

As for Jackie, a cousin recalled, "She did have a tremendous sense of family. After Janet married Uncle Hughdie and they were all together—his children from other marriages, her children—Jackie never once spoke of step-this or half-that. To Jackie they were all her brothers and sisters. There was a great mothering quality about her. She looked after Janet and Jamie when they were babies and when they were young. She was concerned with the welfare of Tommy and Nina when they went through bad times and needed help."[35]

For Jackie in these formative teenage years, Merrywood, Hammersmith and the Auchincloss circle represented home and the stability that had been missing from her life in recent years. "I began to feel terribly homesick," she wrote to Yusha, "just like a dream—I started thinking of things like the path leading to the stables at Merrywood with the stones slipping as you ran up it—and Hammersmith with the foghorns blowing at night—all the places and feelings and happiness that bind you to a family you love . . ."[36]

If Jackie and Lee had hoped that their mother's remarriage would lessen her bitterness toward their father, they were mistaken. "I expected it to change completely but it didn't," Lee said. They suffered, too, when it came to dividing the holidays. Christmas in particular was a difficult time, Lee remembered: "That was always a strain, a big, big strain, and I always remember Christmas Day as being so sad for us because we always spent it at Merrywood and then we knew we only had the few hours in the morning before we had to go up to New York to see our father. And then he was so lonely and we were always the only two people on this plane and we'd have to leave in the middle of this festive lunch . . . I think he counted on us so much, we were his only *raison d'être*—sports, perhaps, came next and the stock market after that. But we always came first. I think the *big* responsibility we felt was ours. Mainly because he was so alone and counted on us totally . . ."[37]

Black Jack's love was indeed focused on his daughters, but his riposte to his ex-wife's remarriage had been to embark on a serious but short-lived affair in the summer of 1942. Ann Plugge was a thirty-three-year-old Englishwoman who had been evacuated to North America with her young son, Frank, in 1940 to escape the Blitz, leaving in London her husband, Captain Leonard Plugge, M.P. for Chatham. Ann was an attractive former actress and model who had a host of influential American friends and, according to her son, probably also had an affair with Bernard Baruch. Arriving in New York in 1941, she took an unpaid job in the offices of British War Relief and found an apartment for herself and her son at 125 East 74th Street in the same building as Black Jack. She and Black Jack probably met in New York, and it was perhaps at his suggestion that she rented a tiny clapboard cottage near the ocean at East Hampton for herself and Frank in the summer of 1942. Frank remembers Jackie "always on a horse—Dad was always around—she and her sister were very close . . . We did lots of things as a family. We would go to horse shows to watch Jackie compete, boat trips, days out at friends' houses and many days at the Maidstone Club where the Bouvier family had a beach cabana. Although I was too young to understand fully adult relationships, I was nevertheless aware that Jack Bouvier was the man around; he was always very kind to me and became a sort of surrogate father figure." In New York he saw a lot of Black Jack, and of Jackie and Lee when they were staying with their father. Frank remembers going with them on the carousel in Central Park.

By early 1943 Jack and Ann were serious enough about each other for Ann to write to her husband saying that she was in love with Jack Bouvier and wanted to marry him. By now she had been welcomed into the Bouvier family and was invited to all their social occasions. No doubt they hoped that Black Jack would marry her and settle down in his middle age. Leonard Plugge, however—who, according to his son, was in London "with armfuls of girls"—refused to consider a divorce and threatened to fight for custody of his son if Ann should try to leave him. Captain Plugge was two years older than Black Jack, an energetic and somewhat eccentric man, a pioneering broadcaster, inventor and scientist. He was also, unlike Black Jack, comfortably rich. He flew to New York and persuaded his wife to return to England with their son, which they did in the late spring of 1943.[38] Black Jack never saw Ann again. According to his niece by marriage, Kathleen Bouvier, Black Jack, by now into his fifties, then "tapered down his associations with girls of East Hampton and Manhattan society, increasingly focusing his attention on women without his social and financial background."[39]

When Janet married Hughdie, Black Jack coined a phrase on the New York Stock Exchange, "Take a loss with Auchincloss," but if anyone was to be the loser it was Jack Bouvier himself. Jackie was moving further away from him in space and time. She now left Miss Chapin's and spent two years at Holton Arms School in Georgetown, where a contemporary remembers her as "a little girl who looked like Bambi."[40]

In the autumn of 1944, Jackie, aged fifteen, enrolled as a pupil at Miss Porter's School in Farmington, Connecticut. Her paternal grandmother, Maude Sergeant, had been a pupil there, as had Jackie's cousin, Edie Beale, but the principal reason for Jackie to go to "MPS" was that Hughdie's sister, Annie Burr Lewis, a former pupil and founder of the first Alumnae Association, and her husband, the bibliophile and collector Wilmarth Sheldon "Lefty" Lewis, a member of the board of trustees, lived nearby. Like Miss Chapin's, Miss Porter's was a Protestant stronghold.

"She was quite a good Catholic," Jackie's school friend Ellen "Puffin" Gates remembered. "We used to tease her about being a mackerel snatcher. Of course, being a Catholic at Farmington they didn't go to the church we all went to, so they peeled off and went to a Catholic church [St. Patrick's]. So it was a teasing thing, but there was also a little element of being different . . ." Here, as elsewhere in society, the Auchincloss mantle, in the form of Aunt Abie—Annie Burr—and Uncle Lefty, protected her but always, lurking in the background, there was the distinctly un-Establishment figure of Black Jack. "And another thing that made Jackie different," Puffin said, "was her father . . ."[41]

When Jackie entered Farmington the school had just celebrated its centenary; it had been founded in 1843 by Miss Sarah Porter, the strong-minded sister of Yale president Noah Porter. *Time* described it as "a rigorous, reticent prep school for rich girls (tuition: $2,700) with rich minds. Steeped in Connecticut charm, it boasts a noted art history department, one teacher for every eight of its 230 girls, and a grade-A milk herd to nourish its grade-A students, who consistently enter Radcliffe, Vassar, Smith and Wellesley." At the time of Jackie's arrival, the school still operated a large farm, geared to produce milk, butter and vegetables for its own use; as war work, the girls helped with the chores like potato peeling.

Jackie attended the Commencement ceremony in the pretty white clapboard First Church of Christ Congregational ("Congo") and was allotted a senior Old Girl to oversee her through her first year. She was given a copy of the school rules for New Girls:

1. New Girls do not wear the school colors, yellow and gray.
2. New Girls hold open the door of Main for Old Girls.
3. New Girls rise when a senior enters the room.
4. New Girls move to the edge of the sidewalk when Old Girls pass.[42]

Although there was no official uniform, the girls wore what amounted to one: they were outfitted by the smart New York firms Brooks Brothers and Abercrombie & Fitch in camel-hair polo coats, gray or plaid skirts, and Shetland sweaters over round-collar shirts, usually worn with a single string of graded pearls. It was all spartan and strictly ladylike: too short sleeves on dresses meant that the girl had to cover up with a school-owned bolero jacket; no sweaters were allowed in church and no slacks were to be worn unless the temperature dropped below 10 degrees. Visits by boys (or "callers") were strictly regulated: girls registered their male visitors in the Callers' Book, which was in the keeping of the school policeman, Officer George Miller. The girl and her caller were then allowed to walk along a prescribed route, finishing with tea at the Headmaster's House, after which the caller was expected to leave. Of course, Jackie's main male caller was Black Jack, who would drive at breakneck speed from New York in his Mercury convertible, bringing presents of stockings and movie magazines and once, romantically, a bunch of gardenias, which he laid in the snow beneath Jackie's dormitory window. Together, father and daughter would tear around in the car like teenagers. Jackie told Yusha that "Daddy" had promised to give her the Mercury when she was seventeen.

To some of the Farmington girls, Black Jack stuck out like a sore thumb among the proper WASP parents: "He used to come to school. There would always be fathers' days and they would play father/daughter tennis matches," Puffin Gates remembered. "And what we liked to do was run around and shake our behinds at him because he was an absolute lecher, absolute ravening, ravenous lecher, and Jackie, of course, knew it, and it amused her, but I don't think she was aware—she might have been, she didn't miss anything—of the extent to which we were teasing her father and making fun of him . . . This man was decidedly repulsive . . . He came through as this sort of cartoon example of a dirty old man and I don't know if Jackie ever realized the extent to which we felt he was."[43]

During her first year Jackie roomed with Sue Norton, a pretty blond girl from California; the two girls etched their names on their dormitory pane with diamond rings—"Jackie Bouvier/44–45/Sue Norton." Once installed at Farmington,

Jackie moved heaven and earth to have Danseuse sent up there for her to ride. The horse's keep would cost twenty-five dollars a month, which she could not afford, but she knew how to get what she wanted. She wrote to Grampy Jack, sending him a copy of her latest poem as a sweetener. The old man replied in his flowery style:

> Dear Jacqueline,
>
> What in one aspect might be viewed as a sumptuary extravagance may, on the other hand, from the mental and physical standpoint, be regarded as a justifiable necessity.
>
> Within this generalization naturally falls Danseuse. Psychologically she aids you. Spiritually she provides a wholesome release from sordid and worldly cares. Therefore will I engage to meet her keep of $25 a month until April next.
>
> Are you or am I in these dreadful days justified in such an indulgence? I think not, but with the necessity for maintaining Danseuse both of us are in concurrence.
>
> Affectionately,
> Grandad.[44]

Jackie groomed the mare every day and stole a blanket to protect her from the onset of the New England winter. She trained Danseuse to pull a sleigh. A photograph shows Jackie standing in it in regal pose, the reins in her hands; standing in the snow behind it, like two handmaidens, are her friends Nancy Tuckerman and Sue Norton. "Tucky," whose family lived in New York, was Jackie's closest friend at Farmington: "We always used to call them Mutt and Jeff," Puffin recalled, "because Tucky would sort of follow her everywhere. It was a strange relationship, but Jackie depended on Nancy."[45]

Jackie blossomed at Farmington, particularly in the English class, where she was the star pupil, often sparring with the teacher, Miss Catherine Watson. As Puffin wrote in her memoir of Jackie,

> No other student so soared in the higher realms of literature. It was our delight when Jackie scored a point to challenge or to reinterpret a reading given by that indomitable teacher. And Miss Watson relished the contest. When the two of them engaged, the classroom became an arena electrified by the excitement of debate. We waited for Jackie to put her particular spin on the comic mode that would convulse us when she punctured pretense in the spoken and written word . . . There were several others in the class as bright as Jackie but what really set her apart was her wide range of reading.[46]

Jackie read the romantic poets and writers, Chekhov, Wordsworth and above all Byron, the prototype of the dangerous, risk-taking, heartbreaking men she was drawn to. She read and reread his poems and his biography by André Maurois. She loved Shakespeare and Longfellow, which she would read at Merrywood beside the Indian-haunted Potomac. In June 1946 she won first prize in the Marie McKinney Memorial Award in Literature, a high honor given for "consistency of effort and achievement, flair and imaginative use of material" in the senior year. Jackie's prize was a volume of Edna St. Vincent Millay's poetry, which she always treasured and kept on a special shelf.

Jackie's interest in art, books and English literature was fostered in the Auchincloss circle. Hughdie, his sister Annie and brother-in-law Lefty Lewis were connoisseurs of eighteenth-century English books, cartoons and manuscripts. (Hughdie's collection is now at the Beinecke Library, Yale; the Lewis collection is at the Lewis Walpole Library associated with Yale at Farmington.) Jackie was fascinated by Uncle Lefty's collection of books, manuscripts, prints, drawings, furniture and objects associated with the writer Horace Walpole, many of them originating from his famous Gothic villa, Strawberry Hill. Lewis was the editor of the Yale edition of Walpole's correspondence and owner of the largest collection of British eighteenth-century satirical and topographical prints, drawings and portraits outside the British Museum. Jackie and her school friends were often invited to the Lewises' charming house in Farmington. A poem by Jackie, illustrated with drawings of poodles and a cake for Aunt Abie's birthday on July 22, 1946, still hangs in the house.

Jackie's yearbook entry records her as known for her wit. "Jackie had a very funny sense of humor . . . she was very irreverent, was wonderful at insults [and had a] raunchy sense of humor. She really had a very dirty sense of humor," Puffin recalled. "I had more fun with Jackie than almost anybody because of that streak in her which was so naughty and irreverent about almost everything."[47]

"Jackie was a legend at Farmington," Isabel Eberstadt, Ogden Nash's daughter, recalled. "She had left a year before [I arrived] and still haunted the place as the 'supergirl.' Even the headmaster of the school was in love with her and all the teachers too . . ."[48]

Jackie particularly enjoyed the drama club, the Farmington Players; she would love to be an actress, she wrote to Yusha, except that she knew she would never want to to starve for the sake of art. She played Mr. Bingley in *Pride and Prejudice*, and Chrysos in W. S. Gilbert's *Pygmalion and Galatea*; she was in charge of the wardrobe for *The Admirable Crichton* and scene-shifter on *The Apple Orchard*. She contributed a poem, articles and illustrations (unsigned) to the school newsletter, *Miss Porter's Salmagundy*, and was on its editorial board in 1947, its second year of publication. She scripted at least one of the four annual school entertainments, known as "Germans," and read a paper at one of the Little Meetings on Sundays in front of the whole school. And, of course, she won prizes on Danseuse at the school horse shows. Her name is inscribed twice on a silver cup awarded for the Miss Porter's Spring Horse Show, now in the MPS archives. Other items relating to her there include a battered stuffed candlewick elephant, handed down, or "willed," by Senior to New Girls, with their name tapes attached.

Yet, much as she admitted she "adored" Farmington, she found some of the old school customs ludicrous, particularly the tradition that at the end of the first year, the New Girls had to ask a Senior to wish on their rings. The passionate crushes and vows of eternal fidelity to the true Farmington spirit involved in this custom moved Jackie to fits of laughter. She vowed to find the ugliest girl in the school, who would know that Jackie couldn't possibly have a crush on her. (The school song emphasized high-minded friendships. It was sung at graduation time. "Farmington, Farmington . . . /There my heart will turn forever, /Be the friendships broken never, /that so lightly were begun . . .") Sue Norton's raptures about the uplifting wonders of Farmington caused Jackie such fits of giggles that she almost choked into her pillow. Sue's sweet innocence made her feel like a sinner; the next term she was going to room with Nancy Tuckerman, which would be a change.

She wrote regularly to Lee as well as to Yusha. Prepubescent Lee was chubby and puppylike; four years younger than Jackie, she suffered more from the changes her mother's divorce and remarriage had made in her life. Although she loved Merrywood and Hammersmith, she missed her East Hampton life. Looking back, she felt she had been "transplanted too soon": "I was always the most alone at Merrywood because everybody else went off to their schools, my mother and stepfather were traveling. I was in that big house, that big place and it was very lonely for me," she recalled.[49] One day, she said, she ran away to an orphanage for company.

As a result of competition with Jackie, who never seemed to put on an ounce, Lee became anorexic. Aged just twelve, she wrote to Jackie at Farmington, asking for advice on how to lose weight. Jackie told her to smoke and try to curb her appetite, in a letter that unfortunately Janet saw. She returned a furious epistle to her elder daughter on "the perils of Nicotine for the Young." "If only she knew Lee took up a cigarette when she put down her first rattle," was Jackie's comment. Jackie and "Tucky," unable to lay their hands on cigarettes, pretended to smoke with pencils and thought of nothing but food, bribing a local boy to buy them chocolate ice cream cones from the drugstore, which they were forbidden to enter.

Jackie's relationship with Lee remained complex, big-sisterly, teasing, dominating. When Lee arrived at Farmington in 1947, the year Jackie graduated, she felt very much in her elder sister's shadow. In September that year, Jackie, now at Vassar, asked Yusha to write to "poor little Pekes" at Farmington, who was feeling bewildered and lonely in an unfamiliar place and, despite her new act of sophistication at home, was really still quite a baby beneath the veneer. Yet she still could not resist teasing her little sister in a way that, a friend said, was "torture" for Lee.[50] At Farmington Lee received letters from college boys she had never met; Jackie would flirt with them wickedly and tell them her name was Lee.

Jackie had a dual personality: there was a dark side to her nature as well as a light side, which became more pronounced as her life became more complex. She would tease Lee cruelly while writing Yusha letters full of gentleness, optimism and wisdom in advance of her years. When he was about to join the Marines in March 1945, she wrote warning him not to let the brutality of the life— "underprivileged men and intolerant race conscious ones and bullying sergeants"—

get him down and to remember that there was good and beauty in the world.[51] Traditionally Jackie has been portrayed as uninterested in politics, but at Farmington she was an active participant in the November 1944 presidential election between Dewey and FDR, writing to Yusha of how important it was, how excited and scared she was about it and boasting that she had done "a beautiful job" for the Republicans. Yet less than six months later she was "dazed" by Roosevelt's death on April 12, 1945, admitting that she thought now that he was really great and the only reason she hadn't liked him was because her father had always grumbled about what he had done to the stock exchange. Poignantly, she wrote of the plight of the President's widow: "I feel sorry for poor Mrs. Roosevelt. It will be awfully hard to leave the White House after all those years."

The Jackie who left Farmington in June 1947 was a bright, confident, imaginative seventeen-year-old looking forward to a world of fresh experiences and limitless possibilities. A short story entitled "Spring Fever," which she wrote for two issues of the *Salmagundy* in February and March that year, is psychologically interesting. Its subject is Daphne, a nymph exiled from Olympus for putting a tack on Zeus's chair; as punishment he turns her into a marble statue with permission to come to life once every thousand years on condition that she do a good deed. "What a stuffy thing to do, a good deed," Daphne mused. "I would much rather do a bad one . . ." Trapped in her statue, which has been transported from the Roman Forum to adorn a fountain in Central Park, Daphne decides that her mission for the day is to inspire a prim young man with spring fever. She steps down from her pedestal and spends a warm spring New York day with him, at the end of which "She climbed up and struck the pose which for centuries had made men wish she were not made of stone. 'Please, oh please,' she whispered to the heavens, 'let me know in some way that I have given him spring fever.' Suddenly the silence of the spring evening was pierced by that most expressive of human sounds, a long, low whistle . . ."[52]

In the spring/summer of 1947, Jackie/Daphne was looking forward to release from the conventional atmosphere of Farmington to become the nymph of Central Park. Under "Ambition" in her graduation yearbook entry she wrote "Never to be a housewife."

CHAPTER THREE

The Education of a Nymph

⌒

The capacity to adapt oneself to his or her environment not only marks evolutionary progress, but discloses a practical philosophy which is more wise to cultivate. With you, happily, this process of adaptation has not been in the remotest degree difficult . . .

—Jackie's grandfather John Vernou Bouvier in a letter to Jackie[1]

It was mid-January 1948, deep winter in New York City. Jackie sat beside the coffin of Grampy Jack in the familiar living room of 765 Park Avenue. The Major had been fading away over the past eighteen months, suffering from cancer of the prostate, of which he had been kept in ignorance, comforting himself by reading and rereading his favorite literature: the works of Macaulay and Shakespeare. The last time Jackie had seen her grandfather before the final stages of his illness had been on his eighty-second birthday at Lasata on August 14, 1947. Perhaps she remembered with a touch of guilt how unwillingly then she had been dragged away from the gaiety of Newport in her debutante season by Black Jack, eager to ingratiate himself with his dying father. She was not shocked by her first sight of death: "I was sitting beside my grandfather's coffin looking at him as he lay in his dark blue suit with his hands folded. I had never seen death before and was ashamed that it made no more impression on me."[2]

What did shock her, however, was the squabbling between her Bouvier aunts and Black Jack over their father's inheritance even before he was buried. "I was glad he couldn't see how his children behaved once he was dead,"[3] she commented. When a workingman arrived with a small bunch of violets for her grandfather, one of the aunts seized it and hid it behind a sheaf of gladioli. Later, when she was alone, Jackie retrieved the violets and put them "down inside the coffin, where the people who came to close the coffin could not see them." It was a private tribute and a protest: for simplicity and against pretentiousness.

To their dismay, his heirs discovered that the old man had run through a great deal more than they had imagined of the $1.3 million he had inherited in 1935. Between 1935 and 1948 some $400,000 had disappeared, and he had left $800,000, of which a third went in taxes. The twins, Maude and Michelle, got the lion's share of the remainder, a quarter of a million dollars plus Lasata and Wild-moor between them; Black Jack, who had been cut out of his father's will until his reinstatement as a result of his assiduity the previous August, received $100,000 plus release from the outstanding debt. Big Edie, who had never compromised the lifestyle of which her father disapproved, received only $65,000 in trust. The Major's mistress was left $35,000; Jackie and Lee got $3,000 each. Within a year, the twins had been forced to put up Lasata for sale; it was finally sold in April 1950.

The precipitate decline of the Bouviers' fortunes provided Jackie with an illustration—if she needed one—of the precarious nature of family prosperity and the importance of money in the social equation. For her, the Bouviers were now history. Just five months earlier she had been launched as a debutante from the secure Auchincloss social platform at Newport with a tea dance held at Hammer-smith, a joint celebration for the christening of her new half brother, the five-month-old James Lee Auchincloss. Three hundred guests had attended the party, described by the *Newport Daily News* as a "reception from 5 to 7 P.M. with Clifford Hall [the regular pianist at the Clambake Club] playing." The coming-out party proper was held on August 16, 1947, with a dinner dance to the music of society bandleader Meyer Davis, who had played at her parents' wedding, at the Clam-bake Club. It was shared with her fellow debutante, Rose Grosvenor. Both girls wore white, with the traditional string of pearls around their necks; schoolgirl Lee, aged fourteen, appeared in a strapless pink satin rhinestone-studded gown, deter-mined to steal her sister's thunder.

Jackie was not entirely popular with her fellow debutantes, and this was not, in fact, her first appearance at a society party. "I knew about her from her roommate, Sue Norton," Priscilla Johnson Macmillan remembered. "And, I remember, my first glimpse of her was at a Long Island coming-out party in, I think, June 1946, when I spotted her in some marble hallway, coming out of the ladies' room. I knew enough about her to know that she was sixteen when the rest of us were seventeen, that she was pushing it a bit going to coming-out parties a year early. Also, I thought she was a little too well dressed for our dowdy fashioned world. She was a wee bit stylish and the rest of us hadn't mastered that yet."[4] A Baltimore girl whose parents summered in Newport remembered, "I used to hear stories from people who were her age who came out with her, found her terribly glam-orous but not particularly nice to other girls who were doing the same thing."[5]

The word "different" crops up again and again in the reminiscences of Jackie's WASP contemporaries: "I remember seeing her once when she was a debutante and I was at the Grosvenor Ball and she was wearing an emerald-green satin dress, which was strapless with a huge hoop in it, and she walked down a flight of stairs and I remember catching my breath because she was so regal, it was as though she was so different from the rest of us, I mean there was something about her that was just amazing. And I've never forgotten that moment."[6]

Jackie had developed an outer shell, a reserve that protected her from people she did not want in her life. Some Newporters of her own age found her shy and aloof, a remote princess descending from her castle on the hill. Asked if she was popular at parties, Columbus O'Donnell, a contemporary who knew her in her early Newport years, said, "Well, she was a bit standoffish, you know, she wasn't a bubbling teenager by any means, she was very serious and she was very bright and she wasn't just interested in men, like a lot of the other girls were at Newport. She was, I think, interested in her family and books and more serious things than just going out on dates."[7] R. "Zup" Campbell James, an Auchincloss cousin, remembers sitting out dances with Jackie at her request so that they could talk about Sartre: "Sometimes," he recalled, "I would have preferred a little less seriousness and a little more partying . . ."[8]

The vein of seriousness in Jackie surfaced in the correspondence between herself and Yusha, her chief confidant in those years, the recipient of her thoughts and feelings. They both kept diaries and compared them. One feature was their shared passion for Merrywood, where they would sit on Lookout Rock above the river at dusk smoking, with the brown river shimmering though the ghostly dogwood trees.

"You really write very well and I feel that I could almost be listening to you," Yusha told her. ". . . It is so much like you that you really are talking from your heart which is one of the many things I love about you."[9]

From New York, where she was staying with Black Jack, Jackie wrote to Yusha of how much she was enjoying her sixteen-year-old preppy social life, going up to New Haven with their crowd for the Yale-Harvard football game, and back to New York to change and dine in the Maisonette Room of the St. Regis, then dance at La Rue.

When it came to dating, Jackie and Yusha, who was now at Yale, operated what Yusha called "our intelligence-gathering system . . . each introducing the other to friends and classmates. . . ." If Jackie happened not to have an escort for a football game or a dance, Yusha would fill in "with the agreement that I might return alone, but she was never left behind. We had lots of mutual friends, and we had a wonderful time and lots of fun later gossiping about who said what to whom, where and why . . ."[10] Jackie loved dancing; she and Yusha used to imitate Fred Astaire and Ginger Rogers, waltzing with a fast spin, doing the fox-trot and the rumba, but failing to master the samba and the tango. She liked to shuffle and tap to "Tea for Two," to listen to records on the big Victrola, pedal out the music on the pianola or listen to the latest pop songs on the radio hit parade. At Newport, after parties, she would bring a favored boyfriend back for scrambled eggs and music on the Victrola, but the flirtation never went beyond a chaste kiss. Her letters to Yusha mention particularly Bev Corbin but there were plenty of other beaux, including Ronnie Dick; the Isham brothers, John and Heywood; Peter Vogt. Jackie, however, found older boys more interesting in the summer of 1945, and was disappointed when her mother refused to let her go out with naval officers at Newport.

Foremost among the "older boys" was Charles Whitehouse, son of the Newport grande dame Mrs. Sheldon Whitehouse. "Jackie was crazy about Charlie Whitehouse when they were young," his cousin Susan Mary Alsop said. "He may have grown fond of her later but I don't think he was in love with her at all."[11] As well as being older than her regular admirers at Newport, Charlie was a great horseman, which made him even more attractive to Jackie. "I was about twenty-four, I was back from the war, and I think it must have been the summer of 'forty-five that I met her for the first time," he recalled. "She was about sixteen. And then I didn't see her much until maybe the summer after that, and then we rode together. They had horses up there [at Hammersmith]. Then I saw her more in 'forty-seven. I finally graduated from Yale and came down to Washington that fall and was hunting down there, staying with family friends—but, of course, on weekends only. And then we used to go to the movies and have dinner together and that kind of thing, down in Washington, 'forty-seven, 'forty-eight . . ." Sometimes Jackie stayed with the Whitehouses at El Destino, their plantation near Tallahassee in northern Florida. Some of her friends thought she would have liked to marry Charlie Whitehouse but he denies there was any serious romance: "I was very fond of her and I don't think she was in a mood particularly to get married, and I wasn't at the time, but we did see a lot of each other and were very fond of each other, and that fondness continued over the years."[12]

Jackie's Newport summer of 1947 was the prelude to the full-blown grandeur of the debutante season in New York later in the year, but before that, she started at Vassar, one of the most prestigious of the women's colleges. Vassar equaled intelligence, money and class. Jacqueline Bouvier of Miss Chapin's and Miss Porter's, Newport and Maclean, Virginia, fitted the bill perfectly. Intellectually, she was more than up to Vassar standard, having scored in the highest percentile in her college board exams. Founded in 1861 by Matthew Vassar, a millionaire local brewer, the institution was intended as "a College for young women which shall be to them what Yale and Harvard are to young men." No expense had been spared on the creation of a magnificent campus with buildings by the most celebrated architects in a variety of styles—Second Empire, Romanesque, Tudor, Arts and Crafts—and beautifully landscaped grounds. Great anxiety had been expressed by the founder that the progressive concept of a boarding college for young women should not imply any stigma on their "purity," a vision aided by the isolation of its position on the outskirts of the small industrial town of Poughkeepsie on the Hudson, far from the fleshpots of New York and, perhaps even more important, from the potential male temptations of Princeton, Yale and Harvard. (This, for Jackie, would eventually prove an unacceptable drawback.) There was a strong feminist streak in the faculty—members never used their married names—and there was a distinct divergence of aims between them and their students: while the staff viewed education as preparation for a career, principally in academic teaching, the majority of the postwar generation of students saw marriage as their ultimate goal. Like so many women of her generation, Jackie was to be faced with the hard choice between her intellect and the safe haven of marriage.

Her initial reaction to Vassar was positive: she enjoyed the freedom and responsibility after the more regimented life at Farmington. She loved all her courses, and extras like dramatics, the college newspaper and, of course, riding.

She was working toward a degree in literature, and took particular pleasure in the Shakespeare class with an inspirational teacher, Helen Sandison. She took courses in studio art and in art history, an area in which Vassar was particularly strong.

Jackie had apparently planned to room with Nancy Tuckerman, who at the last moment did not go to Vassar. Instead, Edna Harrison was put with Jackie—"Someone said to us both that it was because we were both Catholics." They took Spanish together. "I was struggling like mad . . . she whizzed through the class, she got all A's and she was just trying to coach me through it. She was very good at languages." They collaborated on a book: "I was taking child studies and I had to write a children's book—so she did the illustrations and I wrote it." Edna remembers that time with fondness: "She really was great fun and she loved people. I have a lot of letters that she wrote me. I lived in Hawaii in the summers and so she would write me when she was doing her thing and I was doing mine, and I look back on them—they're just so full of humor and such fun."[13]

Jackie took her roommate to spend weekends with her father in New York or with the Auchinclosses at Merrywood. Of Black Jack, Edna said, "He was divine, very dashing, and you could see where she [Jackie] got some of her mischievous sense of humor. If I was dressed up and ready to go out on time, he said, 'Oh, you should never be ready on time, that's just ridiculous, you should always make a young man wait!' He always said, 'Play the game.' And, of course, I was too naïve—this was about my first real date anyway so I was just thrilled to be asked out by this divine Princetonian—so I was all ready and dressed and sitting on the edge of my seat—I'll never forget it, 'You can't be so eager, you must make them wait!' "[14] Staying with Black Jack in his simple New York apartment, she remembered, was much more fun than the grandeur of Merrywood, where maids unpacked your suitcase and the table talk was of horses' bloodlines. Janet and Hughdie she found "rather austere."

Jackie was a star at the debutante balls of the New York winter season, the Junior League and the Grosvenor balls, the Tuxedo Ball. Her launch into the marriage market, which was essentially the object of the debutante season, made her father apprehensive: "I suppose it won't be long until I lose you to some funny-looking 'gink' who you think is wonderful because he is so romantic looking in the evening and wears his mother's pearl earrings for dress shirt buttons because he loves her so . . ." he wrote wistfully, in terms that were more like those of a lover than a father.[15]

His obsession with his daughters, especially Jackie, is recorded by the wife of his nephew Miche. Each night, after the sports and stock market statistics had been thoroughly discussed, Black Jack would "inevitably" get around to talking about them. When he heard Jackie was coming to visit, he would cancel all his previous engagements to concentrate on her. Once when Jackie called from the hairdresser to say that she had just had the latest short "poodle cut," her father was frantic at the thought that she might have spoiled her looks. He raced home from the Yale Club to await her appearance. "He was as obsessed with Jackie's poodle cut as he had ever been with the pursuit of a woman."[16]

As his girls grew up, Black Jack surveyed potential suitors with a stern eye. "He said," Lee Radziwill recalled, "like every time we saw him, 'All men are rats.' I can just hear him now. 'Someday when Lee grows up she'll listen to me, she'll know what I'm talking about. You just remember, Jacqueline, All Men Are Rats. Don't trust any of them.' Of course, there was no young man that was anywhere good enough for his daughters. So I remember staying with him at Christmas vacations and we used to go to various dances that all our friends from school went to and, you know, I'd start to get ulcers a week before about how he was going to look over and question this poor, pimply-faced creature who was coming to pick me up. And so did Jackie, she was very apprehensive about it. Nobody was good enough and, in a way, I think to a very small extent, Jackie took that to heart. I mean, remembered that in the back of her head. And I guess he felt that it was his obligation to warn us."[17] Another mantra was "Play hard to get, play hard to get."

Schooled by Black Jack, the sisters were irresistible to most men: the enthrallment of the male was a game they both played. "All of us used to be amazed," Pamela Harlech, a contemporary, recalled,[18] because these two girls would capture a man, I mean capture a man, and they'd sit on either side and they looked rapturously in this man's eyes but from both sides so he thought, My God, I hit pay dirt, these two glorious women think I'm wonderful . . ." When focused on a man, Jackie's gaze was magnetic: "When she flashed the beam on you it was a beam of great strength and brilliance. Like a lighthouse it could swing around," Lord Jenkins of Hillhead, a friend of later years, said.[19] "I remember that talking with her was very different," recalled George Plimpton, who at one time chased after Lee at Newport. "She sort of enveloped you—rare for someone of that age to be able to learn how to. She had a wonderful way of looking at you and enveloping you with this gaze. Never looking over your shoulder and seeing who's coming up next, you know. I do remember that from the very earliest talking to her."[20]

Jackie was learning the American geisha technique of attracting or, rather, not frightening men. Both sisters, and Jackie in particular, modulated their voices to a soft, whispering coo—"Yesss . . ."—projecting an unthreatening little-girl persona. "She underwent a major voice transformation," Shirley Langhauser, a schoolmate, said. "She didn't speak like that at Farmington. Her voice was quite normal, like everyone else's."[21] Clever women of the time learned to conceal their intelligence. "I remember a man telling Jackie he was afraid he was going to fail his exams," Zup Campbell James said, "and Jackie saying cooingly, 'I have that problem too,' knowing that she had succeeded."[22] A famous art director said memorably that Jackie was "the perfect geisha" because "you never, ever knew what she was thinking."[23] According to the art historian John Richardson, "Jackie was so amazingly winning and attractive. She did have this tremendous charm, that wonderful soft voice—I think pleasing was what she was about."[24] It was a technique she honed to perfection, which was particularly effective after she became famous, as one of her authors, Richard de Combray, whose books she edited at Doubleday, recalled: "She always talked about you, which is part of the geisha syndrome, and it was enormously appealing to sit opposite this woman who with all this baggage she carried, this fame and fortune, whatever, was totally absorbed by whatever it is you were saying to her, as if it was the most interesting thing she had ever heard . . . The trick was," he added, "that she never talked about herself—always about you."[25]

Male reaction to Jackie as a debutante was uniformly favorable. Sam Peabody, grandson of Endicott Peabody, the famous headmaster of Groton, sat beside Jackie when he was at Harvard during her debutante season. "I thought she was wonderful," he said, "beautiful, witty, sweet—and sexy."[26] She attracted even Gore Vidal, who exempted her from the contempt with which he regarded the rest of his Auchincloss siblings. Looking back on Merrywood days, Gore, who first met her in 1949, wrote, "Jackie, whose boyish beauty and life-enhancing malice were a great joy to me . . . a slyly humorous presence when she was in my life." Jackie's body was indeed androgynous: broad-shouldered, flat-chested, with long, muscular legs, large hands and feet. Only half joking, she confessed to him that her aim in life had always been "to be attractive to men." She was a subtle, practiced flirt; Vidal recalled in his memoir a moment of "erotic charge" when Jackie's bare leg (lightly and deliberately) brushed his.[27]

Jackie's attitudes toward both men and women were complex. She seemed to prefer the company of men, and earned the reputation of not liking women. But Black Jack's strictures, and the warning example of his behavior toward women, had taken root: men were there to be captured; they were prey, but they were also the enemy. They were targets to be courted but, in the circumstances of her time, they limited her potential. She needed their admiration and their money, but subconsciously resented that her beauty was directed and her intelligence suppressed to that end. "I think she appreciated men," an ex-admirer said, "but truly understanding them, liking them, is another matter."[28]

"Unlike Lee," said a woman connected with the Auchinclosses, "Jackie really did like some women. Her hostility was taken out on men, not women. Jackie liked to tease men," she continued, remembering their first meeting. "I was about eighteen. This glamorous creature came in. Lots of men wanted to talk to her but she came across to me and said, 'You're so and so and you're a wonderful writer,' and talked to me and ignored them. She'd do this often as a tease. She had so many sides," she went on. "She behaved very capriciously. She'd be very seductive to a man at a party, sitting next to him, and then stub out her cigarette on his hand."[29] Claude du Granrut (the former Claude de Renty), with whose family Jackie spent a year in Paris, commented, "Jacqueline had enormous strength of character, but she also had her weaknesses. It wasn't always easy for her. When you're the kind of person who wants only to be strong—well, she suffered from this. She couldn't accept her own frailties. Nor could she deal with frailties in others. She couldn't tolerate weak men . . . If she didn't esteem and admire a man, if she didn't look up to him, she dropped him immediately."[30]

On January 7, 1948, Jackie became a media celebrity overnight. Igor Cassini, alias Cholly Knickerbocker, syndicated society columnist for the Hearst Press, dubbed her "Queen Debutante of the Year 1947." In an age when Society still counted, this accolade put her almost on the level of a Hollywood star. In an article that first appeared in the *New York Journal-American* and was subsequently syndicated in Hearst publications across America, Cassini described Jackie as "a regal brunette who has classic features and the daintiness of Dresden porcelain. She has poise, is soft-spoken and intelligent, everything the leading debutante should be." Even Cassini was taken in by the aura of Auchincloss and Vassar: "Her background is strictly 'Old Guard,' " he wrote. Privately he stressed that his choice of Jackie did not follow his usual formula: normally he selected one of the prettier, flashier girls, but "I felt something very special in her, an understated elegance. Although shy and extremely private, she stood out in a crowd. She had that certain something, I don't know precisely what word to use to describe this quality: beauty, charm, charisma, style, any or all of the above. Whatever it happened to be, she had it."[31]

With the acquisition of her title as Debutante of the Year, the rise of Jacqueline Bouvier had reached a significant new level. After the heady atmosphere of the New York Season, all-girl Vassar seemed stuffy. Jackie was increasingly irked by the feeling that she was, as she wrote, "a schoolgirl among schoolgirls." She rarely spent a weekend at college and never seemed part of its world. After Jackie's death, when her class attempted to gather reminiscences of her time there, she was remembered as "a member of our class but distanced from it." (One woman, however, who scarcely knew her, recalled Jackie's kindness in lending her notes from their history class when she was in the infirmary so that she could keep up with her academic program.[32]) Contemporaries remarked on her shyness and reserve, the elusive quality that prevented them from getting close to her. She kept a photograph of Black Jack beside her bed, but never mentioned him or her family circumstances. She never took part in the girly conversations about boys that absorbed her classmates.

There were exceptions to Jackie's distancing rule—Edna Harrison, Puffin Gates and Shirley Oakes among others—but to the majority of her classmates Jackie made it clear that shared classes did not mean shared lives. Eugenie Aiguier, who knew Jackie through their mutual friend Shirley Oakes,[33] wrote, "She struck me as exceedingly and deliberately selective of her friends." In the summer of 1951 Shirley and Eugenie traveled to Europe together; in Pamplona for the running of the bulls, they met Jackie and Lee. "It was very clear to me that Jackie wanted to be with Shirley, not me. Shirley was her friend."[34] Six years later Shirley, for some undisclosed reason, was struck off Jackie's list. Jackie's closed circle was difficult to enter: once in, you had lifetime membership but you could be expelled without appeal for some perceived misdeed.

In July and August 1948 Jackie went on her first trip to Europe; significantly, it was a time she usually spent with her father. This trip came, as did everything glamorous in Jackie's life at this time, through the Auchincloss connection. Edward M. Foley Jr., then Under Secretary of the Treasury, was a friend of Janet and Hughdie's, and two of his stepdaughters, whom Jackie already knew, were planning a trip to Europe with another friend. Foley suggested Jackie accompany them, and the efficient Janet persuaded Jackie's former Latin teacher at Holton Arms to act as chaperone. Jackie wrote Yusha an excited letter about going to

Europe with a "heavenly" chaperone who would let them do anything they wanted. Yusha met up with her in Paris and took her to a nightclub at which she was "goggle-eyed"; Paris seemed all "glamour, glitter and rush" and there was hardly time to do anything extracurricular. It was a packed, hurried seven-week excursion—London, Paris, Provence, the Riviera, Switzerland and Italy. For Jackie, the highlight was seeing her wartime hero, Winston Churchill, at a Buckingham Palace garden party: she stood in the reception line twice for the repeated thrill of shaking the great man's hand. Europe, and Paris in particular, were to be high on her agenda for the next three years. Her one idea seems to have been to escape Vassar.

"She was thrilled to be able to get out in the sophomore year [1949–50], which many did," Puffin Gates recalled. Puffin and Jackie, who shared art-history classes and lived on the same hallway at Vassar, planned to join a Smith College course at the Sorbonne but Puffin dropped out of the trip to marry Derry D'Oench. Jackie wrote her a comic poem on the occasion: "Instead of boating on the Seine, alas, Puffin's floating down the drain in Pittsfield Mass," warning her of all she was going to miss of her bachelor-girl life: "She'll remember New York and those nights at the Stork, when she squealed like a deb at the pop of a cork, the train ride down to UVA, when she was met with candy and flowers so gay, football games at Yale, Sunset Lake in May . . ."[35]

Characteristically, Jackie had enlisted the influential help of Uncle Lefty Lewis, who wrote to Smith recommending her as a member of their Paris group: "As you no doubt have gathered from her scholastic record, she has a brilliant mind. What may not appear is that she is an exceptionally attractive girl and one that can be entirely depended on. If you accept non-Smith girls I cannot imagine one more eligible for this privilege."[36] By spring 1949 it was settled. In May Jackie wrote to Yusha that she was planning to spend the early summer rushing around to weddings, and then part of July with her father. Pictures in the *Social Spectator* show her dressed as a gypsy "modeling summertime fashion" at the LVIS Fair at East Hampton on July 29, accompanied by Black Jack, immaculate in a pale gabardine suit.[37] Just under a month later, on August 23, she left for Paris. She did not plan to return until the following July, in time for the exclusive Washington society function, the Dancing Class.

Jackie spent September in Grenoble, where the group boarded with a family of impoverished aristocrats and attended a language course at the university. In October she arrived in Paris to begin the course at the Sorbonne. With two other girls from the group, she lodged with an aristocratic French family living in relatively reduced circumstances at 78 Avenue Mozart at the un-chic end of the smart 16th arrondissement. Both parents had been members of the French resistance; Comte de Renty had died in a Nazi concentration camp. His widow, the Comtesse, had a maid but liked to cook for the household of seven—her three daughters, including divorced twenty-three-year-old Ghislaine, with her "fiendish" four-year-old son, Christian, and the youngest, Claude, Jackie's own age, who became a lifelong friend, Jackie and two other girls from the Smith group.

Not a word of English was spoken in the de Renty household and Jackie saw few other Americans. As usual, she had some excellent contacts and was soon moving in the highest French social circles. "I really lead two lives," she wrote to Yusha, "flying from here [78 Avenue Mozart] to the Sorbonne and Reid Hall [the center for the American students' courses] in a lovely, quiet, gray rainy world or like the maid on her day out putting on a fur coat and being swanky at the Ritz Bar." With her courses late in starting, Jackie plunged enthusiastically into Parisian life. "The most wonderful thing here is all the theaters and operas and ballets and how easy they are to get to," she told Yusha. "You could go out every night all winter and still not have seen everything that is playing." It was just the beginning of her social life. "I think things will get very gay soon and as I know quite a lot of French people the winter should be heavenly . . ."[38]

During the Christmas vacation, Jackie spent some time in London visiting Black Jack's former lover, Ann Plugge, and her family in their handsome, ex-Rothschild house at 5 Hamilton Place. Ann and her husband Leonard, perforce, were reconciled and, since her return to England in the spring of 1943, she had borne him twins, a boy and a girl, on November 4, 1944. Jackie seems to have believed that they were fathered by Black Jack and had written to tell him so on January 6, 1950. "You are dead right about the Plugge twins," Black Jack wrote back on January 10. "They definitely could not be his and there is no question about it . . ."[39] But there was, indeed, no question that they could have been his: the twins were born sixteen months after Ann and her son had left the United States and, at the time of their conception, Black Jack had been going through one of his drying-out spells at the Silver Hill Foundation in Connecticut. Presumably Jackie thought that the five-year-old children, one of whom was dark and the other fair, were a year older than they actually were; she knew how much it would have pleased their father to think they were his. Jackie clearly felt warmly toward Ann, writing to her five years later, after she had missed seeing her on a brief visit she had made to London, that neither she nor Lee would forget the "heavenly times" they had enjoyed with Ann or her gaiety and beauty.[40] According to Frank Plugge, she lunched with them at Cannes in the summer of the year she had just left the Sorbonne.[41]

Jackie unfolded her future plans to her father in her letter of January 6. They made him distinctly nervous: "I see that you say something about going to Belgium next summer and maybe Ireland and all the different parts of France. Don't you ever intend to come home? You had better come home sometime if you know what is good for you, and then I honestly think you could write a book on your travels . . . Don't laugh this off . . . All you have to do is to take the time and you could get out a book that would be a best-seller . . ." He was thrilled that she did not intend hunting in Europe—she had injured a disc riding at home and had been forced to wear a back brace. "It would be such a fatal error to attempt hunting in Ireland or France, and then wind up with a disc that might bring you right back to this Country," he warned. "You will be able to hunt in Ireland someday, and France, especially if you marry a rich husband . . ." Jackie had already determined that she did not want to return to Vassar. Black Jack pleaded with her to change her mind: "You may hate the thought of going back to that damn Vassar, as you call it, but perhaps going back as a senior, and one who can relate all her travels, you may not find it half as bad as you think . . ."[42]

Over the Christmas period, as well as visiting the Plugges in London, Jackie had taken what she described to her father and to Yusha as a wonderful vacation in Austria and Germany, with the fun of traveling on second- and third-class trains, sitting up all night talking to people and hearing their stories. "When I went with Bow [Helen Bowdoin] it was just too luxurious and we didn't see anything," she told Yusha.[43] In Vienna the occupying Russians tried to take her in for questioning after she had photographed their building. They saw Hitler's eyrie at Berchtesgaden, and Dachau concentration camp. At the time, Jackie could not bring herself to mention the effect of Dachau in her letters, although apparently she talked about it to her Newport friend Vivi Stokes, now married to Count Crespi and living in Rome, who was horrified that she had even wanted to go there. "History," Vivi Crespi said. "She wanted to know . . ."[44]

Back in Paris she was going out with French boys from the de Renty circle, indignantly rejecting advice from America warning her not to marry a count, and protesting that she hadn't met any.

But that spring of 1950 Jackie met a number of counts, and one in particular. Through the Newport Whitehouse connection, among the first people she came to know was the dashing young Comte Paul de Ganay, the youngest of four Franco-Argentine brothers, rich aristocrats whose family owned the beautiful Château de Courances thirty-five miles south of Paris. "I was introduced to Jackie by a cousin of mine, Kiko Bemberg, who had known her in Rhode Island," de Ganay recalled, "and as I was studying at the Sorbonne at the same time, we used to go to the Sorbonne quite often together and meet there and have a coffee at the Brasserie Balthasar, which still exists next to the Sorbonne. Of course, as we used to see a lot of each other, we became good friends and I used to take her out to parties and she came out to the country for a weekend and we became intimate friends. She got to know a lot of my friends and was very popular, everybody loved her and she was asked to all the balls and at that time there were plenty of them." Paul de Ganay was described as a "beau" of Jackie's by Letitia Baldrige, Jackie's future White House aide, who was working at the French embassy in Paris at the time, while Demi Gates ventured that she had a "crush" on Paul. De Ganay was more than a little taken with her: "She was an exceptional personality," he recalled. "She had a very good sense of humor. She observed things very well but she always kind of put a bit of fun in the remarks. She used to talk about people . . . she was very friendly and always, always laughing, a very positive personality. She used to enjoy everything, she was very open to beauty and to any new sights she'd see. Sometimes people pass by things without noticing but she was a very good observer."

Once launched on the smart social scene with de Ganay, Jackie was an instant success. "I was going out with her fairly regularly at that time and I was asked to many parties," he said. "She came to these parties and she was invited again there—a good-looking, charming American girl who spoke very good French already. She made an effort so everybody was very happy to meet her and at that time there were very many parties so she was very much in demand." They met up that Easter on vacation in Madrid and visited Toledo together. De Ganay, a member of the international smart set, continued to see Jackie after she left Paris: "We stayed in touch," he said, "we remained very good friends until toward the end of her life. As I spent less time in the States, I saw less of her."[45]

More important, perhaps, for Jackie's future career as the high priestess of White House parties, she was introduced through Jessie Wood, a Vassar classmate whom she also knew from Newport, into the chic, amusing circle of Jessie's mother, the writer Louise (Lulu) de Vilmorin, at Château de Verrières. Louise knew everyone and invitations to her entertainments were sought after. "Everyone who counted wanted to have been there at least once," de Vilmorin's biographer wrote.

> The blue drawing room, a lantern-shaped room, was lit by four windows, took its name from the white-flowered blue material which covered the walls and the curtains. In front of each window there was a banquette and between the windows sofas, bergères and Louis XVI chairs. Tables of ebony carved like bamboo encrusted with blue and white japanese porcelain held paintings by her friends, her collection of malachite, silver birds and candlesticks with lighted candles. The walls were hung with family portraits and a huge equestrian portrait of Louis XIV. No one talked politics; the conversation was witty, champagne and delicious wine flowed. Louise liked to dine by the light of candelabra; sometimes she read her poetry aloud. The food was exquisite and the atmosphere relaxed. Louise invited dancers, painters, writers, the odd foreign millionaire, movie magnates, celebrated directors, only very occasionally politicians.[46]

The parties included people like Orson Welles, Aly Khan and Rita Hayworth, Pamela Churchill (later Hayward, then Harriman) and Elie de Rothschild, Jean Cocteau, Max Ophuls, René Clair, Jean Anouilh and Bernard Buffet. Lulu had recently been the mistress of the British ambassador, Duff Cooper, husband of the famous Lady Diana, and was to be the lover of André Malraux, whom Jackie entertained in her White House days. Jackie often spent the entire weekend there, invited by her friend Jessie. Observant as she was, she absorbed every detail of Lulu's sophisticated, lighthearted parties, experiences she drew upon as hostess in the White House.

Jackie arrived in Paris when high-society Parisian life was bursting gloriously out of the confinements of the war years, when, as de Ganay said, there were parties, parties, parties and spectacular balls with decor by artists like Christian "Bébé" Berard, a member of the Verrières circle. "Never, since the Age of Enlightenment," wrote Prince Jean-Louis de Faucigny-Lucinge, "has society found itself so close to artists."[47] Society leader Comte E'tienne de Beaumont went to enormous lengths in the preparation of great costume balls, even to the extent of rehearsing his guests. At his Bal des Rois in January 1949, costumes for groups of people entering together were designed by artists like Jean Cocteau or Marie Laurencin, and made up by Dior or Chanel. Paul's mother, the Comtesse de Ganay, went as the Empress Josephine in a costume designed for her by top couturier Jacques Fath, and Violet Trefusis (great-aunt of Camilla Parker Bowles) came as Queen Victoria, from whom she claimed (wrongly) to have been descended through her mother Alice Keppel's affair with Edward VII.

Paris was fun at every level; that year brought the first great postwar influx of Americans attracted by the cheapness of the shopping, restaurants and entertainment. The American influence introduced the "cocktail hour" from six to eight-thirty; at the Ritz bar, a favorite of Jackie's, André Guillerin, the barman, was famous for his champagne cocktails. For those who, like Jackie, could understand the language, the Parisian theater in the autumn of 1949 had a great deal to offer. The Ballets de Monte Carlo, produced by the Marquis de Cuevas (father of Elizabeth de Cuevas, one of Jackie's debutante friends and contemporaries) opened its autumn season with Tamara Toumanova and Rosella Hightower. Marlon Brando was in Paris frequenting the nightclub Le Boeuf sur le Toit, with Juliette Greco and Eartha Kitt, and Josephine Baker was making a dazzling comeback at the Folies-Bergère. Parisian nightclubs offered greater variety than anywhere else in the world: female impersonators in fabulous costumes at the Carousel, homosexuals and lesbians at La Vie en Rose (nicknamed the "meat parlor"), White Russian clubs with caviar and gypsy violinists, informal jazz clubs on the Left Bank. Jackie, naturally, had embassy contacts too. The U.S. ambassador, the Hon. David Bruce, and his beautiful, chic wife, Evangeline, became members of Jackie's White House circle in Washington; Letitia Baldrige was then on the embassy staff.

After her exams finished on June 16, Jackie continued her European social life with a party given in London on the nineteenth for her Vassar classmate Shirley Oakes, returning to Paris on June 22 to meet Yusha at Orly. For two weeks they toured Paris, the Louvre, the Eiffel Tower, the banks of the Seine, where, she told Yusha, she used to sit, copying the Impressionists, drawing her own versions of Monet, Manet, Degas and even Picasso, the Bois de Boulogne, the Tuileries, dining at Maxim's and eating pressed duck at the Tour d'Argent. She introduced him to those of her friends who had not left Paris for the beaches, particularly Solange Batsell, an American-educated French friend of Claude de Renty. Solange, practicing as a lawyer in Paris after graduating from Bennington College in Vermont, remained close to Jackie for the rest of her life. Solange and Yusha motored together through the South of France, ending up at St.-Jean-de-Luz, where they were to meet Jackie and Claude.

Jackie spent a few days in the South of France with an aristocratic French family before joining Claude in Lyon for a leisurely tour, sightseeing and staying with Claude's friends and relations before arriving in St.-Jean-de-Luz, where a mutual friend, Gordon Coons, had rented the Château de Borda Berri. He had invited a group of friends to stay—apart from Jackie, Yusha and Solange, there were Diana Vreeland's son, Frecky, who had come across from Pamplona, and Puffin

Gates's brother Demi, was staying in his mother's hotel suite at Zarauz, across the border in Spain. "I came across the border to see the group," recalled Demi, "they were friends of mine, and that was when I fell madly in love with Jackie. There was a summer nightclub in the St.-Jean-de-Luz Casino and—you know—violin music, everything. There was no way I was not going to fall in love with her . . ."[48] It was a romantic summer; inevitably Yusha fell for Solange. Jackie and Claude drove the couple to Bordeaux, then continued their sightseeing *en route* back to Paris to rejoin Yusha.

Jackie had now been abroad for more than a year and still put off her return home to her old life. She and Yusha planned to travel in Ireland, England and Scotland during August, beginning with the Dublin Horse Show, the great social event of the Irish calendar. "I hope you'll say yes," she had written to Yusha in May, "as I'd like to stay over as long as possible as a whole month in Newport would be pretty dull . . ."[49] When they arrived in Dublin, the horse show was ending but the hotels were still full and they had nowhere to stay. They called Father Leonard, a friend of the Wilmarth Lewises', only to be told by "a senile creature in broken Gaelic" that he had left the country. Jackie being Jackie, they called the embassy and another Auchincloss contact found them a room "in the most heavenly little hotel." Father Leonard turned up the next morning clutching three boxes of candy for Jackie and cigarettes for Yusha and took them to see Dublin. They rode in Phoenix Park, lunched at the embassy and were sent sightseeing in the embassy car. Later the chauffeur took them to the theater and came back on his own initiative afterward with his friend Paddy to take them to their pub. After closing time the owner took them down to the cellar and let them pull corks out of the kegs of Guinness to see the dark liquid spurt up into the air and sang them Irish songs. The worldly Father Leonard gave them lunch at Jammet's, the fashionable French restaurant whose chef had been the chef at the Vice-Regal Lodge, with an unworldly but handsome colleague who invited them to stay with him in England to see Uncle Lefty's holy of holies, Horace Walpole's Strawberry Hill. That morning they had visited the Prime Minister, Patrick Costello, who gave them seven signed books on Ireland. They rounded off the day with Shaw's *The Doctor's Dilemma* at the Abbey Theater. They toured literary and Georgian Dublin; Jackie raved about the superb plasterwork interiors and elegant doors. Then they took off for three days in a car loaned by the hotel owner to Limerick, where they had tea with Nellie Curtain, a retired Auchincloss cook, in her thatched cottage by a turf fire, and to Killarney and Cork. According to Yusha, Jackie knew of her Lee family Irish roots and was as proud of them as she was of her French blood. Bewitched, as so many foreigners are, and as Father Leonard had warned them they would be, they didn't want to leave Ireland.

They crossed to Scotland, pursued by a lovestruck Demi Gates, for whom Jackie left teasing and misleading messages. Jackie outfitted Yusha as Sherlock Holmes in deerstalker and Inverness cape, as well as a Royal Stewart tartan kilt. They visited all the usual sights, particularly castles which Jackie loved, Edinburgh and Stirling, then traveled to London, where they went to the Tower and

Windsor Castle. Jackie can hardly then have dreamed that not so many years later she would be entertained to tea at Windsor by the Queen and dine with her at Buckingham Palace.

Together, Jackie and Yusha sailed for home in the liner *Liberté*. With her horizons broadened by her European experiences, Jackie remained determined, to her father's dismay, not to return to Vassar and a further year's exile in Poughkeepsie, and enrolled instead that autumn at George Washington University in Washington. Reverent fans' fingers have blurred Jackie's signature in Vassar's Matriculation Book, rather as the toe of St. Peter's statue in his Roman basilica has been worn down by the lips of generations of pilgrims. It is the only relic of her time at Vassar: by 1975 the file of correspondence pertaining to her was missing. Documents relating to alumnae are carefully preserved in a basement under the supervision of an archivist, the Keeper of the Crypt. It is highly unlikely that Jackie's file would have been lost or thrown away; as Frances Daly Fergusson, the president of Vassar, says, "We tend to keep people forever."[50] The rumor was that it disappeared at the time of John F. Kennedy's nomination as presidential candidate in 1960. Could it be that Jackie regarded her failure to complete her course at Vassar as something faintly discreditable? She never made any secret of her dislike of her time there, perhaps blaming the college rather than herself for what amounted to a failure to fulfill intellectual promise. She never attended class reunions, turning her back definitively on the past, as was her wont.

Part of Black Jack's disappointment lay in the implications of Jackie's decision to return to the Auchincloss fold: he had hoped that she might come and live with him in New York and work in his office. Not only was she now based permanently at Merrywood but Janet had encouraged her to enter *Vogue*'s annual Prix de Paris competition, the prize being a year working as a junior editor for six months in the Paris office and six months in New York.

Jackie's entries for the competition provide an insight into how she saw herself and her lifestyle at the time.

> As to physical appearance, I am tall, 5'7", with brown hair, a square face and eyes so unfortunately far apart that it takes three weeks to have a pair of glasses made with a bridge wide enough to fit over my nose. I do not have a sensational figure but can look slim if I pick the right clothes. I flatter myself on being able at times to walk out of the house looking like a poor man's Paris copy, but often my mother will run up to inform me that my left stocking is crooked or the right-hand top button about to fall off. This, I realize, is the Unforgivable Sin.

The three men she would have chosen to meet reflected her Paris experiences: the poets Charles Baudelaire and Oscar Wilde, and the Russian ballet impresario Sergey Diaghilev, unusual choices for a well-brought-up twenty-year-old American girl. Of Baudelaire and Wilde she wrote, "Both were poets and idealists who could paint their sinfulness with beauty and still believe in something higher." Diaghilev she admired for his ability to represent the interaction of the arts and of the cultures of East and West, his genius for choosing the best and producing a masterpiece, however transient. "If I could be a sort of Overall Art Director of the Twentieth Century, watching everything from a chair hanging in space, it is their theories that I would apply to my period, their poems that I would have music and paintings and ballets composed to," she wrote.

Her choice of clothes revealed the kind of life she had become used to: a gray suit as uniform for traveling, shopping, lunches and art exhibitions; dressed up with a velvet hat with a veil and a huge fur muff, it could go "cocktailing" or out for a "non-dressy evening in the city." A sleeveless plaid dress teamed with a black turtleneck blouse bought for the gray suit could "cope with Sunday afternoons at college followed by dinner in town, or with Sunday lunch at his family's house in the country." The black top and orange taffeta skirt "would see me through after football game dances in fraternity houses when the boys don't dress, and through dinner, theater and dancing dates in the city . . ." Jackie suggested a men's fashion section directed not at men but at women, writing somewhat patronizingly, "It seems to me that any woman would welcome a few pointers on men's clothes. She is eager to brighten up her husband's wardrobe but does not know how to go about it without descending to the robin's egg blue garbardine suit and hand painted tie level . . ."

Attracting and titillating men was the hook for Jackie's perfume promotion: "Perfume was just as effective in piquing the male olfactory glands before our era of adjective-laden advertisements. Why not quote the poetry it has inspired?" she wrote. "It is also analogous to wine. Both are liquids that act upon the closely related senses of taste and smell to produce an intoxicating effect. Wine has had an even stronger appeal in literature . . ." She suggested a layout featuring bottles of perfume in a wine rack, labeled as if they were vintages—most effective in black-and-white photography with the black depths of the compartments pointing up the reflections of the glass bottles. The right-hand page—also with black background—would show some strewn flower petals, a thin stemmed crystal wineglass with the blurred suggestion of a woman (a long neck, an earring—her hand) pouring perfume out of a Diorama bottle into the glass.

Vogue's reaction to her entry was enthusiastic: on April 25, 1951, the Prix de Paris director, Mary E. Campbell, wrote to Jackie congratulating her on being one of the finalists and inviting her to the final selection panel in New York, featuring, among other events, a dinner given for the contestants by *grande dame* and editor in chief Edna Woolman Chase at the Cosmopolitan Club on May 10. Jackie's response was to cable that as her final comprehensive examinations were scheduled for the ninth, tenth and eleventh she would not be able to make it. "Am thrilled at being in the finals and hope this will not disqualify me." Mary Campbell wrote back the next day by return, begging her to fly up to New York at any time within the next two weeks for a meeting at her convenience. "As we all feel that you had one of the most interesting papers submitted, I am sure you can understand our desire to meet the writer." Jackie arranged to fly up on May 3 to see Miss Campbell for lunch. The meeting was a success: on May 15, 1951, Jackie received a letter from Mrs. Chase informing her that she had won first prize out of 1,280 applicants from 225 women's colleges. "Can't believe I have won Prix will be in New York all day Monday may I come in and see you will call you Monday morning," a breathless Jackie cabled on May 18.[51]

On Monday, May 21, she saw Mary Campbell, filled in an application form and posed for studio photographs. She gave her mother's name as next of kin to contact in the event of an emergency, Merrywood as her permanent address, and Virginia as the state in which she had been resident since 1942.

On June 7, 1951, almost immediately after signing up for *Vogue*, Jackie set sail for Europe again, this time with Lee, on the *Queen Elizabeth* (third class, from which they escaped daily to first). The trip was a graduation present from the Auchincalosses to Lee, who had, as she put it, "survived three years at Miss Porter's School only because of the inspiration of my history of art teacher, Miss Sarah McLennan." Lee had conceived a passion for the Italian Renaissance. At the age of fifteen she had written a fan letter to the celebrated art historian and connoisseur Bernard Berenson, to which the great man had replied, and she was determined to go to Florence to meet him.[52] The sisters wrote an account of their trip, "One Special Summer," illustrated by Jackie, as a thank you for Janet and "Unk," who financed it and paved the way with introductions everywhere. In London they went to a cocktail party given by a friend of Janet's, Jane du Boulay, who was married to an Englishman, Guy du Boulay, and bought for £500 a little Hillman Minx car, which they drove to Paris, then on to Poitiers, where Paul de Ganay was doing his military service. The arrival of these two beautiful girls wearing strapless sundresses in the middle of army maneuvers caused a huge stir among the military. "They're sensational, your friends, de Ganay," his commanding officer told him. "Are you engaged?"

"Yes, Lieutenant, to both of them," de Ganay said, saluting back.

Crossing the Spanish border, they made for Pamplona and the bull-running festival among crowds of other Hemingway-inspired young Americans. According to their account, they even got up at 5:30 A.M. to take part, with a vociferous friend, Ace Williams, thundering behind them quoting *Death in the Afternoon* and one of Jackie's favorite books, *The Sun Also Rises*. An English friend of Janet's happened to be there when Jackie caused a sensation at a bullfight: "Somebody'd given them those wineskins and it went all down her shirt, which became rather transparent," Baroness Trumpington recalled, "and somebody made a rude remark about that and someone else defended her and there was a free fight in the bullring, which was quite dramatic."[53] Shirley Oakes, with whom she had spent an Easter vacation on her parents' Nassau estate that year, was also there, as were two other friends, Mike Forrestal (later an aide in the Kennedy White House) and Ed Tuck. Jackie and Lee liked to collaborate in teasing men: they offered Forrestal and Tuck a lift in their car the following morning but when the two men arrived panting at the hotel at the appointed hour, they found that the sisters had left early at eight-thirty.[54]

In Madrid, the Marqués de Santo Domingo—"the only person allowed to walk on the town walls of Avila because he owned them"—showed them his celebrated painting of the Madonna. While Jackie showered him with compliments in Spanish, Lee, characteristically, whispered in her ear, "Gee, if it's worth that much money why doesn't he sell it?" Princes Christian and Alfonso Hohenlohe took them out to their country house, El Quexigal, a sixteenth-century former monastery: "We sat in Columbus' chair—tiptoed around tables full of crown jewels—gaped at pictures signed love George V and just felt we should be taking notes for History of Art 105," Jackie wrote, "but all they wanted to do was make Ma and Pa change the vic[trola] while we jitterbugged to 'Wave the Green for Old Tulane' underneath the Flemish primitives." Then it was over the Pyrenees to Provence and the Riviera, to Venice and Florence, where the awestruck pair made a pilgrimage to visit Berenson at his villa, I Tatti. Lee noted down his conversation, which made a great impression on both of them. "Immediately talked to us of love . . . Never follow your senses—marry someone who will constantly stimulate you—and you him," the sage declared, advice that Jackie followed to the letter.[55]

One less successful visit they made was to Marlia, the spectacularly beautiful villa belonging to the Pecci Blunt family. Count Dino Pecci Blunt was half American and knew everyone (including John F. Kennedy). Lee and Jackie blotted their copybook by slipping out of the villa early without saying good-bye to their hostess, Dino's mother; hoping not to disturb her, instead they offended her. "I remember that Mother was always telling that story that they left without saying good-bye—we all joked about it," said one of Dino's sisters, Contessa Viviana Pecci Blunt.[56] Their youthful gaffe however, was, forgiven; both Lee and Jackie were to be guests at Marlia again. "It's All Over Now. September 15, 1951," Jackie captioned their photograph before the return to New York.

A portrait photograph of Jackie had appeared in the August 15, 1951, issue of Vogue as the first-prize winner of the Prix de Paris. Her resemblance to Black Jack was startling: thick dark, curly hair parted in the middle, heavy dark arching brows over wide-apart eyes, strong nose and finely cut sensual mouth. But it was Black Jack dressed as a deb: double strand of false (not old-money) pearls and a butterfly pin at the neck, dark cardigan outfit, gold bracelets and, the final touch, regulation short white gloves.

According to a friend, Jackie's stint at Vogue was brief. On her first day at work on the nineteenth floor of the Graybar Building, she was told to make herself at home beside the desk of fashion editor Bettina Ballard to get a sense of how the magazine was put together. About midmorning an affected homosexual male editor, with a strong European accent to complement his lofty title, pranced up to Mrs. Ballard's desk, which he dramatically covered with sage-green velvet, theatrically declaiming, "Bettina, darling, this is you!"

"Jackie said that was enough," a friend, who later went on to win second prize in the same Vogue competition, recounted. "Taking her pens out of the pencil cup, she packed up her handbag with the odds and ends that had come out of it, made her way around to the Condé Nast personnel office, and quit, thinking this was not the place to widen her circle of eligible males."[57] To the editors who had chosen her she gave as her official excuse for leaving that her mother "felt terrifically strongly about 'keeping me in the home.' "

The green-velvet episode merely brought to the surface what had already been at the back of her mind: she was not a person given to snap decisions. Jackie would never have given up the *Vogue* job if she had seen it as the way for her to go. The female and gay world of the fashion magazine, which was the most that girls like her could hope for, was not for her. Her European experience was in the past. Washington was rapidly becoming the world's power base. With her connections and the glamour of Merrywood in the background, Jackie would be perfectly placed to explore it.

CHAPTER FOUR

The Daring Young Man on the Flying Trapeze

For herself she foresaw a future as the circus queen who . . . married the [daring] young man on the flying trapeze.[1]

—Jackie's teenage prediction of her future

In the fifties Washington was a small town in which everybody of a certain social and political class knew one another or were bound to meet at some point. From the moment Jackie turned her back on *Vogue*, New York and Europe to focus on Washington, her destiny and that of John F. Kennedy began to converge.

After majoring in French literature at George Washington University, Jackie needed a job both to supplement her meager monthly allowance of fifty dollars and to get her out of the seclusion of McLean, Virginia, and into the center of Washington life. She wanted to make a career in writing and, like other women of that time, saw journalism as the way forward. She had always written poetry for herself and the family circle and recently some short stories based on personal experience, but lacked the confidence to try anything more ambitious. As usual, she used her connections to get what she wanted.

She turned to Arthur Krock, the influential chief of the *New York Times* Washington bureau, who was not only a social friend of the Auchinclosses' but also a paid media "fixer" for Joseph P. Kennedy, patriarch of the Kennedy clan, and totally devoted to his interest. Krock telephoned Frank Waldrop, editor of the *Washington Times-Herald*, a lively newspaper with few intellectual pretensions and a well-known provider of slots for pretty girls who did not need to make their fortune. "Are you still hiring little girls?" he asked. "Well, I have a wonder for you. She's round-eyed, clever and wants to go into journalism."[2] Among previous "little girls" hired by the paper had been John F. "Jack" Kennedy's favorite sister, Kathleen, or "Kick" as she was known, who had been killed in a plane crash in 1948, and his former lover, a beautiful, intelligent Danish blonde named Inga Arvad. Moreover, according to a member of Waldrop's family, old Joe Kennedy "had some long-standing involvements with the paper, mostly covert . . ."[3]

The *Times-Herald*'s hiring policy had been set by its previous proprietor, Eleanor Medill "Cissy" Patterson, a member of a powerful media dynasty, who had bought the paper from her friend William Randolph Hearst and infused it with her own lively style. By the end of the Second World War it outsold the more intellectual *Washington Post* and staid *Evening Star*. Cissy Patterson, who wrote novels and hunted big game, was a major figure on the Washington social scene, famous for the parties she gave at the ornate white marble mansion on Dupont Circle designed for her mother by Stanford White. Her interests—anti-vivisection, cute animal stories, social life and teasing the Roosevelts—were reflected on the pages of her paper. She liked tall beauties to decorate her parties and often employed them as journalists. "We like to hire the pretty girls around town," was the *Times-Herald*'s unofficial slogan, "the ones everybody wonders about: do they? And with whom?" "A steady stream of *ingénues* continued to turn up working for the paper," a contemporary of Jackie's connected with the *Times-Herald* remembered.

Few had newspaper experience. Freshness and style were valued over expertise. A slaphappy lack of skill was no handicap when other qualities were present. Learning on the job was definitely the way to go. Jacqueline Bouvier was certainly in this tradition; with her extremely pleasant, low-keyed manner, she had the gift of not taking herself seriously. Not as devastating-looking as most of the others, she was probably smarter, better educated, and she handled herself with more assurance. Her light touch was absolutely Mrs. P[atterson]'s kind of style, but her looks at that point were not up to the prevailing standard . . . She seemed tall and gawky, with the puppyish charm of feet and hands too big. Her face seemed spotty—not pimples but just a sort of uneven, tweedy look, a little "ridden hard and put away wet." She mocked her looks and complained of those wide-set eyes, saying the oculist could not find frames wide enough to go over the bridge of her nose . . .

Her work at the paper was what was categorized as a "pretty job," the sort held by lots of young women who might be well-connected, clever, pretty, rich, educated, lucky, or any combination of the above. The pay was inadequate so these "Tillie the Toilers" often lived at home and were subsidized by trust funds or Daddy. Jackie lived at home where she was in a pickle. Most of her relatives and extended family were seriously rich but she and Lee were not. That dainty kid sister was the beauty of the family . . . Jackie, as the older sibling, drew the task of all the responsibilities, of being the leader, the thoughtful one, the worrier about others. Her mother's shortcomings hit her hard. Jackie had brains and good taste—no mindless hedonism for her. Her strong religious instinct inclined her to seek a marriage within her church but it was difficult. She was born in a curious time: most of the Roman Catholics of good family had daughters, not sons. These flowers of the flock were going to have to marry down . . . or out. Jackie had figured this out. Like most young women who graduated from college in the early fifties, she expected a lot out of life; and at the top of the list was a suitable mate.

The job ought to serve as a vantage point from which to look. The restlessness of her search was evident. She wasn't desperate, she wasn't undone, but she was always dryly observant and aware of her dilemma. She was not just every young man's cup of tea, either. Her height diminished the number of potential suitors, for in the 1950s, few self-respecting young women were comfortable dancing with a shorter man, much less settling down with one. Her braininess distanced her from many in the "callow youth" category . . .[4]

Jackie's qualifications for the not-very-demanding job of Inquiring Photographer were a photography course she had taken at the Sorbonne and her schoolgirl work for *Miss Porter's Salmagundy*. When Sid Epstein, city editor on the *Times-Herald* detailed to interview her, told her they only employed experienced people, she replied, "I'm also a photographer and used a Leica at the Sorbonne." Epstein laughed: "Kid, we don't have anything that fancy. You'll use a Speed Graphic here. If you can learn how to use the Speed Graphic by tomorrow, I'll hire you." After a crash course with the staff photographer, Jackie came back the next day and was hired at twenty-five dollars a week beginning in January 1952.[5]

She was ambitious and, as she told Frank Waldrop, her editor, serious about making a career in writing. She spent her evenings that spring of 1952 working on a television script featuring a former First Lady, Dolley Madison, whose ghost she pictured haunting the Octagon House, which had been used as a temporary residence for the presidential couple after the burning of the White House in 1812. She envisaged the First Lady holding court at midnight, "in the meridian of life and queenly beauty," the focus of a "gay company" dancing to violins. She managed to interest one television company in the project but it never progressed beyond the proposal stage; the company went bankrupt.

Her inquiring camera-girl column was the type of job that might be dull or interesting depending on the angle the writer took. Jackie made it lively, venturing out on the streets with a list of carefully prepared questions. By March 26, 1952, she was established enough in her job to have earned her own byline as "Inquiring Fotografer." Later, she illustrated some of her pieces or interviews with her own comic line drawings. Her questions were personal, "Do you consider yourself normal?," or topical, "If you had a date with Marilyn Monroe what would you talk about?," often on marriage and relationships: "A Boston University professor said women should marry because they're too lazy to go to work"; "Do you think a wife should let her husband think he's smarter than she is?"; "Chaucer said that what most women desire is power over men. What do you think women desire most?"; "When did you discover that women are not the weaker sex?"[6] She showed an absorbing interest in the White House, according to her dressmaker, Mini Rhea, questioning the members of the press corps about the details of life within its walls. "Everything about the White House was exciting to her," Mini Rhea recounted.

Jackie at work, interviewing ordinary people in the streets and offices of Washington, was a very different creature from the regal vision, the "Dresden shepherdess," of her debutante days. Two of her interviewees, Mac McGarry and Everette Severe, working for WRC (the NBC affiliate in Washington), remember being asked by her, on April 21, 1952, "Are wives a luxury or a necessity?" "Six of us were picked at random," McGarry recalled. "We were all very excited when we heard that Jacqueline Bouvier was coming. She was very well known and her family were very prominent socially. She was slim, wearing her sunglasses on top of her head, and a long skirt, sort of New Look. She was very nice and charming, her voice didn't seem particularly soft. She was very efficient, took the photographs and took notes. I noticed her fingernails were bitten right down to the buff."

Severe remembers that "She was obviously in a hurry, late for her deadline, so afterward she said to me, 'Ev, come and help me compose this.' She sat on my desk with one leg on the floor, one swinging. She had on a long skirt, sort of nubbly tweed, and when she swung her leg you could see more than you normally could in those days. She had dark hair around her face and down to her shoulders but I didn't think she was that pretty—wide eyes and a big wide mouth like a baby bird. What impressed me was her energy and initiative. She had us all organized. I thought she might be worth dating but as she ran down the hall her skirt billowed and I saw her legs were bowlegged and I thought, 'Forget it.' " He also said that her voice was quite normal and that her personality was nothing like the one she later projected when she was in the White House. "When I met her, she was the kind of girl you could play stickball in the street with . . ."[7]

Jackie's Washington friends of the time remember her intelligence and personality rather than her looks. They also remember her ambition. Three had a Kennedy connection. Charles Bartlett, born in Chicago, was a young newspaperman who arrived in Washington in the winter of 1948 as a reporter for the *Chattanooga Times*, a southern newspaper owned by the *New York Times*, to set up his own bureau. He met Jackie and took her out often before she went to France: "She was an awful cute girl, she was a darling girl when she was young," he recalled. "She was smart, she was fresh, she was absolutely unspoiled. She lived as a stepchild in this rather ridiculous household. She had a marvelous sense of humor, totally unaffected by clothes, adornments, drove an old Mustang and she was marvelous fun."[8]

John White, who had been a star feature writer on the *Times-Herald* and was now at the State Department, became one of her escorts after she joined the paper. He had been more than a little in love with Kathleen Kennedy, who had shared an apartment with Inga Arvad, and the two of them had often doubledated with her brother Jack and Inga to screen the affair from father Joe Kennedy's spies. White was attracted to Jackie by what he saw as her "elfin qualities" but it was basically an intellectual friendship: "Jackie enjoyed talking about people and motives from a psychological point of view," he recalled. Although Jackie refused to talk about herself, she would tell him which women in history she identified with. Discussing Sappho, the Greek poet of Lesbos, Jackie admitted that she would "like to have lived long ago, and been unique, the very best in the world at her trade of poetry. And she approved the notion of living on a small re- mote island . . ." The two women she most identified with, he said, were Madame de Maintenon and Madame Récamier; significantly both were women of intelli- gence who derived their position from their hold over powerful men. Jackie liked the idea of holding a *salon* as Madame Récamier had: good conversation was im- portant to her. Also, White said, she "wanted to be the confidante of an important man. Even then her interest in people tended to be in direct proportion to their importance and their ability to amuse . . . Power and charisma seemed to override all other qualities in her estimation of people."[9]

Among John White's friends was William Walton, always known as Bill, the multitalented former war correspondent for Time-Life, who had flown on mis- sions with U.S. and British outfits and been billeted at the same English airfield as Joe Kennedy Jr., Jack's elder brother, and had known Kathleen in London. Among other wartime exploits, Walton had liberated the Ritz bar in Paris with Ernest Hemingway. He was an artist, and at the time he met Jackie—and Jack— divorced and living in Georgetown. He became a lifelong friend of both. Walton charmed everybody: "He was the most fun, absolutely the most fun, very, really brilliant, really sensitive, a total man of the world so that he didn't always take things at their face value and he could have his suspicions of people's reasons for doing things," Mary Bundy recalled.[10] Walton, like most of Jackie's friends, was older than she was. Jackie, he said, "sat worshipfully at the feet of me and a guy named John White . . . John White was a very literary ex-Marine who was just as eccentric as hell and great fun. And she thought we were just the most sophisti- cated men of the world that she'd ever met. He had a little apartment on Dumbar- ton and it was just lined with books. He was a real book freak. To Jackie, it was just a glimpse of another world. We thought she was just a wonderful-looking, kooky young reporter." It was around this time that Walton met both Jack and Jackie, but separately. "I was amazed when I heard they were going to get mar- ried. I didn't know they knew each other. I'd never been anywhere with the two of them at the same time. So it was really a bolt from the blue . . . Of course it was Charlie Bartlett who put them together . . ."[11]

Charlie Bartlett had first met John F. Kennedy in a Palm Beach nightclub at Christmas 1945, when Kennedy was seriously considering running for Congress in 1946. The Kennedy family had a house in Palm Beach, and the Bartletts had one at nearby Hobe Sound. With a similar war background, the two men became friendly, particularly when Bartlett arrived in Washington after Kennedy had been elected to Congress. Charlie Bartlett took it upon himself to play Cupid to Jackie and his friend Jack Kennedy: "I just thought she was a girl with extraor- dinary promise," he said, "and it seemed to me that she'd be a marvelous wife for just anybody. But it had to be somebody with a lot of sophistication even though, as I say, she was totally unspoiled at this point. Really very much a child of nature, as I knew her, with this wonderful imagination and this ability to draw and write and really a sort of basic *joie de vivre*, which was terrific. And I knew our friend Jack was running around—I thought it would be good for him . . . I didn't honestly realize that Jack was as much of a romancer as he turned out to be, I honestly didn't. I knew he liked girls but I didn't . . . I'm not sure I'd have pushed it if I realized that he was . . . that he had this, almost, disease . . ." The marriage, Bartlett was sure, would be the answer for both; it would settle Jack, stop him "running around," and provide Jackie with the sophisticated type of man she needed.[12]

Marriage, however, had not been in the air when she finally met Jack Kennedy at a small dinner party in Charles and Martha Bartlett's Georgetown house the previous summer. Jack muttered about having a drink together after the party but was frustrated by an unnamed beau of Jackie's, who on seeing her Mustang parked outside the Bartletts' home had climbed into the backseat to wait for her, to be discovered with shrill barks by the Bartletts' fox terrier. Shortly afterward, Jackie and Lee sailed for Europe; Jackie and Jack did not meet again for seven months.

For all Jackie's emphasis on her "seriousness" about her writing career, an anxiety about getting married was still there, the pressure increasing as time went on. The standard progression for college girls of her age was to get "the ring by spring," that is, to have a fiancé lined up in your senior year and marry after graduation. Beyond the age of twenty-five you were considered almost "on the shelf." By the time she began work at the *Times-Herald*, Jackie, aged twenty-two, was contemplating getting married, and by early January she was secretly engaged. The man was John Husted, tall, urbane, good-looking and, according to a younger girl who had a crush on him, "a terrific dancer." He had an impeccable WASP background: educated at the smart preparatory school Summerfield in England, then home to St. Paul's before going to Yale. He had done war service with the American armed forces attached to the British in Italy, France, Germany and India, and was now working on Wall Street. He was a member of the Yale Club and the Racquet and Tennis Club; his cousin Carol Husted and both his sisters had been at Farmington with Jackie. It seems that the engagement was a romantic, spur-of-the-moment affair. They met in Washington late in 1951, and by early January 1952 Husted had proposed to her in the Polo Bar off the Westbury and been accepted. Jackie wrote happily to the Wilmarth Lewises before the official engagement, thanking heavens that John wasn't the "sensible boy next door" that her mother thought she needed. With impeccable manners she also wrote to a former beau to tell him the news at first hand, that she had met the love of her life.

That certainty did not last long. By the time her photograph—in which she was sporting the "poodle cut"—appeared in the society pages of the *Times-Herald* on Monday, January 21, 1952, with news of her engagement, an event "of great interest to Capital society," and June wedding plans, she was already having second thoughts. Although Black Jack (whose name had not appeared in the official engagement announcement, although both sets of grandparents had been deemed worthy of mention) was delighted at the prospect of Jackie's marrying a Wall Street man and living in New York, the family at Merrywood was less enthusiastic. Lee remembers receiving a letter from Jackie about her engagement "which went on for an eternity." Of it, she said, "I don't really know what that was all about, if it was for the same reasons as myself of being extremely anxious to leave home at that age and start your own life, which I imagine was the case. And then I think perhaps it was helped by the fact that my mother didn't seem overjoyed by the idea . . ."[13] "Socially the Husteds were a perfectly proper family but they were nothing brilliant or exciting," an Auchincloss cousin said. "Janet was very apprehensive about it. She wanted Jackie to go right to the top. I think she was angry because it was quite apparent that Jackie wasn't very taken with this young man, wasn't in love with him. I think she thought, 'What's this all about?' "[14] Cecilia "Sherry" Parker Geyelin, daughter of Hughdie's partner in his brokerage house, described the engagement party at Merrywood as "a chilly affair . . . there was no warmth there. It was just a social gathering."[15]

Jackie was by now publicly expressing her doubts to friends and relations, including Zup Campbell James, Yusha's cousin, who remembers her sitting at his feet saying that she felt she was unsuited to marry John Husted.[16] The distinguished writer Louis Auchincloss, a member of the family, was told of the engagement with his brother John in Washington, when Jackie came to dinner with Janet and Hughdie: "After dinner, sitting with me in a corner, Jackie expounded to me what her life would be as the wife of a respectable young businessman in New York. She seemed to think it would be peaceful but dull. I had just published a novel called *Sibyl* about just such a woman's life and she kept saying emphatically, 'That's it. That's my future. I'll be a Sybil Husted.' I remember vividly my conviction that the woman telling me this was destined for a very different fate. Only days later we learned that the engagement was off."[17]

In mid-March, Jackie invited Husted to Merrywood for the weekend; at the air terminal where she dropped him for his return flight to New York, she took the engagement ring off her finger and slipped it into his pocket. "She didn't say much and neither did I," John Husted said. "There wasn't much you could say."[18]

"She had Johnny on a string and it was yes and no and yes and no and I will and I won't," a woman who knew Husted well commented. "And then Jack Kennedy came along, and he was dumped. It was that simple. He was devastated, Johnny, at that point. He soon recovered and married someone quite nice. But I remember him when she did dump him and he was really, really depressed. Because she didn't do it in a very nice way."[19] When the first authorized biography of Jackie came out, by Mary "Molly" Van Rensselaer Thayer, a journalist friend of Janet Auchincloss, and based on information provided by Jackie and her mother, Husted's name was not mentioned. Jackie simply airbrushed him out of her life.[20]

Jackie's uncharacteristic revelations of her private doubts about Husted were, no doubt, intended to pave the way for publicly "dumping" him. Her reservations about her future as a New York matron and wife of a middle-earning Wall Street WASP were understandable, given the ambition John White ascribed to her, and that the shining star of Congressman Kennedy had once again come into her orbit, eclipsing Husted. Sometime during the winter of 1951, recorded Rose Kennedy, whose recollections of dates—if not her interpretations of events—were generally reliable, Jackie and Lee were vacationing in Hobe Sound, up the coast from Palm Beach:

> Jackie worked in Washington on one of the newspapers and knew several of our children since by that time Jack, Eunice and Bobby were working in Washington. She was invited to spend a few days at our Palm Beach house while some of them were there. I wasn't there myself at the time; I was detained on other matters and arrived a little later that year. Soon afterward, however, I received a thank-you letter. It was signed "Jackie." I thought it was from a boy, and how extraordinary for a boy to write such a charming letter.
> I wondered, who is Jackie?[21]

Since Jackie by that time was using her own blue stationery with her name "Jacqueline Lee Bouvier" engraved at the top and would, in any case, have been unlikely to have signed herself to a hostess she had never met as "Jackie," the "Who is Jackie" part of Rose's story is possibly a piece of embroidery. The fact remains, however, that Jackie and Lee visited the Kennedys' Palm Beach house in the late winter before Christmas of 1951; it could be surmised also that, as Charlie Bartlett's parents had a house at Hobe Sound, he had had something to do with it.

Charlie did not approve of John Husted as a mate for Jackie and had not given up the idea of matching her with Jack Kennedy. The Bartletts gave another dinner party in Georgetown on May 8, 1952, and Martha Bartlett telephoned to invite Jackie, suggesting that she bring Congressman Kennedy. According to both Jackie and to Kennedy sources, this evening was the key date in their relationship. Jackie told Molly Thayer: "She knew instantly that he would have a profound, perhaps disturbing influence on her life. In a flash of inner perception, she realized that here was a man who did not want to marry. She was frightened . . . in this revealing moment she envisaged heartbreak, but just as swiftly determined that heartbreak would be worth the pain."[22]

Kennedy family tradition has it that the attraction was mutual and, for Jack, serious. "My brother really was smitten with her right from the very beginning when he first [sic] met her at dinner," Jack's youngest brother, Teddy, claimed. "Members of the family knew right away that she was very special to him, and saw the developing of their relationship. I remember her coming up to Cape Cod at that time and involving herself in the life of the family. He was fascinated by her intelligence: they read together, painted together, enjoyed good conversation together and walks together . . ."[23]

At the time of the historic dinner party in May 1952, John Fitzgerald Kennedy was just over two weeks short of his thirty-fifth birthday and already a public figure, author of a widely publicized book, *Why England Slept*, and, as a war hero, the subject of a celebrated piece by John Hersey, *The Story of PT-109*. Now, after five years as a Massachusetts representative in Congress, he was running for senator against the established Republican incumbent, Boston Brahmin Henry Cabot Lodge. Recently he had been voted "America's Most Eligible Bachelor," defeating confirmed bachelor Rock Hudson; in July he was to be chosen as the handsomest member of Congress by the Washington press corps. Kennedy was tall, skinny, with a shock of brown hair, but his attraction came from his personality as much as from his looks. Women—and men—fell over themselves to please him. Inga Arvad, his lover from November 1941 until his father broke up the relationship in February 1942, had written of him at their first encounter: "He had the charm that makes birds come out of their trees . . . thick mop of hair, blue eyes, natural, engaging, warm and when he walked into a room you knew he was there, not pushing, not domineering but exuding animal magnetism . . ."[24]

The writer Gloria Emerson, who later became a friend of Jackie's but was then a young journalist, met Jack Kennedy at a cocktail party in the fifties: "I was almost hypnotized by the sight of this man. He was such a stunning figure. He didn't have to attract women; they were drawn to him in the battalions, by the brigades . . ."[25] Cecilia Parker Geyelin remembered him as "wonderfully attractive and very funny, marvelous sense of humor."[26] Aileen Bowdoin Train recalled the electric charge that seemed to accompany him: "Jack would come into the room and fix you with this little look and it was very exciting . . ."[27]

"When Jack came into a room the temperature would go up a hundred and fifty percent," a male friend said. "Jack *lived* for twenty-four hours a day."[28] He had the boundless family energy but with an extra edge. He had brushed with death at least three times; for him every minute was a race against mortality: "I never met anybody who felt that the minute was as important as it was for him," his longtime friend Charles "Chuck" Spalding said. "He had to live for today. There was this inner pulse and he could find it wherever he went."[29] A recent biographer wrote that the people around Kennedy were like figures in a tableau waiting for him to appear to bring them to life. "He was very impatient, addicted to excitement, living his life as if it were a race against boredom."[30] He was stoical, in constant pain from his back, injured in a college football game[31] and further damaged by his heroism during his days of shipwreck in the Pacific in 1943. His general health was constantly undermined by Addison's disease, yet none of his friends ever heard him complain. Men admired his courage, his humor, his style. "They wanted to be like him," Gloria Emerson recalled, "and they wanted, as did women, to win his favor, but even more important, they seemed to love him. People wanted to please Jack."[32]

John Fitzgerald Kennedy and Jacqueline Lee Bouvier had many things in common. Like Jackie, Jack was immensely well read. Unlike the rest of his family, who had no intellectual or literary pretensions, he had been an avid reader from his childhood, when he spent hours alone through continual bouts of sickness. At three he nearly died of scarlet fever, and he was constantly ill during his schooldays, first at Canterbury then at Choate, a regular patient in the infirmary. In 1934 he was so ill that prayers were said for him in chapel; subsequently he was subjected to tests, humiliating procedures and hospitalization. In 1947 Addison's disease had been diagnosed when he fell seriously ill in London. The English doctor told Pamela Churchill, "Your young friend doesn't have more than three years to live . . ."

A deficiency of the adrenal glands, Addison's disease in its more severe form can lead to physical weakness, and psychiatric symptoms including irritability, nervousness, emotional instability and depression. At the time of the London diagnosis it was considered life-threatening but, fortunately for Jack Kennedy, it was discovered shortly afterward that steroids in the form of cortisone could be deployed to counteract the deficiency and avert the symptoms. Nevertheless, the treatment itself was tricky and could produce serious side effects. A too-low dosage leaves the patient tired and weak, but too much may lead to psychotic symptoms. In the election campaign of 1960 and during the Kennedy presidency, Jack's aides always flatly denied that he had Addison's.[33] Sadly, his condition, the atrophy of his adrenal cortex, might have been precipitated by the emotional trauma of the PT-109 incident.[34]

English and history were his favorite subjects, as they were for Jackie. They shared many of the same heroes—Churchill and Byron among them. Byron appealed to Jackie as a poetic Black Jack—"mad, bad and dangerous to know"—to Jack as a reflection of his own self-image, an element of his inherent narcissism, what his admirer, the political journalist Joseph Alsop, was to call his "snobbery of style." Jack Kennedy's heroes displayed a mixture of wit, cool courage and lack of sentiment. Refusing to be bound by the rules of convention, they were risk-taking, adventurous, never boring or banal. He particularly admired young men who risked their lives on battlefields, paralleling his own Pacific war experience. One of his favorites was Raymond Asquith, a hero of John Buchan's *Memory Hold-the-Door (Pilgrim's Way)*, who died on the Somme in 1915. The book, published in 1940, had impressed him deeply; John Buchan's description of aspects of Asquith might have been applied to Jack Kennedy: "He would destroy some piece of honest sentiment with a jest, and he had no respect for the sacred places of dull men. There was always a touch of scorn in him for obvious emotion, obvious creeds, and all the lumber of prosaic humanity."[35] As Inga Arvad put it, he valued brains over heart. Jack and Jackie shared a biting wit, a black sense of humor, and a clear, often cruel human insight. This was the Jack Kennedy Jackie saw and with whom she fell in love; there were other aspects of his character of which she was not yet aware, rooted in his genes, his childhood experience and, above all, his family.

Jack might have made up his mind, as he later claimed, on that evening at the Bartletts' house that Jackie was "the one," but if he had he showed no immediate sign of it. He invited her to the Kennedy family home at Hyannis Port on Cape Cod; she briefly joined his campaign in Boston, attending an Israel bond rally and listening to his speeches at Quincy and Fall River, Massachusetts, but he was busy on his Senate campaign and continued to see other women. His courtship was sporadic and somewhat furtive; on their first date together at the Shoreham Hotel's Blue Room, he brought along one of his political henchmen, Dave Powers, as a chaperone.

Jackie continued with her job on the *Times-Herald*, her questions reflecting her two Kennedy-related concerns: marriage and politics. A sample on the first included:

Should husbands and wives criticize each other?

Would you postpone your wedding plans if you had to live with your in-laws?

Can you give me any reason why a contented bachelor should get married?

Should engaged couples reveal their pasts?

Do you approve of joint bank accounts?

The Irish author Sean O'Faolain claims that the Irish are deficient in the art of love. Do you agree?[36]

Politically she had now turned her back on her paternal and maternal Republican politics in favor of the 1952 Democratic presidential candidate, Adlai Stevenson, although she was still not involved enough to bother registering to vote. Her questions covered a range of national and international political issues, including the appointment of women to political office. She asked people, "Should a candidate's wife campaign with her husband?" and "Do a candidate's looks influence your vote?" She interviewed Pat Nixon, the vice presidential nominee's wife, and waylaid two of the future President Eisenhower's nieces outside their school. For this piece of journalistic effrontery she earned a complaint to the editor from the girls' mother. Undeterred, she contemplated taking up a suggestion to write a children's book on the White House through the eyes of Eisenhower's niece Mamie: "Now poor little Mamie Moore, whom I bearded coming out of school, just might turn out to be my meal ticket!" she wrote in breathless reply to Bess Armstrong of the *New York Times*. "I'm so in love with all that [newspaper] world now—I think I look up to newspaper people—the way you join movie star fan clubs when you're ten years old."[37] When Jackie herself reached the White House she forgot that she had once been a member of journalism's fan club, and fiercely condemned the exploitation of children of which she had once been guilty with little Mamie Moore.

Jackie attended Eisenhower's inaugural ball in January 1953 as Jack's date but the Senator, as he now was, still showed no sign of proposing. For Jackie, the situation was not comfortable. She was marking time at work; the scope of her job was limited and, if she was serious about a career in journalism, the sprightly *Times-Herald* was not the ideal place for advancement. At home, little sister Lee had beaten her in the marriage stakes by getting engaged in December 1952.

Despite their real affection—"the only woman Lee liked was Jackie," a contemporary said—and a closeness based on childhood experiences and a feeling of "us against the world" that outsiders found hard to penetrate, there was intense, long-standing rivalry between the sisters. As they grew up, the four-year age gap between them seemed to make little difference. "I remember when we were growing up," recalled Jackie's lifelong Newport and New York friend, Vivi Stokes Crespi, "we considered four years' difference in age enormous and yet Lee was so precocious—I mean she had red fingernails and makeup when Jackie and I were still riding ponies, and, if we were sixteen and seventeen Lee was thirteen. She was just very precocious and very beautiful. Yes, Lee was the beauty, but Jackie had the spark and the brains."[38] Indeed, Lee was growing up even more beautiful than Jackie; although her legs, like her mother's, were too short for perfection, her features were so exquisite that people later compared her with Queen Nefertiti. She had determinedly shed her puppy fat and had an ability to wear clothes, a taste in fashion and decoration that outshone her sister's. Yet still Jackie remained the star and Lee the little sister. "I always thought that Lee was more beautiful than Jackie," said a friend noted for his taste in women. "I thought Lee was ravishing. And then you met Jackie. And then you fell for Jackie . . ."[39]

Some people thought that although Lee was less intelligent and less streetwise than Jackie, she appeared more human and appealing in her vulnerability. Both sisters suffered from insecurities and Lee increasingly so, not unrelated to her constant losing battle for equality with Jackie. Jay Mellon recalled, "Lee was a very vulnerable sort of person and a very flawed person. But very attractive as well in a sort of a way . . . As a woman I found her more attractive than Jackie even though if I had to spend the rest of my life on a desert island with one of them it would always have been Jackie because she was so much better company, so much smarter. There was more substance to Jackie, she had read everything. She had an inexhaustible fund of conversation . . . She had a very good sense of humor, she laughed a lot when you were with her . . . Lee was terribly touchy always. Any tiny little joke that seemed to reflect in any tiny little way on her at all, she didn't see the humor of it at all, got very uptight, started defending herself, very insecure, very touchy. Whereas Jackie wasn't touchy at all, not insecure, no way. She knew just who she was and what she was all about and she liked herself basically, which was the feeling I had, which makes a person good company. It's tough to get along with someone who's eating their insides out . . ."[40]

Even in their Newport years, there had been a sexual rivalry between the sisters, on Lee's part at least. "If you made a play for Jackie, Lee was all over you like a rash—that was in our adolescent days," one of Jackie's admirers related. "She [Lee] was better-looking, better figure and all the rest of it [but] it must have been tough for Lee because if Jackie was around you wouldn't really notice Lee . . ."[41]

But in 1952 the balance of power between Jackie and Lee had shifted in Lee's favor. While Jackie was full of uncertainties, not least where Jack Kennedy was concerned, Lee was now a chic, beautiful nineteen-year-old; having returned home the previous summer from several months spent in Rome, ostensibly studying singing, she had dropped out of Sarah Lawrence College and taken a job as special assistant to Diana Vreeland on *Harper's Bazaar*. On December 12, 1952, the Auchinclosses announced her engagement to Michael Temple Canfield (this time Black Jack rated a mention as the bride-to-be's father).

Canfield was the adopted son of publisher Cass Canfield, and it was at the

Canfield houses on 37th Street in New York and at Crowfields in Westchester County that the young smart literary set congregated—young men like Lee's former beau and Jackie's lifelong friend George Plimpton, cofounder of *The Paris Review*, Thomas Guinzburg, son of the founder of The Viking Press, and John P. Marquand Jr., son of the novelist. Canfield was tall—six foot three—blond, and cultivated an English air prompted by the (probably true) rumor that he was the son of the Duke of Kent by Kiki Whitney Preston, a wild young American whom the Duke had met in Kenya and who introduced him to cocaine, to which he was briefly addicted. Lee, like Jackie, was longing to get married and escape from home, and equally eager to beat Jackie to the altar. From friends' accounts it was Lee who fell in love with Michael, pursued him and proposed to him. According to Canfield's stepsister-in-law, when they remonstrated with him, "But, Michael, you can't do that! You don't love Lee!" he replied languidly, "Oh, but the dear girl loves me so . . ."[42]

Lee's marriage to Michael Canfield was celebrated at Holy Trinity Cathedral in Georgetown on April 18, 1953, followed by a reception at Merrywood. Black Jack Bouvier was there and, to everyone's surprise, whirled his ex-wife onto the dance floor. "Everybody watched with extreme interest," a cousin recalled. "I remember saying to someone, 'I suppose it's going to be like Lochinvar. Into the saddle and off they go. She looked as if she'd have gone with him and you contrasted it. He was kind of awful-looking but he was a great deal sexier than Hughdie . . ."[43] As the honeymoon couple left the house Lee, in an irresistible gesture of one-upmanship, threw Jackie her bridal bouquet.

Charlie Bartlett had the impression that Jackie was having difficulties with Janet. "Her mother was a sort of—she was more like Lee than she was like Jackie. She was a sort of tough lady who held no particular charm for me. She had a maintained kind of social position, which wasn't hard in those days if you'd got money. And I don't think she was terribly nice to Jackie. I had that feeling. I think the mother was always pointing to Lee as the model, you know, 'Why aren't you like Lee?' " He thought that she longed to escape from Merrywood: "I think Jackie probably had an anxiety to get out of that house, you know." Bartlett continued, "Yusha was sort of the Crown Prince and there were children. There were so many mixed children—she had Gore Vidal and there were all kinds of mixed blood flowing over there—and the mother talking about how great Lee was . . ."[44]

"I think she felt that time was running out for her," a friend of Jackie's commented.[45]

Within a month of catching her sister's bouquet, Jackie had succeeded in luring the Senator from Massachusetts into proposing marriage. In January 1953 she had been his date for Eisenhower's inaugural ball and in the following month she began translating ten French books on Southeast Asian politics as material for Jack's first major Senate speech. She later joked that she had done this to make him marry her. No doubt her accomplishments in this field did impress him, but there were other factors weighing in her favor. Jack was approaching his thirty-sixth birthday and he had been dating Jackie for over a year. While he was still seeing other women, she was definitely the most suitable girl on his horizon. He was not in love with her. Being "in love" was not a state of mind he had experienced. Ten years later, shortly before his death, when asked by his friend Chiquita Astor whether he had ever been in love, he replied, "No, but I've been *very* interested once or twice."

Jackie certainly came into that category. He was intrigued by her, by her elusive, teasing quality, her wit and sharp judgment of people, her love of history and literature that matched his own. Physically, she was not his type; lean, dark and flat-chested, she was precisely the opposite of the curvaceous blondes he favored, like Inga and later, famously, Marilyn Monroe. Sexually they had little in common: to Jack sex was no more than the satisfaction of a basic urge—"slam, bam, thank you, ma'am" summed up both his attitude and his performance. Jackie was not frigid but she was sexually inexperienced and expected an element of romance. Until then she had kept men at arm's length, following the accepted rule that if you wanted a good husband you had to be a virgin. Sex was not of primary importance to her; she wanted passion, which she was never going to get from Jack Kennedy.

Intrigued by Jackie's adoration of her father, Jack took the trouble to become friendly with him. Jackie introduced them at dinner in New York, where, she recalled, "They talked about sports, politics and women—what all red-blooded men like to talk about. They were very much alike." One might wonder how much Jack, with his interest in history and world affairs, would have liked close comparison with a man whose interest in the world did not extend beyond casual sex and dedicated gambling, but he was amused by the old rogue, and Black Jack, although wary of Joe Kennedy's son and convinced that no man could be good enough for his daughter, was charmed in return, telling a friend that Kennedy was a decent chap: "At any rate, Jackie's madly in love with him."[46] To his credit, Black Jack showed no jealousy of Jack and, after Jackie and Kennedy were married, even became Jack's covert ally where girls were concerned.

It was, as one of Jackie's friends put it, "paging Dr. Freud." Part of Jack's attraction for Jackie was his reckless womanizing, just like Black Jack's. But in equating Jack Kennedy's "red-blooded" male behavior with Black Jack's and thinking she could handle it, Jackie was making a serious mistake. As she was to find out, there was less in common between the two men than she fondly imagined: on the scale of womanizing, Jack was ten to Black Jack's two or three.

Weighing heavily in Jackie's favor as a bride for Jack was the active support of Joseph P. Kennedy, the powerful figure behind Jack's political career, the man who, in Jack's words, "made it all happen." In Joe Kennedy's view, a senator required a wife. Couples married young in the fifties, and a man who reached Jack's age but was still a bachelor risked being branded a "faggot." Even before meeting her, Joe would have had a favorable report on Jackie Bouvier from Arthur Krock, who had helped her get the *Times-Herald* job. At Hyannis Port that summer, Jackie, with her unerring sense of the power source in any gathering, had concentrated her irresistible attention on old Joe and gained her most important ally, for Joe Kennedy was impressed. Jackie had all the qualifications to be Jack's wife, the type of wife a rising politician needed as an accessory to his career. She was beautiful, intelligent and strong-minded enough to cope with him insofar as any woman could. She was a Catholic with an entrée into the WASP world. Against the Auchincloss background of Merrywood and Hammersmith, she had the class conferred by Miss Porter's and Vassar, the Debutante of the Year title—in fact, everything necessary to grace the Kennedys. Joe Kennedy was as unaware as Jackie that the aristocratic Bouvier background was a fantasy, but he was well-informed enough to know that the Bouviers as a family were washed-up and that Black Jack was a financial failure with a reputation as a drunk. But Jackie herself was the perfect package for his son and he was prepared to buy her. "Joe Kennedy not only condoned the marriage, he ordained it," Jack's friend Lem Billings declared.[47]

His father's approval was important to Jack, but it was only one factor among several in his final choice of Jackie. He didn't want to get married but he knew that, sooner rather than later, he would have to, and he wanted children. Of all the women he knew, Jackie, with her cool reserve, humor and intelligence, would be the least likely to bore him. Their shared Catholic religion was important too. This was not because he was intellectually serious about religion, or zealous as his mother and his sisters were. His religion was superficial; although he prayed on his knees every night and went to Mass on Sundays, he found great difficulty in believing most of the tenets of his Catholic faith. "Religion didn't interest him," a Stanford friend said. "He wasn't going to drop his religion. He liked the way it made him special, different in a Protestant world."[48] At least Jackie was more religious than Jack but, like his, her Catholicism defined her uniqueness and commanded her loyalty against the WASP majority. So Jack proposed one evening in early May.

Jackie played hard to get, in the Black Jack tradition, but she knew that this was a decision she could not take lightly. On May 22 she left for England on a trip that would be a perfect opportunity to consider whether, after all, now that she had achieved her objective, she really wanted to marry him. The idea came from Mrs. Bowdoin, mother of Helen, who had accompanied Jackie on her first European tour in 1950. She suggested that Jackie accompany her recently divorced daughter Aileen. "She had got a cabin on the *United States* and they were sailing on Friday, which was six days away," Aileen said. "I said I'd love to go but I'm not going to go by myself. All my friends were married and had children and so forth. And my mother suggested asking Jackie, so I called up Jackie on the Tuesday and I asked her if she would like to go to the Coronation and she said, 'I'll let you know tomorrow morning,' which was Wednesday, and we were sailing on Friday. And she went to the *Times-Herald* and they said they'd be delighted to have her write some stories about the trip."[49]

Jackie and Aileen left New York with a boatload of celebrities, most of them bound for the Coronation of Queen Elizabeth II. Most prominent among those who were not going to London were the Duke and Duchess of Windsor, who, not having been invited to the ceremony, were to land at Le Havre on their way to Paris, which was now their permanent home. Accompanying them were James "Jimmy" Donahue and his mother, Jessie, the Woolworth heiress. Donahue, who had inherited fifteen million dollars from his Woolworth grandfather's estate, was the Duchess's lover, despite his known homosexuality, an affair that was no secret in New York society. Jackie did not interview the Windsors but she talked to the liner's kennelman about their dogs.

Their path smoothed by good connections, Jackie and Aileen spent two weeks over the Coronation celebrations in a Mayfair flat on South Audley Street, courtesy of an old friend of the Bowdoins, Alex Abel Smith, whose wife, Henriette, as one of the Queen's ladies-in-waiting, would be staying at Buckingham Palace. The girls moved in smart social circles, dancing at the fashionable nightclub the 400, and attending Perle Mesta's lavish post-Coronation ball at Londonderry House, where the star of the scene was Lauren Bacall, stunning in a tight white strapless lace dress.

Rumors of Jackie's romance were already spreading: "Henri Claudel spent the whole time telling Jackie not to marry Jack Kennedy," Henriette Abel Smith recalled.[50] They were certainly not encouraged by Jackie, who barely mentioned it, even to Aileen, with whom she shared a cabin on the liner, a room at South Audley Street and at the Hôtel Meurice in Paris, where they spent two weeks. Jack sent her cables—"Articles good but you are missed"—which she kept to herself: "She never read me the cables," Aileen said. "She was probably about the most private person I've ever met. I always felt she was living in a dream world and everything was a kind of a play. As a result of that she was hard to get to know. She was going around collecting books by Aldous Huxley and I said, 'Jackie, who are those books for?' And she had all these extra suitcases—we had to pay two hundred dollars' excess baggage—and she said, 'Oh, for Uncle Hughdie,' but they weren't for Uncle Hughdie, I think they were for Jack."[51]

Jackie might not have discussed her concerns with Aileen but she did over lunch in London with Demi Gates, who was living in Madrid at the time and had come over for the Coronation. He was appalled when she told him she was going home to marry Jack Kennedy. "I said, you know, 'Jack Kennedy, when he comes to New York, he calls up my cousin and all the guys to line up the girls.' I said, 'This guy is a hopeless womanizer,' and and she just laughed and said, 'Look at my father!' I said it—because I felt that she could in her own right be an extraordinary woman, that she would be obscured by this guy because she was a woman. I think basically Jackie was attracted to Jack," Gates said, "not just because he was a senator, he was a good-looking guy [but] because all these flaws of Jack were balanced by the fact that he had money. There was nobody else pursuing her with that kind of money."[52]

She also discussed it with John Marquand in Paris. Marquand was in love with her but for Jackie it seems to have been no more than a flirtation. "People have said that Jackie was really in love with John Marquand," Aileen said. "I don't think that's true at all."[53] Marquand has been credited with having taken Jackie's virginity in an elevator, although Marquand flatly denied the story to Jackie's biographer C. David Heymann. Jackie, when discussing the subject with J. C. Warnecke, a later lover, would say only that "she had come pretty close [to losing it]." It might have been in Paris at that time that the famous elevator incident occurred—

if it did—and it was probably then that the discussion reported by Gore Vidal took place. He recounted the conversation between Jackie's "elevator-lover" ("He came from a better family than hers, as we used, quaintly, to say, but he had no money. He was also a Protestant") and Jackie when she told him she was going to marry Jack.

> . . . he was appalled and said, "You can't marry that . . . that *mick!*" She was coolly to the point: "He has money and you don't." When he asked her how she would like to be married to a *politician* (she had grown up in Washington and had no illusions about the breed) she said, "Of course, I don't like politics and he's a lot older than I am, but life will always be interesting with him, and then there's the money."
> "What on earth is going to become of you in that awful world?"
> "Read," she said, "the newspapers."[54]

For all Jack's glamour and the family money, the Kennedys, as Jackie well knew, were regarded as dubious by East Coast WASP society. There was huge prejudice against the Irish, especially in Brahmin Boston and at Harvard, even among Jack's class of 1940. As one of his classmates told his biographer, it was

> dominated by a WASP atmosphere. And Kennedy didn't fit into that mold at all . . . because he was such an obvious Boston-Irish type. You could tell from the way he spoke—he had a Boston accent as opposed to a Groton accent. And there were those older, more puritanical Bostonians . . . in the class of 1940 at Harvard, who regarded the Kennedys as coarse, loud, *nouveau riche* upstarts. For those people, the Kennedys were just irretrievably Boston Irish . . . The Kennedys were known particularly by the Bostonians as a family on the make. For many of the Brahmin families here, the Fitzgeralds [Jack's maternal grandparents' family] were simply beyond the pale, and the Kennedys also.[55]

As she was an outsider herself, none of this mattered to Jackie. What did matter to her, however, was the money. Attracted to him as she undoubtedly was, she would never have married a poor Jack Kennedy.

Gore Vidal attributed Jackie's obsession with money to the experience of living with wealth in the Auchincloss houses, yet being aware at the same time that she had none of her own. Jackie, Lee and Gore were the poor relations who had five Auchincloss siblings endowed with family trusts. Jackie and Lee had fifty dollars a month from their father and no expectations. But, far from being treated like poor relations, in their mother's new family Jackie and Lee were regarded as the stars. "I think they were both so beautiful and attractive and everybody cosseted them and coddled them," an Auchincloss family member said. "But I think with Jackie's enormous concern about money she must have been aware that she wasn't going to come into Hughdie's fortune. He was a rich stepfather but that goes to his blood. I can't believe that, smart and shrewd as she was, she might [not] have been conscious from the very beginning where that money came from and what it was. But she was no Cinderella. She was the dazzling Jackie of Hammersmith Farm."[56]

Even Jackie's closest friends and admirers could see her obsessive pursuit of money as a fault line in her character. "She was gorgeous, electrifyingly attractive," Demi Gates said, "and as with electrifying people she had one basic terrible flaw, which I identified with because my mother married an extremely rich man and Jackie's mother married an extremely rich man and I could see that she was absolutely obsessed with poverty, absolutely obsessed. In some cases it's very destructive and in other cases it makes people more willing and able to compete in the world . . . She was terrified that she was living in what she considered to be this big house in Washington and she knew that one day she'd be out in the cold. What could she do? How was she going to live?"[57]

"She had a primeval fear of poverty," said a man who knew her in her Onassis days. "She had an insecurity about money, a fear of going back to being poor."[58] "She grew up terrified of not having money—probably induced by Janet," was Arthur Schlesinger's opinion.[59] Lee thought that, for Jackie, money was "insulation. She'd seen enough downfall around her to want that insulation." John White put it more unkindly: "All she was fundamentally interested in was money. That was really the guiding motive of her life."[60] "We were both Depression children," Fred Papert, her friend and mentor at the New York Municipal Art Society, said, "hence at heart parsimonious . . ."[61] Jackie's experience of the hard realities of life so far, the decline of the Bouvier fortunes and the transformation in her mother's position as a result of her marriage to Hughdie Auchincloss, had impressed upon her that marriage to a rich man, preferably a very rich man, was the only true security.

When the plane on which Jackie returned home touched down in Boston *en route* to Washington, Jack Kennedy was waiting for her. The die was cast.

If many of Jackie's friends were appalled, most of his were surprised when their engagement was announced. "We went to the theater," Betty Coxe Spalding, Chuck's then wife, and an old friend of Kathleen and Jack Kennedy's, recalled. "This was before they were engaged . . . My ex-husband and Jack and I were there, and he introduced me to this young girl who was rather sloppily dressed. And black, black, very kinky hair. And I thought, Now who is this, and what's the game here . . . ? She seemed quiet and totally overwhelmed by the group . . . I'd been told that he'd been seeing her and it was getting quite serious . . ."[62] Jackie seems to have been conscious of her lack of glamour: returning from Paris after the Coronation trip, she questioned Zsa Zsa Gabor, who was sitting across the aisle from her. "What do you do for your skin?" "She wasn't the most glamorous nor the most beautiful woman," the actress recalled. "She had kinky hair and bad skin."[63]

Some of Jack's closest friends were as dubious about the engagement as Jackie's had been. George Smathers, the Florida senator who, with railroad lobbyist Bill Thompson and Jack was a member of the Three Musketeers, had firsthand knowledge of the extent of his friend's womanizing, told Jack that he wasn't the type to get married. Others, like Kirk Le Moyne "Lem" Billings, warned Jackie of problems ahead. Lem, having been Jack's roommate at Choate, had known him as long as anyone outside his immediate family. "I took her aside at a party," he said, "and attempted to teach her 'the facts of life.' I described Jack's physiological problems—his bad back, his Addison's disease—and talked about some of the women in his life, emphasizing the dangers of getting involved with somebody older who was already set in his ways."[64]

And if Jackie had had doubts about the marriage, so had Jack. "I never saw a man more depressed than on the day he told me he was getting married," said Alastair Forbes,[65] an English friend of Jack and Kathleen's and a distant cousin of Franklin D. Roosevelt's. In August in the South of France for a last bachelor vacation with Torbert 'Torby" MacDonald, Jack met a ravishing girl, a Swedish version of Grace Kelly, who recorded that he "looked and sounded stricken" as he confessed to her that he was going back to the States to get married.[66]

The wheels had been turning inexorably since the official announcement of the engagement on June 24, 1953. In true Kennedy style, it had been delayed until two weeks after the publication of a profile of Jack in the *Saturday Evening Post*. Featured on the cover, the piece was entitled "Jack Kennedy—the Senate's Gay Young Bachelor." By now he was enough of a celebrity to merit a report of his engagement to "sultry Socialite Jacqueline Bouvier" plus a photograph subtitled "Senator Kennedy and Fiancée" in the "People" section of *Time*. According to the rules of the game established by Black Jack, Jackie kept him waiting until the last moment to catch the flight from New York to Cape Cod to join the patriarch and the clan at Hyannis Port.

Joe Kennedy went to great lengths to extract the maximum publicity out of the celebration of his son's marriage, steamrollering even Janet with the force of his personality and his purse. It was to be his second wedding extravaganza of the year: in May thirty-one-year-old Eunice had married thirty-seven-year-old Sargent "Sarge" Shriver. Shriver, the son of an old Maryland Catholic family who had lost their money in the Depression, was destined to be a Kennedy lieutenant for the rest of his life. Tall, handsome with a Navy war record, a graduate of Yale with some experience of journalism, he had worked with Eunice in Washington and subsequently for her father at the Chicago Merchandise Mart, which Joe Kennedy had recently purchased. Sarge had courted Eunice for more than a decade. According to Laurence Leamer, biographer of the Kennedy women, his attentions to her had become something of a joke among the Kennedy entourage. "It was a minor party game guessing what hoop Eunice would have poor Sarge jumping through next. Sarge had a courtier's solicitousness, toward both Eunice and her father, and he jumped and jumped some more. Joe not only approved of thirty-seven-year-old Sarge, but he actively promoted Eunice's marriage to his business lieutenant."[67]

"I found a man who is as much like my father as possible," Eunice told the wedding guests, a remark that spoke volumes. It was the highest compliment she could pay, but what her groom and his family privately thought of it is unrecorded. In any case, distinguished family as they were, they were losing a son rather than gaining a daughter. Sarge was marrying into the Kennedy family, not vice versa, a state of affairs underlined by the front page of the *Boston Globe*, which featured a wedding photograph not of the newlyweds but of Eunice and her father. The Kennedy press release went into overdrive, calling it "one of the most important and colorful weddings ever held in America." Cardinal Spellman officiated at St. Patrick's Cathedral, attended by three bishops, four monsignors and nine priests; the Pope sent an apostolic blessing. The bride was dressed by Dior and the wedding cake was so tall that Eunice had to stand on a chair to cut it. Seventeen hundred guests attended, "a directory of Who's Who in the nation," according to the *Boston Globe*.

Janet wanted a more sedate family occasion for Jackie and Jack. However, neither Jack nor his father saw it that way. Jack's marriage marked an important stage in his career; the bride was beautiful, the old-money backdrop just what was required, and it had to be a media event whether the Auchinclosses liked it or not. The relatively modest church at Newport could only hold seven hundred but Joe Kennedy saw to it that some 1,400 were invited to the reception at Hammersmith Farm. He flew up for Sunday lunch at Hammersmith on July 12 to finalize arrangements.

Jack had been spending the weekend there with Jackie before what was supposed to have been his last bachelor fling in August. What Jackie thought about this trip has not been revealed. She was, however, noticeably quiet at the pre-wedding get-together at Hyannis Port in September. "Jackie changed since she got engaged," Charles Bartlett mused. "She stopped being as much fun. It was a funny thing. As an engaged girl, she was not the girl who [had] grabbed the prize. I guess at the time she had discovered that she was tying up with a philanderer or something—I don't know what. But she never seemed very happy to me in those days, or indeed over the period she was getting married . . ."[68] According to another source, she telephoned the wife of a notorious Newport womanizer and asked her how she coped.[69] During the four-day house party on the Cape for the groomsmen and bridesmaids, she hardly appeared. "I do think Jackie was worried about marrying—getting into that family and losing her identity—I think it was a big worry," said Aileen Bowdoin, who was to be one of the bridesmaids.[70] Jackie's sense of self, her own uniqueness, was important to her now that she felt in danger of being submerged by a tidal wave of Kennedys.

Aileen was carried along by the supercharged atmosphere: "We had to get up and entertain at night. I mean, I can't sing a note but I had to sing a song with Martha [Bartlett]. It called out the best in you because you had to do it. I'll never forget one day I was playing tennis with Eunice and I haven't played such good tennis since—and it was just because the adrenaline was really going. That happened to you. That family did it to you. I think that's why they all became such strong characters, because they were in that atmosphere all the time. Competition. You had to be better than the next one. They were an interesting family because they were so competitive with each other and at the same time so loyal to each other—the Kennedys against the world." She described Rose as "an enigma, really. She came home from Europe when we were there and the family all gathered around and sang 'For She's a Jolly Good Fellow.'" Joe was another matter entirely: "Mr. Kennedy was very much in control. He used to have appointments with his children scheduled by his secretary. He was a martinet. He was in charge of his children. No question about it. He told them what to do and they did it. He was really not a nice man . . ."[71]

The wedding cavalcade moved on to Newport for further celebrations before the ceremony on September 12. There was a cocktail party for the bridal couple, and two days before the wedding, a bachelor dinner for eighteen given by Hugh Auchincloss at the Clambake Club, at which Jack Kennedy teased his future stepfather-in-law by throwing crystal glasses into the fireplace after each toast in the manner of the Russian Imperial Guard. At the bridal dinner on the eve of the wedding Jack joked that he was marrying Jackie to remove her from the Fourth Estate, where her activities as an inquiring reporter might menace his political career; Jackie riposted by stressing his shortcomings in courtship, holding up the only piece of handwritten correspondence she had received from him, a postcard from Bermuda inscribed, "Wish you were here, Jack." Missing from the bridal dinner was one person who might have been expected to be there: Black Jack had not been invited, although he had been at the wedding rehearsal earlier in the day. Stylishly clad in stiff collar and checkered vest set off by a yellow tie, he had startled onlookers by kissing Janet's hand. "I think that's as close as she's got to an orgasm since she married Hughdie Auchincloss," the prospective bridegroom commented.[72]

What should have been the happiest day of Jackie's life so far, her wedding day, turned out to be one of the bitterest and, in concealing the pain the episode caused her, she showed courage and self-discipline. Black Jack Bouvier had been looking forward to cutting a dash at Jackie's wedding, just as he had at Lee's. He had dried out, taken time to get himself in perfect shape, jogging around the reservoir in Central Park in his special rubber suit. As the father of the bride, he was staying at the best hotel in Newport, the Viking, not far from the church of St. Mary where Jackie was to be married. According to Gore Vidal, Janet sent Michael Canfield, Lee's husband, to the hotel to "tell her ex-husband that he could of course come to the church and give away the bride but he could not come to the reception." Janet, he said, did not tell Canfield to ply Black Jack with alcohol and get him drunk, as one story had it. "Mike Canfield was a gentleman, something which practically none of this cast is, a real gent . . . Mike fulfilled his mission feeling rather guilty about it and he said that old Jack took it quite well, he thought, and he just left him there and of course Jack went straight to the bar . . ." Janet, apparently, had done the same thing to Gore's mother when his half sister Nini was married: "My mother was told she could be in the church—anybody could be in the church—but she couldn't come out to Merrywood . . ."[73]

Lee remembers the episode as a searing experience: "I never saw my father out of it or drunk until the worst day there could have been in his whole life, at Jackie's wedding. It was more than understandable but I think that perhaps I was the only one who knew how he felt in *total* enemy territory, *completely* on his own.

My mother had written him telling him she hoped he realized that he was far from welcome and that he might change his mind and decide not to come, and she felt that this would be a far more appropriate thing for him to do. So then he wasn't invited to the dinner the night before, so that made him feel incredibly low, depressed. Understandably he just got completely drunk the night before, unable to give his beloved daughter away the next day. Right after I went through the wedding, I chartered a little plane and took him back to New York and put him in the hospital for a while. It was particularly heartbreaking because he had been looking forward to this moment for months and sort of had himself in training for it—I suppose one of his greatest weaknesses, far more than alcohol, was that he was very vain. As he adored Jackie this was the moment, the biggest, the most important moment in his life . . ." It was the cruelest thing Janet could have done to both Black Jack and Jackie, a sign of the tremendous bitterness she still felt toward him. Why forbid him to come to Jackie's wedding reception at Hammersmith when only five months before she had danced so animatedly with him at Merrywood? "My mother . . ." Lee said. "A woman's revenge is relentless and she just felt that she would feel extremely uncomfortable if he was in the house. I don't know why—I think it would have added to the festivities enormously and, of course, given my sister the greatest pleasure . . ."[74]

And so, on a clear, bright, windy Newport day, Jackie arrived at the church for the 11 A.M. ceremony on the arm of Hughdie Auchincloss. The local press blithely recorded her as entering St. Mary's Church "on the arm of her father, John V. Bouvier 3rd," and captioned the picture accordingly (an error hastily amended next day with the excuse that Mr. Bouvier had been "taken ill").[75] In the circumstances it is hardly surprising that Jackie looked tense on entering the church or that the couple's wedding vows were "barely audible." The local press devoted the front page and many columns to what it described as "Newport's most brilliant wedding in many years." Special traffic arrangements had to be made; the crowds gathered outside the church to gawk at the celebrities, including the singer Morton Downey and the film star Marion Davies, invited by the Kennedys, who were almost outnumbered by movie and press cameramen. The ceremony was conducted by the Kennedy's friend Archbishop Cushing of Boston, who read out a special blessing from Pope Pius XII before the nuptial Mass. Jackie wore her maternal grandmother's veil of rose point lace, and a dress made for her, at Janet's insistence, in New York, and which, she later told her friend and favorite designer Carolina Herrera, she hated. Made of ivory silk taffeta, it did not flatter her; the "portrait neckline" and tight banding of the bodice emphasized her flat chest, and the circles of tucked taffeta on the skirt looked clumsy. It was a far cry from Eunice's Dior dress, and demonstrated how unconfident of her taste in clothes Jackie still was and how she had allowed herself to be dominated by her mother.

Lee was the matron of honor and Nini Auchincloss the maid of honor, little Janet Auchincloss was the flower girl and Jamie, aged six, the page. There was a huge retinue of bridesmaids to match the army of Kennedy ushers, including the two Bowdoin sisters, Helen and Aileen, Charlie Whitehouse's sister Sylvia, Jean and Ethel Kennedy, Martha Bartlett, Shirley Oakes and Nancy Tuckerman. Robert Kennedy was his brother's best man, and the ushers included Teddy Kennedy, Sargent Shriver, Jack's old friends and boon companions Torby Macdonald, Lem Billings, George Smathers, Chuck Spalding, James Reed and Ben Smith, plus Yusha and Tommy Auchincloss and Charlie Bartlett.

There was a distinct social divide between the Newport, New York and Washington WASPs seated on the bride's side and the more flamboyant Kennedy guests. "All the Newport side were simply dressed," Marion Oates "Oatsie" Leiter, a popular Washington hostess and friend of Janet and of Jack, remembered, "while the Kennedy side were dressed to kill."[76] "It's going to be awful," Janet had told a friend, "everyone in the State of Massachusetts is going to be there."[77] "The Kennedy family breezed in like an army . . . Marion Davies was drunk," recalled a friend of Janet's.[78]

"I remember on the dance floor all the Kennedy friends, political friends, seemed to have bright blue suits on and they all seemed florid and beefy and they kind of arrived on the scene and swamped the place. There definitely was the air of Newport people curling their lips a bit," Cecilia Parker Geyelin, recalled.[79] People in the know wondered about the absence of the father of the bride: "How could you not wonder?" Eilene Slocum of the distinguished Newport family said. "He wasn't there to give Jacqueline away . . . People buzzed, particularly at the reception afterward . . . There were more than 1,300 people at the reception, a strange combination of Irish politicians and many of Hugh and Janet's Republican friends, and a high percentage of both were aware of Jack Bouvier's absence."[80]

> Otherwise it was one of those "perfect" weddings—a sunny windswept day, horses and cattle grazing in the pasture, everybody radiant and fit, several huge tents set up across the back lawns. Meyer Davis, who had played at Janet's first wedding [and Jackie's coming-out party] fiddled madly away. The children—mine, Noreen Drexel's and the two young Auchinclosses—did the Mexican Hat Dance for the benefit of the newsreel cameras.[81]

Jackie was serene, giving nothing away. Sylvia Whitehouse was impressed by her courage, "the splendid way in which she comported herself, her ability to rise above the problems of the day, namely the enforced absence of her father. I was totally unaware, as a bridesmaid, of the fact that he was drunk at the Viking Hotel . . . she certainly didn't cry or let on . . ."[82] Jack and Jackie posed "without stint" for the photographers, Jackie balking only once when she was asked to pose with her husband clinking champagne glasses, pronouncing it "Too corny."[83]

Just as the irresistible tide of Kennedys and their friends had swamped her Newport wedding, Jackie found herself swept irrevocably into a Kennedy future.

CHAPTER FIVE

Clan Initiation

〜

Nemesis is daughter of Night, the goddess of Retribution, who brings down all immoderate good fortune and checks the presumption that attends it.

—Translation of the Ancient Greek interpretation of Nemesis, from *Lemprière's Classical Dictionary*

Even on her honeymoon, Jackie began to sense the roller coaster that her life with Jack would be, the unnerving inability to control events as she had been used to, the compartmentalization of her husband's life and his friends, the range of experience he had passed through that she could not share, the infinite layers of his past and the loyalties that threatened their relationship.

They spent the first part of their honeymoon at Acapulco, on a cliff overlooking the ocean, in a pink-painted house that had attracted Jackie on a previous visit with Janet and Hughdie. Romance and solitude, however, did not appeal to Jack for long: within a few days the newly married couple were in California for a week in Beverly Hills, a favorite hunting ground of Jack and his father, where they stayed in the house belonging to Marion Davies, mistress of William Randolph Hearst, an old friend of Joe Kennedy's. How much Jack had told Jackie of his past exploits there with Gene Tierney, Sonja Henie, and strings of other women "balling at the Bel-Air,"[1] as Paul "Red" Fay put it, is open to doubt. From Beverly Hills they met up with Red, Jack's old naval buddy, and his wife, Anita, to spend a few days on the Monterey peninsula, then drove up to San Francisco, where the Fays lived.

Jackie was beginning to get to know the hard core of her husband's loyal band of friends. Fay, whom Jack usually referred to as "Redhead," certainly qualified for that description. The two men had met at Melville Torpedo Boat Training School in 1942 and served in the same PT boat squadron in the Solomon Islands, where they had become close. Fay, tall, redheaded, handsome and athletic, shared Jack's

Irish Catholic background. He, too, came from a large family dominated by a powerful father, but it was, above all, his warm, fun-loving attitude toward life that had appealed to Jack. Correspondence with Fay had kept up Jack's spirits in the hospital after he was invalided out of the Navy. He had been invited to Hyannis Port in September 1944 in the dreadful days after Joe Jr. was killed and then to Palm Beach later that year. He had been with Jack during his spell as a journalist in San Francisco at the time of the formation of the United Nations in 1945, and helped with Jack's 1946 congressional campaign before his own marriage to Anita in October 1946. He was Jack's loyal companion in arms; even old Joe Kennedy approved of him and he had become practically an honorary Kennedy, particularly close to Bobby and his wife, Ethel.

Jackie had first met Red Fay at Hammersmith Farm before the wedding, when Fay had been struck not so much by her looks as by the softness of her voice. "God, she's a fantastic-looking woman," he told Jack later, "[but] if you ever get a little hard of hearing, you're going to have a little trouble picking up all the transmissions." Jack, he said, "threw back his head and roared." Red's role, Jack wrote to him, tongue in cheek, was to ingratiate himself with Janet—"one fine girl but who has a tendency to think I am not good enough for her daughter . . ." In this mission Fay failed, unsurprisingly, at the first test. In the interest of marital relations Jack refused to play a round of golf with him at the Newport Club. "Can't you see," he said, "how well it will be received by the hopeful bride and her sheltering mother if the ardent husband-to-be spends his first day at her home playing golf with some old wartime buddy?" Jack dropped Fay and a Boston friend, John Galvin—"looking more Irish than Paddy's Pig"—at the golf course. At the end of the round, as he hustled them away in his convertible, he remarked with wry enjoyment, "I hope you two enjoyed your game of golf because as a result of it there was almost a total breakdown of relations between the mother of the bride and her dashing prospective son-in-law. It seems that there is a rule that non-members can play only when accompanied by a member there to sanction the match. I'm afraid that they feel that their worst fears are being realized. The invasion by Irish Catholic hordes into one of the last strongholds of America's socially élite is being led by two chunky redhaired friends of the groom . . ."[2]

Jackie came to understand that Jack's most significant attachments were to men, not women; he preferred the company of men. He was a natural leader, a pole of attraction, and had been since he was a skinny schoolboy at Choate. Schoolmates, college friends, Navy buddies, English aristocrats, political operatives, men of the Secret Service detail guarding him when he was in the White House—all were devoted to him. His male friends gave him their absolute loyalty, which ultimately excluded Jackie, and his loyalty to them was equally unswerving. There was a macho, "jock" side to Jack that enjoyed male comradeship, as Jackie found out on her supposedly romantic West Coast honeymoon. Fay took him to meet Sergeant "the Sarge" Tom Casey, a legend at Stanford University, whom Jack had first met when he was in California in 1945. The Sarge's greeting for Jack was fulsome, not equaled by the response of Fay's old fraternity house when he proudly took the great senator to meet them. Intent on watching the

World Series, they barely acknowledged Kennedy. "I must say that was an alert group," Jack remarked as they left. "When Jack and Jacqueline came to the West Coast on their honeymoon, the pressure of public life—not to mention those of an old shipmate and his wife—too often intruded on the kind of honeymoon any young bride anticipates," Fay wrote.[3] "For example, on Jack and Jacqueline's last day on the West Coast, Jack and I went to a pro football game while his bride of several weeks spent the afternoon being shown the bay area by his old shipmate's wife. I'm sure this didn't seem a particularly unusual arrangement to Jack . . ."[4]

Nor did it seem to Jack an unusual arrangement that he and Jackie should live with his parents for several weeks after their return from their honeymoon, dividing their time between the Kennedy house at Hyannis Port with some nights spent in Boston either at the Ritz-Carlton Hotel or at the rather dismal apartment that was the Senator's Boston residence. Jackie was thrown in at the deep end of the Kennedy maelstrom, learning the realities of life in the family she had described as being as effervescent as "carbonated water," but which her friend John White compared with the pullulating existence of an anthill.

The Kennedy family was a patriarchal hierarchy in a way that Jackie's adopted family, the Auchinclosses, was not. At Merrywood and Hammersmith, Janet's personality was dominant, while Hughdie was a genial, silent presence. The Kennedys were a clan or tribe, united as the Bouviers had never been, despite the Major's predominant position. At Hyannis Port and Palm Beach, old Joe—variously referred to by his children as "Daddy," "Pappy," "J.P." or "the Old Man"—was the King-Emperor at the apex of the pyramid. Tall, well-built and possessed of what one of his son Jack's aides described as "outrageous charm when he wanted to use it,"[5] Joe Kennedy was a coldhearted, brilliant, ambitious and proud man. Both in his private life and in business, he was selfish, single-minded, ruthless and amoral. The grandson of penniless Irish immigrants from County Wexford, he was the son of P. J. "Pat" Kennedy, a tough political ward boss who had been elected five times to the Massachusetts House of Representatives and retired to look after his drinking parlor and liquor-business interests while maintaining behind-the-scenes control of the Boston Democratic Party machine. P.J.'s influence on his grandson was minimal; Jack remembered him with a lack of affection. When he and his elder brother, Joe Jr., were taken for Sunday visits, his grandfather "wouldn't let us cut up or even wink in his presence."[6]

Joe Kennedy had been determined to break out of the Ward Eight, North End Boston, Irish Catholic immigrant ghetto world in which his father operated and into which he was penned by the invisible but nonetheless real anti-Irish prejudice of the Back Bay Brahmin families—Adamses, Cabots, Lowells, Saltonstalls and their web of relations. The disdain of the East Coast Protestant Establishment for the Irish Catholics, from the time of the main flood of immigration in 1847 through to the 1960s, when the election of John F. Kennedy changed perceptions, would be difficult to exaggerate. Nowhere had the impact of huge numbers of Irish immigrants been more noticeable than in Boston, or the determination to stop their infiltration of superior society been more marked. As Stephen Birmingham wrote, a decade after the assassination of John Kennedy, "It is ironic that upper-class Boston, otherwise so culturally and intellectually liberal, could not then—and cannot today—accept the Irish as candidates for social equality."[7] Aged just twenty, young Joe Kennedy had taken the Yankee route toward social acceptability and had come up against that social barrier. He was big enough and tough enough to play football for Harvard but not well-bred enough to be accepted into any of the final clubs—gentlemen's clubs that excluded blacks, women and Catholics. It was the first of many social rebuffs.

> When Joe first went to Harvard [the historian and Kennedy biographer Doris Kearns Goodwin recorded] he fully expected to be accepted by everybody there, just as he had been at Boston Latin. In his family, he was the favorite child. And he was very popular initially. He was a very outgoing, gregarious, vibrant kind of fellow so people liked him. But suddenly, when he started applying for the final clubs, like all his Protestant friends were, he was not allowed in. It was a devastating experience for him. I think really for the first time in his life that he understood what being a Catholic in Boston meant: that he would be perpetually an outsider. And he later said, and told Rose, that that night, when all of his friends got into this fancy final club, and he was denied entrance, he looked at himself in a different way, and from then on he realized that he was going to have to fight that world, that somehow he couldn't just work his way by charm into the world. He would have to mount an attack and in some ways I think his whole career from then on, the money, the kids, the Presidency, was his attack on that Brahmin world.[8]

From the outset of his adult life, Joe Kennedy perceived that money was the source of power and that he could outwit the Brahmins by outbidding them; by 1914 he had become the youngest bank president in Boston. He planned to found his own dynasty to rival the old Boston families, which controlled the financial and social levers in the city. When he was just under eighteen, he had picked out the sixteen-year-old Rose Fitzgerald as a suitable bride.

In Boston Irish circles Rose was a princess, the favorite daughter of John "Honey Fitz" Fitzgerald, one of the most popular and successful of the Boston Irish politicians as a state senator and the first Democratic congressman from Massachusetts, but best known as the five-time Mayor of Boston. Smiling, joking, charming, philandering Fitzgerald was Jack Kennedy's favorite grandparent, whom in many ways he resembled, and whose political heir he had become. A high-energy, high-profile political campaigner (and bitter opponent of P. J. Kennedy), whose attitude toward electoral corruption was far from squeaky clean, he had challenged Republican Brahmin Henry Cabot Lodge for the Senate seat in 1916, the year before Jack was born. Fitzgerald lost, but thirty-six years later, Jack avenged the defeat by winning against another Lodge in 1952.

Fitzgerald's daughter Rose was beautiful, intelligent and ambitious. After a good education at the Dorchester Latin School, she had aimed at the prestigious

WASP Wellesley College, but been deflected by the Catholic Archbishop of Boston and her father's fear of offending his Catholic constituency. Fitzgerald thought P. J. Kennedy's son was not good enough for his accomplished daughter and sent Rose to board at two convents, one in Holland, the other the Sacred Heart at Manhattanville, New York, to keep her away from him. After a huge coming-out party in 1911, Rose acted as her father's hostess on an official tour of Europe representing Boston, and on Democratic Party swings through America. Despite all her father's efforts to distract her, Rose dreamed of Joe Kennedy, mistakenly seeing him as her White Knight who would rescue her from her father's domination.

The couple married in 1914 and, following Joe's determination to move out of Boston, set up house in Brookline, Massachusetts, a largely Protestant suburb where Rose began a married life of successive pregnancies. Joseph Jr. was born on July 25, 1915, nine months after the honeymoon, followed by John Fitzgerald on May 29, 1917, Rosemary (born September 13, 1918), Kathleen (born February 20, 1920), Eunice (born July 10, 1921), Patricia (born May 6, 1924), Robert, "Bobby" (born November 20, 1925), Jean (born February 20, 1928) and Edward, "Teddy" (born February 22, 1932).

For Rose it was a time of emotional and social deprivation. Having been the sparkling daughter of the Mayor of Boston, she became a lonely wife in Brookline, spending more and more time alone as her husband pursued his business and sexual interests elsewhere. "Joe's time was his own, as it had been and always would be," she wrote ruefully. "School and college had once taken much of it before, and now it was business that did so."[9] Her only outlet was as president of the Ace of Clubs, which she had founded, devoted to discussion of educational affairs and, of course, religion. Recoiling from sex, except for the purposes of procreation, she soon came to realize that she had no influence over her husband and that the mutual, civilized social life she had envisaged would not materialize. In 1920, when their second son, John Fitzgerald Kennedy, was in his third year, she left Joe and returned home, where Honey Fitz more or less told her that having made her bed she must lie in it. She went back to the house on Beals Street with no alternative to becoming the archetypal stoic Irish Catholic mother. Motherhood to her was a duty rather than a pleasure; she later wrote of herself and her husband as partners in the family enterprise, a curiously revealing phrase. She became, in effect, the manager of a production-line baby factory, the overseer of the activities of nurses, maids and cooks.

> I had to be sure there were plenty of good-quality diapers on hand . . . There was also the daily supply of bottles and nipples to be cleaned and sterilized. I didn't do much of it myself, but I had to make sure it was done properly, and on a schedule that didn't interfere with another vital schedule. If the nursemaid was in the kitchen boiling bottles and nipples and preparing "formulas" and puréeing vegetables when the cook needed the stove . . . there could be a kitchen crisis,

sharp words and bruised feelings and, from a management point of view, a precipitous drop in morale and efficiency.[10]

Executive Rose kept card indexes of her children's illnesses, treatments and measurements, oversaw their clothes and their daily exercise. Her managerial duty done, she would go out for the day to her Catholic social clubs, returning to direct operations at five in the evening and, if Joe happened to be there, to discuss the children's progress with him. "We were individuals with highly responsible roles in a partnership that yielded rewards which we shared," was her verdict on Kennedy parenthood.

When America finally entered the First World War in April 1917, Joe refused adamantly to enlist and was branded a physical coward for the first but not the last time in his life. It was a stain on his name that his two eldest sons would attempt to erase by their own extraordinary heroism. Instead, he concentrated on making money: bootlegging during Prohibition from 1919, which inevitably put him in contact with organized-crime figures, and on the stock market, learning the secrets of insider trading and stock pooling. By the mid-1920s, though he had had no visible source of income after leaving his brokerage firm in 1922, *Fortune* magazine estimated his wealth at some $15–20 million in today's money. In 1926 he moved on to Hollywood, using the same ruthless expertise to make a great deal more money, and earning himself a reputation as a swindler and double-crosser in the process. Money, however, and in particular the methods he had employed to get it, did not bring Joe the social recognition he craved. Rejected by the Cohasset Country Club, he moved his family to Riverdale, New York, in 1927, claiming that Boston was "no place to bring up Catholic children." While Joe was convinced that his rejection by his country-club peers was prompted by pure prejudice—"because I was an Irish Catholic and the son of a barkeep"—others said it was his bad financial reputation that barred him. Fear of prejudice prompted him to acquire his summer home on Cape Cod in an area he had been assured would accept him. "The basic reason Joe Kennedy came to Hyannis Port," Joseph F. Gargan, Rose's nephew, said, "was that, as an Irish Catholic, he could get into the country club."[11] The Kennedys first rented the Malcolm Cottage, as it was called, in 1925 and bought it three years later.

Early in 1929 the family moved to a six-acre, twenty-one-room colonial-style house in Bronxville, New York, a town apparently notorious for its exclusion of Jews. In that same year Joe had begun a very public affair with Gloria Swanson, then at the height of her celebrity, and succeeded in losing a good deal of her money and some of his own with an expensive flop movie, *Queen Kelly*. Rose's reaction to her husband's affair was to feign ignorance, avoid confrontation and escape by traveling more and more frequently, punishing her husband with extravagant shopping trips. It was a pattern of behavior—denial and escape—that Jackie adopted when confronted with Jack's serial philandering. (Jack's reaction to his mother's absences was hostile. Aged five, he rounded on her: "Gee, you're a *great* mother to go away and leave your children all alone!"[12] At first he used to cry when she packed her bags, but desisted when he discovered that it only irritated her.)

Having survived the 1929 stock market crash by selling short, Joe was soon enriching himself once again through predatory insider trading and in the liquor business, where in 1933, through the good offices of Franklin D. Roosevelt's son James, he obtained the U.S. franchise for Haig & Haig. That year, boosted by an ever-increasing fortune and connections with the new President Roosevelt, Joe bought a house on North Ocean Boulevard, Palm Beach, the winter habitat of the seriously rich. In 1934, declaring, "It takes a thief to catch a thief," Roosevelt appointed him to regulate the stock market through the Securities and Exchange Commission, an organization that aroused the ire of both Jackie's father and her stepfather.

Joe Kennedy's ambitions now soared far beyond Wall Street: with his usual single-minded analytical perceptiveness, he had discerned that, after the crash of 1929, the real seat of power had moved from Wall Street to Washington, from business to government and the highest office in the land. He had supported Roosevelt, both financially and behind the scenes in the 1932 presidential election and cherished hopes of obtaining the Democratic nomination himself in 1940. At the very least he expected to be rewarded with office. He was given the chairmanship of the U.S. Maritime Commission in Washington, and the secret promise of the social summit that both he and Rose craved: the London embassy. Here Roosevelt's hand was forced by Joe's ally, Arthur Krock (paid $25,000 by Joe in 1937 to keep the Kennedy name in the papers), who leaked news of the appointment before it was duly settled. Joe's reason for wanting it was simple: "Don't go buying a lot of luggage," he told Harvey Klemmer, his aide at the Maritime Commission who was to accompany him to London, "we're only going to get the family in the *Social Register*. When that's done, we come back and go out to Hollywood to make some movies and some money."[13] In February 1938 he sailed for England as the United States' first Catholic ambassador to the Court of St. James's. The appointment indeed landed the family in the longed-for columns of the *Social Register* and had far-reaching consequences not only for himself but for three of his eldest children, Joe Jr., Jack and Kathleen.

Jack's interest in world affairs had been sparked the previous year by a trip to Europe with Lem Billings when, among other experiences, he had been spat on by Nazis in Nuremberg. Returning with his family in 1938, he met everybody who was anybody in English social and political life, from the Royal Family downward, and formed close friendships with his own generation among the British upper class. "Jack was the right age to be polished by them," Gore Vidal said, "and he became one of them. I've always thought he was more of a young Whig English nobleman than he was an American. He knew far more English parliamentary history than he knew American history. He and I used to talk about Palmerston and Gladstone's governments and this and that. He was very Englished in a way. Bobby was too young to get the good of it."[14] As an observer of the European political situation in 1939, Jack stayed in Warsaw with Ambassador Anthony Drexel

Biddle, concluding "the Poles will fight," and toured Eastern Europe and Palestine. On the eve of war, gathering material for his Harvard thesis on appeasement, he traveled again to Europe with his college friend Byron "Whizzer" White, and was in Berlin as late as August 20, 1939. On September 3, 1939, he was in the House of Commons to hear Chamberlain's announcement of war with Germany. But while his father was anguished to hear the defeat of his hopes for appeasement of Hitler, Jack was inspired by the fighting words of Winston Churchill, every one of whose books he had read: "It is a war . . . to establish on impregnable rocks, the rights of the individual, and it is a war to establish and revive the stature of man."

Jack was fascinated by the British upper class in the last decade of its power and influence. He enjoyed the sense of history of the great country houses, the historical background for discussion of literature and politics at weekend house parties. He liked the way that political differences had no effect on personal friendships. He enjoyed the jokes, the refusal to take things too seriously, which suited his own cool temperament, and he appreciated the English aristocratic attitudes toward women and sex. Unlike America, where women were put on pedestals and enjoyed power in a real sense, upper-class Englishwomen were luxury objects with a talent to seduce and amuse. In return, the English upper class embraced both Jack and Kathleen—indeed, Kathleen returned to England during the war to marry the heir to the Duke of Devonshire and become Marchioness of Hartington. After his death in action in September 1944, she lived out the remainder of her short life there, until she was killed in a plane crash with her aristocratic English lover, Earl Fitzwilliam, in 1948.

Joe Kennedy's stint as the first Irish Roman Catholic American ambassador to the Court of St. James's began gloriously. For Rose it was perhaps the happiest time of her life. All social doors were open to the Kennedys: they were asked everywhere and even spent the weekend at Windsor Castle with King George VI and Queen Elizabeth. Just over a year later, however, when war broke out in Europe, Joe Kennedy's energetic advocacy of appeasement of Hitler made him deeply unpopular. His craven attitude was exposed when, even before the Blitz, he rented a mansion outside London to escape possible bombing at night, leaving his embassy staff to face the danger. It reinforced his justified reputation for physical cowardice.

In October 1940, on the eve of the presidential election, he virtually blackmailed Roosevelt into recalling him, and on his return gave an interview of such indiscretion that it ended his hopes of a political career. Among other things, he pronounced democracy in England "finished" and declared that the Queen of England would be among the first to make peace with Hitler. Even after America entered the war in December 1941, he continued to voice isolationist views, making himself virtually a social pariah and one of the most unpopular men in America. By 1942, shunned by Roosevelt, with whom he had quarreled, and widely detested by the American people, Kennedy realized that any hope of a future in public life was definitively over. Frank Waldrop met him at a luncheon in Palm Beach in the spring of 1942 and described the ex-ambassador as "in despair emotionally." All his hopes, ambitions, formidable energy and financial clout would be concentrated upon his children, his eldest sons in particular. As Jack's biographer wrote, "In the circumstances, only his sons Joe Jr. and Jack could restore the family honor."[15] And after the death in action of Joe Jr. in August 1944, that responsibility rested solely upon Jack.

At war in the Solomon Islands as commander of a PT (patrol torpedo) boat, Jack had often talked to his mates about his father: "He was very embarrassed by the fact that his father had not served in World War I," recalled one. It caused both Jack and Joe to risk their lives in war: Joe lost his and Jack nearly did, while atoning with heroism for his father's cowardice. In entering politics and succeeding, he would somehow wipe out the humiliation inflicted on his father by Roosevelt. His father's social rejection at Harvard also rankled, and Jack only narrowly escaped a similar experience.

But Jack had one important quality that his father notably lacked: a magical ability to make friends and, perhaps even more remarkable, to keep them. At Harvard, as elsewhere, his friends came from across the social and religious spectrum, Catholics and Episcopalians, rough-diamond Irish football stars like Torby MacDonald, upper-class WASPs. And, with the help of his friends, he got into the Spee Club, where, admittedly, the membership was more liberal New York and less Boston. Eben Pyne, tall, rich, handsome, and in manner and breeding the ultimate WASP, had made friends with Jack during the latter's brief time at Princeton and remained loyal while he was at Harvard. When Pyne asked his mother if he could bring Jack for a weekend in the country she would reply, "You can have one Catholic weekend." Pyne, whom Jack affectionately called "Evil Eben," remembers going to a dance at the Tuxedo Club with Jack and witnessing Jack's amused reaction to prejudice. Jack cut in on a scion of the East Coast aristocracy who was dancing with Charlotte McDonnell, a member of the grand Catholic McDonnell family and a friend of Jack's sister Kathleen. The man in question, wearing the Club emblem while Jack had on an ordinary dinner jacket, had been "pretty rude" in return, along the lines of "Irish peasant." When they came out there was thick snow and his car was stuck in it with Jack's huge limo in front of it. "Why don't you ask Jack?" Pyne suggested. "Kennedy wound down the window a little bit," Pyne recalled, "and asked, 'Have you got a problem?' The other indicated his car. Whereupon Jack revs up his car and rams it backward so that his rival's little car does a flip. The man's face is strawberry and vanilla. Jack goes, 'Have you got a problem?' He shouts, 'Goddam son of an Irish peasant.' "[16]

Jack had the grace, the humor, the wit and the intellect to escape the Irish stereotype and reinvent the Kennedys. After all, he had been the first Irish Catholic to break into the Boston-Harvard set, but his and his father's experience had a strong bearing on his career, as his friend and admirer, the brilliant political commentator Joseph W. Alsop, recalled: "That first part of his political career, the exclusion of the Irish in old-fashioned Boston . . . had a real role in his approach to politics. I think he was bent on showing that here was a man very different from old-fashioned Boston's view of an Irish politician . . . I remember how he was put up for overseer of Harvard while I was on the board, and he was not elected the first time he was put up—it was just after he was elected to the Senate. And he minded very much his failure to be elected and took it—I think not incorrectly—as another proof of that kind of Act of Exclusion against the Irish that the old, cold Bostonians and Harvardians had passed, in effect in the nineteenth century . . . He was proportionally very pleased when he was put up again the next year and was elected by a very large majority. I think that was a real desire to . . . To raise the Kennedy name in Massachusetts, I think, had a real role in his political career."[17]

Jack, his friend Alastair Forbes, wrote, in an article in the *Spectator*, "greatly loved" and to some extent "greatly disapproved" of his father; with his mother he had almost no relationship at all. If anything, their dealings were edged with a thinly veiled hostility. While Joe appeared—and, in most of his relations with other people, was—coldhearted, underneath he was an emotional man, at least as far as his children were concerned. He had been far more stricken by Joe Jr.'s death than Rose was. He loved his children passionately with a demanding love that could at times be fierce and cruel but was always concerned and loyal. Their love for him was partly due to his strength of character, his clarity of intellect and his money, but it was also because of their sense of his total concern and love for them. Even when they thought he interfered too much, as in the case of Joe Jr. and Jack, when he pulled strings (vainly) to keep them out of dangerous war zones, they understood that he did it because he cared for them. If Jack got into trouble at school—he was once nearly expelled from Choate for being the leader of an anarchic gang named the Muckers' Club—Joe would visit and sort it out. Yet when Jack endured one of his prolonged spells in the school infirmary, Rose never came to see him. She was distant from her children's lives, never putting herself to the trouble of writing them individual letters but resorting to round robins, banal résumés of family news duplicated on carbon paper, which she circulated among them. Jack, the great communicator, who kept up regular, witty, scatological correspondence with his friends, was exasperated by her. His biographer quotes a sarcastic response written by him from Washington in 1941:

> I enjoy your round robin letters. I'm saving them to publish—that style of yours will net us millions. With all this talk about inflation and where is our money going—when I think of your potential earning power—with you dictating and Mrs. Walker [Rose's secretary] beating it out on that machine—it's enough to make a man get down on his knees and thank God for the Dorchester Latin High School which gave you that very sound grammatical basis which shines through every mixed metaphor and each somewhat split infinitive . . .[18]

Jack's attitude toward his mother's attempts to turn him into a well-behaved, well-dressed WASP model was both rebellious and mocking. Where she demanded punctuality, he was invariably late; where she expected tidiness and careful adherence to certain rules of dress, he was careless of his appearance. Rose wore notes pinned to her blouse to remind her of things she had to do. She issued strict *ukases* as to dress, "Don't wear white socks with dress suit. Wear dark shoes with blue or gray suit, never brown . . ." and on manners, "Don't say 'Hi!' to people when addressing them." There would be endless instructions on deportment at table, how to use knives and forks in the correct way, where to sit, when to stand and allow the ladies to leave the room first. At Hyannis Port and Palm Beach the children never had individual rooms of their own. "We lived in cubicles in a row," Jack told Bill Walton. "It was like an institution."

"He hardly ever mentioned his mother," Walton recalled. "She was rather a dim figure in his life."[19] "Sometimes when I think about the relationship between Jack and Rose it seems that there was almost a chemical anger between the two of them," Doris Kearns Goodwin said. "From the very beginning he seemed to exasperate her all the time, irritate her. And I'm not sure he meant to but I think after a while he did, it became his modus operandi in that house, to be messy, to drop towels on the floor, to not work hard in school, to come late to meals . . . She was the discipline person in that house and he was always defying the discipline. And I think she always felt, if one kid starts getting out of line then they all will . . . And I think there was real anger toward him and he sensed that and he sometimes played with it and teased her but other times it made him very sad . . ."[20]

Jack's friends, like Chuck Spalding, surmised that his relentless sexual promiscuity had its roots in the lack of physical tenderness in his relationship with his mother. While this might have contributed to his excesses, it would be unfair to lay the blame entirely on Rose, whose social and intellectual ambitions had been blighted by the patriarchal attitudes of both her father and her husband. Her frequent prolonged absences and obsession with clothes were her form of protest against and escape from the demands of unrelenting motherhood, the neglect and flaunted philandering of her husband. It was a pattern that Jackie herself would follow in similar circumstances.

Where women were concerned, Jack Kennedy had inherited his father's genes and absorbed his father's attitudes. The Kennedy approach to women was profoundly misogynistic. This was partly the Irish tradition of regarding women as divided into two distinct groups, for procreational or for recreational purposes, with wives definitely in the former category. This stereotype was reinforced by the acquiescing attitudes of Kennedy women like Rose and Bobby's wife, Ethel, who saw sex primarily in reproductive terms, Rose's nine children being surpassed by Ethel's eleven. More important, it was the result of Joe's particularly crude view of women, whom he considered as no more than sex objects to be conquered, with no other purpose or interest beyond his immediate sexual gratification.

Joe's predatory behavior went far beyond what would normally be considered acceptable: no attractive female was out of bounds, as far as he was concerned, and that included his sons' girlfriends. When these girls were staying at Hyannis Port or Palm Beach he would attempt to kiss them on the lips or persuade them to sleep with him. When in London en route to Chatsworth for Kathleen's funeral in 1948, the supposedly grief-stricken Joe could not resist attempting to grope one of her sisters-in-law in an elevator. Worse, there was competition between Jack and his father over women: each got a thrill from sleeping where he knew the other had gone before. As Inga Arvad's son recalled of "the Ambassador's" attempts to seduce her the moment Jack left the room, "It was a totally amoral situation. There was something incestuous about the whole family."[21] Joe set the pattern for Jack by importing tarts to Hyannis Port and Palm Beach when Rose was not there. On one occasion Jack returned home from school to find his bed covered with sex magazines, "all open to show the female anatomy at its most immodest," left there by his father. Joe showed no loyalty to any of his women; not even to Gloria Swanson. According to one source, he boasted to Jack and Jackie about sleeping with Swanson, and gave coarse details about her genitalia.

Jack was sexually more successful than his father, as he was infinitely more attractive. Women of every age and class fell for him, while Joe went for easier game—showgirls, secretaries or call girls—and Jack was more sexually driven, to the point of satyriasis. Some people have attributed his promiscuity to lack of maternal affection, others to his brushes with mortality, which left him with a desperate need to take all the pleasure he could before death overtook him. Certainly it increased as he grew older until it reached addiction, the full extent of which Jackie never grasped.

At home, which for the Kennedys after Joe sold the Bronxville house in 1941 meant principally Hyannis Port, Joe dominated the family. Compared with him Rose was a cipher in her children's lives. "Old Joe did everything, he practically ran the house, the works," Bill Walton said. "Suddenly I realized that Joe's role in the family was so much more than the conventional father. He was home more than I expected. He ran the house. He hired the servants. He often planned the meals. Mrs. Kennedy was often away. And he had a far greater role in his children's lives than their mother did."[22] The subtext of all this was the old man's paranoia about a hostile world beyond the family. "I think the world outside his house was war for Mr. Kennedy," Chuck Spalding commented.[23]

At the white-shingled house on the Cape Cod shore the Kennedy family lived a hermetic, inward-looking, hierarchical existence, much as if they had been an ancient Celtic clan clustered around their chieftain within their tribal enclosure. They were fanatically loyal to one another, invisibly linked by bonds that no outsider could break. "You belong so wholeheartedly to the Kennedy clan," Inga Arvad had written sadly to Jack after their breakup. "The Kennedys were a like a nation unto themselves," Rose said, "with their own private language and customs. They invited friends into their lives, but there was always a distance between them." The same might be said of their relationships with their marriage partners. "We had such a very good time with each other," Jean reflected. "My family were my best friends, and I was very close to Bobby and Teddy. I mean, we all had such a good time that we didn't really want to marry . . ."[24] The only exception so far was Bobby, who had married Ethel Skakel, his sister Pat's school friend from the Sacred Heart Convent at Manhattanville, which all the Kennedy girls had attended. And Ethel, raucous, bouncy, hyperactive and competitive, was as much like a Kennedy as it was possible to be.

Winning at all costs was the maxim drummed into the Kennedy children.

Winning, winning, winning at everything, even sailing races—under threat of their father's displeasure. Pleasing Dad, competing for his affection and approbation, was the order of the day. (Pleasing Mother had no priority whatsoever.) The Kennedy children were brought up to keep abreast of current affairs; in the war years a map showing the progress of the war was pinned on the wall of the dining room and meals were the occasion for competitive discussion. Charlie Bartlett remembered, "Ambassador Kennedy would sit rather quietly and listen to the children and in some ways guide the conversation but generally let them run on. He was very definitely the overriding figure in the scene. And they were obviously interested in getting his approval or arguing with him. He was a presence, Joseph Kennedy. I always had a feeling that he was a man of strong opinions but he didn't always vent them at these family gatherings. He would sort of let the children talk and let them express their opinions and I think he was more interested in listening to thoughts on their part than trying to dominate the conversation."[25]

In the tribal world where Joe was the acknowledged king and men counted for more than women, Jack was the adored crown prince. After the death of Joe Jr. in 1944, and particularly after Jack's success in the congressional elections of 1946, his sisters regarded him with adoration that verged on idolatry. When a friend told Eunice that she resembled Jack, Eunice was ecstatic, but sister Jean was furious when told she looked like Bobby. "She had a very bitter fight about that. She didn't want to look like Bobby, she wanted to look like Jack," the friend recalled.[26]

~

This was the world that Jackie had first encountered when she had been invited to stay at Hyannis Port in June 1952 while Jack was fiercely engaged in the battle for Cabot Lodge's Senate seat, a campaign in which the Kennedy women were energetically involved. It had been her first taste of the potentially hostile territory with which she had to learn to live. From the start, she captivated the Kennedy men; the Kennedy women were another matter. The girls mocked her elegant manners and soft speech, calling her "the deb" and mimicking her behind her back.

Jackie, however, was tough enough not to be cowed by them. Despite her slimness, she was physically as strong and athletic as they were, with her muscular, slightly bowed legs and large hands. John White gave a revealing glimpse of Jackie in an interview with her biographer C. David Heymann. They had been out of Washington for the day and become snarled in the returning traffic: "I was content to be a bit tardy but Jackie wasn't, and for the first time I saw a streak of real ferocity in her. It was my car and I was driving, but she began to take charge . . . She started giving me all sorts of orders—'Turn right, turn left, stay on your side of the road.' She even put her hands over mine on the steering wheel to make sure I made the turns she wanted, and I thought what a huge, strong, peasant hand that is. That's not a ladylike hand at all. It's a big, strong, powerful hand. And I suddenly realized I was dealing with something I hadn't even suspected. She was one tough cookie, really tough! That undigested, renegade tough-ness lay at the very core of Jackie's personality . . ."[27]

Jackie's method of dealing with the Kennedy tribe was quietly to assert her in-dependence. She stayed out of the relentless activities—tennis, sailing, touch football—but not because she was too delicate for them. Jack's biographer Wil-liam Manchester remembered her "playing touch football like a gazelle." Intellec-tually she could beat them at one of their favorite games, a form of charades called "The Game," in which opposing teams had to act out a given phrase or word for their teammates to guess in a race against time. For the Kennedy women, however, the bitterest pill they had to take where Jackie was concerned was that she had so swiftly conquered the heights of the Kennedy pyramid—the two most important males, Joe Kennedy and Jack.

On his return to the United States from London, Ambassador Kennedy (a title he relished) had imported English trappings. There was an English butler and Jack had a valet, George Thomas (which had caused some ribaldry in the Boston op-position press when Jack was running for congressman—"My dear, a valet . . ." one article began). Yet they hardly lived in the style to which Jackie had become accustomed at Merrywood and Hammersmith. Alastair Forbes, who, although not himself possessed of a fortune, was well connected and accustomed to high living in upper-class Anglo-American circles, was dismayed by the hospitality at Hyan-nis Port, where scant courtesy was shown by the Ambassador to his children's friends even when they were adults. Forbes was ordered to share a room with Jack. (Teddy, as the youngest, frequently found himself displaced to provide a bed for a recent arrival.) He described it as "a horrible place . . . terrible smell of drains as well as bad food. To get a drink you had to go to some relation of Rose who kept a whiskey bottle in a cupboard."[28] Jack himself described the alcohol supplies at the Kennedy homes as "flowing like molasses"; guests were allowed one drink before dinner. Milk was the favored drink for most of the Kennedys. Both Joe and Jack were notably abstemious but Jack resented the lack of hospital-ity in this respect on behalf of his friends and one of the rare times he stood up publicly to his father at home was in defending the right of his friends to have a drink. "Jack and Mr. Kennedy had a fight about the booze in the house . . . Jack insisted upon being able to give his friends a drink. And they had an argument and they didn't speak for a day."[29]

"The thing about Mr. Kennedy, he was so punctual," remembered Nancy Ten-ney Coleman, who as the daughter of the next-door neighbors was a regular at the Kennedy household from the age of nine. "The rest of them were always late, Jack, Eunice, Pat, the whole bunch, but Mr. Kennedy and Mrs. Kennedy—they lived by the clock, they truly did. And I remember my mother and father, living in the house right next to them—we shared the same ocean—and my father would look up and he would see Big Joe and Mrs. Kennedy go swimming and he'd say, 'It's got to be ten minutes to lunch.' " Punctuality was insisted upon, particularly by Rose, whose life was lived to a rigid set of rules. Jackie, by nature unpunc-tual, refused to change her ways, a subtle rebellion against her mother-in-law's insistence on conformity. The Kennedy nation, as Rose said, lived by their own rules, set ultimately by the patriarch, Joe, and Jackie chafed under them. "She seldom complained about Jack himself but she was irritated by the family's rules and regulations," Gore Vidal wrote of a conversation with Jackie in 1956: " 'I wanted this small car, a Thunderbird. I mean what could be more *American?*' The mischievous smile. 'But Mr. Kennedy said, "Kennedys drive Buicks." So I drive a Buick . . .' "[30]

Yet Jackie loved her father-in-law. "She [Jackie] told me that at the beginning she identified more with Old Joe," Doris Kearns Goodwin said, "that she'd sit with Joe and listen to classical music, and he'd tell her not to worry about touch football and that he'd rather talk to her anyway. He really did love classical music and he was an interesting fellow, and probably he was much more interesting to talk to at that stage of her life than Rose would have been. He was worldly, he had adventures, he was a flirt. I can see that she would have liked him."[31]

After all, Jackie had been brought up to cope with dominant males, and she deployed the same methods that she had used on Grandfather Bouvier to win over the Kennedy patriarch. She easily captured Bobby and Teddy, but with the women she did not even try. "She was just never on the same wavelength as the Kennedy women," a friend said. "They didn't get on but it was perfectly civilized."[32] Eunice was the most intelligent of the Kennedy daughters, a woman of deep religious faith and fearless spirit. She shared her brothers' reckless physical bravery and fierce competitiveness and, like them, had her sights set on an active part in the world outside her family. She was the most religious, and when she was young many had predicted that she would become a nun. She would have had to be more than saintly not to resent Jackie's intrusion into her close relationship with her brother. "Jack was the world to Eunice, a gay, witty presence whom she admired beyond admiration," Laurence Leamer, biographer of the Kennedy women, wrote.[33]

By the time Jackie joined the Kennedy family it had already been touched by tragedy. Joe Jr. had died in August 1944, blown to pieces in midair by the high explosives his plane was carrying to bomb rocket silos in France. It was later discovered that the silos were disused and the mission therefore vain. His death had preceded, by less than a month, that of Kathleen's husband, Billy Hartington, killed in action in France in September 1944. She had married him in May against the opposition of both sets of parents, and particularly of Rose, who had retired to a clinic rather than face reporters with the news that her Catholic daughter had married a Protestant aristocrat. Kathleen had been Jack's favorite sister, gifted with his charm and sex appeal, adored by everyone who knew her. "Kick was a shining light of gaiety, pleasure and enthusiasm," said one of her sisters-in-law. When she died in May 1948, she was mourned by her hundreds of friends, men and women, and buried in the Cavendish family plot in Derbyshire. Her wartime photograph, in which she is in uniform, smiling radiantly, hangs in a gallery at Chatsworth alongside the more formal oil paintings of members of the ducal family. "No American, man or woman, who has ever settled in England was so much loved as she, and no American ever loved England more," a friend wrote anonymously to *The Times*, while her mother-in-law, the

Duchess of Devonshire, had engraved on her tombstone, "Joy she gave, joy she has found."

Kathleen had been the only Kennedy woman to break out of the family mold and to take hold of her own life and destiny. For this, and for defying the dictates of the family religion, Rose had threatened her with ostracism from the family and disinheritance. They were not reconciled when Kathleen died; Rose did not accompany Joe to her funeral. Rose had already virtually lost another daughter, her eldest, Rosemary, born the year after Jack. Rosemary had been born retarded and possibly also epileptic, but she had been cherished by her mother and elder brothers, and even presented at Court during her father's ambassadorship. Since Joe's return from England, however, she had been hidden away in a convent in Washington where her behavior had become a matter of increasing concern to the nuns and to her father. Without, apparently, consulting Rose, Joe Kennedy submitted Rosemary to a prefrontal lobotomy, a horrific operation that destroyed her personality. From then on she became a nonperson in the family, dropped from Rose's family bulletins and immured in institutions, ending up at the St. Coletta School for Exceptional Children in Jefferson, Wisconsin, where Joe built her a private house. Almost ten years later he wrote to the superintendent sister at St. Coletta's expressing his gratitude for her help in chillingly practical terms: ". . . the solution of Rosemary's problem has been a major factor in the ability of all the Kennedys to go about their life's work and to try to do it as well as they can . . ."[34]

Rose never revealed how she felt about what her husband had done to Rosemary, but years later, after he was dead, she talked of the deep bitterness she felt at the way he had thrown away his own career: "We had everything," she said, "everything. But Joe didn't have an ounce of humility, and in London he refused to learn anything. After a while I tried to tell him what I felt. He didn't listen, though—Joe never listened—but maybe I should have said even more. Afterward I was very angry at him. I felt that he had not accomplished what we could have accomplished as a couple. He had not accomplished what he should have as a world leader, and I was made to suffer for it. I lost my friendships. We lost our prestige, and within a few years we began to lose our children. And I wonder if he ever knew how much I lost because of him."[35]

It was a heartfelt cry, the stronger and more anguished because it had been repressed for so many years. Yet Rose was tough: there was not a word about Joe's blatant philandering, which most wives would have found intolerable. Her regret was for loss of prestige, for which she so ardently longed—even to the extent of revealing herself to one of Jack's Harvard friends, whom she asked, "When are the nice people in Boston going to accept us?" That prestige had been theirs during the glorious first year of Joe's London ambassadorship; it might still have been theirs had Joe, in his twisted obstinacy, not alienated Roosevelt. In Rose's eyes—and who could say she was wrong?—it was she and her children who had had to pay the price.

According to her memoirs, Rose warned Ethel, Jackie and, later, Ted's wife, Joan, what they had to expect from their marriages: "I made sure to warn them in advance of what they were in for: that they might be hearing and reading all sorts of scandalous gossip and accusations about themselves and eventually even about their children; and they should understand this and be prepared from the beginning . . ."[36] It was only the Kennedy wives who needed Rose's warnings: the sisters had become so accustomed to their father's unashamed display of his women that they accepted this behavior as something to be acquiesced in and not talked about. In the words of Laurence Leamer, they became agents of their father's duplicity: "They learned not to see . . . ."[37] This absolution applied equally to the sexual behavior of their brothers.

Joe Kennedy instillled in his children, and his sons in particular, a sense of entitlement derived from their money and their celebrity. In 1950 *Fortune* estimated the wealth of Kennedy Enterprises, based at 235 Park Avenue, at up to $400 million. As soon as Jack had begun his political career, Joe had liquidated his assets in the liquor business that had made him so much money but might yet prove a political liability. He transferred a quarter of the Chicago Merchandise Mart to Rose and a quarter to his surviving children, enough to take care of their needs for life. He donated another quarter to the Joseph P. Kennedy Jr. charitable foundation and kept the remaining quarter for himself. His biographer, James Landis, claimed that he was one of the few rich men of his acquaintance in a position to write a check for $10 million without having to sell anything. His sons, the beneficiaries of his business acumen, were to concentrate on politics, not business. "Lem Billings once said that to hear the Kennedy boys talking about business was like hearing nuns talk about sex," the distinguished Kennedy historian and former aide, Arthur Schlesinger Jr. recalled. "They didn't know anything about it."[38] At home there were always servants to pick clothes up after them, to take them away and clean them, to shop and cook for them. Bills were simply sent to 235 Park Avenue for payment. Possessions meant little to them; their homes were usually shabby and disorderly, food scarce and basic. Money was not important but that did not mean that they were generous or wont to throw it around. Like most wealthy men Jack rarely carried cash and was notorious among his friends for leaving them to pick up the tab. The Kennedy boys were always the leaders of the pack; friends, however intimate, were subtly relegated to the status of courtiers—and in the Kennedy White House that went for important administration officials as well. During the Cuban missile crisis of October 1962 one Harvard academic, brought in as a consultant, was amazed to see servants bringing in bowls of soup for Jack and Bobby at a cabinet meeting. No one else was offered anything.

To Jackie, her Kennedy sisters-in-law, Eunice, Jean, Pat and Ethel, whom she liked to call the "toothy girls" or the "rah-rah girls," had everything in common with one another and almost nothing in common with her. All of them, unlike herself, had a solid Catholic background and no financial insecurity. All of them had been educated at the Convent of the Sacred Heart at Manhattanville, which Rose had attended and which now enjoyed college status. Ethel, one of seven children of the rich, uproarious Catholic Skakel family of Greenwich, Connecticut, had been Jean's best friend and co-prankster at Manhattanville. At the convent the girls learned about wider social problems, spending time in hospitals and settlement houses. Eunice in particular was attracted by social work—in Washington in 1947–48 she had irritated Jack by bringing home troubled juveniles to be fed by their housekeeper, Mrs. Ambrose. They had also absorbed the good Catholic precept that their goal in life was to marry and raise a family; there was even a "Happy Husband Hunting Club" at Manhattanville. Both Bobby and Teddy found their wives through their sisters' connections with the school. Religion, to the point of zealotry, was important in the lives of both Eunice and Ethel, each of whom had contemplated becoming a nun. Eunice had sided with Rose in the great family row over Kathleen's desire to marry Peter Fitzwilliam, who was not only a Protestant but married, even though her idolized brother Jack had supported their sister. Ethel reputedly kept a picture of the "Bleeding Heart of Jesus" on the wall of the bedroom she shared with Bobby, something that only "bog Irish" Catholics were supposed to do.

When Jackie joined the family, Bobby and Ethel had been married for three years and already had two children, Kathleen Hartington and Joseph Patrick Kennedy II; their third, Robert Francis Kennedy Jr., was born in 1954. Eunice, married in May 1953, was expecting Robert Sargent Shriver in 1954. Pat, who had met the British actor Peter Lawford and had invited him to Palm Beach for Christmas 1953, married him—despite her father's animadversions about hating actors "and British actors most of all"—in April 1954. Two years later, on May 19, 1956, Jean, youngest and prettiest of the sisters, married Stephen Edward "Steve" Smith, who, like Sargent Shriver, became totally subsumed into the Kennedy family. An Irish American and graduate of Georgetown University, he gave up working for the family transportation firm to dedicate himself to the Kennedy interests. He played an important part in Jack's campaigns and acted as his political agent during his presidency. "Steve was a brigand . . . I don't think I would trust Steve with much," Richard Goodwin, special assistant on Latin America in the Kennedy White House, said. "I liked him. I got along fine with him, but he was the hatchet man. He was ultimately ruthless . . ." Shrewd, tough, charming, womanizing, hard-drinking and ruthlessly efficient, Smith fitted perfectly into the Kennedy pattern. "Well, obviously [Jackie's relationship with the Kennedy family] was a multi-layered thing," Goodwin went on. "She maintained certainly correct relationships . . . [but] I don't think she ever felt comfortable with the sisters. I mean, she was very close to Bobby and her relationship with Teddy was fine, he was just a kid anyway, but with the girls—she loved Joe, he was great to her—I don't think she ever felt comfortable with the sisters. They were fiercely competitive women and she wasn't like that—she didn't want to play touch football . . ."[39]

In her relationships with both the king (Joe) and the crown prince (Jack) Jackie, to the Kennedy women, was both an interloper and a threat to their own relationships with Joe and Jack. All of them, headed by Rose, had been closely involved with Jack's recent successful Senate campaign in Massachusetts and could justifiably identify with his success. "It was those damn teas that killed me," Cabot Lodge, the loser, had declared. "What he meant by that," the historian Doris Kearns Goodwin explained, "was that a whole group of women got involved in politics who had not been involved before, Irish Catholic women, and, I mean, this was the silent generation, this was not a politically active generation, but somehow Rose made it legitimate for a housewife with her gloves to get involved with politics. Thousands of women wanted to come to these teas, and what they would do is Rose would talk about the British Royal Family and what it was like . . . my weekend with the King and Queen. And then all the young girls who weren't married wanted to meet Jack, of course, so these teas became not only social events but celebrity events. It was probably one of those times when that power of celebrity and social class and politics combined. And then during the campaign, Rose would be terribly active. There are stories of Rose switching from her fur coat to another coat and going from one thing to another and talking her different languages . . ."

Jackie, the bride, had not shared these experiences and yet she had the Kennedy men on her side. Rose and the sisters were jealous. "Rose had a desire to pull the kids into her orbit," Doris Kearns Goodwin said. "I remember [Jackie talking] about the idea that every Sunday if they were called to dinner at the main house, that's a Sunday she's not with Jack at her house. So the idea that she would piss Rose off by being late, my guess is that wasn't just rudeness or taking too long to get dressed, but psychologically it might have been a sense of rebellion against having to live by somebody else's rules and, more importantly, knowing that if she was ever going to win him over to her she had to pull him to some extent out of that orbit . . .

"Jackie was very insightful into people and she could see through them," Doris Kearns Goodwin went on. She was too intelligent and independent-minded to be dazzled by the Kennedy myth; she could see past the surface glamour and power of the huge, united family to the psychological strains beneath. "What makes you think it was so great being in a large family?" she asked Kearns Goodwin. "And, anyway, then she went through a devastating critique about what impact each kid had in the family on the other ones—that Jack was always in Joe Jr.'s shadow, that Eunice was always in Kathleen's shadow . . . that there were too many kids, too close, too competitive for them to arrive with their own personality . . . I could tell then that she had a really bold ability to analyze people."[40]

"My impression was that the Kennedys were fearfully unsophisticated," an English guest at the Loel Guinnesses' Palm Beach estate in 1954 remembered. "There was something terribly provincial about them—Jackie was the orchid among them . . ."[41] Jackie's achievement would be to remain herself among the Kennedys, not by competing with them but by not allowing herself to be engulfed by them. Eventually she won the respect of the clan, but first she had to win over her husband.

CHAPTER SIX

Twin Icebergs

—

She was in love with him in the beginning and went on to love him. Her care for him showed enormous depths of feeling to which he responded on some levels but never enough to give up the other women . . .[1]

—Wendy Morgan

His love had certain reservations and hers was total.[2]

—Robin Biddle Duke

Jackie was romantically in love with her husband. While they were still on their honeymoon she wrote a poem about him, which expressed the Harvard veneer that hid the sensitive Irishman with his "too proud heart," the present domination of his father and his own restless ambition driving him forward to the presidency:

Meanwhile in Massachusetts Jack Kennedy dreamed
Walking the shore by the Cape Cod sea
Of all the things he was going to be . . .

He thought with his feet most firm on the ground
But his heart and his dreams were not earthbound.
He would call New England his place and his creed
But part he was of an alien breed
Of a breed that had laughed on the Irish hills . . .
That surged in the depth of his too proud heart . . .
On a green lawn his white house stands
And the wind blows the sea grass low on the sands . . .
The lights glowed inside, soon supper would ring
And he would go home where his father was King.
But now he was here with the wind and the sea
And all the things he was going to be . . .
He would find love

He would never find peace
For he must go seeking
The Golden Fleece . . .[3]

Jack was impressed. He read her his favorite poem, Alan Seeger's prophetic "I Have a Rendezvous with Death," which Jackie, whose memory was encyclopedic, memorized and would recite for him.

But romance was hard to sustain in the circumstances of their early married life, living with their in-laws, either on the Cape with the Kennedys, or at Merrywood so that Jack could attend the Senate while Jackie went house-hunting. It was not until mid-December that she found one to rent in George-town, at 3321 Dent Place. Thanksgiving was a rambunctious Kennedy festival at Hyannis Port, after which the house was closed up and Joe and Rose headed south to Palm Beach, where Jack and Jackie joined them for Christmas. Jackie gave her husband a box of paints, hoping to cure some of his restlessness and to give them a mutual interest. In fact, their paintings expressed their very different natures; his were bold and expressive, hers deliberately naïve, almost childlike, showing nothing of her real self. That winter she had written and illustrated a book for Little Janet Auchincloss, entitled "A Book for Janet: In Case You Are Ever Thinking of Getting Married This Is a Story to Tell You What It's Like . . ." "She drew absolutely wonderful pictures of her waving good-bye to Jack as he left the house in the morning and, of course, they were all funny caricatures," Janet Auchincloss recalled. "There was one of the dome of the Capitol all lit up at night, very dark, and there was a rhyme underneath it about when you saw the light burning there late at night and he wasn't home yet, you knew that the coun-try was safe because he was working."[4]

This was hero worship. In the first year of her marriage to a man twelve years older than herself, Jackie seemed young and naïve to some of Jack's women friends who had known him since his Navy days. "I thought she was very, very young," Robin Biddle Duke said of Jackie in Palm Beach. "Even young for a new bride who had worked a little bit in Washington and so forth . . . She used to come and sit around Flo [Pritchett] Smith's pool, and we talked about what we would wear to this party and that. We were all friends of JFK when he had been in the Navy during the war. And I always thought she seemed very young and very inexperienced. I was probably wrong and it was just a façade and she was far smarter than all of us but we were considerably older—and, you know, when there's a gap of five or six years, that much, in those days, was quite a bit. She was a very young, seemingly innocent girl, and I knew JFK to be a very experienced fellow in many ways and so I think she suffered great disappointments."[5]

Among the disappointments was Jackie's failure to follow the pattern expected of a Kennedy wife and bear a child in the first year of marriage. Whether the dif-ficulties she was to suffer both in getting pregnant and in bearing healthy children to full term were on her side or due to her husband's health problems is a moot point. While still at Harvard in 1940 Jack had contracted a venereal disease, de-scribed by his doctor at the time, Vernon S. Dick of the urology department of the Lahey Clinic in Boston, as a mild, nonspecific urethritis. Ten years later, in 1950, Dr. Dick reported him as suffering a "slight burning on urination," the result of "a mild, non-specific prostatitis," which was treated with various antibiotics, painful prostatic massage and sitz baths. Through the winter of 1951–52, he had suffered "recurrent symptoms" and in August 1952 "because of recurrent symptoms" he was hospitalized for rest and tests. Although nothing abnormal was found he continued to suffer "varying degrees of urinary distress," the only abnormality being "a few remaining pus cells in the prostatic secretion." On March 20, 1953, Dr. Dick had referred his patient to Dr. William P. Herbst, a Washington urologist, who saw Jack on March 27. According to Herbst's almost illegible notes, Jack complained of "burning in prostate area" and made four subsequent appointments for treatment with Herbst, the last being on July 24. On February 17, 1954, he visited Dr. Herbst again, and had another appointment on July 28.[6]

According to a recent Kennedy biographer, Richard Reeves, Jack was so concerned that he might be responsible for Jackie's failure to bear a child that he consulted an expert about his sperm count in the first year of their marriage. In fact, Jackie succeeded in conceiving that year but miscarried. The underlying cause of this and her subsequent history of childbearing—a stillbirth and two premature births—was almost certainly chlamydia, contracted from Jack as a result of his gonorrhea. Nonspecific urethritis, which was diagnosed in him in 1950, is now known to be a result of a chlamydial infection.[7] It is unlikely that Jack confessed his medical problems in this respect to Jackie, first, because he hated discussing his various ailments, however serious, and second, although in fairness she should have been the first to be told, he would almost certainly have preferred her to be the last.

As the wife of the Kennedy crown prince, Jackie could not help feeling humiliated by the abounding fertility of the other Kennedy wives. For her, it was a hidden tragedy: if she had succeeded in bearing a child that first year, or even the next, it would have saved her from some of the heartbreak and marital difficulty she experienced over the next few years. Jack had hated giving up his bachelor status and his freedom and had done so for a complex series of reasons of which "having a family" was one. When he was a rich young bachelor his needs had been catered to by a loyal band of retainers: Mrs. Margaret Ambrose, the housekeeper of the Georgetown house he had shared with Eunice; Evelyn Lincoln, his secretary; Boston policeman Muggsy O'Leary, his driver and general gofer; and his manservant, George Thomas. He had the company of his family and many friends, and as many women as he wanted when he wanted. At thirty-six, it was difficult to change his attitudes to accommodate an insecure young wife. He began to feel trapped.

Jackie worked hard to make her marriage a success. "Her adjustment to the Senator had already included catching planes on time and coping with hordes of Kennedys at close quarters," Evelyn Lincoln wrote of her in the spring of 1954. "Now she was going to learn to keep up with the political shop talk."[8] While Jack embarked on a Tuesday night speed-reading class in Baltimore with Bobby and Lem Billings to help him keep up with the mass of Senate work, Jackie studied political science and history at Georgetown University to keep up with Jack. On Sundays they sometimes drove out of Washington to visit Civil War battlegrounds—"My brother and Jackie knew everything about the Civil War," Teddy Kennedy recalled. "She had a fantastic desire for historical knowledge, and she was a sponge once she learned it. She caught every nuance," Jackie's old acquaintance and White House aide Letitia Baldrige recalled. "And she wanted to know American history not just for herself but for her husband. They were almost competitive in the knowledge they consumed . . . in trying to one-up the other on historical facts and so forth . . ."[9] She attended the opening of the Second Session of the 83rd Congress on January 6, 1954. "This time," as Evelyn Lincoln put it, "instead of a lot of awestruck girls watching him there would be his new bride . . ."

She showed her concern for him by asking Evelyn Lincoln to plead with him to come home earlier and stop working such long hours. It worked for a while, but then he returned to his old habit of working until seven or eight at night; Jackie compromised by calling Mrs. Lincoln on the morning of any important evening engagement to ask her to try to get him to leave earlier. She saw to it that he had proper food for lunch, too, either taking it in for him herself or sending it via Muggsy O'Leary in covered china dishes. She took a French cooking course, although cooking was never her forte, and Jack, who had suffered from a weak stomach since childhood, liked the plainest of food. (When he lost weight during his illness and a worried Eunice asked him why he was so thin, Jack joked, "Don't worry. It's nothing serious—just Jackie's cooking.")

But politics and politicians remained for her a largely uncharted area into which she had no desire to venture. Ted Sorensen, Jack's principal speechwriter and closest political aide, who came to work for him in 1953, wrote,

> After their marriage, she interested him slightly in art and he interested her slightly in politics . . . Reared in a world of social graces far from the clamor of political wars, she at first found little to attract her in either the profession or its practitioners. Politics kept her husband away too much. Politicians invaded their privacy too often. "It was like being married to a whirlwind," she was quoted by one reporter in speaking about their early life. "Politics was sort of my enemy as far as seeing Jack was concerned."[10]

To the Kennedy women politics and public life were as natural as the air that they breathed, and Jack had taken it for granted that Jackie would be the same. He was disconcerted to find that she was not. It was a quality in her that he came later to appreciate, but in the early years, it contributed to mutual misunderstanding.

Less than six months after his marriage, Jack was hankering for his old life. He had not forgotten a beautiful blond Swedish girl he had met in the South of France on his prewedding jaunt the previous August. On March 2, 1954, he wrote to Gunilla von Post from his Senate office, Room 362, telling her he planned to return to the South of France that September, and followed it up with a series of telephone calls to Stockholm, never leaving his number. He wrote to her again, twice, hoping to arrange a late August rendezvous, and telephoned her in August, still hoping to meet her in Paris. However, on September 3 she received a cable from Hyannis Port: "Trip postponed . . ."[11]

Jack's letters to Gunilla were based on a desperate optimism: he was trying to hold on to a dream of youthful romance and pleasure when the reality was a daily agony and the prospect of serious invalidism. He had been born with one leg shorter than the other, a condition that would have caused problems even if he had not injured his back playing football at Harvard or ruptured a spinal disk in the wreck of PT-109. (The disk had been removed by neurosurgeon Dr. James Poppen in 1944.) In the spring of 1954 Evelyn Lincoln began to notice that he was having increasing problems with his back. If he dropped something on the floor, he had to ask her to pick it up for him; he even stopped going to his speed-reading class in Baltimore because he thought the car ride would be too much for him. He and Jackie took a brief trip to Palm Beach, hoping that he would recuperate, but he followed this with a journey to Chicago to address the Cook County Democratic Central Committee and then, on April 24, went to New York for the wedding of his sister Pat to Peter Lawford. He was using crutches to walk, but hiding them when official visitors came, to conceal his physical condition from the Massachusetts voters. "Soon his efforts to disguise the agony he suffered, together with his demanding schedule, became a heavy drain on his nervous energy," Lincoln wrote. "He became increasingly irritable . . ."[12] Through the summer the back pain became more and more intense: instead of walking back to his office, he remained in his Senate seat all day and began canceling engagements— "Tell them I am having a little trouble with my back." Loyally, he made an exception for his friend and old Harvard roommate, Torby MacDonald, who was running as a Democrat for Congress in a solidly Republican seat near Boston and needed all the help he could get. Jack went up to Malden, Massachusetts, to speak at a dinner in Torby's honor. When the Senate recessed on August 20, he and Jackie went up to the Cape for September, hoping that a rest would bring improvement and that a threatened back operation might not be necessary.

However, Jack's spinal deterioration had worsened to the extent that drastic surgery was necessary to save him from life in a wheelchair. The danger of the operation, known as a lumbar fusion, was infinitely increased by the Addison's disease, which lowered his immunity to infection. On October 11 he was admitted to the Hospital for Special Surgery in Manhattan for tests and X rays; on October 21 the operation was performed by a team of four physicians headed by Dr. Philip Wilson. Jack survived, but within days, as he had been warned, infection set in. He slipped into a coma; twice his family was summoned to the hospital and the last rites were performed as he approached his rendezvous with death for the third time in his relatively short life. Against all the odds he fought back, as he had when floating semiconscious in the Pacific.

In mid-November, when he was still extremely ill, Charlie Bartlett visited him. He described Jackie as "magnificent with him": "She sat with him for hours, held his hand, mopped his brow, fed him, helped him in and out of bed, put on his socks and slippers for him, entertained him by reading aloud and reciting poems she knew by heart, bought him silly little gadgets and toys to make him laugh, played checkers, Categories and Twenty Questions with him. Once his health improved sufficiently, she encouraged friends to visit as often as possible. Anything to distract him from the pain."[13] A close woman friend was shocked when he telephoned her after dinner in desperation, "Come on down and read me a story . . . I can't stand the pain. I can't stand it." She went to the hospital but when she got home there was another call: "Would you just put the telephone there and read anything you've got, any old thing, any magazine, I don't care. I can't stand it . . ."[14]

While Jackie's care for Jack was unquestioned, the story that she took Grace Kelly to cheer him up is a myth. "I think she [Jackie] lived with a lot of suspicions," Robin Biddle Duke said, "and also over time various things happened that affected her. For example, the time that Flo [Pritchett Smith] took Grace Kelly into the hospital when he was ill, that drove her crazy . . . Flo thought it would cheer Jack up, so she called me up and said, 'What do you think?' and I said I thought it would be more fun and I thought he would be thrilled . . . He had had this terrible back surgery and he was laid lower than a mackerel . . ."[15]

One of the most beautiful film stars of the century, Grace Kelly had been born into a half-Irish, half-German Catholic family in Philadelphia, in November 1929.[16] In 1954, the year of Jack's operation, *Look* had devoted a cover story to her, headlined "Hollywood's Hottest Property," and, in the month that Jack lay in the Hospital for Special Surgery, the *New York Times* had devoted a piece to her "dazzling ascent to success." She was on the verge of winning an Oscar for her role in *The Country Girl*. Most men were in love with, and most women copied, her cool blond high-society looks; in real life, she was not only beautiful but warm and funny. Jack had never made any secret of his admiration for her. Gore Vidal recounts a vignette of Jack and Jackie looking at press coverage of Grace's wedding to Prince Rainier in the summer of 1956, when apparently Jack said, frowning, "I could have married her!" and dates Jackie's well-documented dislike of Grace from then.[17] But, according to Robin Biddle Duke, it was Grace's visit to Jack in the hospital that first raised Jackie's hackles: "Grace Kelly then became somebody in Jackie's life that she could not abide."

If Jackie was jealous, she was too clever to show it. The writer Priscilla Johnson Macmillan, who as a young society girl had worked briefly in Jack's Senate office and whom he sporadically pursued, remembered dropping in at the hospital one Saturday afternoon and finding Jackie there. "She was looking extremely fetching in a black suit, frolicking round Jack's bed, eating his hospital supper, you know at five o'clock, when she was going to meet her old beau, John Marquand, for dinner and Jack knew that . . . I did conclude, that time in the room, when she was frolicking around and looking so attractive and everything, really baiting him . . . it seemed to be working a little bit with Jack. And I concluded that day that what she was was an actress. I concluded it that day and I've never thought anything else. She was one terrific actress . . ." Sometimes Jackie's teasing had an edge to it. "Jackie boasted to me about Teddy," Priscilla Johnson Macmillan said, of that same hospital visit. " 'Have you met Teddy?' she said in her breathy voice. 'He's the real politician in the family,' looking meaningfully at Jack, who was listening the whole time."[18]

There was no cause, apart from Jack's admiration of her looks, for Jackie to be jealous of Grace, who had never had anything even resembling a romance with him. But she was jealous of certain women from his past who remained his friends and close to him long after anything sexual between them was over. She ostracized one of Jack's old friends and confidantes, a beautiful blonde from Boston; this lady had met and become fond of Bobby when he was at Harvard and, with other Harvard men, came over to visit her family, which included three lovely and vivacious daughters, in Boston. Congressman Jack Kennedy had not been welcome at the house. "His father was not liked by the people around Boston particularly," she said. "And my family also were Irish and they were Catholic but my mother couldn't stand Joe Kennedy. The idea even of his children put her in a spin . . . she didn't mind Bobby, as it turned out, because she said he was a lot nicer than she expected him to be. She hated Jack . . . she didn't like him at all because she thought there was a *danger*. She knew Bobby was as safe as a church as far as I was concerned because although I liked him as a pal . . . Joe Kennedy was furious with me because of not marrying Bobby. I wasn't in love with Bobby at all." Jack was another matter. "I did have a wonderfully interesting time with him. He was interesting and he was fun and he was an entertaining and lively person. Very funny. And marvelous-looking. And charming, really charming. Although he had his limitations but one didn't know them . . . I never liked to say that Jack was a beau of mine . . . who else was? A cast of thousands . . ."

She knew Jackie by sight from parties in Newport, New York and Long Island; all she could remember of that period was of thinking how cool and analytical Jackie was: "I can remember dancing at a dance in Southampton at the Cuttings' with Serge Obolensky. And I remember Jackie just sort of sitting there with these cow eyes before she'd gotten to be more beautiful, *watching* as though she was just, you know, piercingly, trying to figure out what was going on . . ." When Jack came up to New York to take her out to dinner and tell her that he was going to marry Jackie, her reaction was: "I thought it's a good idea really in a way because she'll be a good, not too emotional person . . . She wouldn't be emotionally upstrung or upset as much as maybe any other person would be with various things, his time being away, or whatever . . ."

With Jackie, however, feelings ran deep. Jack couldn't understand her moods, her withdrawal and prolonged sulking when she was upset. "He just couldn't stand her. That's all I got. I mean he couldn't understand or stand her at all at that stage," one of his women confidantes said. "And then he came to terms with the whole situation and figured it's better to let this go on, but he had all these other things going on as well which took him out of it, you see, which was a good thing for him, I guess. He didn't have to but that's what he did." He complained about her, that she was cold, a prima donna, a spendthrift, often about her voice. And yet he was fascinated by her and tried to placate her, even to the extent of forbidding an old friend to come to his wedding because of Jackie's feelings about her. "She wanted to have everything in the right place, you see," the friend said. "And she didn't want any interferences, she didn't want any competition. I was invited to the wedding and then I got a call from the bridegroom saying, 'For God's sake don't come. *Don't* for any reason.' He was adamant."[19]

It was a complex relationship. Priscilla Johnson Macmillan remembered an occasion in Washington at a birthday party for Jack's aide, Langdon "Don" Marvin. "It was at some club and I was seated at Jack's right and Jackie was across the table and the whole time he was saying to me, 'I only got married because I was thirty-seven years old and if I wasn't married and in politics, people would think I was queer'—that was his word. He was saying this to me *sotto voce* all through dinner, and I noticed he wasn't eating, which meant that he had stomach problems, and across the table was Jackie, being a perfect spellbinder as always, and he was eyeing her the whole time . . . They had come in a bit late that night. Jackie was wearing a black taffeta dress with a boat neck . . . and she made a real stage entrance, the two of them did, and I thought he was just awfully proud of her. And I think the impression I got that night—and I think it was the first time that he overtly made a play for me—was that because of her extreme attractiveness that he didn't compete with it, he assimilated it and it made him more refulgent. He wasn't eating any food and he was eating her up with his eyes and she somehow enhanced him and made him more of a sun god in his own eyes . . ."

In a curious twist, Jack used his father-in-law, Black Jack, as a cover in his dating game, as a puzzled Priscilla Johnson Macmillan recalled: "Jack Kennedy in, maybe, April of 1957 invited me to come as his date to the dinner of the American Society of Newspaper Editors, at the Waldorf, I think . . . He gave me rather complicated instructions . . . I was to ask for Mr. Bouvier's tickets and sit at his table close to the dais. I was seated with Black Jack, his then mistress, her husband and another couple. Jack made an extremely funny speech . . . And after the speech Mr. Bouvier said to me, 'Stick around. Jack will want to meet you.' " Well, that amused me very much because what state was his brain in? How did I happen to be sitting at his table if I didn't know Jack already? However, taking that cue, I slipped out immediately, went home to the apartment I shared with another girl on East 80th or 81st Street and by the time I got home my roommate said that she had had a rather irascible telephone call from someone who identified himself as Mr. Bouvier and said that they were in the nightclub in the basement of some hotel near the Waldorf, and Jack was quite mad because I hadn't showed up yet. He was apparently using Mr. Bouvier's name. I had no idea what they were up to, and that winter, rumors had more or less swept the East Coast that Jackie and Jack were separated and that the families were choosing up sides and so I had no idea what Mr. Bouvier was doing acting as a 'shill'—if that's the word—for Jack."[20]

Jack's intermittent pursuit puzzled Priscilla. "How did he have time to spend years in pursuit, very intermittent pursuit, of someone with whom the answer was always going to be 'No'? And, furthermore, he always put the question in such a way that no self-respecting girl could possibly have said anything but 'No.' " He was smooth and funny about it. He really was good company but you had to be on your toes all the time . . . I came to the conclusion that he kind of liked talking to women . . . He always tried it on but it was more or less as though he had to go through the motions . . . I did not think he cared for me very much and I was armored with that certainty. He was cute but there was something cold about him. It seemed to me that what he gave off was light but not heat, not warmth. And his great charm was his detachment, his seeming detachment from himself."[21]

Jack was released from the hospital in December and taken on a stretcher to Palm Beach. By mid-January he was well enough to go to the movies with Red Fay, who had been summoned from California to amuse him. "The family was worried about Jack," Red Fay wrote, "and didn't know whether he was going to live. The doctors felt that he was losing interest, and a visit from someone closely associated with happier times might help him regain his usual optimism and enjoyment of life." Fay found Jack in great discomfort but forcing himself to sit still and read for periods each morning and afternoon, taking notes of certain passages and memorizing them for later use in speeches. Two days after Fay arrived, he brightened up sufficiently to drive over to West Palm Beach to see a pirate movie, *Vera Cruz*, starring Burt Lancaster and Gary Cooper. "No one I knew liked to go to movies more than Jack," Fay noted. "Even though you had to stand at the 'ready' to depart if he didn't like the film, which was not infrequent. If the action abated or the dialogue dragged, it was best to be ready to hear, 'All right, let's haul it out of here.' "[22]

The operation had not been a success, and in February 1955, suffering from a near-fatal infection, he was back in the hospital to have another operation to remove a metal plate that had been implanted in his back. Once again his life was at risk and once again he recovered. Back in Palm Beach, Jackie's devotion to amusing and even nursing him impressed everyone. He had an open, suppurating wound in his back, which the nurse had taught her how to dress. When George Smathers visited him there with his brother, he found Jack lying on his stomach and in great pain despite painkillers, the wound in his back oozing pus. "I realized then that I had misjudged Jackie," he told her biographer, David Heymann. "Anybody who could look at that festering wound day after day and go through all that agony with her husband had to have backbone . . ."[23]

Despite the brave face he put on for his friends, Jack's physical discomfort made him difficult with Jackie. Betty and Chuck Spalding visited to cheer him up. "We were all down in Palm Beach when Jack had had this perilous back operation that wasn't working. Awful, because he had a hole in his back. And they had some sort of spat, we were sitting by the pool and the records were playing. Jackie just went off to the other side of the pool, to a little place, went off by herself. So I went over there to talk to her, hoping to make some kind of amends, smooth things over—that was the only time I had ever seen her upset. Jack was just difficult to get on with. It was very difficult for both of them really, because Jack just had a fear of intimacy and I guess Jackie did too . . ."[24] Both of them, she said, seemed to have some sort of emotional block toward each other.

It was easier for them, as ever, to communicate on an intellectual level, at which few women were better equipped than Jackie to deal with his demands. "During his recuperation Jackie did all she could to maintain his spirits and keep his mind occupied," Evelyn Lincoln wrote. "She brought him magazines and newspapers by the armload . . . Somewhere along the line he had decided he couldn't just lie in bed and wait while time did its healing work . . ."[25] During mid-January 1955, he had begun work on the book that was to be published as *Profiles in Courage*, a study of eight senators who had demonstrated particular political bravery.

Jack had conceived the idea for a magazine article early in 1954 but had had no time to develop it. Now, particularly after his second operation, he renewed his interest in it, and bombarded Ted Sorensen in Washington for books from the Library of Congress and for his reaction to drafts he sent him. He reshaped historical memoranda sent him by Professor Jules Davids of George Washington University, whom Jackie had recommended, by his father's biographer, James Landis, and by Sorensen. The book, published on January 1, 1956, acknowledged their help and particularly Jackie's: "This book would not have been possible without the encouragement, assistance and criticism offered from the very beginning by my wife, Jacqueline, whose help during all the days of my convalescence, I cannot ever adequately acknowledge."

There was controversy when *Profiles in Courage* won the Pulitzer Prize the following year. The columnist Drew Pearson insinuated publicly on *The Mike Wallace Show* on ABC television that Sorensen, not Kennedy, was the real author of the book. Jack was furious, and summoned Washington attorney Clark Clifford. Sorensen issued a sworn statement that he was not the author and the network was forced to retract.

Early in May Jack and Jackie returned to Washington; they were homeless again, as the lease on Dent Place had expired. There was, therefore, no alternative to Merrywood, although when Jack returned to his Senate office the couple kept rooms at the Congressional Hotel on Capitol Hill. Jackie was house-hunting again, and for that winter they rented a house on P Street in Georgetown. They thought of building a house on the Merrywood estate, and Jackie had got so far as to draw up plans with George Howe as consultant architect. "She wanted to have a one-story house with a sort of courtyard, perched up on a hill over the river," Janet Auchincloss said. "It all got rather expensive and complicated, bringing in water and heat . . ." Then Janet heard that Hickory Hill, a big white Georgian house two miles from Merrywood on six acres of woodland above the Potomac in McLean, was for sale. The couple fell in love with it, Jackie because the tall trees and the river reminded her of Merrywood and it had stables for her to keep horses, Jack because of its historical connections: it had been a Civil War command post, the headquarters of General George B. McClellan. He finalized the purchase of the house for $125,000 in October, and Jackie set about remodeling it as the family home for the rest of their lives. "I remember all the effort Jackie went to for Jack's bathroom and dressing room," Janet recalled. "The shoe shelves had to be so he wouldn't have to lean over to open them—so that it wouldn't hurt his back. I remember the endless trouble she took over that . . . They spent so much time remodeling it . . ."[26]

Beyond hinting at the couple's temperamental differences—"Often I think he reacted very differently to things than she did because he had a less introverted nature. Sometimes he would look at her with a really puzzled look"—Janet Auchincloss understandably did not refer to the escalating difficulties of their early years of marriage, but by the summer of 1955 Jack and Jackie needed time away from each other. Jackie's arrival in England alone in the first week of July sparked rumors among their social circle across the Atlantic that the marriage was in trouble.

Jackie took refuge with her sister, Lee, and brother-in-law Michael Canfield at their chic but tiny apartment on Chesham Place, Belgravia. Lee and Michael were a popular glamorous couple on the English social scene. They were based in London, where Michael had a pleasant sinecure of a job, wangled by Lee, as special assistant to the American Ambassador, Winthrop Aldrich; his engagement diaries reflect the intensity of their social life. Jackie and Lee were particularly close at that time of their lives: Jackie had few women around her whom she could trust, and Lee never made any effort to make women friends. The two gossiped and giggled together like college girls; intense conversations that outsiders took for discussions of deep personal considerations turned out to have been devoted to gloves. However, the sisters had more important things in common: both their marriages were in trouble; both were intent on enjoying themselves to the hilt. Among Jackie's escorts was an aristocratic young Tory MP, Hugh Fraser, a great friend of Jack's—Jack had campaigned for him during the 1945 British general election. "In the time when Jackie wandered Europe, Hugh had been an escort," a woman friend of Jackie's said.[27] "Jackie and Hugh Fraser had a walk-out when JFK was still a senator, when Lee and Michael Canfield were here, and Jackie's marriage was in trouble," said a friend. On July 6 the Canfields gave a party for Jackie at Chesham Place on the same night as Lady Hulton gave her celebrated annual party. "Everyone dropped by to see the wife of the young senator," said a guest that night, "keeping their cars to go on to the smarter party. Hugh Fraser left to take Jackie out to dinner."[28]

Social weekends in the country and endless parties in London restored her battered morale. Jackie, Lee and Michael spent the weekend with Frankie More O'Ferrall and his beautiful wife, Angela, in Sussex, with the Marquess of Blandford—known as Sunny—at Blenheim Palace, with Jakie Astor and his wife, Chiquita, Jack's friend, at Hatley; they were at a ball given by the Astors on July 13 and at countless cocktail and dinner parties given by, among others, Douglas Fairbanks Jr. At the end of July, Jackie and Lee left for a few days in Paris, en route to the South of France, where Canfield joined them in a flat the couple had rented, 10 bis, rue de Bateau, in Antibes.[29]

Meanwhile, Jack had his own agenda, which he had been planning since the spring, a renewed rendezvous with Gunilla von Post, this time at Båstad, a resort in southern Sweden. He was traveling with Torby MacDonald, now a congressman, a boon companion in Jack's sexual adventures. They arrived in Sweden on August 11, Jack still on crutches, for a week's successful romance with Gunilla, of which Gunilla's mother apparently approved. Although Jack never spoke of his wife, Torby did, "slipping some clues about Jack's unhappy marriage" to Gunilla and telling her that Jackie "was not that concerned" about Jack. If Gunilla is to be believed, Jack had in mind the idea of leaving Jackie and marrying her, or so he told her mother, and later her cousin at the Swedish embassy in Warsaw, Erich von Post. Only Joe Kennedy stood in the way: father and son had an irascible telephone conversation, after which Jack reported, "He doesn't even want to hear about my troubles with my wife—because she likes him and he responds to that . . ."[30]

Jack's Swedish adventure was no secret among the Kennedys' smart English friends. "Jack's going on a f—g vacation to Sweden," one reported.[31] To Jackie the news that her husband was off to Sweden accompanied by Torby Macdonald could only mean that.

From Sweden Jack traveled to Antibes to meet up with Jackie and the Canfields. "Dinner JFK's," Canfield's diary reported laconically for August 18. They were surrounded by their smart social set, English and American, some of whom had more than an inkling of the situation. On August 4 before Jack's arrival, Jackie and the Canfields had lunched on board the Hon. Peter Ward's yacht embarking from Nice. Claire Baring, on a summer cruise on her future husband's boat, remembered Jackie being there with her sister and the rumor that Jackie had left her husband, if not forever then for a trial separation. She recalled thinking "how pretty Jackie was and what a pity . . ."[32] Peter Ward told Lee's biographer, "We were all together in the South of France. Jackie left Jack Kennedy at that time. They were split. Jack was having trouble with his back, and Jackie had rather a bad conscience about that, but that was all. She said, 'I'm never going back,' in my presence several times. She wasn't the least upset and seemed to be having a very good time."[33]

Two things, apart from the Roman Catholic Church, stood between Jackie and divorce from Jack: Joe Kennedy and Jack's ambition. Joe Kennedy refused even to talk about it, knowing that such an early divorce might ruin Jack's political prospects. Jack himself, as he had told Jackie on their honeymoon, had the presidency in his sights, but his recent brushes with death, prolonged convalescence and the writing of *Profiles in Courage* had changed him: he was more focused on the future goal and ready to make personal sacrifices for it. The romance with Gunilla and talk of divorce from Jackie were his last attempts to break free of his destiny.

In fact, that August after Jack's arrival Jack and Jackie were together, sharing part of the young Karim Aga Khan's house, the Château de l'Horizon, overlooking the sea east of Cannes. Jack had invited his old friend, an ex-beau of Kathleen's, the playwright William Douglas-Home and his wife, Rachel, to spend a week with them there. In the fifties the South of France was truly the center of the "jet set": glamorous names congregated in the villas and hotels along the coast or, like Stavros Niarchos and Aristotle Onassis, brought their huge yachts. Before Jack's arrival the party had drinks and dinner on Niarchos's yacht and the next day drove to Lake Como, where George Plimpton was staying in the Villa Baldianello. Back in the South of France they dined with John Marquand and his new wife, Sue. William Douglas-Home remembered sitting after breakfast in the garden at l'Horizon watching a motorboat careering through the waves toward the dock, driven by a "dashing young Italian." " 'That guy isn't coming to pick up you and me, William,' Jack said." It was Gianni Agnelli, handsome heir to the Fiat fortune, arriving to take Jackie and Rachel waterskiing.

The Kennedys and the Canfields spent days lazing in the sea at Eden Roc. "I well remember lying on a raft with Jack and Michael Canfield," wrote Douglas-Home. "In my waking dreams I heard the voice of Michael saying, 'Jack, I just can't understand why you want to be President.' A short silence ensued and then Jack said, 'Well, Mike, I guess it's just about the only thing I can do!' Old Joe Kennedy was staying at the villa he always rented near Cannes, when the party went to lunch with him. As we drove up the drive with what seemed to be a foot-man under every palm tree bowing to us on the roadside," Douglas-Home re-called, "Jack said, 'I see Dad's roughing it again this year.' "[34]

In that sophisticated world, where life was lived on the surface and things were not always what they seemed, the Canfield and Kennedy marriages appeared serene. At the time the Douglas-Homes certainly did not pick up any tensions. Jackie seemed to them unsophisticated compared with her sister: "Lee was the so-phisticated one. The best-dressed and easily the best-looking," one of the party remarked. "Although Jackie had these extraordinary looks, Lee had rather classical good looks. Lee was more the society lady of the two."[35] The Douglas-Homes liked Jackie very much, appreciating her intelligence, which she made an effort to conceal, and her sense of humor. She loved talking about the theater with Wil-liam. Asked whether she and Jack were getting on, a guest replied that it was diffi-cult to answer because the relationship was not demonstrative. "Nothing with Jack would have been like that. So you wouldn't see them hugging and loving each other, holding hands, ever. There wasn't that kind of thing." Jackie appeared perfectly happy to them with Jack. "She wasn't demonstrative but she did love him, and they had this relationship which was fun, you'd have fun in their com-pany, there'd be a lot of jokes and she used to tease him. It was good being with them. It was fun. But, as I've said, they weren't a lovey-dovey couple . . ."[36]

According to Canfield's diary the social life was nonstop. On August 20 the Kennedys, Canfields and Douglas-Homes dined and went to the Juan-les-Pins casino. On August 22 they lunched with Charles and Jayne Wrightsman, the Kennedys' fabulously rich friends from Palm Beach; on the twenty-fourth they were at the Wrightsmans' again, this time for a dinner in honor of the Empress of Iran. On the twenty-fifth Jayne Wrightsman took Lee and Jackie to Venice for the day; on the twenty-sixth Joe Kennedy took a table for the gala night in Monte Carlo, and so it went on until the end of August and the vacations. Black Jack Bouvier arrived on the twenty-third and they dined with him in Cannes on the twenty-seventh. Jackie, according to a guest, used to talk "an enormous amount" about him. "She said he was an absolute cad but he was divine. She adored him and [she said] he was such fun to be with . . . She just loved being with him. I think she felt she was rather sort of . . . not exactly like him but he liked the cos-mopolitan life and so did Jackie, so they had a bond."[37] He was there until Au-gust 30, when he left by train for Paris. The day before, an enigmatic entry records, "Jackie to Lutetia Clinique"; she appears to have remained there for several days since Canfield records dining with JFK, a friend of his and Lee on the thirty-first but without Jackie.

It was at this time, while the Douglas-Homes were staying, that Jackie met Aristotle Onassis for the first time when they went for a drink aboard the *Christina* so that Jack could meet his hero, Winston Churchill, who was staying on board. Sadly, it was not a success. The eighty-year-old Churchill had finally resigned as Prime Minister on April 5, he was depressed, not at his best, and unimpressed by the tall young American in the white tuxedo. "Jack was extremely funny about it," a fellow guest recalled. "When we said, 'How did you get on?' he said, 'Well, I think he thought I was the waiter, practically asked me to go and get him a drink . . .' "[38] The success of the evening was not Jack, but Jackie, who, wearing a simple above-the-knee white A-line dress, her dark hair short, immediately attracted Onassis, and not merely for her ability to speak French. According to Onassis's biographer, he later told Costa Gratsos, his friend and aide (and later a bitter enemy of Jackie's), "There's something damned *willful* about her, there's something provocative about that lady. She's got a carnal soul."[39]

After Jackie had left for Paris and the Lutetia Clinic, Jack sailed down to Capri. He was still hankering after Gunilla von Post and attempting unsuccessfully to persuade her to join him there. He flew to Poland on a fact-finding mission in connection with his service on the Senate Foreign Relations Committee and from there telephoned Gunilla again, promising that he loved her and would tell his father that he was unhappy in his marriage and could not go on "the way things are now," that he wanted to end his marriage and be with her. Not surprisingly, old Joe was furious, as Jack reported to Gunilla. "He yelled at me, 'You're out of your mind. You're going to be President someday. This would ruin everything. Divorce is impossible. Look at what happened with me and Gloria Swanson!' "[40] He planned to join Gunilla in Copenhagen; then Jackie came to Warsaw and the plan was dropped. He joined Jackie and Lee in Rome in mid-September. There they had an audience with Pope Pius XII, who as Cardinal Pacelli had visited the Kennedy home in Bronxville (after which Rose preserved the "Cardinal's Chair" in which subsequently no one else was allowed to sit) and who had sent his blessing for their wedding. At a formal dinner to which they and the French Premier, Georges Bidault, were invited, Jack, whose grasp of foreign languages was minimal, attempted to hold a conversation with Bidault with Jackie acting as interpreter. In the most cynical view, such episodes served to remind him of his wife's undeniable attributes as a high-level politician's wife. It was, after all, this aura of "class," so different from the provincial American directness of the Kennedy women, that had originally appealed to his "snobbery of style," as Joe Alsop had put it. After Warsaw, Jack abandoned his fantasies: he and Jackie traveled from Rome to Paris, Dublin and London, arriving in New York after a transatlantic crossing on October 12. Nineteen fifty-six would be a presidential election year; the die was finally cast in favor of marriage and serious political ambition. As a sign of his decision he finalized the contract on Hickory Hill that month; by Christmas Jackie was pregnant.

By the spring of 1956, Jack's name was already being put forward in the press as a possible vice presidential candidate on the ticket of Adlai Stevenson, the candidate of the liberal wing of the Democratic Party. He had been building up his power base in Massachusetts with a view to his reelection to the Senate in 1958, cleansing the Massachusetts organization of some of its less attractive old-style politics and politicians and enabling him to deliver the Massachusetts delegation for Stevenson. "While the Senator [Kennedy] continued to view the whole subject with more curiosity than concern," his aide Ted Sorensen wrote, "a surprising flurry of newspaper and magazine stories and editorials pointed up his assets with enthusiasm."[41] Despite his long illness and his far from brilliant congressional record, Jack had kept a high public profile: "His best-selling book [*Profiles in Courage*] and growing number of speeches had made him more widely known than most Democratic officeholders. His youthful, clean-cut demeanor, his candid, low-key approach, and his heroic war record gave him a special appeal to both new and uncommitted voters. His television appearances and Harvard commencement address drew national attention . . ."[42]

Jack was interested in the nomination "more out of a sense of competition than of conviction," as Sorensen put it; via Sorensen he put out feelers to influential Stevenson supporters. Neither Jackie nor her father-in-law was happy about the vice presidential prospect, Joe because he saw no point in taking second place on a ticket he regarded as bound to lose to the popular President Eisenhower, Jackie because she thought that his health would not be up to it. In the circumstances, the Kennedy campaign at the Chicago convention in August was a hit-and-miss affair, involving family and friends. Jack narrated the party film, *The Pursuit of Happiness*, and was favored in being chosen to make the nominating speech for Stevenson, but things did not start to get serious until Stevenson, after winning the nomination, threw open the race for the vice presidential nomination. The Kennedy family threw itself into the fight; surprisingly, it became neck and neck between Jack and Senator Estes Kefauver, a battle Jack narrowly lost because of the hostility of the Protestant Midwestern states to his religion and his vote against farm supports earlier that year—"He's not our kind of folks," the Governor of Oklahoma declared, in what must have been the understatement of the year. Jack was disappointed but philosophical, recognizing that his father's diagnosis of the value of the vice presidential nomination that year had been correct. As he told an audience two years later, "I might have won that race with Senator Kefauver—and my political career would now be over." However, his relative success at the 1956 Democratic Convention had shown him one thing: that in the next race for the presidency he might win the nomination.

While he had been undergoing a transformation as a politician, as a husband he was unreformed. Although seven months pregnant, Jackie had gone along with the campaign in Chicago as far as she could. While Jack, Bobby and their aides lodged at the Stockyards Inn in downtown Chicago behind the Convention Hall, she stayed in Eunice and Sargent Shriver's apartment on Lake Shore Drive, but she attended various functions at the convention and elsewhere, an exhausting effort in the Chicago heat. Among them was "a champagne party for the campaign wives" given by Perle Mesta, whose Coronation ball she had attended in London in 1953. Mrs. Mesta found both the Kennedys underdressed, complaining that Jack had worn "brown loafers" with his tuxedo and denouncing Jackie as a "beatnik" for appearing without stockings.[43] (Jackie, whose memory for slights was elephantine, did not forget this when she was in a position to retaliate; Mrs. Mesta was not invited to the Kennedy White House.)

Jackie was exhausted; she had gone beyond the call of duty in supporting Jack in Chicago despite her pregnancy and her miscarriage the previous year. Nevertheless Jack, a creature of habit, never for a moment considered changing his plans for his usual August Mediterranean vacation. Since the other members of the party were to be Teddy Kennedy and George Smathers, there could be little doubt as to what kind of vacation it would be. While Jackie retreated to rest at Hammersmith Farm, Jack took off with Teddy for France, where they were to stay with Joe Kennedy at his rented villa before chartering a boat for a pleasure cruise along the Riviera on August 21.

According to Smathers, the trip had Jackie's blessing. The prospect of asking a restless, frustrated Jack to forgo his vacation in favor of keeping her company at Newport with Janet, Hughdie and the Auchincloss clan would, she doubtless thought, have been both unrealistic and counterproductive in terms of marital harmony. In any case, the baby was not due until September. But on August 23 she hemorrhaged and was rushed to Newport Hospital, where a cesarean was performed to deliver a stillborn baby girl. When she woke after the operation, she saw Bobby sitting by her bedside in Jack's place. Telephoned with the news by Janet at Hyannis Port, Bobby had tried frantically but in vain to contact his brother. Three days later Joe Kennedy spoke to Jack when they moored in Genoa. "I suppose this means the end of the trip," Jack remarked glumly.[44]

It almost meant the end of his marriage. Jackie's family were outraged at his behavior, his failure to be there when Jackie needed him and his apparent unconcern about what had happened. The day after he arrived in Newport and while Jackie was still in the hospital he was reported as being "a charming and jovial dinner partner" at the Clambake Club as if nothing were amiss. Both families began to take sides. A hospital spokesman attributed the stillbirth to Jackie's nervous tension and exhaustion following the Democratic Convention; Rose Kennedy blamed it on Jackie's smoking. For Jackie it was another personal defeat, her apparent inability to carry a child to full term underlined by the successful birth of Pat Lawford's second child two days after she had lost hers. On September 9 Ethel had her fifth child. The emptiness of the nursery she had prepared at Hickory Hill mocked her; all the care she had lavished on the house, the special shoe shelves for Jack, seemed to have been in vain. Jack sold the house at cost to Bobby, who needed a large place for his rapidly expanding family. For Jackie, that particular dream was over.

Jackie once said that she and Jack were like "two icebergs" with only a small part of themselves showing on the surface, and this latest episode in her marriage drove them further apart. "Jack and Jackie's differences in outlook, interests and manner became more obtrusive," Lem Billings said. "They were both bitter, disillusioned, withdrawn, silent as if afraid that conversation would deepen the wound. To her sister, Lee, Jackie confessed that she suspected she was physically incapable of childbearing. But within earshot of Jack, she blamed the misfortune on her grinding participation (Pat Lawford had wisely stayed away from Chicago, at home in Los Angeles) in the 1956 Democratic National Convention. Jack reacted to this kind of talk by turning his back and getting out on the campaign stump for Stevenson and Kefauver."[45]

Jackie reacted as she always did in similar difficult situations: she took off. At the beginning of November 1956 she fled to London to stay with the Canfields in their smart new house at 45 Chester Square and to enjoy the English social scene. In September her beau, Hugh Fraser, had married the Hon. Antonia Pakenham. Jackie and the Frasers spent the weekend with the John Jacob Astors at Hatley, and the two women, sharing the same interests in books and literature—Antonia had just come down from Oxford University—became friends. It was a mutual admiration society rather than an intimate friendship—"Antonia Fraser is a proof that life is unfair," Jackie told Gore Vidal.[46]

"One day the doorbell rang in our flat in Eaton Square," Antonia Fraser remembered, "and there was Jackie bearing a picture of the Duke of Wellington—I had no idea who she was—and there was that whispering voice saying, 'Oh, I think this looks so like Hughie, the nose and everything.' I liked her very much because she was so nice to me. I was very insecure with all these grand people, friends of Hugh's. And she was sweet to me, cooing away and saying, 'You're so clever,' and those sort of things, which I was extremely grateful for because I didn't feel immediately at home in that world and here was someone who was very nice to me, unlike Lee. As far as I know, Lee never spoke a civil word to a female under eighty in her life . . ."[47]

Jackie and the Canfields also spent a weekend shooting with the Lambtons at Fenton in Northumberland, considered one of the smartest places to shoot because of the difficult high-flying birds. Although the weekend was full of jokes and fun—they played charades and the hostess dressed the ultramasculine Polish Prince Stanislaus Radziwill, Jackie's future brother-in-law, in one of her pink lace petticoats—it was an odd time for an American to be in England, a country divided by controversy over the Suez Canal operation, when President Eisenhower refused to support the Anglo-French-Israeli invasion of Egypt and feelings ran high.

Lord Lambton, as parliamentary private secretary to the Foreign Secretary, Selwyn Lloyd, was a member of the government that had ordered the invasion. Lambton, rich, handsome, witty and cynical, the descendant of a family with a radical political heritage, was a Conservative; he found Jackie's politics "a bit pinko," or left-leaning.

Jackie got on better with "Stas" Radziwill, perhaps because his heavy, dark looks and fondness for women and alcohol reminded her of Black Jack. Stas, the descendant of an ancient aristocratic Polish family, had fled Poland at the time of the German invasion. "Stas got a car and somehow made it to Switzerland, where he crossed the border and went to a grand hotel he knew," his friend, Michael

Tree, said. "There was a lot of 'Highness, we're delighted to see you, Highness,' you know—he was a very grand Pole—and he said to the manager, 'Look here, there's one thing that troubles me, I haven't got a penny in the world, not a penny.' And the manager's whole attitude altered and he said, 'Well, I'm afraid we can't help you, and you can't stay here.' So Stas lived in soup kitchens for about three weeks in Switzerland. And then he met woman—he always talked that way, 'I met woman'—who had money, who was Swiss, who he married. He always said, 'Much best wife I ever had, first.' "[48]

At the end of the war, Stas had arrived in London, where he joined a group of Poles who had started a business renovating apartments and selling them. His eccentric charm made him friends who advanced his business career. At first his one well-connected friend was Tony Gandarillas, who lived on opium and was a great friend of the Duke of Westminster, who owned all the most desirable property in London. Through Gandarillas's friendship with the Duke, Stas obtained a magnificent piece of real estate and sold it at a considerable profit.

He was also extremely attractive to women. Divorced from his first wife, he met and married the beautiful Grace Kolin, a shipping heiress, and with her money set up in the real estate business, lending to property developers, among them one of the most successful men in the field, Felix Fenston. They became partners. "Stas made a lot of money, which was quite extraordinary," Tree said. "He practically couldn't write, no one could understand a word he said, he didn't know anyone, and yet the sort of people he got to know were [Charles] Clore and Fenston. And they all had a very soft spot for Stas and put him in the deals."[49]

When Lee met Stas, her marriage was fading fast. Michael Canfield was charming and popular, but he was drinking heavily and was losing his job at the London embassy, as Aldrich was returning to America. Lee had had affairs and taken no trouble to conceal them. It had got to such a pass that, as Canfield told a friend, when he returned home he didn't know "whose hat would be on the hat stand in the hall." Nonetheless, he was desperate at the thought of losing Lee, and turned to Jackie for advice—which, according to Alastair Forbes, although practical, was scarcely helpful. Her response was "Get more money, Michael." When he explained that, with a modest trust fund and a salary, he was able to maintain a more than decent lifestyle, Jackie repeated, "No, Michael. I mean *real* money."[50] In Jackie and Lee's world women could not make "real" money: they either inherited it or married it. Michael Canfield, with his charm and elegance, his mysterious royal parentage, had given Lee what she had wanted: the entrée to the heart of English and international society. Men liked her for her exquisite looks, her taste and her wit. Women, for whom she never made an effort, did not. Lee's glamorous European life did not make her happy: when she was in England she longed for America and vice versa. For Lee, as one of her friends remarked, "The grass was always greener on the other side of the fence."[51] In her own mind she had reached the limit of where Canfield could take her; it was time to move on.

On November 25 Jackie and Lee left for four days in Paris before Jackie returned to the United States. She had been away from Jack for over a month, but even before she left she had barely seen him. "Autumn 1956 was a time of campaigning for the Stevenson-Kefauver ticket," Ted Sorensen wrote. "The Massachusetts Senator emerged from the spectacular Vice Presidential balloting more sought after by party members than any Democrat other than the two nominees. Covering more than thirty thousand miles in twenty-four states, he made over 150 speeches and appearances in the course of six weeks."[52] On September 18, 1956, Jack and Sorensen had begun a series of tours, which over the next few years would take them into every state, seeking votes for Stevenson in 1956, votes for senatorial, state and local candidates in 1957, 1958 and 1959, making friends for Kennedy at every stop.

That autumn of 1956 the evidence that Jack and Jackie had spent hardly any time together provoked ever stronger rumors that they would divorce. A particularly persistent story was that Jackie had been offered a million dollars by Joe Kennedy to stay with Jack, which, as Jackie joked, was hardly a huge bribe—"Why not ten million?" she asked Joe, when the story came out in *Time*. There was no doubt, however, that she had talks with Joe, whom she knew to be overwhelmingly on her side. In realistic terms, the stronger the Kennedy ambitions for the presidency became, the more the strength of her hand increased. At Thanksgiving 1956 while Jackie was in Europe, Jack and Joe held a conference at Hyannis Port, during which they agreed that Jack would run for the presidency in 1960. Joe, no doubt reiterating the personal sacrifice he had made in ending his affair with Swanson, a favorite theme, pointed out that Jack must give up any fantasies about ending his marriage. In the coming campaign, image would be all. "It's not what you are it's what people think you are," as the Kennedy mantra ran. In appearing as a serious candidate for the vice presidency that year, Jack had gone a long way toward shaking off the irresponsible-lightweight reputation that he had had as a congressman. Image and money, unstinting quantities of Joe's funds, could swing him the prize.

When Jackie returned to America in early December, accompanied by the Canfields, her marital situation was far from ideal. The couple were homeless: having sold Hickory Hill because Jackie could not face returning there, they had nowhere to go. An attempt to rent Joe Alsop's house, 270 Dumbarton Avenue, fell through while they were vacationing with the Canfields at Round Hill, Jamaica. In January they rented 2808 P Street from Joseph Bryan while Jackie went househunting for a suitable family house, eventually finding the delightful Federal-style 3307 N Street, which was to be their home for four years. Joe Kennedy, apparently anxious to placate Jackie and cement the marriage, put up the money.

As long as Jack confined his extramarital activity to the campaign trail, and to a room at the Mayflower Hotel when he was in Washington, his philandering affected Jackie less than did his lack of consideration for her and her relegation to second-class female status within the Kennedy clan. She could accept the infidelity, à la Black Jack: it was standard behavior in the international circles in which she now moved. What she found difficult to deal with was that, in his eyes, she was not number one, a position she had been accustomed to occupy practically since birth with the men of her family and circle of friends.

She was soon to lose the man with whom she had always been number one:

her father. James "Jimmy" Rousmaniere, one of Jack's Harvard friends, heard of Black Jack's "slow but visible" decline from the Kennedy side: "He was pretty bad. His drinking was legendary. There was a sense of buried drama about him, brewing clouds."[53] Black Jack had recently made a habit of visiting Havana, where he would spend nights going from casinos to nightclubs with Cuban friends. By day he went gambling at the racetrack and jai alai matches, often with air stewardesses from the Pan Am service to Cuba. These episodes masked his loneliness at home: he had quarreled with his sisters Maude and Michelle over the sale of Lasata, while his unstable third sister, Edith "Big Edie" Beale, blamed him unfairly for mismanaging the stocks left her by the Major. He rarely saw Jackie and Lee. From 1952 he had lived a more or less reclusive life in his New York apartment with the Bouvier housekeeper, Esther Lindstrom, who shared his obsessive interest in gambling, cooked his invariable dinner of lamb chops and lima beans, and vetted his women. On January 27, 1955, he sold his seat on the New York Stock Exchange for $90,000, a fraction of what it had been worth at the time of the Crash. The next day he drew up his will. He became reconciled with his sisters, burying the bitterness of the wrangles over his father's estate, but he was a sad and disappointed man with a deep sense of personal failure, which he would assuage by complaining to his sisters that it was all Janet's fault. Unsurprisingly, given his lifetime of hard drinking, his liver was in poor shape. He complained of his daughters' neglect, although Lee was living in England and Jackie, based in Washington, had her own problems to cope with. Apparently he had been mortified to hear of Jackie's new pregnancy from the evening papers and took it as one more instance of her neglecting him. Yet in April 1957 at the age of nearly sixty-six, as Priscilla Johnson Macmillan's account shows, he could still attract women and was not averse to a night out with his son-in-law, "acting as a shill for Jack."

Neither Jackie nor Lee was aware that Black Jack was seriously ill, or that he had cancer of the liver when he checked into Lenox Hill Hospital on July 27 for a series of tests that apparently revealed nothing. Jackie, who had been spending the summer at Hyannis Port, flew down to see him but, thinking there was nothing seriously wrong with him, spent her birthday with her mother at Hammersmith. Lee was with Michael Canfield in Tuscany. "You see, he was a big hypochondriac," Lee explained, "and he always had a bad back and he always had serious sinus and, once again, like 'all men are rats,' you got so used to hearing it that you never paid attention after a while. When he did complain of a bad back again I was living in England and Jackie was here but, I guess, she didn't take it too seriously . . ."[54] On August 3 he lapsed into a coma and died, riddled, apparently, with cancer. Jackie, this time accompanied by Jack, arrived too late to say good-bye.

For Jackie, Black Jack's death was the worst emotional shock of her life so far. She took charge, dry-eyed, of her father's obituary and funeral arrangements. Lee and Michael arrived from Italy on August 5 for the funeral on the sixth. The sisters and their husbands dined together that night. Black Jack's funeral in St. Patrick's Cathedral was for family and a few of his former business associates; his circle of friends had dwindled to the vanishing point. There were no more than two dozen mourners, including his ex-lovers, dressed and veiled in black, all to-gether in the back pew. Jackie saw to it that, instead of funereal flower arrange-ments, there were white wicker baskets filled with colorful summer flowers. Before the coffin was closed she placed a bracelet her father had given her as a gradua-tion present in his hand. The coffin was covered with yellow daisies and corn-flowers, Jackie's favorite flowers.

The family traveled to East Hampton for the burial near the Bouvier family church, St. Philomena's, where "the Major" had worshipped every summer Sun-day, roaring up in his red Nash convertible, and where Black Jack and Janet had been married just under thirty years before. Black Jack was buried in the family plot, presided over by two large crosses, beside his father, mother and brother Bud. Jackie heaped his grave with cornflowers. "I want everything to look like a summer garden, like Lasata in August," she said.

CHAPTER SEVEN

Seeking the Golden Fleece

⌒

He would find love. He would never find peace. For he must go seek the Golden Fleece.

—Jacqueline Kennedy on JFK, September 1953[1]

As Black Jack's death signaled the passing of an era in Jackie's life so the birth, four months later, of her daughter opened a new phase in the Kennedy marriage. She delivered the longed-for baby, weighing seven pounds two ounces, by cesarean section in New York's Lying-In Hospital, at the Cornell University Medical Center, on November 27, 1957. The birth had been planned for the Wednesday before Thanksgiving and this time all went well. She named her daughter Caroline Bouvier after Lee and Black Jack. The first time Jackie saw her daughter was when Jack wheeled her in. He had been sitting in the waiting room with Janet and Hughdie to wait for the birth. "I'll always remember Jack's face when the doctor came into the room and told him that the baby had arrived and that it was a girl and that Jackie was fine and the baby was fine," Janet said. "I will always remember the sweet expression on his face and sort of a smile . . ."

Lem Billings came to the hospital and Jack showed him the newborn babies through the glass screen. Janet went on, "He didn't point the baby out and just said, 'Now, Lem, which one of the babies is the prettiest?' And Lem got the wrong one and Jack didn't speak to him for three days . . ."[2] (Jack had learned his lesson; that autumn as he went on his travels again he had instructed Evelyn Lincoln "to keep in close touch with Jackie in case you need me in a hurry . . .")

Caroline was christened on December 13, 1957, at St. Patrick's Cathedral in New York City, in the robe her mother had worn at her christening; her godparents were the two family members closest to her parents, Bobby Kennedy and

Lee. She had been taken home to the Kennedy Park Avenue apartment by her father and her new English nurse, Maud Shaw, eleven days after her birth, and was four months old before they moved back to Washington, to the sunny third floor of the N Street house and the nursery bedroom Jackie had decorated for her in pink and white with a dado of red roses.

Maud Mercy Ellen Shaw was a trained baby nurse. Aged fifty-four when she came to Caroline, she was tiny, only five foot two, with what a relative described as a "pouter-pigeon bust" and a quiet, firm, reassuring personality. "Miss Shaw," as the children were to call her, had traveled widely and led an adventurous life; she placed great stress on teaching her charges not only manners but about the world around them. She was immediately struck by Jackie's reserve and shyness, her consideration for others and good manners. She was not strong after the cesarean birth and did not breast-feed her baby. While she remained in bed she was undemanding. Maud Shaw wrote of her:

> It was not simply because she is an independent person, but because she never likes to put other people out, even the tiniest bit. In fact, through the seven and a half years I was with her and the children, she never asked me to as much as pick up a pin for her . . . Mrs. Kennedy was always a little reserved and withdrawn. It took time before she was completely friendly with me, even though I saw her every day and was entrusted to look after her children. It is not that she is the least bit unfriendly by nature—just shy.[3]

In September 1964 Jackie told Joan Braden that she still remembered the day Caroline was born as "the very happiest day of her life." For the first time in her marriage she felt she was winning. She had a baby to tie Jack to her and to end the Kennedy sneers about her childbearing ability and Jack was showing patience and restraint with her, humoring her whims. She had a home to go to, at 3307 N Street, a three-story house in Georgetown that had belonged to Marion Oates Leiter.

Jackie was euphoric over their home, decorating and redecorating to make it just right. "It was a house with a lot of feeling to it and a lot of charm," Janet Auchincloss recalled at the time, "but she did that double living room downstairs over at least three times in the first four months they were there. I remember you would go there and there would be two beautiful needlepoint rugs, one in the little front drawing room and one in the back one toward the garden. The next week they would both be gone . . .

"We were having dinner there one night and Jack didn't get home, until quite late, after we had finished dinner. He was having dinner on a tray. At that moment the room was entirely beige: the walls had been repainted a week or so before, and the furniture had all been reupholstered in soft beige, and there was a vicuna rug over the sofa that Jackie still has . . . rugs, curtains, upholstery, everything was suddenly turned lovely different shades of beige. I knew how wildly expensive it is to paint things and upholster things and have curtains made, but I can remember Jack just saying to me, 'Mrs. Auchincloss, do you think we're prisoners of beige?' "[4]

But Jack found Jackie's extravagance painful. "I do remember one scene when we were first married and Jackie was spending money," Betty Spalding said. "Jack, you know, was so cheap, never carried a nickel, always borrowed from his friends—he was furious at the way she was spending . . ."[5] Jackie used to wheedle Mrs. Lincoln into slipping through checks for her decorating so that Jack wouldn't notice.

The two rugs mentioned by Janet were a case in point. "I remember two new expensive rugs that she had in the Georgetown house," Bill Walton recalled, "that she hid in her budget, and paid a little bit each month. She didn't ever want him to know how much they had cost because they'd been wild extravagances. He was crazy about them, of course. Eventually he found out how much they were, and liked them . . ."[6] Encouraged by Lee, Jackie liked the best in clothes and decoration, and knew she was married to a very rich man who, although tight, had no grasp of money. She rightly considered it her job to provide the ambitious senator with the kind of backdrop her wealthy friends considered necessary and give her house the touch of class that Kennedy homes notably lacked. Now that she had more power within the family, she knew what she wanted and she was determined to have it. "I guess after she had Caroline, she kind of came into her own as an individual," Betty Spalding said. "There was a different kind of scene from the one by the pool where she ran off and stayed by herself . . ."

Jack came to appreciate what Jackie was trying to do and how she was transforming his life, putting him on the level his WASP and European friends enjoyed, taking him away from the meat-and-potatoes Kennedy family style. "He was always terribly proud of the Georgetown house and admired what Jackie had done there," Bill Walton said. "He was a nonvisual guy in most respects, but he learned a great deal from her and was perfectly aware that he'd learned it from her. And he was quite blind to houses earlier in his life, you know, wouldn't notice, could live anywhere, paid no attention. But it was as he grew older that he began to like houses, and to compare them, and notice other people's houses. He got so that he noticed everything. Women's clothes, he was an absolute expert on . . ."

Jackie succeeded also in transforming Jack's attitude toward his own clothes; the untidy, casual congressman became a sophisticated senator. "He did become far more dapper, in the better sense of the word, neater and had many more clothes as time went along," Walton said. "He [became] the most clothes-conscious man I think I've ever known. Always disapproved of mine, was always giving me advice. I remember going there to dinner with them—not dressed but business suits—and he looked down. I had very very dark brown shoes and he pointed and he said, 'Brown at night? Never . . .' And he really just always thought about his own clothes too, very conservative except in the sports field . . ." Jackie, once the sloppily dressed girl reporter, understood the Cinderella-like transformation of the public image: the Kennedy boy was being groomed for President.

Lord Harlech, a close friend of Jack and Jackie's, thought that Jackie had brought out Jack's innate good taste: "I suppose he always had it naturally—he liked the best when he saw it but in certain areas the family did not pursue excellence in style . . . Until he married Jackie he really had no idea about how you should decorate a room or what was the difference between a pretty house and an ugly house, and he certainly had no great feeling about good food or good wine . . . I think she found it rather tough going in the early stages, because most of the others who had married into the family by then, or married subsequently into the family, really went along with the Kennedy atmosphere . . . She wouldn't go along with the Kennedy atmosphere. She had certain standards of her own, which she insisted on in her own house. They were standards about the manners of the children, about having good food, about having beautiful furniture, the house well done. In the early days he was apt to be pretty impatient with this. You know, he was very happy just to have a steak and some ice cream . . . Certainly he had no worry about furniture. I remember him saying when Jackie had gone off and bought some French eighteenth century chairs or something, 'I don't know why, what's the point of spending all this money? I mean, a chair is a chair, and it's perfectly good the chair I'm sitting in. What's the point of all this fancy stuff?' Well, that was his first reaction but gradually he came to appreciate good taste in these and other matters, and really cared about it by the end. I think that this marriage to Jackie did add a whole new dimension to his life and gave him all kinds of new pleasures in life which he hadn't had before."[7]

The Kennedys led a relatively informal social life in Georgetown, going to the movies, seeing a small circle of close friends, giving dinner parties for eight or twelve people when Jack's busy schedule permitted it. Both of them preferred conversation, wit, jokes and—Jack at least—serious political discussion to the pompous round of Washington diplomatic dinners and socially exclusive evenings like the Dancing Class, a white-tie-and-tails ball held three times a year at the Sulgrave Club. Bill Walton remembered seeing Jack there, "really rather miserable, he didn't like this kind of a party," and as for dancing, "He sort of walked around the room pushing somebody. You'd nearly always see him on the couch in a corner, talking to somebody with great intensity." The people they saw included Charlie and Martha Bartlett—Jack liked to play backgammon with Charlie because he could beat him. Above all, he liked conversation—"He was a great player on words, and it's a wit of conversation," said Walton, "the exchanged remark, keeping the ball bouncing—you make a remark, he picks it up, makes it better, you pick it up, he picks it up, until it gets to some ridiculous end. So that the dinner table is just about his best conversation, he's fishing people, and he'd play on the dinner table, you know, goading, kidding, laughing." Lem Billings, whom Jackie described as her "permanent houseguest," was often the butt of Jack's teasing.

Jack enjoyed the quick wit of Ben Bradlee, then a political reporter in the Washington bureau of *Newsweek*, and later on the *Washington Post*, and his beautiful wife, Tony Pinchot, friends and N Street neighbors. Jack liked journalists as much as Jackie was suspicious of them; he reveled in the quickfire repartee, the earthy language, the sense of being plugged into what was happening, and he loved gossip, political, social, sexual.

Another journalist or, rather, political commentator in their social circle was Joseph Alsop. Alsop was different from the macho Bradlee, sophisticated, with a refined taste in antiques and decoration, the friend of grand ladies throughout the Anglo-Saxon world, his dinner parties celebrated for the excellence of the food, wine and conversation. He was also one of the most influential and best-informed journalists of his day. Early on Joe had talent-spotted Jack Kennedy as presidential material, and in 1958 he confided this to a surprised Katharine (Kay) Graham. Kay's husband, Phil Graham, was a Lyndon B. Johnson supporter and, as the publisher of the *Washington Post*, one of the most influential figures on the Washington scene. He was surprised and impressed by Jack's political instinct and the coolly rational way in which he had worked out his future when they met at a dinner party given by Alsop in the spring of 1958. Challenged by Graham as too young to run yet for President, Jack replied, " 'Well, Phil, I'm running and this is why. First, I think I'm as well qualified as anybody who is going to run, except for Lyndon Johnson. Second, if I don't run, whoever wins will be there for eight years and will influence who his successor will be. And third, if I don't run I'll have to stay in the Senate at least eight more years. As a potential candidate in the Senate, I'll have to vote politically and I'll end up as both a mediocre senator and a lousy candidate.' I was thoroughly impressed by this," Kay Graham recorded, "and each time I saw Senator Kennedy I grew more impressed."[8]

Jackie and Joe Alsop had been close friends since 1956 when she had thought of renting his house on Dumbarton Avenue, even to the extent that he addressed her as "Darling Jackie" in December 1956 when, embarrassed, he wrote to tell her that the deal was off because his precious "couple," Jose and Maria, were apprehensive at the prospect of change.[9] By the spring of 1958 Alsop had become thoroughly disillusioned with the sclerotic Eisenhower administration, writing to his future wife, Susan Mary Patten: "I see no hope whatever, of any kind, or anywhere, as long as Mr. Eisenhower remains President."[10] Just under a year later, after dinner at the Kennedys', he was writing to Evangeline Bruce, wife of the American Ambassador to West Germany, David Bruce, describing Jack as "the perfect candidate."[11]

Among the closest of their political and social friends were the wise, liberal Republican Senator from Kentucky, Judge John Sherman Cooper, and his vivacious wife, Lorraine. Lorraine Cooper had been a friend of Jackie's before they married their Senators. "She used to ask me to dinner parties when I was still either in my last year in college in Washington or the year or so I worked on the newspaper," Jackie later recalled.[12] They had met frequently at the Bartletts while courting: "We used to go to Charlie Bartlett's for dinner . . . Senator [Albert] Gore was often there. We were always about the six of us, maybe eight, and that's where you became friends . . ." she added, and went on, "She's such a sophisticated, elegant, decorative person," Jackie said of Lorraine, and of John Sherman Cooper, "You always felt that great kindness coming from him."

From 1957 to 1960 the Coopers were frequent guests at the Kennedys'

N Street house. Jackie described their social life: "Well, you know, you always hear about Washington, all this going out and party circuit. We never did that. We didn't like it. Then Jack would be traveling a lot so we just liked to stay home and there were a couple of houses that you'd go for dinner or else you'd have your close friends over rather informally." Jackie outlined her philosophy as hostess: "If you put busy men in an attractive atmosphere where the surroundings are comfortable, the food is good, you relax, you unwind, there's some stimulating conversation. You know, sometimes quite a lot can happen. Contact can be made, you might discuss something . . . a whole lot of things. It's part of the art of living in Washington . . ." The Sherman Coopers' lives intertwined with the Kennedys' in curious ways: Lorraine Cooper's first husband had been Thomas Shevlin who subsequently married Durie Malcolm Desloge, rumored to have had a brief secret first marriage to Jack Kennedy in 1947. According to Seymour Hersh, Lorraine Cooper told Maxine Cheshire, then a society reporter for the *Washington Post*, how Jack would laugh at a dinner party and say, "Lorraine and I are related by marriage." And then the two of them would die laughing and nobody else knew what they were talking about."[13] In 1963–4 John Sherman Cooper was appointed to sit on the Warren Commission, inquiring into the circumstances of his friend Jack Kennedy's assassination.

Jackie was prepared to fight a long battle to be number one with Jack. Politics, which at first she regarded as "the enemy" because it took Jack away from her, was in fact a strong weapon. Once Jack started to run for the presidency, his need for her acquiescence in the image they were creating became an important factor in their relationship. Jackie had learned the power game in family relationships a long time ago and in that sense their marriage was a trade-off.

Jack was by now widely acknowledged, although it had not been announced officially, to be running for the presidential nomination in 1960. An article in *Time* dated December 2, 1957, devoted a lengthy piece to him: "In his unannounced but unabashed run for the Democratic Party's nomination in 1960, Jack Kennedy has left panting politicians and swooning women across a large spread of the U.S." Apart from the new harmony in his private life, 1957 had been a good year for Jack. He had won the Pulitzer Prize for *Profiles in Courage* (and forced journalist Drew Pearson to back down over claims that others had written the book for him), and he had beaten Senator Estes Kefauver for a seat on the prestigious Foreign Relations Committee. For Joe Kennedy, however, Jack's most impressive achievement had been his election to Harvard's Board of Overseers. "Now I know his religion won't keep him out of the White House," he told Dave Powers and Kenny O'Donnell, leading members of Jack's political circle. "If an Irish Catholic can get elected as an Overseer at Harvard, he can get elected to anything."[14]

Jack was not only running for President, as an immediate step he had to win re-election as Senator from Massachusetts in 1958. To help Jack, Jackie even agreed to allow *Life* into Caroline's nursery for photographs early in 1958. Then after traveling with him on a Senate Foreign Relations Committee trip to Europe, she went campaigning with him that autumn. They were in Omaha, Nebraska, for their fifth wedding anniversary that year, and she also accompanied him to Massachusetts. As Dave Powers wrote, somewhat ingenuously, "She was always cheerful and obliging, and to me a very refreshing change from the usual candidate's wife because she did not bother to put on a phony show of enthusiasm about everything she saw and every local politician whom she met. The crowds sensed that and it impressed them. When Jackie was traveling with us, the size of the crowd at every stop was twice as big as it would have been if Jack was alone."[15]

She also took part, at November election time, in a stagy Kennedy family television show orchestrated by Rose, *At Home with the Kennedys*, intended to introduce Massachusetts viewers to the senatorial candidate's wife. Jackie sat primly in the Kennedys' Hyannis Port living room, the image of submissive wife and daughter-in-law, parroting the cloying script, her soft, breathy voice contrasting oddly with Rose's harsh, flat Boston tones. "I've enjoyed campaigning so much, Mrs. Kennedy," she fibbed, in response to Rose's introduction. "Since September fifteenth Jack and I have been traveling through the state trying to meet as many people as we can. Your son, Teddy, who as you know is campaign manager, set up the schedule for us last summer. We visited 184 communities . . ."

"Well, congratulations, Jackie," Rose rasped, "and congratulations to Jack for having found a wife who is so enjoying the campaign."

Jackie even put in a slot for Caroline: "I'm surprised that Jack hasn't insisted on taking Caroline on this trip," she cooed. "She's back in Boston now but she was very lucky to be with you on the Cape . . ." Home-movie footage of the Kennedy families and their respective children followed, narrated by Eunice and Jackie. The grand finale was the appearance of Jack, a tall, handsome figure standing behind the women, reminding the audience to vote for him on November 4. The program, scheduled for a workday morning, was deliberately aimed at women, Jack's major constituency.

He won reelection by an overwhelming majority, more than 850,000 votes, the largest total vote ever recorded by a Massachusetts politician. It was one more key step along the road to the White House.

Family values were again to the fore in a *Time* piece at the end of the month, featuring presidential hopefuls. Jackie, darkly exotic-looking in silk dress and triple strand of pearls, posed with eleven-month-old Caroline on her knee, seated beside her handsome, tanned husband dressed in a sober suit, polka-dot tie and white shirt, his formerly tousled hair closely combed, flashing the great Kennedy asset: a row of movie-star teeth. The glamorous couple, pictured in their Georgetown drawing room against a background of leatherbound books and expensive china bibelots, presented a complete contrast to the down-home Hubert Humphreys, photographed cornily holding hands with their average-looking teenage children in front of a simple shingle cabin.

Their image, as far as Jackie was concerned, was not far removed from reality. Mary Barelli Gallagher, who had once worked for Jack, then Janet Auchincloss and was now Jackie's unofficial but full-time secretary, was taken aback by the huge gulf separating Jackie's way of living and that of the average American housewife and mother. Gallagher's impression was that Jackie did not lift a finger at home. The maids took care of the household chores; George Thomas, the valet, took care of Jack's clothes, while Jackie's personal maid, Providencia "Provi" Paredes looked after hers; Maud Shaw was in charge of the nursery; and Muggsy O'Leary drove and did emergency shopping. There was a cook—or, as Gallagher cattily put it, "a parade of cooks" until they discovered Pearl Nelson—to prepare all the meals. As she had declared in her Farmington days, Jackie had no intention of being a housewife; her function was to provide a mise-en-scène for Jack's entertainment.

Glamour was a commodity singularly lacking in contemporary American politics and, indeed, in American life east of Hollywood. The image that Jack and Jackie projected, of beauty, sophistication, taste and intelligence, offered the public something new, something that satisfied the American desire for change. As politics entered the visual age, their image was in tune with the times. Jackie made no attempt to dress down or be ordinary; backslapping bonhomie was not her style. And Mary Gallagher was wrong to criticize her for never doing the chores. Jackie was a star, an American princess and it was that image the public wanted.

Some things, however, had to be concealed: English nannies, chauffeurs, personal secretaries were deliberately kept out of sight by Jackie. As the campaign progressed after Jack's official announcement of his candidacy in January 1960, so Jackie's control of the visual and spoken image increased. Her distaste for the bread and butter of politics, the physical contact, the jostling, shouting crowds, never left her. With that gift for publicity, which was half instinct, half intelligence, she knew that part of her allure was her inaccessibility. Remoteness and mystique were the principal ingredients of her appeal.

Jackie's lack of enthusiasm for the vulgarities of the political process was all too evident to the staff in N Street. Because she wanted to please Jack, she held Press Teas for newswomen in her Georgetown drawing room, but in private she made it plain that it was all a great bore and an inconvenience. With few exceptions, she did not like women reporters, which she had made evident since the day at the Chicago Convention when, although heavily pregnant, she had picked up her skirt and made off at speed to escape from Maxine Cheshire, the ambitious and inquisitive reporter from the *Washington Post*, who became her chief bugbear.

Jackie's household rule was to handle things herself when photographers were around. At the teas, Mary Gallagher would "pour" for the reporters until it was time for pictures, when she would disappear and Jackie would be photographed with teapot in hand. When *Life* turned up to do a feature on the candidates' wives for the preelection issue in October 1960, a scene was set to show Jackie answering her mail with Gallagher. When the pictures appeared in the magazine, Gallagher's name and photograph had been eliminated and the caption ran: "Reading the 225 daily letters; Jackie answers each with help of a part-time secretary. 'I could use one of these full time these days,' she says." She did; her "part-time" secretary was working six to seven days a week.[16] The same stratagem produced the famous photograph of Jackie leaning over Caroline's crib and the caption, "Tucking her daughter in for an afternoon nap, Jackie, who does not have a nurse for Caroline ..." Maud Shaw, the full-time live-in nanny, was not mentioned.

"Maud Shaw and I continued to learn that the way to stay on the good side of Jackie was to stay on the side *away* from the cameras . . . I could manage, but it didn't always work for Miss Shaw, who had to scramble away from the children, cameras or no cameras. And her mistress would be annoyed. 'What does she expect me to do?' Miss Shaw would grumble to me. 'Just leave the children there and hide?' "

"When you talked to her one felt that she had a very good relationship with President Kennedy," Maud Shaw's nephew said of his aunt. "Whether it was quite so good with Mrs. Kennedy is a debatable point but of course you're talking about a mother, and a mother who wanted everything to be perfect and to seem—to be seen—to be perfect, that she could do everything . . ."[17]

On October 28, 1959, a key meeting of the Kennedy political inner circle was convened by Jack and Bobby at Bobby's house in Hyannis Port to lay final plans for Jack's assault on the presidency the following year, of which the first phase would be to win the nomination of the Democratic Party at the Los Angeles Convention in July. In essence, Jack had been running for the past three years, working in tandem with his political alter ego, adviser and chief speech writer the tall dark Nebraskan, thirty-one-year-old Theodore C. "Ted" Sorensen, whom he described as his "intellectual blood bank," a gut liberal who was responsible for Jack's most important speeches and acted as a filter for all major policy decisions. Bobby was to act as full-time campaign manager. Steve Smith was in charge of logistics, financing and recruitment. Lou Harris, pollster supreme, would carry on running analyses of public opinion, while Pierre Salinger was brought in to handle the press. An American of French descent, like Jackie, Salinger was a war veteran, *bon viveur* and gifted pianist. Eternally good-humored, shrewd and quick-witted, he was universally popular, managing simultaneously to remain on good terms with the inquisitive press corps and the resolutely private Jackie. Then, like a Praetorian Guard around Jack, there were his devoted Boston politicians, Kenneth O'Donnell, Lawrence O'Brien and Dave Powers—Kennedy's Irish Mafia, or "the Murphia" as they were sometimes called. (In private, Jackie was adept at mimicking them, although she rarely did so within earshot of Jack.)

While Ted Sorensen defined the major obstacle facing Jack as the fact that the country had never elected a Catholic, let alone a forty-three-year-old, as President in the twentieth century, the Kennedy circle regarded French-speaking, couture-clad, foxhunting Jackie as another problem. The campaign staffers, like Kenny O'Donnell, Larry O'Brien and Jack's brother-in-law Steve Smith, failed to appreciate that Jackie might be an electoral asset. "There was a conscious decision, as I remember, to keep her in the background," Richard Goodwin recalled. "They wanted to keep her away from the campaign because they were political experts and they thought that the American people's idea of a First Lady was Bess Truman—nice, matronly, dowdy, Midwestern American mother—and that someone like Jackie would just turn people off, which showed how much they understood the American people!"[18]

Whatever the Irish Mafia, the Kennedy family and their friends thought of Jackie's potential as a campaigner, Jack himself was well aware of the effect her gift for languages had on voters for whom English was only a second language. In

October 1959 he invited her to help him campaign in Louisiana. They met in St. Louis, where campaign worker Edmund Reggie noted that they were anxious to be left alone for an evening out together in the French Quarter. The following day Jackie got up too late to accompany Jack to an appointment at the Knights of St. Claver Hall in the heart of New Orleans's black district, where a group had been waiting with a bunch of roses for her. Then they flew together to Lafayette, where Jackie was presented with two camellias and confronted with a cavalcade of twelve 1958 white Cadillacs to carry the party to lunch at the Oakborn Country Club, where Jackie surprised the guests by saying a few words in French. Later that day, at the crowning of the Queen of the Rice Festival, a huge crowd estimated at some 100,000 people had gathered to see them. Jack wanted her to address the crowd. When she stepped forward and said, in her soft voice, "Bonjour, mes amis," the crowd of French-speaking Cajuns went wild. "You could just hear the screaming," Reggie recalled. "When I tell you screaming, it was just unbelievable, the applause, the shouting . . . She went on to tell the crowd in French that she was very happy to be in south Louisiana because her father had told her as a child that Louisiana was a little corner carved out of France, that she loved France because of her own French ancestry—and that she was glad to see for herself that what her father said was true that this was the beautiful part of France . . ." When the couple rode at the head of the parade afterward in another Cadillac—this time the latest 1959 model—the screaming of the crowds was deafening; women ran out of the crowd to speak to Jackie in French, one presenting her with homemade pralines she had brought with her. Afterward in the car going to the airport, Jack and Jackie had eyes only for each other. According to Reggie, who later went on to manage the Kennedy presidential campaign in Louisiana, "[They] were sitting in the front seat and, I swear, they were just like little love birds. They were really . . . almost to the point of embarrassment on my part . . . I mean, you can't go around just whispering to your wife and chuckling, pecking her on the cheek . . ."[19]

Earlier that year, as plans for the presidential campaign of 1960 gathered pace, Jackie had felt extreme misgivings about its effect on their lives, which she had confided to Joe Alsop. She wondered whether it was really worth it to have Jack run for the presidency when she never saw him and Caroline together in the same place two days running, and when she did see him they were usually too tired to speak to each other. "It's the only game that's worth the candle," Alsop had told her, words she thought about again and again. Gradually she had come around to his point of view and begun to feel happy about the situation.[20]

Jackie responded to Jack's political requests, but not entirely with enthusiasm. Her native caution and reserve made her as wary of biographers as she was of journalists. This applied even to sympathetic writers like historian and politician James McGregor Burns, who with the Kennedys' agreement was writing a profile of Jack during the 1960 campaign. McGregor Burns interviewed Jackie, among other members of the family, and found her the least forthcoming. "To me she was rather an elusive person," he said. "She was very polite. She was proper about the whole thing but I never felt that I really made a connection there."[21] When Burns sent the manuscript of the book to the Kennedy family in October 1959, they were deeply upset at his portrayal of Jack which, although sympathetic, expressed understandable doubts about the depth of his commitment to the liberal cause. The author received what he described as a "lovely but unhappy" letter from Jackie. Where Jack was concerned she was like a tigress in her concern for his image and reputation. The least of her complaints was his referring to her not as Jacqueline but as Jackie "a name which I loathe and never use anymore." More important, she objected to his draft account of Jack's Addison's disease, which was a well-kept Kennedy secret, and the string of illnesses from childhood onward. She did not like the description of Jack's efforts to win his father's approval and thought that Burns had presented Jack as "pathetic" and "not up to the job."

Burns responded by pointing out the benefit Jack's campaign might derive from an honest, informative and nonadulatory, although favorable, book that would show undecided readers "what a really tremendous career he has had, and above all—my main point—the growth and development he has shown." Jackie showed this letter to Jack and wrote back in conciliatory vein, agreeing with all his points, and saying, "I am sure it will be something that we will all be proud of." Privately, however, the Kennedys remained offended. Burns had tried to remain neutral and objective but, as another biographer who experienced the weight of the family disapproval commented, "In the context of the Kennedys, neutrality was a sin."[22]

Jackie was concerned to protect Jack against the most damaging charges then doing the rounds: principally that he was the puppet of his dominant father. Joe Kennedy, of course, was then a controversial figure. "There was talk that old Joe was really running the show, and buying his son's election, and that he had great influence on Jack," Laura Bergquist, a bright *Look* journalist who followed Jack on the campaign, remembered. "A lot of important people I knew in Washington—political types or journalists—discounted Kennedy because they thought he was a kind of 'golden boy' dominated by Big Daddy . . ."[23] It was an open secret that Joe had "loaned" the owner of the financially precarious *Boston Post* half a million dollars to support Jack in the 1952 senatorial race, and Jack, with his characteristic candor, admitted frankly to reporter Fletcher Knebel that "we had to buy that paper."[24] In an article on presidential hopefuls written in November 1958, *Time* listed among Kennedy's handicaps first his Catholicism, and then the "rumor that his millionaire father, Boston financier Joe Kennedy, is willing to spend any amount of money to get him elected—an idea forcefully denied by Kennedy and carefully spread by his opponents." Jackie, *Time* reported a year earlier, had indulged in "masterly oversimplification in defending father Joe against charges that he runs his children's careers, 'You'd think he was a mastermind playing chess . . . when actually he's a nice old gentleman we see at Thanksgiving and Christmas,' she said demurely."[25] Burns did agree to suppress evidence of Jack's Addison's disease, rumors of which surfaced and were spread by Lyndon Johnson's supporters at the 1960 Democratic Convention. In 1959 Jackie was in the forefront of the defense; it was the first of even more bitter battles.

Asked why Jackie had objected to his book, James McGregor Burns replied, "She thought that I did not emphasize enough the seriousness of Jack Kennedy, that I made him out to be not just a playboy but a kind of superficial person, really not capable of drawing leadership. She felt I did not do justice to him, she felt that I exaggerated the role of the father and exaggerated the role of the family generally, and left an image of someone who again did not have the steadfastness, the stamina, the resolution that would be needed for presidency."[26] She felt, too, that, despite Jack's public commitment to the Supreme Court's resolution on civil rights, made during the Lousiana campaign, Burns's questioning the extent of Jack's emotional commitment to liberal causes played into the hands of the pro-Stevenson wing of the Democratic Party. Jack's relative youth and his "playboy" reputation were, indeed, serious handicaps, particularly when compared with the experience of Stevenson and of Lyndon Johnson, who liked to refer derisively to Kennedy as "the boy."

Then, as Jack was rolling up the votes in West Virginia, on May 1, 1960, Francis Gary Powers, piloting an American U-2 spy plane on a mission over the Soviet Union, was shot down by Soviet fighters and captured alive, precipitating a major crisis in U.S.-Soviet relations. The Paris summit between Eisenhower and Khrushchev collapsed, and with it the disarmament negotiations between America and the U.S.S.R., while in newly Communist Cuba, deteriorating relations with Fidel Castro reached permanent hostility when Castro expropriated American interests and turned to the "rocket-rattling" Khrushchev for support. Anarchy in the newly liberated Belgian Congo involved the United Nations in crisis action that escalated through the summer. It was a dangerous world—too dangerous, some people thought, to entrust to a forty-three-year-old untried in government.

"Loyalty was characteristic of the whole Kennedy entourage," Laura Bergquist said. Discretion in return for friendship and private candor was a condition; any breach was greeted by accusations from the Kennedys and their entourage of "breaking a trust." In 1957 Bergquist had been working on a story, "The Rise of the Brothers Kennedy." In conversation with Ted Sorensen she raised the rumors circulating in Washington—it was apparently common gossip—"that the Senator and his wife were not getting along, that they've separated." Heatedly Sorensen denied any rift, telling Bergquist that the reason Jackie wasn't traveling with Jack was because she was pregnant (with Caroline)—"That's in confidence," he added. "However," Bergquist said, "between our talk and the time my story appeared, there were all kinds of items [about it] in the papers. So in one two-line caption, along with a picture of the then Senator kissing Jackie good-bye at the airport . . . I wrote the reason Mrs. Kennedy wasn't campaigning with him was that she was pregnant. By the time that caption appeared, I figured it was common knowledge." Yet even as late as the summer of 1964 Sorensen brought up the subject— "the fact that I had broken his confidence about Jackie's pregnancy. That one caption. He was still protecting the Kennedy interests."[27] Ben Bradlee, who with Charlie Bartlett was the closest to Jack of the Washington press corps, felt the punishment of withdrawal of friendship when they deemed him to have transgressed. An article in the August 1962 issue of *Look*, entitled "Kennedys vs. Press" by Laura Bergquist's husband, Fletcher Knebel, landed Bradlee in hot water when it quoted him as saying, "It's almost impossible to write a story they like. Even if a story is quite favorable to their side, they'll find one paragraph to quibble with."[28] From regular contact with the Kennedy White House, dinner once or twice a week, and regular telephone calls, the Bradlees were cut off for three months. In 1975 after Bradlee published his memoir of their friendship, *Conversations with Kennedy*, Jackie cut him dead.

In the spring of 1960, Jackie knew she was pregnant again, yet she still went out on limited excursions on the campaign primary trail for Jack, accompanying him on a discouraging visit to snow-covered Wisconsin. She was with him at the Hotel Pfister ("Pfistula," Jackie had dubbed it in a letter to Joe Alsop) in Milwaukee to hear the unsatisfactory result of the primary. Jack had overwhelmed Humphrey with his superior organization but obtained only an indecisive 56 percent of the popular vote, with the electorate splitting on the Catholic/Protestant divide. He had tried to dodge the religious issue but would now have to face it head-on in the next crucial primary: West Virginia, where the population was 95 percent Protestant and 5 percent Catholic. He was running in West Virginia against his father's advice: "It's a nothing state and they'll kill him over the Catholic thing," had been Joe's view. "Dad, I've got to run in West Virginia," Jack had responded.[29] News that the religious issue had surfaced, confirming the insider's Washington view that a Catholic could never win the presidency, brought reporters swarming into West Virginia, and with them, Joe Alsop reported, in response to desperate appeals from the Kennedy camp, "Kennedy operatives . . . carrying bags bulging with greenbacks."[30]

While old Joe pulled strings behind the scenes, deluging the state with money and calling on his dubious mafia contacts to provide the carriers, Jackie too concentrated her best efforts on West Virginia. "I remember Jackie in the campaign in West Virginia," said Nuala Pell, wife of Claiborne Pell, the Rhode Island senator and close friend of the Kennedys. "The staff were always grumbling that she wasn't interested in campaigning and didn't . . . and that they would have to get her to do something, but I must say, the times she came out and talked to those coal miners or whatever, she was fabulous and they all just sort of oohed and aahed at her . . . she just did it in that breathless way."[31] Jackie herself could see the humor in the situation, describing to Gore Vidal how she would have to go into supermarkets and talk to unwilling voters: "There I am, stationed by the cash register in a supermarket and must shake the hands of the women coming out, and they will do anything to avoid contact with me—they hide behind things, they race up the aisles, they cower in corners."[32] West Virginia was Jackie's—and Jack's—first true encounter with real, grinding poverty, due to widespread unemployment among the miners. Cocooned as the Kennedys had been in their wealthy world on the eastern seaboard, the misery and hunger of the Appalachian families came as a shock to them; when Jackie came to the White House she remembered it and ensured that every contract for the presidential glassware went to West Virginia.

Jackie's pregnancy curtailed her active participation in the 1960 campaign but that did not prevent her doing her best privately to help Jack. She personally oversaw the deployment in Jack's campaign of Teddy's wife, Joan, the youngest and most beautiful of the Kennedy women. Joan might have been tailor-made as a Kennedy bride; she was Catholic and a virgin, convent-educated at the Sacred

Heart at Manhattanville. At twenty-one, she had been introduced to the twenty-five-year-old Teddy at Manhattanville where, at his mother's instigation, he had been asked to open the new gymnasium, an occasion attended by no less than seven other members of the family. Jean Kennedy Smith, who had been responsible for recruiting Ethel as a bride for Bobby, introduced Joan to "my little brother," six foot two, two-hundred-pound handsome Ted. Joan had been brought up in Bronxville, as had the Kennedys in their earlier years, and the family knew all about her. Rose—who, as she later told Joan, had been saying her rosary hoping that Ted would meet and marry a nice Catholic girl—took the precaution, after interrogating Joan herself, to check her out with Mother Elizabeth O'Byrne, president of Manhattanville. It was, Joan reflected bitterly, almost an arranged marriage, driven by inevitable momentum rather than passion. Ted's mumbled proposal was followed by his prolonged absence campaigning for Jack's reelection to the Senate and studying law in Virginia, until he turned up late for their engagement party at Joan's parents' house in Bronxville. Yet, Joan said, "Everyone thinks this is a marriage made in heaven . . . my mother- and father-in-law, my parents and me, and all my girlfriends and Ted's friends."[33]

When Joan hesitated over marrying a man she hardly knew, Joe Kennedy refused to consider canceling or even postponing the wedding plans. She could not escape her chosen role; nor was it conceivable that a Kennedy could be publicly jilted. Teddy himself had doubts, which he confided to a friend on the eve of his wedding. It was too late: the couple were railroaded up the aisle by family expectation. Jack, the best man, was recorded giving his youngest brother an extremely frank talk on marriage, which contrasted strangely with the public exhortations on the subject. "Here was Cardinal Spellman talking about the sacredness of the marital vows," Leamer wrote, "and behind the altar Jack giving a different sort of sermon on what marriage meant to a Kennedy man . . ."[34] In their way the couple loved each other, but Ted Kennedy, for all his charm and real sweetness of character, could not escape his heritage while Joan, a gentle, cultured spirit, was not tough enough to withstand the demands of Kennedy family life. In Jackie, always sensitive to the vulnerability of the young, she found a friend and protector.

Jackie was especially protective toward Joan when it came to life in the Kennedy pack. Joan, a gifted pianist, could not compete athletically with the Kennedys but, as Jackie remarked wickedly, "All Joan needed to do was to go out on the tennis court in her leopardskin swimsuit and she needn't worry about Eunice's forehand or Jean's backhand."[35] She was Joan's ally against the mass sporting onslaught: "We can be different together," she told her. Joan said, "In the summers, everybody else in the family would do everything together from morning to night—the touch football, the sailing, the tennis, the waterskiing—all day long they'd play together *en masse*. And Jackie would go to her house and read and paint, and I would go to my house and I would read and play the piano. And then sometimes we'd take walks together on the beach between the compound and Squaw Island where Ted and I had our house. She was wonderful, she made me feel like it was OK to be myself."[36]

In the eighteen months since their marriage Teddy and Joan had been living with their in-laws at Hyannis Port and Palm Beach, or out of suitcases as Teddy traveled around the western states drumming up delegates for Jack. In the spring of 1960 Jackie stepped in to help Joan after the birth of her daughter Kara, in Bronxville. She rented a house for the young Kennedys in Georgetown, two blocks from her own, hired a couple to help and found an Irish nanny who was an old friend of Maud Shaw. "It was like having an older sister who was looking out for me," Joan Kennedy said. "When I came down [to Washington] with my new baby girl she met me, took me through the house, and made sure everything was fine and went out and did some grocery shopping for me."

Jack liked to campaign with one of the photogenic Kennedy women to escort him, and two weeks after her arrival in Washington Joan was co-opted for West Virginia. Jackie lent her clothes for the campaign trail and debriefed her when she returned. "We'd chat, talk about campaigning, and I'd ask her questions and she'd say, 'Seems to me you're doing the right thing,' or she'd make suggestions about how to work the room." Joan was being used, although she did not realize it, as a chaperone for Jack. "I remember her [Jackie] saying to me, 'Stay *very* close to Jack. Just glue yourself to him. Don't let anybody else wiggle in, specially when they're taking those pictures.' " Jackie wanted to keep the rumors at bay: if any attractive woman was to be photographed with Jack, it was going to be a member of the family. She encouraged Joan—'They'll love meeting you because your name is Kennedy," she told her, "whereas Jean Smith is Jean Smith even though she's his sister." Joan, with her beautiful figure, long blond hair and fashionably short skirts, drew wolf whistles from the West Virginia miners. "Jack really got a kick out of it that all these guys were whistling at me [but] he wasn't sure that that was good for his candidacy to take me places where I got whistled at. And at the end of the campaign he gave me a cigarette box, it was a silver one and on it was engraved, 'Too beautiful to use on these occasions, Love Jack.' "[37]

On May 10, the day of the West Virginia primary, Jack returned despondent to Washington to sit out the results with Jackie, who had invited the Bradlees to dinner. He was far from certain of the result. After dinner, when no clear picture of the voting had emerged, the Kennedys and the Bradlees, after a quick call from Jack to Bobby, who was holding the fort at the Kanawha Hotel in Charleston, went to the movies. Jack's attention was far from the screen: he kept popping out to call Bobby, returning to his seat to sit edgily tapping his teeth with the nail of the middle finger of his right hand, a sure sign of preoccupation. When they were back at N Street, Bobby telephoned to announce an amazing victory. Champagne was drunk and the Kennedy private plane prepared to take them down to the victory celebrations in Charleston. It was a notably bumpy ride; Bradlee remembered Jean Smith screaming for her husband Steve all the way down.

When they arrived, the women were pushed into the background. Bradlee remembered,

> Kennedy ignored Jackie, and she seemed miserable at being left out of things. She was then far from the national figure she later became in her own right. And this night, she and Tony [Bradlee's wife] stood on

a stairway, totally ignored, as JFK made his victory statement on television. Later, when Kennedy was enjoying his greatest moment of triumph to date, with everyone in the hall shouting and yelling, Jackie quietly disappeared and went out to the car and sat by herself, until he was ready to fly back to Washington.[38]

Bradlee recorded from 1959 Jackie's distaste for noisy, mindless political gatherings, when she had attended one in a motel convention hall in Maryland.

I remember most watching Jackie, and the almost physical discomfort she showed, as she walked slowly into this crowded hall to get stared at—not talked to, just simply stared at. Her reaction, later to become so familiar, was simply to pull some invisible shade across her face, and cut out spiritually. She was physically present, but intellectually long gone . . .[39]

Jack's neglect of Jackie at moments of political triumph was symptomatic of his basic disregard for women when it came to the business of politics. "Maybe it was the Irish mick in him," Laura Bergquist meditated, "but I don't think he took women seriously—as human beings that you work with. He married Jackie, who had her own special kind of intelligence, [yet] as Bobby once said about her to me, 'She's good for Jack because he knows that she's not the kind of wife when he comes home at night who's going to say, "What's new in Laos?" ' " Bergquist admired Jackie's mental toughness and sense of self. "She was a very strong person," she said. "She had a very definite mind of her own. I think that's how she survived in that family, just by being very private and stubborn and saying no, and carving out her own existence. He [Jack] was a very tough character to get along with, I would think, as charming as he was. But she was not railroaded. She could have been."[40]

Asked whether Jackie was interested in politics and whether she ever discussed them with her husband, John Kenneth Galbraith claimed that "On some great issues Jackie was both informed and articulate, but on the day to day business of Democratic politics she took no part, no part at all. She listened to campaign speeches with almost total detachment." One morning in Georgetown the Kennedys were about to set out campaigning outside Washington. Galbraith remembers them leaving after breakfast, "he with his campaign speeches for the day, and she with the memoirs of Saint Simon"—"which she read throughout the motorcades," Kitty Galbraith interjected. She was not, Galbraith said, particularly interested in politics, but in one area she was "absolutely indispensable" to Jack: "First of all on her judgment of people, and this is something on which I think JFK depended. And that's been very little mentioned. He tended to take people at their face value, she looked at them much more scrupulously to see what they were up to, to distinguish between those who had something from those who were promoting themselves. Jackie's critical view, sometimes favorable, sometimes unfavorable, was something that was extremely important. For all the people that I have known, she had the shrewdest eye for a phony or somebody who was engaged in self-advancement, and she didn't conceal it."[41]

During May and June, the run-up to the Los Angeles Democratic Convention, which was to choose the party's presidential candidate, Jackie barely saw her husband as he shuttled across the country. At the end of June he returned home for a ten-day rest before leaving for Los Angeles in July. Three thousand people waited at the international airport to welcome him, banners waving, bands playing, girls screaming. On Friday July 16, with the candidates he had defeated—Stevenson, Johnson, Humphrey and Symington—sitting on the platform with him, he addressed 80,000 people in the Los Angeles Coliseum, accepting his party's nomination. It was a young man's speech:

"Today our concern must be with that future. For the world is changing. The old era is ending. The old ways will not do . . . we stand today on the edge of a New Frontier—the frontier of the 1960s—a frontier of unknown opportunities and perils—a frontier of unfulfilled hopes and threats . . . The New Frontier of which I speak is not a set of promises—it is a set of challenges. It sums up, not what I intend to offer the American people, but what I intend to ask of them. It appeals to their pride, not their pocketbook—it holds out the promise of more sacrifice instead of more security . . ."

A phalanx of Kennedys flanked Jack as he spoke, but two of the most important members of the family were not there. Joe Kennedy, holed up in the Beverly Hills house of his friend Marion Davies, had kept out of sight all week, as he had during the long months of the campaign hitherto, working behind the scenes to swing delegates to Jack—in New York City, New Jersey, Illinois and elsewhere. That Friday morning he flew to New York to witness his son's triumph on television. At the deserted Hyannis Port compound, a tanned Jackie, who had spent the week of the convention alone with Caroline and Maud Shaw, watched on a rented seventeen-inch television set with Janet and Hughdie, Little Janet and Jamie Auchincloss, who had come down from Newport to be with her. Two reporters from *Life* were also there to see her take calls from Jack before and after the nomination. "Isn't it wonderful?" Jack apparently asked her, and then, as if seeking reassurance, "Do you think so?" At 2:45 A.M. she stepped out into the glare of floodlights and the barrage of questions from newsmen and broadcasters waiting outside for brief impromptu press conference. "I thought I was all alone in the country," she quipped, and admitted she was "soo . . . excited," before seizing on Jack's acceptance speech as a chance to escape inside. The following morning she gave a press conference to forty reporters and cameramen in the living room of Joe Kennedy's house, fielding their questions with her usual shy reserve.[42]

She had been working on a painting, a present for Jack to celebrate his triumphant return home. It depicted him in a three-cornered hat marked "El Senatore," striking a Napoleonic pose in their small boat, the *Victura*, crowded with Kennedys. Meanwhile the compound was under siege. Three cars invaded Joe Kennedy's grounds, their passengers swarming out over the lawns, snapping cameras and stripping flowering shrubs as souvenirs before being told by the police to leave. Other souvenir-seekers had stripped the rambler roses from behind Jack and Jackie's front fence before a protective stockade could be erected. Low-flying airplanes took photographs of the compound, while other photographers zoomed in their lenses from the sea.

Jack was due on Sunday evening. That afternoon no less than two hairdressers arrived at Jackie's house to style her hair for her airport rendezvous with Jack. Driven by Muggsy O'Leary and accompanied by Little Janet, she rode in a white Cadillac to the airport, at which wave upon wave of Kennedys arrived, accompanied by a large press plane. Jack appeared last, to be met by Jackie in the airport building before taking a motorcade in the open convertible through "undisciplined" crowds to the compound. Wearily acknowledging them, Jack told them he had to get inside his house before Caroline went to sleep, but emerged five minutes later with her in his arms. Later, admiring Jackie's painting, Jack joked, "I wonder where she ever got the idea I had a commander-in-chief complex." In return, his present to her on her thirty-first birthday at the end of the month was a painting he had made for her of the family's favorite news store in Hyannis Port. The next morning he and Jackie picnicked aboard the family cruiser, the *Marlin*, with Bobby and Ethel. They went sailing again the next day, but the promised vacation lasted a bare two weeks as Jack reconvened his campaign team for the next phase: the bid for the presidency against the Republican nominee, Eisenhower's Vice President, Richard M. Nixon.

Early in August, Norman Mailer, clad in an ill-pressed washable black suit and "sweating like a goat," waited among a crowd of newspapermen, politicians and policemen to interview Jack for his *Esquire* article, "Superman Comes to the Supermart." Apart from the swarms of people on the lawn and politicians "immortalizing" their visit to Hyannis Port by having flash photographs taken on the terrace of the house, Jackie's yellow and white living room was crowded with guests— Arthur and Marian Schlesinger, *Saturday Evening Post* writer Peter Maas, campaign photographer Jacques Lowe, and Kennedy press aide Pierre Salinger. Mailer sensed Jackie's controlled exasperation at the invasion of her home. Offering him a cool, non-alcoholic drink, Jackie teasingly told him, "We do have something harder, of course . . ." This was typical Jackie, an attempt to trip up the already nervous writer; it was a reference to his trial the previous month in Provincetown, Cape Cod, for "drunkenness and rude and disorderly conduct," following an incident when Mailer had emerged from a local bar and hailed a police car with cries of "Taxi!"[43]

Mailer noted her "saucy regard" and her "surprisingly thin but not unfeverish" calves. Jackie appeared unnerved by Mailer with his intense perceptions; as an interviewer, his probing questions could not be swatted away as easily as the usually inane female reporters' "candidate's wife" queries. Her covering tactic was physical retreat; while they sat together she got up at least half a dozen times, disappearing for two minutes and returning for three. "Since there was an air of self-indulgence about her, subtle but precise," Mailer wrote, "one was certain she liked time to compose herself."[44] Jackie was wise to be wary: Mailer's observations that day were the most penetrating ever written about her. Like most men he was seduced by her, by her elusiveness and "concealed cruelty." His first impression of her as a nice, clean, merry college girl changed as he perceived her reactions to the mob invasion of her home. "Jackie Kennedy was a cat, narrow and wild, and her fur was being rubbed every which way." As she taunted him over the verbena tea, "something droll and hard came into her eyes as if she were a very naughty eight-year-old indeed." While noting that this "saucy regard" was something he had already detected in photographs of her, there was another quality about her that surprised him, "of shyness conceivably. There was something quite remote in her. Not willed, not chilly, not directed at anyone in particular, but distant, detached . . ." She was very obviously the center of the group: "There was a natural tendency to look at her and see if she were amused . . . she had a keen sense of laughter, but it revolved around the absurdities of the world. She was probably not altogether unlike a soldier who had been up at the front for two weeks. There was a hint of gone laughter." He concluded, "I liked Jackie Kennedy, she was not at all stuffy . . . she had perhaps a touch of that artful madness which suggests future drama . . ."[45]

Mailer's impressions of the candidate he had come to interview were equally perceptive. He noted Kennedy's "excellent, even artful" good manners, "better than the formal good manners of Choate and Harvard." Behind the courteous façade, Mailer observed, as he had with Jackie, that Jack's most characteristic quality was "the remote and private air of a man who has traversed some lonely terrain of experience, of loss and gain, of nearness to death, which leaves him isolated from the mass of others." He went on,

> Kennedy had a dozen faces. His personal quality had a subtle, not quite describable intensity, a suggestion of dry pent heat perhaps, his eyes large, the pupils gray, the whites prominent, almost shocking, his most forceful feature: he had the eyes of a mountaineer. His appearance changed with his mood, strikingly so, and this made him always more interesting than what he was saying. He would seem at one moment older than his age, forty-eight or fifty, a tall, slim, sunburned professor with a pleasant weathered face, not particularly handsome: five minutes later, talking to a press conference on his lawn, three microphones before him, a television camera turning, his appearance would have gone through a metamorphosis, he would look again like a movie star, his coloring vivid, his manner rich, his gestures strong and quick, alive with that concentration of vitality a successful actor always seems to radiate.[46]

A steady stream of official visitors interrupted Jack's boating trips on the *Marlin* and *Victura*—among them two of his principal opponents at the Los Angeles convention, Adlai Stevenson, longtime hero of the liberal wing of the Democratic Party, and Lyndon B. Johnson, Jack's surprise choice for his running mate as Vice

President after a bitter round of infighting between their respective supporters. Kennedy was not a fan of Stevenson, who was a particular favorite of Jackie. Politically he regarded the former Governor of Illinois as something of a wimp while on a male level he was unable to comprehend the charismatic appeal that Stevenson, although balding and paunchy, exercised over a number of beautiful women other than Jackie.

Lyndon Baines Johnson, the tall gangling senator from Texas, as Majority Leader in the Senate, had been a powerful figure on the Washington scene; it had been a surprise to many that he had been prepared to accept the political nullity of the vice presidential nomination at the behest of Jack, who was many years his junior in years and status. For Jack, Johnson represented important southern votes; beyond that he respected Johnson's political ability and was amused by what he called his "riverboat gambler" characteristics. Jack was detached enough to ignore Bobby's detestation of Johnson; there was a visceral antagonism between the two. Johnson was a larger-than-life character, insecure, driven and unpredictable: "an actor, a role player, in turn courtly and crude, gentle and overbearing, magnanimous and vindictive," as his latest biographer describes him.[47]

Johnson had been born in the hard Texas hill country west of Austin to a family down on their luck. Unlike Jack, he had experienced poverty at first hand, and had an insight into an America unseen from the comforts of Georgetown. Ruthlessly ambitious, brilliant and manipulative, he had carved his way to the top of the American political scene. His crudity was both macho and deliberate—his dismissive "Adlai Stevenson squats to piss" amused both Jack and Jackie. The Harvard intellectuals, and particularly the Hickory Hill circle around Bobby, affected to despise him as a hick, but Jack appreciated his unrivaled political skills and knowledge of the workings of Capital Hill.

Jackie already knew his wife, Claudia Taylor Johnson, always known as Lady Bird, from her earliest days as a Senate wife when she had attended the introductory lunches Lady Bird held for the wives of new senators. Lady Bird was a remarkable woman, capable, controlled and strong. She had none of Jackie's sophistication, glamour or chic, but she had shrewdness, wisdom and understanding of people. In background and outlook the two women were poles apart and would never become close, but they shared a mutual respect and sympathy. Almost the only thing they had in common was devotion to their husbands, and gallantry in the face of their habitual philandering. Lady Bird was a political wife through and through, upon whose support and help Johnson was absolutely dependent, however roughly he might appear to treat her.

To Lady Bird, who had met Jackie as a Senate wife, Jackie had an appealing vulnerability despite her glamour. "She had a most charming quality to me of being a little girl . . . she looked vulnerable, she looked like you wanted to help her and she remained that throughout the period I knew her."[48] Later Jackie recalled how impressed she had been by Lady Bird's calm efficiency, noting everything down in a spiral pad: "When she'd hear a name she'd jot it down. Or sometimes if Mr. Johnson wanted her, he'd say, 'Bird, do you know so-and-so's number?' and she'd always have it down. Yet she would sit talking with us looking so calm . . ."[49] Jackie won over Lady Bird by appealing to her for help—"I don't know how to do anything . . ." she said, in her little-girl voice. Both Jack and Jackie were concerned about the effect that the strain of the final run for the presidency might have on her pregnancy: she was terrified of having another miscarriage. Immediately after the Los Angeles Convention, Jack had telephoned the Johnsons to ask if Lady Bird would "carry the load on the women's end of the campaign."

For Jackie the future held other fears. In conversation with Walter Reuther, president of the United Auto Workers, during his visit to Hyannis Port, Jackie expressed her concerns about the presidency in general and assassination in particular. Gunmen had attempted to kill Walter Reuther in 1948 and his brother Victor Reuther in 1949. "She really was obsessed," Reuther's companion, Jack Conway, recalled, "with this whole idea of the change in her life, the change in Kennedy's life, and how do you protect against assassinations. She wondered what security precautions did to family life. 'Don't let the precautions ruin your life,' Reuther said; 'you can't stop living.' "[50]

Intensely private as she was, Jackie was deeply concerned about the demands that public life would make on her and her family. She had expressed her fears to Joe Alsop when he visited Hyannis Port after the convention. (As a cousin of Eleanor Roosevelt, Alsop knew the White House well and had an insider's perception of the demands of the First Lady's role; as always Jackie had chosen the right person to consult.) She had given a party for sixty members of the press, which had given her an unpleasant foretaste of things to come. Alsop had advised her to regard the problem unemotionally, to see the distasteful press party in the same light as if it had been a charity affair to raise money.[51] Jackie told him that she had been appalled at some of the personal questions women reporters had asked her, "and on the defensive about poor little Caroline whom they want to chase around with flashbulbs and turn into a ghastly little Shirley Temple if I'd let them." Irritation with "the Kennedy girls' adoration of publicity" had contributed to her outburst, while Jack, she said, "couldn't explain it [the publicity/privacy problem] properly."[52] Alsop had helped her to overcome her ambivalence to the purpose of politics and to respect power, which she never had before possibly because it had come so suddenly without her having had to work for it—through marriage. But if things turned out right she would welcome it and use it for the things she cared about.

The press, stirring up rivalry between the two candidates' wives, had been making an issue of Jackie's fondness for Paris couture. Coming as it did in the opening stages of the final contest for the presidency between Kennedy and Nixon, the Kennedys had been concerned, Jackie upset and on the defensive, as she told Alsop. A Kennedy suggestion that she should hold a press conference to counter the criticism had enraged her. Alsop advised her in a letter, "It is well known that you are a faithful and admiring customer of Givenchy. It will probably help if there are some pieces in the papers about your buying your maternity dresses at Bloomingdale's."[53]

Jackie had followed his advice and invited a group of fashion reporters to see her try on maternity dresses. She let them know that she had been upset at a recent Sunday *New York Times Magazine* article reporting that many American women were annoyed by her "devil-may-care chic" and thought she looked, as one put it, "too damn snappy." It quoted from a *Women's Wear Daily* report that Jackie spent some $30,000 a year on Paris couture. Jackie complained, "They're beginning to snipe at me about as often as they attack Jack on Catholicism, I think it's dreadfully unfair," and expostulated, "I never buy more than one suit or coat from Balenciaga and Givenchy. I couldn't spend that much unless I wore sable underwear." Rather unwisely she went on, "I'm sure I spend less than Mrs. Nixon on clothes. She gets hers at Elizabeth Arden, and nothing there costs less than $200 or $300." Her comment backfired: "Miss Arden," it turned out, was "very Republican" and often sold Mrs. Nixon clothes at cost. Tracked down at Atlantic City, Pat Nixon, wearing a turquoise wool jersey dress (Lord & Taylor "about $49") was able to take the high line: "I have no comment on what Mrs. Kennedy wears or says. I don't criticize other women and never have. I buy my clothes off the racks of various stores around Washington and sometimes in New York. I don't think clothes are an issue."[54]

Jackie enlisted the help of Diana Vreeland, doyenne of the fashion world, former editor of *Vogue* and now of *Harper's Bazaar*, who explained that she must now begin ordering American clothes, and let it be known where, in order to counter press reports of her wearing Paris clothes, and comparing her fondness for French couture with Mrs. Nixon's homespun thriftiness. David Dubinsky, the head of the International Ladies Garment Workers Union, had complained to Jack about it. To forward her "Dress American" initiative she needed some American clothes for a press release on October 1 to combat "Pat Nixon Week" when she feared she might be portrayed as a "let-them-eat cake fiend who buys Paris clothes!"[55]

Fashion trivia aside, Jackie was determined, despite her increasing immobility due to her pregnancy, to make "every effort for dear Jack," as she told her friend Eve Fout, and took a greater interest in the run-up to the presidential election in November than she had in the campaign for the nomination earlier that year. J. K. Galbraith had underestimated her interest in the campaign. Once she had been reassured by Joe Alsop that gaining the presidency was the "only game worth the candle," she was committed to Jack's victory. In the autumn of 1960, in the run-up to the general election, she wrote a memorandum to Ted Sorensen, enclosing memoranda from a friend, the medical lobbyist Florence Mahoney, in case they might prove to be of use in composing speeches for Jack. She stressed the particular importance of a Polish memorandum from Michel Cieplinski for Jack's Polish speech on October 1 in Chicago and a suggested speech by another prominent Pole. The Poles, it appeared, were not solidly pro-Kennedy, and influenced by dislike of the Irish clergy and Nixon's popularity after his trip to Poland.

Joan Braden, a leading Kennedy campaign worker in California, who worked closely with Bobby, gave him a list of her suggestions. "Draw Jackie into the campaign as much as possible," she advised. People had criticized Jack for not mentioning his wife in his Los Angeles acceptance speech. She should write a weekly "Campaign Wife" column for the newspapers. Bobby called Jackie, and Joan Braden, also heavily pregnant, moved to Washington to liaise between Jackie and campaign headquarters, and to protect her against too heavy demands on her. Jackie and Joan together wrote the "Campaign Wife" column, and Jackie started the "Coffee for Kennedy" campaign, asking women to invite ten friends for coffee to be drunk from "Coffee for Kennedy" paper cups, each friend to donate ten dollars to the campaign. She held meetings of medical-care-for-the-aged experts and the Women's Committee for New Frontiers, chaired by Joan Braden, at N Street, to appeal to women voters to support the Kennedy–Johnson ticket. She was present at the final meeting of the Kennedy campaign in New York City, held in front of the "Freedom Hotel" in Spanish West Harlem, addressed by a bizarre collection of speakers: Eleanor Roosevelt, the liberal Jewish Senator Lehmann, the Reverend Adam Clayton Powell, the demagogic local black congressman, and Jack. "Visually, however, it was Mrs. Kennedy, at once demure and dazzling, who stole much of the show," recalled an observer.[56] To the delight of the crowd, she spoke a few sentences in Spanish and, later that day, in Italian to an Italian group.

There were problems, however, Joan Braden recalled, when Jackie's "sense of good taste" clashed with the Kennedy family's wishes. There was an acute difference of opinion between them over the Sinatra Rat Pack. "Jackie did not like the Rat Pack trio of Frank Sinatra, Dean Martin and Peter Lawford for whom the Kennedy family had an almost star-struck regard," Braden recalled. "After all, Peter Lawford was a member of the family and they were famous; so use them. Use them whenever possible. But Jackie was certain that the Rat Pack was the wrong image; at least, she didn't want to be associated with the Rat Pack, didn't want to appear at campaign rallies with them, didn't want to appear on television with them, and though she was less demanding on this point, she didn't want her husband to appear with them either. I was Jackie's liaison with campaign headquarters and I was to make her wishes known; and I dreaded what might be the confrontation. But it was done. The Rat Pack disappeared from the campaign. I have ever since credited Martin, Lawford and Sinatra as possessing a quality not many people associate with their names. They showed understanding. They wanted very much to help. And if they could help best by staying away, so be it."[57]

Jackie had every reason to advise Bobby to keep Sinatra away from the campaign and, even more, the candidate. Publicity had linked the singer with the Mafia since 1947, when a February visit by Sinatra to Havana in the company of Joseph Fischetti and his brother Rocco, members of Al Capone's Chicago gang, and Lucky Luciano, "father of the modern Mafia," was reported in the press. Sinatra and Luciano were seen together in a casino and at racetracks and parties. Scripps Howard columnist Robert Ruark, in Havana at the time, wrote a story about it, headlined "Sinatra Is Playing with the Strangest People These Days," which was repeated by other columnists, one of whom, Lee Mortimer of the *New York Daily Mirror*, earned a punch from Sinatra outside Ciro's in Hollywood as a result. In 1951 Mortimer further alleged that, on that Havana trip, the Fischetti brothers had brought with them two million dollars "in the hand luggage of an entertainer." This particular allegation remained unproven, but the fact that rumors about Sinatra's links with the mafia were being aired in New York's press would have alerted Jackie to the dangers of any connection with him. She continued to be wary of Sinatra even after Jack became President, telling her staff there to refuse any donation the singer might make to the White House restoration project because it was "dirty money."[58]

She was intelligent enough to know that the games played by the Rat Pack, Sinatra and Peter Lawford were far from innocent. No doubt she suspected that when her husband was with Sinatra he liked to play them too. Sinatra's participation in Jack's campaign had been solicited by Joe Kennedy in the winter of 1959, when he invited the singer to lunch to ask him to contact the Chicago mobster Sam "Mooney" Giancana to help in Illinois and West Virginia, "getting the numbers out, getting the unions to vote."[59] Sinatra, who liked and admired Jack and believed he would make a good President, was more than willing to help. His song "High Hopes" was adopted by Jack as his campaign theme and, until the ukase by Jackie against the Rat Pack, he stopped off several times that spring on the campaign trail to party with Sinatra either in Las Vegas or at Sinatra's house in Palm Springs. One of the singer's attractions for the Kennedys was that he was a source of girls. On February 7, 1960, Jack left the campaign plane at Las Vegas, en route from New Mexico to Portland, Oregon, to catch a Rat Pack show at the Sands. It was on that occasion, according to Blair Clark, Jack's old friend as editor of the *Harvard Crimson*, now a reporter for CBS on the campaign trail, that Jack met Judith Campbell, a beautiful Elizabeth Taylor lookalike. "She turned up at our table while Sinatra was doing his act," said Clark.[60] Within a month he had embarked on a two-year affair with her, which involved him in dangerous connection with the mafia, for she was also a girlfriend of Giancana. According to later statements by Campbell, on April 6 she slept with Kennedy at his Georgetown house shortly after Jackie had left for Florida. At Kennedy's request, she effected an introduction to Giancana, and thereafter in April 1960, she said, she acted as a courier between Kennedy and the mafia leader, carrying a satchel of money for deployment in the Illinois primary. On March 22, 1960, the FBI had received information that *Confidential* magazine was investigating a rumor of an "indiscreet party" at Sinatra's Palm Springs house, attended by Jack Kennedy and Peter Lawford. As Sinatra's daughter, Tina, admitted, "It's not as though Dad and the President would meet and play golf . . ."[61]

However, the most potent weapon in the Kennedy armory in the 1960 campaign was not the superiority of the Kennedy political machine, oiled by vast amounts of Joe Kennedy's money, but television, which Jack was the first politician to deploy with devastating effect. By 1960, 88 percent of American families owned a set, as compared with only 11 percent ten years before. "Within a single decade," Theodore E. White wrote in his definitive book on the 1960 campaign, "the medium has exploded to a dimension in shaping the American mind that rivals that of America's schools and churches." On September 26, the first of the four "Great Debates" on television between Kennedy and Nixon was broadcast.

It was a key moment in the campaign, which pitted the young, untried senator, against Eisenhower's vice president. As White wrote,

> Until the cameras opened on the Senator and the Vice President, Kennedy had been the boy under assault and attack by the Vice President as immature, young, inexperienced. Now obviously in flesh and behavior he was the Vice President's equal. Not only that, but the contrast of the two faces was astounding. Normally and in private, Kennedy under tension flutters his hands—he adjusts his necktie, slaps his knee, strokes his face. Tonight he was calm and nerveless in appearance. The Vice President, by contrast, was tense, almost frightened, at turns glowering and, occasionally, haggard-looking to the point of sickness. Probably no picture in American politics tells a better story of crisis and episode than that famous shot of the camera on the Vice President as he half slouched, his "Lazy Shave" powder faintly streaked with sweat, his eyes exaggerated hollows of blackness, his jaw, jowls and face drooping with strain.[62]

It was unfair: Nixon suffered from the televisual defect of having an unusually transparent skin so that every hair follicle showed up on camera, even if he had just shaved. He was tense, unnerved by technical complications in the studio during the day, while Kennedy was relaxed after a brief, anonymous sexual encounter shortly before the debate. Those who heard it on radio thought that the candidates had come off equal, but polls of those who had watched it indicated that Nixon had come out of it poorly or even very poorly. Alsop, in the audience at Chicago, thought Nixon had won. His confidence in Kennedy's chances was only restored when he telephoned his cousin, Theodore Roosevelt's daughter, Alice Roosevelt Longworth, an expert political handicapper, who based her predictions on television watching. Her reaction was decisive. "Well, Joe, your man's in, my man's finished. I don't see why they bother to go on with the election. Dick has finished himself off."[63]

"It was the picture image that had done it," White noted, "and in 1960 television had won the nation away from sound to images, and that was that." He noted also the "quantum jump" in the crowds that greeted Kennedy on the morning after the debate: "Now, overnight, they seethed with enthusiasm and multiplied in numbers, as if the sight of him, in their homes on the video box, had given him a 'star quality' reserved only for television and movie idols."[64] The networks estimated the total audience for the debates at 115–120 million Americans, the largest in history. Pollsters concluded that in the final analysis two million of Kennedy's final vote count came from the impact of television. Since his final popular vote margin over Nixon was a mere 112,000 votes, this was a significant figure. Jack Kennedy's skillful use of television had counteracted the weight of religious prejudice against him, and after the Chicago debate he had vastly increased his chances of being elected the first Catholic President of the United States.

On the morning of election day Jackie got up early to be driven to Boston to meet Jack and cast her vote, before returning with him to their house to begin the long wait for the result. Jack was edgy, his response to the welcoming crowd at Hyannis airport perfunctory and his smile halfhearted and strained. Posing with Jackie for photographs he looked tired, his face puffy with fatigue, squinting in the cold bright sunlight, and unsuspected lines appeared in his "perpetually young-looking face." "And," an observer noted, "though he walked with the same long, brisk stride as always, some watchers detected a limp."[65]

At the compound, he checked in at his father's house for a family breakfast, had a quiet word out of earshot on the lawn with Joe, then lunched later with Jackie on baked ham and apple brown Betty. At intervals during the day he visited the communications center set up in Bobby's house, supervised by Kenny O'Donnell and Larry O'Brien on the ground floor. In a pink and white child's bedroom on the upper floor, poll expert Lou Harris was ensconced, evaluating results as they came in from dispatches and teletypes collected by Peter Lawford, while in another child's bedroom Teddy Kennedy and Steve Smith commanded a battery of telephones. The house was crowded with Kennedys and campaign workers, while the servants' bungalow behind Joe's house was occupied by a select group of press, including the ubiquitous representatives of *Life*.

Hopes rose and fell through the evening as conflicting reports came in. Early exuberance at favorable results from Connecticut turned to gloom as at 7:15 P.M. CBS announced that their computer analysis of returns predicted a Nixon victory by 450 electoral votes. Within an hour the CBS computer had switched sides, predicting a narrow Kennedy win by 51 percent of the popular vote. Kennedy, beaming, lit a big cigar.

While increasingly elated Kennedys munched tuna, chicken, lobster and egg salad sandwiches, the simple food they liked provided by a local caterer, Jack slipped back to his own house to say good night to Caroline and relax over a daiquiri, his favorite cocktail, with Jackie and their houseguest Bill Walton. The three dined in the large formal white dining room punctually at eight, heroically dispensing with the presence of television for the duration of the meal, then returned to watch the results. At ten thirty, when a Kennedy landslide was predicted, Jackie exclaimed, "Oh, Bunny, you're President now!" Jack knew better. "No," he said. "It's too early yet." At eleven thirty, optimistic, Jackie went to bed and Jack crossed the lawn to Bobby's house where, with apparent victory in sight, the mood was uproarious. As the night wore on the euphoria faded: early results from the Kennedy strongholds in the northeast were gradually overtaken by Nixon voters in the Midwest and far west. At 1:00 A.M. the White House mistakenly released a congratulatory telegram from Eisenhower to Kennedy, indicating, the Kennedys thought, that Eisenhower might have advance information that Nixon would concede, because despite the decline of his popular vote, Kennedy was adding to his total of electoral votes. With 262, he needed only seven more to achieve the required 269. At 3:30 A.M. Nixon appeared at the Ambassador Hotel in Los Angeles to make a statement, with his wife Pat in tears at his side; everyone expected a surrender. But Nixon was cautious: he limited himself to saying that if the present trends continued Kennedy would be the next President of the United States. "Why should he concede?" Jack commented. "I wouldn't." Then, after stopping off at his father's house, he returned home to wake Jackie with the latest results, and read for a while before going to bed himself at 4:30 A.M.[66]

Shortly before six, while Jack and Jackie were asleep, Secret Service men, a sure sign of official recognition of the transfer of power, joined the police manning the cordon point outside the compound. At nine thirty Ted Sorensen arrived to confirm what the Secret Service men already knew. Jack had been elected thirty-fifth President of the United States.

Shortly afterward Pierre Salinger turned up to confer and agreed that there could be no public celebration yet as Nixon had not conceded. Jack breakfasted with Jackie and Caroline, then took Caroline for a walk on the beach with Teddy, trailed by members of the family and Sorensen, with the Secret Service men following at a discreet distance. At noon, he returned home for lunch. Just after twelve thirty he officially won Minnesota, and clinched his victory. Twelve minutes later Nixon conceded, in a statement read by his press secretary. Jack found graceless his opponent's failure to appear in person to thank those who had voted for him. "He went out the way he came in," he said, "no class."[67]

He crossed the lawn to Bobby's house. "When Jack came into the room he was no longer Jack," an aide said. "He was President of the United States. We all stood up—even his brother Bobby. It was just an instinctive thing."[68] Dazed, Jackie put on raincoat and headscarf and headed for the beach for a solitary walk as the other members of the family were dressing for a victory photograph at Joe's house. Symbolically, Jackie was plowing her own independent furrow. "Where's Jackie?" Jack asked, then went down to the beach to fetch her.

With admirable self-restraint, Joe Kennedy had earlier stated his refusal to attend the celebration at the Hyannis Armory, which would be the occasion for Jack's acceptance speech. He had made two vital contributions to his son's success with his money and his silence; even in this moment of triumph, of the fulfillment, if vicarious, of his lifelong dream of a Kennedy presidency, he intended to keep out of the limelight. It was only at Jack's insistence that, at the last minute, he agreed to go along.

At the Armory Jackie, at last, appeared radiantly happy, in contrast to her father-in-law, who was described as looking "somewhat grim and pale."[69] After his speech Jack introduced his father first of his family to the audience. The two stood there, their arms round each other's shoulders. Jack may have been at pains during the campaign to underline that his father's political views were not his but now he drew him out of the shadows in a public, if unspoken, demonstration of affection and deep gratitude.

Jack had closed his speech with the words "My wife and I look forward to a new administration and a new baby," but childbirth, as far as Jackie was concerned, was never easy and the birth of John Jr. was no exception. Jackie had planned to remain quietly in Georgetown until December 15 when she was scheduled to go into New York Hospital for the birth, stay in there until Christmas Eve, then fly down to Palm Beach to recuperate until January 19, when she would return to Washington for the Inauguration. Instead, on November 27, just after Thanksgiving and three hours after Jack had left the house to fly to Palm Beach, an ambulance was called to 3307 N Street. Yet again Jackie's child arrived prematurely. John F. Kennedy Jr., weighing six pounds three ounces, was born around 1 A.M. as his father was dashing back from Florida. It was the perfect ending to a triumphant year.

CHAPTER EIGHT

Queen of the Circus

She said, "You know, being in the White House is like being in the French Court. All these people are sycophants hanging around," but it amused her in many ways. Secretly she loved the service and she loved the followers . . .

— Betty Spalding[1]

Jackie spent twelve days in the hospital after the cesarean. John Jr., almost a month premature, was tiny—"a dark-haired mite," as Maud Shaw described him— and spent his first five days of life in an incubator with a minor respiratory infection. Although she gave every impression of recovering quickly and taking control as usual, sitting up in bed writing long memos on her favorite yellow foolscap legal pads, she was both physically and mentally weak. Jack's formal inauguration as thirty-fifth President on January 20, 1961, was less than two months away. Under her habitual calm exterior Jackie was feeling the pressure of unavoidable problems both public and private.

Early on December 9 Jack went to the hospital to bring Jackie and John Jr. home. That morning she had the long-awaited appointment at the White House for a tour with Mamie Eisenhower. Her doctor, John Walsh, had only permitted this on condition that she went around in a wheelchair but when she arrived no chair was to be seen. The suggestion had not been welcomed by Mrs. Eisenhower, whom White House chief usher J. B. West described as "the grandest of First Ladies."[2] She had wanted to give Jackie a private tour and seems not to have contemplated abandoning her dignity to push her guest around. "We'll get a wheelchair, but put it behind a door somewhere, out of sight," she ordered. "It will be available *if she asks for it.*" To West, Jackie appeared "very young . . . thin and quite pale." Walking with him to the elevator to meet Mrs. Eisenhower on the second floor, Jackie appeared ill at ease, her "wide, uncertain eyes" taking in everything around her.

An hour and a half later, the two women descended. Mamie Eisenhower departed regally in the back of her limousine to her daily card game; Jackie walked slowly to her three-year-old station wagon. West caught up with her to give her photographs and plans of the rooms and saw that her face was drawn with pain. Two months later, when touring the White House again, Jackie asked him why a wheelchair hadn't been available. He told her that it had been there, waiting for her request. "To my surprise, she giggled. 'I was too scared of Mrs. Eisenhower to ask,' she whispered. Mrs. Eisenhower's feelings about the young Mrs. Kennedy were never spoken, only intimated," he wrote. "She's planning to re-do every room in the house," she told him. "You've got *quite* a project ahead of you." Then, in a voice she reserved for disapproval: "There are certainly going to be some changes made around here!"[3]

Mrs. Eisenhower would have been even more disapproving had she known of Jackie's plan to smuggle in her decorator, Sister Parish—Mrs. Henry Parish II— telling Mrs. Eisenhower that Mrs. Parish was her aunt. Mrs. Parish responded cautiously, rejecting the idea as unsafe. "First of all I think I must tell you that for your sake I think it would be wrong for me to be your aunt. I am so afraid you might get into trouble—I assume they take names etc. and probably go so far as checking. I may be wrong but the last thing that should happen would be for you to start wrong . . ."[4] Jackie had to make do with her own memory plus photographs and plans, which she took with her to work on in Palm Beach.

Later Jackie told friends that her White House tour had led to a "two-hour crying jag." Physically exhausted and on the verge of postpartum depression, she went down to Palm Beach to spend nearly two weeks in bed. From her point of view, there was indeed plenty to cry about. The transformation of the White House, as she envisaged it, would be a daunting task. Her recently appointed social secretary, Letitia "Tish" Baldrige, had sent her the bad news in a long, dispiriting memo after a meeting with Mrs. Eisenhower's social secretary, Mary Jane McCaffree. The main problem was lack of funds: "The White House budget is TOO small," she stated, in a paragraph under the heading SHOCKING FACTS. Therefore it could not afford proper linen, flowers, containers for flowers and plants, or "worst of all" champagne and cocktails at big dinners and receptions. No alcohol had been served by the Eisenhowers at their "big musicales," only punch, coffee and sandwiches. The house had been run "like a military camp the past 16 years or so and lacks female taste (real)." In the State Dining Room, for example, the only plant or flower container to be seen by the public filing through was "a cheap $2.98 heavy white porcelain jardiniere with 3 sick ivy plants in it on the great marble mantelpiece." She reported that the Eisenhowers had eaten off trays in their sitting room every night while watching television. "The food must be plenty cold when it reaches them since it is prepared two floors below in another part of the house." And she continued, "Anyone who knows anything about cuisine says the food at State Dinners is nothing short of *awful* . . ." Rigid convention made even the logistics of moving in a performance worthy, Tish said, of Alfred Hitchcock: "It's tradition that you can't move in until 12 noon Jan. 20th. I asked Mrs. McCaffree if we couldn't smuggle a lot of stuff over without the

E[isenhower]s knowing and she said yes, the Chief Usher could store cartons, suitcases etc. out of sight and then whisk them into sight on the stroke of 12 noon . . ."[5]

Even before the birth of John Jr., Jackie had been laying plans for her White House campaign. As far back as July 1960, a week after Jack had won the nomination at the Los Angeles Convention, Jackie had focused on what would be one of the key posts in her entourage, that of social secretary. She had contacted Tish Baldrige, older than she was but, like her, educated at Farmington and Vassar; Tish's parents were Washington friends of the Auchinclosses. Tall and distinguished-looking with great self-confidence, energy and a strong sense of humor, Tish had all the qualifications for a First Lady's social secretary. She was fluent in French and Italian, having worked in both the Paris and Rome embassies. Recently she had worked in public relations for Tiffany's and had accepted a job with the firm in Milan before receiving Jackie's telephone call. She knew who was who and had great drive and determination—too much, Jackie later came to think.

Tish had made her first public appearance in Washington on November 23 at the Sulgrave Club where her intended lecture on the jewelry of Schlumberger had turned into a press conference for the women reporters of Washington's press corps, most of whom were her friends. Exhilarated by the attention her new position attracted, Tish was flippant when asked what she really thought of Jacqueline Kennedy: "She is a woman who has everything, including the next President of the United States," she quipped, and followed it up with a series of gaffes. She referred to the numbers of clubwomen who would be anxious to meet Jackie as "those great hordes of females . . . er, I mean those large groups of very interesting ladies," and implied that Mrs. Eisenhower had not yet had the courtesy to invite Mrs. Kennedy to the White House.

Her anxiety to put across Jackie's intention to make the White House "a showcase for great American artists and creative talent" was interpreted by the press to mean that Jackie would be covering the walls with modern art. She thus offended the clubwomen of America, Mrs. Eisenhower and the Fine Arts Commission (who issued a statement denying that permission for such a sacrilege would be granted in the historic house), and enraged Jackie by announcing that Mrs. Kennedy would be giving regular press conferences. More importantly, perhaps, with her quip about Jackie as "the woman who has everything," she had affronted the Kennedys' view of the dignity of the presidential office. On November 23 Jack, treated to columns of this in the Washington press, darted out of his office, waving the offending papers "with some pretty strong words." To no one's surprise, Tish later announced that Mrs. Kennedy had said there would be no more Social Office press conferences.

Tish's assurances that Jackie would be wearing American clothes merely served to highlight a potentially controversial issue in which the press had already demonstrated an intense interest. After Jack's election as President, the problem of the source of Jackie's clothes became acute. David Dubinsky and the women of America had to be reassured that the First Lady would not be patronizing foreign designers and clothes made overseas. It seems to have been Joe Kennedy who came up with the solution in Oleg Cassini. Oleg and his brother Igor, nicknamed "Gighi" but always referred to by the Kennedys as "Gigi," were naturalized White Russian aristocrats and international playboys. Igor, the "Cholly Knickerbocker" who had singled out Jacqueline Bouvier as Debutante of the Year 1947, was married at the time to Charlene Wrightsman, the daughter by his first marriage of Charles B. Wrightsman, the oil millionaire and neighbor of the Kennedys in Palm Beach. He claimed to have coined the expression "jet set," to reflect the glamour of the new jet-propelled airliner used by the international rich and social set to ferry themselves to their ritual destinations. Both he and Oleg were golfing partners of Joe at his Palm Beach Club and his guests in New York, where he held court at Le Pavillon, in which he had a financial interest. "The old patriarch . . . treated both Oleg and myself as his protégés, often advising us financially," Igor wrote. "Ambassador Joseph Kennedy liked beautiful girls, and so did we. When he came to New York, he often did the rounds of the fashionable clubs and restaurants . . ."[6]

Igor was a member of the Kennedy Palm Beach circle, which caused Jack's liberal friends and sympathizers some disquiet. The circle included Porfirio "Rubi" Rubirosa, the most successful of all twentieth-century playboys, who launched his career as the son-in-law of the right-wing Dominican dictator Rafael Leónidas Trujillo, and went on to marry two of the richest American heiresses, Doris Duke and Barbara Hutton. Earl E. T. Smith, former U.S. Ambassador in Cuba, a strong Batista supporter, who was married to Jack's close friend and former lover Florence "Flo" Pritchett Smith, with whom he had stayed in Havana in the winter of 1957–58, was also in the group. Both Igor and Rubirosa had financial connections with the Trujillo regime, an undeclared link that proved disastrous for Igor. Oleg had Hollywood connections, which the Kennedys shared; he had been married to Gene Tierney, with whom Jack had had an affair, and engaged to Grace Kelly.

When the future First Lady's potential dress problem loomed in the late winter of 1960, Oleg presented the answer. He was a designer and, as Joe Kennedy's friend, he could be trusted. Joe Kennedy was prepared to finance the image of his son's presidency, as he had the reality of his presidential campaign, and told Cassini: "Don't bother them at all about the money, just send me an account at the end of the year. I'll take care of it."[7] He told Cassini to be "discreet" about the cost, which might hurt the President politically. Subsequently Oleg received a call from Evelyn Lincoln while Jackie was still in the Georgetown hospital after the birth of John Jr. and visited her there, finding her surrounded by sketches from top American designers—Norell, Sarmi, Andreas of Bergdorf Goodman—sent through Diana Vreeland.

For controlling, image-conscious Jackie, who liked to have her own way working behind the scenes, Oleg was the perfect solution. While he represented an American-based designer, she could have the clothes she wanted, paid for by Joe Kennedy without recourse to Jack and without attracting hostile publicity. It was a trade-off: he would be her official designer, she would make him famous. On December 8, the day before she left the hospital with John Jr. for Palm

Beach, she wrote a note of benediction for Oleg. As a quid pro quo for all the help Vreeland had given her, *Harper's Bazaar* was to have exclusivity to the first photograph of Jackie as First Lady–elect by Avedon in clothes by Cassini. She had just chosen all her evening clothes from him: "He knows what I like," she told Vreeland.

Later Cassini gave a press conference to announce his appointment at the Pierre Hotel in New York. John Fairchild of *Women's Wear Daily* described the occasion as "hysterical," and Cassini's claims to be Jackie's exclusive designer were met with skepticism by the fashion press. "I had letters from her," Fairchild went on, "which said she would never wear French clothes and everything was Oleg Cassini."[8] But Fairchild remained skeptical. "She always wanted the best of everything." In fashion terms then, the best was Paris, where Jackie's favorite designers were, of course, Givenchy and Balenciaga. She had known Hubert de Givenchy since 1952, when she attended the opening of his couture house and she had been a client since her marriage.[9] The Givenchy look, spare, sleeveless A-line dresses as worn by Audrey Hepburn—Givenchy's muse at the time—was the one that most appealed to her. It suited her lean figure, while her own doe-eyed, dark, fawnlike looks resembled those of the gamine star of *Sabrina*, *Roman Holiday* and *Funny Face*. "She liked that look," Fairchild said. "It was very neat and conservative and it suited her." He dismissed claims that Cassini had shaped her image. Jackie had a clear vision of herself and what she wanted—regal without being dowdy, modern but not extreme, a look of understated glamour to suit America's First Lady. "No one could shape her image," Fairchild said. "She shaped her own image."

Jackie was a passionate follower of fashion: she read all the international fashion magazines, knew exactly where to buy the best shoes in Florence. Through Lee—whose taste was unerring and who in 1960 made the Best-dressed List for the first time—and Diana Vreeland, she was in touch with all the latest trends. In 1960 she had secretly ordered an outfit from Princess Irene Galitzine in Rome, the designer whose palazzo pajamas of heavy silk with jewel-encrusted embroidery at neck and hem had become the indoor uniform of the international set. According to her secretary, Mary Gallagher, she had fashion scouts in New York, Paris and Rome. The latter was Irene Galitzine. "Jackie herself also kept track of what the couturiers in Paris and London were featuring," Gallagher wrote, "and would get in touch with her scouts to order the items she liked without anyone knowing they were for her. She would sometimes fall in love with the material a famous designer had used and order something in the same fabric to be made by another designer."[10] For hats she used Marita O'Connor, "Miss Marita" of the custom-hat department at Bergdorf Goodman (often by the future star Halston). Like Jack, Jackie detested hats but while he remained hatless—the despair of the American hat trade—she knew that for her hats, on certain occasions, were inevitable. "Here goes—an order for a million hats," she wrote to Marita, after Jack's election. "Oh dear, it was so pleasant when I didn't have to wear hats!" she wailed. "They will pauperize me & I still feel absurd in them . . . Can you find me some hats in future at downstairs hat bar—the easy to wear back of head pillbox ones."

This was the origin of the hat that became Jackie's trademark—the hat that suited her large head and bouffant hairstyle best. Miss Marita was also to act as Jackie's "personal shopper" for gloves and shoes to match various outfits, including the keynote inaugural dress and coat: "Please order me a pair of alligator shoes size 10A—medium heel—slender—pointed toe but not exaggerated—no tricky vamp business . . . you know what I like—elegant & timeless . . ."[11]

The deal suited both Jackie and Oleg Cassini, but for Cassini, the rewards were social as well as commercial. Jackie knew that Jack was amused by him, and in her never-ending quest to keep her husband entertained, she made him one of the White House social circle, a regular at the private parties for the Agnellis and Lee and Stas Radziwill, who had married in a civil ceremony on March 19, 1959, in Virginia. "Plan to stay for dinner every time you come to D.C. with sketches—& amuse the poor President & his wife in that dreary Maison Blanche," she wrote, adding significantly, "& be discreet about us—though I don't have to tell you that—you have too much taste to be any other way." They worked together on sketches and swatches of material to produce the look she liked. He turned a blind eye to the odd outfit from a couture house other than his own, and she used him as cover to counter stories about her purchases of foreign clothes. "I refuse to have Jack's administration plagued by fashion stories of a sensational nature & to be the Marie Antoinette of the 1960s," she wrote under the heading PUBLICITY in a letter of instruction to Cassini on December 13, "so I will have to go over it with you before we release future things—because I don't want to seem to be buying too much—You can make the stories available—but with my approval first— There may just be a few things we won't tell them about!"[12]

Jackie's choice of Oleg as her official couturier ruffled feathers in New York, particularly at Bergdorf's, where they had been working under Diana Vreeland's supervision for Jackie's Inaugural Ball gown. Ben Zuckerman had already designed a coat to be worn on Inauguration Day. Somehow with consummate tact, Jackie smoothed things over immediately, as she told Oleg in her letter of December 13: "Thank heavens all the furor is over—and done without breaking my word to you or Bergdorf's. Now I know how poor Jack feels when he has told 3 people they can be Secy. of State." Her solution was to divide Inaugural Day between Cassini and Bergdorf's, which was to go ahead with the ballgown, while Cassini created a stunning white satin dress to be worn for the Inaugural Gala. Diana Vreeland continued to help from the sidelines, as principal shopper and adviser.

After Tish, Jackie's next office appointment was a press secretary, Pamela Turnure, a small, fine-boned brunette with blue-green eyes and a creamy complexion, who had something of Jackie's look and, oddly for a press secretary, reflected her qualities of quiet reserve. She was only twenty-three and had had no previous experience of such a job, apart from three years' spent in Jack's office as receptionist and secretary to Timothy "Ted" Reardon, the Senator's administrative assistant.

Jackie had rejected Pierre Salinger's suggestion of a seasoned woman reporter: her idea of her press secretary's role was precisely the opposite of Salinger's. "You will be there as a buffer," Jackie wrote, in one of her classic memoranda of instruction to Pam, "to shield our privacy not get us in the papers . . . I think you are rather like me & so will answer questions the way I would. I feel so strongly that publicity in this era has gotten so completely out of hand—& you must really protect the privacy of me and my children . . . just know you can't discuss us— JFK, me & infants." Even in Pam's private life, Jackie instructed, she was not to answer any questions as to what it was like working for the Kennedys—"Everyone exaggerates so—& some tiny insignificant thing you say goes from one person to another & ends up horribly in some gossip column a week later." Jackie went on to assure her that "None of this is meant to sound reproachful—it's just that I have suddenly realized what it means to completely lose one's privacy . . . My press relations will be minimum information given with maximum politeness—you are great at that anyway. I won't give any interviews—pose for any photographs, etc. for next four years. Pierre will bring in *Life* and *Look* or Stan Trewick [*sic*] a couple of times a year & we'll have an ok on it."[13]

Pam took Jackie's point perfectly. "I must say I always look at my job as one to help preserve Mrs. Kennedy's privacy and not to create publicity," she was quoted as saying.

The principal victims of Jackie's resolutely impenetrable stance on publicity would be the Washington women reporters. Initially promised a press conference by the First Lady, all they got was a tea party. While Jack's West Wing of the White House would be easily accessible to the press, both via the amiable Pierre Salinger and through the President's regular press conferences, the inner workings of Jackie's East Wing would be as difficult to penetrate as the Kremlin. Among the few areas that Pamela Turnure listed as of legitimate news interest to the press were the White House restoration project and State entertainments. Family life, and the children in particular, would be strictly off-limits.

"They were as different for a journalist as night and day," Laura Bergquist Knebel said. "The President, if he had known you for some time and you were a friend or whatever—especially in the first year or two—was among the most accessible VIPs I knew in Washington. Jackie was the remote fairy queen in that other wing who didn't want to have much truck with us journalist types. All the time she was in the White House, I was often in Dutch with her because I was trying for the stories she wanted least. Like stories on her children . . . she gave the press a hard time, she managed to surmount all of us. The working press in the White House, particularly, had a great deal of resentment for Mrs. Kennedy. For instance, two women reporters, Helen Thomas of the UPI [United Press International] and Frances Lewine of AP [Associated Press] were professional, competent newspaper types. Their job was to cover what goes on in the White House, especially in the First Lady's domain. Jackie would never have anything to do with them. She wouldn't even recognize their existence, which was, I thought, unnecessary. You don't have to give them big exclusive interviews, but you can be polite . . ."[14]

"She waged a three-year war of independence with the press," Helen Thomas recalled. "Looking back, I would say it ended in a draw. We won a few, she won a few, but her army included the secret service." Jackie, she said, "treated the press like so many foreign invaders."[15] Traveling back to Washington from Hyannis

Port with her new dog, a German shepherd puppy named Clipper given to her as a birthday present by her father-in-law, the press sent her a note asking what she would feed the dog. Jackie sent back a one-word reply: "Reporters."

Jackie did not bother to hide her preference for stylish journalists and reporters over what Bergquist called the "working stiffs": "If you were stylish and foreign, an Italian or French photographer or a writer like Romain Gary, these people interested her. They had much more open entrée; they got invited to dinner; they talked to her . . . She had her favorites. There were people she liked and trusted, a different set of people than the President's circle." A year after Jackie left the White House, Laura Bergquist and she had a long talk at Hyannis Port, what Bergquist called "a sort of reconciliation meeting." Jackie told her, " 'You know, you were always part of *his* wing,' indicating that she had concerns in her domain that sometimes worked at cross-purposes with what the President was up to. And you were either in one camp or the other . . ." She had not always been like that: Laura had first met her when she was the Senator's wife and Bergquist and her husband, Fletcher Knebel, were working on a joint book, *Candidate 1960*. "I liked her very, very much," Laura Bergquist remembered. "She was very funny and wry and off-beat . . ." The White House froze Jackie into a regal ice sculpture. Charlie Bartlett's wonderful free spirit became buried behind a façade of suspicion, mistrust, and a deep rage at her own imprisonment, and manifested itself in a black contempt for human pretensions and frailties. According to Bergquist, the façade melted after she left the White House. "She said to Stanley [Tetrick, *Look* photographer] once, 'Oh, Stanley, remember how all the time in the White House I used to hate you so much? And now we are such good friends . . .' "

Jackie's concern for the right image was expressed in her collaboration with her first—and last—official biographer, Mary "Molly" Van Rensselaer Thayer, a friend of Janet and a former editor of the *Washington Post*. It was at Janet's suggestion that she telephoned Jackie at Hyannis Port shortly after the election to propose a series of biographical articles on the new First Lady. Surprisingly Jackie agreed, and cooperated, handing over to Thayer her scrapbooks, family letters and photographs. She even communicated with Thayer from the Georgetown Hospital, answering questions sent in to her on long handwritten sheets from the legal notepads. According to Mary Bass Gibson, who bought the serialization rights for the *Ladies' Home Journal*, "Jackie did a lot of the writing in bed and then Molly would take it over and rewrite it. The proofs were mailed to Palm Beach that winter by the Kennedys' daily courier plane to be checked over by both Jackie and the President."[16] Serialization began in the *Journal* on the day of the Inauguration; *Jacqueline Bouvier Kennedy* was later published as a book.

Thayer's book is interesting in that it presents Jackie as she wanted to be seen. There were her early poems, written when she was ten and fourteen, letters from Grampy Jack, records of her successes at Long Island horse shows, and a photograph album, a history of Danseuse's life put together by Jackie after the horse died. The Bouviers and the Vernous were still presented as "ancient" and "noble" families—but Grampy Jack's genealogical pretensions had not yet been exposed. Black Jack and Janet's divorce was smoothed over—"the children's normal routine was not unduly upset . . ." Jack Bouvier was described as the dashing, handsome, larger-than-life figure that Jackie had created; Janet received less attention; the Lees were hardly mentioned at all, and John Husted was left out altogether. Jackie's wedding was "wonderful," the absence of the bride's father not noted. The Kennedys were all "fantastic"—"The love and security of being part of such a close-knit clan was bliss to Jacqueline . . ." Thayer wrote. Jackie singled out two Kennedys for special mention: old Joe "whom she adores" and Bobby, "the one I would put my hand in the fire for."

The overall tone of the book is rosy—Jack and Jackie's early troubles in their marriage, his health, her difficulties in childbearing were "shared troubles [which] helped bring them closer." According to Thayer, Jack was "lost without" Jackie. Caroline was a paragon: aged three, "She talks about Le Roi Soleil as if he were Peter Rabbit." Servants, secretaries, nannies—with the exception of the man-servant, George Thomas—do not make an appearance to interrupt a seamless tapestry of joy and elegance. Jackie was pleased with the book, so much so that some eighteen months after Jack Kennedy's death, when Molly Thayer proposed that she should chronicle Jackie's White House years as a sequel, Jackie willingly agreed.

Her concern about the effect the presidency might have on her private family life was underlined by a letter she received from Eleanor Roosevelt congratulating her on the birth of John Jr. "I know there will be difficulties in store for you in this White House life," Mrs. Roosevelt wrote, "but perhaps also you will find compensations. Most things are made easier, though I think on the whole life is rather difficult for both the children and their parents in the 'fish bowl' that lies before you."[17] Politics had been their own reward for Eleanor Roosevelt, who had survived four terms in the White House. Her dedicated public life had compensated for an incompatible marriage, but she must have been aware of the damage that both factors had inflicted on her children.

For Jackie herself, escape from the "fish bowl" was essential to her personal survival. She had no intention of being crushed by the demands of public life, any more than she had been defeated by politics or the Kennedys. For her, escape meant country life and horses, the congenial company of her riding friends around Middleburg, Virginia. Chief among them at the time were Eve Fout and her husband Paul, a racehorse trainer. Jackie had known Eve since her Merrywood days when she and Janet had gone to Virginia to hunt and take part in the local horse shows. Early in the summer of 1960 she had asked Eve to put her up for membership of the local Orange County Hunt; news of her acceptance had leaked out in September. Since Jack was by then the Democratic presidential nominee, there was a furor in the New York and Boston papers, to the discomfiture of the Kennedys who had always seen Jackie's foxhunting as an electoral disadvantage. Jackie, however, worried more about the effect her membership would have on the Orange County Hunt rather than Jack's prospects: she assured Eve Fout that if Jack won she would never hunt if it caused a fuss and changed Orange County from being the "joyous thing" it was for their friends, something which she treasured.[18] She planned to start hunting the following March on her horse

1. Mummy, Jackie and Lee, 1933

2. Jackie, aged five, with pony Buddy

3. Lee, Janet and Jackie, 1939

4. At Farmington: Jackie holding the reins with Danseuse between the shafts. Sue Norton (far right) and Nancy Tuckerman in attendance

5. With Black Jack at graduation, Miss Porter's School

6. Jackie, aged thirteen, with Black Jack

7. Jackie holding a daylily in the Olmsted garden at Hammersmith Farm, 1943

8. The Auchincloss clan, Newport, 1945. Clockwise from top left: Jackie, Hugh D. "Yusha" Auchincloss III, Lee, Hugh D. Auchincloss II, Janet holding Little Janet, Nina and Tommy

9. Jackie on the stairs at Hammersmith Farm before her coming-out party, August 16, 1947

10. Christmas Day at Merrywood, 1948. From left: Lee, Jackie, Little Janet, Nina, Yusha, Jamie, Tommy

11. Jackie and Yusha wearing their newly acquired Scottish costumes, Scotland, August 1950

12. Jackie on the moors, Scotland, August 1950

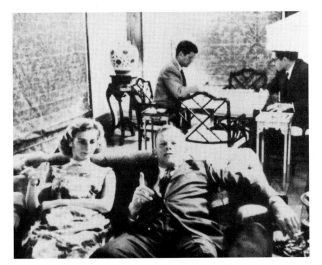

13. Georgetown life: Jack playing backgammon with Claiborne Pell. In the foreground are Nuala Pell and William Walton

14. Engaged couple: Jackie and Jack at Hyannis Port, July 1953

15. Jackie and Jack leave St. Mary's Church, Newport, after their wedding, September 12, 1953

16. Jackie, Jack and groomsmen at the wedding reception, Hammersmith Farm

17. Jackie and the "toothy girls" at a party at the Stork Club, May 1956, in honor of Jean Kennedy's engagement. From left: Jackie, Pat Kennedy Lawford, Ethel Skakel Kennedy, Jean Kennedy, Eunice Kennedy Shriver

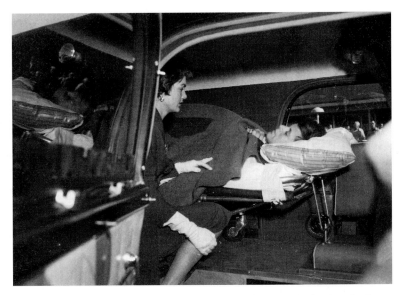

18. Jackie with Jack in an ambulance *en route* to Palm Beach after his discharge from the hospital following his first spinal operation, December 21, 1954

19. The Senator's wife: Jackie working with Jack in his Senate office, autumn 1958

20. The presidential campaign, 1960

21. The clan: the Kennedys at Hyannis Port, November 10, 1960. Standing, from left: Ethel Kennedy, Stephen Smith, Jean Kennedy Smith, John Fitzgerald Kennedy, Robert Kennedy, Pat Kennedy Lawford, Sargent Shriver, Joan Kennedy, Peter Lawford. In the foreground: Eunice Kennedy Shriver, Rose Kennedy, Joseph P. Kennedy, Jacqueline Kennedy, Edward M. Kennedy

22. Letitia "Tish" Baldrige in the White House, October 25, 1961

23. Pamela Turnure, winter 1960

24. Nancy Tuckerman, just after joining Jackie's staff, Washington, June 1963

25. Jackie and John Jr., photographed by Richard Avedon, West Palm Beach, January 3, 1961

26. Glittering in the snow: Jackie leaves 3307 N Street for the inaugural gala, January 20, 1961

27. Inauguration Day: President Kennedy and First Lady in front of the White House, January 20, 1961

28. Jack with Caroline and
John Jr. in the Oval Office,
November 1962

29. Jackie with Caroline in the
White House school,
May 24, 1961

30. Jackie with Premier Nikita Khrushchev in Vienna, June 1961

31. Jackie and Jack with the Queen and the Duke of Edinburgh before a dinner at Buckingham Palace, June 1961

32. Watching Alan Shepard's first U.S. space flight, May 5, 1961. From left: Tazewell Shepard, Lyndon B. Johnson, Bobby Kennedy, Richard Goodwin, Paul Nitze, Arthur M. Schlesinger Jr., Jack

33. The White House restoration project: the Blue Room. Jackie shows one of the old candleholders from the Monroe furnishings purchased in Paris, July 1, 1961

34. Jackie and Lee riding an elephant in Jaipur on their tour of India and Pakistan, March 1962

35. Ravello, 1962. From left: Gianni Agnelli, Benno Graziani, Prince Stanislaus "Stas" Radziwill, Jackie

36. Frank Sinatra, Peter Lawford and Bobby Kennedy, Los Angeles, July 1961

37 (*left*). Marilyn Monroe posing as Jackie, June 1962

38 (*above*). Judith Campbell Exner, c. 1962

Bit of Irish, which was stabled at the Fouts'. Her mother encouraged her: she wrote to Eve Fout from Merrywood on December 7, 1960, while Jackie was still in Georgetown Hospital, that the thought of hunting again was getting Jackie through "lots of intricate things," adding, "I feel it would be a great escape for her at times . . ."

Even before John Jr.'s birth, she had taken Jack down to Middleburg at weekends to view country houses to rent. She had dismissed out of hand, without seeing it, the official presidential country retreat, Camp David, presumably on the grounds that because the Eisenhowers had enjoyed it so much, there must be something wrong with it. Jack went along with this, even though Camp David would cost him nothing and anything in which Jackie was involved in Virginia would be liable to cost him a lot—as, indeed, it turned out. Too late, he discovered how much he preferred Camp David.

Bill Walton came up with Glen Ora, the property of his friend Gladys Tartière, a four-hundred-acre estate near Middleburg in the heart of the Virginia hunt country, just over an hour's drive from the White House. It consisted of a square, French-style country manor house of buff stucco with white shutters, farm cottage, guest cottage, stables and large swimming pool. Jackie was still in the hospital when Walton brought her photographs of the place; she liked it and rented it sight unseen.

The countryside around Middleburg, Virginia, is an idyllic landscape of oaks, gums and chestnuts laced with dogwood blossom in spring, green pastures fenced with wooden palings, the fields dotted with horses and brown cattle, threaded with streams and springs, blue hills ranging on the horizon. The woods are full of wild turkey, geese, foxes, skunks and deer. The roads are dirt or laid with stones, and there are few signposts, for this is a country of private estates with all the beauty and peace that money can buy. Then owners included the very rich, like the Averell Harrimans and the Paul Mellons. Rachel Lambert Mellon, always known as "Bunny" became one of Jackie's closest friends and her principal mentor from her earliest days at the White House. The Mellon stud farm at Oak Spring, Upperville, near Middleburg, was a haven for Jackie in hunting country at a later phase of her life.

The renting of Glen Ora was a huge concession on Jack's part: he loved the ocean, not the deep countryside. Horses bored him, and Jackie's horsy friends were not a part of his world, but he understood his wife's need for escape and physical exercise. To keep her happy he was prepared to pay a stiff rent, but the amount of money Jackie and her fashionable decorator, Sister Parish, spent on redecoration of this temporary home enraged him. The two swept through Glen Ora to the tune of $10,000, including wallpaper, paint, rugs, curtains and furniture. At first Jackie tried to put this down as an official expense and sent Sister Parish to ask Chief Usher West for the money but since the government was already paying the "enormous cost" of running Camp David as a perfectly good presidential retreat, the answer was a firm negative. The result was a presidential explosion, as Jackie's official chronicler admitted: "President Kennedy disliked spending money unless he considered it essential: he was surprised and annoyed."

When he met his landlady, Mrs. Tartière, for the first time he put her back up by telling her crossly, "Your house cost me a lot of money!"[19]

"Jackie hadn't hunted in Virginia since her marriage to Jack; she was either pregnant or traveling," her old friend, Charlie Whitehouse said. "Jack . . . wasn't interested one darn bit so it wasn't until she got to the White House that she suddenly curiously had the freedom to come down here."[20] But keeping Jackie happy and away from the White House had its own rewards for Jack: it left him free to enjoy himself with his own coterie of like-minded men and compliant women.

The thought of Jack's "women" lay like a shadow across Jackie's life, and there were times when privately she nursed agonizing doubts about her ability to sustain the reality behind the family façade. In February 1958 she had opened her heart to Walter Ridder, newspaper publisher and Merrywood neighbor. "She said to Walter," his widow, journalist Marie Ridder recalled, " 'I don't know if I can stay with him, he is so unfaithful.' And Walter said to her, 'The terrible thing for you, Jackie, is, it's not a decision you can make on a personal basis. If you should leave him and divorce him, there is no way that he can be President, and I doubt that you want that mark on your life.' He said, 'Let's just put it out realistically. My sympathy is with you. We have all known that Jack is difficult in ways of women, but, A, you knew that from the beginning, and B, I'm sure there are many moments that make up for it.' And she said, 'Yes, there are. When he's around, he's just an enchantment from my point of view.' He said, 'But now you are in the public domain and the decision you have to make involves a great deal more than your personal relationship with Jack.' And she said, 'I know that, I know that and that terrifies me . . .' "[21]

Jackie learned about the women in Jack's past—from Jack. "You know, in the end, Jackie knew everything," William Walton said. "Every girl. She knew her rating. Her accomplishments . . . I mean, everything that was worth knowing, she knew. And she always had that kind . . . she will get it out of you so you might as well give in quickly because you're going to." Jackie learned that just as Jack compartmentalized his male friends so there were different categories for his women: "The way his male friends are in cells, there are women who simultaneously [had] different statuses in the hierarchy of his love," Walton said.

Walton gave one example: Frances Ann Cannon, a woman Jack had desperately wanted to marry in 1939 but who had turned him down and chosen John Hersey instead. By the late fifties the Herseys were divorced and Frances Ann came to Washington for the opening of a show in which she was involved. Walton asked her who she would like to see for dinner. "She replied, 'For me that's terribly easy. There's only one person I want to see and that's Jack Kennedy.' So I called up Jackie," Walton went on, "and I asked if Jack would like to see Frances Ann Hersey. And she said, 'I don't know whether he would but I'll tell you I would. I have never seen this lady and I have all her letters. I've read them all and we'll be there if I have to drag him by the hair.' So I thought that with just the four of us it might be a little embarrassing so I asked Jack who else he'd like to have. He asked me if I thought I could get Phil Graham [of the *Washington Post*] to come to dinner. So it was us six. It was a glorious moment when Frances Ann made her entrance in a short black dress that was all covered up in front but all open at the back. And he gave her about ten minutes and paid no attention to her for the rest of the evening . . . Who Jack was concentrating on was Phil Graham. They fell for each other that night like a ton of bricks. They were both at their best and it was a really important evening for both of them. And Jackie was in heaven because she saw her old rival being rejected."[22]

The women whom Jackie seems to have most resented were those who, like his Boston friend, were close to Jack in a way that she seemed unable to achieve. She found these close platonic friendships more difficult to handle, more wounding and intrusive into her life with Jack than any of the sexual liaisons. Jack kept in touch through the loyal Evelyn Lincoln, his conduit to all his women friends and mistresses. "He would be in touch no matter where," one of them said. "You'd get a call from her [Evelyn Lincoln] saying, 'Would you call this number? It's in Chicago . . .' 'Why?' 'No, he really is counting on you. Please. Please. I can't put you through on this but would you call . . .' He called every week of his life almost . . ."[23]

Just as Jackie had barred her from her wedding, so she and her then husband were struck off the invitation list for Jack's inauguration. Two days before the Inauguration the telephone rang. It was Jack: " 'I just heard that you were not coming and that you were not invited and you were on the list to be invited and I'm not getting inaugurated unless you come down. And you're going to get on a plane which I've already arranged leaving La Guardia . . .' " She learned later that there was a "list of the people that weren't coming—not that weren't invited, but that weren't coming. I don't know if it was Jackie or Jack's father . . ." The last blow came after Jack's death. Fifi Fell and her daughter Natasha, both friends and belles of Jack's, called her up: " 'Now, there's no bitterness, you can come down to the funeral with us.' And they were asked *not* to bring me to the funeral . . . Fifi had to call me back and say, 'Well, maybe, I don't know . . . you know.' I said, 'I'm not going . . .' That's how things were," she added. "Something was there. There was a cloud there, there was a definite *barrier* there. And there was no real reason at all that I could ever find. I mean, I talked to him when he rang but that was it."[24] Years later, in the eighties, she happened to be living in the same apartment building as Jackie, 1040 Fifth Avenue; Bill Walton was coming in to dine with her when Jackie met him in the lobby and asked him where he was going. When he told her, she said, "You *traitor*, going to the enemy like that."

"She couldn't handle the idea that he would call the girls on the phone in New York," Robin Biddle Duke said. One of those she most resented was Flo Pritchett Smith, whom she had formerly accepted as an old friend of Jack's from his navy days. It had been a serious romance but had ended long since. "But . . . when Jackie found out that Flo had been an old girl of Jack's . . . then Jackie resented it because Flo was still very much in the picture because they used to have the New York crowd down for dances . . . Jackie was beginning to stiffen up more and more with Flo, because when she realized that her husband was a bit 'naughty,' then she wondered if he was still fiddling around with Flo—but he wasn't the least bit interested in Flo. He enjoyed Flo because she had the most incredible sense of humor. Jack used to call her and ask her what were the latest jokes in New York, plug into the gossip and he had that side of him which he got fun out of. It was a relief—and Flo used to tell him funny stories and who was sleeping with who and who was doing this and that or the other, and JFK would get a big hoot out of it. But Jackie began to stiffen against her and eventually told Jack she wasn't welcome at the White House . . ."[25]

Jackie's jealousy of the women with whom Jack kept up close platonic friendships was mental rather than sexual. They existed in a compartment of Jack's life that excluded her; her pride was wounded by the fact that these relationships reflected on her. Jack *needed* to talk over his life with his women friends; he was getting something from them that he could not get from her.

Her pride made her resent invidious comparisons, jealous of the blameless Grace Kelly and even of Ethel. "She was jealous of Ethel," one of Jack's close friends said, "because Ethel was so outgoing and the President had so much fun when Ethel was around . . . The President loved being with her, loved all her enthusiasm and her jokes and her stories . . ." Once when the same friend was "raving" about Ethel's qualities in front of Jackie, Jack took him aside and told him to cut it out.

When it came to Jack's sexual affairs, she closed her eyes to those she did not see. Apart from casual sexual encounters, Jack was regularly sleeping with at least three women in the year before he entered the White House—Judith Campbell (later Exner), an unnamed Radcliffe student, and the woman whom Jackie was to name as her press secretary, Pamela Turnure.

Pam had been introduced to Jack at Nini Auchincloss's wedding to Newton Steers in the summer of 1957 and been offered the job in his office from that autumn. Some time after that, they began an affair that involved indiscreet late-night and early-morning arrivals and departures, noted by Pamela Turnure's landlady, the owner of the Georgetown house, Florence Kater, who was well aware of Jack's identity since he had subleased the apartment for Pam. Florence Kater, a Catholic, became obsessed by the married Catholic senator's adultery, and when Pam Turnure moved to another apartment nearby, her husband ambushed Jack leaving the apartment in the early hours of the morning of July 11, 1958, and photographed him. In May 1959 Mrs. Kater mailed the photograph, showing a guilty Kennedy attempting to hide his face behind a handkerchief, with a letter describing the episode to fifty influential people in New York and Washington, where in June it reached the office of the FBI. Her letters were ignored but on May 14, 1960, four days after Kennedy won the West Virginia primary, she appeared at his political rally at the University of Maryland, carrying a placard with the photograph. A photograph of Mrs. Kater and the placard appeared in the following afternoon's *Washington Star*. The story was spiked although several reporters interviewed Florence Kater and believed it to be true. Even when Mrs. Kater picketed the White House with her placard following the Inauguration, the loyal Washington press corps refrained from mentioning it.[26]

It is inconceivable that Jackie should not have seen or heard Mrs. Kater's story when it first surfaced but, characteristically, she showed no sign of being aware of it. "I'm not so sure that Jackie knew about any of that until very late in the game," Robin Biddle Duke, wife of the White House Chief of Protocol, said. But according to another White House insider who worked closely with Jackie, housekeeper Anne Lincoln, known as "Linky," Jackie did know about it. "Linky was intrigued," a friend of hers recalled. "She said, 'Mrs. Kennedy well knows what the relationship is here but she [Turnure] became Mrs. Kennedy's press secretary and did a damn good job.' And Linky, who, as I said, was a very partisan friend of Mrs. Kennedy, was not someone who spared a caustic remark at somebody else's expense if there was one to make, and she liked Pam Turnure. She said she was a good friend, someone you could talk to and rely upon her discretion. She just said, 'She does a damn good job.' And she was amazed because this relationship was allowed to continue in the White House when so many people knew . . . I think it went off and on for quite a while. And she [Turnure] behaved with personal dignity, so her presence was never an embarrassment. She was just a very pretty young girl. She contributed a great deal to Mrs. Kennedy's period at the White House and people knew that she represented her and she handled some very difficult situations with great ease and dexterity . . . She did a lot to help Mrs. Kennedy and to make her introduction to the White House as smooth as it was."[27]

Jack's relentless womanizing represented an unexploded bomb under the Kennedy White House. Although at one point he had seemed to envisage the curtailment of his adventuring when he reached the presidency—"I suppose my 'poon' [womanizing] days are over," he had scribbled idly, while on the campaign plane—the scale of his sexual risk-taking actually increased during his years in the White House. In the ultimate analysis, Jackie's loyalty and strength of character, and her sense of the dignity of the American presidency, were Jack's only real insurance against disaster.

His other arm of defense was the appointment, at his father's insistence, of Bobby as Attorney General, an act of blatant nepotism that at first he had resisted. Bobby had been even more strongly against the appointment, principally on the grounds of the criticism it would bring: nepotism, youth, inexperience. But "Jack needs all the good men he can get around him down there," Joe said. In the loneliness of his exalted position, he would need someone he could confide in, someone with no axe to grind, someone he could trust absolutely; only Bobby could fit that bill. Bobby was tough, ruthless and unforgiving (his father said admiringly of him, "Bobby's a better hater than I am"), unswerving in the pursuit of his aims and utterly loyal to his brother. Not only could he guard Jack's back from any political threat, but as Attorney General of the United States, he would be in authority over the FBI where, as Joe well knew, damaging information about Jack's sexual escapades would be gathered in the special files kept in two standard metal cabinets behind the desk of Helen Gandy, secretary to J. Edgar Hoover, the director of the FBI.[28]

As the President's brother, the Attorney General was not only Hoover's superior in the bureaucratic hierarchy but he also behaved like his superior in fact as well, far more than any previous Attorney General. He had a direct line installed to a telephone on Hoover's desk and a buzzer to summon Hoover to his office—trappings of rank that Hoover, thirty years Bobby's senior in age, deeply resented.[29]

There were no fewer than six files involving Jack Kennedy's "sexual misconduct," according to Hoover's aide, dating back to his affair with Inga Arvad. When Kennedy was being considered as the Democratic vice presidential nominee in 1956 Hoover had asked for a name check; on being told what was in the files, he had been "shocked," according to his aide, Cartha "Deke" DeLoach. "Hoover was a close friend of Ambassador Kennedy and . . . did not want to be responsible for a report that would damage the political career of old Joe's promising son." Hoover and Joe Kennedy were on first-name terms; since September 1943 Joe had been designated a "Special Service Contact" for the Bureau. In 1953 he was reported as having provided information for an FBI investigation into Henry Luce III, and as being "very profuse in his admiration for the Director and for the FBI." Joe had invited Hoover to Eunice's wedding, while Boston Special Agent William Carpenter had attended Jack and Jackie's wedding. A photograph of Joe with Carpenter, accompanied by a laudatory report, had even appeared in the Bureau's staff magazine, *The Investigator*. Joe believed that information was power, and it pleased him to be on intimate terms with the head of one of the most powerful and secretive organizations in the United States. "Dear Edgar," Joe Kennedy had written to Hoover in 1958, "I repeat what I have said so many times before: This is the greatest organization in the Government and you have performed the greatest public service of any man that I know."[30]

The Kennedys had every reason to placate Hoover: by 1960 his Bureau held enough explosive material on Jack to blow his presidency out of the water. In a memo of July 13, 1960, when it seemed likely that Jack would be nominated the Democratic candidate for the presidency, an FBI biographical summary about him included:

> allegations of immoral activities . . . reported over the years . . . They include data that (probably in January 1960) Kennedy was "compromised" with a woman in Las Vegas; and that Kennedy and Frank Sinatra have in the recent past been involved in parties in Palm Springs, Las Vegas and New York. Regarding the Kennedy–Sinatra information, "Confidential" magazine is said to have affidavits from two mulatto prostitutes in New York. Allegations have also been received concerning hoodlum connections of Senator Kennedy.[31]

A further section raised allegations of electoral fraud by the Kennedy campaign in West Virginia, which included not only vote-buying but the relocating of voting places and even the operation of handles on voting machines by local officials in place of voters.

A report to Hoover from the Los Angeles office of the Bureau, dated January 4, 1960, detailed a conversation one of its agents had had in Las Vegas with "Senator Kennedy's campaign manager," whose name he did not recall, the boxer Rocky Marciano, and Belden Katelman, identified as "a prominent Las Vegas investor":

The campaign manager bewailed KENNEDY'S association with SINATRA, stating something to the effect that the Senator is vulnerable to bad publicity only because of his association with Sinatra. [He] . . . added that there are certain sex activities by KENNEDY that he hopes never are publicized. CI [the FBI's Los Angeles operative] said he learned that these parties involving the Senator and Sinatra occurred in Palm Springs, Las Vegas and New York City.

BELDEN KATELMAN . . . made the point that KENNEDY had stayed at the Sands with SINATRA while in Las Vegas. KATELMAN said it is a known fact the Sands is controlled by hoodlums and that while the Senator, Sinatra and [Peter] Lawford were there, show girls from all over town were running in and out of the Senator's suite.[32]

Just as Jack would have Bobby as his trusted ally in the White House, so Jackie, isolated as First Lady and wary of trusting women, would rely upon Lee. "Jackie was happiest when her sister was around," Mary Gallagher wrote, "because Lee was the one person with whom she could relax and pour out her feelings They were like schoolgirls together, sharing confidences and telling how some frustrating or dense person 'drove me up the wall—screaming and knocking things over.' Or, how someone had 'a knack for being interested in and remembering the dullest details.'" The White House years were the closest of their adult relationship. Jackie needed Lee and rewarded her with the highest favors at her court; in return, Lee was happy to act as lady-in-waiting and to enjoy them.

The Jackie-Lee relationship was as competitive as ever. At the time of Jackie's engagement to Jack, friends had reported Lee as jealous that her sister had captured the handsome, rich young Senator. Lee and Jack found each other attractive and during his early troubles with Jackie, he had been heard to complain that he had "married the wrong sister."[33] Getting into bed together was bound to happen, at least once. Michael Canfield told Gore Vidal that the first time had been in the South of France and that Lee had made no effort to conceal it from him.[34] Jackie found out, quite when nobody knows, but during the late seventies in long talks with her sister-in-law, Joan Kennedy, she confessed that she had known about it.

By 1960 Canfield was out of the picture, as far as Lee was concerned. In February 1958 she had left him for Stas Radziwill, with whom she had been having an affair, and Stas left his wife, Grace, and two children for her. London society, in which Grace was popular, took sides and at parties her women friends ostracized Lee. Stas was nineteen years older than Lee and in some ways, therefore—apart from his resemblance to Black Jack—represented the father figure she sought for security. That he was rich, a prince and popular with the international set made him a desirable prospect. Stas was a curious mixture of the cynical and the noble; he used his social connections, as he was later to use Lee, for money, but he had his own code. "Stas's social life was one thing, but he had depth and a great sense of people and values," his niece, Isabel, Comtesse de Ornano, told Lee's biographer. "He knew exactly what was right and wrong, he really had values, which made him original in the world he lived in, a world which can be very superficial."[35] Above all, Stas cherished his family in Poland, his upright, gallant father, Prince Janusz, whose wife, Princess Anna, had died while both were imprisoned in a Soviet concentration camp, and who, after refusing to head a postwar puppet government, had lost all his possessions and lived in a two-bedroom Warsaw flat. Stas supported him, despite his painful awareness that his father regarded him as the black sheep of the family.

Lee had been trying to obtain an annulment of her marriage to Michael Canfield, from whom she had obtained a quick divorce. Her first attempt had been through the Kennedys' friend Cardinal Spellman. Later that year, however, the Westminster Tribunal in London began hearing Lee's case, after interrogation of various witnesses, including Jackie, had been carried out in New York. While this was under consideration, Lee and Stas made an incredible faux pas in the eyes of the Church: they married in a civil ceremony in Virginia on March 19, 1959, their reason being that Lee was pregnant. Their wedding was celebrated with a dinner given by Jackie in her N Street house. Outraged, the ecclesiastical authorities suspended the London judgment and sent the case to Rome for secret consideration by the Supreme Tribunal of the Holy Office. In the spring of 1961 Lee's petition was refused with no right of appeal. By then, however, Jack's election as the first Catholic President of the United States offered new possibilities for the Radziwills in Rome.

"Where Stas was clever," said a friend, "was that he sensed that the important man was Kennedy, long before anyone else he saw this. He divorced Grace, gave her all her money back with interest and married Lee. And this was a clever thing to do because he got right into all the connections, and they [the Kennedys] adored him. Bobby in particular adored him."[36] Jackie, too, loved her eccentric Polish brother-in-law and was loved by him in return. "He liked Jackie because I think Jackie had this feeling for him," a friend said. "I don't mean physically but she really liked him."[37]

"Stas used to say about the Bouvier sisters, 'These girls are frightfully greedy,' but he was dazzled by Jackie," remembered an intimate friend of his.[38]

Stas and Lee had been very visible during the 1960 campaign. Stas played an active part in helping to attract the Polish vote, particularly in Chicago where there was a large Polish population; Jackie later gave him a map showing him crisscrossing the country, inscribed, "You really did do it, Stas." Lee was pregnant with her second child, whose birth was, like John Jr.'s, expected that winter. She already had a son, Anthony, born in August the previous year, but this time there were complications, and Lee, like Jackie, did not find childbirth easy. Both women dieted rigorously despite their pregnancy; Janet was particularly worried about Lee, who had been anorexic as a teenager. Nonetheless, Lee went to Los Angeles with Stas for the July convention, and telephoned Jackie daily with news from the Beverly Hilton.

After the convention the Radziwills had returned east, basing themselves with Jackie at Hyannis Port. Lee was on a visit to New York when on August 18 she was rushed to the hospital to give birth to a daughter, Christina, three months premature and weighing only two and a half pounds. Afterward she was racked by postpartum depression, which affected her badly for some months; she took refuge with Jackie until September when she traveled back to England, accompanied by the Kennedys' masseuse. The Radziwills' marriage, hitherto happy and successful, deteriorated abruptly as a result of Lee's traumatic childbirth experience, to Stas's great unhappiness. "Lee was the great love of Stas's life," a friend of his said. "She went off Stas physically after their daughter was born. She had a bad time and closed shop on him—therefore he became even more in love with her."[39]

Jackie, like Lee, was suffering postpartum problems, which lasted until well into the spring of 1961 when Jack expressed himself to Dr. Max Jacobson as "very much concerned about Jackie's condition following her last delivery. She suffered chronic depression and headaches." The headaches were so debilitating that Jackie herself described them as "severe migraine."[40] Jackie was as stoical as Jack about concealing what she saw as weaknesses from everyone except those closest to her, like Jack and Lee. Despite her serene appearance she was highly strung, bit her nails and chain-smoked at difficult moments throughout her adult life, despite promising Jack to limit herself to five cigarettes a day. She was always conscious of the strain of alcoholism running through the Bouvier blood. Her uncle Bud had died of drink; her father's life had been shortened by it. She might drink champagne late at night but alcohol was never to become a habitual release. Only in her private moments with Jack did she reveal her underlying vulnerability and occasional crises of confidence. The little-girl act, which she used to disarm people and obtain their help, had real roots in her psyche, relating to her need for strong older men on whom she could lean.

At Palm Beach after John Jr.'s birth Jackie kept to her room, away from the mayhem in the house, only emerging for official appointments, like giving an interview to *Time*. Rose Kennedy was irritated by her daughter-in-law's seclusion. "I suspected that the two women did not understand each other too well," recalled Mary Gallagher, who had been imported, incognito, to help Jackie with her correspondence. Rose saw her daughter-in-law surrounded by helpers—the Kennedy maternity nurse, Luella Hennessy, to look after her, and a friend of Maud Shaw's, Elsie Phillips, to take care of John so that Miss Shaw could concentrate on Caroline—and thought her spoiled and malingering. The nadir in their strained relations came one day when Rose came to ask Gallagher if Jackie would be getting out of bed that day. When Gallagher responded that she didn't know, Rose said, with some asperity, "Well, you might remind her that we're having some important guests for lunch. It would be nice if she would join us." Jackie merely mimicked Rose and did not appear for lunch. She was following doctor's orders and sensed that her mother-in-law had little patience with weakness after childbirth. To Gallagher, her mood seemed withdrawn and subdued; she showed no reaction or excitement even when the Bergdorf Inaugural Ball gown was sent down for her to try on, merely remarking that she preferred the one designed by Cassini for the gala.[41]

Only Jack seems to have been aware of the severity of her depression. He showed unusual consideration for her, as Evelyn Lincoln recorded.

While he was eating breakfast, Jackie came out to see him and said she wanted to see him in her bedroom. As soon as he finished, he went through the living room and into her bedroom. In a little while I had to take him a message that Douglas Dillon wanted to talk to him. He came to the door and said he would talk to Dillon, but he didn't want to be disturbed for a while. He did not like to ask Jackie to share their moments together with his public responsibilities and demands.[42]

The state of Jack's own health, however, was a secret worry, which he went to considerable length to conceal from people around him. He instructed his doctors not to discuss his medical problems with his wife, saying, "I don't want her to think she married an old man or a cripple." He could not conceal from her his back problems and their physical manifestations—the canvas lower-back brace, which he wore at all times except when swimming, the rocking chair he had used since 1955, the hard mattress made of woven cattlehair (horsehair could not be used as he was allergic to it) with a bedboard beneath it, or the eighth-of-an-inch lift he always wore in his left shoe. (According to his personal physician, Dr. Janet Travell, Kennedy had been born with the left side of his body smaller than the right: "The left side of his face was smaller, his left shoulder was lower . . . and his left leg was appreciably shorter . . ."[43]) He suffered from "persistent and recurring attacks of skeletal muscle spasm—painful and debilitating," which Dr. Travell, whom he first consulted in New York in May 1955, treated with injections of procaine (novocaine). At times the pain was so bad that he was forced to use crutches to walk; he hated being seen to use them, even by Evelyn Lincoln.

In the autumn of 1960, suffering from extreme exhaustion during the election campaign, Jack had been introduced by Chuck Spalding to Dr. Max Jacobson, known by his clientele as Dr. Feelgood. Jacobson was patronized by several people in Jack's circle including Chuck Spalding, Stas Radziwill and Alan Jay Lerner, who relied on him for shots of his magic potions, based apparently on amphetamines mixed with other ingredients including, it was rumored, sheep placenta. Shortly before the Nixon-Kennedy debates, Jacobson recorded in his unpublished memoir, he received a call from Chuck Spalding requesting a private and confidential consultation for Senator Kennedy. Jack appeared without his Secret Service details. According to Jacobson, he was suffering from stress and increasing back pain. "After treatment, he [Kennedy] reported that his muscle weakness had completely disappeared and he felt cool, calm and very alert." Obviously Jack felt the need for an additional boost on top of the Novocaine and cortisone he was already taking. Jacobson's injections galvanized him in time for the ordeal of the Nixon debates. People were then largely unaware of the addictive qualities of amphetamines, which seemed like wonder drugs. Although not addicted, like many of Jacobson's clients (including, at one time, Truman Capote, who was severely affected), Jack—and Jackie—came to rely on his "treatments" at times of stress.

To counteract his adrenal insufficiency Jack injected himself with 35 milligrams of cortisone daily, doing it with apparent calm, so much so that Paul Fay asked him casually if it hurt, and received an agonizing jab in the thigh as an answer. He also had DOC (deoxycorticosterone acetate) tablets of 150 milligrams, which were replaced several times a year, implanted in his thigh. There were rumors that the Kennedys kept supplies of DOC and cortisone in safe-deposit boxes around the country to be available in an emergency wherever Jack traveled.

Jackie would have been unaware of the intricacies and dangers associated with the regular administration of steroids, which were not widely known at the time. There is a risk of what is called "hypomania" with psychotic symptoms—paranoid delusions, hallucinations and disordered thought—and Kennedy is reported to have suffered one such "psychotic episode" before his marriage. Less drastically, this is associated with high energy, confidence and "supernormal social functioning." More serious from Jackie's point of view was the possible effect of the drug on her husband's already supercharged sex drive. Steroids accentuate normal characteristics: in Jack's case they might have contributed to what in medical terms would be defined as his "hypersexuality."

Rumors had been spread by Johnson allies at the 1960 Los Angeles convention that Jack had Addison's; one Southern Democrat, India Edwards, had gone so far as to claim that "Kennedy was so sick from Addison's disease that he looked like a spavined hunchback"[44] and that only cortisone was keeping him alive. Johnson's campaign manager claimed that Kennedy wouldn't be able to serve out his term since "he was going to die." Despite a flat denial by the Kennedy camp, backed up by a bland statement by Drs. Travell and Cohen that a checkup in December 1958 had shown that Kennedy's adrenal glands did function, the Addison's issue had continued to rumble beneath the surface through the subsequent general election campaign. An attempt was made to steal his medical records and a prominent Republican challenged the Kennedys to admit or deny that an article describing an operation on an anonymous patient with Addison's published in the American Medical Association's *Archives of Surgery*, volume 71, referred to Jack.

Unsurprisingly, therefore, in the week of the Inauguration, the loyal American Medical Association, devoted an article in its magazine, *Today's Health*, to the incoming President. The article detailed his medical history and dealt with the Addison's disease allegations with the sophistry that Kennedy did not have classical Addison's disease but "nontubercular, nonfatal adrenal insufficiency." According to the report reproduced in *Time* on January 27, 1961, Kennedy's health problems—back pain and adrenal insufficiency—were all in the past. He still took corticosteroids by mouth, the magazine reported, "although his last tests showed his adrenal function to be normal." His 1960s chart showed "a couple of colds, a touch of laryngitis, and a short-lived bout with sinusitis." At forty-three, the President was a "trim, tanned, 6ft., although a recent gain of 10 lbs (to 175) showed in his plump cheeks [a side effect of the cortisone]. His blood pressure is a normal 112/80." The doctors gave President Kennedy a warm welcome to the White

House: "Your health is excellent. Your vitality, endurance and resistance to infection are above average. Your ability to handle an exhausting workload is unquestionably superior."

This was only partly true, but Jack Kennedy did present an image of glowing health. The mature Kennedy had the figure of an athlete, broad-shouldered, deep-chested (although he was sensitive to what he called "the Fitzgerald breasts"), tapering to narrow hips and long, elegant legs. The bronze tint that Addison's gave to his skin was accentuated by regular nude sunbathing in the walled "bullpen" at the Kennedy Palm Beach house, his muscles toned by frequent swimming in the ocean or the pool. His hair was as thick as ever, his teeth as white, despite his penchant for cigars. Ambition, willpower and the Kennedy genes gave him a restless vitality, beside which other people paled in comparison. Pain was his constant companion, but he was used to it. He cared much more about his physical appearance; he had a strong streak of vanity about which Jackie teased him mercilessly and publicly. The cortisone had the effect of sometimes making his face look puffy, which he much resented. One day at Palm Beach in front of his adoring fan club, Evelyn Lincoln and Mary Gallagher, he glanced at himself in a mirror, slapped his jowls and said, "If I don't lose some of this weight before the Inauguration, we'll just have to call the whole thing off."[45]

Through the months of November and December Jack assembled his administration, the "best and the brightest," top businessmen and financiers like Robert S. McNamara as Secretary of Defense and C. Douglas Dillon as Secretary of the Treasury, brilliant academics like McGeorge Bundy, former head of the Harvard Faculty, and special advisers Walter C. Rostow, Burke Marshall, historian Arthur M. Schlesinger and rising legal star Richard N. Goodwin among them. As the Inauguration approached they symbolized the dawn of a youthful, self-confident era, the New Frontier.

CHAPTER NINE

Coronation

⌒

Let the word go forth from this time and place, to friend and foe alike, that the
torch has been passed to a new generation . . .

—John F. Kennedy, Inaugural Address

Snow fell on Washington in large, soft flakes as Jackie, shimmering in her white
satin Cassini gown, the glitter of borrowed Tiffany's emeralds and diamonds on
her ears and at her throat, stepped out of the N Street house bound for the Inaugural Concert and Gala on the night of January 20, 1961. The events of the next
two days would project her on to the world stage as the wife of the thirty-fifth
President of the United States, an international celebrity at the age of thirty-one.
"Turn on the lights so that they can see Jackie," the President told Bill Walton, as
they drove away from the concert hall heading for the gala. From now on the
lights would always be on her.

The gala had been organized by Frank Sinatra and Peter Lawford apart from
the official program. Technically it was a hundred-dollar-a-head fund-raiser to
pay off the Democratic National Committee campaign debt; the stars gave their
services free but the incidentals such as chauffeured limousines and luxury hotel
suites were rumored to have swallowed up the money raised by the sale of seats in
the Armory. In practice it was a huge personal celebration for the Kennedys
and their friends in the swinging style they enjoyed with show-business stars
and pretty usherettes wearing rhinestone crowns serving drinks in the intermis-
sion. Frank Sinatra came out of his self-imposed purdah to lead a radiant Jackie
into the hall. Mahalia Jackson sang "The Star-Spangled Banner"; Sinatra turned
"That Old Black Magic" into "That Old Jack Magic"; Laurence Olivier, Jimmy Du-
rante, Harry Belafonte and Bette Davis performed; even Eleanor Roosevelt joined
in, reading with Fredric March and Helen Traubel "A Moment with Lincoln,"

based on the farewell address Lincoln delivered when leaving Springfield for Washington.

After the gala ended and Jackie went home to spend her last night in N Street, the Kennedy party continued with family, cast and friends at a "private dinner dance" for three hundred given at Paul Young's restaurant by Joe and Rose. Paul "Red" Fay, in Washington for the Inauguration, was staying with Bobby and Ethel at Hickory Hill. On the way to the gala, Ethel turned to Fay and said, "I hope you are going to constantly be thinking of things you can do for old Eth because I have really got a prize for you when we get to the gala . . ." The "prize" turned out to be film star Angie Dickinson. "If she'll have you," Ethel said, "here is your date for the evening." Writers have alleged—and Paul Fay strenuously denied—that Fay was Jack's cover for sexual encounters that evening and the following night with Angie Dickinson.[1] Mary Van Rensselaer Thayer's authorized account of the gala evening simply says, "Jack enjoyed himself immensely, and it was 3:28 A.M. when the Secret Service agents clocked him in at home."[2]

Jack and Jackie breakfasted together in the library of the N Street house for the last time on the morning of Inauguration Day, a day of brilliant blue sky, sun dazzling off the snowdrifts and piercing cold. As usual he ate off a tray on a stand in front of his chair—orange juice, lean bacon with two poached eggs, toast and marmalade, and coffee. Jackie sat opposite with orange juice, toast and honey, coffee with skimmed milk. Jack devoured the newspapers as he always did before going to Mass at 8:55 A.M. at Holy Trinity Church nearby. Later, both dressed for the Inaugural ceremonies. Jack, instructed by the venerable eighty-four-year-old Senator Carl H. Hayden of Arizona—"Tell that young fella he should wear a cutaway coat and silk hat. I want him to come down looking like a President"[3]—struggled with the stiff wing collar that no longer fitted his more substantial jowls. Jackie put on the simple beige wool dress and coat that she had ordered from Oleg Cassini and matching pillbox hat. The coat, with a circular sable collar to match her muff, had had to be hastily fitted with a warmer lining to protect her from the cold. With her instinctive sense of theater she had planned this pale outfit with its slim simple outline to stand out among the rows of women huddled in their furs.

At precisely 11:03 A.M. the Kennedys drove to meet the outgoing Eisenhowers at the White House: Jack, at forty-three, the youngest of thirty-five presidents to be inaugurated, the first Roman Catholic President and the first to have been born in the twentieth century; Ike, at seventy, the oldest man to have served as President of the United States. Jack, who had mocked Eisenhower as an old man past his time who did nothing but play golf, had changed his opinion of the thirty-fourth President since their briefing meeting earlier that week. He had been impressed by Eisenhower's shrewdness and mental toughness. In return, Eisenhower had found Kennedy to be more than the young whippersnapper he had expected him to be, so it was with cordiality that he welcomed his successor inside the door of the North Portico of the White House that morning, a cordiality not evident between the presidential wives. The atmosphere as Jackie and Mamie Eisenhower shook hands over the coffee and cakes was painfully strained; and Pat Nixon ignored her when she sat down on the same sofa. Later, as they rode down Pennsylvania Avenue to the Capitol, Jack asked the former Supreme Commander of the Allied Forces in Europe if he had read Cornelius Ryan's blockbuster on the Normandy invasion, *The Longest Day*. When Eisenhower replied dismissively that he hadn't, Jack realized belatedly that Eisenhower, having been in command of the entire operation, had had no need to. In the second car Mamie Eisenhower, traveling with Jackie and Senator Styles Bridges of the Joint Congressional Inaugural Committee, was scarcely seated before she remarked brightly to the Senator, "Doesn't Ike look like Paddy the Irishman in his top hat?"[4] Senator Bridges looked "visibly distressed" by the outgoing First Lady's Freudian slip. Jackie said nothing.

The fact that this was the inauguration of the first Roman Catholic President was underlined by Cardinal Cushing, who delivered a lengthy invocation, apparently oblivious to wisps of smoke from a short circuit that drifted up from the base of his lectern while Secret Service men and workmen scrambled at his feet seeking the cause. "In my opinion," Paul Fay wrote, "the chance for the Catholic clergy to leave a favorable impression with the broad American public upon the election of the first Catholic President was shattered by Cardinal Cushing. He went on and on in an endless monotone as though he had been plugged into the wall and wouldn't stop till somebody disconnected him."[5] He was followed by the octogenarian poet Robert Frost, who, blinded by the sunlight, decided not to read the Inaugural dedication he had composed but to recite instead his popular hymn to America, "The Gift Outright." Jack Kennedy became the thirty-fifth President of the United States fifty-one minutes late, as he swore the presidential oath, placing his hand symbolically on a copy of the Catholic Douai version of the Bible, which had belonged to his grandfather Honey Fitz.

When Jack, bareheaded and coatless in the bright cold, stepped forward to deliver his Inaugural Address, he seemed the epitome of youthful vigor set against the ranks of elderly men and middle-aged women huddled in their coats in the presidential stand behind him. People were surprised by his eloquence, unaware of the hours he had spent studying Churchill's speeches, or of how he had honed his speaking skills over the four long years campaigning for the presidency and, more recently, practicing voice exercises with a drama coach every morning. He stood out as an inspirational leader, his impressive oratorical cadences ringing though the cold bright air before the dome of the Capitol. For millions of Americans it seemed as if a new era had begun. "Let the word go forth from this time and place, to friend and foe alike, that the torch has been passed to a new generation of Americans. Let every nation know, whether it wishes us well or ill, that we shall pay any price, bear any burden, meet any hardship, support any friend, oppose any foe to assure the survival and success of liberty . . . Now the trumpet summons us again—not as a call to bear arms, though arms we need—not a call to battle, though embattled we are—but a call to bear the burden of a long twilight struggle year in and year out . . . And so, my fellow Americans: ask not what your country can do for you—ask what you can do for your country . . ." Afterward, Jackie laid her finger on his cheek and whispered, "Jack, you were so wonderful."

It was Kennedy Day in Washington. The family had finally made it to the top. The dream of the old patriarch, Joe, which had seemed shattered with the death of Joe Jr. had been fulfilled by Jack. No less than sixteen Kennedys sat on the Inaugural platform. During the Inaugural Parade that afternoon, there was one symbolic moment which passed unnoticed by everyone but the Kennedys. As the presidential car passed the reviewing stand, Ambassador Joe doffed his top hat to his eldest son. Eunice, sitting behind him, was overcome. It was the first time she had ever seen her father defer to one of his children. Jack was already returning the compliment; standing up in the car he took off his hat to his father, the man who, in his words, "had made it all possible." In the White House later, Eunice jumped up and down on the Lincoln Bed, shouting, "Man, we made it!."

Jackie was all Kennedy now. The Bouviers metaphorically took a backseat on what should have been, also for them, a day of triumph. At the luncheon at the Mayflower Hotel given by Joe Kennedy, Rose and Janet Auchincloss acted as co-hostesses but, apart from introductions, there was little contact between the clans. The Kennedys sat together on one side of the room, the Bouviers, Lees and Auchinclosses on the other. At the White House reception for the families at five that afternoon, it was much the same. The Ambassador showed none of his legendary charm, particularly when "Little Edie" Beale sashayed up and reminded him that she had once been "semi-engaged" to Joe Jr., and that if Joe hadn't been killed Joe would have been President instead of Jack. Joe Kennedy was heard to comment in a contemptuous aside, "Jesus Christ, I didn't know Jackie had so many goddamned relatives."[6]

The new President radiated energy and charisma. It was as if the act of inauguration had given him a real sense of the presidency, of being the elected head of the most powerful country in the world, much as the coronation of a king or a queen endows an ordinary human being with an almost mystical sense of the qualities of kingship. Jackie, however, was upstairs. She had left the reviewing stand early in a state of collapse from emotional and physical exhaustion; it was less than six weeks since her cesarean and the birth of John Jr. Resting on the huge bed in the Queen's Bedroom, she had found herself unable to get up. Jack's doctor, Janet Travell, summoned from the reviewing stand, gave her a Dexedrine pill and ordered her to stay in bed. Jackie felt she could not face her relatives, with the exception of her favorite cousin and godfather, Miche Bouvier, whom she asked up to chat with her for half an hour.

Still mentally not strong, she had suffered a panic attack. It was as though her Bouvier relations had been ghosts from a less glittering past who had come back to haunt her on her most glorious day. She needed to put on her regal act for the public and the cameras, to be queen of the circus, to hide her insecurities and self-doubt behind her carefully applied makeup, the magnificent coiffure by Kenneth, the white chiffon sheath from Bergdorf, with its bodice embroidered with silver and brilliants. While she had dinner in bed and prepared for the evening, Jack went out to a New Frontier dinner given by Mr. and Mrs. George Wheeler for the members of the "Kennedy Caravan"—Ethel and Joan Kennedy, Arthur Schlesinger Jr., actor Jeff Chandler, Angie Dickinson, Stan Musial, James Michener and

Byron "Whizzer" White, Jack's old friend and former Harvard football star. Jack then returned to the White House to pick up Jackie. He sensed that she needed reassurance. "Darling, I've never seen you look so lovely," he told her. "Your dress is beautiful."[7] He called for champagne and raised his glass to Jackie before leaving with her, arm in arm, to do the rounds of the five Inaugural Balls.

At the first, Jackie sat bolt upright beside Lady Bird Johnson, enduring the stares of the other guests. No one danced; the crowd stood, those at the back pushing and shoving to get a closer look, just staring at the guests of honor. Jack, hyped up and having the time of his life, left Jackie there to make an unscheduled stop at his kind of party, a dinner hosted by Frank Sinatra, before returning to escort her to the second ball at the Washington Armory. Jackie never made it to the third, fourth and fifth balls: exhausted, she went back to the White House leaving Jack to enjoy the rest of the night without her. At the last ball Jack cunningly made sure that Red Fay, not himself, would be photographed with Angie Dickinson. Fay was in a party with Angie, Kim Novak and the Kennedys' Acapulco friend, architect Fernando Parra. Just as Jack left the party, he called Fay over to his car. "Why don't you jump in here and come out to Joe Alsop's with me?" he asked.

"It's great with me," Fay replied, "but is it all right if Angie comes along with us?"

"Fine, but let's get out of here," Jack said impatiently. Fay asked if Kim Novak and Fernando Parra could come along too, at which Jack's sense of self-preservation came to the fore: "I can just see the papers tomorrow," he said. Fay recalled, "The new President concluded his first day speeding off into the night with Kim Novak, Angie Dickinson, architect Fernando Parra and an old ship-mate." With a tone of resignation and loneliness, he said, "Well, Redhead, for a moment I almost forgot that I was President of the United States. It has its advantages and its restrictions, and this is one of the latter. Good night . . ."[8]

Leaving the last ball too were Peter Duchin and Pamela Turnure. Duchin recalled, "Pam was my date and she had a car and it was snowing, she had chains so we could get around. We started off and then we saw this figure in the snow who turned and looked at us and recognized us. It was Joe Alsop, who said, 'Oh, my God, could you give me a lift home?' and we said, 'Sure,' because it was really hard getting around, you can't imagine a city totally engulfed in snow which wasn't prepared for it . . . So we took Joe Alsop home to his house and he said in his typical, rather arcane, exotic way, 'Why don't you come up for some turtle soup? I'm having some people over,' so we said OK and we went in. I knew that meant I would be the bartender, and so we went up to Uncle Joe's for turtle soup and whatnot and there were maybe twenty-five, thirty people. All of a sudden the doorbell rang and the President walked in. It was the damnedest thing, that I could not believe. There was Jack, I mean looking absolutely terrific, and he sat down, and of course we all stood up and applauded, and he sat down and started telling stories about the changeover and the whole thing, which was just fantastic."[9]

Joe Alsop described Peter Duchin as "a godsend." On reaching home in Dumbarton Street, he recalled, "I was horrified and instantly reminded of my own weakness for scattering invitations, for there, in full ball-going regalia, were Flo

Smith and Afdera Fonda beating on my door knocker in a determined manner . . . Indeed, it soon became clear that Flo and Afdera had told all sorts of people, including the about-to-be-inaugurated President, that there would be champagne at my house if the lights were on. Consequently, a line of cars delivered what seemed to me an endless stream of guests. Peter, who had assumed the role of co-host, was beginning to worry about the supply of champagne when I heard a storm of very hard knocking on the front door. I rushed to open it. The scene in the open doorway was unforgettable. Dumbarton Street was solidly blocked by a vast Secret Service cortège of black cars and limousines. Every one of my neighbors' windows was open and lighted, and in every window people in their dressing gowns were clapping and cheering.

"I can still summon the picture of the new President standing on my doorstep to my mind's eye. He looked as though he were still in his thirties, with snowflakes scattered about his thick, reddish hair. Exhilaration always rejuvenated him, and he had been greatly exhilarated by his Inauguration and all that surrounded it. The burdens of his office had not yet settled heavily across his shoulders, and there was a bounce in his manner, a light in his eye that would not be so prominent later. He explained that Jackie had been so tired after her last visit to one of the several Inaugural balls that she had simply fallen into bed in the White House. He, however, had become hungry, but could find no one in the White House who could give him anything to eat."[10]

Returning to the White House in the early hours where Jackie slept, exhausted, in the Queen's Bedroom, Kennedy climbed into Abraham Lincoln's vast bed and slept, wrapped in the arms of American history. Next morning Charlie Bartlett asked him if he had used Lincoln's bed. "Yes," Jack replied. "I jumped in and just hung on!"

CHAPTER TEN

The House of the Sun King

I want to make this a grand house.

—JBK to Chief Usher J. B. West, on moving
into the White House, January 1961[1]

Jackie loved John F. Kennedy; he was the center of her life as—sadly, perhaps, for her—he was for so many other people. He was the sun around whom the planets, political, social and personal, revolved. The presidency gave her love for him a different dimension. She was determined to give the Kennedy White House an aura and a glamour that had never been seen before. On the private side, perhaps her hardest task was to keep that restless, most easily bored of men amused. The Kennedy White House had to be not only beautiful and dignified, a fitting setting for the head of state, it had also to be a glorified private house, fun, informal, with good food and wine, and witty, elegant people, an American version of Louise de Vilmorin's Château de Verrières.

The task would not be easy. The White House was a gaunt, unloved mansion on which little money had been spent since the Truman years, when it had been found to be structurally unsafe. Rebuilding had left nothing for redecoration beyond the most basic. Mrs. Eisenhower, as the wife of an army officer, had been used to a peripatetic life, running a series of households within a military context that focused on efficiency and order rather than beauty. Households of which she was in charge ran like clockwork and within strictly defined limits: maids at the White House were not allowed to step on the carpets and spent a good deal of time on their knees erasing careless footprints. Tall brass spittoons of the kind that furnished messes and saloons all over the country lined the White House reception rooms. Depressed palms drooped in corners. The furniture was of a style that Jack Kennedy defined disgustedly on his first day as "Sears Roebuck," and the connoisseur Joe Alsop denounced as "Statler Hilton." "On the third floor, which was supposed to be the guest rooms, they had public drinking fountains set in the walls, and it was just institutional," recalled William V. Elder III, curator of the White House during Jackie's regime.[2]

Joe Alsop, who with Bill Walton, Franklin and Sue Roosevelt, Leonard Bernstein and his wife dined at the first private dinner Jackie gave on the Sunday night after the Inauguration, had known the White House in the days of Franklin D. Roosevelt, remembering it as a

> very large, old-fashioned, American gentleman's house. The interiors were what the French would call *"dinge"*—full of suitable, handsome, and very odd objects, all mingled together in a comfortable, timeless sort of way, as if a happy and mildly curious family had lived in them for many years. In short neither the fell touch of fashion nor the fancy touch of the interior decorators had been anywhere apparent in the feel or design of the place, and in my old-fashioned way I had always found this delightful.
>
> The Eisenhower White House, after its evacuation by its occupants, presented a stark contrast from the White House I remembered from the Roosevelt years . . . Indeed, the place looked like an enormously enlarged and not quite as attractive version of the Presidential suite at the Muehlebach Hotel in Kansas City . . . I can recall the peculiar combination of vomit green and rose pink that Mrs. Eisenhower had chosen for her bedroom and bathroom . . .
>
> By Sunday night Jackie had rummaged through the entire house, encountering a good many surprises. "Do you know," I remember her exclaiming, "I've found a whole room of calligraphers busily at work in the cellar." These were . . . the skillful people who used to spend their days writing out White House invitations and place cards in perfect script . . .
>
> Other more contemporary features proved just as surprising. Among these were a pair of large, porthole-like contraptions built into the wall on either side of the door leading from the oval sitting room into the main upstairs hall. I had never seen anything like them and I asked what the devil they might be. The President rang, one of the ushers appeared as though by magic. The President asked the usher by name—he had already learned by name all the members of the White House staff—what the portholes concealed. The usher opened one of them to show a television screen, and he explained that in their last year or so the President and Mrs. Eisenhower liked to dine on television suppers, each watching a different television show. Two portholes were necessary because the President preferred Westerns and Mrs. Eisenhower preferred soaps.

Jackie had selected an enormous gold bucket, as big as a milk pail, and this was waiting for us in the oval sitting room upstairs filled almost to the brim with ten pounds of fresh caviar, which a vague Palm Beach acquaintance of the Kennedys had sent for no reason at all except that he was delighted by their move into the White House. I had never seen ten pounds of caviar—much less fresh caviar—in one bucket before and I have never seen it since . . . But since the caviar was accompanied by bottle after bottle of Dom Perignon, it seemed good while it lasted, and the party was jolly indeed . . .[3]

Privately the Kennedys ate off trays as the Eisenhowers had, with two butlers apiece hovering around them. When Jack complained about the food, Jackie brought in Pearl Nelson, their N Street cook, to prepare the food—particularly clam chowder—that the President liked. When they had guests, however, they had to use the Family Dining Room, with its gloomy high ceilings, burgundy-colored carpet and curtains, and nondescript walls. It was also extremely chilly: the White House central-heating system was antiquated and the fireplaces unused. When, on that first evening, Jackie had taken her two women guests into the Green Room for coffee after dinner they found three straight-backed chairs placed in a semicircle in front of an empty fireplace. Meanwhile the President and his guests wandered around the main floor of the White House in search of a bathroom—there was none. A related problem had plagued the President on his first day in the White House. Sister Parish and her young assistant, Richard Nelson, working in the Oval Room that morning had noticed on a side table a note in the President's hand. It read, "Jackie, let's declare war on toilet paper. Where the hell is it?"[4]

Jackie was determined that their personal social life should be much the same as it had been before the White House, so the next night Charlie and Martha Bartlett came to dine, to find Jack and Jackie already bursting with plans for the beautification of the White House and the saving of the federal architecture of Lafayette Square nearby, which the Eisenhower administration had had plans to demolish. Bill Walton, who was to be a key figure in the plans for the square, turned up impromptu the following night, bringing with him the writer and war correspondent Martha Gellhorn. On Saturday John and Lorraine Sherman Cooper gave a dinner for the Kennedys and twenty other guests. When Jack and Jackie walked into the romantic candlelit house out of the snow-laden street, even those who had known them before caught their breath at what seemed to be a transformation in the couple. "Everyone thought they looked out of this world," Lorraine Cooper recalled, "so beautiful, both of them, and enveloped in radiance which seemed almost tangible." As Joe Alsop was later to write, "The first period of the Kennedy era was downright exhilarating . . ."[5]

At the weekend Lem Billings came to stay as he had almost every weekend of their lives. "When the Kennedys first moved into the White House," J. B. West, chief usher, recorded, "Lem came down every weekend and just moved into his room without anybody ever knowing that he was coming." Billings, along with Dave Powers, said West "was court jester at the Great Hall." Lem, who worked in advertising in New York, was one of the few people the Kennedys asked to join them also on their country weekends. Jackie's family, however, was kept at arm's length. Janet Auchincloss came to the White House on special occasions; in the first week that the Kennedys moved in, she and Hughdie were invited to tea. "Mrs. Kennedy seemed to me to be rather formal with her mother," West wrote.[6] Nor was she close to Rose, who annoyed her by pointedly sending prayers, rosaries and religious artifacts to the President and his family. It was noticeable that Rose was to be seen in the White House more often when Jackie was away, when she enjoyed acting as the President's hostess. "There would have been some jealousy on Rose's part during the White House [period]," Doris Kearns Goodwin said. "I remember Lem Billings talking about that, that Rose had expected to be the Queen Mother and she was obviously outdistanced by Jackie."[7] Her Kennedy sisters-in-law were never invited to drop by for lunch; like Rose, they were called in to act as hostess when Jackie was away. "One exception to the arm's length distance between Jacqueline Kennedy and her family was her feeling for the 'Ambassador,' Joseph P. Kennedy," West recalled. "When the President's father came to visit, she fairly danced down the halls, arm-in-arm with him, laughing uproariously at his teasing. Her face was animated and happy, as it was when she was playing with her children."[8]

Lee and Stas were other exceptions to the no-family rule. Lee, now as permanent a fixture on the Best-Dressed List as Jackie herself, and Stas with his title and international connections fitted in perfectly with the Kennedy White House. To make up for the inequality in their relative positions, Jackie seems to have been determined that Lee and Stas should capitalize as much as possible on her new-found greatness. "When she entertained her sister," West wrote, "it was always a production, as if entertaining a visiting dignitary. Princess Radziwill slept in the Queen's Bedroom, her husband in the Lincoln bedroom."[9] The parties Jackie gave in honor of Stas and Lee were glamorous and sought after, with international celebrities flying in from Europe and socialites down from New York. "I have boxes of letters from Jackie," Lee Radziwill said. "Most are from 'sixty on—I have her life then, imploring me to come over, what pleased Jack or didn't please him, what would make him happy and a lot about our children and trying to keep them together and seeing each other every summer. Those letters showed great anxiety to keep us together and the children together as often as possible. We did spend those first three Christmases in the sixties in Palm Beach together with our children and a large part of every summer as well."[10]

With Jack, increasingly, what Jackie wanted she got, even if it meant cutting an old friend out of his life. Alastair Forbes had quarreled seriously with Stas over some "matters that I thought good and sufficient," a quarrel that ended his old relationship with Jack. "It was borne in upon me," Forbes said, "that part of his rapprochement with his wife involved a very strong rapprochement with her family. There were two considerations. One that Jackie had behaved extremely well, and had proved herself to be an asset, and had not in anyway impeded his political career, and that the debt of gratitude to her was both in his mind and in his heart, and that one of the things which made her happy was to allow her sister to enjoy as much as possible the trappings of being involved with the White House."[11] For the Radziwills, the "trappings" were not merely social; there was good business to be done through closeness to the Kennedys.[12]

On Sunday January 29, 1961, the Kennedys gave a reception for the cabinet and subcabinet, the fifteen members of the administration. Wives and children were also invited, as was the White House press corps. Accustomed to the reception lines and stiff, smoke-free, alcohol-free receptions in chilly State Rooms of the Eisenhower era, reporters were astounded at the changes. "Now the White House Is a Home" ran a headline the following day. There was a bar in the State Dining Room, and guests were allowed to smoke—ashtrays were strategically placed. There were glowing fires in the fireplaces and glorious flower arrangements in silver bowls—tulips and red carnations in the Red Room, white tulips and yellow carnations in the Blue Room. The informal, welcoming atmosphere was the result of a week's frantic work by Mrs. Paul "Bunny" Mellon, Jackie's friend and new mentor, Sister Parish and Tish Baldrige. To cheer up the gaunt mansion, Sister Parish toured the rooms every day that week, checking that the fires were properly laid, the newly purchased Lowestoft ashtrays in position. Bunny Mellon, a gardener of genius and a trained horticulturalist, brought with her not only the flowers from her Oak Springs estate near Upperville, Virginia, but her garden supervisor and a maid to create arrangements in the informal style of a Flemish still life, quite unlike the previous stiff florists' displays. The sad palms were banished. But as well as the compliments, there was outrage that alcohol had been served on a Sunday in the house of the head of state. Kennedy, always sensitive to image, was angry with Tish, whom he blamed for installing the bar. "You got me into trouble the first day," he complained.

Jackie's chief instrument in running the White House was the chief usher, J. B. West, virtually the CEO of the White House, who had served three previous presidents—Roosevelt, Truman and Eisenhower. His working with Jackie over the thirty-four months during which she transformed the White House was an entirely new experience for him. As he wrote,

> I would have to adjust White House management from a regimented, stylized, order-of-business to that of running an informal household. I would find myself dealing with Empire tables and rabbit cages; housing Maharajahs and ponies; steaming down the Potomac and wearing disguises; and thoroughly enjoying the most creative and challenging work to which the Chief Usher had ever been put.
>
> The new First Lady turned the White House inside out, and she imprinted her own rarefied lifestyle upon the mansion. But the greatest change in the White House was brought about by the presence of Jacqueline Bouvier Kennedy herself. She was thirty years younger

than any of the First Ladies I had served, and, I was to discover, had the most complex personality of them all. In public she was elegant, aloof, dignified, and regal. In private she was casual, impish and irreverent. She had a will of iron, with more determination than anyone I have ever met. Yet she was so soft-spoken, so deft and subtle, that she could impose that will upon people without their ever knowing it . . .[13]

While she was recuperating in Palm Beach Jackie had done her homework well: by the time she arrived in the White House she knew every inch of room space, exactly what furniture she would bring with her, and every detail of how she wanted the seven family rooms on the second floor. A crew of painters, plumbers, carpenters and electricians moved into the family part of the house on the day after the Inauguration. As soon as each room was finished, furniture was moved in, rugs rolled down and pictures hung. Meanwhile Jackie roamed the house discovering "treasures" and banishing "horrors." The "Mamie pink" disappeared from the walls of the upstairs rooms, the "hotel suite" decor of the Truman guest rooms became Caroline's pink rosebud paper with white canopied bed and rocking horses, and John Jr.'s blue and white nursery. A dressing room became Maud Shaw's bedroom. "She won't need much," Jackie commented. "Just find a wicker wastebasket for her banana peels and a little table for her false teeth at night." A new family dining room was installed with a kitchen nearby designed by the new French chef, René Verdon, and Sister Parish. The room had previously been used by President Eisenhower's mother-in-law. "I want my children to be brought up in more personal surrounds," Jackie said. "That 'Family' Dining Room is just too cavernous."[14]

The Kennedys' sleeping arrangements were different from the Eisenhowers'. The latter had shared the biggest bedroom, which Jackie designated as principally hers. She vetoed the first design made with the President in mind as "too severe as it is mainly my room." She took a four-poster canopied bed from one of the old guest rooms and had it fitted with the special cattlehair mattress for the President's back. She ordered an extra one for him to take on his travels and another for one side of the queen-sized bed in her room. By the end of two weeks, Jackie had used up the entire $50,000 appropriation for the redecoration of the White House on the family quarters alone. There was no money left for the State Rooms. "I know we're out of money, Mr. West," Jackie said, "but never mind! We're going to find some way to get real antiques into this house."[15]

"I want to make the White House the first house in the land," Jackie told Clark Clifford, lawyer and presidential fixer, whom Jack invited to lunch with them on February 6 to discuss her plans. "How many people do you think come through the White House every day? We must make this building something they can be proud of."[16]

Clifford warned Jack and Jackie that the pursuit of her dream would involve taking the greatest care not to give offense to the American people to whom the White House was "a sacred cow." He reminded them that the White House was government property, occupied only temporarily by whoever was President. He told them that the legal groundwork had to be carefully prepared to avoid any political problems, a warning that touched Jack's always sensitive political nerve. He asked Clifford to draw up an "airtight legal framework" for Jackie's work in the White House. "On February 23, 1961, only a month after the Inauguration," Clifford wrote, "Jackie unveiled the first result of our efforts, the Fine Arts Committee for the White House, established for the purpose of locating 'authentic furniture of the date of the building of the White House and the raising of funds to purchase this furniture as gifts for the White House.' "[17]

Since everything relating to the White House was innately political, Jackie's project needed not only to be clothed in cast-iron legality but also to be seen to have the backing of the most prestigious names in the American art and antiques world. Henry du Pont, multimillionaire owner and creator of the Winterthur Museum near Wilmington, Delaware, the supreme authority on American furniture and decorative objects of the 1640–1840 period, was the name everyone pressed on Jackie. Jayne Wrightsman, Jackie's adviser on antique French furniture and decoration whose contacts in the museum and dealing world were unrivaled, was a prime mover in recruiting him. Uncle Lefty Lewis had had the same idea. On February 4 Jackie wrote to him saying that "Mummy" had told her of his plan to involve du Pont, and joked that so many people had told her that they would approach du Pont on her behalf as soon as he returned from a Caribbean cruise that the "poor man" would be flattened by a horde as he stepped off the boat.

When du Pont returned from the Caribbean to his winter home at Boca Grande, Florida, Jackie flew down from Palm Beach with Jayne Wrightsman to meet him, in the hope of persuading him to be chairman of her Fine Arts Committee. Although Jackie and Jayne arrived casually dressed in slacks, while the ladies invited to meet them for lunch wore smart dresses and hats, du Pont was "captivated" by Jackie and impressed by her organized approach to the project. She had brought with her files and books from the Library of Congress, which she had been studying all winter, and together they discussed possibilities for the restoration and plans for the Fine Arts Committee, which was to oversee it. As Jackie said, "Without him on the committee I didn't think we would accomplish much—and with him I knew there would be no criticism. The day he agreed to be chairman was the biggest red-letter day of all."[18]

Janet Felton Cooper, whom Jackie invited to become secretary to the Fine Arts Committee, underlined what Jackie had said. The du Ponts moved in the dizziest heights of WASP Republican old-money society with which even Jackie was not totally familiar. Janet Felton, as she then was, remembered coming to the White House long before she took the job later in 1961 and being present when Mr. du Pont made his first tour, or "walk-through" as he called it, of the White House on April 29, 1961. "We went through the White House and truly there were about two or three antiques, and one of them was a pair of card tables in the Green Room and Jackie said, 'That's one of the few antiques and they were given by Mrs. Crowninshield,' and he said, 'That's my sister.' That had been in the Roosevelt era; she didn't realize that Mrs. Crowninshield was his sister. It was rather dear . . ." "But I promise you," Janet Felton Cooper added, "his support lent legitimacy to the whole thing—it would have collapsed in seconds, because I think Jackie was considered a bit of a flighty young thing, the wife of a Democrat and Joe Kennedy's daughter-in-law."[19] "And to all the Establishment," said William Elder III, later the White House curator, "all those people would have looked at the Kennedys as kind of enemies, political enemies, wrong party, wrong place."[20]

"Wrong class," added James Roe Ketchum, who later succeeded Elder as curator.[21] Henry du Pont was regarded as not only the greatest collector of Americana but also "the highest-qualified authority on the subject of American historical decoration. By enlisting him in the White House project, Jacqueline Kennedy had fulfilled two critical requirements for success: historical and artistic legitimacy in the public's eyes, and the support of a powerful network of dealers and collectors in the field of American antiques."[22]

It was a part of Jackie's genius and an important quality in her role in restoring the White House that she not only had an instinctive feel for what was right for the house but also knew exactly where to go for advice and who to approach for help. Mr. du Pont may have been the doyen of American connoisseurship but two of her most important mentors were women: Bunny Mellon and Jayne Wrightsman. Both had access to unlimited quantities of money—Bunny in her own right as a Listerine heiress and through her husband billionaire Paul Mellon; Jayne through her husband, the rude, irascible, autocratic Charles Wrightsman. Bunny was generally considered to be an arbiter of good taste in everything to do with houses and gardens, a perfectionist with an unerring eye for beauty. Jayne, whose own beginnings were humble, had made herself an acknowledged expert on French eighteenth-century furniture. Her house at Palm Beach and New York apartment were the settings for a remarkable world-famous collection. While Bunny Mellon took charge of everything to do with plants and flowers at the White House, remodeling the Rose Garden at President Kennedy's request, creating what was one day to be called the Jacqueline Kennedy Garden and revolutionizing the style of the flower arrangements in the house, Jayne Wrightsman was an indefatigable tower of strength in the organization of the White House interiors.

The appointees consulted a committee of wealthy and knowledgeable people: along with Bunny Mellon, Sister Parish, and Jayne Wrightsman were Charles Francis Adams, Mrs. C. Douglas Dillon, Mrs. Charles W. Engelhard, David E. Finley, Mrs. Albert D. Lasker, John S. Loeb, Gerald Shea, John Walker III and Mrs. George Henry Warren. It was assumed that these twelve influential people, through their network of affluent friends, would find donors of money and furnishings to the project, alleviating the need to petition Congress for more appropriations. Their money-raising work was to be supplemented by the scholarship of an advisory committee of curators and academics who were in touch with collectors and dealers all over the country. In a letter to Jackie, du Pont wrote of his hopes that these two committees would "achieve your desire of making the White House a symbol of cultural as well as political leadership . . . Believing as we do that an understanding of America's cultural past is a prerequisite to a real understanding of our country today, we shall strive to obtain those tangible evidences of the skill of the early craftsman and the taste of his patron which will make the White House . . . an historic document of cultural life in the United States."[23]

In a *Life* interview with Hugh Sidey in September, Jackie was anxious to emphasize the seriousness of her plans. "Everything in the White House must have a reason for being there. It would be sacrilege merely to redecorate it—a word I hate. It must be restored, and that has nothing to do with decoration. That is a question of scholarship."[24] It was not to be confined to one period only but to cover the entire past of the American presidency. The whole project was given legal protection by Congress in September when Public Law 87–826 declared the White House to be a museum and its contents inalienable. The passage of this act allowed the Fine Arts Committee to assure potential donors that their gift to the White House would not end up at public auction or in the private collection of a future president. Nor would a future first lady be able radically to change the character of the White House as it was now envisaged: "Primary attention shall be given to the preservation and interpretation of the museum character of the principal corridor on the ground floor and the principal public rooms on the first floor of the White House."[25]

A White House curator's office was established, with the first curator nominated by du Pont. The appointment of Lorraine Waxman Pearce, a graduate of the Winterthur Program, to the part was announced in late March. William Voss Elder III was appointed registrar of the growing collection of furnishings. The carefully orchestrated publicity for the White House project resulted in a flood of donations, which were vetted and either accepted or politely returned. Jackie had tapped a vein of patriotic generosity. Skillfully, by appealing to the rich, she avoided the political pitfall of deploying taxpayers' money, and by operating within a framework of professionalism and scholarship her plans were seen as a national project and not as a rich woman's whim.

There were soon to be interior-designer wars behind the scenes. Sister Parish, forthright, upper-class WASP creator of the Anglo-American style, had in 1958 redecorated the N Street house with the simple printed cotton and canvas things that she liked and was initially recruited to do Glen Ora and the White House, but found herself displaced as decorator of the State Rooms—and later for the private rooms as well—by Stéphane Boudin, of the renowned Paris house Jansen, introduced by Jayne Wrightsman. Boudin's client list had included such illustrious names as the Duchess of Windsor, the Shah of Iran, Lady Mendl, Babe Paley, C. Z. Guest, Jayne Wrightsman herself and Lady Olive Baillie at Leeds Castle in England. He had been responsible for the restoration of several great European houses and palaces, including the Empress Josephine's Malmaison, which Jackie was to see on her visit to France in June 1961. Above all he had transformed Jayne Wrightsman's Palm Beach house into a French château, designed her Fifth Avenue apartment, and formulated the concept of the Wrightsman galleries and period rooms at the Metropolitan Museum. Jackie had fallen under Boudin's spell when introduced to him by Jayne in around 1955, when Jack was still a senator and, as always, a tightwad when it came to expense on decoration. (In those days New York antiques dealers had often refused to deal with Jackie because anything they sent for her approval was inevitably returned on the grounds that she could not afford it.)

Now, with the support of her rich friends, she could afford Monsieur Boudin. Jackie was deeply impressed by his ideas for the White House, which incorporated designs from European interiors, and by his knowledge of architecture, always one of her chief interests. She was impressed too by the Jansen historical archives and expert artisans. Within a few weeks of the Inauguration, on February 9, 1961, Boudin visited Jackie at the White House.

Jackie's fondness for French decoration was as politically sensitive as her passion for French couture; and Boudin, like Givenchy, would have to be concealed from the American public. The extent of his influence was also better kept hidden from Henry du Pont: the decorator's views often clashed with those of the connoisseur. Boudin disliked seeing too many legs on furniture about a room, preferring to cover them with skirts—"like a brothel," his opponents muttered. He had the temerity to say that the legs on Daniel Webster's revered sideboard should be shortened to improve the proportions. Such views did not go down well with du Pont. "They had to hide Mr. Boudin in the pantry when Mr. du Pont came around," a member of Jackie's Fine Arts Committee commented.[26] Janet Felton recalled, "Mr. du Pont was aware of Monsieur Boudin and I think he resented it." Du Pont rightly considered Boudin ignorant on the subject of Americana: "I shudder to think what Mr. Boudin would do with American furniture," he snorted to Lorraine Pearce, after one session with the Frenchman.

Jackie's tact and charm were an important factor in ensuring du Pont's continued cooperation, despite his suspicions about Boudin. Susan Mary Alsop, wife of Joe and a member of the White House Paintings Committee, recalled, "We had meetings and Mr. du Pont would come down occasionally from Winterthur in rather a Jove-like fashion. We had been given two little pictures which we liked a lot. And before one of Mr. du Pont's visits we hung them in the Red Room and we thought they looked absolutely marvelous. They were tiny little still lifes and they were sweet. And Mr. du Pont came into the room and we all stood up and he looked around, and Jackie said, 'That is our most recent acquisition, Mr. du Pont.' He gave them a look and turned to us and said in an icy tone, 'Surely you are aware that still lifes are only for dining rooms.' And Jackie said, 'Oh, Mr. du Pont, how awful of us not to know and how difficult, we're so ignorant. Thank *goodness* you've told us. They'll be down right away.' And she had someone take them off the wall. About a month later I went to the White House on a purely social occasion with Joe, and I went into the Red Room by chance and there I saw Mr. du Pont staring at the wall and on the wall were the two little flower pictures exactly where they had been before. I said nothing and he said, 'Susan Mary, I do think we've done well. The Red Room has never looked better. Everything is perfect.'"[27]

The new curator, Lorraine Pearce, was a du Pont appointee and revered him as her Winterthur mentor. According to the historians of the White House restoration, the two kept in regular touch about new and prospective acquisitions and their placement, and about other ideas. This quickly proved uncomfortable as Pearce received contradictory instructions from Jackie and du Pont. Naturally she secretly agreed with du Pont, which contributed to the end of her White House career. As Abbott and Rice saw it, she viewed Boudin as a threat to the historical accuracy of the rooms that she and du Pont were working to create. In a letter after a visit he made in late 1961 she wrote:

> After all of our good work on that famous Tuesday, Mr. Boudin arrived fresh and vigorous the next day and promptly undid the Entrance Hall. The two French pier tables were moved around to the Cross Hall, Mrs. [Cornelia] Guest's settee slated for the entrance hall, Miss [Catherine] Bohlen's card table was removed entirely, as were the Lannuier tables, so that the hall is terribly barren and worse than ever . . . The hall is thus empty of anything but the two pier tables which are out of sight of the entering visitor. I suppose we should keep this entre nous and see if we cannot improve things a bit on your next visit.[28]

Nothing in fact was changed. William Elder recalls that after du Pont's furniture-moving visits, Jackie would tell him to go through the house replacing things in the position they had occupied before du Pont's arrival. Jackie was willing to let du Pont feel that he was responsible for arranging the White House furnishings but ultimately she retained the final control. She viewed Lorraine Pearce, however, as an obstruction. "Lorraine Pearce didn't really get along with Jackie Kennedy, I guess," said Bill Elder, "but she was very capable and she did an excellent job in the beginning. I think it was just a clash of personalities."[29]

Personality clashes were enhanced in Jackie's eyes by what she saw unfairly as publicity-seeking. Like any other museum curator, Lorraine Pearce accepted speaking invitations and wrote articles on the White House historical furnishings for antiques magazines. This, to Jackie, was the cardinal sin; discretion was imposed on everyone concerned with the project from members of the committees to antiques dealers and craftsmen. She became unreasonably upset when the persistently inquisitive Maxine Cheshire of the *Washington Post*, ferreted out and published details of the White House restoration in a series of articles in September 1962. Cheshire revealed that a Baltimore desk, which Jackie in her televised tour of the White House had highlighted as "one of our finest pieces," was a fake and, even more to Jackie's consternation, revealed the secret existence of Monsieur Boudin. Lorraine Pearce was quoted as saying, "We NEVER introduce Mr. Boudin . . ." Jackie's angry tears induced Jack to telephone Phil Graham, editor of the *Post*, and berate him for upsetting his wife.

Jackie found herself bombarded with cross notes from her social staff complaining about Lorraine Pearce's demands, and, when she asked what was wrong, received a twelve-page memo from the curator which, as she told West, convinced her that Pearce had "come down with White House-itis." Gradually Lorraine Pearce was eased out: she was given the important task of writing the text of the White House guidebook. After its publication in August 1962, she resigned her position and was replaced by William Elder. James Roe Ketchum, a young employee of the National Park Service, was brought in as registrar. Pearce wrote to du Pont of "her relief at being free of the pressures of the White House and her frustration at the near futility of trying to uphold the high standards set for the project in such a confusing atmosphere."[30]

The simple truth, though, was that Jackie was in charge, and the public image of the restoration as a professional project under the control of a committee was a façade. She was perfectly prepared to butter up du Pont and Sister Parish to preserve the façade, then carry on doing what she wanted behind what Maxine Cheshire called her "velvet curtain." In an article for *Newsweek* on September 17, 1962, Cheshire perceptively described the restoration project as "a tale that encompasses scholarship, wrangling over prices, discreet pressure, petty jealousies, and a cast of influential characters who keep well behind the velvet curtain Jackie has drawn around the inner workings of her program." Three days later an enraged Jackie scribbled a furious letter to du Pont from the deck of a destroyer off Newport while awaiting the start of the America's Cup Race, denouncing the Cheshire articles and Lorraine Pearce's desire for publicity.[31]

The employment of Monsieur Boudin on the more spectacular of the White House rooms displeased Sister Parish. Although she was prepared to defer to the authority of du Pont, Boudin was a different matter entirely. In the summer of 1961 when Jayne Wrightsman asked Boudin to provide period textile documents for the Red Room, which Sister Parish regarded as her most important project, Sister intimated resignation and was soothed only by a ten-page letter from Wrightsman written on June 28, 1961, from the Ritz in Paris: "You must *never* think of resigning from the committee! It would break Jackie's heart + mine, too . . . The White House is so lucky to have you."[32] Sister's strength lay in her social connections and her own devoted client list; both Jackie and Jayne recognized this, and Jackie in particular was aware of the importance of stressing her contribution as an American decorator in the concealment of Boudin's influence. Sister Parish, with her new partner Albert Hadley, had free rein in the Family Dining Room because the costs were underwritten by Charles and Jane Engelhard, who were both friends and clients. Jack Kennedy, who used the room for numerous congressional breakfasts, was pleased with the transformation, Jackie less so: "For Jacqueline Kennedy," Mary Van Rensselaer Thayer wrote, "this alienation of Boudin assured a lack of enthusiasm for the proposed scheme and helped to define the completed space as 'her most unfavorite of all White House rooms.' "[33]

Sister Parish won most of the game over the second-floor Yellow Oval Room, the Kennedys' semiformal drawing room in their private quarters. Annoyance over Boudin-inspired incursions into the design for this room was partly responsible for her threatened resignation in June 1961; she had, after all, begun work on the concept of this room on the day of the election. Her trump card, however, was the assurance that the completion of the room would be paid for by her friends on the Fine Arts Committee, New York banker John Loeb and his wife, Frances. On hearing the news, the ever-tactful Jayne Wrightsman, enthused from Switzerland, "You really are a wonder! Bravo!" and Jackie deflected Sister's anger by writing her a most conciliatory letter on June 30 designating the Yellow Oval Room as exclusively her territory and acknowledging that the wishes of the Loebs would be respected over her personal preference for Boudin's drapery suggestions for the room.

Jackie, however, was nothing if not persistent. Eighteen days after this letter, she returned to the charge, telling Sister Parish that Jayne Wrightsman had secured Boudin's permission for Parish-Hadley to use his window designs as their own. Wisely, Mrs. Parish decided not to stand and fight on this one; the eventual room was principally her work and acknowledged as such, although furniture and objects suggested by Boudin and placed in it were screened as the ideas of Jackie or Jayne.

The move from Parish to Boudin for Jackie's personal living quarters symbolized the evolution of her personal aesthetic. To begin with, Mrs. Parish had worked with Jackie on transferring the general feel of her Georgetown bedroom to the much larger and more formal scale of 1600 Pennsylvania Avenue. By 1962 Boudin began to plan a reinterpretation of Jackie's bedroom: the country-style fabrics were to be replaced with Parisian silks, the upholstered headboard provided by Mrs. Parish with a Louis XVI-style in painted wood. As James A. Abbott and Elaine M. Rice put it:

> This room was in the process of becoming another example of Boudin's worldly style—familiar to the likes of Jayne Wrightsman, C. Z. Guest, and the Duchess of Windsor . . . the true expression of Boudin's style was the adjoining dressing-room. From this small corner room, the Frenchman removed all traces of Parish's casual Southampton vocabulary, replacing them with Paris-born silk and trompe-l'oeil sophistication . . .[34]

Jackie's wardrobe doors were painted by a Paris-based artist, Pierre Marie Rudelle, to represent the most important events of her life—significantly they included a 1935 photograph of Jackie with her father after she won a rosette in a Long Island horse show, *Profiles in Courage*, and a *Look* picture showing Jackie taking a tumble in Virginia from her horse, Bit of Irish. Prints and color plates on the walls illustrated the grandeur of France past, which Jackie and Boudin were re-creating in the White House. Among Jackie's favorites was an early nineteenth-century engraving of the Empress Josephine, whose French Creole blood, love of beauty and faithless, brilliant, powerful husband probably had resonances in Jackie's own experience.

The Oval Office, heart of the presidential White House, was initally redecorated according to the ideas of Jackie and Mrs. Parish in 1961, keeping the Truman-era green curtains and carpets, with the addition of the historic "Hayes Desk," which was to become almost a symbol of the Kennedy presidency. Found by Jackie on the ground floor of the White House, the desk, made from the timbers of HMS *Resolute*, had been a gift from Queen Victoria to President Rutherford Hayes, a poignant token of Anglo-American friendship ideally suited to one of the most Anglophilic twentieth-century American presidents.[35] By mid-1962 the Parish scheme had been superseded by plans for a new layout, a cooperation between Jack, Jackie and Boudin, epitomizing the increasing sophistication and internationalism of the Kennedy outlook—the "Imperial Presidency."

The gradual ascendancy of Boudin coincided with Jackie's own evolution from relatively unknown Georgetown wife to glamorous First Lady, wife of the most powerful man in the world and celebrity in her own right. Sister Parish's chintzes for the American rich gave way to the specially woven silks and moirés fit for Versailles and the Sun King.

Jackie's fury at the Maxine Cheshire articles (one was entitled "They never introduce M. Boudin") was undoubtedly caused by the "outing" of Boudin: it sparked fears that her use of a foreign designer might harm Jack politically and reflect badly on her whole project. Having run the press gauntlet over her Paris clothes, she was sensitive to possible anger from the American public at the employment of a foreigner to decorate the house of the American Head of State. Du Pont and Sister Parish were both knowledgeable and talented, but in Jackie's eyes their high-profile connection with the White House restoration project provided a useful cloak of concealment for her increasing deployment of Stephane Boudin. The Boudin affair was typical of the subtle, secret ways in which Jackie liked to operate, the almost Machiavellian skill with which she got what she wanted while avoiding political fallout.

Even Maxine Cheshire never found out that fabric had been specially ordered from a Parisian firm, not from the New York–based Scalamandré, for the Blue Room—which, after Boudin's redesigning, was in essence no longer blue. The fabric in question was an eagle-patterned silk for the Monroe-period gilt chairs. The chairs presented a problem: the only evidence of the original appearance of the upholstery for the Bellanger suite, ordered by President Monroe in Paris, was in a portrait of Monroe: the suite featured in the background. Scalamandré studied the portrait in New York's City Hall and came up with a reproduction of the motif, an eagle clutching a sheaf of arrows and surrounded by a laurel wreath. It was not a success, as William Elder wrote, forwarding the Scalamandré sample to Jackie, who was on vacation with the Radziwills at Ravello in August 1962. "As you can see, the eagle for the chair back looks more like a plucked chicken and the weaving is very coarse . . ."[36] Jackie rejected it, and wrote to du Pont when she returned in September to tell him of her disappointment at the American-manufactured samples. Then she instructed Boudin to find another manufacturer.

Boudin chose the Parisian firm of Tassinari and Chatel with whom he frequently worked, and Jackie went to great lengths to conceal that a foreign manufacturer would produce the fabric for one of the White House's most important rooms. Jansen, not the White House, placed the order with Tassinari and Chatel. When completed, it was shipped to the U.S. embassy in Paris, from there to the State Department under diplomatic cover, and hence to the White House. The Paris firm also produced, undetected, the green silk moiré for the Green Room. Until the 1980s the common belief was that Scalamandré had supplied these Kennedy-era textiles. The Wrightsmans funded the decoration of the Blue Room, so Boudin had felt he had more of a free hand in this room than anywhere else in the mansion, where the feelings and opinions of du Pont and Sister Parish had to be taken into account. (Sister Parish had had the upper hand with the President's Dining Room and the Family Dining Room funded by her friends the Loebs, the Engelhards and Mrs. Vincent Astor.)

The prestige of the White House, combined with the glamour of the First Lady, proved an irresistible lure for wealthy donors. When approached by Boudin and Paul Manno, director of Jansen's New York office, the financier André Meyer eagerly underwrote the purchase of an exceptional and extremely expensive Aubusson carpet for the Red Room in exchange for an introduction to Mrs. Kennedy. The American Institute of American Designers paid for the ground floor Library, the decoration of which was entirely under the expert guidance of du Pont; its walls were enlivened by five rare portraits of Native Americans, painted in 1821 on the occasion of their visit to President Monroe at the White House. The pictures were discovered by Vincent Price, the celebrated actor, connoisseur and a member of the White House Paintings Committee, and their purchase funded by Sears, Roebuck & Company. Books for the Library were chosen by a scholarly committee, which included Harvard's Lyman H. Butterfield, editor of the Adams Papers at the Massachusetts Historical Society, Princeton's Julian Boyd, James T. Babb, librarian at Yale, and Jackie's favorite Kennedy adviser, Arthur Schlesinger Jr. "As at present envisaged," Schlesinger wrote, "the Library would consist of 2000 or so volumes considered essential to an understanding of the American experience."[37] Jackie wrote that she wanted "a library of significant American . . . & writings that have influenced American thinking—Locke etc. & all books by Presidents . . . —just what a gentleman's library should look like—"[38]

On November 3, 1961, Jackie's permanent protective umbrella for the White House, a nonprofit organization called the White House Historical Association, was incorporated, with David Finley, John Walker and Clark Clifford as founding board members. To raise money for it, Jackie came up with the brilliant idea of the White House guidebook. Jackie herself oversaw every stage of its production, the text, pictures and layout. The book was an instant success, and over the years sales of some eight million copies have funded the Historical Association and acquisition of furniture and works of art for the White House, as well as paying for the official portraits of the presidents and first ladies that hang there.

Jackie was ruthless in pursuit of objects she wanted. Walter Annenberg, the wealthy Philadelphia publisher and later ambassador to London, was the happy possessor of a portrait of Benjamin Franklin by David Martin, which he had recently purchased for $250,000 a considerable sum in those days. One day he heard the soft voice of Jacqueline Kennedy, whom he had never met, soliciting a favor in terms of the most outrageous flattery: "Mr. Annenberg, today you are the first citizen of Philadelphia," she whispered, "and in his day Benjamin Franklin was the first citizen of Philadelphia. That is why, Mr. Annenberg, I thought of you. Do you think that a great Philadelphia citizen would give the White House a portrait of another great Philadelphia citizen?"[39] Annenberg, a Republican, thought for a few days, then waved good-bye to his quarter of a million dollars. The Franklin portrait was on its way to the White House.

People who tried to say no to Jackie found that she would go to great lengths of outwit them. Early in December David Finley was dispatched to the Capitol to tell George Stewart, architect of the Capitol, "of Mrs. Kennedy's desire to secure one of the chandeliers which had hung in the White House and had been sold at the time of the Theodore Roosevelt Restoration in 1902."[40] A month later Stewart told Finley that there might be difficulties over this and an Act of Congress might be required, adding, "This office is of the opinion that the 3 known White House chandeliers should remain in the Capitol as they conform to the period of the Wings and do not conform to the period of the restored White House."[41] Jackie resented being lectured to on what did or did not conform with the "restored White House" but she bided her time until after her highly praised TV tour of the restored White House and her return from her successful solo visit to India and Pakistan before broaching the chandelier question in a six-page handwritten letter with the one man who really knew his way around the Capitol: the Vice President, Lyndon B. Johnson. She was just asking, she said, for three out of the hundreds of chandeliers in the Capitol for the White House, but even this modest request was being thwarted by the bureaucrats in charge, notably Mr. Stewart, who had also seen off the senators whose help she had enlisted. Could "dear Lyndon," with his legendary powers of persuasion, accomplish this for her?[42]

Johnson tackled the Senate Majority Leader, Mike Mansfield, on Jackie's behalf, only to receive a discouraging memo from him on May 8, all too clearly dictated by the obdurate Mr. Stewart who, it said, could pinpoint only three chandeliers as having definitely come from the White House, and stating "factors which would suggest the inadvisability of transfer." Johnson forwarded it to Jackie on May 22 and promised to discuss it with her. On June 5 he received a determined, even subtly threatening, letter from Jackie. She would reduce her demands to just one chandelier, for the Treaty Room—but that she was determined to have, even if it meant bringing in the press who were to be shown the Treaty Room on June 29 and would ask awkward questions if they didn't see the chandelier there. She suggested Johnson charm Mr. Stewart into lending it for that one day and then leave it to her to keep him from getting it back.[43] The result of Jackie's combination of cajoling and veiled threat was a letter from Mansfield to Stewart of June 15: "You are hereby authorized and directed to loan to the White House, on a temporary basis, the crystal chandelier now hanging in the connecting corridor, Principal Floor, Senate Wing of the United States Capitol . . ."

James Biddle, scion of a famous Philadelphia family and assistant curator in charge of the American Wing of the Metropolitan Museum of Art, was another victim of Jackie's tenacity. Jackie wanted an important early American silver table centerpiece for the Family Dining Room; Biddle refused it on the grounds that it was too valuable for such use. Then he went on vacation—to find on his return the platter gone and a note from Jackie couched in blunt Anglo Saxon terms: "Darling Jimmy, I've got it. F— you!"[44]

By her staff, however, Jackie was adored. "She was such a fantastic, interesting, fun person that you never knew what was going to happen the next day," Janet Felton Cooper recalled. "I can't think of any unpleasant situation that we ever had. Sometimes she would give you the devil for not answering her memos, but there really weren't any unpleasant incidents. I think she was very protective of the office too. I remember the people who used to come in and give us a hard time and she would then say 'Don't pay any attention to So-and-so . . .' And during that time at the White House we had the complete run of it—we could go anytime, any place, upstairs, downstairs . . . —and she would say, 'Janet, you can take people up to the second floor, but just don't go in when Jack is taking his nap!'"[45]

James Ketchum said, "I remember her saying to me in 'sixty-three, 'Have your parents been here? Have they been upstairs?' And I thought to myself afterward, She wasn't allowing Ethel up but she was allowing my mother!"[46] William Elder remembered going to a cocktail party at Janet Auchincloss's Georgetown house when Jackie was away: "She asked me if she came to the White House would I take her to the second floor to the private living quarters? She had never been there."[47] Ketchum remembered Mrs. Auchincloss coming into their office to buy guidebooks, "which I always thought odd. And I also remember when we were told that if a certain woman called Ethel called to make sure that she paid more for her guidebooks than anyone else . . ." He went on, "I don't know how to get across the fact that her sense of humor was absolutely the most delicious, wonderful part of her being and for the rest of us her saving grace. She absolutely could turn any situation and find a laugh line no matter what was going on . . . And her language could be very colorful . . ."

J. B. West was impressed by Jackie's skill at running a large, sophisticated household. She had learned a great deal from her mother's handling of Merrywood and Hammersmith, and from the luxury and beauty of houses like the Aga Khan's Château de l'Horizon, Gianni Agnelli's La Leopolda and Lulu de Vilmorin's Verrières. She knew how to handle a large staff of domestic servants— what to expect from them, how to evaluate them and how to get a polished performance from them. On the morning after the Inauguration, she asked West to arrange a meeting with the indoor house servants. Wearing jodhpurs, a shirt and boots, her hair tousled from exercise, the First Lady perched informally on the edge of a desk as the various squads were paraded before her—the three ushers, housekeeper Mabel Walker, Charles the maître d' who supervised food preparation and service, four butlers, the kitchen staff, three cooks and their assistants ("who plainly were startled by the sight of a First Lady in pants," West commented), the five second- and third-floor maids and two upstairs housemen, Filipino Navy stewards. Jackie memorized all their names. "Is that all?" she whispered, as the housemen left. "Well," West replied, "there are three men in the flower shop, two women in the laundry, five downstairs housemen, three plumbers, three painters, two in the storeroom, twelve engineers, seven carpenters and eight gardeners." "How much is our operating budget?" Jackie asked. "Five hundred thousand dollars a year, not including your personal expenditure," was the reply. Jackie's staff, whom she had brought with her, all had to be added to the White House payroll. Of them, only Miss Shaw could have no official designation. "Well, just remember this," Jackie told West, "I want you to run this place just like you'd run it for the *chinchiest* President who ever got elected. We don't have nearly as much money as you read in the papers!"[48]

First to go to make way for Jackie's new regime was the White House housekeeper who, after their first meeting, had remarked sniffily to the staff, "How could she [Jackie] tell what she was looking at, with all that hair falling in her face?" Jackie was in the habit of leaving West notes, with her latest thoughts on staff. Many read, "Could someone please rev up Miss Walker?" She decided to bring in Anne "Linky" Lincoln from the Social Office to replace Miss Walker, who was moved to making an inventory in the warehouse. Jackie tended to surround herself with women of her background, who would instinctively understand the way she wanted things done. Of Anne Lincoln, Jackie said, "She knows how I want cigarette boxes placed, and everything else about the kind of house this should be . . ."[49]

There were changes specifically in the kitchen, where Jackie had hired French chef René Verdon, formerly at Le Pavillon, and his assistant, Julius Spessot. She decided that Spessot, whose speciality was ice sculpture, her least favorite form of table decoration, should depart in favor of Ferdinand Louvat, the pastry chef.

The President, always ultrasensitive where the press and public relations might be concerned, became nervous when he heard of the staff dismissals. "Aren't you afraid he [Julius] might want to write something?" he asked West. Several days later, Jackie telephoned West to tell him that the Kennedy attorney James McInerney (who handled their private affairs and awkward customers like Pamela Turnure's landlady, Florence Kater) had drawn up confidentiality pledges for the White House staff to sign. When Pierre Salinger disclosed the existence of the pledge, there was uproar. He had to deflect it toward Jackie: "We just felt that it is a step to ensure that the President's wife will have privacy," he explained. Jack, the real author of the pledge, realized that the deflection had to go further: neither he nor his wife should be implicated in it. He left his office in the West Wing and made a private visit to West. "I want you to help me, Mr. West," he said. "This 'pledge' business is causing me a lot of trouble. Would you take blame for it? We'll put out a statement saying it was your idea, and you initiated it. It will look more official and less of a personal thing coming from you."[50]

For Jackie the couple's private life was as important—if not more so—than the public trappings of the thirty-fifth presidency. She was determined that her children should lead as normal a life as possible in the White House, with its imposing rooms and flunkies on every floor. "I don't want them to think they are 'official' children," she told West. "When I go out with them or when they go out with their nurse, please ask the doorman not to hover around to open the doors for them."[51] On the day the children arrived at the White House she had asked the gardeners to build a snowman for them, with carrots for eyes and an apple for its mouth to amuse them and distract them from the strangeness of their new big house. But Caroline was a little in awe of the huge rooms and the height of the ceilings, and always kept her bedroom door ajar so that she felt closer to Miss Shaw.

Press attention and security made it difficult for Caroline to go out to her Georgetown playgroup so Jackie made the White House the venue for the group so that she could see her friends. "The first year it was a co-operative nursery school with the mothers, and Mrs. Kennedy included, taking turns as teachers and helpers each week," said Pamela Turnure, "and then the next year it became more formal and they got regular nursery school teachers and kindergarten teachers. It went into two classes while it was there . . ."[52] Jackie designed the playschoolroom in the third-floor solarium, complete with sandbox, rabbit cages, guinea pigs, goldfish and plants, and selected hundreds of schoolbooks from the list the teacher had prepared. It soon became a full-fledged nursery school with ten pupils, whose parents paid the teachers' salaries between them with the Kennedys. "It looked like a lovely little nursery school," said Susan Neuberger Wilson, one of the mothers whom Jackie had asked to organize the school and recruit the teachers. "It had blackboards, paint suits, dress-up clothes, sand tables, all the correct equipment."[53] Nelson Pierce, who worked in the Usher's Office, was surprised one day to receive a request for a pregnant rabbit from Jackie—"She thought it would be nice if the children could see a mother rabbit and her babies." A white rabbit with pink eyes named Annabelle was produced by the president of the local Rabbit Breeders' Association and duly gave birth to four babies. There was also a homemade hatchery for chicks. The children had a playground hidden underneath the trees near the President's West Wing office, with a treehouse, a swing, a slide and even a trampoline. The Kennedy menagerie was kept there— the ponies, Macaroni and Tex, dogs, lambs and guinea pigs.

"The school was very much in her [Jackie's] mind," Susan Wilson said. "It wasn't just something that somebody had organized and two very competent people ran, she was always thinking about it and how she could supplement the curriculum . . . When guests came to the White House or a helicopter landed on the South Lawn, the children all went down to watch the VIP who was arriving . . . I remember once there was a delegation of Native Americans who came to the White House in their full regalia and Jackie arranged for them to come and see the children . . ."[54]

The children always came first with their parents when they were in the White House. As John got older both of them would run into their father's room while he was having breakfast; afterward Caroline walked with him to his office, carrying her brown paper lunchbag before she took the elevator up to her school on the third floor. At quiet moments in his office, if he heard the children on the lawn, Jack would clap his hands and they would run in for the candy he always kept for them. In the evenings when he finished work John and Caroline would swim with him in the White House pool; John was just learning but according to her nurse, Caroline was "a wonderful swimmer." Her father "took great pride in

her when she came home with prizes for swimming. Especially if she beat someone a little older than herself, which she often did . . ."[55] Jackie often joined the
children for lunch, and if she and Jack had a quiet dinner together they would
have the children with them. Jackie always kept an hour for them at six thirty and
Jack made sure that he saw them, however briefly. "No matter what big or small
function that the President had," Maud Shaw recalled, "he always made time to
visit his children to say goodnight and if possible to hear their prayers. He never
missed."[56]

Equally sacred to Jackie was "nap time," when Jack came upstairs after his ritual
1:30 P.M. swim to rest. "Mrs. Kennedy dropped everything, no matter how important, to join her husband," West wrote. The bedroom doors were closed, no telephone calls put through. Jackie had her husband to herself. As she spent less and
less time in the White House, such occasions became increasingly rare.

Jackie revolutionized entertainment at the White House, cutting down on the
state dinners of the Eisenhower years and limiting them to visiting heads of state
or important foreigners. The huge E-shaped formal dining table was replaced with
round tables with organdy cloths and beautiful table settings of vermeil flatware,
informal flower arrangements in vermeil baskets and simple stemware specially ordered from the Morgantown Glassware Guild in West Virginia (in the interests of
West Virginian poverty, Jackie even refused the offer of free glassware from a big
east coast manufacturer). Black tie replaced white tie, pomp and circumstance
gave way to an atmosphere of informality and—carefully planned—spontaneity.
Instead of being stiff affairs state occasions became glamorous and imaginative,
like the alfresco dinner given on July 11, 1961, for the President of Pakistan, Ayub
Khan, at George Washington's former home, Mount Vernon, romantically situated above the Potomac.

Jackie's imagination had been fired by the idea of holding a summer fête at the
founding father's house. She led a reconnaissance party there and discovered apparently insurmountable difficulties: the house was open to the public during the
day but no official function had been held there since a small luncheon party for
Queen Marie of Romania in 1926. Kitchen and toilet facilities were rudimentary;
lighting and refrigeration virtually nonexistent. The White House party—except
Jackie—were prepared to rule out the idea but, Tish wrote in her memoir of the
occasion, "one look at Jackie's animated face and I knew we were all doomed . . ."[57]
The food would have to be cooked at the White House and transported on Army
trucks along the Memorial Parkway; Jackie and her chef worked out a simple meal
with a main dish that would improve on standing, and other courses and side
dishes that would be easy to assemble in primitive conditions. Generators, tables,
chairs, china, linen, crystal and staff, including twenty-two butlers, would have to
be transported from the White House to Mount Vernon; the guests were to arrive
by boat along the Potomac. A thirty-by-fifty-foot open-sided marquee was to be
erected on the lawn in case of rain, portable lavatories provided, and the foliage
sprayed against bugs. "As those around her doubted that we could pull it off,
Jackie remained serene and confident in her staff's abilities. Her innate control of
endless details and superb sense of organization were accompanied by a quiet lit-

tle phrase of iron, '*Of course* it can be done . . .'" Tish wrote. Even the President took an interest, with a memo about the flowers: "See that they have all the Lowestoft bowls in the house filled with flowers—very low—"[58]

On arrival, guests were served mint juleps in silver cups (orange juice for the Muslims in the party), treated to a reenactment of a Revolutionary War drill, including a barrage of blanks fired at an unsuspecting press corps (the *New York Times* correspondent waved a white handkerchief in mock surrender), then served dinner in the blue and yellow tent decorated with garlands of smilax, white and yellow ribbons by Tiffany's window designer, at tables with yellow cloths and centerpieces of delphiniums, yellow carnations, lemon lilies and cornflowers from Bunny Mellon's garden. After dinner the National Symphony Orchestra performed in the concert area, which was lit with citronella candles to end an enchanting evening.

Other memorable dinners included one that winter given for the Governor of Puerto Rico, at which the great Pablo Casals played in the White House. Leonard Bernstein was among the guests. He compared it with a dinner under the previous administration,

> when the food was ordinary, and the wines were inferior and you couldn't smoke . . . [At] the Casals dinner in November 1961, you were served very good drinks first . . . there were ashtrays everywhere . . . When you do line up you are in a less querulous mood because you have a drink and a cigarette; when the moment comes for you to greet the President and First Lady, two ravishing people appear in the doorway who couldn't be more charming if they tried, who make you feel utterly welcome, even with a huge gathering . . . The food is marvelous, the wines are delicious, there are cigarettes on the table, people are laughing, laughing out loud, telling stories, jokes, enjoying themselves, glad to be there . . . You know, I've never seen so many happy artists in my life. It was a joy to watch it . . .[59]

Only the Kennedys could have assembled under the same roof Casals, who had not performed in America since 1928 because of American support for Franco, and Charles Lindbergh, ostracized for his support of the totalitarian regimes in the Second World War. One equally extraordinary evening was the dinner for all living Nobel laureates, the first ever at the White House, on April 29, 1962. The actor Fredric March gave readings from Hemingway, General George Marshall and Sinclair Lewis. Among the guests was writer William Styron, a friend of the Kennedys, who recalled, starstruck, the moment when to a fanfare of trumpets and the sound of "Hail to the Chief," the couple appeared. "Jack and Jackie actually *shimmered*."[60]

Jackie admitted the great American public to her project but on her own terms—and at a price. In the summer of 1961 she collaborated with Hugh Sidey, one of her husband's favorite journalists, on a big feature for *Life* describing her plans, which contributed to the restoration project. Possibly inspired by *Life*'s incursion, CBS producer Perry Wolff suggested a TV tour of the White House to show the nation what was being achieved there. "Perry Wolff came to me with the idea," Blair Clark, then general manager and vice president of CBS and a Harvard friend of Jack's, recalled. "He was saying he had run into an obstacle, which was that she [Jackie] didn't want to do it. He knew that I knew Jackie and JFK— we were in the same class at college and belonged to the same despised Spee Club. [Neither Clark nor Jack, he said, were 'crazy about their club mates at the Spee,' who blackballed Torby MacDonald because he was Irish.] I went down to Washington to see her, talked with her and then with JFK, who had doubts as to whether she should do it. I said she would do it well and it would be good for them . . . I thought she did it fine. We had to amplify her voice so people could understand what she was saying . . . JFK turned up while we were filming. He was pleased with it and it was a big hit."[61]

By today's standards, Jackie's performance was amateur: she moved stiffly, her manner was demure and her voice ever more girlish by the minute. Norman Mailer wrote an extremely critical piece for *Esquire*. Derogatory as it was, though, it was really, as Diana Vreeland told Cecil Beaton "a violent love letter" to Jackie. Mailer himself admitted that his pride had been hurt by what he saw as a series of rebuffs from her. She had liked his favorable article on Jack published three weeks before the presidential election and had written to him to tell him so, "a nice letter, generous in its praise, accurate in its details." Mailer, "in Napoleonic mood," wrote back to her of his hopes to do a biography of the Marquis de Sade and "the odd, strange honor of the man."[62] Jackie, seeing the perils of involving herself in discussions about de Sade with Mailer, wisely did not reply.

Over the New Year 1961–62, *Esquire* suggested Mailer do a story on Jackie; his request for an interview was turned down. Mailer acted like a rejected lover. He admired her, saw her as a potential ally against reactionary philistinism and prudery: "I liked her and thought she would understand what one was talking about, because as First Lady she was queen of the arts, she was our Muse if she chose to be." He had already thought she had "an odd public voice," unlike when he had heard her in her Hyannis Port sitting room, when it had been "clear, merry and excellent." "But the voice I was hearing now," he wrote, "the public voice, now after a year in the White House, had grown undeniably worse . . ." He called it "self-conscious parody." (Watching newsreels of Jackie in the White House, the voice ever more like the little-girl whisper of Marilyn Monroe, one is tempted to shout out loud, "Come off it, Jackie.") ". . . she was a phony . . . a royal phony. There was something very difficult and dangerous she was trying from deep within herself to do, dangerous not to her safety but to her soul. She was trying, I suppose, to be a proper First Lady, and it was her mistake."[63]

"He was right about the voice," Jackie later admitted.[64] But Mailer was also right about the phoniness of Jackie's First Lady act; he was right, too, about the danger that the White House act did to her soul. The persona she was presenting to the public had little to do with her real self. Charlie Bartlett's wonderful, eager, intellectual girl reporter was being submerged by the trappings of queendom.

CHAPTER ELEVEN

America's Queen

~

She looked beautiful, she was the best asset he could ever have had and on that Paris visit, my husband said, "The deck has shifted. We are now listening to the other side because the weight has changed." I mean it was a different ball game—de Gaulle and the French, really, that did it. And then I think gradually a lot of things changed . . .

—Robin Biddle Duke, wife of Angier Biddle Duke,
Chief of Protocol in the Kennedy White House[1]

It took only about three weeks [Tish Baldrige wrote] for those of us in the White House to realize that in Jacqueline Kennedy we had a huge star on our hands. Women were writing to the White House asking for the name of her brand of shampoo and exactly how many rollers she used when she went to bed, and did the President object? . . . The letters and gifts poured into the East Wing by the vanload, nine thousand a week . . . But we didn't realize the degree of Jackie's rising stardom until the state visit to Canada in May 1961. It was the Kennedys' first official foreign trip . . .[2]

Only a month before the Canadian trip, in mid-April 1961, John F. Kennedy had suffered the first major defeat of his political career in the disaster of the Bay of Pigs, the lowest but perhaps also the defining moment of his presidency. Since Fidel Castro's initially socialist revolution in Cuba at New Year 1959, the specter of a Communist-dominated island so close to America's shores had become an increasing factor in American defense thinking. Eisenhower had approved a CIA-inspired plan for an invasion force of Cuban exiles to topple Castro, a plan Kennedy inherited and which he cautiously approved. Since he had repeatedly attacked the Eisenhower administration during the election campaign for its apparent failure to do anything about Castro, he had in fact painted himself into a corner on the issue. He was concerned also about the possible effect of the spread of Cuban-style left-wing revolution in Latin America, undermining his cherished Alliance for Progress with the governments in the area. Just a few weeks before Kennedy's inauguration, Khrushchev had given a new Cold War dimension to the Cuban question in a speech on January 6, 1961, signaling his welcome to Castro as a new member of the Soviet bloc.

The Kennedys had spent the weekend of April 15–16 at Glen Ora. On Monday April 17, 1961, they returned to the White House where they were due to welcome the Greek Prime Minister to lunch. At 4:45 A.M. that same morning 1,400 CIA-trained Cuban exiles landed on the south coast of Cuba in an area known as the Bay of Pigs. By the next day, the messages from the beachhead were desperate. That evening a congressional reception was held as planned at the White House. Jack and Jackie appeared just after ten as the Marine Band played "Mr. Wonderful." Just before midnight, the President slipped away to attend a grim meeting of the inner circle in the Cabinet Room. The operation had been botched from start to finish; recently declassified documents reveal that the Soviets knew of it by "around April 9,"[3] a leak of which the CIA was aware but let the invasion proceed nonetheless. By 1 P.M. on April 19 the U.S. chiefs of staff had concluded there was nothing left to be done but rescue as many of the invaders as possible. Even that attempt was a failure; they succeeded in getting only 14 men away; 1,189 surrendered to Castro's forces.

Kennedy blamed himself for the fiasco and bravely took the responsibility for it at a press conference a few days later. "There's an old saying," he said, "that victory has a hundred fathers and defeat is an orphan. I am the responsible officer of this government." Privately he blamed not only himself but those he saw as having poorly advised him. The two leading CIA officials, Allen Dulles and Richard Bissell, were quietly removed from their jobs and from then on Kennedy distrusted the military top brass—with the exception of General Maxwell Taylor: "Those sons-of-bitches with all the fruit salad just sat there nodding, saying it would work," he complained. From now on the man whose loyalty and judgment he knew he could depend upon, his brother Bobby, would be present at all crucial meetings. The humiliation of the Bay of Pigs meant that Castro and Cuba became an obsession with the Kennedy brothers.

Jack and Jackie were scheduled to make their visit to Canada on May 17. On May 11 they flew to Palm Beach, and it was there that on May 12 Jack summoned Max Jacobson to tell him of his concern about Jackie's mental and physical condition, "chronic depression and headaches," and whether she would be able to take the strain of the forthcoming Canadian trip followed in June by their visits to Paris, Vienna, for the summit with Khrushchev, and London. Jacobson, who administered to her the same treatment he gave Jack, described her as "very unhappy" and complaining of a severe migraine.

Her moods and health seem to have been volatile. In February and March she had spent a great deal of time at Glen Ora and was certainly well enough to hunt. After the Kennedys' first weekend there in mid-February, she had complained that a cold prevented her going back to Washington on Monday but she had been seen riding that Saturday and hunting with the Orange County Hunt on Monday.

On Tuesday, showing no signs of a cold, she returned to Washington in time to attend a pre-wedding dinner at Joe Alsop's to celebrate his forthcoming marriage to Susan Mary Patten, the chic, well-born widow of diplomat Bill Patten. In February, *Time* noted, she had spent nine days in Virginia, with only a brief trip back to Washington to pick up John Jr. In March she spent every weekend at Glen Ora, apart from one in Florida with the Wrightsmans when she lunched with Henry du Pont. The Radziwills arrived on March 12 and went to Glen Ora; on the fifteenth Jackie gave a glamorous dinner for them with seventy-eight guests, and the following week she and Lee went on a three-day jaunt to New York, where Diana Vreeland gave a party for them and a radiantly smiling Jackie was photographed escorted to the City Center ballet by Adlai Stevenson. Easter was spent in Palm Beach. By April 4 Jackie was back in Washington to meet the British Prime Minister, Harold Macmillan, and his wife, Lady Dorothy, and for a consultation with Clark Clifford, no doubt about her White House restoration plans, before going down to Glen Ora for a long weekend. She returned to Washington for the visit of Chancellor Adenauer of the Federal Republic of Germany and a private dinner before escaping to Virginia once again.

Then the Bay of Pigs crisis intervened; not only did Jackie have privately to support her husband, shattered by unaccustomed failure, but with him she had to maintain the public façade: dinner at the Greek embassy on the fateful April 19, followed the next day by the kind of occasion Jackie most dreaded, a tea at the White House for more than three hundred women, the wives of the American Society of Newspaper Editors. The event was made more distasteful by the circumstances of the aftermath of the Bay of Pigs. Once again Jackie retreated with Caroline to Glen Ora on the weekend, while on Sunday her husband helicoptered down to Camp David to confer with ex-President Eisenhower.

The following week there was a state dinner for the President of Tunisia and Madame Bourguiba, at which Jackie looked stunning in a one-shoulder draped chiffon dress, then the usual Glen Ora weekend, a private dinner; superficially there was nothing in Jackie's schedule to indicate a period of unusual stress.

Jackie's regal mask concealed a personality subject to great strain and periods of collapse. There were times when she felt inadequate and unable to cope, leaning heavily on Jack. As Arthur Schlesinger revealed, she would cry, "Oh, Jack, I'm so sorry for you that I'm such a dud." and he would reply, "I love you as you are."[4] Robin Douglas-Home, nephew of the Kennedys' friend William, a young man intensely sensitive to women and the lover, among others, of Princess Margaret, had several long, intimate conversations with Jackie during the White House years and after. He first met her at a small dinner party. The contrast between Jackie's behavior and her husband's was marked. "He was mixing easily with the guests, looking as if he were enjoying every minute, sparkling, throwing probing questions at everyone, aggressive, handsome, while his wife sat mainly in the shadows, not mixing much, preferring to sit and talk at length with one person rather than mingle with her guests . . ." Jackie appeared to him as an enigmatic, slightly distant, reticent, politely attentive, almost chocolate-box figure. It was only some months later in hours of late-night conversation that he discovered the tensions and frustrations raging beneath that smooth surface. He described those hours with Jackie, pouring out her heart, as "the most emotionally disturbing I have ever had . . ." It seemed to him that she had been "literally projected into a position where she could rarely, if ever, be completely herself, or do anything, go anywhere, say anything, laugh, cry, drink, or even *talk* as she wished, without the fear of becoming the subject of public comment, political gossip or social tittle-tattle . . . And that although all this sickened her, she was forced to put up with it because of her loyalty to her husband. She seemed the original 'bird in the gilded cage,' too intelligent, too proud and too stubborn to accept her captivity as part of the price she must pay.

"At one moment she was misunderstood, frustrated and helpless. The next moment, without any warning, she was the royal, loyal First Lady to whom it was almost a duty to bow, to pay medieval obeisance. Then again, without any warning, she was deflating someone with devastating barbs for being such a spaniel as to treat her as the First Lady and deriding the pomp of politics, the snobbery of a social climber . . ."[5]

He sensed the conflict within her, the difficulty of trying to "reconcile her deep, personal distaste for her public role as 'First Lady and First Mother' with her overwhelming private devotion to her husband and children and her determination not to fail them." The day before Jack had telephoned from Washington; Douglas-Home had heard all the rumors about their marital difficulties but he believed that "the delight with which she recounted their conversation was not simulated. It was a touching, almost childlike demonstration of a magnificent passion which she could, it seemed to me, describe more easily to me than she could to her husband . . ."[6]

Jack and Jackie remained emotionally twin icebergs, as she had originally described them. Her inhibitions in her closest relationships led both her husbands to complain of her "coldness"; she found it easier to express herself on paper, as a love letter she wrote to Jack in October 1963, in the last few weeks of his life, demonstrated. Jack himself, although superficially more outgoing, was reserved in return. Her failure to communicate with him, and he with her as easily as he appeared to with other women, was a source of real frustration, as was his unconscious relegation of her to a domestic level when she was clearly intellectually capable of so much more. He treated her, she later wrote, as "a Victorian wife." And then there was the pain his infidelities caused her, which she gallantly concealed. She only confessed the hurt in the last decade of her life to her friend Carly Simon.[7] Yet in her long-running battle to be number one in her husband's life, she was aided, ironically, by the huge celebrity she both loathed and enjoyed.

The first indication that Jackie was becoming a star of the first magnitude outside her own country came on the Canadian visit for which Jack and Jacobson had so anxiously prepared her. The Canadian ambassador to Washington had warned that the Canadians were not a demonstrative people; even Queen Elizabeth II was habitually disappointed by the cool reception she received in Ottawa. Yet the route along which the Kennedy motorcade drove from Ottawa airport to the

Governor-General's residence, Rideau Hall, where they were to stay, was lined with cheering, applauding crowds, and, like a groundswell, rhythmic chants of "Jack-ie! Jack-ie!" At a formal state dinner for a hundred guests "every head snapped around as though at a parade-ground command to admire the entrance of Jackie Kennedy in her pure white silk sheath," *Time* reported. The next day the massed members of the Canadian Parliament banged their desks in a traditional salute as she entered. Given the sensitive undertones of normal relations between the U.S. and Canada, the Kennedys' reception was extraordinary.

It was just one month after the Bay of Pigs disaster; Jack, eager to demonstrate his vigor, overexerted himself planting a ceremonial tree and damaged his back. By the time he was on the way home he could barely move and his aides radioed ahead for crutches to meet the plane. Dr. Jacobson's renewed ministrations were needed to prepare the President and his wife for the demands of their forthcoming European tour to Paris, Vienna and London. Summoned to Washington on May 23 he flew down that night with Jackie's friend, Mark Shaw, and at 11 A.M. drove to the White House with his medical bag disguised in an attaché case. He saw Jackie first in the private quarters; she was in comparatively good spirits but "apprehensive about the impending European trip and its strenuous schedule." Jacobson administered "her treatment," presumably the accustomed dose of amphetamines mixed with vitamins and other mysterious substances. Then he went to the President, whom he found lying on his bed, resting his back, worrying about how it would withstand the hours of standing and sitting he would have to undergo in Europe. Dr. Travell had been numbing it with ethyl chloride spray, a technique Jacobson dismissed as out-of-date and ineffective: "I demonstrated an exercise to strengthen the back muscles," he wrote. "I then administered the treatment, not only to relieve his local discomfort but to also provide him with additional strength to cope with stress." The President got up and claimed instant improvement, telling Jacobson he wanted him to accompany them to Europe next week.[8]

Driven by pain and the demands of his life, Jack Kennedy was reckless with drugs, using numbing sprays and Novocaine administered by Dr. Travell, dosing himself with cortisone, using Jacobson's injections "to relieve stress," and secretly obtaining other drugs as well. A worried Jackie showed Jacobson a phial of Demerol she had found in her husband's bathroom. Demerol, a powerful painkiller mixing pethidine with paracetamol, was highly addictive, Jacobson told Jackie, and asked who had prescribed it. It turned out that Jack had gone behind the backs of his regular team of doctors and obtained it through a Secret Service man. Jacobson remained in Washington for four days, treating Jack and Jackie "several times" before returning to New York.

On May 31, fortified by Dr. Feelgood's treatments, the first President of the jet age and his First Lady flew off in their sleek new plane, Air Force One, designed for the Kennedys, for whom only the best would do, by the famous Raymond Loewy. Booked as the only passengers on an Air France plane for Paris, unmentioned among the official Kennedy party, went Dr. Jacobson, his bag of secrets, and his wife. Even before they left, Jacobson had been called to attend the

President, who had felt severe twinges in his back on the flight from Washington to New York. On Saturday evening, the day of their arrival, he was called to attend Jackie after the gala evening at Versailles. The whole Kennedy entourage was in high spirits after their magnificent reception by de Gaulle. As for Jackie, who had achieved a triumphant success, Jacobson said, "It was most unusual to find her so loquacious in contrast to her usual reserved attitude toward me." After treating her, he went in to the President, who told him he wanted to see him early next morning.

It was, as Angier Biddle Duke who accompanied the Kennedys to Paris said, that trip which really impressed on Jack Kennedy his wife's star quality and the huge political asset she represented for him. Kennedy himself was a clumsy linguist so he was all the more in awe of Jackie's ability to speak French, and the blend of historical knowledge and charm that captivated her European hosts. In France, awareness of Jackie's French ancestry and the year she had spent at the Sorbonne warmed the hearts of ordinary Parisians, while the French upper classes, notoriously dismissive of Americans, knew of her as the delightful Jacqueline Bouvier. Among the guests at the gala dinner at Versailles, was Jackie's "flirt" from her student days, Paul de Ganay, invited at her special request.

Jacqueline, Vicomtesse de Ribes, the most elegant woman in Paris, arranged for the world's top hairdresser, Alexandre, to do Jackie's hair. Jackie had laid careful undercover plans for clothes to dazzle the French. According to Givenchy, she had instructed him, via Mary Gallagher, "to prepare a complete wardrobe for this special trip. And this had to be kept a secret . . . Only at the last minute—that means one hour before Mrs. Kennedy left for Versailles, were we allowed to say that Mrs. Kennedy's wardrobe was made by us." Givenchy had made one coat and one dress in pink wool, and the beautiful evening dress which she wore to the banquet at Versailles, which, as Jackie later told him, de Gaulle had greeted with the words, "This evening, Madame, you are looking like a Watteau . . ."[9] Wearing French couture on this occasion could be excused as "a compliment to her French hosts." The stunning pink straw lace gown in which she appeared at the official reception at the Élysée Palace was also, secretly, French in inspiration. When the press released a sketch of her official Cassini-designed gown for the occasion, the wife of a high French official discovered that she had ordered the identical dress from Pierre Cardin's spring collection, "so identical that the Paris couture couldn't believe their eyes," as the watchful *Women's Wear Daily* remarked. But the time for criticism was past. *Time* dubbed her "First Lady of Fashion." In the one hundred days since Jack had taken office, Jackie had taken the world by storm. She had shown the world that the wife of an American president could be beautiful, stylish, intelligent, cosmopolitan, elegant. Not for the last time, she made America proud of her.

For the young American President visiting the towering General de Gaulle on his home ground was somewhat akin to Daniel stepping into the lions' den. The French were the most anti-American of the European peoples: the CIA-inspired Bay of Pigs attack on those icons of the left, Fidel Castro and Che Guevara, had enraged the intellectuals and the French left, while the impression of presidential weakness and indecision left by the disaster needed to be counteracted to shore up the Western Alliance in the face of the threat represented by the Soviets, principally over Berlin. Khrushchev had described the city as "a running sore." Surrounded by Communist East Germany it had been divided into East and West, with the West occupied by the three western powers, America, Britain and France, the East by the Soviets. The eastern sector was hemorrhaging through emigration to the capitalist West; to counteract this Khrushchev threatened to sign a peace treaty with the East Germans and cut off western access to the city. He did not exclude armed confrontation with its concomitant specter of nuclear war. The defense of Cuba against U.S. invasion was also high on his agenda.

From the British embassy, Sir Piers Dixon reported to the Earl of Home, British Foreign Secretary, on the first day of the visit:

> President Kennedy's visit to Paris got off to a good start. His speech at the airport on arrival, though perhaps a little too fulsomely flattering for English tastes, has gone down well with the French press. There has been a genuine surge of popular interest. Most people, despite the normal widespread tendency to criticize America and American policy, have been impressed with the charm and spontaneity of the young President and his wife. Mrs. Kennedy is, of course, receiving full press treatment with frequent references to her student days on the Boulevard St. Michel.[10]

Politically, not much was achieved, but on a personal level the visit was a success. "It is rapidly becoming known," the British Minister, Anthony Rumbold, reported to the Foreign Office, "in official circles and in society that General de Gaulle was impressed by Mr. Kennedy's intelligence, lucidity, and grasp of international affairs . . . It is recognized that he [de Gaulle] is a severe judge of character and that it is no mean achievement to have impressed him."[11]

"Thanks in large part to Jackie Kennedy at her prettiest," *Time's* political editor reported, "Kennedy charmed the old soldier into unprecedented flattering toasts and warm gestures of friendship." Acknowledging his wife's triumph, Jack famously introduced himself to the French press as "the man who accompanied Jacqueline Kennedy to Paris."[12]

For Jackie, the crowning moment of the visit was the magical evening at Versailles, with the banquet in the Galerie des Glaces, followed by a ballet, first performed for Louis XV, in the restored theater of the palace, with flaming torches as spotlights—just as it would have been in his day. As the motorcade drove home through the gardens of Versailles, the lead car stopped by a magnificent illuminated fountain. Jack and Jackie got out and walked to it, standing there romantically hand in hand, unconscious of the distant presence of their entourage.

The Kennedy entourage left Paris on June 3 for Vienna, where the future, not the past, was uppermost. Kennedy had come to the summit to meet Khrushchev with high hopes of achieving a détente in relations with the Soviet Union, over nuclear arms, and, above all, Berlin. Through Bobby he had expressed as much, using a private channel to Moscow. He wanted to prove to the Soviet leader that he was his own man, not in the clutches of the Pentagon hawks but also determined enough to stand up for Berlin. He wanted, too, to improve his image as a world leader with the American people, which had been so dented by the Bay of Pigs failure.

It was, therefore, with high hopes that Kennedy, fired up by Jacobson's recent treatment, "burst" out of the front door of the U.S. embassy in Vienna and ran down the steps to greet Nikita Khrushchev at 12:45 P.M. on May 3. Discussions on the first day did not go well: Khrushchev was firm over his plans for Berlin and did not intend to back down, even as Kennedy made clear American commitment to the occupied city. "If you want war," Khrushchev concluded, "that is your problem."[13]

Jackie, however, met no difficulties with either Mr. or Mrs. Khrushchev. After touring Vienna with the homely Mrs. Khrushchev, she charmed the Russian leader at the state banquet at the Schonbrunn Palace while enthusiastic crowds chanted her name outside. Khrushchev complimented her on her pink-beaded white evening gown and drew his chair noticeably close to her as they chatted about horses, Ukrainian folk dances and Russian space dogs. Khrushchev promised to send her a puppy and he did.

At the meeting the following morning Khrushchev's bullying and aggressive stance shook Kennedy to the core. The Soviet Chairman threatened the American President over Berlin, without a thought to ways of decreasing tension, in the hope of which Kennedy had come to Vienna. The possibility of war over Berlin was raised with neither side backing down. "It will be a cold winter," Kennedy told Khrushchev as he left.[14] Not only was Kennedy now looking at the prospect of an apocalyptic nuclear war, but he felt personally humiliated, certain that the Soviet leader thought him weak, indecisive, inexperienced. Ten minutes later he told James "Scotty" Reston of the *New York Times*, "He savaged me."[15] He was still reeling from the experience when he met Harold Macmillan in London the following day: "The President was completely overwhelmed by the ruthlessness and barbarity of the Russian Chairman," the British Prime Minister told the Queen. "It reminded me in a way of Lord Halifax or Neville Chamberlain trying to hold a conversation with Herr Hitler. For the first time in his life Kennedy met a man who was impervious to his charm."[16] Bobby thought that, in many ways, this had been a revealing moment in his brother's political education, that for the first time he had met someone with whom he could not exchange ideas in a meaningful way, and that it had been a salutary shock.

Joe Alsop, who spoke to Kennedy in London where the presidential party arrived on June 5 from Vienna, thought the same. Much as he admired Kennedy and had supported his bid for the presidency, he had always had the reservation that, as he told Elspeth Rostow, the brilliant wife of Kennedy's special adviser, Walt M. Rostow, Kennedy had exhibited an "apparent failure prior to his election to calculate the real dimensions of the burden he was seeking. I think that he didn't really face up to the appalling moral burden that an American president now has to carry until Vienna when he met with Khrushchev who asked for surrender and threatened war."[17] In London, at the party to celebrate Christina Radziwill's christening, "the President, barely back from Vienna, sort of shoved me into a corner and talked for fifteen minutes in a tense, new way about what he had just been through ... After that, it was when, I think, he really began to be president in the full sense of the word."[18]

At the party Susan Mary Alsop, dazzling, according to her husband, in a bright pink silk Dior dress she had just bought in Paris, remembered that neither Jack nor Jackie betrayed the slightest sign that anything had gone wrong—"They had such style."[19] Yet Jackie, on the flight over to London, had appeared very down, like the rest of the Kennedy entourage. Jacobson's ministrations to both Kennedys at the Radziwills' Buckingham Place house enabled them to put on a brave face for the top British officials and London society, who crowded the Radziwill house after the christening.

The plan for the London visit had been cooked up by the President and the Prime Minister at the time of Macmillan's visit to the White House in April. It had been planned to include a private aspect in order not to offend America's European partners—particularly de Gaulle—who had always been suspicious of the Anglo-American relationship. The centerpiece was to be the Radziwill christening and subsequent party; the Prime Minister would give an informal luncheon and the Queen a dinner at Buckingham Palace. The Macmillan lunch for twenty at Admiralty House was almost a family affair, crowded with cousins, who would have been Jack's relations by marriage had Billy and Kathleen Hartington not been killed: the Duke of Devonshire and his wife, Deborah, with Kathleen's mother-in-law, the Dowager Duchess of Devonshire, and the Ormsby-Gores, David and Sissie (David, also a cousin, was soon to be announced British Ambassador to Washington). Macmillan was related by marriage to all of them, through his wife, Lady Dorothy, the Duke of Devonshire's sister. The Foreign Secretary, the Earl of Home, was the elder brother of William Douglas Home.

The dinner at Buckingham Palace that evening was, Macmillan recorded in his diary "a very pleasant party," this time with royal relations: the Duke of Edinburgh's sister, Princess Margarita of Hohenlohe-Langenburg, and her husband, Earl Mountbatten of Burma with his daughter and son-in-law, Lord and Lady Brabourne, and friends of the Kennedys the Ormsby-Gores, the Homes, the American ambassador, David Bruce, and his wife Evangeline, with Eunice representing the Kennedy side. Lee and Stas were also invited—after some huffing and puffing about protocol, as Macmillan, who persisted in called them the Radzinskis, recorded.

> After much hesitation the Queen waived her rule about divorce. Prince and Princess Radzinski were invited, although they had two or three partners apiece to date. She was very unwilling to do this, or to put their names in the Court Circular. I think had the Kennedys been staying at the American Embassy, I could have advised the Queen to omit the Radzinskis. But since the President and Mrs. K. were actually staying with the Prince and Princess, it seemed impossible to do so ...[20]

According to Gore Vidal, Jack and Jackie were aware of the Queen's proposed veto on Stas and Lee. They had been asked beforehand by the Palace whom they would like to be invited. Jackie proposed the Radziwills, Princess Margaret, whom she wanted to meet, and Princess Marina of Kent, whom Jack remembered from his father's embassy days. The Palace had intimated that "Mr." and "Mrs." Radziwill, as divorcees, could not be invited, then—presumably at Macmillan's urging—backed down. "Anyway," Jackie joked, "the Queen had her revenge. No Margaret, no Marina, no one except every Commonwealth minister of agriculture they could find. The Queen was pretty heavy going." Jackie thought the Queen "resented" her—in all probability Her Majesty was somewhat intimidated by Mrs. Kennedy's famous sophistication—and that Prince Philip was "nice but nervous." "The Queen was human only once," Jackie said. She had been telling Her Majesty about the Kennedy state visit to Canada and the rigors of being on view at all hours: "The Queen looked rather conspiratorial and said, 'One gets crafty after a while and learns how to save oneself.' Then she said, 'You like pictures?' And she marched Jackie down a long gallery, stopping at a Van Dyck to say, 'That's a good horse.' "[21]

The Queen's Lord Chamberlain, Lord Scarbrough, who at that time still exercised the right of theater censorship, vetoed a skit in a forthcoming revue, with a young actress in pillbox and bouffant impersonating Jackie and singing:

> Well, I'm doing my best to be everyone's choice,
> Playing Caroline's mother with Marilyn's voice . . .

Jack returned to the United States after the dinner at Buckingham Palace. Jackie stayed on for two days in London, then left for a private trip to Greece with Stas and Lee, where they stayed at the villa of shipping magnate Markos Nomikos and cruised around the Aegean islands aboard his yacht. She was back in Washington by June 15, Jack having returned on crutches from a weekend at the Wrightsmans' house in Palm Beach.

⁓

Jackie's Paris state visit made her an international superstar. She was, as a UPI reporter put it, "news twenty-four hours a day," and *Women's Wear Daily* could have been rechristened *What Jackie Wears Daily*. In the three years she spent in the White House, barely a day went by when the American woman's Bible did not report her clothes, accessories, even shoes. The "Jackie look" was a regular selling point on Seventh Avenue, where everything she was photographed wearing was translated into cheaper copies. Even behind the Iron Curtain a Leningrad fashion magazine carried advertisements for "Jackie look" clothes, and the Polish magazine *Swait* wrote that she had "entered the group of a few women in the world who, today, as in times past, set the style and tone of their epoch . . . but never before has her influence been so far-flung or so quickly disseminated. The face and silhouette of Jackie are known to all people all over the civilized world."

It was at this point that the Kennedy Chief of Protocol, worldly, sophisticated

Angier Biddle Duke, told his future wife, Robin, "The deck has shifted."[22] The balance of power within the White House and the Kennedy family had tilted subtly toward Jackie, both in the eyes of her husband (which was all important to her) and the Kennedy entourage. If Jack was the Sun King, Jackie was by now most definitely America's Queen.

Gore Vidal recalls that Jackie had said, " 'I never saw Jack until we got to the White House. He was always away and gone.' I don't even think he thought anything about her until they got there and he began to see pictures of her in the paper, this glamorous woman who happened to be married to him. And he started—I remember up at Hyannis Port, calling her 'the sex symbol'—'Will you tell the sex symbol lunch is ready?,' you know. He found that pretty funny and I think it awakened his interest."[23]

Interest—but not passion. By re-creating her image as regal and glamorous, Jackie had achieved a new importance and respect in her husband's eyes. Once, shortly after her marriage, she had overheard old Joe, Jack and Bobby discussing Jack's career: "They spoke of me," she told George McGovern later, "as if I weren't a person, just a thing, just a sort of asset, like Rhode Island . . ."[24] Jackie-as-asset had turned out far bigger than they had envisaged.

Their relationship remained complex. Jack was coming closer to Jackie's idealized Black Jack—the dashing womanizer who still came home to envelop his family with love. The birth of his children had awakened a strong paternal streak in him, not only for Caroline and John but for his Kennedy nephews and nieces, his godchildren, all children. He spoiled Jackie, propping her up when she felt vulnerable, allowing her the freedom to do as she liked. But he would not, and could not, give up his sexual habits; nor did he feel the least bit guilty about them. As Lee was to tell Cecil Beaton in June 1968, after the news reached London that Bobby had been shot in Los Angeles: "Jack used to play around & I knew exactly what he was up to & would tell him so. And he'd have absolutely no guilty conscience & said, 'I love her deeply & have done everything for her. I've no feeling of letting her down because I've put her foremost in everything.' "[25]

Jack had anticipated that he would have to restrain his sexual adventures when he became President, but protected by his loyal staff, his wife and the press, his office merely added to his attraction and meant that he could have virtually any woman he wanted. Jackie's frequent absences gave him plenty of opportunity. A study of the Secret Service logs over the period of the Kennedy presidency shows that Jackie spent a great deal more time away from the White House than she was there, mostly alone or with the children at Glen Ora or Hyannis Port, or on overseas trips with Lee. As Lee said, Jackie regularly left the White House on Friday afternoon for Virginia and did not return until Monday or later. Jack never left the White House until Saturday. Jackie spent almost all the steamy summer months out of Washington. For instance, the first part of June 1961 was devoted to the state visit to France, Vienna and London, followed by the vacation in Greece. She returned to the White House for one night before going down to Glen Ora with Jack for the debutante ball given by Bunny Mellon for her daughter at Upperville on June 16. She was back in Washington for the following week, conferring with

Henry du Pont about the White House restoration and entertaining the Japanese Prime Minister, Mr. Ikeda. She was at Glen Ora for the first ten days of July, returning in time for the dinner in honor of President Ayub Khan at Mount Vernon on July 11, a private dinner on the twelfth at the White House for old friends— Senator and Mrs. Gore, Bill Walton and Charlie Bartlett—and a dinner at the Mayflower Hotel on the thirteenth. She was away for the rest of the month, including her thirty-second birthday, celebrated with Jack at Hyannis Port, then throughout August and for over half of the first part of September until the eighteenth when she returned for a week before leaving with the President for Newport until the beginning of October.[26]

Jackie was a rebel and a free spirit at heart, and the White House seemed claustrophobic over extended periods. "You're never alone there," she told Gore Vidal. "You sit in a room and try to write a letter and someone comes in."[27] Schooled by Black Jack she could close her eyes to what Jack was up to when she was not with him, but his blatant pursuit of women in her own circle at their private parties was different. "He did it. It's amazing, he used to do it in front of her," said a well-known New York debutante several years younger than Jackie. "In New York his great friend, one of his ex-girls, his age, organized an after-theater party. And he obviously had said to this Flo Smith, 'Can you get me a bunch of young nice girls?' Not tarts but nice girls and so Flo Smith, to my astonishment, rang me and I had the flu—she rang me and said, 'The President and Mrs. Kennedy are coming. Would you like to come to the party?' And I thought, This is strange but why not? There must be a reason, you see. And I thought, Flu or no flu, I'll go." And another great friend of mine was asked and the two of us were riveted so we both went. And there were about four or five other friends, single girls we knew also. And then Jack and Jackie came in and Flo came up to each one of us—I remember this like yesterday—and said, 'The President would like to speak to you.' And there was one of those pouffe things next to him, he was sitting in a chair, and Jackie was over there, and Flo said, 'Would you go and talk to the President?' So each one of us was led over for about ten minutes . . . I wasn't as enamoured of him as other people were. I mean, I didn't dislike him but I didn't think he was this great sex symbol. I got no message but I have to say equally he got absolutely no message from me. So it was mutual. But we got on and he started saying—teasing, 'I don't know why you continue with *Vogue*, it's such frippery.' And I said, 'Well, I notice you wrote an article for us recently and you got paid for it, so it can't be that tacky.' So, of course, my interview was finished and I was hauled back by Flo. And he asked for—I know exactly who won, who shall be nameless. But what fascinated us all was that Jackie was sitting there and he actually said to Flo, 'I'll take that one.' It was perfectly obvious and this was a very shy, divine girl really, heavenly girl, very shy, very pretty, very tall girl we all knew.

"So the next time I saw Jackie was when they asked me—to my astonishment again because I thought I hadn't made a very good impression—to a party at the White House, which was the last party before he was killed. I went with a great friend who still lives in Washington, a much older man, and we just sat there riveted by the whole thing because, again, she was waltzing around, and he would dance with somebody—he didn't dance with me, I got Lyndon Johnson—and he would dance with a girl for five minutes, he couldn't dance because of his back, and then they would disappear up in the elevator and then they'd be back in twenty minutes. We just sat there, my friend and I, just sat there watching this for a while. I was astounded. And she paid no attention . . .

"I think life with Kennedy must have been total hell because he never stopped, none of those [Kennedy] boys do. And they have to have every woman in the room. I remember when Kennedy was assassinated—I had this tiny flat just off Fifth Avenue and 80th Street. And the day after he was killed and everybody was watching the funeral I had four what you'd call 'widows' in my tiny sitting room— all married—because they couldn't cry their eyes out in front of their husbands, all of whom thought they had been the only one. I swear to you, and this is absolutely true, at this point it was chic-er not to have slept with the President than to have slept with him . . . So every time she [Jackie] walked into a room she must have known that half the women there had slept with him.

"One of the 'widows' who was in my apartment talked about it the whole time to anyone who would listen. She was snuck—I don't know if that's the word— into the White House in the back of a car, in the trunk of a car, and she was taken down to the swimming pool and he would join her for a swim . . . Then there was the famous Angie Dickinson who used to go up and down in the elevator at the Carlyle, you know, at the back, service elevator, and Marilyn Monroe . . . What I couldn't understand about all these women was that they must have known that they were the lollipop for the day and who wants to be used as a lollipop?"[28]

Demi Gates remembered how Jack Kennedy made no attempt at concealment of his pursuit of women in their social circle. "The one night I was there [at the White House]," he said "it was a party for Eugene Black. I think he [Jack] did the double—when you boff the mother and the daughter. Anyway, he leaves the room with the mother, then he leaves the room with the daughter like twenty minutes later . . . And at a party at Peggy Bancroft's in New York, where she had a little foyer going into this duplex, my friend comes out of the elevator and there is Jack Kennedy soul-kissing an Italian princess."[29] The woman in question moved in the highest stratosphere of the international jet set which so appealed to both Jack and Jackie. Another of Jack's high international society lovers, also an Italian princess, used to visit him at weekends at the White House when Jackie was not there.

People thought that Jackie did not mind Jack's infidelities because she showed no signs of doing so. Indeed, the President's notorious swimming pool frolics with the two secretaries known as "Fiddle" and "Faddle" did not worry her, but sleeping with her friends and women in her circle, did. As Robin Biddle Duke, who married Angier in May 1962, said, "She had a lot of reasons to be fragile and to feel fragile because it hurts . . . She marries Jack and he is the love of her life and he really does like, you know, fiddling around with other girls. I felt very sorry for her. Because public humiliation is devastating anyway. Everybody knew that Jack was naughty. I mean, it was something that wasn't talked about but I think this woman was put through a very great deal. I think she loved JFK and she always thought he loved her. In his way he did, but his love had certain reservations and hers was total."[30]

At this point in her life, isolated on her regal peak at the White House, Jackie was unable to unburden herself to anyone except Lee. Occasionally the sphinx-like front cracked. According to Anne Lincoln: "Mrs. Kennedy's mood swung rather more widely than one would have expected and there were times when she became quite confessional and would tell you things that in any other frame of mind she wouldn't give you any sign that she knew about. I mean that she had these sort of two faces . . ."[31]

She had little patience with women in general and with official women and newspaper women in particular. "She was not responsive to the other cabinet wives," Robin Biddle Duke recalled, "and she made it very tough for me because I was the wife of the Chief of Protocol and at receptions before big dinners there would only be the wives of cabinet ministers and of the cabinet ministers of the visiting chief of state. And if it was a head of state that interested her, like Haile Selassie, everybody was in a cluster on one side of the room and she would be on the other side with the big wheel, hopefully speaking French because she loved to speak French, and I would have to go over and take Mrs. Ball and say, 'Mrs. Kennedy, Mrs. Ball has not had a chance to speak to His Majesty,' and I'd try and be gracious about it and I knew she was just looking daggers at me. So it was kind of hard and I found those days very difficult and it was because really she thought they were all a bunch of dowdy dames."[32]

Jackie was not fond of what Tish Baldrige had called "hordes of women," and was repelled by what she saw as their intrusive interest in her. En route to a Senate Ladies Lunch in her honor, to which she had invited Puffin d'Oench, she told Puffin of her experiences as a Senator's wife at one of these functions when she and the other Senate wives were traditionally expected to change into Red Cross uniform. "She truly disliked those occasions," Puffin recalled. "Because the room in which they took their clothes off had no privacy, and some of the women crowded around to feel the material with their fingers, or stole glances at her to inspect her underwear. They were looking at her slip and the lace and the rest of it and she just felt that this was unspeakably awful . . . It must have been quite a sight," Puffin added, "since I suspect Jackie wore especially flossy things in anticipation of being seen partially undressed. At school and college, Jackie, unlike many others, was always modest, although I often saw her in a slip. We all teased her about having the flattest chest of anyone we knew."

On their return to the White House, Puffin recorded a touching instance of Jack's delight in his wife's appearance and his interest in what she wore. "We got back and Jack Kennedy came upstairs from the Oval Office because he liked to see what she was wearing. And he said, 'But you've taken your hat off, go get your hat and put it on.' So she did and she put on her little pillbox hat and he was delighted . . ."[33]

Deep down Jack Kennedy would probably have liked to be as good a husband to Jackie as he was a father to Caroline and John and, in his own way, he tried.

When asked by a friend why he played around, he replied seriously, "I can't help it." He shocked the eminently respectable, self-controlled British Prime Minister, Harold Macmillan, by confessing to him that if he didn't have sex at least once a day, he had a headache.[34] To the far less respectable Bobby Baker, secretary to the Senate Democrats and provider of favors for senators, he said, according to Baker, "I get a migraine headache if I don't get a strange piece of ass every day."[35] To Jack, easily bored in this as in everything else, variety was the spice of life: he not only liked different women but three-in-a-bed sessions, sometimes with hookers. "Dave [Powers] was involved in getting them. Dave would bring the girls in," recalled a Kennedy White House aide.[36] According to the Secret Service logs, appointments with women were made through Jack's old friend and closest personal aide, whose name appeared in the official record. When Teddy Kennedy was being publicly unfaithful, Jackie told a disconsolate Joan, "All Kennedy men are like that."

Jackie, however, kept hoping against hope that one day he would calm down, as she confessed to her friend Adlai Stevenson at the White House dinner for Eugene Black in March 1963: "I don't care how many girls [Jack sleeps with] as long as I know he knows it's wrong and I think he does now," she said, adding, more optimistically than the evidence for that evening warranted, "Anyway, that's all over for the present . . ."[37]

Jackie also revealed how traditionalist her husband was. "At night he won't let me ask questions—brushes them aside, gets irritated even when I talk with Tish on the phone and try and sneak in a little work—and sends me to the end of the corridor to the other phone." Being treated like the little woman was clearly not something she enjoyed; according to Stevenson, she went "on and on" about this aspect of their life.

Jackie liked publicly to needle Jack: her fits of pique and willfulness, her refusal to be nice to Senate wives, White House newswomen and obscure statesmen, her rebellion against "doing her duty" as other people saw it were her way of getting back at him. Earlier in the difficult years of her marriage she had had brief affairs—including, according to Gore Vidal, one with the actor William Holden—motivated by revenge as well as "plain stamp-collecting. Celebrities are invariably celebrity-mad." Vidal, and many of Jackie's friends, testify that she was "very interested in sex":[38] "Jackie was always fascinated by gossip about sex," Puffin d'Oench recalled.[39] She liked to flirt—"She liked to capture men," said a fellow New Yorker, not her friend. As she had told Nini Gore Auchincloss on the occasion of Nini's first marriage in the taboo-ridden fifties, "The great thing about marriage is you can have lunch with men."

She did not, however, as rumor had it, take sexual revenge on her husband while they were in the White House. "I can swear now that she didn't," said Benno Graziani, a close friend of Jackie and Lee and, despite working for *Paris-Match*, popular with their high-level international friends. "She was too afraid to. She was very dignified, she took her job very seriously and she didn't want to make some scandal . . . No, no, she was very serious when she was in the White House."

Asked how Jack and Jackie were getting on together in the White House years, Graziani replied, "Good. They loved each other, I must say . . . they like . . . they were very fond of each other. I think sexually something was wrong . . ."[40]

Jack's unsatisfactory sex life with Jackie was confirmed by another Kennedy intimate, with whom she had an affair after Jack's death. "I don't think she was ever really happy that much." Then, talking of the relationship between Jack and Jackie: "I don't think it was a terribly intimate and intense [one] ever . . . I think things got a lot better for her because she had a role in life and he admired that. She made a contribution as they went around the world but I don't think on a personal level . . . I mean, how could they when he was fucking other women every weekend? What are you talking about in terms of a close relationship? The guy's sexual appetite was too large for it ever to have worked . . ."[41]

Jack encouraged his staff to have sexual relationships, whether they were married or not. "Everybody on earth had an affair in the White House," recalled Marian Schlesinger, an artist and Arthur Schlesinger's first wife.[42] When a friend of Jackie's escorted the wife of one of Jack's aides into the room where they were having dinner at a White House party, he heard her take a sharp breath as she saw the woman with whom her husband was having an affair seated beside the President, with the aide in question on her other side. Jackie's friend later questioned her, "How did that happen?" Jackie thought for a moment and then said, "Oh, I think Jack fixed it for him." Pierre Salinger said, "During the time I was the press secretary I was concentrating on what we were doing politically, I was not looking at his private life. However, I did have a couple of things that happened which made me feel that he was having mistresses because he was grabbing me to have mistresses. OK? But I didn't know any of them, I didn't know who he was having affairs with."[43]

Jackie was apart from this sexually charged circle yet, at the same time, a part of the cover-up for the President. She never tried to catch her husband out in his infidelities, always cabling when she was returning from Europe and making a point of telling him if she might be coming back a day earlier. In return Jack indulged in his more outrageous activities when she was not there. If she had not played the heroically self-controlled role that she did, if she had reacted emotionally to the perpetual betrayal, the presidency would have come crashing down around the Kennedys' ears. Her attitude toward Jack and his political life had changed since the 1960 campaign: she was totally committed to him and to his career. She thought she saw the capacity for greatness in him now; the success of his presidency was all-important to her and nothing should be allowed to jeopardize it. For all her European veneer she was intensely patriotic. "She cared about the country," as Richard Goodwin put it. "That feeling was at the sort of center of her life and it was important to her."[44] She saw the inspirational side of Kennedy, envisaging him as a leader in the mold of her heroes, de Gaulle and Churchill. She was the fierce guardian of his presidential image in life as she was to be after his death.

Yet the self-control she imposed on herself, the demands made on her as First Lady, Wife and Mother, took its toll, emphasizing the blacker sides of her character. Robin Douglas-Home spoke of "the nagging fear that that razor brain suddenly, upon a whim, would be turned on me . . . the fear that the merciless mockery she could direct at other people and customs and protocols and institutions, would be suddenly flung in my own eyes like gangsters' ammonia . . ." He talked of her "shifting moods," "biting wit," "flares of aggression."[45] Occasionally, the "merciless mockery" would be turned on Jack. "He used to be brutal to her in public," Bill Walton said, in the late summer of 1961. "But now it's the other way around; she needles him too much. I find myself saying, 'Come on, you can't say that to him. After all, he's the President, give him a break.' "[46]

Jackie's antidote to the pressures upon her was to spend Jack's money. It was perhaps the only area in which she paid no attention to either his feelings or his remonstrances, apart from going to considerable lengths to conceal the extent of her extravagance. The unfortunate Mary Gallagher had been given the job of bookkeeping for Jackie and presenting her expenses to the President. "My battle with the President's budget—or, I should say, his wife's—became so serious that I would take the long way around in the White House halls to avoid meeting him. I just couldn't stand the reproachful look on his face," she wrote.[47] In July 1961 she reported that Jackie's personal expenses for the second quarter of the year totaled $35,000, almost half of which was spent on clothes. Givenchy's bill alone came to $4,000 of the total. Back in March, the President had instructed Tom Walsh to set up a new bookkeeping system for Mary Gallagher and Jackie had obediently attempted to economize—but only as far as household expenses were concerned. Staff were ordered to cut back wherever possible and to keep itemized accounts of food and liquor, with the names of the stores where they were purchased. More and more bills were sent to Evelyn Lincoln in the President's office to be concealed among his expenses so that they would not show up on Jackie's. Jackie, as Gallagher noted, "seemed to be a compulsive buyer."

She liked to check the top New York department store advertisements in newspapers and tear out items that took her fancy. She would then ask Gallagher to order them for her on the "Mary B. Gallagher—Special" account. At one point she had a boots craze, ordering pair after pair. When, occasionally, she asked Mary Gallagher where most of the money went and Mary replied, " 'Clothing' she would seem not to hear me, and would go on questioning how she could economize, picking up such other areas as food and liquor and usually ending up with the little items in Miscellaneous."

When it came to economizing, clothes were a blind spot, but so also were paintings and house furnishings, especially antiques. If Jackie liked something she ordered it and coped with the bills later. Animals—and particularly the cost of Jackie's hunting in Virginia—were another major item. One year, expenditure in veterinary bills, feed and accessories, including a horse vacuum cleaner, totaled almost three times the expenditure on the children. Jackie attempted to lay off the costs of the animals at Glen Ora by asking Tom Walsh whether the Texas cattle kept there, which had been given to her and the President by Lyndon Johnson, might enable them to get a tax deduction on Glen Ora as a farm. Lyndon had also, kindly but somewhat embarrassingly, presented them with a Texas pony, nicknamed "Tex," for the children to ride, which proved unsuitable for them. She tried to balance the bills for her art purchases by selling off items she had bought earlier.

In October 1961 Jackie had Ted Kahn of Kahn Furs come to the White House with a selection of coats. The original idea had been that she would swap one of her old mink coats and that Kahn, a Harvard classmate of Jack's, would give her a good price for it. Jackie was torn between a new mink and a rare Somali leopard; Jack was summoned from his office to help her choose. He chose the mink, but Jackie liked the far more expensive leopard. She got the leopard and, according to Kahn, caused a mad rush for leopard and a steep decline in demand for the much more easily available mink. The President's attempts to persuade her to accept the offer of free hats from a manufacturer in the interests of the hat industry were unavailing. Jackie stuck to Marita at Bergdorf.

The "Battle of the Budget" reached its height in mid-November 1962. On the evening of November 15, the President had taken a look at the "Black Book," Mary Gallagher's carefully annotated record of Jackie's personal expenses. The following morning he descended to Gallagher's office, looking "as serious" as she had ever seen him. "The President was on the financial warpath again—but good!" Gallagher recorded. Carmine Bellino, she was told ominously, the Kennedy "figures expert," would be put on to the matter of Jackie's expenses. Gallagher had never seen the President "look more distraught." A week later, after the family returned from Thanksgiving at Hyannis Port, on November 28, 1962, "the Budget storm hit." Jackie had clearly received a tremendous lecture from her husband on economy; as usual, she listened with only one ear when it came to her clothing expenditure. All other areas were to be blitzed and the yellow memos came thick and fast. Tish was told in no uncertain terms that liquor in the White House was flowing as though it were the last days of the Roman Empire; the drinks were too strong and the supply too unlimited. No one should have too much to drink at official functions; at private parties no limits were set, but Jackie came up with the unhygienic solution of refilling glasses that were unfinished. They were to be passed around again, unless they had obvious lipstick marks, Jackie instructed, "even if a few people get hepatitis." Anne Lincoln was to be in charge of all food and drink from now on; only she would have the key to the drink cabinet. On the same day the President sent over a note via Evelyn Lincoln that from now on he wanted to see all the monthly bills before Gallagher wrote out the checks.[48]

On December 11, as Christmas approached, Jackie hit on another bright idea for economizing. Presents sent to the children from the general public were to be dispatched to Palm Beach in time for her to check them for suitability as presents for John and Caroline and the Radziwill children who would, as usual, be spending Christmas with them. "This," commented Gallagher, "was in itself unusual because gifts to the White House were ordinarily sent to charitable organizations. I could see that this would lighten her load in the 'Miscellaneous' column of her budget." She wanted Kenny O'Donnell to suggest liquor as presents for the President, if asked, as that was the item where expenditure was heaviest. Food gifts for the White House were to be used instead of being forwarded to orphanages.

Then Jackie lit upon a wonderful idea, completely new to her—trading stamps. "I don't think I'll ever forget the day," Gallagher wrote, "I walked into Jackie's bedroom and found her propped up in bed, looking at a picture catalog for trading stamps! 'Oh, Mary, do you know what I've just learned from Anne Lincoln?' she exclaimed. 'You know all the food we buy here at the White House? Well, she told me that with the stamps the stores give us, we can trade them for these marvelous gifts!' " The effect of all these budget-saving schemes, however, was offset by a long, descriptive letter to her favorite clothes scout in Paris, Mrs. John Mowinckel. Mary Gallagher was forced to report to the President in her Annual Statement of Expenses for 1962 that Jackie's personal and family spending had not diminished over the previous year. Her total for 1962 came to $121,461.61 as against $105,446.14 for her first year in the White House.[49]

At the time of the Battle of the Budget in November 1962, Fletcher Knebel wrote a seven-piece series for the *Des Moines Register* and the *Minneapolis Tribune* estimating that John F. Kennedy was worth about $10 million, mostly in a trust fund set up by his father. Kennedy, he wrote, had never owned a credit card, rarely carried cash with him and maintained separate checking accounts for himself and Jackie. Ever since he had become a congressman he had been turning over all his government salaries to charity, a total of about $400,000 from 1947 to October 1962; since his wealth placed him in the 90 percent income tax bracket, his taxes on that amount would have been $360,000. Thus, presuming that Kennedy took tax deductions, his donations cost him $40,000 out of pocket. In 1962 his taxable income was projected as probably topping the $450,000 mark. Aside from his presidential salary of $100,000 plus $50,000 for expenses, he stood to receive at least $250,000 from a $500,000 trust fund, another $160,000 or so from $5 million dollars received on his forty-fifth birthday that year and invested in municipal and federal bonds, only a third of which was taxable, plus income from personal investments, royalties, etc.

As Ben Bradlee noted in his diary, for November 15, 1962,

> We served as insulation tonight for a family squabble over finances. Jackie had just learned (remarkably enough) that her husband was giving his salary to charity, and had told him early that day that she sure could use the money herself. A series of questions had evidently ensued, which led to a request for information from the President about the state of the family finances. He had [received] the information in a letter, which he had with him and which had him boiling, not so much mad as amazed and indignant. The item which really had him bugged was "Department Stores . . . $40,000." No one had an explanation, much less Jackie. No furnishings for the White House, and, as Jackie pointed out, "no sable coat or anything."[50]

Jack said he had called in Carmine Bellino, a longtime Kennedy friend and an expert on deciphering Mafia finances for Senate committees, to sort things out in the White House as he had recently been called in by Bobby to investigate Ethel's extravagance at Hickory Hill. He also said, which Jackie denied, that his valet George Thomas and Jackie's maid Provi had been put on the civil service pay bill. Jackie, probably to bug Jack and express her defiance over the expenditure row, put her portable record player on "going full tilt" during an important conversation Jack had with Adlai Stevenson about a meeting the U.N. ambassador had just had with the deputy Soviet foreign minister. She also had what Bradlee called an unfair dig at her husband. When Jack said how much he had admired Adenauer's energy, at eighty-six, in throwing little John Jr. into the air, she "couldn't resist saying that it was the first time anyone had ever thrown little John into the air."[51]

Certainly no expense was spared at the Kennedys' parties, either State or private. The Kennedys made Washington, hitherto considered stuffy, boring and too political by American and international smart society, into the social center of the world. As Bradlee put it,

> The Kennedys were changing the face and character of Washington. Nothing symbolized this change more than the parties, for the Kennedys were party people. He loved the gaiety and spirit and ceremony of a collection of friends, especially beautiful women in beautiful dresses. They liked to mix jet setters with politicians, reporters with the people they reported on, intellectuals with entertainers, friends with acquaintances. Jackie was the producer of these parties. Jack was the consumer. They gave five or six dances during their time in the White House, and that's where it all came together. The crowd was always young. The women were always stylish. And you had to pinch yourself to realize that you were in the Green Room of the White House, and that that chap who just stumbled on the dance floor [actually fell over dancing with Helen Chavchavadze, reducing Jackie to helpless giggles] was . . . the Vice President of the United States, Lyndon Baines Johnson.
>
> The guest lists rarely included members of the Irish Mafia, the Irish Catholic political friends and associates, generally from Boston, who were in many ways closer to Kennedy personally and professionally than the Beautiful People or the intellectuals. There was a fundamental dichotomy in Kennedy's character; half the "mick" politician, tough, earthy, bawdy, sentimental, and half the urbane, graceful, intellectual "Playboy of the Western World" . . .[52]

In a piece entitled "New Frontier's New Order," *Time* highlighted Jackie's social dominance of the capital. The other Kennedys occupied first rank below, particularly Bobby and Ethel, whose poolside parties at Hickory Hill were boisterous affairs. At an outdoor dance given by the Kennedys in June 1962 in honor of Pat and Peter Lawford, with the Ormsby-Gores and a roll call of New Frontier names, Arthur Schlesinger and Ethel ended up, fully dressed, in the pool. On previous occasions Teddy had purposefully dived in and Pierre Salinger had been seen bobbing in the water, cigar carefully held aloft. Astronaut John Glenn, "who has been something of a fixture at the Hickory Hill lunching pad since he got back from outer space," was there, and Harry Belafonte did the Twist, the social signature of the New Frontier.

Time named as the inner Washington circle the Charlie Bartletts, the Chuck Spaldings, the journalist Rowland Evans Jr. and his wife (the Ben Bradlees were not mentioned as representing the magazine's rival, *Newsweek*), the Ormsby-Gores, the Sherman Coopers, the Joe Alsops, Bill Walton, the Paul Fays, Stas and Lee, Mrs. John R. "Fifi" Fell, Flo Pritchett Smith and her husband; and the favored members of the administration who were invited to inner circle White House occasions, were the Bob McNamaras, Marian and Arthur Schlesinger, Walt and Elspeth Rostow, and the McGeorge Bundys. Even as far as Washington was concerned, the list was too restricted: it should have included Secretary for Commerce Franklin D. Roosevelt Jr. and his wife Sue, and Oatsie Leiter. Lem Billings was a permanent fixture for weekends and the best parties. Oleg Cassini, cofounder of Le Club, the temple of the Twist in New York, was an essential social ingredient. Arkady Gerney, Jack's friend from Harvard days and an occasional business partner of Stas, was another insider. For Jackie's private parties for international friends, like the Radziwills and the Agnellis, the jet set and smart New York turned up in force. Usually, the Kennedys would invite a select few upstairs to their apartment afterward to carry on the party where Cassini would demonstrate the Twist, or the latest dance rage from Paris, the Hully-gully, with Benno Graziani, or take on Howard Oxenberg and others in a push-up competition.

The food, prepared by René Verdon, was delicious, and the music, often featuring Peter Duchin and his band, the best. Alcohol flowed freely, the cause of more than one incident. On March 15, 1961, Jackie's dinner dance for seventy-eight guests in honor of the Radziwills was the first of her glamorous private parties, invitations to which were the most sought after in international society. At a dinner for Lee, Franklin Roosevelt, somewhat overcome by alcohol as he tended to be on occasion, mistook one mustachioed foreigner, Oleg Cassini, for another, the absent Stas Radziwill, and toasted Cassini instead of the guest of honor. Jack Kennedy followed this up with the toast "To Stas, wherever you are." On November 11, 1961, Jackie gave a party for eighty guests in honor of Gianni and Marella Agnelli, at which Gore Vidal's much discussed quarrel with Bobby occurred. Recollections of the skirmish vary, clouded by time and champagne. By his own account, Vidal's temper was up by the time he encountered Bobby; he had already had aggressive encounters with Janet Auchincloss, and Lem Billings, the "court fag." According to Vidal, he was kneeling beside Jackie who sitting in an armless chair and put her hand on his shoulder as he got up. Someone pulled it away. It was Bobby. Enraged, Vidal followed him and they had what he later described as a "macho chat" on the lines of "What the fuck do you think you're doing?"—Vidal. "What's wrong, buddy boy?"—Bobby. Blair Clark saw "the pushing and shoving" from thirty feet away. "Gore, who had had quite a lot to drink, came up and said, 'Do you think I should take a swing at that bastard [Lem Billings]?' and conjectured Billings had got between Gore and Bobby and threatened Gore."[53] Gore left with Arthur Schlesinger and George Plimpton; it was his last evening at the White House.[54]

Until the row with Bobby Kennedy ended his White House social career, Gore Vidal, whose sardonic humor both Jack and Jackie shared, had been in high favor in the late summer and autumn of 1961. He had dined with the Kennedys at Hyannis Port on August 27, 1961, while the Berlin crisis was still simmering. Jackie, wearing capri pants and a windbreaker after waterskiing, was at the bar making daiquiris. Jack wore chinos and a blue shirt, looking trim and boasting of his weight—"172 pounds before I got here and started eating Jackie's cooking." A few days later Bill Walton told Vidal that "Jack is now rigorously dieting, exasperated by newspaper accounts that he has aged in office. The problem is lack of exercise since his last back ailment."[55]

The talk was all of politics and politicians, world affairs. Jack was reading aloud to Betty Spalding a letter from de Gaulle about the recent Berlin crisis and the possibility of a meeting with Khrushchev to discuss the situation (the Berlin Wall had just been erected, paradoxically defusing the danger of a confrontation). Vietnam was not mentioned. The great issue of the 1960s was not yet at the top of Kennedy's agenda although it was soon to become so, as later that autumn he pondered the possible consequences of direct U.S. military involvement in Vietnam to prop up the regime of the Catholic Ngo Dinh Diem against the Communist Viet Cong. Torn between the damage to his reputation as a hard-nosed cold warrior, which would result from total withdrawal, and the dangers of venturing further into what looked like a quagmire, he hesitated, stepping gingerly. Pressure came from ex-President Eisenhower, still an influential figure, who proclaimed the "domino theory," that without U.S. intervention the whole of Southeast Asia would fall to the Communists. Kennedy compromised by increasing the number of "military advisers." By the end of December more than two thousand were authorized to use their weapons "in self-defense." On December 21, 1961, the first American was killed in the jungle. But in the summer of 1961 few people could have imagined that that far-off country would be the site of a major American war, which would claim the lives of almost sixty thousand Americans and three million Vietnamese.

Bobby came in, slender and vivid in an orange shirt, with a cold greeting for Vidal. Caroline was dutifully passing round canapés; her father snapped his fingers and wiggled his hips, "Buttons, you want to dance for us?" She giggled and shook her head. Pat and Peter Lawford came by before flying to the South of France, leaving their latest child, six-week-old Robin, in Los Angeles. (The Lawford marriage was not going well, mainly due to the extramarital activities of Peter who, since the Kennedy banning of Sinatra, acted as what Vidal called "Jack's Plenipotentiary to the Girls of Hollywood.") Over cold Spanish soup, lobster and mousse, Jack, as always, was curious about the theater and the movies. Jackie urged him to tell Vidal about a plot he had thought up for a movie involving a Texas coup to remove him from the presidency. He talked, as he often did, of assassination. He was fatalistic. "If the assassin is willing to die, it couldn't be simpler . . ."[56]

Jackie's principal opportunity for political input, where her husband was concerned, came on the foreign trips. Just as she had translated ten books on French Indochina when courting the Senator, so, on Latin America in particular, he regarded her as an asset. Richard Goodwin, Kennedy's Special Assistant in the South American area, remembered, "Kennedy made three trips to Latin America and I went with him and so did she. And she would always read the briefing books in the aircraft and sit and discuss it. And I would know because he would call up certain phrases I had put in the briefing memo and talk about it and that kind of thing. She was involved, she knew what was going on. Her looks and her Catholicism and her Spanish were a pretty potent combination—very potent for both of them. He didn't speak Spanish, he used to practice those words 'I'm so happy to' and 'Viva.' We tried to get it right so that he could get off the plane and shout a few Spanish words. In private it was horrible! He had no gift for pronouncing but he did work at it and he did use them . . ."[57]

The Kennedys left Washington on December 15, 1961, for a three-stop tour of Puerto Rico, Venezuela and Colombia, returning to spend Christmas at Palm Beach with the Radziwills at the house loaned them by C. Michael Paul and his wife, Josephine. On the morning of December 19, Jack left for Washington, en route to confer with Macmillan in Nassau. Joe Kennedy went to the airport to see him off, returning with Caroline who had traveled in the car with her father. He then went to the Palm Beach golf course to play his customary round with his niece, Ann Gargan. At the sixteenth green he felt faint and was chauffeured home, where Jackie and Caroline were enjoying a swim. He spoke briefly to them and went up to his room, where, alone, he suffered a massive stroke.

At 2 P.M. he was taken to the hospital, where an arteriogram revealed the thrombosis to be in the left cerebral hemisphere and inoperable. He was practically paralyzed down his right side, unable to move his arm or leg. The facial muscles on the right side of his face were frozen, giving him a lopsided look. He dribbled. Worst of all, he could not speak. Of all the blows that Joe Kennedy had suffered—and was still to suffer—this was one of the worst. The former king of the clan, the all-powerful ambassador, already sidelined by his son's presence in the White House, became a prisoner in his own body, locked up with his thoughts and fears, unable to communicate. The man "who had made it all possible" was helpless, impotent in the grip of a terrible fate.

As Jackie told Dorothy Schiff, owner of the *New York Post*, three years later, she thought that when the brain had been damaged, it was as if nature allowed the person to become a complete vegetable so that they would not know what was happening. To have only partial functions was a terrible thing.[58] Jackie, tough and worldly as she often seemed, was tender, sensitive and loving toward the raging old man within his shell, wiping the saliva from his chin, kneeling beside his chair, sometimes laying her head in his lap. It was harder for Jack, who had to telephone his father daily and try to hold a normal conversation with the grunts that were all Joe could produce. For Jackie, it was as if another pillar of her life had foundered, leaving her more than ever on her own. For the Kennedys as a clan, the patriarch's stroke began the next phase in the Greek tragedy, as nemesis stalked the golden family.

In Venice on board his yacht the *Christina*, Aristotle Onassis, superstitious and a student of Greek myth, remarked of Jack and Jackie, "Those two are in for bad luck."[59]

CHAPTER TWELVE

Salad Days

The thirty-odd months at the White House were indeed her "salad days" and she described the galas with Proustian rapture. Proust would indeed have studied her, admired her and put her into his fictions.

—Edna O'Brien[1]

At the 1962 Women's Press Club show, Helen Thomas, one of the two principal women reporters of the White House press corps, to whom Jackie regularly gave what her friends called her "PBO" (Polite Brush Off) treatment, got back at the First Lady. Dressed in a pink evening dress, with her hair in a Jackie bouffant style, she performed a skit in "that breathy, little-girl voice that America's ears often strained to hear":

> If I want to give a ball
> For just me and Charles de Gaulle,
> I have absolutely all the gall I need
> I'm . . . Jahh-kee!
> If I like to water-ski
> And maintain my privacy
> Am I to blame?
> You would do the same
> If you were me
> I'm Jahhh-keeee!
> If I want to fly away, without taking JFK
> Or if I'm fond of French champagne
> And I'd rather not campaign
> That's me . . . Jahh-keeee!

According to Thomas, Jack Kennedy came up to her in the Rose Garden the next day with a huge grin on his face, saying, "I've been reading all about you. Some party."[2]

Nineteen sixty-two was to be Jackie's Getaway Year: while Jack campaigned industriously for the congressional elections that year, she undertook a triumphant solo visit to India and Pakistan, taking in Rome and London on the way, followed by a prolonged international jet set vacation in Italy, far away from the touch football and clambake simplicities of Hyannis Port.

John Kenneth Galbraith, the celebrated liberal Harvard economist, recently appointed ambassador to India by Kennedy, and a great favorite of Jackie, had brought up the possibility of a visit by Jackie to India when he visited the President on September 13, 1961. Later he talked on the telephone to Jackie at Hyannis Port; she was "enchanted" at the thought of the trip and wanted to make it in October or November. Galbraith asked her to wait until the Berlin situation had cooled. On November 5 he visited Jack and Jackie at Hammersmith Farm; the trip had now been officially announced. He dined that night with the two of them. While Jack played backgammon with Lem Billings, they watched the recently arrived Prime Minister of India, Jawaharlal Nehru on *Meet the Press*. Next morning Nehru, with his daughter, Indira Gandhi, and B. K. Nehru, flew up to Newport where they boarded the *Honey Fitz* for Hammersmith Farm. Nehru was amused when Kennedy pointed out the "beach house" palaces of the American rich with the remark, "I want you to see how the average American lives."[3] After a long lunch dominated by serious political discussion, Jackie told Galbraith she was having "new doubts about her journey to India." Flying to Washington on Air Force One, Galbraith noted that, while the President flicked through the newspapers at the rate of one a minute, Nehru read the *National Geographic* and Indira looked at *Vogue*. Jackie was immersed in Malraux.[4]

That night at the White House there was a dinner for Nehru at which the Indian Prime Minister, who had earlier been monosyllabic and unresponsive in his meeting with Jack, sat between Jackie and Lee—"and with the light of love in his eyes, was obviously delighted."[5] The evening ended at about midnight; two hours later the President called Galbraith to tell him that Jackie had decided to postpone her trip until January, giving no reason. The following evening she gave a dinner in honor of Galbraith and David Ormsby-Gore, who had recently arrived as British ambassador. Jack described Ormsby-Gore, with McGeorge "Mac" Bundy, who was also there, as the two brightest men he knew.[6] At a reception at the Indian embassy the following evening, where the Kennedys were out in force, Eunice Shriver asked Nehru why he did not have bags under his eyes as he did in photographs and would he increase the size of the Peace Corps? Her brother called Galbraith afterward to say he "thought she had probably set back Indian-American relations about five years."[7]

Galbraith worked on drawing up a schedule for Jackie's Indian visit. "It promises to be fun," Galbraith wrote. "The Indians are worried about a trip to Kanarak lest she be photographed in the middle of a set of highly pornographic statues." On December 20 the Indians invaded the then-Portuguese territory of Goa.

On February 26, possibly because of the international repercussions to this dé-marche, possibly for genuine reasons, Galbraith received a telegram from Tish Baldrige referring "vaguely to health" and postponing Jackie's arrival by a week. Galbraith hurried to Nehru who, "deeply in love" with Jackie and having a photo-graph of himself strolling with her hung proudly by itself in his main entrance hall, was "entirely agreeable."[8]

Jackie, accompanied by Lee, arrived in Delhi on March 13 "looking a million dollars in a suit of radioactive pink." Official functions with excellent photo-opportunities managed by Galbraith followed, but a press briefing concentrated, to his disgust, almost exclusively on Jackie's clothes—"far too much attention to the subject of clothes, designer, dress, handbag and so forth." Once again, this, for Jackie, was a sensitive subject; her Cassini wardrobe was supplemented by clothes made secretly for her by the fashionable Rome-based designer Princess Irene Galitzine. Despite the attempt to soft-pedal attention on clothes, the dress Jackie wore at the Prime Minister's evening party, of a pale turquoise fabric that caught the light, caused a sensation among the brightly colored saris worn by the Prime Minister's other women guests. On the following day a leisurely journey by the splendid former Viceroy's train—scarlet outside, fawn within—equipped with drawing room, dining room and bedrooms, ended in a visit to Fatehpur-Sikri, the great red sandstone city built by Akhbar the Great in 1569 and abandoned after only fifteen years. Then the party went on to Agra, where Jackie posed for a riot of photographers at the Taj Mahal. Another semi-riot took place at a Benares silk factory: "With her excellent sense of theater," Galbraith reported, "J.B.K. had put on a lavender dress which could be picked out at any range up to five miles."[9]

For Galbraith, anxious not to offend the Indian Government which classed the maharajahs as political enemies, the visit by Jackie to Udaipur and particularly to Jaipur was fraught with pitfalls. In Udaipur, "the boat trip had been very heavy with princes so [at the evening reception] I got J.B.K. around to chat with various modern officials. Jackie was polite but bored, 'What is your annual rainfall?' being all she could come up with in conversation with the dean of a college of agricul-ture."[10] The Maharajah was even more sensitive. He and his wife, the beautiful Ayesha, who were both involved in politics, were personal friends of Lee, and were, according to the ambassador, suspected by the Indian government of trying to make political capital out of Jackie's visit. Various stratagems were deployed by the civilian government and frustrated by the Maharajah; to Galbraith's despair, the magnificently caparisoned royal elephants at the Amber Palace provided an unmissable photo opportunity; Jackie and Lee climbed aboard and the camera-men had a field day. The Maharajah had planned a party for Jackie at the palace, which, no doubt, Jackie knew about beforehand but of which Galbraith was un-aware until she telephoned to ask his permission to go. Delhi had to be consulted before the party went ahead.

Jackie and Lee were in their element, the intellectual Galbraith less so. "The conversation was on horses, mutual friends, social events and polo," he com-mented, "scarcely my particular social speciality."

"At dinner a whole lot of polo players were there and then they put on the gramophone and she said, 'Do you know the Twist?' and then she was teaching them," the Rajmata of Jaipur recalled. "She was good fun."[11] Around midnight the party drove to the City Palace, spending hours exploring the courts and audience chambers and gardens with illuminated fountains. "It was all most romantic, and it was plain that Mrs. Kennedy enjoyed it enormously."

Escorting Jackie on her foreign travels was no sinecure. Earlier Galbraith had written, "The President warned me with great good humor that I had as yet unexplored experiences in traveling with Mrs. Kennedy . . ." Even on official trips such as this, Jackie did more or less as she wanted, and if she didn't feel like doing something—within reason—she didn't do it. After the party at the Maharajah and his wife's she was tired and stayed in bed until noon. On her last day, after a parting visit to Nehru, she begged off recording a farewell message, which Galbraith had to do in her stead. The President, he decided, had been accurate in his warning that "the care and management of Mrs. Kennedy involved a good deal of attention. I found myself worrying constantly either about the Indian press reaction, the American press reaction, that of the people she was visiting and her own state of contentment. The last perhaps was most important because if she had become tired and unhappy, the rest of the effect would certainly have been poor."[12]

Jackie's trip to India had a remarkable effect both on her and upon her hosts. "Jackie's effect on the Indians was just wonderful," Galbraith remembered, "[and] she developed her interest in Indian art and architecture . . . [and her] visit was the high spot of Indian-American relations. Nehru was by all odds the strongest figure in India and he was captured by Jacqueline Kennedy . . ."[13] Kitty Galbraith remembered that after the final dinner at the residence they went down to the embassy garden: "I watched Jackie and Nehru sitting on the steps and they were laughing together and he had his white jacket with a red rose on it and she had on a red and white dress . . . and they were acting like schoolchildren, they were just talking back and forth and laughing."[14]

"I think Nehru was particularly delighted to be the host for an American who didn't feel obliged to talk about politics at every suitable moment and was so obviously interested in Indian art," Galbraith said. Asked if Jackie's visit had a helpful effect on Indian-American relations, he replied, "Oh, sure. It established Nehru—as I said India had a strong government at that time and the epitome of strength was Nehru. [He] was greatly attracted by Jackie, and this led to a more amiable view of the U.S. without much doubt."[15]

By the time she reached Pakistan, Jackie was visibly tiring. After a spectacular horse show featuring dancing horses and a camel doing rock and roll, President Ayub Khan, to Jackie's delight, presented her with a ten-year-old bay gelding named Sardar. She saw the famous gardens of Shalimar, created by Shah Jehan, and the Khyber Pass, but canceled a sightseeing tour of Lahore and a lunch among the ruins of Taxila. One day she overslept and thousands of Pakistani children waited for three hours to see her.

To the worshipping crowds Jackie was "Ameriki Rani"—Queen of America—and, as befits a queen, she had a lady-in-waiting in the form of Lee. Outwardly Lee put on a brave face over her sister's astonishing success. Jackie not only had the man whom Lee had always fancied, but that man had become the most important man in the world and Jackie a star of international magnitude. Never had the balance of competition between them weighed so heavily in Jackie's favor; increasingly, from the day Jack became President it was a battle that Lee could never win, however hard she tried. In return for the glamour and privileges conferred by the White House connection, Lee had to act as Jackie's lady-in-waiting, help her keep Jack amused, accompany her on flying visits to New York for shopping, parties, the ballet. As Lee's marriage to Stas faltered, she spent more and more time in Jackie's company, and only a saint or a fool could have endured such imbalance without rancor. Lee was neither. "Had lunch today with your new friend Princess Lee," Truman Capote wrote to Cecil Beaton, from Verbier on February 9, 1962, "(my God, how jealous she is of Jackie. I never knew), understand her marriage is all but finito."[16]

The pain that Jackie inflicted on Lee, simply by existing, Lee took out, or tried to, on Stas. Since Lee had barred her bedroom door to him, Stas had had other women, but he was still in love with Lee and almost admiring of her extraordinary extravagance, particularly on clothes. "You've no idea how much that tiny little body costs me," he would tell his friends. Lee was inwardly as tense as a bowstring, while Stas had a Polish aristocrat's short-fuse temper, drank heavily and was reliant on Dr. Jacobson's shots. According to friends, the result was "a Punch and Judy show" of rows and insults. While the Kennedy presidency endured, the Radziwill show stayed on the road as long as it suited all parties to keep it there.

The Bouvier sisters' extraordinary capacity to maintain a façade concealed their deep rivalry from almost every observer. Benno Graziani, a trusted friend of both, was on the India trip for *Paris-Match*. "I saw them for twenty-five years," he said, "so sometimes they got on very well together. I was in India and Pakistan with them . . . They were very friendly at this moment."[17]

Kenneth Galbraith, also a close friend of both sisters, remembered how helpful and self-effacing Lee was on the India/Pakistan tour. "Lee was wonderful, Lee was very good," he remembered. "She was the ideal sister." Kitty Galbraith added, "She had some times she wanted to do on her own but that was OK. She kept Jackie [happy]. [When] they wanted autographs, hundreds and hundreds of autographs, Lee's handwriting is exactly like Jackie's so I watched them [signing]." Galbraith said, "There was no serious question that Lee enjoyed it too, but she was also a very important person on the trip because she was not only wonderfully visible in her own right, but she was the retreat for Jackie . . . when the time came."[18]

"I was so proud of her," Jackie told Joan Braden. "Nothing could ever come between us . . ."[19] She was careful to compensate for Lee's so obviously inferior position, being relegated to the back of motorcades, overlooked and sometimes even left behind. At Fatehpur-Sikri, when Lee failed to arrive in time to see boys diving from over a hundred feet into a tank, Jackie asked if they could repeat their act for her.

En route to India Jackie had done her best to help her sister in the important matter of her annulment by a personal appeal to the Pope. In July 1961 Lee had drafted a petition to John XXIII, which was submitted personally to him by Philippe Etter, a former president of Switzerland, in November 1961. The Pope refused angrily to consider it, telling Etter that it was not for him to interfere with the competent authorities. The Kennedys and Radziwills had not, however, given up. Cardinal Cicognani, the Vatican Secretary of State, a contact of the family from his days as Apostolic Delegate in Washington, visited the White House at the end of the month where he had a "long and amicable" discussion of Lee's case and was informed of the plan for Jackie and Lee to visit the Pope on the first stop of their Indian tour. After pressure from cardinals favorable to the Kennedys, the Pope agreed, two days before Jackie arrived in Rome on March 10, 1962, to allow the reopening of Lee's case. The following day Jackie, with Lee in tow, had a private audience with the Pope. On November 24, 1962, after prolonged secret negotiations, Lee's marriage to Michael Canfield was declared annulled. In the eyes of the Church, which did not recognize divorce, she was now free to marry Stas, whom she had already married in a civil ceremony four years earlier, and to take the sacraments. They were married in a religious ceremony on July 3, 1963, shortly after the death of Pope John XXIII, to whom the whole affair had been personally distasteful. It was important for Stas, a devout Catholic, that his marriage to Lee should be recognized by the Church to placate his saintly father, Prince Janusz.[20]

On the journey back from Pakistan, Jackie, exhausted, spent three days in London recuperating with Lee and Stas; a luncheon with the Queen at Buckingham Palace was her only official engagement. She had asked Jack to call Galbraith back to Washington earlier in order to give her an excuse to cut short her trip to the subcontinent.

At Wartski's in London she fell in love with an antique eighteenth-century sunburst diamond clip. Among the major events that spring would be the visit of the Shah of Iran and his beautiful young third wife, Farah Diba. The Empress was bound to be loaded with jewelry, a contest that Jackie could not possibly win, so she planned to wear in her hair this simple, beautiful pin, which would be quite unlike anything the imperial jewel box was likely to provide. Instead of asking Jack for the money, she decided to trade in some of her jewelry to make up the price of the pin, which was just over six thousand dollars. Mary Gallagher listed the jewelry to be appraised: a big aquamarine given her by the Brazilian government, a diamond clip that had been a wedding present from her father-in-law, a sapphire and diamond bracelet from Van Cleef and Arpels, a gold and emerald pin given to her during her visit to Greece in 1961, and assorted pieces of gold jewelry. After checking with the Kennedy New York office, she handed over these pieces and $2,000 for the diamond sunburst.

Her canniness and acquisitiveness sometimes overstepped the mark. That spring she persuaded the President to let her have a diamond-encrusted sword, which had been given him by Ibn Saud of Saudi Arabia, with the idea of taking out the diamonds and substituting them with fakes. The jeweler entrusted with the work was to be told that the sword was an old thing of Ambassador Kennedy's that she wanted to remodel. Tom Walsh of the New York office was summoned to take charge of the affair but reported to Jackie that the cost of taking out the diamonds and substituting them would make the stratagem prohibitively expensive.

A week relaxing at Glen Ora was followed by a punishing schedule of Washington events: a congressional reception for some eight hundred guests on April 10, a dinner for the Shah and Empress of Iran on the eleventh, out to dinner at the Iranian embassy on the twelfth. On the eighteenth the Kennedy family left for Easter at Palm Beach; Jackie remained there until the twenty-eighth when she flew back for the visit of Harold Macmillan, and the dinner for the Nobel Prize winners on the twenty-ninth.

The main event of mid-May was the arrival of the French Minister of Culture, André Malraux. His visit had been instigated by Jackie, who had pressed Jack to issue a formal invitation. The dinner in his honor was intended by her to focus attention on the importance of the arts and subtly to underline that in France an entire ministry was devoted to cultural interests. Her secret hope was that America should have a Secretary of State for the Arts. Malraux had been fascinated by Jackie on her visit to Paris; she, for her part, was already a fan of his novels and admired him as a hero of the French Resistance in the Second World War. After dinner, with a Gallic flourish he promised to loan the Louvre's *Mona Lisa* to the National Gallery in Washington as a personal favor to her. In return, Jackie persuaded the Smithsonian Institution to lend the famous Hope Diamond from their gem collection to an exhibition of historic French jewelry in Paris (a loan that the Smithsonian had hitherto refused). The following year Malraux returned to Washington for the unveiling of the *Mona Lisa*.

Earlier on the day of the Malraux dinner, Jack and Jackie had attended a more personal function, the wedding reception of Angier Biddle Duke and the beautiful Robin Chandler Lynn, but even this private event had political undertones.

In the background was the battle of the McLean riverbank. Janet and Hughdie had sold Merrywood to a developer, leaving their neighbors up in arms. The neighbors fought the development and eventually won, but in the meantime the atmosphere there was poisonous. Janet Auchincloss became extremely upset and Jackie loyally took her side. "We fought it badly enough," Marie Ridder, Janet's McLean neighbor, said, "so that Mrs. Auchincloss and for a moment, I thought Jackie, [were offended]. I went to the Malraux dinner during this fight and for a moment I thought Jackie wasn't going to speak to me, but the President said, 'Jackie, you really agree with Marie and not with Hughdie.' And then he said to me, 'Just keep it quiet that she does.' And during this fight," she went on, "we were to give a wedding party for Robin Duke and Angier, and the party was supposed to be here and the President was supposed to come. And [my husband, newspaperman] Walter Ridder called him [Kennedy] up and said, 'You know, I really think all this is unwise. I'm a journalist and I'm a friend of yours and I think the headline is going to be 'President and Mrs. Kennedy go to friend's house that's in a suit against [his in-laws] and very nasty stories.' And the President said, 'I can go wherever I want to. Hughdie and Janet don't control me.' This was at 11:00 A.M. At 11:05 he must have tried this out on somebody and called back and we moved the reception to the Pells [Senator Claiborne and his wife, Nuala] . . . and as the President came in he said to Walter, 'Well, Walter, remind me to get your advice on other things!' which was so sweet."[21]

The citizens of McLean, Virginia, were outraged and protested, demanding that their bucolic neighborhood be saved. Coast-to-coast environmentalists joined the cause, urging that the land be preserved for its scenic and historic value. Irate neighbors picketed the house with signs saying, "Her daughter beautifies the White House and she desecrates our neighborhood."

Despite the protests, the bulldozers arrived to break ground—at which point the Attorney General, Bobby Kennedy, also a Merrywood neighbor, took action. He discovered an old scenic easement, rarely if ever used, and slapped it on the gates of Merrywood. Construction stopped, and a legal battle ensued. Eventually Congress appropriated over $750,000 to buy the air rights to Merrywood in perpetuity. This meant that nothing could ever be built there over forty feet high— the height of the house—and that no trees over a certain diameter could be cut down. The developers were left with a big mansion and fifty acres of land zoned not for high-rise apartments but for one-acre houses. It was bought by C. Wyatt Dickerson, whose wife Nancy was a high-profile reporter for CBS.[22]

Given Jack's predilections for Hollywood stars, it was only a matter of time before he met Marilyn Monroe, the world's greatest sex symbol. Marilyn, divorced from Joe DiMaggio and deserted by her second husband, the playwright Arthur Miller, her career nose-diving, was very much involved with the wild Frank Sinatra–Peter Lawford ("Brother in Lawford" as Sinatra called him) set. Sinatra introduced her to what Monroe's biographer described as "the alcohol-drenched scene" at Peter Lawford's oceanside home in Santa Monica, with pool parties and all-night card games. When the President headed west, he would inevitably stay with his sister Pat and her husband. Sinatra, besotted with the Kennedys, was determined that his Palm Springs home would be an unofficial western White House, and the Lawfords were such regular guests that they kept clothes there for their weekend visits. Sinatra, in anticipation of a presidential visit, had built a heliport and other facilities for "Chicky Boy," as he liked to call Jack.

It was at the Lawfords' Santa Monica house that Marilyn had first met Jack on Sunday, November 19, 1961. The President, who had been speaking at the Hollywood Palladium the night before and was due to meet Konrad Adenauer later, changed into jeans and relaxed with the Lawfords' guests, slipping back easily into a scene he knew well from earlier years. According to Lawford's second wife, also called Pat, Marilyn was virtually living in the Lawfords' house at the time. "There were times that Jack would be there having sex with Marilyn, separated from the Lawfords only by a dividing wall. Yet this was tolerated and, seemingly, encouraged. Peter also acted as the official recorder of these events. There was a beautiful marble-and-onyx bathroom serving the extra bedroom. Jack liked to get into the tub, then have Marilyn climb on top of him while they had sex in the water. Peter would be asked to take photographs, the President delighting in having his activities recorded. Such semivoyeuristic tendencies on Jack Kennedy's part were an open secret among some family members. After the President's death, as many of the photographs as could be found were destroyed . . ."23

Jackie was at Glen Ora when Jack had his first encounter with Monroe at the Lawford's west coast house. She was at the White House on December 5 that year when Lawford smuggled Marilyn into the Carlyle for a New York assignation with Jack. "Peter told me how he used to dress Marilyn in a brown wig, dowdy clothing and glasses, then hand her a legal pad and pen. She would be sneaked into the Carlyle as Peter's personal secretary," Lawford wrote. Several years later, a report sent to Hoover at the FBI by a Special Agent Contact in Newark alleged that "sex parties took place at the Hotel Carlyle in New York, in which a number of persons participated at different times. Among those mentioned were the following individuals, Robert F. Kennedy, John F. Kennedy . . . [two names blacked out] Marilyn Monroe."24

Monroe began to fantasize about her relationship with Jack. Far from seeing herself as just another "lollipop," she even believed he would leave Jackie and marry her. By the early spring of 1962, deeply upset by the remarriage of her ex-husband, Arthur Miller, she had turned again to pills and alcohol, and was in dreadful shape: she arrived drunk at the Golden Globe Awards in Los Angeles, unsteady on her feet and with a Mexican lover in tow. When it was time to collect a gold statuette as the World's Favorite Female Star, she could barely get to the podium, while her slurred acceptance speech at such a major film event led to rumors that she was finished. Later that month, as Jackie arrived in London on March 25, 1962, on the last leg of her India trip, Lawford took Marilyn to Palm Springs for a weekend rendezvous with Jack.

They were not to stay with Sinatra, who had even erected a flagpole, copying the Kennedy Hyannis Port compound, in anticipation of the presidential visit, but at the rented house of Bing Crosby, Sinatra's longtime singing rival and a Republican to boot. When he heard the news, Sinatra personally took a sledgehammer to break up the concrete helipad. He also threw the Lawfords' clothes into the swimming pool and cut Lawford out of his life. But it had hardly been Lawford's fault.

The reason behind Kennedy's switch of plan was a memo sent by the head of the FBI, J. Edgar Hoover, to the Attorney General in Washington the previous month, dated February 27, 1962, officially informing him that Judith Campbell Exner, known to be in contact with gangsters including Sam Giancana, had made two telephone calls within a week to Evelyn Lincoln (which Bobby already knew). 'The relationship between Campbell and Mrs. Lincoln or the purpose of these calls is not known," Hoover wrote guardedly. Copies of this memorandum were sent to two of Bobby's aides in the Justice Department. Apparently Bobby did not dare tell his brother about this, but Hoover had no such reservations. On March 22, 1962, he had a lunch appointment with the President during which he allegedly informed Kennedy that Judith Campbell, with whom the President was still carrying on an affair, had connections with the well-known hoodlum and friend of Sinatra, Sam Giancana, the head of the Chicago mob, and Johnny Roselli, both of whom had been involved in the assassination plots against Castro. According to Judith

Campbell's later account of his telephone call after the lunch, Kennedy was furious at Hoover's audacity and implied blackmail. "He was well aware that Hoover knew every move that he made, and he did not care. That's the reckless side of Jack— that he would allow himself to be in that position. I mean he should never have been involved with me. They wanted to get rid of Hoover and they couldn't, because of the information that Hoover had on the Kennedys—not just Jack."[25]

Bobby, however, was less reckless than Jack and concerned as ever to protect his brother's back. He told Jack that, as President, he could not go to Sinatra's house and sleep under the same roof, possibly in the same bed, as Giancana had. The superficial excuse, Bobby decided, was to be that Sinatra's house was a security risk. Lawford was given the unwelcome task of conveying this message to Sinatra. The President only called Sinatra with the same excuse after his arrival at Crosby's house. This failure, in Lawford's opinion, ruined Lawford's relationship with Sinatra and to some extent his career. There were to be no more Rat Pack movies, or shows at the Sands with Sinatra, Dean Martin and Sammy Davis.

On May 11 Jackie entertained Marilyn's ex-husband Arthur Miller in the White House at the dinner in honor of André Malraux. Miller was surprised to find himself seated at Jackie's table with Malraux. It was a symbol of the Kennedy's liberal policy toward the arts that Miller, stigmatized as a Communist sympathizer in the McCarthy days of the Eisenhower administration, should have been given a place of honor by Jackie. There seems to be little doubt that she was aware of Monroe's obsession with her husband; according to one biographer, Marilyn had the number of the private apartments at the White House and on one occasion, woozy, no doubt, with drink and drugs, had told Jackie of her desire to marry the President. It was hardly surprising, therefore, that Jackie was pointedly absent from the New York gala at Madison Square Garden in honor of the President's forthcoming forty-fifth birthday, at which Marilyn was to be the star attraction, singing "Happy Birthday, Mr. President." She was at Glen Ora, attending the Loudon County Horse Show with Caroline.

Wearing a skintight flesh-colored gown encrusted with rhinestones, Marilyn was high when she wiggled on stage at Madison Square Garden to be introduced by master-of-ceremonies Peter Lawford. Her act was so provocative that Broadway columnist Dorothy Kilgallen described her as "making love to the President in the direct view of forty million Americans." Kennedy grinned as he reflected publicly that he could now retire from politics having had "Happy Birthday" sung to him "in such a sweet, wholesome way," but privately that evening was to be the end of his relationship with Monroe. Her over-the-top performance had set everybody talking about the President and the Movie Star; it was only a matter of time before rumors might appear in print. His aides were instructed to deny everything and kill the story.

Frantic at the thought he was abandoning her, Marilyn bombarded him with calls at the White House; eventually he refused to take them. Desperate to keep the Kennedy connection, she telephoned Bobby instead. In June during a photo session with *Vogue* photographer Bert Stern, she put on a brunette Jackie wig, pearls, white silk top and black palazzo pants and posed as the First Lady. Obviously this underlined her yearning to *be* Jackie, to be married to Jack. Marilyn never saw Jack again but she did see Bobby at a dinner party at the Lawfords on June 26 and again alone at her house on the following day. Under his ruthless, tough exterior, Bobby had a compassionate heart: according to Marilyn's biographer, another disturbed Hollywood star, Judy Garland, also used to telephone him to cry on his shoulder.

On the night of August 4, 1962, Marilyn took an overdose of sleeping pills, nembutal and chloral hydrate. The last person known to have spoken to her was Peter Lawford, who was concerned that she had not turned up at their house for dinner. She sounded drunk or drugged, which was not unusual. He shouted into the telephone, hoping to wake her and persuade her to come out. According to his recollection, she then said, "Say good-bye to Pat. Say good-bye to Jack. And say good-bye to yourself because you're a nice guy . . ." Worried, Lawford called her back and got a busy signal; his manager contacted her lawyer Milt Ebbins who rang and was told nothing was wrong. At about 3 A.M. the following morning, Eunice Murray, Marilyn's housekeeper, saw Marilyn sprawled facedown on the bed; she was naked, one hand resting on the telephone receiver. She was dead at the age of thirty-six. The coroner, after a "psychological autopsy," declared her death to be a "probable suicide." This was not her first overdose but this time it could only be conjectured as to whether it had been a failed cry for help or a genuine attempt to end her increasingly desperate life.[26]

Jackie, who had admired Arthur Miller enough to seat him at her table at the Malraux dinner, turned on him for his betrayal of Marilyn in his play *After the Fall*, which opened in New York on January 23, 1964. For her, loyalty was the ultimate test of character, and in portraying Marilyn as a self-destructive slut whom he had abandoned for her own good, Miller had dismally failed it. "Gene Black Jr. told me this wonderful story," said Demi Gates. "He called her up and said would she support the American Theater and he set up a meeting with Elia Kazan and Arthur Miller and all sorts of other people. They were meeting for lunch and let's say it was on a Thursday—he calls her up on the Tuesday to make sure that everything was all right and she says, 'Tell me something, you are currently doing a play by Arthur Miller, is that correct?' And he said, 'Yes.' And she said, 'I won't have anything to do with that theater because of the way he treated Marilyn Monroe . . .' "[27]

Marilyn was simply the biggest celebrity "lollipop" Jack Kennedy had enjoyed. Forty-eight hours later, on the night of August 6 when her death was still the headline story in the newspapers and Jackie was in New York on the eve of departure for Italy, he was entertaining another woman in the White House. In January 1962 he had begun an affair with Mary Pinchot Meyer, the beautiful artist sister of Ben Bradlee's wife Tony, and ex-wife of CIA man Cord Meyer. Jack had known Mary for many years since meeting her at the San Francisco Conference in 1945 when he was reporting for Hearst and the Meyers were there on honeymoon. More recently, Mary Meyer had been included in the Kennedys' Georgetown set. She had also provided an apartment for Pamela Turnure to carry on her affair with Jack after Florence Kater's surveillance had made her previous apartment too risky for them. In those Georgetown days, Mary used sometimes to walk with Jackie along the Chesapeake and Ohio canal towpath, where she met a mysterious, still unsolved death on October 12, 1964.

Mary's background was very different from that of either the middle-class Judith Campbell or Marilyn, who had been brought up in foster households and a Los Angeles orphanage. The Pinchots were east-coast aristocracy with a huge estate, Gray Towers, at Milford, Pennsylvania, and Mary, like Jackie, was a Vassar girl. For a woman of her time and background, Mary was comparatively free-thinking and, like Jack, curious and adventurous about the boundaries of her life. Like him, she was a risk-taker; beginning in the spring of 1962 she had sessions with Timothy Leary, high priest of LSD, to learn how to "run an LSD session," telling him she was part of a group of women who planned to influence men through LSD and that she wanted to use it on "this friend who's a very important man." Leary was fascinated by this tough, cool lady, whom he saw as a Mata Hari of drugs: "Flamboyant eyebrows, piercing green-blue eyes, fine-boned face. Amused, arrogant, aristocratic . . ."[28]

Kennedy was attracted to both Pinchot sisters. Phil Geyelin of the *Washington Post*, married to Sherry, remembers him sitting between Mary and Tony at a White House party: "We went to the White House twice, once for Eugene Black and once for Lee, and whichever one it was the wife of whoever it was honored should have been sitting at his right side. As it happened the Pinchot girls were on either side of him, I remember I thought that was a little odd." He propositioned Tony, who was, Sherry Geyelin said, "outraged that Kennedy would do this to his best friend's wife."[29] Mary, who at first turned him down, succumbed on January 22, 1962, while Jackie was at Glen Ora. The affair continued through the summer of 1962 when Jackie was away from Washington. On August 6 at 7:50 P.M. while Mary Meyer was in the White House, Jackie rang Jack from New York, presumably for a last-minute conversation before she left for Italy, and was told that the President was out. Judith Campbell had also called that day and been put off by Evelyn Lincoln; her affair was over.[30]

Mary was later reported as having smoked marijuana with Kennedy and even introducing him to LSD. No one, not even her sister, seems to have been aware of their affair, beyond Dave Powers and Kennedy's womanizing coterie, until in January 1963 the brilliant Phil Graham, suffering from then-untreatable manic depression, apparently revealed the name of the "President's new favorite" at a convention of newspaper editors in Phoenix, Arizona. According to the unwritten conventions of the day, nothing appeared in print but for Kennedy, already preoccupied with the prospect of the presidential election in 1964, any public risk was unacceptable. The relationship ended, but they remained friends. Mary was still regarded as a member of the inner circle; Jackie invited her to the birthday party she gave for Jack on May 29, 1963, even though Mary told a friend that Jackie "did not particularly enjoy the fact that her husband was so fond of both Mary and Tony." Mary described Jackie as "impenetrable" and her relationship with her as "not warm";[31] evidence, perhaps, that Jackie suspected, even if she did not know, the possibility of a relationship with Jack.

Jackie continued to be a potent asset abroad for Jack. Every year he took a trip to Latin America, preaching "democratic—as opposed to Communist—revolution" and reinforcing the Alliance for Progress. In late June 1962 they made a high-profile three day visit to Mexico for which Jackie had been polishing her Spanish with the help of Linguaphone records. On their arrival in Mexico City, he saluted the Mexican revolution, adding that "the revolution of this hemisphere" would be incomplete until "every child has a meal and every student has an opportunity to study, and everyone who wishes to work can find a job, and everyone who wishes a home can find one and everyone who is old can have security . . ."

After a recent buffeting at home, where the U.S. business community, nervous after Kennedy faced down U.S. Steel over its unilateral inflationary price rise, accused him of running an anti-business administration, and the American Medical Association and a recalcitrant Congress opposed his Medicare plans, the President was delighted to find himself so popular south of the border. "By the uncounted millions," Time reported, "Mexicans gave him and his pretty wife the warmest abrazo and the greatest outpouring of goodwill he had yet seen on his travels."

No one had been sure of the kind of welcome the Kennedys would receive from their prickly and often anti-gringo neighbor but it had been "tumultuous," surprising both the Mexican government and the White House with the intensity of its emotion. Jackie looked beautiful and won hearts by her ability to answer TV reporters' questions in Spanish. At a banquet given by the Kennedys she gave a speech, which was broadcast, speaking for ten minutes without notes and with an excellent accent, a bravura performance.

Jackie was enchanted with her husband's reception, as she told Arthur Schlesinger in an enthusiastic letter, thanking him for sending her Mexican magazine reports of the trip. She was touched by the Mexicans' love for JFK and bitter against everyone who had treated them like servants for years when they didn't deserve it."

But while she was prepared to do her utmost for husband and country abroad, she was still not interested in campaigning at home. Kennedy, however, took these midterm congressional elections very seriously; his failure to win votes in a Democratic Congress was damaging his presidency and his credibility. According to Schlesinger, he traveled more miles in the 1962 campaign than Eisenhower had covered in 1954 and 1958 put together. His central theme was to establish the difference in domestic policy between the two parties: "We have won and lost vote after vote by one or two or three votes in the Senate, and three, four or five votes in the House of Representatives," he would say, "and I don't think we can find jobs for our people, I don't think we can educate our younger people, I don't think we can provide security for our older citizens, when we have a party which votes 'no.' " He would conclude with sharpening voice and stabbing hand: "And that's why this election is important."[32]

Kennedy's domestic problems were in the House of Representatives, where southern Democrats held the balance of power and were almost unanimously opposed to the agenda of northern liberals, the basic national Democratic platform, which included increased foreign aid, civil rights, federal aid to education and medical care for the aged. The trouble was with the radical right, always strong beneath the surface of American life. "The fury of the right-wing response to Kennedy was a measure of his impact on the nation," Schlesinger wrote. "If the intellectuals did not always recognize a friend, the reactionaries lost no time in recognizing an enemy."[33] In the spring of 1961 Major General Edwin A. Walker had been relieved of his division command in West Germany for spreading ultra-right-wing political material through the forces under him. He later retired to Dallas to promote the John Birch Society, an organization of isolationists, nationalists and racists living, as Schlesinger put it, "in a dreamworld of no communism, no overseas entanglements, no United Nations, no federal government, no labor unions, no Negroes or foreigners . . ."[34] In a typical outburst, E. M. Dealey, chairman of the board of the *Dallas Morning News*, told the President, "We need a man on horseback to lead this nation, and many people in Texas and the southwest think you are riding Caroline's bicycle."[35] Significantly, that spring saw the publication of the best-selling *Seven Days in May* by Washington newspapermen Fletcher Knebel and Charles Bailey, a thriller about an attempted military coup against the President. "Could it happen here?" Paul Fay asked Kennedy, as they were cruising off Hyannis Port. The President's reply was, "It's possible . . ."[36]

Everything about Kennedy fed the resentment of the right: he was young, rich, good-looking, Catholic, intelligent, Ivy League, Yankee, with a large, ambitious Irish Catholic family and a beautiful wife who wore foreign clothes and spoke foreign languages. (In Georgia, it was reported, the film *PT-109* was advertised as "See how the Japs almost got Kennedy.") In the two years after November 1961 the Secret Service investigated thirty-four death threats against Kennedy from the state of Texas alone. That autumn Bobby Kennedy told his Russian contact Georgi Bolshakov that he feared for his brother's life: "In a gust of hate, 'they' may go to any length . . ." Bolshakov assumed that the Attorney General was talking about American right-wingers.[37]

At Hyannis Port in July the normally camera-shy Jackie was prepared—and even seemed to enjoy—taking part in a Kennedy propaganda show, using as a prop the formidably clean-cut astronaut John Glenn. Glenn had provided the first real success of Kennedy's space program aimed at fulfilling his pledge to put a man on the moon before the end of the decade. On February 20, 1962, Glenn had succeeded in orbiting the world three times, narrowly risking death as the heat shield on his capsule began to break up before successfully bringing it down on manual control. The Americans were well behind the Russians in the space race— Yuri Gagarin had orbited the globe in April 1961—and after ten attempts Glenn represented their first success. Glenn was the ideal man to have made it: a daring pilot and war hero, all-American boy and churchgoing family man from a small town in Ohio. Lyndon Johnson had been practically counting the votes his success would produce. "If only he were a Negro," he said wistfully.

On July 22, as the *New York Daily News* put it,

Star athletes of the John F. Kennedy family and the John H. Glenns teamed up today to stage a dazzling 3-hour water show in Lewis Bay. Undisputed star was Jacqueline Kennedy, wearing a skin-tight, one piece black and white bathing suit and then a flaming pink one. "Jackie" was in the pink number when she skied in tandem with grinning spaceman Col. John Glenn. Both were on mono-skis and put on a show for a flotilla of boats including the *Marlin* with the President, his father and senatorial candidate Ted aboard, two press boats, and a crowd of sightseers, a Coast Guard cutter carrying Secret Service agents, and speedboats loaded with local constables. Jackie even skied holding Caroline in an orange life preserver in front of her.

The *New York Daily News* reporter Gwen Gibson was astounded at the way in which Jackie "seemed to delight in performing for the cameras." She added, "It was most unusual for the Kennedys to allow the press boat to idle alongside as they did today . . ." The family was also there to help Teddy, who was running for Jack's former Massachusetts Senate seat, which had been kept warm for him by Jack's old friend Ben Smith. Election-time politics was one thing; obscure Latin-American presidents quite another. Jackie refused to leave the beach to return to Washington to greet the visiting President of Ecuador so Jack took Rose to serve as his hostess in the White House—"an unusual arrangement" was the press comment.

For Jackie, August was a month of pure pleasure, far away from domestic politics in Italy with Stas and Lee. The Radziwills had rented the twelfth-century Villa Episcopio from the Duca Riccardo di Sangro, founder of the Corviglia Club at St. Moritz. The villa, situated in the enchanting hill town of Ravello, stood on the edge of a cliff eleven hundred feet above the sea with spectacular views across the Gulf of Salerno. Jackie left New York with Caroline on August 7 for Naples via Rome and arrived at Ravello on the eighth. The party consisted of international friends—all of whom knew each other and were invited because they were fun—who arrived and left at various times during the month: Gianni and Marella Agnelli, Benno Graziani and his wife Nicole, Robin Douglas-Home and his wife, the ex-model Sandra Paul, Frankie More O'Ferrall, Harry Hambleden, Arkady Gerney and Stas's partner Felix Fenston, among them. Anything more different from the hearty, frenetically athletic Kennedy compound would have been impossible to imagine. Days were spent down at the beach where Agnelli's friend and lawyer, Sandro d'Urso, had a beach house, nights speeding by boat for dinner in Positano or at *palazzi* in Naples and villas on Capri.

Harry Hambleden, a great friend of Stas, whose country house in the Thames valley, Turville Grange, was ten miles down the road from Harry's estate, spent two weekends there: "It was an amusing group. Gianni Agnelli had organized special little open cars, and we went down the hill to Amalfi (a highly dangerous precipitous narrow road with hairpin bends) at a terrifyingly dangerous speed to board the boats. Felix Fenston had a stick with a rifle inside and he used to let it off and all the Secret Service were electrified and terrified.

"Jackie was very, very good at the job. I mean, when she had to do a tour around Ravello it was [he imitated Jackie's breathy voice], 'Oh, Mr. Mayor . . .' interspersed with amusing asides if I happened to be next to her. It was 'Oh, Mr. Mayor . . .' and that sort of thing, and then I suddenly heard, 'Oh, Harry, what a cute little bottom you've got . . .' All said *sotto voce* . . .

"That weekend we went from one farce to another," Hambleden remembered. Through Gianni Agnelli they were invited to dinner with a Neapolitan count in the garden of his *palazzo* serenaded by a famous Neapolitan singer. "Then we went into the house and the Conte, I think, was with his mistress not his wife, in true Neapolitan fashion. I was lagging a bit behind—as I remember there were glass cases with the odd old gun—muskets and that sort of thing. There was a crack, a loud crack, and suddenly the mistress came rushing back screaming "O, la moglie del Presidente è morte, è morte." What had happened, I think, was that Gianni Agnelli had picked this gun up and said, 'Oh, that's very boring,' and put it back. And Benno Graziani picked it up and it went off. These bullets, or whatever they have in there, went whizzing into the wall where Jackie was standing there, three feet away from her. There was consternation and then everyone laughed and made fun of it. Next day, I happened to see Mr. [Clint] Hill [Secret Service man assigned to Jackie] and he was looking pale. I said, 'Mr. Hill, how are you feeling this morning?' And he said, 'Lord Hambleden, I'm not feeling well.' He had it up to here, poor man."[38]

Jackie wanted to meet Princess Irene Galitzine, creator of the palazzo pajamas, which were now the uniform of the international set. A beautiful Russian who worked in Florence and Rome, Galitzine was the hottest fashion designer of the moment and had made several things for Jackie for the trip to India and Pakistan. She and her husband, Silvio Medici, had a villa on Capri; Jackie arranged a meeting through Gianni Agnelli. To avoid the press, Agnelli's boat had sailed backward and forward among rumors that Jackie would be landing in the port of Capri. Instead, wearing bathing suits and carrying their evening clothes, the party anchored undetected beneath the Medicis' rented villa. Irene Galitzine escorted Jackie to what she described as her "minuscule" bathroom where Jackie, totally relaxed, asked for a vodka as she sat on the toilet before putting on her green Thai silk palazzo pajamas.[39]

After dinner, which had been accompanied by three singer-guitarists, Jackie expressed a wish to walk around the streets of Capri. The party, including Mario d'Urso (then a banker, now an Italian senator and a lifelong friend of Jackie), drove down to the piazza where there were the accustomed scuffles between police and photographers, while the delighted inhabitants opened their shops in anticipation. Jackie walked the length of the via Quisisana and bought two pairs of sandals before going to the Number Two nightclub. There she danced the Twist and the cha-cha before leaving to board the Agnellis' yacht for a trip back to Amalfi, serenaded under the moonlight by Scarola, a celebrated local singer-guitarist. On August 29, shortly before her return home, she paid a second visit to Capri, buying twelve silk ties for Jack, two bracelets and a pair of pants for herself. The following evening Irene Galitzine and her husband were invited back to a farewell dinner at the Villa Episcopio. The next day Jackie and Caroline flew back to the United States to join Jack and John Jr. at Hammersmith Farm.

By now whatever Jackie did was international news. Photographs and reports depicted her leading the jet set life in newspapers and magazines all over the western world. Complaints about the dangers of her taking the four-year-old Caroline waterskiing were voiced in a popular English Sunday paper, while there was a running debate in the United States as to whether she should allow herself to be photographed in a bathing suit at all.

The President, who had been enjoying what *Time* called his "bachelor summer"— to an extent of which it was probably unaware—became increasingly concerned about the effect on the voters of the increasingly critical press coverage of Jackie's Italian vacation. "More Caroline, less Agnelli," read the cryptic but graphic cable he reportedly sent to Jackie at Ravello, and was prompted not by sexual jealousy but political concern. He ordered Jackie to come back before the end of the month. Friends witnessed his irritation "when Jackie went to Italy and didn't come home when she should have come home." Jackie was giving Middle America and right-wing America plenty of ammunition to fire at the Kennedy presidency. The *New York Daily News* syndicate published a report of her nightclubbing activities, headed "Jackie's Big Night in Pirate's Den," which described her arrival in Capri after a "four-mile moonlit boat ride from Amalfi" at a "beach-level cave decorated like a pirate's den" with Lee and four others "including an Italian duke and two counts," with whom she danced the highlife to calypso music.

Reading the reports, the columnist Drew Pearson jotted furious notes: "How can a man handle the problems of the nation when he can't handle his wife? Wife off dancing with red blouse, red slacks & red shoes with some aristocrat 4 in the morning. Doesn't she have enough respect for her husband to be good wife?"[40]

On August 31 Jack, Jackie and Caroline were reunited for the Labor Day weekend at Newport, where John Jr. and Miss Shaw had spent the summer with the Auchinclosses. When Jack was there Hughdie and Janet moved out to the eighteenth-century house known as the Castle down the hill from Hammersmith to allow the President space for his inevitable entourage. Otherwise it was very much a family party. With the younger Auchinclosses in attendance, they would go swimming at Bailey's Beach, or cruise round Narragansett Bay on the *Honey Fitz*. Jackie and the children spent the entire month of September at Hammersmith Farm, apart from a brief visit by Jackie and Jack on September 8 to Hyannis Port to see Joe, who had been released from New York University's Institute of Physical Medicine and Rehabilitation in July.

Earlier the entire family had attended his admission to the residential Horizon House in a bustle of noise and activity, which so disturbed the old man that he erupted in a shriek, banging his feet on the ground. His daughters and Ethel fled. A few hours later Jackie came quietly into the room:

> At times the First Lady was a woman of the most willful manipulativeness, selfish and self-absorbed. There was also a Jackie who was a woman of exquisite sensitivity and concern. It was this woman who

knelt on a footstool in front of Joe and whispered, "I'm praying for you every day, Grandpa, so you work hard while you're here." She knew how Joe had dominated the world around him, and she placed her head in his lap, as if she needed his solace. Then she kissed his crippled hand and his crippled face. As she whispered to Joe, he grew peaceful and relaxed, until his face did not look contorted at all. The rehabilitation was painful for Joe to experience and his family to watch; in his frustration he would flail out with his arm, screaming incomprehensibly. Once again Jackie had an ability to calm him which his own family did not. She brought him a handsome walking stick and, using it, he walked for the first time. When he sat down, exhausted by the effort, Jackie took his hands and kissed them, saying, "Grandpa, remember when you told us that you didn't believe in coming out in second place? You came out first today, Grandpa. You had yourself a victory . . ."[41]

Jack flew back from Washington to Newport to be with Jackie on their ninth wedding anniversary on September 12. Ironically, as the couple celebrated the occasion, long-rumbling rumors were surfacing about a previous marriage between Jack in 1947 and a beautiful blond Chicagoan named Durie Malcolm—subsequently Bersbach Desloge, Shevlin, Appleton. The source of the rumor was an obscure tract, *The Blauvelt Family Genealogy* compiled by Louis Blauvelt over a period of thirty years from 1926 to 1956, and published in 1957 by the Association of Blauvelt Descendants. According to the genealogy, Durie's mother, Isabel Cooper, married her father, Fred Kerr, and divorced him, subsequently marrying George H. Malcolm in 1929 and moving to Palm Beach, where Durie, who took her stepfather's name, married as her third husband John F. Kennedy. Blauvelt's information was inaccurate in several respects and apparently based on a cutting from a Miami newspaper reporting that Kennedy had been seen in a Miami nightclub with Durie Malcolm. Subsequent press digging revealed a cutting from the *New York World Telegram* by Charles Ventura, dated January 20, 1947:

> Jack (John F.) Kennedy, who won the Navy's highest award for heroism by swimming through a sea of flame to rescue two of his PT crew, has just been voted another decoration. Palm Beach's cottage colony wants to give [him] its annual Oscar for achievement in the field of romance . . . giving Durie Malcolm Desloge the season's outstanding rush. The two were inseparable at all social functions and sports events. They even drove down to Miami to hold hands at football games and wager on the horses . . .

On November 22, 1961, Hoover had dictated a memorandum for his personal files to the effect that he had mentioned the affair to Robert Kennedy when he called and asked him if he had seen it. Bobby replied that he had and that a number of newspapermen had spoken to him about it:

The Attorney General stated the fellow who put it together is dead, and the executor of the estate went through the material to find out where he got the information and all he found was a newspaper clipping saying the President had gone out with the girl. The Attorney General stated that the girl used to go out with his brother, Joe, and that the President, Jack, took her out once. He stated the newspaper people contacted the girl and, in fact, a lot of the facts regarding her were incorrect . . . I stated what impressed me was that all of a sudden there is circulation of it. The Attorney General stated the newspapermen come in and he tells them he hopes they print it because then "we" could all retire for life on what "we" collect.[42]

That, however, was not the end of the matter, as far as Hoover and the FBI were concerned. According to a Washington hostess and friend of the family, Durie and her husband at that time had taken a house in Newport that first summer of Kennedy's presidency. "Durie Desloge [Shevlin] called me up one morning and said, 'What do I do?' The Secret Service, somebody official, would call her and ask her whether she'd been married to him or not. And she said, 'What do I do?' And I said, 'There's only one thing you can do and that is to keep your mouth shut.' She did not come out and say, 'I was married to Jack for one night,' [but] I don't doubt for a minute that there was some sort of relationship . . . She was very upset by this call . . . maybe they were drunk, I don't know. There were only big rumors."[43]

On January 15, 1962, Jackie wrote to Clark Clifford, the Washington attorney, thanking him for his help: "You always come to the rescue whether it is Profiles in Courage or the Blaufeld [sic] case . . ." Earlier that month the President had summoned Clifford and told him the story that was circulating. He said that he had indeed known Durie Malcolm and that they had had two dates together. "One may have been a dinner date in which we went dancing. The other, to my recollection, was a football game." He repeated the story Bobby had told Hoover, which was that she had been a date of his brother Joe some years earlier. Clifford, who had known Durie Malcolm in St. Louis when she was married to Desloge, called her and quizzed her about the Blauvelt story. "Good God," she said. "Married to President Kennedy. That's a laugh."[44] Her story matched the President's—a dinner date in New York and a football game. She denied there had ever been anything serious and signed an affidavit stating that she had never been married to John F. Kennedy.

The story continued to circulate, surfacing in May 1962 in the *Thunderbolt*, the right-wing publication that later printed Florence Kater's allegations about Pamela Turnure. Four months later, on September 2, 1962, *Parade*, a nationally distributed Sunday newspaper supplement, printed a letter asking if the rumor was true, and on the same day it appeared in the British press. The President felt it was time to react. He commissioned Ben Bradlee to write a piece for *Newsweek*, to be published in the September 24 issue, discussing the rumor and dismissing it. *Newsweek* research showed Blauvelt's record to have been wrong in several respects: Durie Malcolm's first husband had been not Desloge but Bersbach, whom she divorced in the summer of 1938; she had subsequently married Desloge in January 1939; on January 24, 1947, they were divorced and on July 12, 1947, she and Thomas Shevlin, former husband of Lorraine Cooper, were married and had remained so for the last fourteen years. According to Bradlee's calculation, the only time Durie was legally free to marry Jack had been between the summer of 1938 and January 1939 when he was a junior at Harvard, and late January to July of 1947, the first six months of his first term in Congress. When he raised the question, the President told him, "She was a girlfriend of my brother, Joe, and I took her out a couple of times, I guess. That's all. You haven't got it, Benjy," he added. "You're all looking to tag me with some girl, and none of you can do it, because it just isn't there." Jackie listened "with a smile on her face."[45]

Jackie could afford to sit there with a smile on her face as Jack told Bradlee that the evidence wasn't there. He knew it had been destroyed. His friends the Spaldings had been in Palm Beach at the time of the 1947 newspaper report by Charles Ventura, after Durie was divorced from Firmin Desloge on January 24 and before she married Shevlin on July 12, 1947. Betty Spalding remembers "that there was some sort of marriage ceremony at 2 A.M."[46] She also recalls Eunice telling her that "the Old Man was furious" about it. Her ex-husband Chuck told Seymour Hersh that at Jack's request he had gone and "got" the marriage papers with the help of a Palm Beach lawyer. Apart from not being a Catholic, Durie Malcolm had already been twice divorced; Joe Kennedy was well aware that a marriage like that could ruin his son's career. So it appears that there was a marriage, but once the documentary evidence had been removed, it could be denied. Since Jack had not been married in a Catholic church, it would have been easy enough for Joe to acquire a nullity declaration from the Church through his high level contacts like Cardinal Cushing. When Clark Clifford obtained Durie's affidavit, Jack—and probably also Jackie—knew that he was safe.

That September, Jack and Jackie, with old Joe in a wheelchair and three hundred guests including Bill Walton, the Spaldings and the Fays, watched the America's Cup yacht races from the deck of the destroyer *Joseph P. Kennedy Jr.* Oatsie Leiter was there too: "It was the first time I heard in the history of the U.S. Navy that there was a full bar set up, because you're not allowed to have any alcohol on a naval vessel. It was so impressive. There were tables and chairs set out on the deck and we all sat there—absolutely divine . . . And Jack was in seventh heaven because he really did love the Navy and love the sea . . ."[47]

Jackie left Newport briefly after entertaining President Ayub Khan of Pakistan to lunch at Hammersmith Farm to take him down to Glen Ora to see Sardar. On September 25 they took a party to the National Theater to see the pre-Broadway opening of *Mr. President*, a gala evening organized by Ethel and Jean in aid of the family psychiatric charities. The play itself was described as "a sorry, soggy musical by Irving Berlin," but the evening was "the sveltest, splashiest, most scrambled-after social affair that the nation's capital has seen in years." The theater was followed by a dinner dance for six hundred at the British Embassy. By the evening of the following day Jackie was back in Newport to resume her vacation, only returning to Washington with the children on October 9.

"Jackie does as she likes," Drew Pearson scribbled, adding, with journalistic license, "has spent the past three months out of Washington," "wife of Pres. can't do this. No one can especially not wife of Pres. Twist parties—Peppermint Lounge [New York nightclub and home of the Twist]. Skiing when Pres. Ecuador here—refused see visiting Russian peace bodies."[48] Jackie even tried to get out of going to Eleanor Roosevelt's funeral in November in favor of a hunting weekend at Glen Ora. An entry in Mary Gallagher's diary for November 8 read: "JBK does not wish to attend the funeral of Mrs. Eleanor Roosevelt." On this occasion, however, the President put his foot down. Gallagher's entry for the following day read: "JBK *will* attend funeral!"[49] Jackie blithely hosted a small dinner dance for fifty people on Friday, the eve of Mrs. Roosevelt's funeral, then flew off next day with the official party to attend the service on Saturday, November 10, at the Roosevelt estate on the Hudson River, in Hyde Park. Immediately afterward she and Jack returned to Washington and took off for Glen Ora by helicopter.

Pearson's criticism of Jackie was unfair. Although she had spent relatively little time in Washington that year, when she was there she had concentrated on things that interested her, principally her determination to make not just the White House but Washington itself a showcase for the arts. "I think a lot of people do not realize what a serious working side there was to her," Lady Bird Johnson said. "I just think she chose what she wanted to do and didn't veer off that path. You get so many appeals in that position . . . but you really don't get much time and you have to choose what really makes your heart sing."[50]

Liz Carpenter, Lyndon Johnson's press secretary, whose admiration for Jackie was not unqualified, said, "I appreciate terrifically what she did for the arts. She started this series of White House–sponsored performances and one of them was the play *Our Town* which is a classic by Thornton Wilder. He was alive then and he came up—and even then she didn't come. That's the kind of thing that Lady Bird would never do—she'd be there in the first row. And Thornton Wilder said that Mrs. Kennedy had given the arts a beacon light, and that's true. Because we're not a country that used to subsidize the arts and Jackie helped make that happen, very much . . ."[51]

It was Jackie who had initiated the appointment of August Heckscher as "Special Consultant to the President on the Arts" in 1961. Heckscher's presence in the White House ensured official backing for his arts projects, and not simply painting, ballet, opera and theater but "the whole environmental condition of the nation's life and that architecture and city planning were very important."[52]

Yet Jackie, Heckscher recalled, was "a somewhat ambivalent figure in all this: in the first place she was devoted to the private life that she could keep for herself and her children and yet, on the other hand, she found that she was becoming more and more the representative of a bright flame of cultural interests in this country. Sometimes she seemed to draw back as if she didn't want to get too much involved in all this. The public had the impression, for example, that Mrs. Kennedy was doing an enormous amount for the arts, was busy every moment. But Mrs. Kennedy herself was much too wise to be busy every moment promoting the arts. She would do one thing with superb taste and it would have a tremendous impact . . . We were always—I was working very closely with Tish Baldrige—trying to get Mrs. Kennedy to do things which she wouldn't do; to receive people at the White House or to ask certain people for dinner, and she would plead that she was busy or that she wasn't having any state dinners at that time, or one thing or another. I remember being disappointed, for example, when I finally did persuade Mrs. Kennedy to invite some poets who were gathering in Washington for a convocation at the Library of Congress to come to the White House for sherry, and she agreed to do that. And that fell just at the time of the Cuban crisis and she canceled it. I always regretted that because I think it would have been a glorious thing if we could say that, now at the moment when the President was facing this supreme crisis in the nation's life, the White House was filled with a great gathering of leading American poets . . . That same moment when Mrs. Kennedy was canceling the visit of the group of poets to the White House, pictures appeared in the papers showing Khrushchev going behind the scenes at the opera in Moscow and greeting American singers who were there . . ."

Typically, Jackie had said to Heckscher, "Mr. Heckscher, I will do anything for the arts you want." Then, equally typically, she qualified it by saying, "But of course, I can't be away too much from the children and I can't be present at too many cultural events." Then, with a sort of smile, she said, "After all, I'm *not* Mrs. Roosevelt." Tish, Heckscher said, was always full of enthusiasms. "But she was always getting her ears pinned back a little bit . . . Tish would send up some idea to Mrs. Kennedy and Mrs. Kennedy would just write 'No!' on it." As Jackie told leading Washingtonian Kay Halle, she hated committees and public lobbying, even for the arts.

Jack and Jackie, with Bill Walton, were involved from the beginning with the saving and restoration of Lafayette Square. The very first week he was in office, Jack entrusted Walton with the examination of a project left over from the Eisenhower administration waiting for a decision. It involved plans for modern government office buildings to replace the old federal houses of Lafayette Square near the White House. "I thought they were wildly unattractive plans," Walton said, "and I showed them to Jackie, and she agreed with me, it wasn't the kind of architecture we wanted facing the White House." Jackie, Walton said, played a key part in saving the square: "She said, 'Until the bulldozers move, we're ahead and you can't give up.' And she meant it, and we didn't. She was really riding us there." The President became deeply interested: "It was his pet project," said Walton. "In Hyannis in the summer I brought up there a little model of the square and a set of paper façades in different styles to put on this and he got down on the floor and just loved it . . . And played with it. And Jackie came in and said, 'You two . . .' And later, another time she caught us on his bedroom floor [in the White House]. He was supposed to be taking a nap, meaning he just had on his underpants, and it was like two thirty in the afternoon. I'd been let in because I'd had a crisis and something that had to be decided that afternoon. We're on the floor with another model and she got up and went out and got her camera and took a picture and sent me a copy. And it said, 'The President and the Czar,' because the newspapers had started calling me the Czar of Lafayette Square."

As with everything in Washington, there were political complications. "It got to be a very tough problem," Walton remembered. "We had certain requisites back from Congress for the amount of floor space that had to be worked into these areas. And the architects found it insoluble, if we preserved the buildings facing the park. But Jackie said, 'No. Until the bulldozers move, I will not let this happen,' so we kept sending the architects back and back until finally the President himself asked Jack Warnecke to look over the matter."[53]

J. C. "Jack" Warnecke, son of another famous architect, John Carl Warnecke, based in San Francisco, had first come to Jack's attention as an All-American football player at Stanford. "We were on a team that astounded everybody," Warnecke said, "because we had lost every single game the year before . . . Much to his [Jack's] astonishment we turned around and won every single game including the famous Rose Bowl, which made us national champions." They had first met in 1956 when Jack was out campaigning for Adlai Stevenson on the west coast. Paul Fay organized a date for Jack with Warnecke as the cover. "I had to take a very beautiful lady who was a blind date for Jack, who needed to be with somebody, so I got pulled in," Warnecke recalled.

In March 1962 Warnecke happened to be in Washington. "I phoned up Red [Fay]," said Warnecke, "who was then Under-Secretary for the Navy and he said he was having a party and would I like to go see Jack. And I said, 'Sure, I'd love to,' and so I went to the White House. Red and the PT boat boys were in the Oval Room telling locker-room stories, so there I was with all these ladies in this great big room, and Jack comes in, leading the pack, looks at all these ladies, and then looks over and sees me and comes right over to me, and he said, 'Rosebowl, what the hell are you doing here?' "

They chatted for a few minutes and the next night at dinner Jack asked Fay, "What does Rosebowl do?"

"He's a very successful architect," Fay replied.

After a moment's thought, the President said, "Have him call me tomorrow morning at nine thirty. Jackie is very upset about the plans for the new building to be put up on Lafayette Square. She feels that what they are planning will ruin the beauty and historic charm of this area, and I agree with her."

"Jackie had left for India," Warnecke said. "The two of them had been working together on this ever since he was President . . . Jackie had left and she had written this letter to the GSA [General Services Administration] which I didn't discover until twenty years later, strong words telling the head of the GSA that the President of the U.S. had made a mistake, his friend Bill Walton had approved his plan and it was wrong. She had made a last-ditch stand."[54]

"I've got a terrific architectural problem," Jack told Warnecke. "Call up Bill Walton and find out about it."

"So he did," Walton recalled. "And I spent two or three days with him outlining all the things we'd been through, and he closeted himself, and a couple of days later came up with the idea that was the germ of what we're doing now. And the

President was just overjoyed with it. It just fitted everything he wanted. We got the floor space, we saved the old buildings."[55] Warnecke's idea was what he called a "new concept of contextual designing." His idea for Lafayette Square was based on the London squares with central gardens; to gain the required space he placed the new buildings behind the old, instead of replacing them. Warnecke was getting on a plane back to the west coast when he was telephoned by an architect friend at the GSA: " 'What the hell went on [at that meeting] in the White House today?' 'Well, the President asked me for my advice and I gave it to him.' 'He doesn't want your advice now, he wants you to do it.' So, quick as hell, I got off the plane."[56]

Jackie forged a strong alliance with Bernard L. Boutin, the Kennedy-appointed head of the GSA, and therefore, as overseer of public works, a key figure in her plans for Washington. "I so strongly feel that the White House should give the example in preserving our nation's past," she told him. "Now we think of saving old buildings like Mount Vernon and tear down everything in the nineteenth century—but in the next hundred years there will be none of it left, just plain glass skyscrapers . . ."[57] Not only did she tell Boutin firmly that the President's agreement to Bill Walton's plans for Lafayette Square had been wrong, but she outlined her own vision for the square and its surroundings. Nor had she forgotten an old enemy, George Stewart, the Capitol architect, whose reappointment was imminent and who she was determined should be replaced. He had already torn down so many lovely old buildings near the Capitol, and she hoped Boutin would prevent him from destroying the remaining old houses for the Library of Congress annex. The new Capitol architect, she said, should have a thorough knowledge of architecture and be a preservationist, and she could secretly get a few suggestions.

Later that year Warnecke met Jackie. At a British Embassy dinner dance he cut in on her, tapped her on the shoulder and said, " 'I'm the man you're going to meet tomorrow, would you like to dance?' The next day there she was, on her way to New York, and she came in to see all our models. So basically she took over—with the President. Right after we had the final approval for everything, she had a nice dinner party for me upstairs in the family quarters. That was the end of 'sixty-two. I went to all these parties. I was swept into the middle of Camelot."

⌒

As September 1962 ended, the United States and the Soviet Union edged toward a military confrontation in the Caribbean over Cuba. Over the following month a crisis developed that brought the world to the brink of nuclear war. Kennedy had believed he could topple Fidel Castro without military force; he and Bobby had pushed the CIA to use whatever means necessary—probably including assassination—to remove Castro and Che Guevara from power. He was now considering a military invasion, using conventional weapons, unaware that Khrushchev was preparing simultaneously to envisage the use of nuclear weapons in defense of Cuba. On August 29 a U-2 spy plane flying out of Texas had detected eight SAM (surface-to-air missile) sites on the island only a week or two away from being operational. On September 4 Kennedy issued a warning statement backed up the next day by a call-up order for 15,000 reservists. As yet he did not believe that the Russians had any aggressive intent, but on October 14 another U-2 plane photographed missiles much longer than the SAMs. They were MRBMs (medium-range ballistic missiles), capable of being armed with nuclear warheads and of reaching the United States.

At 9 A.M. on the morning of Tuesday, October 16, McGeorge Bundy brought him the news. "It was a hell of a secret." The President held two secret crisis meetings that day, before taking Jackie to the Alsops' house for a farewell dinner for Charles "Chip" Bohlen on the eve of his departure for the Paris Embassy.[58] According to Alsop, Kennedy was "in the first deep brown study I had ever seen." Hardly saying a word after greeting his hosts, he took Chip Bohlen, who as one of the administration's principal Soviet experts was aware of the crisis, down the garden for a heated discussion. At dinner he said barely a word. Afterward Alsop took the men out into the garden for a drink, the President still noticeably preoccupied. Talk turned to history and its unforeseen chances. "Our . . . Kennedy suddenly looked up and said quietly, 'Of course, if you think simply about the chances in history, you have to quote the odds as somewhere near even that we shall see an H-bomb war within the next ten years.'" Over the next few days the secret meetings of Ex-Comm continued while the President, for security reasons, otherwise kept to his usual schedule. After an early-morning meeting on Friday, October 19, he left at 10:35 A.M. for a long-planned campaign tour to Cleveland, Springfield, Illinois and Chicago. That afternoon Jackie took the children and Joe Kennedy down to Glen Ora.

By lunchtime on Saturday, October 20, Kennedy was back in the White House, summoned urgently by Bobby for another tense meeting to discuss action options and a presidential statement on the crisis. Kennedy, coming down between the doves and the hawks on action, decided on a naval blockade of Cuba, coupled with a demand that Khrushchev remove the missiles, and the preparation of an air strike should Khrushchev not comply. Although the major newspapers on Sunday, October 21, headlined the Chinese attack on India, Salinger told Kennedy that the press would soon be aware of the crisis.

That day Jackie and the children were called back from the country. David Ormsby-Gore recalled, "He wanted her and the children to be there when he was making these awful decisions."[59] Jack had called him in, too, that Sunday morning, and after the President had held an off-the-record cabinet meeting, the two men sat discussing the crisis and waiting for Jackie to arrive, which she did at about half past one. The Ormsby-Gores were back in the White House for dinner again that Sunday evening, with their guests the Duchess of Devonshire and Robin Douglas-Home. At dinner no one mentioned the crisis. With their incredible self-control, neither of the Kennedys betrayed any sign of strain. Jack, although fidgety and constantly called to the telephone, carried on conversation with his usual "batteries of questions about people in whom he was interested . . . their behavior, their motives and secret ambitions; all the tiny facts about people which he fitted into the jigsaw of his mind." Jackie, Douglas-Home noted, was "more restrained." As she explained to him the next day, "She was very conscious of the strain the President was under, but could say nothing about it at the time."[60]

At 7 P.M. on Monday, Kennedy revealed the seriousness of the situation to the American people, who were as yet unaware that they were truly on the verge of a nuclear war, and appealed to the Soviet Union to "move the world back from the abyss of destruction." A fleet of Soviet missile-bearing ships was steaming toward Cuba, while the U.S. Navy set out to enforce the blockade around Cuba that was intended to stop them. The risk of war had never been greater.

Jack did not discuss the mechanics of the crisis with Jackie. "She must have had a terrible time that week," Susan Mary Alsop said, "because one of the junior assistants at the White House at that time was a young man called Mike Forrestal, a great friend of ours . . . After the crisis was over, I saw Mike and said, 'How did you manage to get through that week?' And he said, 'Well, it was all right but I was awfully sorry for Jackie.' 'Oh,' I said. 'Why?' And he said, 'Because nobody ever told her anything. I'd come on her wandering sadly around the halls and she would say to me, "Mike, what's the news?" and I, of course, could tell her. But nobody took the trouble to tell her.' I suppose the President didn't want to talk about it, the last thing he would want. He probably wanted a stiff martini and a little food and a little gossip. News about what the children's day had been, that sort of thing . . ."[61]

On Tuesday, October 23, Jackie had to cancel a dinner for twenty-five to celebrate the arrival of the Maharajah of Jaipur and his wife; but, according to Secret Service logs, fourteen people dined at the White House anyway. They included the Maharajah and his wife, Benno and Nicole Graziani, David Ormsby-Gore and Charlie Bartlett. Around midnight Nicole Graziani made scrambled eggs for the party. "He [Jack] took her hand," Graziani recalled, "and he said, 'You know, maybe tomorrow we will be at war . . .' "[62]

Just over twenty-four hours later, at 2 A.M. on Thursday morning, Kennedy received an angry four-page letter from Khrushchev. The Soviet ships were going ahead. Tensions continued to rise over the following days until Sunday, October 28, when Khrushchev agreed to withdraw the missiles in return for an American pledge not to invade Cuba. Ormsby-Gore, a shrewd firsthand observer of Kennedy's handling of the crisis, thought it represented his finest hour: "He was very remarkable during that week. I think that everybody who worked with him during that week conceived this fantastic admiration for him; the way he kept his humor, the way he could make decisions at the exact time they were needed, the way he could listen to a vast quantity of contradictory advice and come out with what everybody at the end of the day decided was exactly the right action."[63]

As if the continuing missile crisis was not bad enough, John Jr. was ill with a temperature of 104°. Jackie kept her cool, concerned not to add to Jack's worries. On Thursday, October 25, one of the worst days, she went ahead with her social schedule as planned. The Maharajah of Jaipur and his wife came for a drink that morning; in the afternoon she had invited Robin Douglas-Home around while she was being filmed by NBC for a program on the new National Cultural Center, a project in which both she and Jack took special interest and for which Janet

Auchincloss was helping with the fund-raising.[64] Douglas-Home found her surrounded by TV paraphernalia—glaring lights, switchboxes, cables, squads of technicians. "Outwardly, she was the calm, dignified First Lady, an oasis of controlled, glamorous equilibrium in a jungle of mechanical chaos," he wrote. "But inwardly she was mocking . . . her muttered asides to me during the TV session made it almost impossible for me to keep a straight face . . . Like her husband, she invariably deflated any attempts at glorification." After tea Caroline came bounding in with a huge hollow pumpkin, on which she asked Douglas-Home to carve a face for next week's Halloween parties. As Jackie was taking photographs of the pair kneeling on the floor, the President walked in and immediately became engrossed in their activity. Douglas-Home was asked to stay for dinner. Beforehand Jackie instructed him, "For God's sake don't mention Cuba to him." After dinner, in the intervals between urgent telephone calls, Kennedy, cigar in hand, chatted "about such diverse subjects as Lord Beaverbrook's way of running his newspapers, Frank Sinatra's handling of women, and why *Queen* magazine had published a fashion picture of a model (Celia Hammond) lying on a white bearskin sucking her thumb." He made no reference whatsoever to the crisis, apart from saying meditatively of the Russian attitude at the Vienna talks, "It's like trying to talk to people who've spent all their lives in a cellar . . ." Around 10 P.M. he went to bed, appearing later in his nightshirt to say good night.[65]

The first weekend in November, Jackie went with Lee, who had been staying at the White House, originally for the Maharajah of Jaipur's dinner, to Glen Ora. Janet Auchincloss and Robin Douglas-Home traveled with them. The principal object of this particular weekend was Jackie's latest project: a house of their own in Virginia since Mrs. Tartière had refused to extend the lease on Glen Ora. The site on Rattlesnake Mountain had been chosen by Paul Fout; initially called Atoka, Jackie rechristened the house "Wexford" to please Jack (the Kennedys had originally emigrated from County Wexford). In vain: Jack never liked Atoka/ Wexford and never felt at home there. "What am I doing in a place like this?" he said exasperatedly to Ben Bradlee. In November 1962, as the Atoka project was under way, the worst Battle of the Budget took place. The cost of building, furnishing and decorating the Virginia house did not endear it to Jack—and, in any case, it came on top of restoring Glen Ora to its original decoration, as Mrs. Tartière had understandably insisted. He far preferred Camp David, with its spectacular views of the Cactoctin Mountains, where that year he, Jackie and the children had spent the Fourth of July. Wexford, enclosed in woods in the rolling Virginia countryside, did not have the same appeal.

Jackie, however, loved it. The house was modeled on Charlie Whitehouse's, a one-story block with two wings at the back and a terrace in front, with a view down over the trees to the blue hills in the distance. It had three master bedrooms, two children's and a nurse's room and two maids' rooms. It had a three-acre pond where the children could swim and fish, and Jackie had deliberately planned a no-maintenance garden, the house sitting on a ledge with a terrace and no lawns needing mowing, just a big field sweeping away in front. It would be ready in May, she told the Pells on April 8, 1963, and she would be moving their furniture in on April 24 when they returned from Florida. Understandably eager to make economies, with Jack always hounding her, she asked Claiborne if he could find someone who might like to rent it from June. "We got $400 for renting Glen Ora last summer," she told them.[66]

Nineteen sixty-two closed for Jackie on the same note of fashion and pleasure that it had held for her throughout. Celebrating New Year's Eve in Palm Beach as usual at the Wrightsmans' were no less than six of the World's Best-dressed Women: Jackie herself and Lee, plus four others who were on her international social circuit—Jayne Wrightsman, Gloria Guinness, Marella Agnelli and Nicole Alphand, wife of the French ambassador in Washington.

CHAPTER THIRTEEN

Rendezvous with Death

~

I have a rendezvous with death . . .
At midnight in some flaming town . . .

—John F. Kennedy's favorite poem, "I Have a
Rendezvous with Death," by Alan Seeger[1]

For Jackie, lazing away the days at Palm Beach, 1963 promised to be the best year yet. On January 1, with Jack and Lee, she sailed along the Florida coast to Fort Worth marina, where they disembarked for lunch at the Vanderbilt. Much of the rest of the week was spent on the ocean cruising on the *Honey Fitz* with Lee and Peter Lawford among others, and visiting Palm Beach friends like the Earl T. Smiths. She had every cause for satisfaction. Her White House restoration project was well under way and would be almost complete by the end of the year; she had saved Lafayette Square, lighting a beacon for the restoration of old city centers that would be followed down the succeeding years. The new house in Virginia would be ready in May. Most importantly, she knew she was pregnant.

Her present life seemed under control. The White House no longer worried her. She intended to relax and enjoy herself while waiting for the birth of the baby. On January 8, with Jack and Caroline, she returned to Washington by helicopter. Two days later, as she was dictating to Mary Gallagher in her White House sitting room, she asked casually, "Mary, would you say I've done enough till now as First Lady?" It was a rhetorical question and her secretary, suspecting Jackie was pregnant, answered, as expected, that she had done more than enough and should only do what the President felt she must do. Then she called Tish to announce, "I am taking the veil," and ordered her to cut off all outside activity and limit her engagements to only the most important things. She did not see enough of her children, she said, and felt she had done enough as First Lady. She concentrated on family, household affairs, varying the children's menus, instructing the assistant housekeeper on how to make the perfect daiquiri for the evening pre-dinner drink she always had with Jack—two parts rum, three parts frozen limeade, one part fresh lime juice and a few drops of Falernum as a sweetener—and added new recipes to the chef's repertoire—since the previous autumn Jack had suffered a recurrence of his stomach trouble and had been ordered on to the blandest of diets.

With Lee she attended a few inescapable official functions—the President's State of the Union message, a $1,000-a-head Second Inaugural Salute dinner and reception, a dinner for the Vice President and other dignitaries at the White House—and a few private dinners given by the Douglas Dillons and the Franklin Roosevelts, before flying with Jack to New York for a week's shopping, gallery hunting and the theater. The three dined at Le Pavillon before going to a perfor-mance of the British satire *Beyond the Fringe*, then on to a fund-raising party given by the Steve Smiths. Stas Radziwill and Chuck Spalding joined them for a leisurely Sunday lunch at Voisin before Jackie, Jack and Caroline flew back to Washington on February 11. There were dinners and receptions for the President of Venezuela and for the King of the Belgians, and a last weekend at Glen Ora to check on progress at Wexford.

Jackie returned to Glen Ora with mixed feelings: decorating Glen Ora for a two-year lease had been a complete waste of money. The President had some cause for annoyance at Jackie's extravagance, but he continued to indulge her, even paying for two paintings she bought in New York as a late Christmas pres-ent. At the end of March the President ordered Mary Gallagher to show Jackie "the latest clothing figures." Jackie looked at the books without comment, then left that evening for another jaunt to New York. "I knew it wouldn't be long be-fore we'd be re-enacting this little scene again . . . ," Mary Gallagher sighed.[2]

"We are frantic with Congress re-opening, Mona Lisa unveiling, and State Visitors popping up from every country known to man, as well as some that aren't!" Tish Baldrige wrote to her friend, Clare Boothe Luce on January 8, 1963.[3] She was leaving the White House on June 4; the Kennedys, she told Mrs. Luce, had been understanding about her reasons for leaving, including "my desire to STOP BEING POOR. I will cherish every memory of this fantastic experience . . . I feel touched and very humble to have had a hand in the shaping of events. A tiny hand, but nevertheless, the satisfactions are gigantic. And I have loved the Ken-nedys with all my heart—with increasing respect and admiration as the months have passed."

Tish's letters to Clare Boothe Luce disprove rumors that Jackie fired her. She admits that Jackie sometimes resented the way Tish bombarded her with memos, trying to get her to do things she didn't want to do, but she admired Jackie greatly as First Lady: "She had real class, the way she dealt with the house, the maids, the Secret Service, her maid—always the boss, complimenting them when they did right, kind and considerate."[4] Tish's farewell party was held on May 27 in the China Room, where the Marine Band played and Jackie, who had composed a parody of "Arrivederci Roma" as "Arrivederci Letitia," sang it along with the staff.

Tish, to whose work Jackie paid tribute as "invaluable," remained in favor with the Kennedys: she was given a job with the family's Merchandise Mart in Chicago.

Tish was replaced as social secretary by Nancy Tuckerman, Jackie's old friend of New York childhood days and Farmington roommate. Nancy was Jackie's Praetorian Guard, totally devoted and utterly loyal, a selfless buffer against the outside world. Her calm manner was a complete contrast to Tish's whirlwind way of doing things. Jackie, Tish said, "had Nancy anesthetized." "One advantage Nancy had," J. B. West, the White House Chief Usher, wrote, "was her personal friendship with Mrs. Kennedy. She knew all the First Lady's foibles, and how she wanted to operate. She knew exactly what to send upstairs, when to send it, what to discuss with her, and what subjects to avoid. When Nancy approached her with an idea, she sometimes said, 'Oh, Nancy, I don't want to *do* that,' and that would be the end of it."[5]

"She's completely Jackie's slave," said a cousin of Jackie's, and Nancy devoted her life to Jackie, remaining with her until the end, never marrying. "One day I said to her," John Fairchild recalled, " 'Why don't you go out and have some life? Why are you devoting your life as a slave? What is the future for you?' She said nothing."[6]

When Jackie offered her the job at the White House, Nancy objected that she had had no training for it. Jackie couldn't see that that mattered. "It's a very simple job," she said. "It's mostly fun."

"While I never thought the job simple," Tuckerman said, "Jackie did more than her share to make it fun. And fun was when she'd put on a disguise and we'd venture outside the White House gates unescorted. Or when the Goodyear blimp came to Washington and we took Caroline and John on a spur-of-the-moment jaunt over the Virginia countryside, while the Secret Service, with no advance notice, were forced to follow the blimp's course by car, weaving through the roads at breathtaking speed."

Nancy's first major task was to mastermind an evening in honor of the King of Afghanistan. Jackie made sure that Nancy's press debut as organizer of state entertainment would be a spectacular one with fireworks on the South Lawn. On the evening of the dinner, Jack Kennedy gave instructions that the time allotted for fireworks should be cut. As a result, the fireworks supplier packed eight minutes' explosives into four—with stunning results. The first blast was so huge that the President's Secret Service agent and the King of Afghanistan's bodyguard leaped forward to protect them; subsequently the White House switchboard was inundated with calls from Washingtonians wondering if a bomb had dropped or a plane had crashed. Next day the fireworks and Nancy got rave reviews, the King a passing mention. " 'See, Nancy?' Jackie said. 'You upstaged the King of Afghanistan.' She gave me the credit that was due to her, a typical act of friendship," Tuckerman commented.

Nancy, a New Yorker with a distinguished family tree, had been working in a New York travel agency, with Janet and Hughdie Auchincloss among her clientele, and occasionally helping her mother in her party-organization business before taking up the White House job. For Jackie, she was the ideal helper, reserved, efficient and discreet. According to her ebullient mother, she was the quiet one of the family, the middle child between an extrovert older sister and boisterous younger brother. "She has terrific tact," her mother said of her. "She handles details with superb efficiency. And she keeps her mouth shut!"[7] With the arrival of Nancy, Jackie had the rock she needed in her turbulent life.

After the official announcement of Jackie's pregnancy at Palm Beach on April 18, both Kennedys were thinking ahead to post–White House days. Privately Jackie worried about Jack's future, and had confessed her fears to Benno Graziani in late-night talks on her trip to India in March 1962. "Jackie was a little worried, because she said, 'In two years maybe he won't be President, what will he do? And he's crippled . . .' I remember exactly the words she said, because he was always in pain. She said, 'What will he do?' "[8] The President also talked about his post–White House future, but not with any great seriousness.

Both were particularly concerned about the siting and design of the John F. Kennedy Presidential Library. After a note on the subject from Jackie in January, Boutin wrote to reassure her that they had been "working very quietly with Harvard on a site and some early planning for the President's Library up at Cambridge . . . As these plans progress, I would certainly appreciate any ideas you might have that would be helpful to us . . ."[9] Thanking him for his letter on January 30, Jackie replied, ". . . the thing I really care about is the President's Library; he says you suggested some brilliant changes and, before any design is picked, I would have to see that."[10] Jackie, Warnecke and Boutin had been working closely together on the plans for Lafayette Square; she had already asked Warnecke "long ago" "to do a bit of research and give us some ideas on the Pres. Library in Boston."

Both Kennedys saw the restoration of Lafayette Square and Pennsylvania Avenue as future monuments to the JFK Presidency in Washington. In the summer of 1963 Jackie had the imaginative idea of placing an ancient Egyptian temple on the Potomac, where its situation on the river would mirror its original site on the Upper Nile, soon to be flooded by the reservoir of the Aswan Dam. One Sunday evening in the White House, Dick Goodwin had brought in a loose-leaf folder of monuments that had been designated by the Egyptian Department of Antiquities as worthy of being saved for posterity. She and Goodwin had gone through the book and she had chosen the Temple of Dendur.

The initiative had indeed come from Jackie, Dick Goodwin recalled. Gianni Agnelli had spoken to her about it and she got the President interested. The United Nations had run a big campaign to raise money to save the monuments that were going to be destroyed by the Aswan Dam. "If you made the biggest contribution you got a temple, that was the prize," Goodwin said. "So I put together a book. I had to get a lot of pictures of these monuments, with quotes from Malraux about saving the Pyramids and I looked into different plans of how to save it. Kennedy, he had a problem, he had to go to Congress to get $65 million— that's a lot of money and Rooney, who was Head of the Appropriations Committee and you had to go through him, an Irishman from Brooklyn, said these are nothing but a bunch of rocks. Obviously he [JFK] wanted to do it but it was the political issue, congressional relations. And finally, when I saw he was wavering, I said to him, 'Mr. President, Napoleon only brought an obelisk back to Paris and you could bring a temple back to Washington.' And he said, 'Let's do it.' "[11]

Nineteen sixty-three was to be the year of the growing profile of the civil rights movement. On the afternoon of February 12, Lincoln's birthday, Kennedy had accepted a 246-page report on the Negro struggle for civil rights over the hundred years since the Emancipation Proclamation in 1863. It did not make for happy reading. "A freedom more fictional than real" was the inheritance of the modern Negro, as the report put it. "The legally free Negro citizen was denied the franchise, excluded from public office, assigned to inferior and separate schools, herded into ghettos, directed to the back of the bus, treated unequally in the courts of justice and segregated in his illness, his worship and even in his death . . ."

That same day the President gave a reception at the White House for black leaders. Among the guests was Sammy Davis Jr., whom he knew as a member of Sinatra's Rat Pack. Davis was a controversial figure because of his marriage to Swedish actress Mai Britt, considered shocking in an era in which interracial marriages were rare. Jack wanted to avoid the potential political fallout from a photograph of the couple together in the White House and told one of his aides to tell Jackie to take Mai Britt aside so that she would not be photographed with Davis. Jackie refused furiously to fall in with the suggestion or to go downstairs at all. It took all Jack's persuasive powers to bring her down to the reception where, after being photographed with the Johnsons, Ethel and eleven black leaders, she left in tears. She was outraged by what she saw as insulting political subterfuge.

Burke Marshall, the distinguished Yale law professor who worked prominently in the Kennedy administration on civil rights, said that Jackie was, "in common with most of her political friends, and many personal ones as well, in sympathy with the civil rights movement in the 1960s."[12] Jackie's personal contribution was to ensure that racial segregation played no part in the White House. She changed the social pattern by ensuring that blacks were invited to all official entertainments.[13] Black writers, like James Baldwin, and singers—Marian Anderson, Grace Bumbry—were honored guests. The son of Jack Kennedy's press aide, Andrew Hatcher, attended the White House school. According to contemporary sources, blacks saw her as genuinely unprejudiced in her determination that the White House should be a symbol of racial integration and social inclusion, and accorded her the ultimate accolade. She was "tough." A 1964 article in *Ebony* was entitled "The Lady in Black—U.S. Negroes look with nostalgia on former First Lady's White House reign."

On April 9 Kennedy presided over the ceremony to make Winston Churchill an honorary American citizen. His hero had been his father's enemy, and old Joe happened to be staying at the White House that night. Jack teased him, "All your old friends showed up, didn't they, Dad? Bernard Baruch . . . Dean Acheson . . ."

There was a family dinner in the old man's honor, with the three Kennedy brothers, Eunice, Ann Gargan and the Bradlees present. Later Bradlee wrote:

> The old man is bent all out of shape, his right side paralyzed from head to toe, unable to say anything but meaningless sounds and "no, no, no, no" over and over again. But the evening was movingly gay, because the old man's gallantry shows in his eyes and his crooked smile . . . And because his children involve him in their every thought and action. They talk to him all the time. They ask him, "Don't you think so, Dad?" or "Isn't that right, Dad?" And before he has a chance to embarrass himself or the guests by not being able to answer, they are off on the next subject. Bobby and Teddy sang a two-part harmony for him: It was calculatedly bad and off-key, but the ambassador leaned forward in his armchair, tilted his head back to see them better, and was obviously delighted with their performance . . .[14]

Caroline and John Jr. careered around the room and at one point John knocked his grandfather's drink into his lap. Going in to dinner, Jackie supported her father-in-law as he struggled along; at dinner she wiped the drool off the paralyzed right side of his mouth, "rattling on and on, talking to him about many things, especially reminding him how he and Judge Morrissey had worked on JFK to marry her."[15] Bradlee found these scenes of the Kennedys and their crippled father "touching, simple and moving." The Kennedys were at their best in these simple family situations, especially, Bradlee thought, the Kennedy brothers. "It was common knowledge how much the Kennedy men depended on each other, especially how much the President depended on Bobby; but their private behavior reminded me of some rambunctious game, almost like roughhousing . . . full of wit, sarcasm, and love. The times I saw them together, they were relaxing, teasing each other, bantering, making each other laugh . . ."[16]

As far as Jackie was concerned, however, that closeness between the brothers did not extend automatically to the sisters and in-laws. One night, when the Bradlees were waiting upstairs for Jack and Jackie to come up from a cocktail party they were giving for the astronauts and their wives, Steve and Jean Smith came in. They said they didn't dare gate-crash the astronaut party and, apparently, they hadn't been invited to dinner, which was a foursome of Kennedys and Bradlees. "As a result," a surprised Bradlee commented, "strangely, we thought, they had one drink with us and left."[17] Even at Hyannis Port Jackie had insisted on moving out of the compound, renting first Morton Downey's house and then the Louis Thun house on Squaw Island about half a mile away across a narrow causeway. She saw the Kennedys on her own terms.

Caroline and John were always around, running in and out as if it were just an ordinary home and not the White House. Once, when the Bradlees came out of the private elevator on their way to dine with Jack and Jackie, they met Caroline "naked as a jaybird," laughing, pursued by an embarrassed Maud Shaw. Jack kept urging Ben to pick up John Jr. and throw him in the air, because he loved it so and

Jack's back prevented him doing it. "He doesn't know it yet," Jack said wistfully, "but he's going to carry me before I carry him."[18] Jack had a close relationship with both his children. "Caroline thought her father was a God," Maud Shaw said. "She had such faith in him. She adored him just as much as he adored her." Jack would telephone Caroline any night she was away from the White House at Hammersmith or Palm Beach. As John Jr. grew up, Maud Shaw recalled, he became "a boy that every man would be proud of. John is one hundred percent boy. He is very intelligent and very enquiring, and the President began to be so very proud of him because he was a little man to take around. There was no silly nonsense that you have with a child . . . He was a great companion to his father and at this age—about two and a half—he was a great talker . . . they had a wonderful time together." John, she said, was "really fascinated by mechanical things and airplanes."[19] His father would often sit with him inside the helicopter, putting the helmet on for him and showing how things worked.

One morning, shortly before the President's departure for Europe in June 1963, Evelyn Lincoln received back the copies of speeches she had left for him to check marked "Daddy" and "CBK" in red and blue. Caroline had been sitting on his lap while he read them and had initialed them for him. Jack's relations with his outgoing son were more robust—"John-John and JFK quite simply break each other up. Kennedy likes to laugh and likes to make people laugh, and his son is the perfect foil for him."[20] Both Jack and Jackie were careful to treat the children equally. Jack got into the habit of keeping toy airplanes in a cupboard in his office, so that he could hand them out as treats to John Jr.; a cache of toy horses was quickly ordered so that he could do the same for Caroline. The President was careful to explain to the children, particularly Caroline, when they were going away on official trips: "He would tell her where they were going and what they were going to do and what they [the trips] were for," Maud Shaw remembered. "And through these conversations Caroline learned more of the history of the United States than any child of her age. She seemed to know every state around the United States."[21]

Jackie seemed especially anxious this year to please Jack. For the state dinner in honor of the Grand Duke and Duchess of Luxembourg on April 30, she decided to ask the English actor Basil Rathbone to recite Shakespeare, accompanied by Elizabethan music. Rathbone left a covering note with his correspondence with Jackie: "I cannot help wondering if any 1st Lady in the White House has ever corresponded with a comparative stranger, in her own hand and with a simplicity and sincerity that will remain a treasured memory for me all the days of my life . . ."[22] There was some confusion over the exact program: Tish Baldrige told Rathbone that the President was particularly anxious that the St. Crispin's Day speech from *Henry V* should be included. Rathbone was doubtful. Jackie wrote a tactful letter: "Is it not funny how things become overcomplicated?" she said. "I am sorry you thought the President 'would accept no other' speech but St. Crispin. It is just one of his favorites for whatever lovely dreams of leading or being led on to victory lurk in his soul! He also knows it by heart and I suppose wanted it for the same selfish reasons I asked for so much Donne and other things I love. He also loves Henry V (and he reminds *me* of him—though I don't think he knows that!) . . ."[23] When Rathbone delivered the St. Crispin speech in the "velvet-covered jewel box" setting, especially designed by Lincoln Kirstein for the evening in the White House East Room, it had a special resonance for the New Frontiersmen. The phrases "we happy few . . . we band of brothers" encapsulated their sense of togetherness, united in their cause.

May 29 was Jack Kennedy's forty-sixth birthday. Jackie had arranged a birthday party on the presidential yacht, the *Sequoia*, as the *Honey Fitz* was deemed unsafe ("rotting in the timbers, like us,"[24] Jack said). As usual when the Kennedys and their intimates assembled, Paul Fay did his rendition of "Hooray for Hollywood" to the background of Kennedy catcalls, boos and cheers. A veteran Boston politician, brought along by Teddy, got drunk and put his foot through a rare engraving of the War of 1812, which had been Jackie's present to Jack, everyone was soaked by violent storms and Teddy mysteriously lost one leg of his trousers. Jack, apparently unaware that by 1963 the Twist was going out of fashion, ordered more Chubby Checker tunes every time the band played anything else. As usual, Jackie was cool and impeccable, greeting the destruction of her carefully chosen present, Ben Bradlee observed, with "that veiled expression she assumes" and saying, "Oh, that's all right. I can get it fixed."[25] She did not participate in the boisterous Kennedy yelling. When Jack saw the ruined present the next day at Camp David, he seemed to have forgotten what had happened, putting it aside and remarking, "That's too bad, Jackie, isn't it?" "Jackie was almost as unemotional about what would have been, we felt, a disaster to most people," Ben Bradlee recalled. "They both so rarely show any emotion, except by laughter . . ."[26]

The summer of 1963 marked the beginning of a particularly violent time in America. NBC ran a TV series *The American Revolution of 1963* documenting the struggle for civil rights. Pictures of policemen urging their dogs to attack black schoolchildren in Birmingham, Alabama, shocked the world. In June civil rights leader Medgar Evers was shot dead in Jackson, Mississippi. Thousands of miles across the world, a Buddhist monk burned himself to death in Saigon. It was no doubt with a feeling of relief that Jack, accompanied by Eunice and Lee, said good-bye to Jackie and the children at Camp David on June 22 and flew to Europe, to make his famous speech at the Berlin Wall (it made no difference to the cheering thousands that when he said, "Ich bin ein Berliner," it meant that he was a local doughnut), to make a homecoming visit to County Wexford, to confer in England with Macmillan, who was deeply troubled by the Profumo sex-and-spy scandal that had recently erupted, and to meet the Pope in Rome. He also stopped at the Villa Serbelloni on Lake Como for a private rendezvous with an Italian woman friend.

Jackie was at Squaw Island when Jack returned to spend the Fourth of July with his family. Both he and she loved the isolation of the large house at the end of the road, on the point directly on the ocean. At the back of the house grass ran down to a twenty-foot cliff that fell straight into the water. "It was a big, rambling house with that kind of New England charm," remembered Paul Fay, "with gray, darkened shingles. They were wood shingles but with the sea spray they'd become almost gray—really a beautiful old house." Jack considered buying it, but once again was deterred by the price and the fear of bad publicity.

Jackie spent her days reading, painting, resting for the birth of her baby and planning, just as she had in 1960, in the weeks before the birth of John Jr., either in her bedroom or the adjoining closed-in porch that she used as an office. She was looking ahead to autumn at the White House, selecting menus for State visits, ensuring that, in response to press criticism, there should be less French and more English on them—Eggs Mollet, for instance, instead of Oeufs Mollets. She was even drawing up lists of Christmas presents—J. B. West was to receive a cushion embroidered, "You don't have to be mad to work here but it helps." Jackie herself wanted a fur bedspread as a present from all the family—the choice ranged from rabbit at $350 to chinchilla at $4,000. Caroline was to have a party for her cousins around the time of Jackie's birthday—there were ten in Caroline's age group, and ten in John Jr.'s. With Oleg Cassini Jackie was already working on a postnatal wardrobe; she planned to use an exercise machine in Morton Downey's basement to work on getting her figure back in shape.

On July 19 there was yet another Kennedy christening, of Bobby and Ethel's eighth child, Christopher George Kennedy. Jack and Jackie were there with Lem Billings. On the weekend of August 2, the Fays were staying at Squaw Island with the Kennedys, when Paul Fay walked into Jack's bedroom at his invitation and found Jack and Jackie in bed together: "She was lying there with him and I guess felt uncomfortable, but she just wanted to be with him, so they were lying there in each other's arms and chatting . . ."

But August, instead of being a joyful month as Jackie had anticipated, was destined for tragedy. On Saturday August 3, their friend, the brilliant Phil Graham, publisher of the *Washington Post* and *Newsweek*, still suffering from depression, shot himself on his first day home from the hospital. His funeral was held on Tuesday, August 6, in Washington National Cathedral. Jack attended the service, walking by himself up a side aisle after everyone else was seated and taking his place. "The sun shone through the stained-glass windows, somehow illuminating him," Phil's widow, Kay, remembered. Jackie had written her an eight-page letter—"one of the most understanding and comforting of any I received . . ."[27]

Phil Graham's death was the second suicide in their circle that year. In April Charlene Cassini, daughter of Charles Wrightsman by his first marriage and wife of Igor, died of an overdose of sleeping pills at the age of thirty-eight. Her death touched the Kennedys, not because they were close but because they were indirectly involved. In February, Igor's Dominican connections came back to haunt him and he was indicted, at Bobby's instance, for failure to register his position as a foreign agent, among related charges. On March 31 Charlene had written Jack a long, desperate letter, appealing to him to restrain Bobby. The President did not reply, but discussing Charlene's death a few days later he was "obviously upset, and wondered out loud about the virtue of prosecuting Cassini."[28] In the autumn, he told Cassini's lawyer that if Igor pleaded *nolo contendere* (no contest), he "won't be punished."[29]

The next day, Wednesday, August 7, Jackie was rushed to the hospital of Otis Air Force Base after an emergency call at 11 A.M. Her baby, due to arrive at the end of the month, was evidently on the way. Patrick Bouvier Kennedy, weighing only four pounds ten ounces, was born by Caesarean section at 12:52 A.M. The President, called from a meeting in the Cabinet Room about the ratification of the Nuclear Test Ban Treaty, was told of the birth and hurried down to Cape Cod, arriving at the hospital at 1:30 P.M. Elspeth Rostow arrived at the White House to meet him that morning and found everything in confusion. "I've never seen anything so disorganized," she recalled. "Evelyn Lincoln wasn't there and the Secret Service, as I checked in, said, 'We don't know what's happened.' But then we suddenly saw the chopper going off and it was the President going to what was Patrick's death. It was the beginning of the end . . . an ominous prefiguring of what would happen later that year."[30]

There was tension and silence on the plane flying down to Otis, Nancy Tuckerman and Pam Turnure remembered. "At that moment on the trip up, really not knowing whether her life was in danger, he was very withdrawn," Tuckerman recalled. "He just kept sitting and staring out of the window, and obviously his thoughts were completely with her and getting there as soon as possible, rushing to the hospital." Pam Turnure said, "I had seen that look once before. It was time again back to when John was born. I remember that look on his face when he got the word 'Come back.' They had been through some terrible, terrible times together."[31] At the hospital baby Patrick was fighting for breath, having been born with hyaline membrane disease. He was transferred to Boston Children's Hospital later that afternoon, accompanied by his anguished father.

Meanwhile Jackie had no idea how ill her baby was and remained in ignorance until well after he had died at 4:40 A.M. on the morning of August 9. Jack had come back from Boston to be with her the previous day, returning to Boston for the last vigil on the night of the eighth. Jackie was told the news of Patrick's death by Dr. Walsh. Jack returned to her, bringing Bobby, later that morning. At the Boston hospital, the President had sobbed at the death of his son, and back at Otis, although Jack and Jackie put on a brave face for each other, there was a sadness beyond words. The next day a funeral Mass was held in the private chapel of Cardinal Cushing in Boston. A stricken Jack had to be prized away from the little white coffin containing his son's body, before returning to Jackie. On Sunday and Monday he brought the children to see her.

Afterward, neither Jack nor Jackie spoke much about Patrick's death, which had a profound effect on their relationship, bringing them closer together— unlike the stillbirth of 1956. While Jack once confessed to Paul Fay, "It would have been so nice to have had another son, but there's nothing I can do about it," and never discussed it again, his concern was for Jackie. "It's much harder on Jackie than it is on me," he said.[32]

By August 12, Mary Gallagher noted, "JBK pulling herself together."[33] Her first thought was of Jack and their tenth wedding anniversary, which they would be celebrating at Newport in just a month's time. She wanted a St. Christopher medal for him that could be used as a money clip and drew the design for it to be made up by a New York jeweler. It was a curious present for a man who disliked carrying cash.

Jackie left the hospital with Jack for Squaw Island on August 14; unusually, for the nontactile Kennedys, they were hand in hand as they walked out of the door. He flew down from Washington to be with her on the Cape several times each week. According to Evelyn Lincoln, "Each time he wanted to take her something that would let her know he had been thinking about her and to share with her something of his life in Washington. Sometimes he would ask that a bouquet of flowers be gathered from those blooming in his garden . . ."[34] The people of Ireland had given the President two dogs, a pony and some deer. Jack decided to take a dog down to Jackie as soon as it arrived. It was a cocker spaniel, with drooping ears and mournful eyes. "God, he's sad-looking, don't you think?" he said. But the next day the spaniel, named Shannon, went with him to the Cape.

The President flew up to Hammersmith to join Jackie for their wedding anniversary, bringing the Bradlees. The sky was lowering and overcast. Ben Bradlee thought the scene reminiscent of *Wuthering Heights*—"The light was that dark yellow light of a New England fall evening, and that great barn of a house could have been brought over intact from a Brontë moor." But now, after ten years of marriage, the Kennedys' relationship was warm and obviously glowing. This was the first time the Bradlees had seen Jackie since Patrick's death; they were surprised by the change in the couple toward each other. Jackie "greeted JFK with by far the most affectionate embrace we had ever seen them give each other. They are not normally demonstrative people, period."[35]

In the hall, Jack teased his mother-in-law by giving her the "tacky" silver bowl just presented to him as an anniversary present by the Republican Governor of Rhode Island, John Chafee, saying that he had long wanted to give her a token of his undying affection. Janet, taken in by Jack's deadpan humor, "cooed like a dove," even while looking askance at the hideous bowl. Then there were cocktails—daiquiris—in the Deck Room overlooking Narragansett Bay, just as there had been ten years ago when Jackie and Jack were engaged. Yusha and Little Janet were there, and Sylvia Blake, Charlie Whitehouse's sister, who had been one of Jackie's bridesmaids. Presents were exchanged. The Kennedys had chosen them for each other with taste and care. For Jackie, Jack read out a list of desirable objects from Klejman, the New York antiquities dealer, for her to choose from, with humorous asides—"Got to steer her away from that one"—at the most expensive items, although he didn't read out the prices. Jackie chose a simple coiled serpent bracelet.

Jackie's principal present was typically original, following her taste for carefully composed, evocative, often amusing historical records. It was a before-and-after album of pictures of the White House Rose Garden, which Bunny Mellon had created for Jack: for each day there was a photograph, plus a copy of his schedule that day and a quotation in her own handwriting, often from Joe Alsop's celebrated gardening column. Jack read aloud all the quotations, "pausing to admire Joe's ornate prose."

"Dinner was on the dicey side," Bradlee wrote. "Jackie's stepfather is not exactly a swinger, and the toasts were pretty much in his image." There was a good deal of wine, caviar and champagne, and everybody went to bed early. Jackie, unsurprisingly considering the occasion, the wine and what she had recently been through, had one of her rare emotional moments. "Just before we retired Jackie drew me aside," recalled Bradlee, "her eyes glistening near tears, to announce that 'You two really are our best friends.' It was a forlorn remark," he commented, "almost like a lost and lonely child in need of any kind of friend."[36] Ordinarily she would never have said that. (In truth, the Bradlees were more Jack's friends than hers. As they were to discover on an uncomfortable weekend after his death, he had been the one thing they had in common with Jackie, and when Ben finally published his memoir of days with Kennedy, Jackie regarded it as a betrayal of confidence and cut him dead.) Now she embraced the Bradlees as she was willing to embrace everyone and everything that pleased Jack. And more than ever, after ten years of misunderstanding, heartbreak and a personality-wrenching iron self-control, she was convinced, as she had told Adlai Stevenson in March, that she was winning the battle for Jack. His tenderness after the death of Patrick seemed to her a significant change of heart. She thought she had finally become his number one.

As she had after John's birth, Jackie was suffering from postpartum depression. When Lee heard of Patrick's death, she was on board Aristotle Onassis's yacht with, among others, the ballerina Dame Margot Fonteyn. She immediately flew to Boston to attend the baby's funeral and to comfort Jackie in the hospital. Later she spent a week with her sister at Squaw Island. Returning to Onassis in August, she had told him about Jackie's sadness and suggested she should join them on a cruise on the *Christina*.

Onassis had had several run-ins with the U.S. government, and had been divorced by his first wife, Athina "Tina" Livanos, because of his blatant behavior with Maria Callas, although Tina had not named Callas in her suit, saying, "I'm not going to give that old bitch the satisfaction." Callas had left her husband for Onassis, and their affair had been blazoned over the world's press for the past four years. But Onassis had a reputation for tiring quickly of his women, and in the spring of 1963 he had begun an affair with Lee, making Stas a director of his Olympic Airways as a consolation prize. That summer the news of the Lee-Ari relationship had reached America, reported by Drew Pearson in the *Washington Post*: "Does the ambitious Greek tycoon hope to become the brother-in-law of the President?" he asked. Such a jet set adventure would not go down well with Middle America.

That Jack, always so sensitive to adverse publicity and with an election year coming, was none the less prepared to let Jackie go was a measure of his concern for her. He was aware of the potential political fallout that might result if Jackie were to accept hospitality from the buccaneer Greek, and so were his advisers. Pam Turnure was brave enough to voice her concerns to him. He told her, "Well, I think it'll be good for Jackie, and that's what counts. I think it will be beneficial for her." Salinger and O'Donnell backed her up, telling Kennedy, "You know, you have an election year coming up, and it may not look right to have this sort of trip." Jack was unmoved. "We will cross that bridge when we come to it, and that's final. I want her to go on the trip. It will be good for her, and she has been looking forward to it."[37]

It was announced that Jackie would not be engaging in any official activities until the end of the year, apart from greeting Emperor Haile Selassie of Ethiopia on the eve of her trip to Greece. Onassis's name was kept under wraps, and Jackie's forthcoming vacation, according to UPI, was billed as "a visit to Greece with her brother-in-law and sister, Prince and Princess Stanislaus Radziwill."

Jack, however, had persuaded his Secretary of Commerce, Franklin D. Roosevelt Jr., and his wife Suzanne, to go with Jackie as chaperones, while Jackie herself had asked Princess Irene Galitzine to join them. Characteristically, she had not mentioned Onassis's name in her invitation to Irene Galitzine, who only discovered the truth when she met Stavros Niarchos, Onassis's great rival in business and women, who was married to Eugenie Livanos, his former wife's sister. "Do you know whose yacht you're going on?" he asked her. "Ari's, for sure."[38]

Jackie and the Radziwills spent several days with her previous Greek host, Markos Nomikos, at his villa near Athens before boarding the *Christina*. Also aboard, to lend an air of respectability, were Onassis's sister, Artemis Garofalidis, and her husband. Arkady Gerney was also there. The Roosevelts were under no illusion as to their role: "We were supposed to make it respectable," Suzanne said. "So he [Kennedy] had to be thinking up things for Franklin to be doing. He dreamed up a trade fair on Somalia for him to be there."[39] As they often did when they were together, Jackie and Lee behaved like schoolgirls. "There was a good deal of levity—I thought there was something rather sophomoric about Jackie and Lee sometimes," Suzanne said. "They were quite childish together, giggling in corners."

There have been allegations that the bitterness between Jackie and Lee had its roots in October 1963, that Onassis and Jackie slept together, that Onassis was quoted as saying, "I'm going to get her . . ." Suzanne Roosevelt, now Mrs. Ernest Kloman, absolutely denies that this was so. "He [Onassis] wasn't especially paying attention [to Jackie]. He was being a very good host, he wasn't courting her." Asked if Jackie and he had gone off by themselves together, she replied, "No . . . The only time that Ari went off with anybody that I knew was with me and Franklin." At the end of the trip, Onassis gave all his guests presents, graded in order of importance—a gold *minaudière* (evening purse) for Suzanne, diamond-studded bracelets for Lee, and a ruby choker for Jackie. Lee later told Jack that while Onassis had showered Jackie with rubies he had given her only "dinky little bracelets" of a type that she might have given Caroline. That she was able to joke about it indicates that she did not see the Jackie-Ari relationship as a major romance. It was more the kind of thing to which she had already become accustomed, like the gifts of a head of state to the wife of the President of the United States, and less glittering objects to the First Lady's entourage.

Yet Onassis had been out to charm and impress, and he succeeded. Much of his spectacular success in business was due to his ability to stay ahead of the game. "Like Richard Nixon, he would never do things spontaneously," a relative by marriage said. "He would sit back and think and have the vision to see what was happening and why. He was very perceptive."[40] With Lee and now Jackie, he was in touch with the most powerful family in the world, the Kennedys, the wielders of political power. Onassis loved publicity, and the presence of the U.S. President's wife on his yacht as his guest was publicity beyond anything that mere money could buy. In his running battle to get the upper hand over his rival Stavros Niarchos, this was a coup. Lee's Kennedy connection had been a factor in his attraction to her, and it was paying off.

The party disembarked at his birthplace, Smyrna (now Izmir), where Onassis told Jackie some of the details of his amazing life. Aristotle Socrates Onassis was born on January 20, 1904, in Karatass, a suburb of Smyrna. He was the son of a wealthy Greek trader, a Turkish citizen, named Socrates Onassis. He inherited his business ability from his father, and from his uncle Alexander came an essential Greekness in his ideas of passion, love, loyalty and revenge. "No matter how seemingly sophisticated and civilized he was to become," wrote his biographer, "there remained inside him an atavism that could never be tamed."[41]

Onassis survived the sacking of Smyrna by the Turkish army in 1922 by pretending to be sixteen and becoming the lover of the Turkish officer who requisitioned the family villa. He escaped and, after living on his wits in Constantinople, Athens and Naples, emigrated to South America. As the ship steamed westward, the young emigrant saw the lights of Monte Carlo, the playground of the international set, which would one day be part of his empire. In Buenos Aires he made a fortune in tobacco, then simultaneously moved into shipping, traveling between London and Athens, Buenos Aires and Paris. He was the first to foresee the future for ever bigger tankers to carry the burgeoning trade in oil. By 1940 he was in New York, already a millionaire, then moved to California, where he lived the life of a Hollywood playboy, promoting his image as a great lover and having a brief affair with Gloria Swanson, Joe Kennedy's mistress. In New York, he set his sights on Athina, daughter of Stavros Livanos, the biggest shipowner of them all, an aristocrat of business in comparison with whom Onassis was an upstart.

Tina, aged seventeen when Onassis married her (he was forty-six), represented sex and commercial advantage. She was also, in traditional Greek eyes, a good childbearing prospect. (Niarchos also coveted her but married her elder sister Eugenie; the personal and business rivalry between him and Onassis began around this time when they became brothers-in-law.) Marrying Tina was also an act of revenge for Onassis, revenge on Livanos and the exclusive union of Greek shipowners who had refused to let him in on a profitable deal with the U.S. government over Liberty Ships. "You've got your revenge now," his old friend and associate Costa Gratsos told him at the wedding reception, attended by all Onassis's shipping rivals. "It's not enough, Costa," Onassis had replied. "I'm looking to beat the shit out of these sons-of-bitches. I'm at *war* with these gorillas."[42] It was the kind of language Jack Kennedy himself would have used and, like Jack Kennedy, Onassis knew how to cultivate the press, who began to call him "the Golden Greek." In 1952 he went into whaling, inviting guests on board his *Olympic Challenger* to live in luxury, watch the slaughter and even fire the harpoon gun. In 1953, just thirty years after he had seen the distant lights of Monte Carlo from the deck of the emigrant ship, he gained control of the company, the SBM (Société des Bains de Mer at Cercle des Étrangers), which virtually controlled Monaco, owning the casino, the Hôtel de Paris, the yacht club and about one-third of the real estate.

Taking over the SBM brought Onassis worldwide fame. Now he was more than just another rich Greek: he was established in the public consciousness as a major celebrity, a multimillionaire both mysterious and flamboyant. Not content with this, though, his next big deal was to muscle in on Aramco's exclusive deal with the Saudis to exploit and transport their oil. When Niarchos heard of this through a private investigator, he scuppered the plan by warning the Americans. As if that was not bad enough, Onassis was indicted on virtually trumped-up charges in New York for conspiracy to defraud, which left an unpleasant shadow over his reputation in the United States. Socially, however, he went from strength to strength; from his base in Monte Carlo, he captured the biggest fish of all, Winston Churchill. Then, in 1956, the Suez crisis made his fortune unimaginably larger: when the war caused the closing of the Suez Canal, Onassis was the only major independent shipowner with the fleet available, deployed to cash in on the rush for vessels to carry oil around the cape. A year before, he had entertained Jack and Jackie aboard the *Christina*. It was a meeting that neither Onassis nor Jackie had forgotten.

Pictures of the First Lady walking through the streets of Smyrna with an attentive Onassis at her side were publicized worldwide, causing anguish to Maria Callas, discarded in Paris. "Four years ago," she told a friend, "that was me by his side, being beguiled by the story of his life . . ."[43] Jackie was impressed, drawn by the potency of Greek myth, seeing Onassis as Odysseus, the captain, forging his way over those same seas. He was dangerous, a pirate in the Black Jack mold. The experience provided, perhaps, the germ of an idea that stayed in the back of her mind. The images also brought Onassis to the attention of the American public— too much so, in Jack Kennedy's view. He telephoned Jackie and told her about the press stories—"brilliantly lighted luxury yacht, gay with guests, good food and drinks," "lavish shipboard dinners," "dancing music," "a crew of sixty, two coiffeurs, and a dance band."[44] He did not order her home, but she was to keep to the agreed date of October 17.

However, he told Bradlee that he had insisted that Onassis must not come to the United States until after 1964, which was "the best evidence that he thinks the trip is potentially damaging to him politically,"[45] Bradlee commented. According to Taki Theodoracopoulos, there were other reasons why Kennedy wanted to keep Onassis out of America, which related to the tangled love lives—if you can call them that—of the international set: "There was a period when Stas Radziwill was going to marry Charlotte Ford and Lee was going to marry Onassis. JFK had told them, 'You have to wait until after the '64 election.'" Asked how he knew this, Theodoracopoulos said, "Well, Lee told me. Lee dropped hints and cross-referenced with Charlotte Ford because I was having a little flirt at the same time. And then, of course, Dallas happened and Onassis went for bigger fish . . . I figured that Lee and Stas's marriage had run out of steam completely. I don't know if Onassis would have married Lee but Lee would certainly have married Onassis."[46]

That Jackie suffered from "guilt feeling" about the damage her pleasure cruise might be doing her husband politically is confirmed by Irene Galitzine, who said that she "agonized over it." One night she encountered Jackie, who occupied the cabin opposite hers, coming down from the deck, champagne glass in hand, about to go into her cabin. "I'm not going to sleep, I'm writing to Jack," Jackie told her. Every evening, Galitzine said, she would write to her husband. Her letters were not just travelogues but love letters, in which she told Jack the innermost feelings that she could not express to him in spoken words. They showed the little-girl vulnerability that was a part of her relationship with him; she spoke of her shyness and insecurity and her reliance on him, her concerns about their life after the White House.[47]

"The letter showed a tremendous love of Jackie Kennedy for John Kennedy," said Robert White, the collector of Kennedy memorabilia.[48] It showed a frail First Lady saying things like 'I loved you from the first moment I saw you . . .'" Seeking, as so often, his approval, she wrote of her hopes that Caroline would follow her example in putting into marriage what she herself had. In another letter, she told him how very much she missed him, fantasizing about the perfect state of their marriage: "I think that I am lucky to miss you—I know I always exaggerate—but I pity everybody else who is married . . . I have never realized the enormous stress you are under—but there I can't help you, therefore I shall give you the only thing I can give you: I think of you . . ." She ended, "I'll show you how much I love you when I get back. I hope you're not making a speech in Arkansas . . ."[49]

Jack was not making a speech in Arkansas the day Jackie got back (via a visit to the King of Morocco). He was at the air force base with John Jr. and Caroline to greet her when she landed aboard the Kennedy's private plane, the *Caroline*. Coates Redmon, whose husband was in the Pentagon, was at a military party at the base that evening and joined the watching crowd. She noticed that Kennedy adjusted his back brace as he got out of the car and walked stiffly as he went to the plane. "You could see them embrace, a very stiff, formal embrace . . . the children, of course, were jumping up on her. She had her hair cut straight, blunt, all the pouffe was gone so that was the new style. The next day everybody went to the hairdresser and had their hair cut straight."[50]

Jack needed Jackie and his family more that autumn than ever before. Beneath the glamour of the Kennedys' life, the parties, the ocean cruises at Hyannis Port and Newport, the jokes with friends, the sands were shifting dangerously for him both in his public and his private life. His secret world was in danger of rising to the surface. The distinguished diplomat George Kennan saw him that autumn and found him "terribly alone with the loneliness that is known only to people in supreme position . . ."[51] On the political front the news was almost invariably bad, and fraught with danger as election year, 1964, grew closer. His great foreign policy triumph, the Nuclear Test Ban Treaty, threatened to be engulfed by domestic difficulties. On May 18, his poignant appeal for civil rights at Vanderbilt University in Tennessee had been answered by the murder of Medgar Evers. Congress remained unmanageable, humiliating him with savage cuts in his foreign aid program. In Vietnam a crisis was threatening as his advisers quarreled, divided over policy toward the present unpopular regime. "My God, my government's coming apart," he exploded to Charlie Bartlett.[52] In late August the civil rights march on Washington alarmed white voters everywhere. He was in constant, agonizing pain from his back. And, from the spring of 1963 an ever-increasing stream of reports about his entanglements with women began to surface, threatening to engulf him in a sex-and-spy scandal similar to the Profumo affair in England.

Since that spring both Jack and Jackie had enjoyed the titillating reports of the Profumo scandal sent to the President from London by David Bruce, the U.S. Ambassador, and described by him as "one of the juiciest scandals in modern political history."[53] John Profumo, defense secretary in the Macmillan government, had been involved in an affair with a nineteen-year-old call girl, Christine Keeler, who was simultaneously sleeping with Evgeny Ivanov, an intelligence officer attached to the Soviet embassy in London. Profumo denied the affair, but resigned in June after admitting that he had lied to the House of Commons, bringing the scandal into the open. On his trip to Europe in June, Jack had arrived to stay at Birch Grove, Macmillan's country house, in the third week of the Profumo crisis. Jackie had described her husband as "very depressed at the prospect of what he considered to be a great hero brought down; so Jack wanted to do something really nice, and give him a nice present, and to hell with the State Department budget—so he gave Lady Dorothy a golden dressing-table set . . ." Despite his own troubles and Kennedy's brave face in public, Macmillan had been concerned at his appearance: cortisone had affected his face, which was "very puffed-up, very unhealthy. He suffered agony, he was a terribly brave man; I had no idea how much he suffered. He couldn't sit for very long without getting up."[54]

The tentacles of the Profumo affair reached across the Atlantic, where J. Edgar Hoover was aware of it. On June 29 the *New York Journal-American* printed allegations under the headline "High U.S. Aide Implicated in V-Girl Scandal" that call girls Susy Chang, "a beautiful Chinese American girl," and Maria Novotny, "London party girl," had been mixed up in a vice ring run by Harry Alan Towers in New York in 1961, and were linked with Christine Keeler and Mandy Rice-Davies "in a web of international vice activities." Keeler and Rice-Davies had apparently spent eight days in New York in July 1962, allegedly in connection with "an international ring of call girls operating on the U.N. premises." "Like our Mr. Profumo, your man also has access to government secrets," Miss Novotny told American reporters in a telephone interview.[55] There were rumors, too, that Jack Kennedy had met Keeler in New York between July 11 and 18, but there is no hard evidence that he did, although a study of the Secret Service gate logs and other sources shows him as absent from the White House—and not at Hyannis Port with his family—on July 17. Keeler and Rice-Davies flew home to London the next day, July 18. On July 1, two days after the publication of the *Journal-American* article, Bobby Kennedy had a meeting with the two journalists concerned, Dom Frasca and James Horan, of which he forwarded a memo to Hoover: ". . . the Attorney General brought up the article published in the New York Journal American on June 29, 1963 which contained a statement that a highly elected U.S. official is connected with the Profumo matter. In response to a question as to the identity of this official, the reporter said that it was the President of the United States; that the activity occurred prior to his election to this office . . ."[56] The tape of the conversation between Frasca and Peter Earle of the London *News of the World*, in which Maria Novotny took a brief part, was played, after which Bobby asked Frasca if this was the only source of his allegations about the President. Frasca "contended that he had other sources of a confidential nature" but "did not volunteer anything further."

In the summer of 1963 the Ellen Rometsch affair threatened to provide Washington's own Profumo-type scandal, which touched the presidency.[57]

Through the summer of 1963 the Attorney General's office was flooded with allegations about John Kennedy's behavior with women as the 1964 election loomed, most of them concerning call girls or former call girls. Nothing was substantiated. The FBI picked up a story by a call girl informant named Gloria that featured a threesome between herself, another girl and the President at the Waldorf Towers.[58]

On July 3, two days after his unsatisfactory interview with Frasca and Horan, Bobby was informed by Hoover of another allegation, this time about Ellen Rometsch, born in East Germany, who was having "illicit relations with highly placed government officials." In a letter to Hoover, thanking him for the FBI's discreet handling of the matter, Bobby dismissed the Rometsch matter as one of the usual allegations about prominent people. On August 21, however, Rometsch was deported to Germany at the request of the State Department, escorted by a former associate of Bobby's.

That, however, was not the end of the matter: in September the press began reporting stories of financial and sexual corruption in the Senate, centering on Bobby Baker, a protégé of Lyndon Johnson and genial operator of the Quorum Club on Capitol Hill. The Senate Rules Committee began investigations into every aspect of Baker's operations, and on October 26 reporter Clark Mollenhof revealed that the committee was planning to hear testimony about Ellen Rometsch and her deportation from the United States. According to investigative biographer Seymour Hersh, Bobby contacted Hoover for help in heading the committee away from Rometsch, and particularly from causing her return to the United States. Several days later, Hoover lunched with the President and the two discussed the Quorum Club and Rometsch. They speculated also on "who might be the hidden Profumo in the Kennedy administration . . ."[59]

According to Seymour Hersh, in *The Dark Side of Camelot*, one of Jack Kennedy's old friends had procured Rometsch from Baker for the President, or so Baker alleged to Hersh. Baker also told Hersh that Rometsch had gossiped to him about naked pool parties at the White House and estimated that she had gone to the President at least ten times that summer. If Baker was telling the truth, then Kennedy had been indulging in the most dangerous risk-taking of his career.

Jackie had returned invigorated from her Greek vacation. At dinner with the Bradlees in the White House on October 22 shortly after she returned, the President had taken advantage of what he called Jackie's "guilt feelings." "Maybe now you'll come with us to Texas next month," he had said, with a smile. Jackie answered, "Sure I will, Jack." She was prepared to do anything to help, even attend the Army-Navy football game with him after Thanksgiving. "We'll just campaign," she told him. "I'll campaign with you anywhere you want."[60] And with that she flipped open her red leather appointment book and scrawled "Texas" across November 21, 22 and 23.

The following weekends, October 27–28, November 2–3, 1963, were the first that she had induced Jack to spend with her at Wexford. She also persuaded Irene Galitzine, on a flying visit to the U.S.A. to see her clientele, to join them there on October 27. "You know," she said, "Jack detests the country and adores the sea and doesn't want to come."[61] During the weekend they ran a movie of the Onassis cruise, and then a rerun of the Kennedy-Nixon debates. Kennedy was transformed. "He was no longer the fascinating, joking playboy," Galitzine recalled. "He seemed like a fighter before he gets into the ring—face tense, his look concentrated, he held on to my glass of champagne and drank out of it without realizing what he was doing, lost in his thoughts."[62] The Bradlees were down there on November 10 for a relaxed weekend. Jackie rode Sardar, the horse given her by Ayub Khan, while the President made the Bloody Marys. At dinner they talked about the forthcoming campaign trips the President was to make—to Florida and then, the week after, to Texas. On the fifteenth Robin Douglas-Home flew down from New York at Jackie's invitation to spend the afternoon with her. He found a great change in her: she was more relaxed, outwardly composed and happy than in their previous meetings. "Gone was much of the bewilderment, the repressed frustration, the acidity, and . . . the bitchiness . . . she had clearly 'grown up a lot' in that year . . . Some of the arrogance had gone: there was a new humility in its place. The moods were less shifting, the wit less biting, the flares of aggression dimmed and deeper . . ." He attributed the change to her new relationship with Jack: the birth and death of Patrick had acted as a catalyst to bring them closer than ever before, transforming their marriage. "She had never been happier," he wrote.[63]

In contrast, that November there was a seriousness, even a somberness, about Jack Kennedy that struck close observers. "I think what you felt in him as his life came to a close," Charlie Bartlett said, "was a gathering political tension toward the election. I don't think he thought it was going to be easy at all."[64] Laura Bergquist had interviewed him a month or six weeks earlier for a *Look* piece on John Jr. "He seemed very serious, very sober," she recalled. "There was a quality, it was a somberness about him, in fact. Kind of an edge of sadness." Nine months later, talking to Jackie about the memorial issue for Jack on which they were working together, she mentioned this. "Oh, you caught that," Jackie said. "Because that was true about him."[65]

Vietnam had become a major worry for the President. Despite the commitment of some 16,000 "military advisers" in Vietnam, the U.S. ambassador in Saigon, Henry Cabot Lodge, had reported to Kennedy on October 14 that, in the contest with the Viet Cong, the U.S. was "doing little more than holding our own." Kennedy and his advisers had come to the conclusion that the government of Ngo Dinh Diem, corrupt, unpopular, militarily ineffective and now even hostile toward Washington, must be removed and had surreptitiously encouraged a military coup against it. Nonetheless the murder of Diem and his brother, Ngo Dinh Nhu, after the coup in Saigon on November 1 had shocked him. Assassination and death were on his mind. On November 11, Veterans' Day, Kennedy attended the annual ceremony at the Tomb of the Unknown Soldier in Arlington National Cemetery. Afterward, walking among the war graves on the hill above the Potomac, he told Robert McNamara, the Secretary for Defense, "This is one of the most beautiful places on earth. I think, maybe, someday this is where I'd like to be . . ." Bobby Kennedy later told William Manchester, author of *Death of a President*, that on November 19 he had spoken seven times on the telephone to his brother and that Jack's manner was then, and had been for the past ten days, "rather gloomy." To Pierre Salinger, off to Honolulu with Dean Rusk and McGeorge Bundy for a council of war on Vietnam, Kennedy said, simply, "I wish I weren't going to Texas." At the judicial reception that night, a watching Ethel Kennedy

> realized that something very grave must be on his mind. He had leaned back in the rocker, his hand cupped under his chin, and was gazing out with hooded gray eyes. The Chief Justice, Douglas, called over jocularly that Texas would be rough. There was no reply; Kennedy had withdrawn into a private sanctuary of thought. *Why*, Ethel wondered, *is Jack so preoccupied?* Just before the group prepared to drift toward the stairs, she crossed over and greeted him herself. In the past, no matter how complex his problems, the President had always responded. Not now. For the first time in thirteen years he was looking right through her.[66]

Jack called his Boston friend just before he went to Dallas: "He said to me something so queer just before he left," she said. "He said, 'You know the reason I have to talk to you all the time is you're always so interested in what's going to happen tomorrow and then the next day and you have these little plans and things. You may not think I should be interested but I am because I don't have that. I don't feel that way at all.' I said, 'Jack, that's ridiculous, you have so much of your life in front of you . . .' 'I don't see it,' he said, 'I just don't see it . . .' "[67]

Dallas would certainly not be friendly territory: a week before the November 1960 election, Lyndon Johnson and his wife had been severely jostled by a group of Republicans, including top socialites, and Lady Bird had been spat upon. Just the previous month, October 1963, Adlai Stevenson, in Dallas to make a speech on United Nations Day, had been jeered by a crowd and hit on the head by a woman with a placard. Both Stevenson and his host, Stanley Marcus of Neiman Marcus, had advised Kennedy not to make the trip. Contrary to rumor, Johnson had not encouraged the Kennedy visit, not wishing the President to see how little influence he exercised over the rival Democratic factions in Texas, which were represented by bitter enemies in the conservative Governor John Connally (a personal friend of the Johnsons) and liberal Senator Ralph Yarborough. Three days before the scheduled presidential arrival on Friday, November 22, Connally, unwilling to give the Kennedys too much public exposure, was arguing vociferously against a motorcade and for the couple to be driven directly from the airport to the hall where the luncheon was to be held. "The President is not coming down to be hidden under a bushel basket," Kenny O'Donnell told Bill Moyers, a member of the advance guard. "Otherwise we can do it from here by television." The finalized motorcade route was released that day. Although it had been mooted as early as November 15 by the *Dallas Times-Herald*'s Washington correspondent, Elizabeth Harris, a Peace Corps worker acting in the political advance party, hoping to attract maximum crowds, saw to it that the two Dallas papers published the map of the route on Thursday afternoon, November 21, and Friday morning, November 22.[68]

At dinner in the White House on October 23 with the Alphands, Franklin Roosevelts and Irene Galitzine, Jackie had not seem perturbed when the Dallas trip was discussed, even though Stevenson had warned her against it. She and Jack had spent a good deal of time considering her wardrobe for Texas: he wanted her to choose something simple and elegant, particularly for Dallas where, he told her, "There are going to be all these rich Republican women at that lunch, wearing mink coats and diamond bracelets . . . Show these Texans what good taste really is."[69] They had selected her shocking pink Chanel suit with navy trim and blouse, and matching pink pillbox hat.

On the morning of Thursday, November 21, the day of departure, Evelyn Lincoln said that Jack "seemed edgy when he came to the office." The first thing he asked was what the temperature would be in Houston where cool weather had been predicted the previous day. Evelyn Lincoln called the Air Force office. It was going to be warm. Unusually, Kennedy lost his temper. "He was furious—he really raved and ranted," she remembered, and he bawled out the Navy man on the other end of the line. "This was all very unusual—first, his getting so angry, and second, bawling out this Navy man." He swore at Kenny O'Donnell. "Hot. *Hot.* Jackie's clothes are all packed and they're the *wrong* clothes."[70] In the hours before Dallas he was touchy where Jackie's comfort was concerned. That evening when they reached the hotel in Fort Worth he was furious with Mary Gallagher, standing in for Provi, who had joined the motorcade and arrived after Jackie, instead of being there before her and unpacking her clothes. As usual, Jackie kept the party waiting, having her hair combed before scrambling aboard Helicopter No. 1 in a two-piece white bouclé coat and dress. It had been drizzling and the sky was overcast as the helicopter wheeled away toward Andrews Air Force Base.

Jack's mood cleared as they took off in Air Force One, and he worked on papers taken from his worn black alligator briefcase while across the aisle Jackie rehearsed her Spanish speech for the League of United Latin-American Citizens in Houston with Pam Turnure. Both Kennedys were wearing glasses, which they always concealed from the public; Jackie had been wearing them for reading since her teens, Jack only more recently as middle age crept up on him. (At Wexford, the previous month, when Irene Galitzine had tried to take a farewell photograph of him wearing them, he had turned on her, good-humoredly: "For God's sake, Irene, spare me. You'll lose me all my women [voters] . . .")[71]

It was going to be hot in San Antonio. Jackie went into the bedroom to change into a white dress with a black belt, assisted by Mary Gallagher in her new role as lady's maid. Gallagher had swiftly changed the hair grip from the planned mink hat to a black beret. There was a tap on the door. It was Jack, probably concerned to see that Jackie would be ready on time. Jackie was brushing her hair. "Yes, Jack, what is it?" she called. "Oh, Jackie," he answered, without coming in, "just thought I'd check to see if you were all right." Pressed for time, her hairbrush in midair, she answered impatiently, "Yes, Jack, I'm just fine. Now, will you just go 'way?"[72]

That evening, at the Rice Hotel in Houston, she dressed for the dinner in honor of Congressman Albert Thomas, dictating answers to press questions to Pam Turnure as she did so. As usual, she was thinking ahead. When Jack came in she asked him what he would like for lunch on Sunday when Ambassador Lodge would join them on the Cape, no doubt to report on the increasingly serious situation in Vietnam. "Quail" was Jack's verdict. Jackie immediately dictated a menu based around her husband's choice to Mary Gallagher with instructions to pass it on to Evelyn Lincoln: "Crab Meat mousse—in a ring—with sauce, casserole of quail, wild rice, green vegetable—purée of peas—or other, currant jelly. Something light for dessert—can't think of anything, but have something nice." There would be five for lunch, she said, and would Mr. Rodham, their Secret Service agent guarding Wexford, "get enough quail in Virginia."[73]

Before descending to the hotel's grand ballroom for the LULAC's meeting, where she was to make her speech, Jackie heard raised voices from the next room. Jack was apparently putting his point of view on the feud between Governor Connally and fellow Democrat Senator Yarborough, which threatened to overshadow the presidential tour, forcefully to the Vice President. "What was that about?" Jackie asked, after a furious Lyndon Johnson had left.

The President looked amused. "That's just Lyndon," he said. "He's in trouble." Jackie came out vehemently against Connally: "I just can't bear him sitting there saying all these great things about himself. And he seems to be needling *you* all day." Jack was calm. "What he was really saying in the car was that he's going to run ahead of me in Texas. Well, that's all right. Let him. But for heaven's sakes, don't get a thing on him, because that's what I came down here to heal. I'm trying to start by getting two people in the same car. If they start hating, nobody will ride with anybody."[74] They went downstairs and Jackie, extremely nervous, followed up Jack's speech with her own words in Spanish. "They loved and cheered her," Dave Powers wrote. The Kennedys "exchanged eyes" as they left the ballroom. Lady Bird thought the President "looked beguiled" by his wife; he went out of his way to collar a bilingual spectator and relayed to Jackie that the man thought she had been wonderful. What else could the poor man say? she thought. "But," she told William Manchester later, "she was pleased by the gesture, touched that he was still waging an all-out Kennedy campaign to sell Texas to her."[75]

Then it was on to the Coliseum for the Albert Thomas dinner, and to the airport to fly to Fort Worth, touching down just after 11 P.M. Before going to bed in her own room, Jackie joined the President. "You were great today," she said. "How do you feel?"

"Oh, gosh, I'm exhausted," he replied. Later, as she left, he called, "Don't get up with me, I've got to speak in that square downstairs before breakfast, but stay in bed. Just be at the breakfast at nine-fifteen." She said good night. Before turning out the light she carefully laid out tomorrow's navy blouse, navy handbag, low-heeled shoes, pink suit and pillbox hat.[76]

Crowds had been gathering in the rain outside the hotel since 5 A.M. George Thomas woke the President and, while he showered and shaved, laid out his clothes for the day, blue-gray two-button suit, dark blue tie and white shirt with narrow gray stripes, specially ordered from Cardin in Paris. Striding down to the street, he mounted a flatbed truck to address the crowd. There were scattered shouts of "Where's Jackie?" He pointed to her eighth-floor window. "Mrs. Kennedy is organizing herself." He grinned. "It takes her a little longer but, of course, she looks better than we do when she does it."[77]

Jackie seemed to have forgotten about the breakfast, or else she was preparing carefully to make one of her late, shy entrances. She checked her appearance in the mirror critically. "Oh, Mary," she said, "one day in a campaign can age a person thirty years." She held out her wrists for Mary Gallagher to button up her short white kid gloves.[78]

Downstairs Kennedy was getting impatient. "Where's Mrs. Kennedy?" he asked an agent. "Call Mr. Hill. I want her to come down to the breakfast." He went into the dining room without her. Jackie did not appear for another twenty minutes, ushered through the kitchen doors into a pandemonium of klieg lights and cheering Texans, startled, half blinded, stunned by the noise, fawnlike. Jack had been right in wanting her to come along. Her presence defused the violent political atmosphere. She was so evidently nonpolitical, simply a star whom everyone wanted to see. Only the newspapermen were interested in the poisonous Connally-Yarborough-Johnson triangle; the public simply wanted to see Jackie. As Kennedy finished his breakfast speech, three New York reporters approached Dave Powers: "Wasn't Jackie sensational?" he asked them. "Did you ever see a greater ovation?" "When are you going to have her come out of a cake?" the *Wall Street Journal* man asked sarcastically. "She's not that kind of bunny," Powers snapped back.

But if Jackie wouldn't exactly have stepped out of a cake for Jack, she was prepared to do some more campaigning with him. There was an hour's respite before they had to leave for Dallas. "Do you mean we have a whole hour to just sit around?" she asked incredulously. "Oh, Jack, campaigning is easy when you're President. Listen, I can go anywhere with you this year." "How about California in the next two weeks?" Jack said. "Fine, I'll be there," Jackie promised.[79]

There was a less happy moment when O'Donnell, leafing through the *Dallas Morning News*, came upon a large black-bordered advertisement, grimly aping a death notice. Full page, it bore the sardonic heading "WELCOME MR. KENNEDY TO DALLAS." The *News* publisher, E. M. "Ted" Dealey, was the man who had publicly told Kennedy to his face that he was a "weak sister," and that instead of leading the nation like a man on horseback, the people of Texas thought he was "riding Caroline's bicycle." His father's statue dominated a small area of green in downtown Dallas known as Dealey Plaza. (The ad in question had been placed by a local branch of extreme right-wing John Birch sympathizers.)

O'Donnell showed the advertisement to Jack, who read each ranting word, his face grim, then handed it to Jackie. She felt sick. Slowly, Jack said to her, "Oh, you know, we're heading into nut country today . . ." She watched as he paced the floor, pensive. "You know, last night would have been a hell of a night to assassinate a president," he said casually. She took it lightly as his way of shaking off the advertisement, demonstrating what she called his Walter Mitty streak, fantasizing about another of his assassination scenarios. "I mean it," he said. "There was the rain, and the night, and we were all getting jostled. Suppose a man had a pistol in a briefcase." He gestured vividly, pointing his rigid index finger at the wall and jerking his thumb twice, imitating the action of the hammer. "Then he could have dropped the gun and the briefcase"—in pantomime he dropped them and whirled in a tense crouch—"and melted away in the crowd . . ."[80]

It was a sunny morning in Dallas when Air Force One touched down at Love Field at 11:38 A.M. A smiling Jack and Jackie appeared at the top of the ramp, descended and made for the fence to touch the hands of the adoring, cheering crowd. She was presented with a bouquet of long-stemmed red roses, a contrast to the yellow roses of Texas that had greeted her elsewhere. Asked by a *Newsweek* reporter how she liked campaigning, she replied enthusiastically, "It's wonderful!" Her inexperienced eye did not register, behind the organized welcome reception, the sour note of hostile, misspelled placards and a group of high-school kids who had taken the day off to hiss at the President. She and Jack boarded the familiar presidential Lincoln SS 100 X. They took the rear seats, the red roses between them, with John and Nellie Connally on the jump seats facing them. Dave Powers appeared with a characteristic last-minute instruction for Jackie: "Be sure to look to your left, away from the President. Wave to the people on your side. If you both wave to the same voter, it's a waste."[81]

The crowds along the route were screaming, "Jack! Jackie!" In the Mexican section every flutter of her white-gloved hand raised hysterical shrieks, "Jack-eee!" It was hot, blindingly hot, Jackie thought. She put on her sunglasses, only to have Jack tell her to take them off. She kept them in her lap, sneaking them on again through the empty sections where there were only billboards to wave at. Again Jack told her, "Take off the glasses, Jackie."[82] They were the last words he ever spoke to her. At 12:30 P.M. the Lincoln turned off Houston on to Elm Street, five minutes away from their destination, luncheon at the Trade Mart. Moving slowly at just over 11 m.p.h. it made for the dark underpass beyond the grass of Dealey Plaza. Nellie Connally pointed to it, saying to Jackie, "We're almost through. It's just beyond that."[83] Jackie thought gratefully of the cool darkness of the underpass ahead. Beside her, Jack smiled and made as if to raise his hand to wave at a small boy.

Then it happened, a sharp, shattering crack.

Jackie's evidence to the Warren Commission:

> . . . And in the motorcade, I usually would be waving mostly to the left side and he was waving mostly to the right, which is one reason you are not looking at each other very much. And it was terribly hot. Just blinding all of us . . .

Q: Now, do you remember as you turned off of the main street on to Houston Street?

MRS. KENNEDY: I don't know the name of the street.

Q: That is one block before the Depository Building.

MRS. KENNEDY: Well, I remember whenever it was, Mrs. Connally said, "We will soon be there." We could see a tunnel in front of us. Everything was really slow then. And I remember thinking it would be so cool under that tunnel.

Q: And then do you remember as you turned off Houston on to Elm right by the Depository Building?

MRS. KENNEDY: Well, I don't know the names of the streets, but I suppose right by the Depository is what you are talking about?

Q: Yes; that is the street that sort of curves as you go down under the underpass.

MRS. KENNEDY: Yes; well, that is when she said to President Kennedy, "You certainly can't say that the people of Dallas haven't given you a nice welcome."

Q: What did he say?

MRS. KENNEDY: I think he said—I don't know if I remember it or I have read it, "No, you certainly can't," or something. And then you know the car was very slow and there weren't very many people around. And then—do you want me to tell you what happened?

Q: Yes; if you would, please.

MRS. KENNEDY: You know there is always a lot of noise in a motorcade and there are always motorcycles beside us, a lot of them backfiring. So I was looking to the left. I guess there was a noise, but it didn't seem like any different noise really because there is so much noise, motorcycles and things. But then suddenly Governor Connally was yelling, "Oh, no, no, no."

Q: Did he turn toward you?

MRS. KENNEDY: No; I was looking this way, to the left, and I heard these terrible noises. You know. And my husband never made any sound. So I turned to the right. And all I remember is seeing my husband, he had this sort of quizzical look on his face, and his hand was up, it must have been his left hand. And just as I turned and looked at him, I could see a piece of his skull and I remember it was flesh-colored. I remember thinking he looked just as if he had a slight headache. And I just remember seeing that. No blood or anything.

And then he sort of did this [indicating], put his hand to his forehead and fell in my lap. And then I just remember falling on him and saying, "Oh, no, no, no," I mean, "Oh, my God, they have shot my husband." And "I love you, Jack." I remember I was shouting. And just being down in the car with his head in my lap. And it just seemed an eternity.

You know there were pictures of me climbing out the back. I just don't remember that at all.

Q: Do you remember Mr. Hill coming to try to help on the car?

MRS. KENNEDY: I don't remember anything. I was just down like that.

And finally I remember a voice behind me, or something, and then I remember the people in the front seat, or somebody, finally knew something was wrong, and a voice yelling, which must have been Mr. Hill, "Get to the hospital" . . . someone yelling. I was just down and holding him [reference to wounds deleted].

Q: Do you have any recollection of whether there were one or more shots?

MRS. KENNEDY: Well, there must have been two because the one that made me turn around was Governor Connally yelling. And it used to confuse me because first I remembered there were three and I used to think that my husband didn't make a sound when he was shot. And Governor Connally screamed. And then I read the other day that it was the same shot that hit them both. But I used to think that if only I had been looking to the right I would have seen the first shot hit him, then I could have pulled him down, and then the second shot would not have hit him. But I heard Governor Connally yelling and that made me turn around, and as I turned to the right, my husband was doing this [indicating with hand at neck]. He was receiving a bullet. And those are the only two I remember.

And I read there was a third shot. But I don't know.

Just those two.[84]

The first shot had hit Kennedy in the back of the neck, bruised his right lung, ripped his windpipe and exited at his throat, nicking the knot of his tie. The bullet traveled on through Connally's back, chest, right wrist and thigh; in delayed reaction, he was not aware of it. Recognizing it as a rifle shot, he was glancing over his right shoulder to identify the source. Kennedy's wound was not fatal but the actions of the Secret Service agents in the front of the Lincoln made it so. Both agent and driver failed to react; the driver even slowed the car down further when he saw what had happened, making it inevitable that an experienced marksman, as Lee Harvey Oswald was, would have another chance. He was just eighty-eight yards away when he fired the second shot. Jackie was leaning toward her husband:

His face was quizzical. She had seen that expression so often, when he was puzzling over a difficult press-conference question. Now, in a gesture of infinite grace, he raised his right hand, as though to brush back his tousled chestnut hair. But the motion faltered. The hand fell back limply. He had been reaching for the top of his head. But it wasn't there.[85]

William Manchester's description of the scene is lurid and in italic:

The Lincoln continues to slow down. Its interior is a place of horror. The last bullet has torn through John Kennedy's cerebellum, the lower part of his brain. Leaning toward her husband Jacqueline Kennedy has seen a serrated piece of his skull—flesh-colored, not white—detach itself. At first there is no blood. And then, in the very next instant, there is nothing but blood spattering her, the Connallys, Kellerman, Greer, the upholstery, Clint [Hill] running behind, the curb alongside. Gobs of blood as thick as a man's hand are soaking the floor of the backseat, the President's clothes are steeped in it, the roses are drenched, Kennedy's body is lurching soundlessly toward his wife, and Motorcycle Police Officer Hargis, two feet from her, is doused in the face by a red sheet . . . [the Connallys] are overwhelmed by matter, saturated in Kennedy's bright blood; and one fragment, larger than the rest, rises over the President's falling shoulders and seems to hang there and then drift toward the rear, and Jackie springs up on her stained knees, facing toward the sidewalk, crying out, "My God, what are they doing? My God, they've killed Jack, they've killed my husband, Jack! Jack!" she cries and sprawls on the sloping back of the car, defeated, tumbling down toward the street . . .[86]

What Jackie did next is a source of controversy. Abraham Zapruder's film of the scene shows her jumping on to the trunk of the car, reaching out her hand. Was she trying to escape in a moment of self-preservation? She told the Warren Commission she had no recollection of doing any such thing. She later told some people she was trying to rescue a piece of Jack's skull. William Manchester, who from his extensive interviews at the time, must have had the best idea of what actually happened, limits himself to the dramatic description alone, adding that Hill tried to jump on the accelerating Lincoln, grabbed Jackie's hand and vaulted up pushing her back down into the car. "It is impossible to say who saved whom," he wrote. "Neither remembers and the Zapruder film is inconclusive."[87]

In shock, Jackie crouched over her husband's body, futilely trying to hold his head together, his blood and gray brain matter caking her white kid gloves. She knew he was dead. A man had died. A legend was about to be born.

CHAPTER FOURTEEN

Profile in Courage

⌒

She gave the world an example of how to behave.

—General de Gaulle

In the confusion outside Parkland Hospital, Jackie sat oblivious, bent over Jack, cradling his head to her breast as if to hide the spectacle from the outside world. She was making soft "little weeping sounds." Hustled by the Secret Service out of the third car as they arrived, Lady Bird Johnson caught a glimpse in the President's car of "a bundle of pink, just like a drift of blossoms, lying on the backseat. It was Mrs. Kennedy, lying over the President's body . . ."[1]

Her Secret Service agent, Clint Hill, touched her shoulder. "Please, Mrs. Kennedy," he said. Jackie controlled her sobs with a single violent spasm and lifted her head. "Please," Hill repeated. "We must get the President to a doctor."

"I'm not going to let him go, Mr. Hill."

"We've got to take him in, Mrs. Kennedy."

"No, Mr. Hill. You know he's dead." From this moment on, according to William Manchester, who interviewed not only Jackie but every possible eyewitness, her recollection was total.[2]

Hill realized her concern, to conceal the President's shattered head. He whipped off his jacket, and she wrapped it over Jack's head as they drew his body onto the stretcher, clutching it to make sure it did not slip off. She ran beside the stretcher, holding on as if she could hold Jack back from death. At the threshold of Trauma Room No. 1, she released him. There was nothing more she could do.

She sat on a folding chair just outside the room. Godfrey McHugh and Betty Harris fetched chairs for the three Kennedy women staffers, Evelyn Lincoln, Mary Gallagher and Pam Turnure, who had just arrived from the Trade Mart.

Betty Harris recalled, "Mrs. Kennedy was sitting there, the epitome, the total epitome of forlornness, she was totally traumatized . . . She was immobilized . . . I can't think of the right word. There was total confusion, nobody knew exactly what had happened . . . And all this time, Jackie was just sitting there. People would try to speak to her, she didn't want to talk to anybody—she just simply did not respond. And I looked at her and she was sitting with her hands like this . . . and had on short white gloves, and I looked at the gloves and they looked polka dotted, and I remember thinking, 'She wouldn't wear polka dot white gloves with a pink suit'—you do think ridiculous things at a time like that—and suddenly I realized that the polka dots and the spots on her suit were his brains . . . and she wouldn't let anybody touch her and she wouldn't let anybody clean her up . . . She wouldn't take her gloves off."[3]

The doors of Trauma Room No. 1 opened and a tall man came out. He was Dr. Kemp Clark, senior neurologist at Parkland. "He leaned over Jackie," Betty Harris said, "and said something to her, and she, if anything, got a little bit smaller . . . He was a tall man and he pulled himself up and walked over toward me and I walked over toward him and I said, 'How bad was it?' And he said, 'It was lethal . . .'"[4]

Manchester's account varies in detail both from Betty Harris's and from the oral history that Kennedy's doctor, Admiral Burkley, gave to the Kennedy Library. In the confusion and shock at Parkland, most witnesses remembered things slightly differently, others confused memory with what they had subsequently read. According to Manchester, at one point Jackie, hearing voices and movement from within the Trauma Room, had a fleeting hope that Jack might still be alive. She got up and tried to enter the room, but was barred by a nurse from doing so. She struggled with the nurse. "I'm going to get in that room." Again, according to Manchester, Admiral Burkley came over to her and offered her a sedative. Jackie told him, "I want to be in there when he dies." Burkley escorted her in. Briefly, she knelt and prayed in a corner, unable to get past the doctors tending her husband.[5]

Jack was naked except for his undershorts, white from loss of blood. Burkley, who had been in the room previously, recorded that as soon as he saw the President, he realized that "for all intents and purposes life did not exist or could be sustained. I talked to the doctors who were busily engaged in doing what was indicated and would have been indicated had there been any hope of salvation of the President. I gave them some hydrocortisone [for Kennedy's adrenal insufficiency] to put in the intravenous which was being given, and told them his blood type. There was no need for doing anything in my estimation . . . he was essentially no longer living." Burkley then went out and saw Jackie. They stood together as the doctors continued their hopeless resuscitation attempt until one came over "and said that they felt the President was dead. I went over and checked him myself, and I pronounced him dead, and I came back to Mrs. Kennedy and said, 'The President is dead.' And we went over to the President and we said the prayers for the dead . . ."[6] Officially, John F. Kennedy died at Parkland at 1:00 P.M. In reality he was dead from the time that Oswald's second bullet smashed through his skull into his brain in Dealey Plaza half an hour earlier.

Jack's body was too long for the emergency room gurney and his feet, white as marble, protruded from under the covering sheet. Jackie kissed them, she kissed his lips—his mouth looked "beautiful" she later said. His terrible wound was concealed from her by bandaging. His face was unmarked, showing no signs of his ordeal, apart from his eyes, which were fixed and staring with pupils dilated, with an expression, Jackie told Manchester, of "compassion." She slipped off her wedding ring and placed it on his little finger. Then she held his hand, standing at his shoulder, looking down lovingly at his face. A priest, Father Huber, from Holy Trinity Church, appeared to give the last rites to the dead President. As the bronze casket ordered from the local undertaker was brought in, she went outside the room to wait.

Lady Bird Johnson arrived to see Jackie before she left the hospital, and found her standing beside the closed door behind which her husband was being prepared for his coffin. "You always think of someone like her as being insulated, protected," she recalled. "She was quite alone. I don't think I ever saw anyone so much alone in my life. I went up to her, put my arms around her, and said something to her. I'm sure it was something like 'God, help us all,' because my feelings for her were too tumultuous to put into words."[7]

"Hysteria was hanging like Spanish moss from that basement ceiling [at Parkland]," said Jack Valenti, who had recently joined the Johnson entourage.[8] Conspiracy fears ran wild—it was the Communists, it was the John Birchers. Johnson's Secret Service men, fearful of another assassination attempt, hustled him and Lady Bird off to the airport. Meanwhile, the Dallas bureaucracy was making efforts to keep the President's body in Dallas until all procedures had been followed. Nor was Jackie aware that from the moment Jack's body had arrived in Parkland, two camps had formed and hostilities had begun that would carry on into the new administration. "In the hospital I knew that the Kennedy people not only hated the simple concept that their beloved Jack had been killed in the land of the hated LBJ—but also literally blamed Johnson for his death," Betty Harris asserted. "The emotion was raw, irrational, and hating . . ."[9]

She went on to observe, "God knows what was going through her [Jackie's] mind. I don't even want to try and guess but the thing was that she was much better behaved and much more in control of herself than either Larry [O'Brien] or Kenny [O'Donnell]. Traumatized as she was, she was at least thinking—the wedding ring was one example—and then when the coffin was brought in, she finally stirred, and as soon as it came out of that little tiny room, she got up and then put her left hand on it and never took it off. When they walked through the door, she walked with them and never took her hand off the casket. She wasn't going to be parted from him at that point. There was this feeling that you got from her that she was almost fixed, tied to him, tied to the casket . . ." Jackie got into the hearse with the coffin, locked in her own world with Jack, oblivious to the pandemonium around her.[10]

Admiral Burkley, Clint Hill and another agent were squeezed in behind her and in the front three more Secret Service men. En route, Burkley handed her two dying red roses from her welcome bouquet that he had retrieved from the waste-bin in the Trauma Room. She took them and put them into her pocket. Reaching Air Force One, parked in an obscure corner of Love Field, the Kennedy men damaged the coffin, which weighed nearly half a ton, as they wrestled it from the ambulance housing and up the rear steps into the plane.

Later, in the bedroom, Jackie washed her face and combed her hair. She ignored the fresh clothes that someone had laid out meaningfully on one of the twin beds for her. Then, still wearing the pink, bloodstained suit, she stood beside President Johnson as he took the oath with his hand on the small black Bible Jack had kept in his bedroom. Jack Valenti, who was there, described her as being "in a catatonic trance almost . . . She came forward for this historic photograph, it shows her eyes cast downward, opaque, unseeing. It was a tragic scene but she stood there beside the President and so that historic photograph, which was flashed around the world, was mirrored in President Johnson's words four days later. He said, 'John Kennedy said, "Let us begin," I said, "Let us continue." ' The photograph was all part of this embrace of both the past and the future."[11]

Not everyone was willing to embrace the future.[12] Even if there was no overt hostility, there was definitely a feeling of two camps: that of the new leader in the main body of the aircraft and the fallen leader in the rear compartment. Jackie sat in the back beside Jack's coffin with the members of his Irish Mafia, Powers, O'Brien and O'Donnell. It was like an Irish wake as they drank whiskey and talked about the past. "Jackie listened, entranced, while Dave described to her President Kennedy's last visit to his father at Hyannis Port on Sunday, October 20, after he had appeared at a Democratic fund-raising dinner in Boston the night before. The President spent the whole day with his father."

Early the next day, when the helicopter was waiting to take him to Air Force One at Otis air base and the ambassador was on the porch in his wheelchair to see him off, the President went to his father, put his arm around the old man's shoulders, and kissed his forehead. Then he started to walk away, turned and looked at his father for a moment, and went back and kissed him a second time, which Dave had never seen him do before. It almost seemed, Dave said to Jackie that night on the way back from Dallas, as if the President had a feeling that he was seeing his father for the last time. When the President and Dave were seated in the helicopter, waiting for takeoff, he looked out of the window at the figure in the wheelchair on the porch, and for the first time in all the years that Dave had known John Kennedy, he saw that his eyes were filled with tears. The President said to him sadly, "He's the one who made all this possible, and look at him now." Powers and O'Donnell told Jackie of their visit on the Saturday afternoon of the same weekend to Patrick's grave in Brookline, and told her how the President had said to them, looking at his baby son's burial place, "He seems so alone here." Jackie listened, nodded slowly, and said, "I'll bring them together now."

As she sat there, Jackie was visualizing details of Jack's funeral. She remembered how he had told her about his visit to Ireland that summer—"the most enjoyable experience of his whole life"—and how impressed he had been by the Irish military cadets at a wreath-laying ceremony. "I must have those Irish cadets at his funeral," she said. Only nine days before he died, Jack had enjoyed the performance of a band of the Black Watch pipers at the White House. "And he loved the Black Watch pipers," she added. "They must be at the funeral, too."[13]

There were other decisions she had made and had to make. The first was her refusal of all suggestions that she should change her skirt, stained with Jack's blood and brains. "No," she said fiercely, "let them see what they've done." She vetoed a secret arrival with Jack's body carried off the plane out of sight of the press and television cameras for the same reason. "We'll go out the regular way," she said. "I want them to see what they've done."

On the plane Admiral Burkley had told her that there would have to be an autopsy and that he was perfectly willing to perform it wherever she wanted it done. "Well, it doesn't have to be done," she replied. He told her it was mandatory. She had then chosen the naval hospital at Bethesda, Maryland, because Jack had served in the Navy.

As Air Force One taxied to a halt under the November moon, Bobby Kennedy rushed up the steps to the front entrance. Haggard, he brushed past the Johnsons and their party. "I want to see Jackie," he muttered. He put his arm around her. "Hi, Jackie, I'm here." "Oh, Bobby," she breathed. Bobby was always there when she needed him. Together, hand in hand, they stood in the glare of the floodlights at the head of a ramp. In front of them, the light glinted on Jack's red bronze coffin, showed the ugly stains on Jackie's skirt and legs. There was dead silence from the three thousand odd crowd gathered there. She had made the effect she wanted.[14]

This was a Kennedy moment, and the new President, Lyndon Johnson, was ignored, as he later told a colleague. "When the plane came in . . . they paid no attention to him whatsoever, that they took the body off the plane, put it in the car, took Mrs. Kennedy along and departed, and only then did he leave the plane without any attention directed or courtesy toward him. But he said he just turned the other cheek . . . He said, 'What can I do? I do not want to get into a fight with the family and the aura of Kennedy is important to all of us.' "[15]

Sitting with Bobby on the other side of the coffin in the back of the ambulance as they drove to Betheseda Naval Hospital where the autopsy was to be performed, Jackie spoke without stopping for twenty minutes, describing everything from the motorcade to the aftermath. By her express wish, Bill Greer, driver of the Lincoln in Dallas, was at the wheel; she wanted to show him she did not blame him for what had happened. At Bethesda, she and Bobby were ushered to the suite on the seventeenth floor to join a vigil by family and friends, as Burkley and the naval team performed an autopsy in the morgue below. There was a horrified silence as Jackie stood there, as Ben Bradlee described it, "this totally doomed child, with that God-awful skirt, not saying anything, looking burned alive."[16] Bobby was in charge: "He was the strongest thing you've ever seen. He was subdued, holding Jackie together, keeping everyone's morale up when his own couldn't have been worse." It was Bobby who broke the news to Jackie that the assassin had been found. "He says he's a Communist." Oh, my God, but that's absurd, Jackie thought. It even robs his death of any meaning. She turned to Janet

Auchincloss: "He didn't even have the satisfaction of being killed for civil rights—it had to be some silly little Communist."[17] Ethel arrived. Her strong Catholic faith moved her to tell Jackie that she was sure Jack had gone straight to heaven. "Oh, Ethel," Jackie said. "I wish I could believe the way you do." Then she told her, "Bobby's been so wonderful." "He'll always help you," Ethel replied, with a generosity she was not always to feel.[18] Over and over again, to Tony Bradlee, to Robert McNamara, Jackie recounted the terrible final events in Dallas, as if she could purge herself of the nightmare by bringing it out into the open.

Janet Auchincloss took charge of Caroline and John, who had been taken with Miss Shaw to her Georgetown home when the news broke. She learned that Jackie wanted them back at the White House, their routine disturbed as little as possible. It was Janet who took the decision that Maud Shaw should tell Caroline that night what had happened to her father. John could wait until the morning.[19] Maud Shaw wrote,

> Feeling overwhelmingly sad, I put John in his bed, said his prayers with him, tucked him down and went in to Caroline. I sat on the edge of the bed and felt tears well up in my eyes. I started reading to her from one of her books—she loved this moment of the day—but after a few paragraphs I could no longer see the words. Caroline looked up at me, her little face frowning with concern.
> "What's the matter, Miss Shaw? Why are you crying?"
> I took her gently in my arms. "I can't help crying, Caroline, because I have some very sad news to tell you."
> Then I told her what had happened. It was a dreadful time for us both.[20]

That was Maud Shaw's brief account. According to what she told William Manchester, she said to Caroline, "Your father has been shot. They took him to the hospital, but the doctors couldn't make him better." She paused. "So your father has gone to look after Patrick. Patrick was lonely in heaven. He didn't know anybody there. Now he has the best friend anyone could have."

Caroline cried herself to sleep, with Miss Shaw sitting beside her on the bed. Later, in answer to Caroline's question whether God would give her father something to do, she told her, "God is making your father a guardian angel over you and John and Mummy, and his light will shine down on you, always. His light is shining now, and he's watching you and he's loving you, and he always will."[21]

At Bethesda, Bobby was making all the decisions. Jackie was too absorbed in her assassination "talkathon" to think ahead now. When he asked her what should be done when they left there with Jack's body, she answered simply, "It's in the guidebook," where an illustration showed Lincoln's body lying in state on a catafalque.[22] A chain of command ran down through Bobby to Arthur Schlesinger, Richard Goodwin and William Walton. Illustrated accounts of Lincoln's funeral were found for Walton to study. There was to be a lying-in-state in the East Room on Saturday, transferal to the rotunda of the Capitol on Sunday, the funeral Mass and burial on Monday. Through the night Walton, with Sargent Shriver and a bevy of assistants including the presidential dog handler, worked to get the East Room ready, draping the chandelier with black crepe, cutting huge branches off Andrew Jackson's magnolias to provide greenery.

At Bethesda, the autopsy completed, Burkley retrieved Jackie's wedding ring from the President's finger and returned it to her. While cosmeticians worked on his body, the Irish Mafia went down to Gawler's to purchase another expensive coffin, in five-hundred-year-old African mahogany, to replace the damaged one. Upstairs Jackie was arguing with Bobby and McNamara as to whether the coffin should be open or closed. She couldn't bear the idea of an open coffin; they insisted that it was the custom for a head of state. Later, when the coffin arrived at the White House East Room, a succession of friends gave their opinion after looking at the body. Most of them thought it "appalling," "a wax dummy" with "no resemblance to the President."[23] To Jackie's relief, the decision was made to keep it closed. "It wasn't Jack," she said. "It was like something you would see at Madame Tussaud's."[24] Kneeling beside the coffin, she buried her face in the veterans' flag draped over it.

Hughdie and Janet Auchincloss slept in the President's bedroom for what was left of that night at Jackie's request. At seven that morning, Caroline came in pushing a big toy giraffe her father had given her. John followed her, pulling a toy behind him. "She came over to the bed," Janet Auchincloss remembered, "and pointed to the picture of her father which covered the front page of the newspaper and said, 'Who is that?' I said, 'Oh, Caroline, you know that's your daddy.' And she said to me, 'He's dead, isn't he? A man shot him, didn't he?' And her little face was so extraordinary. She's a very, very affectionate little girl and a very thoughtful child . . ."[25]

In Jackie's bedroom Dr. Walsh administered his second sedative shot of the night. The first had had no effect. This time he injected a full half gram of Amytal. She cried for a while until it knocked her out. But not for long: by 8 A.M. she was awake, her mind working furiously over the coming events. Shortly before ten she went to fetch the children to take them down to pray in front of their father's coffin. Then there was a Mass, attended by weeping family and friends, the Bradlees and Bartletts, the Spaldings, Sissie and David Ormsby-Gore, among others, and celebrated by Joe Kennedy's old friend, Father Kavanaugh. Afterward Sargent Shriver noted Caroline's sensitivity: "Jackie and Caroline were kneeling side by side, and when they had finished praying Jackie rose and turned; her face was a mask of agony. Caroline took Jackie's left hand in her right hand and patted her mother's hand and looked up with an expression of intelligence and compassion and love, trying to comfort her mother." Afterward, with incredible self-control, Jackie thanked everyone for coming, with an individual phrase for each. She told Sissie Ormsby-Gore that she and Jack had planned to ask her to be a godmother to Patrick. Then mechanically, as if she were still in charge, she took J. B. West, the Chief Usher, on a tour of the redecorated rooms, particularly the Oval Office, which had been finished as a splendid surprise for Jack when he returned from Dallas.

But now the most urgent choice to be made was the site for his grave. The Kennedys and the Irish Mafia were for the family plot in Brookline, Massachusetts. "We're all going to be buried around Daddy in Boston," Eunice, up on the Cape with her father and Teddy, pronounced.[26] Bob McNamara, remembering Kennedy's remarks to him at the last Veterans' Day celebration at Arlington, argued for the national cemetery. Jackie agreed, perhaps stirred by the memory of her first visit there with Yusha over twenty years ago. Various Kennedy groups visited the cemetery in the pouring rain and were converted by the magnificence of the site just below the Custis-Lee Mansion, with a view over the whole of Washington. Jackie herself visited it for fifteen minutes. The decision was made: Arlington was the place.

That day the weather was abominable: cold rain, wind, thunder and lightning. Bunny Mellon flew up from Antigua to New York, then down to Washington in a Mellon plane. Through the windows she looked down on "flashing lightning and whipping rain and terrifying gusts—the storm was like the horribleness of the occasion," she recalled. She visited the catafalque in the East Room. "The tears would not stop. It was like the fall of all the hopes of youth—as though youth had tried and been thwarted. It seemed to me that this country had symbolically killed something." J. B. West told her that Jackie wanted her to do the flowers for the lying-in-state at the Capitol, at St. Matthew's Cathedral where the funeral service would be held, and at the graveside at Arlington.

On Saturday night, November 23, Dr. Walsh gave Jackie another shot of Amytal. Before she slept she called for Bobby, sleeping in the Lincoln Room. "I have to see Jack in the morning," she told him. "I want to say good-bye to him— and I want to put something in the coffin." Bobby promised to come and fetch her on Sunday morning so that they could go down together. Before she went to bed, Jackie sat down and wrote her last love letter to Jack, page upon impassioned page, and sealed it in an envelope. Notwithstanding the Amytal, she had what Bobby said was "another bad night," twisting and turning on her bed and calling for Jack. Bobby telephoned the Ormsby-Gores and asked them to come over and spend the day with her. Sunday, when Jack's body was to leave the White House for the last time, was another dreadful step in her separation from him. Before the coffin left, Jackie asked Caroline to write her own letter to her father; then Caroline guided John Jr.'s hand as he scrawled his illegible note. The children's letters were put in separate envelopes for Jackie to take down to the coffin. She took with her a pair of extravagantly expensive cufflinks she had given Jack and, one of his favorite things, a piece of scrimshaw with the presidential seal carved on it, her present to him last Christmas, 1962.[27]

Down in the East Room beside the opened coffin, Jackie put her gifts inside. Bobby added his PT-109 tiepin and a silver rosary that Ethel had given him at their wedding. Jackie took a lock of Jack's hair and left to watch the departure of the coffin. Mary Gallagher thought she had never looked worse. "Bobby was leading her by the arm, holding her up; she was limp, with her head down, weeping. She looked as though she was ready to fall."[28]

Jackie was not yet aware that as she was preparing to go down to her husband's coffin, the "silly little Communist," Lee Harvey Oswald, was shot by Jack Ruby, in the garage of the jail in Dallas, and was taken to die in Parkland Hospital in Trauma Room No. 2. The scene of the shooting was televised on NBC. As a grim-faced President Johnson told Bobby when they met in the Blue Room before leaving for the Capitol, "It's giving the United States a bad name around the world."[29]

At the White House, Jackie appeared on the steps of the North Portico holding John and Caroline by the hand. Her sense of theater carried her along. Although she usually did all she could to avoid publicity for the children, now she needed them for this tragic triptych, the widowed mother and the two fatherless children, for all the world to see. With the eyes of the world upon her, Jackie stood, as her friend, Joe Alsop put it, "in the glare of history."[30] At the Capitol, after the eulogies, Jackie again took Caroline's hand, telling her, "We're going to say good-bye to Daddy, and we're going to kiss him good-bye, and tell Daddy how much we love him and how much we'll always miss him."[31] Caroline copied her mother as they knelt and kissed the flag covering the coffin, her hand creeping underneath it as if she wanted to touch her father one last time.

Back at the White House, which Stas Radziwill, arriving there while everyone was at the Rotunda, described as "Versailles after the King had died," Jackie had recovered enough to take all the important decisions for the next day's funeral and for her own family's immediate future. After the White House she would have nowhere to go. Friends stepped in to help. David Ormsby-Gore volunteered to house Caroline's school in the British embassy. Kenneth Galbraith discussed a house for Jackie with Averell Harriman, who said he would give up his own home for her and move with his wife, Marie, into the Georgetown Inn. Meanwhile Jackie had to settle the funeral Mass card, the graveside eulogies, the Bible readings and who should deliver them—it was decided, Bobby and Teddy. McGeorge Bundy, who was consulted, said, "It came out right—as did just about everything that Jackie touched those days—and she touched nearly everything." It was Jackie, too, who decided that there should be an Eternal Flame burning beside the grave. She discussed the flowers for the cathedral and the grave with Bunny Mellon. Bunny had already decorated St. Matthew's with two simple blue vases from the White House on pedestals filled with daisies, white chrysanthemums and stephanotis. She had anticipated Jackie's wish as to what should be done with the countless wreaths sent by the public at the graveside: "Please see that they're put far, far from the grave," Jackie told her. "When Patrick died you sent such a nice, simple basket. So there's one thing I want at the grave. A straw basket with just the flowers he had in the Rose Garden. Only those flowers and nothing else at the grave."[32]

Lee Radziwill flew in from London; Stas arrived in Washington the following day. Another foreign guest was Aristotle Onassis, invited to join them by Lee. He had been in Hamburg for the launching of a tanker on the day of the assassination and immediately telephoned Lee. When she invited him, he reminded her that he had been told to stay out of the United States until after the 1964 election but, as Lee pointed out, that was hardly relevant anymore. The following day he received an official invitation to the funeral from Angier Biddle Duke; he was to be a guest at the White House during his stay in Washington. That weekend Mary Gallagher was surprised to see Jackie walking through the Center Hall on the arm of a gentleman she did not recognize and was later told by Provi that it was Onassis. In the general outpouring of grief, his presence in the bosom of the Kennedy family passed almost unnoticed. However, he rated a brief mention by the meticulous William Manchester.

On that evening of Sunday, November 24, after Jack's body had been removed to the Capitol to lie there in state, family and friends dined at the White House. Rose Kennedy had dinner upstairs with Stas Radziwill; Jackie, Lee and Bobby ate in Jackie's sitting room, while the remaining Kennedys were in the family dining room with their houseguests, McNamara, Phyllis Dillon, Dave Powers and Onassis. The family party quickly became an Irish wake, with lots of drink, silly jokes and wigs being passed around. Onassis became the target for jokes about his yacht, where the bar stools had been upholstered with fabric made from a whale's scrotum. Even Bobby joined in later. He drew up a formal document stipulating that Onassis must give half his wealth to help the poor in Latin America. Onassis signed it in Greek.

On Sunday night, after a private visit to the Capitol, Jackie had another Amytal injection, and lay on her husband's side of her bed with the hard bed board for four hours' disturbed sleep.

Monday morning, November 25, the day of the funeral dawned clear and crisp. Jackie had made the momentous decision to walk behind the gun carriage carrying her husband's coffin. The tradition for funerals was that men should walk and women ride in cars behind them. Jackie's decision was a security nightmare: it was not just herself and the Kennedys who would be an easy target for yet another assassin's bullet but the heads of state and of government from all over the world who had arrived for the funeral: General de Gaulle, Emperor Haile Selassie of Ethiopia, Prince Philip, Duke of Edinburgh, the Soviet Foreign Minister, Mikoyan, to name but a few. The new President, Lyndon Johnson, had absolutely refused to be deterred by his advisers from walking. There had been numerous assassination threats, but if the widow was going to head the march, no one was going to back out. Also in the procession was a shining, sweating black gelding, bearing the sheathed sword and reversed boots of a dead commander-in-chief. His name, curiously, although Jackie did not know it, was Black Jack.

Once again, Jackie stood out, the widow veiled in black, flanked by her two brothers-in-law, while the pack of dignitaries twelve abreast, sixteen ranks of them, followed her. "Jacqueline Kennedy walked with a poise and grace that words cannot convey—as regal as any emperor, queen or prince who followed her," a reporter wrote. Lady Jean Campbell wired the London *Evening Standard* that Jackie had "given the American people from this day on the one thing they always lacked—majesty."

In the cathedral little John Jr., whose third birthday this was, was heard to cry "Where's my daddy?" Twice during the Mass, Jackie shook in a spasm of uncontrollable sobs; both times she was comforted by Caroline. "You'll be all right,

Mummy. Don't cry. I'll take care of you." Even Cardinal Cushing was in tears as at the end he broke from the ritual Latin into English: "May the angels, dear Jack, lead you into Paradise . . ." Jackie wrestled for self-control. Then John was brought up to her as she stood outside watching the coffin strapped to the gun carriage for the last journey. She remembered how he had loved playing soldiers with his father, even to the extent of disrupting the Veterans' Day ceremony at Arlington earlier that month with his marching and saluting. "John," she said, "you can salute Daddy now and say good-bye to him." The image of the three-year-old boy, standing to attention, executing a perfect salute was etched on the minds of everyone who saw it.[33]

Air Force One flew over Arlington as the President was buried, the pilot dipping its wings in tribute. At the graveside, Jackie clutched to her the flag that had covered his coffin. "The end of the service in Arlington," Mac Bundy wrote, "was like the fall of a curtain, or the snapping of taut strings . . ."[34]

CHAPTER FIFTEEN

The Knights of Camelot

Rarely, if ever, has hagiography been so skillfully managed by and on behalf of a 33-year-old widow in a democracy.

—Nigel Hamilton[1]

Jackie wrote to Lyndon Johnson on the morning after Jack's funeral:

Dear Mr. President, Thank you for walking yesterday—behind Jack. You did not have to do that—I am sure many people forbid you to take such a risk—but you did it anyway.

Thank you for your letters to my children [on Friday night, the night of JFK's assassination, the new President had sat down to write two handwritten notes individually to John and Caroline, praising their father] . . .

And most of all, Mr. President, thank you for the way you have always treated me—the way you and Lady Bird have always been to me—before, when Jack was alive, and now as President.

I think the relationship of the President and Vice Presidential families could be a rather strained one. From the history I have been reading ever since I came to the White House I gather it often was in the past.

But you were Jack's right arm—and I always thought the greatest act of a gentleman that I had seen on this earth—was how you—the Majority Leader when he came to the Senate as just another little freshman who looked up to you and took orders from you, could then serve as Vice President to a man who had served under you and been taught by you.

But more than that, we were friends, all four of us. All you did for me as a friend and the happy times we had. I always thought before the nomination that Lady Bird should be First Lady—but I don't need to tell you here what I think of her qualities—her extraordinary grace of character—her willingness to assume every burden. She assumed so many for me and I love her very much . . .[2]

Relations between Jackie and the Johnsons had never been closer than at this time. Jackie did not share the feelings of antipathy toward Lyndon felt by Bobby and the Kennedy crowd gathered around him, the heir to the crown, at Hickory Hill. Jack's friend Hugh Sidey, *Life* correspondent in Washington and a frequent visitor to Hickory Hill, had been horrified by the gang's ridicule of Johnson, which he called "just awful" and "inexcusable." In October 1963 friends, amid much merriment, had given Bobby a Johnson voodoo doll.[3] Both she and Jack had been aware of the humiliation and frustration involved in the vice presidency—"a bucket of warm spit"—as one holder of the office had described it.

While Jack had specifically tried to involve Johnson as closely as possible in the administration, Jackie had gone out of her way to ensure that he and Lady Bird were included in every social function and that their daughters, too, were invited on suitable evenings. Jackie had written personally to Lyndon asking him to give the welcome speech at the dinner in honor of André Malraux on May 10. Jack and Jackie, according to Arthur Schlesinger, regarded Johnson with a "certain fondness," seeing him as "an American original, a figure out of Mark Twain," and Lady Bird had uncomplainingly done her best to fill in for Jackie at functions the First Lady could not be bothered to attend.

Jackie may have mocked Lady Bird's total subordination of her own wishes to her often difficult and demanding husband ("Lady Bird would crawl on her hands and knees eating grass down Pennsylvania Avenue if Lyndon asked her to," Jackie is reported to have said) but she respected and liked her for her integrity and strength. She appreciated, too, the Johnsons' kindness in letting her stay on at the White House as long as it suited her. Reporters stationed outside The Elms, the Johnsons' Washington home, irritated Lady Bird with their persistent questions about when Jackie was going to move out. She turned on them: "Would to God, I could serve Mrs. Kennedy's comfort. I can at least serve her convenience."[4] Lyndon Johnson described Jackie's behavior as "graceful."

What Bobby saw as Johnson's "abuse" and "mistreatment" of Jackie on board the plane at Love Field, his keeping her waiting on the ground for the swearing-in and "forcing" her to take part, added fuel to the fire of his hatred of his brother's "usurper," Jackie herself never complained about it, and the evidence is that she understood the importance of her affirming presence beside Johnson during the oath. Both the Johnsons and Jackie were concerned to keep their relationship as warm as possible. She found the strength to telephone Lyndon with her good wishes on the night of Thanksgiving, November 28, a gesture to which the President responded with a handwritten note from the White House: "You have been magnificent and have won a warm place in the heart of history," he told her. "I only wish things could be different and I didn't have to be here. But the Almighty willed differently, and now Lady Bird and I need your help. You have now and for *always* our warm, warm love . . ."[5]

"Jackie loved Lyndon," Charlie Bartlett said. "Lyndon was very sweet to her . . . As she said, he couldn't have been nicer, more thoughtful and more compassionate . . . Bobby had a running feud, a deep, deep, deep feud with Lyndon . . . She was funny about Bobby. 'Bobby would make me put on my widow's weeds and ask Lyndon Johnson to rename Cape Canaveral.' The Kennedys were pushing for everything they could get out of the situation. Jackie was their foil. She was very funny about that."[6] (On November 27, five days after the assassination, Jackie had paid a half-hour's visit to Johnson in the Oval Office, when she had asked him to do something to commemorate Jack's support for the space program. The result had been his decision to rename Cape Canaveral. Later, Jackie said she regretted having asked Johnson to rename it Cape Kennedy—"If I'd known that that had been its name since the time of Columbus, I wouldn't have done it."[7] But for the politically minded Kennedys, the renaming of Canaveral was important in the light of Jack's pledge to have a man on the moon before the end of the decade.)

Jack had wanted for his library a replica of his office in the White House, the chief feature of which was the elaborately carved Hayes desk. (The desk became part of Kennedy iconography with the photographs of a two-year-old John Jr. crawling out of it as his father worked in the Oval Office.) "On the day of the assassination," White House curator James Ketchum recalled, "I was doing something which Mrs. Kennedy had asked me to do about three weeks before and that was to get a hold of some people from the Smithsonian and have them come with a fabricator who would talk about a process of casting so that the desk could be reproduced for the Kennedy Library." Now, the Kennedys made strenuous efforts to take the original for the library. As Ketchum remembered: "On November 22 you no longer have a President Kennedy, you have a President Johnson, who says to Mrs. Kennedy in the earliest days of his administration, 'Little lady, anything you want in this room is yours.' And she said, 'Well, I don't think there's anything I want, Mr. President.' And then about six weeks later there's a phone call in which I was told the plans were made for a traveling Kennedy exhibit, and that the desk would be requested and I should assume that it would never return to the White House." Outraged, Ketchum ensured that papers were drawn up to show it was only a loan, but when the desk returned, battered and in need of restoration, from worldwide exhibition, a renewed battle was joined. "Archives had taken possession of it," Ketchum recalled. "And what I did was make a phone call to the archivist, didn't say I wanted it, just said I'd send a truck over for it, and so we took possession of it. In the meantime Bobby Kennedy got into the act and Bill Moyers got into the act and I was getting phone calls that were quite tense and bitter about what was going on. My only point was to see the desk put back in its original state and also that it did belong to the White House. I had talked to Mrs. Johnson about it when the desk was coming back and she talked to the President about it, and it was suggested that I go and talk to Clark Clifford . . . Clifford spent about forty-five minutes saying, 'Maybe we should reenter the copy sweepstakes and look at that whole process.' But I was at that point hopeful enough that possession would be nine-tenths of the law, and the fact that we did have it, and that I had to point out along the line that it was really not President Johnson's desk to give away to begin with any more than it was Mrs. Kennedy's desk to ask for. And yet who would say no to the widow of our martyred president? It was a very uncomfortable position."

This time the tenacious young curator won the war: the desk was repaired and put back in the Oval Office, where, since Kennedy's time, it has been used by every President as Queen Victoria had originally wished it to be.

Jackie was obsessively anxious to ensure that Lady Bird preserved her legacy, the restored White House, and to help her do so in every way she could. From Hyannis Port, where she had spent Thanksgiving, she wrote Lady Bird a long letter dated Sunday, December 1, on her usual legal pad. She had always been afraid that the next First Lady would not care about the preservation of the White House, and she thanked Lady Bird for making sure that the house would always be cared for.

That day she also wrote a ten-page memo on the operation of the White House, which she instructed West to forward to Lady Bird. When she returned to the White House, she had two last requests for West. The first was to have a plaque made for the mantel of her bedroom: "In this room lived John Fitzgerald Kennedy with his wife, Jacqueline, during the two years, ten months and two days he was President of the United States: January 20, 1961–November 22, 1963." It was to be placed near the brass plate recording that Abraham Lincoln had slept in the room. The second was the hanging of the Kennedy family present to the White House in memory of JFK, a Monet entitled *Morning on the Seine*. "Can you have it hung in the Green Room?" she asked. "That was his favorite room . . ."

Lyndon Johnson's courtship of Jackie continued unabated. He and Jackie cooed at each other over the telephone, the President's Texan drawl as warm as honey, Jackie's voice soft and breathy. "I just wanted you to know you are loved by so many and so much," Johnson told her on December 2. "I'm one of them." Breathlessly Jackie thanked him for the letter he had written her the previous day. "I didn't dare bother you again," she said. "Listen, sweetie," Johnson replied, "one thing you gotta learn is that you don't bother me. You give me strength. You just come over and put your arm around me. That's all you do. When you haven't anything else to do, let's take a walk around the backyard . . . You've got this President relying on you . . ."[8] "I love you," Johnson began another conversation with Jackie on December 21. "You just kept away from this town, I ought to have you arrested. You almost made me mad at you, leaving without coming by and hugging me and telling me good-bye . . ."[9] Two days later he told Pierre Salinger that he was thinking of appointing Jackie U.S. Ambassador to Mexico and expressed his affection for her: "I talked to her a while ago," he said, "and she just oohed and aahed on the phone and she was just the sweetest thing, she was always nicer to me than anybody in the Kennedy family. She always took my children and made me feel like I was a human being . . ."[10]

Jackie responded with almost wifely concern to Lyndon's appeals to her: "Will you please start to take a nap after lunch?" she told him. "It changed Jack's whole life. He was always sick and when we got to the White House he did it every day . . ." "You come down here and see me and if you don't I'll come out there and see you," Johnson responded. "Oh, Mr. President," Jackie breathed. But there was one thing she could not bring herself to do: "I can't come down there, I wanted to tell you, I've really gotten hold of myself. You know I'll do anything for you. I'll talk to you on the phone. I'm just scared I'll start to cry again . . ."[11]

Yet underlying the cordiality of Jackie's relations with the Lyndon Johnsons was her obsessive fear that the new President's achievements might obscure Jack's reputation. "Already without him it is disintegrating," she wrote to Harold Macmillan on January 31, 1964. She was determined not only that Jack should not be forgotten, but that he should be remembered in the heroic light in which she now saw him. She had heard that Teddy White, author of *The Making of the President 1960*, a writer Jack had admired, was to do a piece for *Life* on the assassination. She wanted White to hear what she had to say, to see Jack as she saw him, to have it there on the pages of *Life* for millions to read. She was about to create a myth: the myth of Camelot.

White was summoned to Hyannis Port on Friday, November 29, the day after Thanksgiving. It was a stormy night as he was driven down to the Cape, arriving at eight-thirty. He stayed until 2 A.M. as Jackie talked, talked and talked. She was not alone: Chuck Spalding and Franklin Roosevelt Jr. were there, with Dave Powers and Pat Lawford. "The chief memory I have of her is of her composure," White recalled, "of her beauty (dressed in black trim slacks, beige pullover sweater), her eyes wider than pools; and of her calm voice and total recall."[12] She told him that she knew Arthur Krock and Merriman Smith were going to write about Jack as history, and that was not the way she wanted him remembered. She was not interested in the myriad theories as to who might have been behind Jack's murder. "What difference did it make whether he was killed by the CIA, the FBI, the Mafia, or simply by some half-crazed misanthrope?" White recorded. "He was gone, and what counted for her was that his death be placed in some kind of social context."[13]

" 'But there's this one thing I wanted to say,' she said, '. . .one thing kept going through my mind, the line from a musical comedy. I kept saying to Bobby, I've got to talk to somebody, I've got to see somebody. I want to say this one thing. It's been almost an obsession with me . . . At night, before going to bed . . . we had an old victrola, he'd play a couple of records. I'd get out of bed and play it for him when it was so cold getting out of bed. It was a song he loved, he loved Camelot. It was the song he loved most at the end . . . on a victrola ten years old. It's the last record, the last side of Camelot. "Don't let it be forgot that for one brief shining moment there was Camelot . . ." When I came home I looked for it again. I wanted to say, "There'll never be another Camelot . . ."

" 'Jack loved history; but history isn't something that bitter old men write. History made Jack what he was. You must think of him as this little boy, sick so much of the time, reading history, reading the knights of the round table, reading

Marlborough. For Jack, history was full of heroes . . . if it made him this way, if it made him see heroes, maybe other little boys will see . . . Jack had this hero idea of history, the idealistic view, and then the other side, the pragmatic side.' She did not want them to forget John F. Kennedy, or read of him in dusty or bitter histories. *For one brief shining moment . . . this was Camelot.*[14] And all she could think [Jackie added] was tell people there will never be that Camelot again."

"She put it so passionately that, seen in a certain light, it almost made sense," White recalled. "I realized it was a misreading of history, but I was taken with Jackie's ability to frame the tragedy in such human and romantic terms. There was something extremely compelling about her. All she wanted was for me to hang this *Life* epilogue on the Camelot conceit. It didn't seem like a hell of a lot to ask. So I said to myself, Why not? If that's all she wants, let her have it. So the epitaph of the Kennedy administration became Camelot—a magic moment in American history when gallant men danced with beautiful women, when great deeds were done and when the White House became the center of the universe."[15]

The whole concept was evidence of Jackie's power as an image maker. Like all myths it was a distortion of the reality, and reality would catch up with it one day. Alan Jay Lerner, author and lyricist of the musical *Camelot*, was as puzzled as Teddy White had been. "He didn't understand about all that Camelot business—he went to boarding school and Harvard with John F. Kennedy so he knew him going way back and he knew Jackie well—he said neither President Kennedy nor Jackie had ever said anything to him about their great love for *Camelot*," recounted his wife, Karen Lerner. "Which leads me to believe," she added, "that Jackie when she spoke to Teddy White in her first interview for *Life* after the assassination, had maybe created this."[16] No one would have been more derisive of the Camelot concept than Jack himself.

From now on, Jackie had two concerns: to glorify Jack's presidency and to ensure her children's future. "Two days after Kennedy was assassinated," Pierre Salinger said, "she walked into my office and said something which I think was her complete future because she said, 'Listen, I only have one thing to do now—I have to take care of these kids. I have to make sure they grow up well, they have to get intelligent, they have to move forward to get good jobs, they have to have a whole very important life because if I don't do that for them, they'll spend all their time looking back at their father's death and that's what they shouldn't be doing.' "[17] But she was determined they should not forget him. Maud Shaw recalled, "She was firmly of the opinion that, having had such a wonderful man for a father, they should grow up knowing all about him . . . It was Mrs. Kennedy's aim to make her children proud of their father, so that they were always aware of what he was and who he was. And I think she has succeeded well in substituting pride in his achievements and his memory for lingering sorrow at his death."[18]

On that stormy night on Cape Cod, Jackie spoke of her children to Teddy White, of Caroline's wonderfully supportive behavior at the funeral—"She held my hand like a soldier, she's my helper, she's mine now . . ." Of John Jr. she said, "I want John to grow up to be a good boy. He loves planes, you know. Maybe he'll be an astronaut when he grows up, or maybe he'll be plain John F. Kennedy fixing somebody else's plane on the ground . . ."[19]

Jackie held a delayed third birthday party for John Jr. on December 5, brightening their last day in the White House. The next day, wearing the same black suit she had worn at Jack's funeral and holding the children by the hand, she left the White House for the Harriman house in Georgetown, accompanied by Lee, Ethel and Bobby. "There was a lump in my throat as I walked down the corridor," Maud Shaw wrote, "knowing that we would never retrace these footsteps. At the elevator, I looked back toward the nursery rooms, where I had shared three such happy years with the children. The rooms were quite silent now. A pall of sadness hung like a dust sheet over everything . . ." It was a sad occasion for all of them.[20]

Once in the Harriman house, 3036 N Street, Jackie's self-control deserted her. Spiraling down into depression, she rarely left her bedroom on the second floor. Coming in on the following Monday, Mary Gallagher went up to her bedroom to take dictation and found her in "a lonely, depressed mood . . . She wept, saying how very lonely she was. 'Why did Jack have to die so young?' she moaned. 'Even when you're sixty, you like to know your husband is there. It's so hard for the children . . .' Her suffering pervaded the house. She spent a lot of time going up to Arlington Cemetery to Jack's grave and praying alone in St. Matthew's Cathedral."[21]

Meanwhile Jackie and Miss Shaw did what they could to make life normal for the children. Their favorite toys came out first—for Caroline, a doll carriage, a dressing-up doll called Mary, her beloved Raggedy Ann, and a toy poodle, Tinkerbelle. John had his usual armor of guns and swords, and the Marine uniform he had been given for his birthday, which he wore almost constantly. Dave Powers came to drill John Jr. just as he had at the White House. Caroline was still attending school at the White House, where the Johnsons had kindly allowed it to continue until Christmas. "John and I carried on our lives more or less normally," Maud Shaw wrote. "He played and scampered and chatted as much as ever, but I could not help noticing his bright little face clouding over sometimes as he struggled to understand what had happened to him. He often asked why we were not still living in the 'other house' and similar questions, and it was with some relief that we eventually traveled down to Palm Beach and away from Washington."[22] There they joined the Radziwills in the house that Jack and Jackie had always rented.

"Mrs. Kennedy did very well that Christmas in making it a good time for the children," Maud Shaw recalled. "She was a sad figure, and I felt a tremendous sympathy for her and admired her a great deal for the effort she made for John and Caroline. The house was so full of memories for us all, though, that when the children went to bed in the evening it was difficult to prevent that sadness from spreading through the house again."[23]

Aware that her children must have a home and that the Harrimans could not be expected to stay much longer at the Georgetown Inn (where Marie complained that the bathtubs were too short), she bought a house on the same street, 3017, planning to move in there in February. At first she clung to familiar places.

She would never go to live in Europe, she had told Teddy White. "That would be a desecration." She was going to live in the places she had lived with Jack—her first hope, expressed during a talk with Bob McNamara, had been to get back their original Georgetown house, but it was not for sale. She would also be with the Kennedys at the Cape—"They're my family now," she told White.[24]

Jackie returned to Washington in January, bringing Lee for company. Although she put on a brave face for the children, she was still distraught. The decorator Billy Baldwin came down from New York to discuss plans for the new house. Showing him the collection of Greek and Roman antiquities that Jack had begun, she broke down. "It's so sad to be doing this. Like a young married couple fixing up their first house together . . ." She wept. Then pulling herself together, she told him, "I know my husband was devoted to me. I know he was proud of me. It took a very long time for us to work everything out, but we did, and we were about to have a real life together. I was going to campaign with him. I know I held a very special place for him—a unique place." Haunted by what might have been she talked on and on about Jack, about their life together, about what could have been and should have been. "Can anyone understand how it is to have lived in the White House and then, suddenly, to be living alone as the President's widow? There's something so final about it. And the children. The world is pouring out terrible adoration at the feet of my children and I fear for them, for this awful exposure. How can I bring them up normally?"[25]

The new house on N Street, into which they moved on January 27, was not a success. Jackie had looked forward to it as a new beginning, but Mary Gallagher described it as "silent and lonely."[26] For Jackie the most difficult moments came when she unpacked cartons that had remained unopened since the move from the White House—photographs, records, scrapbooks, the couple's personal library, all of them haunting reminders of her life with Jack. For a while she could not even bear to put up his photograph. One morning, going through a file of cuttings about Jack, she asked Gallagher to sit with her. "It's so much easier doing it while you're here than at night when I'm alone. I just drown my sorrows in vodka . . ."[27]

In her depression, Jackie began to panic about money, although she had a government appropriation of $50,000 for her expenses plus about $150,000 per year from a Kennedy trust in her name and $50,000 that Bobby provided from the Kennedy funds. She began to be uncharacteristically mean with her staff. "I really can't *afford* to pay all my help from the $50,000," she said, "what with having to pay for the new house, and Provi, and all the other expenses." The valet, George Thomas, was still on the payroll, but was finally offered a job by Jack's former assistant, Ted Reardon. The two Navy stewards provided for her by the White House requested transfer back to the White House and their normal duties. Jackie was furious. "She showed no signs of recognizing that her small staff did not like being called on to provide all the services, accommodations, conveniences, and comforts that she had grown so used to receiving from a much larger staff during her White House years . . . ," Gallagher wrote.[28]

She even upset the loyal Evelyn Lincoln who, with Ensign George Dalton, was working on the late President's papers in the Executive Office Building and preparing the traveling exhibition. Jackie told her petulantly, "All this shouldn't be so hard for you because you still have your husband. What do I have now? Just the library . . ." She wanted to know why Lincoln needed such a large office, and when she replied that it was necessary to display memorabilia for people to see, Jackie burst out, "But these things are all mine!" and forbade her to give anything to anyone as a souvenir. She questioned her closely as to what exactly she had been doing over the past few weeks, then said, "Why, Mrs. Lincoln, I could sit down and in a half-day index all these items on cards myself!" Going through the household accounts with Gallagher, she was even sharper, accusing the staff of taking food home with them, objecting to Provi being paid overtime for working late in the evenings and at weekends. "Do you mean that for every little thing extra someone does around here, I have to pay them?" She objected to paying Provi her full salary while she and the children were away for the summer and told Gallagher to get the employment agency to find extra work for Provi to make up the amount.[29]

Jackie was emotionally disturbed, subject to violent mood swings, irrational behavior, guilt feelings about Jack—how she had not helped him enough, how she might have saved his life. Lee told Cecil Beaton that she had been "through hell" trying to calm her sister's hysteria. "You don't know what it's like being with Jackie. She really was then half around the bend! She can't sleep at nights—she can't stop thinking about herself and never feeling anything but sorry for herself! 'I'm so unprotected,' she says. But she is surrounded by friends, helpers, FBI [Secret Service men] . . . She gets so she hits me across the face when I've done nothing . . ."[30] In turn Lee was being comforted by Onassis, as Diana Vreeland told Beaton: "Jackie Kennedy is moving into the house Rex & Leslie had during the war in Washington & Billy Baldwin helping her. Lee is with her & Onassis in tow . . ."[31]

In fact, as Lee pointed out, Jackie was rarely alone. The knights of Camelot, led by Bobby, rallied around their widowed queen. Old friends, friends she had shared with Jack were not included in this tight-knit band of brothers, tending the Eternal Flame. The Bradlees spent a "couple of emotional weekends" at Wexford in the weeks immediately after the assassination, "trying with no success to talk about something else, or someone else. Too soon and too emotional for healing, we proved only that the three of us had very little in common without the essential fourth." On December 20, just under four weeks after Dallas, Jackie wrote them an emotional, almost angry and hurt letter:

Dear Tony and Ben,

Something that you said in the country stunned me so—that you hoped I would marry again.

You were close to us so many times. There is one thing that you must know. I consider that my life is over and I will spend the rest of my life waiting for it really to be over.[32]

"Jackie talked of staying in Washington," Ben Bradlee recalled, "even enlisted Tony to look at houses in Georgetown for her, and eventually bought one. But by the time she moved in, we felt that she was not long for the city where her life had been ruined."[33]

Although Jackie's first instinct had been to cling to the past, to her life with Jack, psychologically she was already exercising that instinct to move on and leave the past behind her. Charlie Bartlett experienced the same feeling: "After she left Washington we saw very little of her. We accompanied her on a trip to Cambodia in 1967, but otherwise we saw her only in the Far Hills–Peapack–Bernardsville area, where she had her weekend house and my in-laws had theirs. I had the feeling she didn't want to be reminded of the past."[34]

"Washington wasn't for her," her friend William vanden Heuvel said. "Washington is the President's town and she knew that."[35]

Jackie's penchant for married men—without their wives—alienated old friends like the Bartletts. "It annoyed Martha that she would pick up husbands—Franklin Roosevelt and whatever—and sort of assume them. Martha wasn't going to have any of that," Charlie Bartlett said, chuckling. "So I didn't see much of her [Jackie] because I didn't want to have any trouble at home. And Martha kept seeing her because she was godmother to the little boy, John, and she made a big effort. She made a big effort to see her but Jackie changed a lot, Martha didn't find her so much fun down the road. She was pretty full of herself. Jackie changed. Jack never changed . . ."[36] Indeed, old friends, like the Bartletts and Bradlees, reluctantly came to the conclusion that they had been invited to the White House because Jack had wanted to see them and not from any initiative of Jackie's.

Later Tony Bradlee felt ambivalent about Jackie: "There was a kind of disconnectedness on her part as to what a best friend is supposed to be. I don't think she probably ever had a very close friend . . . I'm not sure she ever really experienced the need for an intimate friend. She had social friends—Bunny Mellon, Jayne Wrightsman, Nancy Tuckerman—but there are friendships and then there are friendships . . ."[37]

"She did not have any intimates, Jackie," Robin Biddle Duke said, "that was one of the tragedies when he died. Angie said to me, 'There's no one to send in [to comfort her]' in effect. Lee was on her way back from London but . . . so Chuck Spalding's wife went in, I think. But Jackie was not close, didn't have any intimate women friends and never really liked women. As a consequence maybe because of her experience with her husband . . ."[38]

By the time of the assassination Betty Spalding and her husband Chuck were going their separate ways. Jackie, however, invited Betty down for a couple of weekends at Wexford, probably because Betty's twin girls would be company for John and Caroline. To Betty, Jackie seemed to be drifting, uncertain how or where to anchor her life. "I saw her there and she just didn't know where she was going to go or . . . she was drifting, really. She did not get on with Mrs. Kennedy. The old man, of course, by that time was incapacitated, and she didn't want to go, she didn't know whether to bring the kids up near—to go back to the Cape in the summer time—because they did not want to be involved, to stay in Mrs.

Kennedy's house. She wanted to keep them all away from Ethel's children as much as she could—they were really quite dangerous. One of them threw a pitchfork at one of my twins. Can you imagine that?"[39]

Wives were not admitted to Jackie's circle in Georgetown. Robin Biddle Duke remembers that when her husband was appointed ambassador to Spain by Johnson, "he called Jackie and said, 'I'd love to come and say good-bye, we're off to Spain,' and she explicitly said, 'Do come to tea, and don't bring Robin.' And lots of the girls never really expressed their scorn," she went on. "I know Ros Gilpatric's wife, Madelin, did—but Phyllis Dillon didn't and she was very graceful, Marg McNamara didn't and she was very graceful. But behind the scenes we all played tennis together and knew each other and they didn't like the fact that their husbands were going out with Jackie Kennedy. And she would always call the men and say, 'Help me, I feel desperate about this or that.' It was a bit childish but on the other hand I forgave her everything because that woman had been put through something, the experience of which has no parallel I know of . . ."[40]

"She had a kind of *droit de seigneur* about men," a woman friend said. "I think it didn't matter to her whether men were married or not. And in addition to that I think perhaps if she had romantic feelings or even sexual feelings it was safer for her to be with a married man . . ."[41]

Jackie had "deep depressions, suicidal feelings," a woman who had known Jackie since her debutante days said. "Some things that seemed inexplicable were attributable to that."[42] In the period after Jack's death, Jackie was capable of doing things that were quite out of character. She drank, sometimes too much, and the sudden sexual deprivation she suffered with the disappearance of Jack manifested itself in some peculiar episodes, the oddest of which was her encounter with Marlon Brando in January/February 1964. The meeting was engineered by Lee through her friend the film director George Englund, Brando's best friend. The foursome dined at the Jockey Club, drinking martinis and having a hilarious time until photographers appeared in the restaurant. Englund, Brando, Lee and Jackie fled through a back door to carry on the evening at Jackie's house. Dancing with Brando, Jackie made it obvious that she was physically attracted to him, pressing herself close and whispering in his ear. "I think they both wanted it to happen but it didn't happen," a friend of Englund's recounted, "because Marlon was so drunk."[43] Realizing that the evening could well turn out to be a fiasco, the actor fled.

Initially, Jackie's bond with the knights of Camelot was founded on one connection, mourning for Jack, which she shared with the men, not the wives. As Joe Alsop wrote:

> For a time after Jack Kennedy's death the sense of emotional loss was so staggering among those who had known and worked with him that the Washington landscape seemed to me to be littered with male widows. McNamara's Deputy Secretary, Roswell L. Gilpatric, a man with long experience in the world, and not given to easy emotion, told me days after the event: "You know, Joe, when the President died, I

suddenly realized that I felt about him as I've never felt about another man in my life." Mac Bundy admitted to me that President Kennedy's death struck him more deeply than the loss of his own father who had passed away some months before. I felt much the same way . . . After that bright, blustery November day, nothing would be quite the same in my life again or . . . in the life of this country.[44]

Averell Harriman, aged seventy-two, told Susan Mary Alsop late in 1963, "When Kennedy was alive was the last time I felt young . . ."[45]

All this pent-up emotion in the Kennedy circle (not to mention the hundreds of thousands of letters of condolence that flooded into the office designated for Jackie in the Executive Office Building) focused on the thirty-three-year-old widow. It induced an abnormal atmosphere of suppressed hysteria, emotion, catatonic grief that marked Jackie for life. Even in her private life she became someone extraordinary, touched by fate and celebrity. No one would ever be able to react normally to her again; nor would she ever, however hard she tried—and she did try—be able to escape her golden cage.

Of all the knights of Camelot gathered around the widowed queen, Bobby was by far the closest. In a distortion of the myth, he increasingly played Lancelot to Jackie's Guinevere. In their grief they clung together, Bobby acting as a husband substitute for Jackie, a father substitute for her children. He had always been the one member of the Kennedy family who was always there for her—at her bedside after the stillbirth of her daughter in 1956, when Jack was vacationing in Europe, with Jack after the death of Patrick, and, finally, first to the plane when she brought Jack's body back from Dallas. Bobby was with her constantly on N Street, coming around immediately if she called him, stopping by in the evening. In order to avoid attention, he parked his car some distance away from the house on another street. But Washington, and Georgetown in particular, is a small place and it was not long before gossip began about Bobby "spending a lot of time with the widder," as Eunice is reported to have put it. The rumors ran through the top hairdressing salons. "Yes, there was lots of talk in those days, after Jack was shot and Bobby was around a lot and taking care of her," a Kenneth employee admitted, "when it was supposedly happening those were the Kenneth days, and that was in the late sixties."[46]

Bobby had been closer to his brother than to any other human being and consequently suffered the most. More deeply religious than Jackie, he found this random death more difficult to accept in terms of faith. On the night of Jack's death, Chuck Spalding heard him weeping in the Lincoln Bedroom, crying out in agony, "Why, God?"[47]

Jackie and Bobby had instructed Bill Walton to go ahead with his prearranged trip to Moscow, ostensibly to meet Soviet artists (in his position as head of the Fine Arts Commission). He left on November 29. Soon after his arrival he met the unofficial Kennedy Soviet contact, Georgi Bolshakov, in a Moscow restaurant where he explained that the Kennedys believed there had been a large political conspiracy behind Oswald's rifle. Despite Oswald's connections to the Communist world, the Kennedys believed that the President had been felled by domestic opponents. A KGB analysis confirmed this theory. According to their intelligence, Kennedy had been killed by a conspiracy of three wealthy Texan oilmen, opposed to his policy on civil rights and rapprochement with the Soviet Union, and angered by recent tax reforms. According to information from the respected diplomatic correspondent of the *Baltimore Sun*, this group, headed by Harold Lafayette Hunt, had instructed Jack Ruby (who had murdered Oswald in the Dallas police garage) to give Oswald a large sum of money to kill Kennedy. Afterward, when the conspirators learned through their Dallas police sources that, under interrogation, Oswald had said he would tell all at his trial, Ruby was instructed to silence him.[48] Walton was a Johnson hater, like most of Bobby Kennedy's circle; a primary objective of his mission was to undermine Johnson and boost Kennedy in Soviet eyes by representing Johnson as opposed to Jack's détente policy and Bobby as the man most likely to continue it.

Jackie—and Bobby in particular—had their own reasons for wanting to believe the right-wing conspiracy theory. Jackie had cried out in dismay when told that Jack had been killed by "a silly little Communist." If that was so then for her Jack's death had no meaning. Both she and Bobby—and the Kennedy circle—passionately wanted to believe that the president had been martyred for his liberal policies. When Jackie defiantly displayed her suit spattered with her husband's blood and brains, saying she wanted "them to see what they've done," she was aiming it at the right-wingers of Dallas whom she believed had killed him.

Bobby himself was haunted by the fear that he himself had been indirectly responsible for his brother's death. "Assuming that Oswald was not the lone assassin," Richard Goodwin, Bobby's friend and political aide, said, "the only other people who it could be would be from the mob. Also they were the only organization at that point that could have kept it secret. And Bobby always thought that. And part of it was because of his . . . he felt guilty. His going after the mob, they had to get rid of him. One of the mobsters is reputed to have said to his boys, 'We shot the wrong one.' But I always thought and he always thought, and he said to me, 'If anyone else is involved it was the mob.' "[49] As Attorney General, Bobby had ruthlessly pursued the Mafia, despite his alleged involvement with them as instruments of the CIA operation to eliminate Fidel Castro. They were also said to have been resentful that the help they had provided in the 1960 election had been rewarded by persecution from the Kennedys.

All the authorities on Oswald and the assassination have agreed with the eventual judgment of the Warren Commission, which investigated the death of Kennedy, that the President was shot by Oswald acting alone. This does not mean, however, as Richard Goodwin testifies, that Bobby did not believe that it might have been an act of revenge on the part of the Mafia for his pursuit of them. His deputy at the Justice Department, Nicholas Katzenbach, who handled matters relating to the Warren Commission in his stead, said of Bobby, "He never really wanted any investigation."

In the days and months following Jack's death, Bobby Kennedy was like an empty shell of his former self. "It was much harder for him than for anybody," Lem Billings said. "He had put his brother's career absolutely first . . . And I think the shock of losing what he'd built everything around . . . aside from losing the loved figure . . . was just absolutely [devastating]—he did not know where he was . . . Everything was just pulled out from under him."[50] Pierre Salinger recalled, "He was the most shattered man I had ever seen in my life. He was virtually non-functioning. He would walk for hours by himself." Another friend said that everything Bobby did was through "a haze of pain."[51] Just over three months after the assassination, William Manchester, meeting Bobby in Washington, was "shocked by his appearance. I have never seen a man with less resilience. Much of the time he seemed to be in a trance, staring off into space, his face a study in grief."[52]

Jackie and Bobby had to bear the brunt of making decisions on the design of Jack's grave at Arlington with architect Jack Warnecke. "About two days after the funeral," Warnecke said, "I got this call saying that Bobby and Jackie wanted to take me over to Arlington. At that time there was a little white picket fence and there was a flame at the grave . . . Jackie and Bobby went down on their knees and crossed themselves, and when they stood up I realized that they were all upset so I said, 'Let's walk around, let me take you for a walk.' So we walked above, we walked up the hillside to the Lee mansion and looked down. And when Jackie, she was very silent going over, as was Bobby of course—but when she got up near the top and saw the axis, that's where you really see the spirit, you look down on the grave and you feel . . .

"In the design team we had a hard time—Jackie would come to meetings and I think she was very good. She just had to deal with it . . . As compared, for instance, when Bobby would come to a meeting, he'd come in and see models and drawings, and Jackie was there, and he just stood there. He was knocked out, cold, and he eventually left—Teddy came back and apologized for his brother . . ."[53]

On March 26 Jackie and Bobby flew off together for a skiing vacation in Sun Valley, Idaho. For Easter 1964 Jackie traveled down with Bobby, the Radziwills and Chuck Spalding to Bunny Mellon's house on the Mill Reef Estate on Antigua. It was there that she changed his life by introducing him to the Greek philosophers. She showed him *The Greek Way*, by Edith Hamilton, a former pupil at Miss Porter's. "I'd read it quite a lot before and I brought it with me," she told Arthur Schlesinger. "So I gave it to him and I remember he'd disappear. He'd be in his room an awful lot of the time, reading that and underlining things."[54] For her, as for Bobby, Aeschylus on tragedy gave meaning and dignity to the random point-lessness of Jack's death.[55]

Jackie had always felt a tenderness for Bobby and he for her. Perceptive as she was, she sensed the kindness, humanity and sensitivity that lay beneath his tough, uncompromising, often ruthless exterior. Lacking Jack's easy charm and cool objectivity, Bobby had an unrivaled capacity to make as many enemies as he had devoted followers. "Bobby was a pain in the ass," was George Smathers's view of his friend's younger brother, an opinion shared by many, including Gore Vidal, whose friendship with Jack and Jackie had been ended by his famous row with Bobby. Years later, looking back on his time with the Kennedys, Vidal reflected, "As I let the drama idle away in my mind, I suspect that the one person she ever loved . . . was Bobby Kennedy . . . There was always something oddly intense in her voice when she mentioned him to me . . ."[56]

Jackie and Bobby were almost inseparable during that spring and summer of 1964. Both were planning to turn their backs on Washington for New York. According to Bobby's biographer, David Heymann, Bobby confided to Jackie early on (but to no one else) his plan to run for Senator from New York. Neither of them wanted to remain in a town that reminded them every moment of Jack and, worse, that Jack's dominion had been replaced by that of Lyndon Johnson's. Jackie moved out of N Street in June. She had spent precisely four months there. The house had become a tourist attraction, turning the quiet tree-lined street into a sightseers' thoroughfare. The traffic never let up until nine or ten at night, said Joe Kraft, a Washington reporter and Kennedy friend, who lived two doors away. Sightseeing buses made the narrow street a regular port of call; people even went so far as to set up picnic tables outside the house opposite Jackie's, equipping themselves with binoculars to keep watch for a glimpse of her or of the children. Someone stole the board with the house number on it as a souvenir. Despite the presence of a policeman on guard, people were always snapping off twigs of the shrubs within reach. "If you didn't have a policeman here," said the officer on duty, "you wouldn't have a house there."

Jackie's last public appearance in Washington was with the children at Arlington on May 29, the day that would have been Jack's forty-seventh birthday, when they laid flowers on his grave and attended a memorial mass at St. Matthew's Cathedral. She was at Hyannis Port when on the night of June 19 Teddy Kennedy, flying to a political dinner in Springfield, Massachusetts, crashed in thunderstorms over the Connecticut valley. The pilot and another passenger were killed; Teddy survived with damaged vertebrae, broken ribs and a punctured lung. "Somebody up there doesn't like me," Bobby said after visiting his brother in the hospital.[57]

Lyndon Johnson's paranoia about Bobby extended to an obsession about Jackie. For Johnson, Bobby across the Potomac, surrounded by his court at Hickory Hill, was like the King over the Water, the legitimate pretender to his throne. He suspected Bobby of a burning political ambition to replace him. In this he was correct. Before his death Jack Kennedy had told Charlie Bartlett that Bobby intended to run against Johnson in 1968. Since Johnson could never hope to win over Bobby, he needed Jackie's support to gain the legitimacy he craved. He telephoned her constantly, adoring, flirtatious conversations. He contributed to the fund for the Kennedy Library. He not only agreed to the renaming of Cape Canaveral but also of New York's Idlewild Airport, and the National Cultural Center in Washington, one of Jack's most cherished projects. He made repeated attempts to lure her back to the White House but in vain.[58] Jackie returned once to see Caroline's school Christmas play on December 17; she had intended to call on Johnson but discovered he was at the United Nations. She promised to visit him after Christmas but never did, refusing all his invitations. (She eventually went to the White House in 1971 when the Nixons invited her and the children to view her and her husband's official portraits.)

Her refusals enraged Johnson and he complained about it in no uncertain terms to Pierre Salinger, as the two men bobbed about in the White House swimming pool. On one occasion Johnson attempted to use Jackie for his own publicity purposes when he made a Christmas telephone call to her on December 23 when several newspapermen were in the room. One of them, Frances Lewine of UPI, reported the call, as a result of which Pierre Salinger tackled Johnson about it. Alarmed, ten minutes later, Johnson called Lewine and told her, "I just don't want to be carrying on my private conversations in public and have her [Jackie] think I'm using her or something. All I want to do is just be to as sweet [as I can] and wish her a Merry Christmas and I hope you didn't say any more than that . . ."[59]

He was obsessed with fear of the effect that Jackie's actions might have in winning support for his hated rival Bobby, particularly at the Democratic National Convention to be held in Atlantic City. He was determined not to have Bobby as his vice presidential running mate. He voiced his anxiety as early as the beginning of July after the passage of Kennedy's Civil Rights Act in a telephone call to his friend, Governor John Connally: "I think we gotta give a little thought to our vice president," he told Connally. "You know who's campaigning for it [i.e., Bobby], and that's gonna be a knock-down drag-out probably. With Miz Kennedy [Jackie] nominating him and all the emotions . . . you can't tell what'll come there . . ."[60] Yet the next day, as if anxiety about Jackie's support for Bobby could not have been further from his mind, Johnson sounded ebullient, laughing, cheerful as he telephoned Jackie to wish her a happy Fourth of July.

None the less he was determined to preempt any attempt by Bobby to launch a campaign for the vice presidential nomination by telling him at a meeting at the White House on July 29 that he would not choose him as running mate on the ticket. The exclusion of Bobby was masked by the ploy of explicitly eliminating any cabinet members—even "those who meet regularly with cabinet"—from consideration for the vice presidential nomination. He was extremely worried by a news broadcast by Nancy Dickerson on July 30 that Jackie would be attending the convention, allegedly to urge delegates there to place Bobby in the vice presidential slot. On August 1 he spoke to McNamara, one of his most important links to the Bobby camp, and discovered to his relief the plan for Bobby to run for Senator from New York. Two days later, on August 3, he had another conversation with McNamara about Jackie and the convention. McNamara attempted to reassure him that she wouldn't be "got at" by Kennedy partisans. "She's leaving [on vacation with the Wrightsmans] day after tomorrow and she's gonna be gone during this critical period," McNamara told Johnson. "And I hope she'll stay away a little longer than she planned . . . and that will keep her out of it. And, furthermore, she just doesn't want to do it." A week later Johnson and McNamara had another telephone conversation about Bobby's candidacy for the New York Senate seat: McNamara told the President that he had been encouraging Bobby to run, "And I talked with Jackie about it before she left and asked her to push him . . . I, I don't think they're going to have trouble at the convention from either one of them."[61]

The question of Jackie and the convention continued to preoccupy the President. The Kennedy family wanted the occasion to be a massive celebration of the Kennedy Presidency, with a memorial film to be introduced by Bobby, an undoubted boost for his chances in New York. Averell Harriman, a keen Bobby supporter, had been persuaded to act as front man for a reception at which Jackie would be the draw. The limelight would conspicuously not be on Johnson. A nervous Teddy Kennedy telephoned the President to sound him out about the setup. "Mr. President, we had a very nice invitation from Governor Harriman to have a reception at the convention on Thursday after the selection of the, uh, presidential and vice presidential candidates, on Thursday afternoon, for Mrs. Kennedy. And, uh, she would come to the convention for that afternoon. And have a reception that would be for Mrs. Kennedy and the members of the family, and the, uh, of course, the presidential and vice presidential candidates. And she was, uh, uh, Jackie has indicated that she would be delighted to accept this, but of course we wanted to do, uh, we wanted to have this in complete accord with your wishes on the arrangements . . ."[62]

Johnson, naturally, was not fooled. He spoke to Harriman and discovered that the Kennedys had asked him to host the reception and that the initiative had definitely not come from him. Both he and his Secretary of State for Foreign Affairs, Dean Rusk, believed that, in Rusk's words, the Harriman reception, graced by Jackie, was "a send-off for Bobby in New York." Johnson continued to treat Jackie with kid gloves. He extended invitations to her via Kenny O'Donnell so that it would not appear that he was putting pressure on her or using her to advance his cause.

Jackie might refuse to allow Lyndon Johnson, for all his blandishments, to bask in the reflected glory of her political aura, but Bobby was quite a different matter. Probably to Johnson's relief, she did not attend the convention hall or sit in his box. Johnson had planned to keep the Kennedys away from the spotlight by insisting that the Kennedy commemorative film, *A Thousand Days*, to be introduced by Bobby, would be shown on the Thursday after the balloting for the presidential and vice presidential nominations was over.

"I don't think Jackie would have come to that convention at all but for the fact that Bobby was going to be a candidate for the Senate," William vanden Heuvel said. "There was some controversy about it because of her position. But she did come to Atlantic City and she was an extraordinary attraction to the delegates. She was the guest of honor at a reception for New York Democrats. Well, that was the centerpiece of the convention."[63]

Jackie arrived in Atlantic City aboard the *Caroline* with Eunice, Jean and Pat in time for the reception given by Harriman on Thursday evening. Crowds surrounded her at the hotel, many of them in tears at seeing her. Emotion ran high that evening. At the reception, Fredric March and his wife, Florence Eldridge, read passages of John Kennedy's favorite poems and some of his best-known speeches. There was hardly a dry eye in the room as March recited Seeger's "I Have a Rendezvous with Death." Bobby and Jackie had concentrated particularly on the delegations that had helped Jack win the nomination in 1960. Jackie's contribution to the evening was a short whispered speech: "Thank all of you for coming—all of you who helped President Kennedy in 1960. May his light always shine in all parts of the world."

She made another significant contribution by providing Bobby with a peroration for his introductory speech, a quotation from Shakespeare. Wild cheering and a standing ovation that lasted thirteen minutes greeted Bobby as he stepped up to the rostrum. "The demonstration, entirely spontaneous," *Time* reported, "proved . . . the magic of the Kennedy name and memory." After thanking the delegates "for the encouragement, the strength that you gave him after he was elected President of the United States," he went on. "When I think of President Kennedy," he said, "I think of what Shakespeare said in *Romeo and Juliet*:

> 'When he shall die,
> Take him and cut him out in little stars,
> And he will make the face of Heaven so fine
> That all the world will be in love with night,
> And pay no attention to the garish sun.' "

The "garish sun" could only have been taken to apply to Johnson. Kennedy loyalist Arthur Schlesinger wondered if either Bobby or Jackie had "consciously noted the thrust of the last line," adding that he never knew. The kindest thing that could be said is that Jackie, whose suggestion it was, was so carried away by the beauty of the words that she ignored their implications. Curiously, Lyndon Johnson himself, always so sensitive to Kennedy slights, does not seem to have taken it badly, probably because he did not hear it. He was absent during Bobby's ovation and the showing of the film, appearing in the hall only after the emotion had subsided for his own and vice presidential candidate Hubert Humphrey's triumphant acceptance speeches.

Jackie turned her back on her previous life at the same time as Bobby headed for New York. She left Washington in mid-June for the fund-raising dinner held at the St. Regis Hotel for the Kennedy Library. From the Cape on July 2 she telephoned Mary Gallagher to tell her and Evelyn Lincoln that she was moving permanently to New York. The news was released on July 7, with the announcement that Pam Turnure and Nancy Tuckerman would be staffing her office there (the costs of which, including franking privileges, would be borne by the government). The next day Jackie telephoned to tell Mary Gallagher that she would not be needing either her or Provi—who could not leave her family anyway in Washington—in New York. She returned briefly early in August, and again on September 10 to pack, then left the house for good. Her Washington life was definitely over.[64] She put both the N Street house and Wexford up for sale, and after a spell at Hammersmith in September she moved to New York, staying at the Carlyle Hotel while her fifteen-room apartment at 1040 Fifth Avenue was being decorated. Bobby bought an apartment at United Nations Plaza and rented a large house in Glen Cove on Long Island's North Shore, Scott Fitzgerald's Gold Coast. Some ten minutes away, Jackie rented a cottage on the estate of J. P. Morgan's daughter-in-law, Louise Converse Morgan.

⁓

That first year of mourning had been a roller coaster of emotion for Jackie, plunged into the depths of depression as she agonized over the loss of Jack, racked with guilt that she might have saved him, and might have done more to help him during his presidency. On January 31, her last night in the Harriman house, she had poured out her heart in a letter to Harold Macmillan, the British Prime Minister whom Jack had held in such warm affection despite the wide gap between their ages. She told him of her agony of soul as she sought to come to terms with the death of her husband and how lost she felt without him . . .[65]

The pain was inescapable. In March she was forced to relive the horror of Dallas in giving evidence to the Warren Commission. Alone with Kitty Carlisle Hart, when both were staying with her friends James and Minnie Fosburgh, at around the same time, "she began to talk about those last three minutes in Dallas. Could she have—if she moved this way—have deflected the bullet? If she had moved that way, what would have happened? And she went over and over those last three minutes. It was agonizing, just agonizing . . ."[66]

Within a month of historian Teddy White's departure, clutching his hastily scribbled notes, from storm-lashed Hyannis Port, Jackie had taken a further step toward enshrining her beloved Jack's memory and, at the same time, cutting out unauthorized interlopers on her sacred turf. Jim Bishop, author of *The Day Lincoln Was Shot*, was rumored to be turning his attention to Kennedy's assassination. Bishop had incurred Jackie's displeasure that autumn when he had visited the White House for a day to write an article for *Reader's Digest* and, in her view, had asked too many personal questions. He had interrogated Provi as to the presidential sleeping arrangements, and George Thomas about the contents of the President's wardrobe. The President had laughed off Jackie's objections on the grounds that Bishop's access to millions of *Digest* readers would provide much-needed publicity. Jackie, however, had not forgotten. If anything was going to be written about the dreadful events surrounding Dallas, it was going to be under her control.

William Manchester, respected professor of history at Wesleyan University and an unqualified Kennedy admirer, had produced a book about John F. Kennedy, who, he wrote, "was brighter than I was, braver, better-read, handsomer, wittier and more incisive. The only thing I could do better was write." He had even submitted proofs of his book to Jack for verification. "Bob Kennedy subsequently told me that after one of my evenings alone with his brother at the White House the President had told his wife of his regard for me, and that she had recalled that in the days which followed his funeral." However, Manchester was under no illusions as to the reason for Jackie's choice: "It is a good story, but I don't believe it. President Kennedy hadn't liked me that much. I think Jackie picked me because she thought I would be manageable.[67]

" 'Mr. *Manchester!*' she said, in that inimitable, breathy voice as she stepped into the living room, closed the sliding doors behind her with a sweeping movement, and bowed slightly from the waist. It was a few minutes before noon on April 7, 1964, the date of our first meeting. She was wearing a black jersey and yellow stretch pants, she was beaming at me and I thought how, at thirty-four, with her camellia beauty, she might have been taken for a woman in her mid-twenties. My first impression—and it never changed—was that I was in the presence of a very great tragic actress. I mean that in the finest sense of the word. There was a weekend in American history when we needed to be united in our sadness by the superb example of a bereaved First Lady, and Jacqueline Kennedy—unlike Eleanor Roosevelt, a more extraordinary woman in other ways—provided us with an unforgettable performance as the nation's heroine. One reason for this triumph was that her instincts were completely feminine. If she met your plane at the Hyannis airport, she automatically handed you the keys to her convertible. Men drive, women are driven; that was the logic of things to her, and it is impossible to think of her burning a bra or denouncing romantic love as counter-revolutionary."[68] Manchester was given a full dose of Jackie's irresistible feminine helplessness, and implied vulnerability and submissiveness.

Almost half of the hundreds of interviews Manchester undertook for the book were emotionally deeply disturbing, but none so affecting as the hours he spent with Jackie. Background noise on the tapes features the clinking of ice cubes and the noise of matches being struck. (Manchester, who had given up smoking for two years, could not survive the experience without chain-smoking; it was another eight years before he could give up again.) Jugs of daiquiris and packs of cigarettes were devoured as he questioned and the widow bared her soul over hours of tapes, which today lie sealed in the JFK Library at Columbus Point, embargoed until the year 2067. The undertaking of William Manchester's book, begun in tears, ended in tears.

There was to be no escaping occasions for emotion in the months that followed Dallas. Public memorials were a particular strain. On May 25 Jackie flew to New York for the opening of the JFK Library Exhibit. May 29 would have been his birthday, and he was commemorated in an international television broadcast via Telstar in which prominent world leaders participated. A memorial service at St. Matthew's Cathedral in Washington was, as David Ormsby-Gore (now Lord Harlech) told Macmillan, "an agony to her. She now feels she is no nearer being reconciled to what has happened than she was last November."[69]

There was no letup for Jackie. The summer of 1964 she was at Hyannis Port, busy cooperating with Laura Bergquist and photographer Stanley Tetrick on a memorial issue of *Look* to coincide with the first anniversary of the President's death. "We went up to Hyannis to take pictures of her and the children," Bergquist recalled, "and I also persuaded her to write that tribute to JFK for the memorial issue. She really worked on that. She wrote it and rewrote it . . ."[70]

It is nearly a year since he has been gone.

On so many days—his birthday, an anniversary, watching his children running to the sea—I have thought, "But this day last year was his last to see that." He was so full of love and life on all those days. He seems so vulnerable now, when you think that each one was a last time . . .

Now I think that I should have known he was magic all along. I did know it—but I should have guessed that it could not last.

So now he is a legend when he would have preferred to be a man . . .

For the memorial issue she chose quotations from his favorite authors, as she had scripted the passages to be declaimed by Fredric March and Florence Eldridge at the JFK Library dinner and again at the Democratic Convention: Tennyson's "Ulysses"—the passage she had memorized for him and used to recite to him—lines from Shakespeare's *Richard III* and *Henry V*, Pericles' funeral oration, Robert Frost's "Stopping by Woods on a Snowy Evening," Stephen Vincent Benet's "John Brown's Body," Thomas J. Davis's lament for the Irish patriot Owen Roe O'Neill. She wrote out the lines from John Buchan's *Pilgrim's Way*, lamenting the death of his brilliant friend, Raymond Asquith, killed in the First World War, a passage Jack had liked so much and which to Jackie seemed to capture Jack himself:

> . . . for the chosen few, like Raymond, there is no disillusionment. They march on into life with a boyish grace, and their high noon keeps all the freshness of the morning. Certainly to his cradle the good fairies brought every dower. They gave him great beauty of person; the gift of winning speech; a mind that mastered readily whatever it cared to master; poetry and the love of all beautiful things; a magic to draw friends to him; a heart as tender as it was brave. Only one gift was withheld from him—length of years.

She worked closely with the *Look* editors on layout, suggesting particular photographs of her husband to fit in with particular quotations, underlining "the lines that meant most—to him—and some now to me—" Of Seeger's "I Have a Rendezvous with Death" she wrote, "This is the most shattering of all the poetry he loved."[71]

Bergquist described Jackie's mood that autumn as one of "sad longing": "She said that she would wake up in the morning and find it incredible that her husband was not there. She would not believe that she would never see him again and felt that there must be an afterlife. She wondered how she would keep going, and she commented that speaking of him, in taped interviews for the Kennedy Library . . . had been an excruciating experience."[72]

In reality, for the whole of that year following the assassination, Jackie was going through what amounted to a nervous breakdown, depending on Bobby to pull her through. She had moods of black despair, feeling that her life was over and that all she could do was get through one day after another until the children were adults. Once she thought of turning them over to Bobby, because she felt her agony was infecting them. She described herself as "a living wound." Everything seemed to remind her of Jack—especially at Hyannis Port. She would cry and Caroline would try to comfort her, saying, "You're crying about Daddy, aren't you?" Caroline herself became withdrawn and moody; her father's death affected her far more than it did little John. Only with Bobby did she relax, whispering secrets into his ear as she had with her father.

Jackie and Bobby had always been close; after Jack's death, they became emotionally and spiritually entwined. Jackie's old friend from Paris days, Solange Barsell, recently divorced from the Comte de la Bruyère, was a New York neighbor and saw a good deal of Jackie in the first year after she moved to New York. She described her as being "very sad": "She was really in her shell then and Bobby made her give dinner parties. And she wore the same old yellow dress—it was practically unraveling—for every single dinner party she gave at 1040 Fifth. I don't think she cared much about herself in those days, like wearing a pretty dress or a new one."[73]

Even in her depression, Jackie was dedicated to helping Bobby in whatever way she could. One favor he asked her was to meet Dorothy Schiff, who as the influential publisher of the *New York Post* was a key figure to capture for Bobby's campaign to become Senator from New York. Dorothy had mentioned to Bobby how much she would like to meet Jackie and he promised to arrange it. On October 10, a Saturday, she met Jackie in her apartment at the Carlyle, 18E. Jackie, simply dressed and looking "beautiful," was unconsciously regal. When Schiff, a guest and an older woman, hesitated as they were about to go into another room, "to allow her to go first, as one does in the White House for the First Lady," Jackie walked through ahead of her. Dorothy Schiff noticed that she "talks in the third person a great deal": "When talking about Jack, tears came into her eyes," Schiff recalled. " 'People tell me that time will heal. How much time? Last week I forgot to cancel the newspapers [this was a reference to the publication of the Warren Report], and I picked them up and there it was, so I canceled them for the rest of the week. But I went to the hairdresser and picked up *Life* magazine, and it was terrible. There is November to be gotten through . . . One is expecting someone to come home every weekend, but no one . . .'

"The phone rang," Schiff noted. "I had the feeling it might be Bobby . . ."[74]

CHAPTER SIXTEEN

La Dolce Vita

~

She said to me once that a few of us should be forgiven for some of the things we did in the years immediately following the President's death. I think she was not only excusing me but also excusing herself.

—Theodore C. Sorensen[1]

Jackie's return to life began early in the summer of 1965. "I don't know if she was ever really happy that much," said a Kennedy aide and personal friend of Bobby's, who had been in love with Jackie. "But I think a few years after he [Jack] died, sort of 'sixty-five to 'sixty-eight, it was much better for her, emotionally better. Her life had settled in, and Bobby was around, I think that was a pretty good period."[2] Chuck Spalding, who remained close to the family, told Kennedy biographer Nigel Hamilton that Jackie and Bobby were lovers, and that he was good for her.

"She had a real depression after Jack Kennedy died," Richard Goodwin said. "It took her quite a while to get out of it. She really got out of it by getting out and seeing people, doing some work, and doing things like that."[3] Some people have conjectured that Bobby and Jackie's love for each other was morbid, as if being together was somehow sharing a piece of Jack. "On Jackie's side it was genuine, real passion," another friend confided. "For him it was more complicated. It might have been—I don't know. He would have said no, obviously, he would have said it was an insane thought. This doesn't mean it's not true, just because he wasn't aware of it . . ." Asked how long the relationship had gone on, he said, "Close to when he died."

Bobby was Jackie's great love; a secret rock at the center of her life. Their romance was all the stronger because it was an impossible one. Bobby would never have divorced Ethel, intensely loyal as she was to him and the mother of their nine children. (The tenth, Matthew Maxwell Taylor Kennedy, was born on January 11, 1965.) Even if he had wanted to, both his religion and his political career presented insurmountable obstacles. Nor would Jackie have wanted to go over all the old territory again, the politics, the infidelities. She was under no illusion that Bobby was capable of physical fidelity. When she told Joan Kennedy at the time of one of Teddy's most public affairs, "All Kennedy men are like that," she meant it. Bobby was less chauvinist in his attitude to women than the other Kennedy men; he liked talking to them and in that sense he was not a user to the extent that his brothers (and father) were. He had a long relationship with a Boston-born woman in New York, but he had shared some of Jack's women and had many relationships out on the campaign trail.

Jackie and Bobby were not discreet, meeting frequently alone in public places, as if the unbelievability of their relationship was a shield against the reality. Peter Lawford, a pariah as far as the Kennedys were concerned since the death of Jack, his patron, and his divorce from Pat early in 1966, particularly hated Bobby, whom he largely blamed for the break with Sinatra over Jack's 1962 visit. As he walked with Taki Theodoracopoulos and a girlfriend into the Sherry-Netherland Hotel (where both had apartments), they saw Bobby and Jackie sitting close together in the bar. "There was ice between them [Lawford and Bobby]," Taki recalled. "And he turned around and said to the girl—I overheard—he said, 'See, I told you. The son-of-a-bitch is doing her . . .' "[4]

During the later years of her marriage to Jack, Jackie's life had been sexless, apart from the routine brief marital encounters. Now, hiding behind her trademark dark glasses and her untouchable reputation, she did more or less as she liked. As America's Queen, the newspapers protected her—never printing an unflattering photograph or unseemly speculation about her private life. She was never shown smoking a cigarette, although she was virtually a chain-smoker. If she was reported as dancing the Twist or the Frug, she was always said to have done so "in a dignified manner." She was more than aware of this: as she hubristically told William Manchester, no one would believe anything against her "even if she eloped with Eddie Fisher."[5] She believed that, after all her self-restraint in the White House, the suffering she had stoically endured after the assassination, she had earned the right to enjoy herself. Not for her the boring women's committees, the charity work that was part of upper-class, moneyed New York life. Only two good causes engaged her interest: one, the saving of the doomed old Metropolitan Opera House; the other, Bobby's Bedford-Stuyvesant Development project in a deprived section of Brooklyn. Beyond that, she still took a passionate interest in the funding and building of the Kennedy Library and the completion of Jack's grave at Arlington.

As Women's Wear Daily put it, she was, without question, "the most elegant New Yorker," and "the most outstanding woman in the world." Outstanding for what, you might ask? Apart from her performance after the assassination, when she "broke the nation's heart and held the country together," she did nothing of substance. And yet, through her looks, her style, her mysterious personality, she had a hold on the world's imagination in a way that no one else had. "Culturally something happened between her and the decade that she lived in," said Doris Kearns Goodwin, "and that is what is really interesting to try and figure out."[6]

There was a string of escorts, public cover for more private relationships. Her first sexual affair lasted for eighteen months and was over before it was even hinted at in the press. Jackie had met Jack Warnecke over his plans for Lafayette Square; in the year after Jack's death, she had worked closely with him on the design for Jack's grave. At forty-seven Jack Warnecke was a very attractive man—six foot three with the athletic physique of the ex–football star—a brilliant and successful architect and, since his divorce in 1961, the lover of a succession of beautiful women. That autumn Janet Auchincloss had invited him up to Hammersmith to see the work of a famous local stonecarver, who was to execute the inscriptions for Jack's grave. Jackie was there. "I can recall at that time, after this full year of me working with Jackie, me looking at Jackie, Jackie looking at me . . . all the things we were struggling through. And I remember saying, 'Why don't you let me drive back to Hyannis Port, let me take over from the Secret Service?' And she said she'd be delighted. So we got rid of the Secret Service. It was a beautiful open-top car she was in, so we had a very nice drive back to Hyannis Port, and then . . . it all started, right then and there, after all the looking at each other, listening to each other, going through all the grieving and the tension and the time . . . That's where it started. I spent the weekend with her. I can't for the life of me remember where the children were, I just remember us. So that's how it all started, and then I began seeing her all the time, every weekend . . ."[7]

"Bunny Mellon had a little surprise thing for us, a little cottage all dolled up for Halloween, and by Thanksgiving I was there at Hammersmith, with my children, her children . . . We spent the whole weekend with the family."

Warnecke reminisced, "She was witty, she was charming, she was fun, she was beautiful, she was passionate, she was all the things we dream about. We talked about intimate things, about how she almost lost her virginity to John Marquand." Jackie also talked tenderly about Bobby, but when she telephoned him to tell him about her new love, Bobby, a political Kennedy to the fingertips, warned her that it was "too soon" after Jack's death. With his political career in New York to consider, and beyond that the inevitable bid for the Presidency, his public interest decreed that Jackie remain the priceless Kennedy asset. Jack Warnecke was to be kept under wraps and was not to be seen publicly as her escort until the autumn of 1965, when he was reported as taking her home after the New York party she gave for Kenneth Galbraith.

Just as Jack had, Jackie compartmentalized her life and her loves. Warnecke could not believe that she and Bobby were closely involved in the autumn of 1964. Yet she certainly saw a great deal of Bobby while maintaining her relationship with Warnecke and other men. She spent Christmas 1964 in Aspen with Bobby, Pat, Jean and the children, but no Ethel, who was expecting their tenth child in January. In the first week of February 1965 she was at Puerto Marques, near Acapulco, with the Radziwills as guests of their old friend the architect Fernando Parra Hernandez, but on February 13 she and Bobby took the children skiing again to Lake Placid, and again in Vermont on April 20. At around the same time, she rode in Central Park with a handsome Italian count, whom she met through Kennedy friend Arkady Gerney. The man, who was working for U.S.

Steel, spent a good deal of time in New York; his relations with his wife were not close and they later divorced. With gentlemanly reticence, he refused to divulge more about Jackie than to say that she was "not so interested in sex." Another admirer and constant escort through 1965 was Mike Nichols, the brilliant theater and film director. Several years younger than she was, he was fascinated by Jackie, and remained a constant friend and support to her in difficult times. "They were friends and they shared some intimate moments," as a friend put it. Jackie was not promiscuous—sex was something that happened in the course of a friendship. "She clearly inspired a very romantic feeling in many men," her friend Antonia Fraser said. "I tend to think that all people sleep together once or twice if they're the appropriate sexes . . ."[8]

In May Lee gave a party ("a teeny, tiny dance for less than a thousand") at her superbly decorated duplex at 969 Fifth Avenue, to cheer up Jackie, who appeared in a white silk crepe dress by Yves Saint-Laurent, on the safe arm of Averell Harriman. Guests included Mike Nichols, Sam Spiegel, Leonard Bernstein and Bobby, with Camelot loyalists Kenneth Galbraith, Pierre Salinger and Franklin Roosevelt Jr. But underneath the glamorous exterior Jackie was still in pain, still feeling sorry for herself, searching for another man to validate her as Jack had. In London for the Runnymede memorial dedication in May 1965, she opened her heart to her old English friends, Hugh and Antonia Fraser, who gave a huge party for her. Afterward, alone with the Frasers (Jackie had acquired the habit of drinking whiskey late at night), she was in confessional mode. "She talked about being a widow and how if you were a widow, you were a cripple, [perceived as having] something wrong with you," Antonia Fraser remembered. "I just thought it was such an extraordinary reaction—she had this horror as if she herself had done something wrong . . . she felt blighted by this state."

But even in the middle of the dinner party, Jackie had the thoughtfulness to thank the Frasers' old Scottish cook, who was staying with them in London on a semi-holiday and who had taken it upon herself to make tea and sandwiches for John and Caroline the previous day. "She was in the middle of what was virtually a State visit" Antonia Fraser said, "yet she insisted on meeting this lady, Mrs. Hepburn, thus transforming a rather sad life into a life of splendor so that Mrs. Hepburn went back to Scotland forever after boasting about it . . . In those days I don't think English people did go about congratulating cooks . . . That to me was extremely characteristic of Jackie. I do think she had, I think she probably developed these extraordinary sort of spiritual good manners as a defense really. Because people with wonderful manners actually protect themselves from a lot of things . . ."[9]

Harold Macmillan spoke at the ceremony at Runnymede when the Queen dedicated the simple white stone monument to John F. Kennedy on an acre of British soil given by the British people to the United States. Runnymede had a special significance, which would have appealed to the historically minded Jack, as the "birthplace of constitutional government," where King John had signed the Magna Carta in 1215. On the following Sunday the Kennedys descended on the Macmillans' country house, Birch Grove. Later, on May 17, Jackie wrote a thank-you letter, wryly referring to all the Kennedys and all the inevitable confusion which accompanied them when they traveled. Macmillan's speech, she told him, had been emotionally the hardest part of the Runnymede ceremony for her: "For everyone else Jack has receded and it was a beautiful memorial—but he has not receded for you or for me—"[10]

Those days in May were the last the children were to spend with Maud Shaw, although they were unaware of it. Jackie and Miss Shaw had agreed not to upset their trip by telling them. Quite apart from Miss Shaw's age—she was fifty-nine—and the needs of her own family, both Kennedy children were now enrolled in school. The trip to England was a huge adventure for them—they went in Air Force One, "Daddy's airplane"—and saw all the things Miss Shaw had told them about, the Changing of the Guard, the Regent's Park Zoo for a chimpanzees' tea party ("Oh, Miss Shaw, what table manners!" Caroline gasped, clapping her hand over her mouth in a characteristic gesture). At the Tower of London John surprised the Beefeater assigned to guide them by his bloodthirsty interest in the executions that had taken place there, and his agility at wriggling through an ancient cannon.

Carefully coached by Miss Shaw they managed their respective bow and curtsy when presented to the Queen, and had tea at Windsor Castle after the Runnymede ceremony. Then Miss Shaw took them off to stay at her simple terraced house in Sheerness, Kent, the home of her brother and sister. "I like this dumpy little house, Miss Shaw," John said. "I'm glad you have only one flight of stairs. I'm tired of stairs." (At the Radziwills' London house he had to go up four flights to his bedroom.) "Where's the cook and the butler?" he asked Hettie Shaw. "I'm the cook and the butler around here," Hettie replied. "You can't be the butler too," John said. "You're not a man."

"Of course," Miss Shaw wrote, "he made himself completely at home from the moment he walked in. Caroline was a little more shy, but she got on famously with Hettie and Jack, proudly telling them that she was my blood sister for life." Caroline, suspecting something was wrong, was particularly upset. She followed her nanny around all morning on the last day, with her arm around her. Jackie was moved to try to persuade Miss Shaw to go back with them. Torn between her own family and the children she loved, Maud could only sadly shake her head. As she wrote in her book, which Jackie condemned, "No words can ever really tell how closely bound I felt toward these two and their parents." She never saw them again.[11]

Jackie was to regard Maud Shaw's affectionate book, *White House Nannie, My Years with Caroline and John Kennedy, Jr.*, published later that year, as a gross betrayal. Even though Miss Shaw had not signed a confidentiality agreement, Jackie reacted with the same cold fury as had Queen Elizabeth the Queen Mother to the syrupy reminiscences of Marion Crawford, the former governess to Princesses Elizabeth and Margaret. Although continuing to pay her a pension ("She will live up to the promises made to you even if you have broken the trust she and President Kennedy had put in you," Nancy Tuckerman told Miss Shaw, in a cold letter of November 19, 1965), she cut off relations. Caroline, however, continued to write loving letters to her former nanny. "I miss you very, very, **very much**," she ended a letter to Miss Shaw that Christmas. A year later it was still "I MISS YOU!" Two years later, in March 1967, she was still sending the same message.

Evelyn Lincoln, who published her *My Twelve Years with John F. Kennedy* in September 1965, escaped unscathed, possibly because, as keeper of the Kennedy secrets, she was untouchable. Jack's true friend and old Navy mate, Paul Fay, felt the weight of Kennedy disapproval over his memoir, *The Pleasure of His Company*, which he had begun writing at Jack's behest in September 1963. ("You know, Redhead," he told Fay, "you have had an exposure of [*sic*] the Presidency that few people have ever had. You have the obligation to write it.") Fay began the memoir but dropped it after his friend was assassinated. Six months later he took it up again with Bobby Kennedy's agreement. Bobby, however, suggested that it should be a history of the "major issues affecting the Navy and the President," to which Fay replied that he wasn't a historian and that "mine was kind of the human side of it." He did not realize that his memory of his witty, macho, "jock" friend, whose conversation was littered with the four-letter words every ex-serviceman used, was not the image of Jack that the Kennedys wanted put across to the public. Nor did he realize the extent to which the image of John Kennedy was regarded as a Kennedy copyright, and paid the price of family displeasure when the manuscript was finished in the summer of 1966.

It was sent to Bobby, who ripped it to pieces, taking out at least a third, with bitter marginal comments. "He really turned on me as a result of this," Fay told an interviewer. He was then informed that "Jackie wants to get in the act," and that she, rather than Bobby, would have the ultimate say. Jackie, however, refused to read the manuscript herself, telling Fay that Kenneth Galbraith should read it as "He's the official censor for the family." Galbraith made a couple of minor comments but Fay heard nothing further from either of the Kennedys until he sent a wire to Bobby informing him that he had given *McCall's* the go-ahead with the magazine serialization of the book.

"Boy, he just came unglued," Fay said. "Then Jackie came in and I spent an hour and forty minutes with Jackie on the telephone. She called me and, gee, we went over step by step on this book. And her comments were fascinating, just fascinating, in the things she wanted deleted." Among other things, she would not let him mention the story of the President's anger with Arthur Schlesinger over an interview he gave implying that his advice had prevailed over the Bay of Pigs. To please her, Fay took it out. "She demanded that she always be referred to as Jacqueline, never Jackie, that John-John should be John. She said, 'The President never called him John-John.' I said, 'Jackie, you've got to be kidding. He called him John-John all the time.' She said, 'He did not call him John-John. He called him John.' Well, now, how do you argue with something like that?" a despairing Fay asked.

"I didn't realize what a locker-room relationship you had with Jack," Jackie told him, with barely concealed contempt.[12] Fay's portrait of the human Jack, with all his profanity, irked her; his refusal to have his book totally emasculated infuriated her, as it did Bobby and Ethel. Jackie even objected to one proposed revision on grounds of pure vindictiveness. She wanted the anecdote left in because she thought it made Fay look bad. Jackie returned to him the check for $3,000 he sent to the Kennedy Library fund, but after a few years he was forgiven.

Even Jackie's cultural mentor, most devoted courtier and Kennedy loyalist historian Arthur M. Schlesinger, author of *A Thousand Days, John F. Kennedy in the White House*, did not escape her censorship. Both he and Ted Sorensen had embarked almost simultaneously on accounts of Camelot. Sorensen, the Nebraska intellectual who had been Kennedy's speechwriter and political alter ego, wrote a personal recollection drawing on eleven years of political intimacy with the late President, the book he might have helped Kennedy write as his political memoir. Sorensen had no problems with Jackie over *Kennedy*—"in part because I showed her the manuscript and she gave me some suggestions," as he told the author of the book. When he was writing his book on Cape Cod in the summer of 1965, he got what he described as a "sad call" from Jackie. It was her birthday, so he went over to Hyannis Port to see her, taking with him as a birthday present some doodles drawn by Jack during the Cuban missile crisis, which he had found among his papers. "Khrushchev," "Submarines. Soviet submarines," "Serious," "Guantanamo," "Missiles 16-2-32," Kennedy had scribbled. According to Sorensen, she was very moved by the gift, and for Christmas 1966 she gave them back to him, framed with a note of thanks "for all you were to him."[13] Sorensen's book was published in the autumn of 1965 with an enthusiastic endorsement of its historical value as an account of the Kennedy Presidency in a foreword by David Harlech. It was serialized in *Look* and remained at number one on the *New York Times* best-seller list through the Christmas season.

Schlesinger, however, whose history of the Kennedy Presidency, *A Thousand Days*, contained more personal detail, encountered rougher waters with Jackie. On April 2, 1965, he sent her and Bobby the first twelve chapters of his book. "Please do not spare my feelings in your criticisms," he wrote, "for I will be everlastingly grateful for your help in making the book a faithful account of the greatest man I shall ever know." Jackie sent it back with painstaking and—in many cases—revealing comments. She did not like his portrayal of Jack as the archetypal Roman senator, cool and unemotional, as compared with the depiction of his former mentor Adlai Stevenson as Greek in feeling. To her, Jack, with his passionate defiance of fate, was truly a classical Greek.

She took exception to Schlesinger's assertion that Kennedy had come to the Presidency "knowing more about domestic than foreign affairs," arguing passionately that his book *Why England Slept* and Senate speeches on Indochina and Algeria, his travels to Poland, Czechoslovakia, the Near and Far East showed that he knew as much about foreign as domestic affairs and certainly more than any other American President coming into office.

And at her behest Schlesinger altered a sentence about how Joe Kennedy had been "determined" that Jack should make Bobby his Attorney General: "The President-elect's father hoped that Robert Kennedy would become Attorney General."

She was concerned that he should cut down on all references to herself and particularly to her married life with Jack, which Schlesinger had apparently based on her own recollections in her oral history for the Kennedy Library (which is still under embargo). Jackie was upset when Schlesinger permitted pre-publication serialization of the book in *Life* containing what she considered to be unpardonable intrusions upon her private life with Jack. Schlesinger bowed to her wishes. When submitting the final manuscript of the book for Kennedy approval he had "practically cut Jackie out of the book . . ."[14]

On November 23 he received his reward in the form of a gushing letter of praise and gratitude from Jackie.

⁓

For the first time since Jack's death, Jackie, to her surprise, had enjoyed a happy summer at Hyannis Port and Hammersmith Farm. From Hammersmith on September 14, the day before she left with her children for them to start school in New York, she wrote a long letter to Macmillan, describing the joys of returning to loved, familiar houses, cooking fires on the beaches and American summer food—lobster and corn, blueberries and peaches—and being barefoot all the time. It had all been like so many other summers "except that Jack didn't come on weekends."

She had been reading Kazantzakis's *Report to Greco*. Since Jack's death she had been increasingly drawn toward Greece and the Mediterranean life of sun and physical sensation. She felt that she had recovered her strength and determination to survive and carry on toward a higher plane of peace or resignation, and she had done it for the sake of her children who had given her a reason to live. Yet there was still a deep anger at the heart of her, anger against the world that had killed Jack, and to bring up their children in his spirit would be her defiance of that world.

"And there is Bobby with his compassionate and unconquerable soul . . . ," she had written. By 1965 Bobby, too, was emerging, like Jackie, from the pall of grief. Everyone noticed the change his brother's death had wrought. The tough, ruthless, uncompromising Attorney General, John F. Kennedy's hatchet man, had evolved. Under Jackie's direction, and following in his brother's footsteps, he read history and biography, but most of all he loved poetry, one of his favorites being Tennyson's "Ulysses," as it had been Jack's. While Jack's favorite verse had included the line "To sail beyond the baths of all the western stars until I die . . . ," Bobby's included the passage that ended "Come, my friends, 'Tis not too late to seek a newer world." He loved to recite poetry with Richard Burton, or with the Russian Yevgeny Yevtushenko. He discussed it with the poet Robert Lowell, Jackie's obsessive admirer, who had given her a copy of Plutarch and written a poem about her. He wrote about Bobby too, after his death, which Arthur Schlesinger called the best poem written about Robert Kennedy—"Doom was woven in your nerves . . ." People noticed a thoughtfulness in him, a vein of sadness, or "resident melancholy," that had not been there before. Norman Mailer, that most perceptive and articulate of Kennedy observers, wrote of him, "He had grown modest as he grew older, and his wit had grown with him," noticing a "subtle sadness [that] had come to live in his tone of confidence. He had come into that world where people live with the recognition of tragedy and so are often afraid of happiness."[15]

39. Jackie, radiant and heavily pregnant, cruising off Cape Cod three days before the birth of Patrick, August 4, 1963

40. The assassination, November 22, 1963

41. Jackie stands by President Lyndon B. Johnson as he takes the oath on board Air Force One, November 22, 1963, with Lady Bird Johnson on her husband's right

42. Farewell: John Jr.
salutes his father's coffin,
backed by Caroline and
Jackie, Ted Kennedy and
Bobby Kennedy. Peter and
Pat Lawford are partially
glimpsed behind them.
November 25, 1963

43. Jackie and Bobby take
a last look after Jack's
interment at Arlington,
November 25, 1963

44. Ethel and Bobby Kennedy leave Jackie at the Harriman house in Georgetown after accompanying her from the White House, December 6, 1963

45. Jackie, followed by Joan Kennedy and Sargent Shriver, descends the steps of the aircraft bringing Bobby Kennedy's body back from Los Angeles, June 1968

46 (*left*). Jackie picking up Caroline and her niece after school, September 17, 1964

47 (*above*). Stas Radziwill with Lee in her dressing room after her Chicago debut in *The Philadelphia Story*, June 1967

48. Jackie riding with Caroline and John Jr. in County Waterford, Ireland, 1967

49. With Lord Harlech

50. With Roswell "Ros" Gilpatric

51. John Carl Warnecke: by the time this report of their impending engagement appeared, Jackie's romance with Warnecke was over

52. Aristotle Onassis with Maria Callas, 1961

53. Aristotle Onassis with Jackie

54. Jackie and Aristotle Onassis after their
wedding on Skorpios, October 20, 1968,
with Caroline clinging close to her mother.
In Greek tradition, sadly wrong in this case,
rain on a wedding day brings luck

55. The Onassis children, Alexander and
Christina, at their father's wedding

56. Jackie pursued by photographer Ronald Galella, New York, October 1971

57. October 7, 1971. "Late one afternoon I saw Jackie walking up Madison Avenue in New York City without her sunglasses on. I was behind her, so I hopped a cab to get in front of her so she couldn't see me. 'Follow that woman!' I told the cab driver. For once, Jackie's instincts were all wrong: instead of turning away, she turned right toward me after hearing the first click of the camera from the cab window. Spotting me, she turned and immediately put on sunglasses. This is my favorite photo because it captures the qualities of the paparazzi style: off-guard, unrehearsed, spontaneous; the dramatic soft backlighting and the over-the-shoulder composition show her at her sexiest...Da Vinci had his 'Mona Lisa' and I have my 'Windblown Jackie,' my favorite, most famous photo of Jackie." —Ronald Galella

58 (below). Ronald Galella pursues Jackie through Central Park, October 4, 1971

59. Jackie and Aristotle Onassis with Pierre and Nicole Salinger and Solange de la Bruyère on their transatlantic cruise on *Christina* after Alexander Onassis's death, early 1973

60. Jackie and Aristotle Onassis in Egypt, March 28, 1974

61. Jackie with Christina Onassis, arriving in Athens for Onassis's funeral, March 1975

62. John Jr., Jackie, Caroline and Ted Kennedy at Onassis's funeral service on Skorpios, March 1975

63. Jackie at Viking with her mentor, designer Bryan Holme (seated), and colleagues, January 17, 1977

64. Caroline Kennedy and her uncle, Ted Kennedy, gesture to the press to be quiet before Caroline walks down the aisle to marry Edwin F. Schlossberg at Our Lady of Victory Church, Centerville, Massachusetts, July 19, 1986

65. Rachel "Bunny" Mellon, June 3, 1982

66. Charles Whitehouse and Jackie, riding Frank, in
Virginia

67. John Jr. and Caroline at the dedication of the John F. Kennedy School of Government at Harvard University, October 27, 1978

68. Caroline with Edwin F. Schlossberg

69. Red Gate Farm, Martha's Vineyard: Solange Herter outside Jackie's house, August 1993

70. Jackie and Maurice
Tempelsman

71. Jackie walking with Maurice
Tempelsman in Central Park,
April 24, 1994

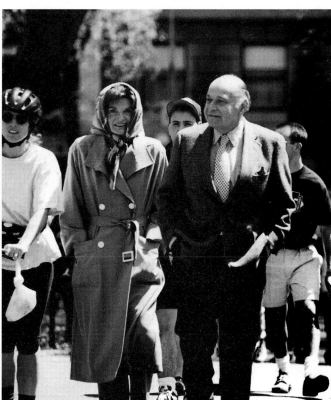

72. With her grandchildren, Tatiana and Rose, in Central Park. Note Rose's striking resemblance to Jackie as a child

73. John Jr. at Jackie's funeral, May 23, 1994

The concept of his brother's legacy haunted him, driving him on in his political career to help the poor and underprivileged. He began to make foraging trips abroad, preparing himself to use that legacy. In November 1965, he toured South America with Ethel, Richard Goodwin and William vanden Heuvel, facing down left-wing students who spat on him as a representative of Yankee imperialism, going down dismal mines to meet Communist workers. A photograph taken of him at the time, tanned, his shirt open to the waist revealing a well-muscled torso, showed how "the little runt" had developed into a charismatic, physically attractive man.

Like his brother, he indulged in serious risk-taking, testing his courage to the limit, climbing mountains, white-water rafting, diving into stormy seas. To Bobby, as to Jack, courage was the most important quality a man could have.

The change in him was even more startling to outsiders who had known him before 1963. "Bobby was really nasty, vicious," said Sam Peabody, brother of Endicott Peabody, the Governor of Massachusetts whom Bobby and his henchmen had attacked as part of their plan to erase WASP liberalism on their home turf and replace it with their own machine. "But afterward he changed completely, he really *cared* about people . . ." Joseph Alsop said, "So many people have him [Bobby] absolutely wrong. They think he is cold, calculating, ruthless. Actually, he is hot-blooded, romantic, compassionate." Averell Harriman said, "It was impossible for him not to tell the truth as he saw it. I think that is why some people thought he was ruthless. At times the truth is ruthless."[16]

Shortly after her return to New York Jackie, with William vanden Heuvel, gave a party for Kenneth Galbraith on his return to the United States at the restaurant called the Sign of the Dove. Jackie intended it as a thank-you for all the Galbraiths had done for her on her trip to India. She did some of the decorations for the party herself: "She had a paper doll, sort of blown-up photograph of him in a white jacket—as you walked in, there he was," Kitty Galbraith remembered. "And she had wonderful Indian paintings [in the style of Mogul miniatures] which she had done herself but with Kenneth's face, as a maharajah riding an elephant, scenes like that, hung in old gilt frames."[17] The Galbraith party was an example of how much care and thought Jackie put into pleasing people she loved. The Galbraiths still have the paintings in their Cambridge, Massachusetts, home and the fondest memories of Jackie as "one of the most intelligent and elegant people I have ever known, with such a creative imagination and a gift for using just the right phrase. And with everything else very kind and thoughtful, loyal to her friends."

It caused a sensation in the press simply because it was the first public party she had given since the assassination. Jackie had hired "Killer Joe" Piro to teach the guests the newest dance, the Frug; Andy Warhol and Edie Sedgwick were among the guests. The party was so late and so noisy that neighbors called the police. There was a certain amount of criticism: this was not how mourning queens were supposed to behave.

As a sign that her life was truly returning to normal, Jackie took up hunting again in the autumn of 1965, renting a house in Far Hills, the New Jersey horse country near Bernardsville. Pleasant Valley, where Jackie first rented then bought a converted sheep barn, was—and is—a secluded green enclave, despite being only a little over an hour's drive from New York City. Like the Virginia horse country near Middleburg, it is an area of rich, privacy-oriented estates and dirt roads. Pleasant Valley itself is deceptively hard to find, which particularly appealed to Jackie. Her clapboard house on a knoll was near the home of the Murray McDonnells, a well-known New York Irish family, whose eight children provided instant company for Caroline and John. There, Jackie spent her time reading, resting, riding. She stabled her horses there, exercised them and practiced jumps. Caroline was becoming a fine rider like her mother but John, although brave, was "hopeless," according to a neighbor, "just clinging on for dear life." Jackie applied for membership of the local Essex Hunt but, as had originally happened in Virginia when she was First Lady, a few people objected that her celebrity would destroy their privacy. Douglas Dillon, Jack's former Secretary of the Treasury, a close friend of Jackie, simply threatened to close his land to the hunt if Jackie was rejected. The objectors backed down.

"She always hunted Thanksgiving Day," said John Pierrepont, a friend and fellow horseman, whose family owned a big property in the Far Hills area. "I remember her son used not to ride at all, and once a year she put him on a horse and she put on this tiny little saddle. And I thought he was so gutsy sitting in this ghastly saddle and riding all day. It was very uncomfortable but it didn't seem to bother him. She took such pleasure out of it. She really enjoyed her children . . . I respected her enormously in the way she brought up her two children without the glare of publicity. I think that was a real miracle. I remember when they were small children there would be helicopters sent out to New Jersey to follow her on her horse and then the children playing. But they lived across the road from a wonderful family called McDonnell and the Kennedy children just disappeared into the mass of children. And Peggy McDonnell said, 'Well, you know, my children were terrible muggers and they couldn't wait to get out in front of the cameras.' In other words it was the perfect medium to hide them in." Jackie, he said, was "extraordinary on a horse. The bigger the fence, the higher the jump, the more she liked it. She got such a big kick out of it."[18]

Jackie's most important financial mentor was a French-born New York investment banker, André Meyer, one of the most successful venture capitalists of the postwar era. Meyer, confidant to the world's top politicians and tycoons, lived in a two-bedroom apartment on the thirty-third floor of the Carlyle, surrounded by his collection of French furniture and paintings. He loved the rich and powerful, and they in turn respected his acumen and turned to him for advice. Katharine Graham said of him that he was "a tremendously gifted high-level gossip, very interested in people: who is doing what to whom; is he good or isn't he good? He would *grill* me about that kind of thing. He was interesting, funny, warm, companionable, interested. He was tremendous good value." According to his biographer, Meyer took a particular interest in wealthy women in trouble, and foremost among them was Jackie, for whom he managed one of his special "AM" accounts at Lazard Frères.[19]

Meyer was also close to Bobby. It might well have been at Jackie's suggestion that, early in 1964, Bobby (who, like his elder brother, had no financial acumen whatsoever) approached Meyer to act as a trustee for the huge family trust funds established by Joseph P. Kennedy, totaling some $100 million, providing $500,000 a year for Rose and the surviving Kennedy children. Meyer also became a member of the board of the John F. Kennedy Library, serving as key fund-raiser and managing the $60 million building fund. According to Gianni Agnelli, Meyer "*really* liked" Bobby, and Bobby in turn was close to the old man, turning to him for advice as he would have to his father.[20] "André was one of the relatively small group of people whose judgment Robert Kennedy would trust," a Kennedy aide said, "not only in things relating to the business world, but things in general. It was a very close relationship."[21]

For Jackie, too, André Meyer represented the father figure that old Joe had been for her. All her life, for all her outward independence, she had needed someone to lean on, and Meyer fulfilled that role to perfection. "He was a very respected and admired close friend or personal adviser," said Robert McNamara who was close to both, "on both financial matters and more broadly on other matters. She had the most immense admiration and respect for him." Eugene Black, the former World Bank president and an old family friend of Jackie's, put it more bluntly: "Jackie had money and Jackie liked money, and she felt André would be a pretty damn good fellow to handle the money for her. It's that simple." Moreover, Jackie resented her financial dependence on the Kennedys and the family office in Park Avenue, run by her brother-in-law, Steve Smith. "I don't recall her ever going to Steve Smith for advice," a friend said. "It was always André."[22]

Meyer was almost certainly in love with her, captured by her beauty and vulnerability, the breathless little-girl-lost manner in which she would approach him for advice. "He thought she was *extraordinary*," said a member of his circle. Jackie's beauty and coquetry captivated him. He was hurt and angry when she married Onassis—a union he bitterly opposed—but Jackie was clever enough to win him back later and to remain on close terms with him.

In 1966 Jackie traveled frenetically, visiting the "Beautiful People" on both continents. After Christmas she went skiing in Sun Valley with Bobby and the children, returning to New York to go nightclubbing with Mike Nichols before flying off to spend time in Gstaad with the Galbraiths. On January 28 she flew to Rome to stay with her old friend Antonio Garrigues y Diaz Cañnabate, formerly Spanish ambassador in Washington during the Kennedy Presidency, now representing Spain at the Vatican. Her arrival was an occasion for nonstop shopping and parties with the Roman aristocracy. Pursued by paparazzi, she visited Irene Galitzine's showroom and bought items from her new collection, and in the evening Galitzine gave a dinner for sixteen close friends. Galitzine's seamstresses worked through the night to make Jackie a black dress for an unscheduled visit to the Pope, which provoked rumors that she intended to marry handsome widower Garrigues. She went hunting with Dino Pecci Blunt and visited the studio of her friend the sculptor Pericle Fasini, where she and Lee had spent so many hours on their visit to Rome in 1951. Now Fasini was working on a bust of Jack. After yet another high-society dinner, given by Prince Aspreno Colonna, she flew back to New York with a stopover at Lisbon, where a quick sightseeing trip turned into a longer one. For Jackie's convenience, SwissAir delayed the plane's takeoff.

While in Gstaad, Robin Biddle Duke, whose husband Angier was now U.S. ambassador in Madrid, had suggested she must see the *feria* in Seville, an idea enthusiastically taken up by Jackie's host, Antonio Garrigues, in Rome, but before that she had promised Chiquita Astor to take the children for their Easter vacation to San Francisco de Vittoria, the Cárcano family's magnificent ranch in the Argentine. For Jackie the visit was a family pilgrimage. Jack had stayed there in May 1941, riding and hunting in the Sierra with the Cárcano children, Miguel, "Baby" (Stella) and "Chiquita" (Anna). "When he [Jack] died," Miguel's widow, Teresa, said, "she wanted to go to the remotest place she could. Our custom is when you go riding in the mountains you place a stone on top of this most beautiful mountain, which means you will come back. There's quite a big pile now from all our friends."[23] Jackie and the children added their stones to the pile where Jack had placed his just under twenty-five years before.

Later that month Jackie took off for Spain to stay with Angier and Robin Biddle Duke at the U.S. embassy in Madrid, arriving on Sunday, April 17, before flying down to Seville to stay with the Duke and Duchess of Alba at the Duenas Palace. She attended the annual Red Cross Ball at the magnificent fifteenth-century Casa de Pilatos, the palace of the dukes of Medinaceli. The evening was flawed for her by rumors that she was to marry Antonio Garrigues and that the ball was officially presided over by Prince Rainier and Princess Grace of Monaco. When Grace had called at the White House after Jack's assassination, Jackie had stayed in bed and refused to see her, and there was a frostiness between them because of her unfounded jealousy. Things were not helped by Grace's arrival forty minutes late at the ball. The two famous Americans sat stony-faced on either side of the Duke of Medinaceli, prompting international press stories of their mutual hostility. At the subsequent bullfight, three of Spain's leading bullfighters, El Cordobes, Paco Camino and El Viti, bypassed Grace to offer their hats and dedicate their bulls to Jackie—outraging American animal lovers. On another day Jackie, dressed in Andalusian riding costume, rode through cheering crowds. Rumors of an engagement between Jackie and Garrigues became so persistent that Angier Biddle Duke felt compelled to issue a statement denying them and pointing out that Garrigues had been a Kennedy acquaintance ever since Joe Jr. had visited Madrid during the Spanish Civil War.

In June she set off for a carefully planned seven-week sojourn in Hawaii, the culmination of her romance with Jack Warnecke. The couple had contemplated marriage, and when Warnecke confessed to Jackie that he had never been baptized, she was delighted: " 'Maybe I can make you a Catholic,' and I said, 'I don't mind, it doesn't mean anything to me!' So I said I would find out, we had to be sure." Bobby, however, absolutely vetoed the plan. "I was in the middle of an airport once when he called her up about Warnecke. He was not hesitant," Richard Goodwin recalled. "He was at the damn airport ticket counter and nobody knew what he was talking about, but I did. I mean he was polite, nice, gentle enough in tone, but the message was clear . . . Remember they always had one thing in common, apart from their feelings, and that was to protect Jack's good name. John F. Kennedy's reputation and name and historical position. And I think that therefore if Bobby thought a marriage might somehow have jeopardized that he would have called much quicker than anything else." According to Warnecke, Jackie told him, "Bobby says it's too soon."

Warnecke had an important architectural commission in Hawaii, the beautiful new State Capitol with its columns and reflecting pool, and huge open courtyard four stories high, which was to be completed in 1968. He had bought a house at Diamond Head and spent part of the summer there while working on the Capitol. "She [Jackie] wanted to come to Hawaii," Warnecke said, "so what I did was to arrange for a lady called Cecily Johnston, who is a very well-established social lady in Hawaii, [to] become the person who was inviting Jackie to Hawaii. Cecily rented the house for her down the beach from where I was, and that's how she came to Hawaii."24

Additional cover was provided by Peter Lawford who came with his children, Christopher, aged eleven, and Sydney, nine, one of Caroline's closest friends among her Kennedy cousins, and a Honolulu bachelor friend John Spierling. Cecily Johnston gave a big party for the children at which Don Ho, the popular Hawaiian singer, pushed Jackie into the pool, and Jackie retaliated by pitching him in. Jackie watched the King Kamehameha Day parade, flew to Laurence Rockefeller's Manua Kea Beach Hotel a hundred and fifty miles from Honolulu, bought pareos and ventured into bikinis, something she had not hitherto been seen to do on the mainland.

At first Jackie had only intended to spend four weeks in Hawaii but Henry Kaiser, for whom Warnecke was designing a master plan for a huge development at Hawaii Kai, offered her their guesthouse. "We went to all kinds of places in Hawaii," said Warnecke. "We spent a week or ten days on the island of Kauai, through friends. They gave us a beautiful piece of native land and a private bay and a little house which Jackie and I took over. We had my two younger sons, Fred and Rodger, my daughter Margo and her best friend, Nina Nichols, who came over to Kauai to join us with Caroline and John. We had a camp. The Secret Service would arrange tents for themselves and the kids, cook out under the palms, and we had a little house overlooking their camp." Jackie fantasized about buying a house in Hawaii where she felt totally at home and at ease. "We could go any place we wanted and nobody bothered us," Warnecke said. Before she left, Jackie thanked the Hawaiian press for their restraint. "I had forgotten, and my children have never known what it is like to discover a new place, unwatched and unnoticed," she said.

Jackie's Hawaiian dream remained just that: a dream. Bobby's veto on marriage to Jack Warnecke had had its effect. And in the end Warnecke, although successful and well-off, did not have the kind of money that Jackie's friends like Pamela Harriman would have called big bucks—private planes, yachts and the trappings of a billionaire. For all her longing for privacy, Jackie could not step down from her pedestal into ordinary life. She had to return to the stratosphere of the superrich, the high altitude to which she had become accustomed. For Warnecke, too, reality hit with an unpleasant bump when his accountant informed him that he owed the bank a million dollars. "I had big offices and a big staff but I guess I didn't have a lot of new work. My accountant was talking about what amounted to a two-year absence from my practice, designing the [Kennedy] grave and being carried away with this romance, or letting that play a dominant role. I said to Jackie that I realized that I had my children, my name and my practice and I couldn't see her as much. I worked seven days a week for almost two years. I would see Jackie but I couldn't really see her."[25]

Jackie was on the Cape again on July 28 for the thirty-seventh birthday party Bunny Mellon gave for her at the Mellon home in Osterville. The next day she was in Newport for the prewedding dinner at the Clambake Club given by Janet and Hughdie before Little Janet's marriage to Lewis Polk Rutherfurd on July 30. Janet, Jackie's pretty and much-loved twenty-one-year-old half sister, had been working since her 1963 debut at Sotheby's in London, where she had almost become engaged to an Englishman before suddenly deciding to marry Rutherfurd, whom she had already known for nine years. Rutherfurd had recently majored in Oriental Studies at Princeton, which he was to follow up with a fellowship at Chung Chi College of the Chinese University in Hong Kong where the couple were to live. Their engagement had been celebrated with what Janet's mother described as "a quiet family party" in May before Jackie left for Hawaii. Her wedding, thanks to the presence of Jackie and her children, was anything but quiet.

"Although the 21-year-old brunette should have been the star of the show," the *Providence Sunday Journal* reported the next day, "it was her famous relative who stole the show." A crowd of five thousand started gathering two hours in advance of the ceremony outside St. Mary's Church in Newport, where Jackie and Jack had been married just under thirteen years before. When the first black limousine containing the bridesmaids and pages arrived, the screaming crowd besieged it, with middle-aged women jumping up for a sight of Caroline and John as hysterically as they had once greeted their father. Caroline looked frightened as she made her way into the church through the screaming mob; John and the other pages jumped out and bolted up the steps to escape the crowd that was reaching out to touch him. Jackie's arrival provoked a frenzy with screams of "Jackie, Jackie." A policeman had to force himself in front of the crowd to open her car door and bulldoze a path for her to the church. Jackie appeared composed in a yellow two-piece suit, paused, smiled slightly as if to acknowledge the crowd, before disappearing into the church. "Help me, somebody help me," the terrified bride was heard to appeal, as she struggled to get to the church door.

The noise outside was such that the wedding guests could hardly hear the service. Twenty people broke into the church and had to be ejected, others climbed the walls to take pictures through the windows, which had to be closed despite the heat. Afterward a policeman was injured as they tried to clear a path for the couple as they left the church, and some of the crowd burst into the church to steal the flowers for souvenirs. This was Jackie-mania at its height. No queen or movie star—with the possible exception of Rudolph Valentino—had been greeted with the hysteria that surrounded the thirty-seven-year-old widow. No wonder she felt endowed with superhuman powers as she faced William Manchester at Hyannis Port later that summer.

Jackie's easy ride over Arthur Schlesinger's book might have encouraged her to be tough with William Manchester, whom she had anointed as the historian of Dallas. Jackie's attempts to censor *Death of a President* proved, in public relations' terms, to be one of her worst mistakes. As has been noted, Manchester was an ardent admirer of John Kennedy, and the book was a hugely long twentieth-century version of Arthurian legend in which Kennedy was cast as the lost leader, the dead king of Camelot, with the unfortunate Lyndon Johnson almost in the role of Mordred.

On March 25, 1966, Manchester had boarded the Middletown–New York bus staggering under the seventy-seven-pound weight of a suitcase containing five copies of his 1,201-page manuscript. Both Bobby and Jackie had been too busy to read it—Bobby in keeping a high political profile, traveling and campaigning, Jackie, fully emerged from mourning, in a life of pure enjoyment. Probably, too, neither of them could bring themselves to relive the pain of Dallas. Instead the book was read critically by Kennedy aides and friends: Edwin Guthman and John Seigenthaler, Arthur Schlesinger and Richard Goodwin. Evan Thomas, the Kennedys' ever-loyal editor at Harper & Row, perceived Manchester's hostile depiction of Lyndon Johnson as potentially harmful to Bobby's political position, since the book had been originally authorized by him. After sixteen weeks of textual revision a final version was agreed upon. On July 29 a telegram arrived from Bobby stating that the Kennedy family would place no obstacle in the way of the book's publication but clearly indicating that this did not cover serialization. He appeared to raise no objection when told of the huge sum—$655,000—offered by *Look* for serial rights.

Then Jackie stepped in. The news of the serialization, with the consequent publicity the book would receive, shocked her. She had thought that what she was getting was a simple historical record, as she later told Manchester, "bound in black and put away on dark library shelves." She did not want those intensely—for her—private and traumatic events recalled to the public gaze. Her pressure on Bobby to stop even the publication of the book increased, resulting in a shocked telegram from him to Evan Thomas stressing that publication of the book could only take place on the proviso that "Mrs. Kennedy and I must give permission for publication of the book and that has not been given." During the tense weeks that followed, Richard Goodwin, whom Jackie trusted and whom Manchester regarded as eminently qualified to understand editorial problems, attempted to reach a solution. A meeting was set up for the pair of them with Jackie at Hyannis Port in September.

Looking stunning in a green miniskirt, Jackie met them at the airport. After iced tea on the porch, she indulged in a spell of power play with Manchester, showing off her athletic body and her acrobatics as she waterskied, with the apprehensive author in the boat in front. Eventually she tired of it, but instead of returning the boat to shore, she dived into the ocean far out. Strong swimmer as she was, and wearing flippers, she soon left Manchester, wallowing out of breath, in her wake. "I momentarily wondered whether I would make it," he remembered.[26]

Back at the house and joined by Goodwin, Jackie was bitter, hectoring, in what Manchester described as a "completely unrealistic" frame of mind: "hostile toward *Look*, bitter about [Mike] Cowles [publisher of *Look*], and scornful of all books on President Kennedy including Schlesinger's . . . She was going to fight, she said savagely, and she was going to win: 'Anybody who is against me will look like a rat unless I run off with Eddie Fisher.' " The atmosphere was one of hysterical emotion. Any attempt to raise factual discussion was met with "tears, grimaces and whispery cries of 'Jesus Christ,' abrupt retreats into the house to compose herself, returns with boxes of Kleenex." According to *Look* editor William Attwood, Mike Cowles had had an even worse time at Hyannis Port: "She called Mike a son-of-a-bitch and a bastard . . . and she became quite hysterical and violent, verbally violent, to the point that Mike came back a little amazed, you know, that the great lady of the funeral and all that could talk just that way . . ."[27]

To be fair to Jackie, this was not something she could contemplate rationally. She was all too aware of how far she had revealed herself to Manchester in those ten hours of daiquiri-fueled tapes, of how much she had said that she now never wanted to see the light. She had showed him two letters she had written to Jack: one from Greece on her October cruise, the other a copy of the one she had placed in his coffin. Apparently Manchester had paraphrased them. Although he later claimed that he had not used the tapes, it is difficult to see how else he could have obtained the information on the Kennedys' last evening together, or on Jackie dipping her dead husband's finger in Vaseline before slipping on her wedding ring without her having told him. As he said, "She had withheld nothing during our interviews . . ."[28]

Early in December Jackie decided to sue, charging Manchester and his publishers with disregarding "accepted standards of propriety and good faith," of violating "the dignity and privacy my children and I have striven with dignity to retain" and of "inaccurate and unfair references to other individuals [Lyndon Johnson]." Richard Goodwin, called in by Bobby to defuse the situation, had sympathy for Jackie's point of view: "She had felt that she could review it [the book] and that she could take out anything she didn't like. And that was the condition on which she had sat down and given this frightfully emotional interview. I mean she was in a real emotional state even then. And she would get going and she would have a couple of drinks and all this stuff would pour out and you never knew how much was real and neither did she. And so when the book finally came out and she had done the interview and hadn't been allowed to change it. It didn't matter at that point what the substance was . . . even from a political point of view it [suing Manchester] was a stupid thing to do. But she wasn't coming from a political point of view. She wasn't trying to censor history because most of the stuff she was concerned about might have been the description of the kids' reaction—them also he kept talking about. I don't think there was anything she said . . . she wasn't sitting down and thinking, Is this harmful or not?—She just said this guy had betrayed her and she had poured out her heart of hearts to him and she said she just had to do something. It was sad. I remember the night the decision was made up in the apartment on Fifth Avenue and she just wanted to do it, and I guess I could sympathize. Sure, Bobby didn't want to do it . . . I was deeply involved, up there at 1040 the night she decided and Bobby going backward and forward to the bedroom saying, 'I guess we're going to have to do something.' He was dead set against it. Everybody with any sense was dead set against it. I just said, 'If she wants to do it, let's do it.' Bobby was right against it . . . and he would have been most sensitive to the Johnson thing. But her feelings were so irrational and emotional and not rounded that people preferred to find a rational reason for her wanting to censor the book. She didn't calculate the impact on Johnson. She wouldn't have cared if Lyndon Johnson had been dropped in the middle of the Atlantic in concrete overshoes!"[29]

She had still not read the book. Meanwhile, the *Look* serialization went ahead. In mid-January Jackie finally read *Death of a President* and, according to its author, found it fascinating. By that time the Kennedys, aware of the enormous damage the quarrel was doing to the public image of both Bobby and Jackie, decided to settle. The book was finally published on April 7, 1967, with a publishers' statement saying that Harper & Row wished to make it clear that "neither Mrs. John F. Kennedy nor Senator Robert F. Kennedy has in anyway approved or endorsed the material appearing in this book . . ." Just over a year later, Jackie and William Manchester were reconciled when the author generously not only offered his support to Bobby's campaign but also donated the book royalties of *Death of a President* to the Kennedy Library.[30]

News headlines after the settlement agreement proclaimed Jackie the winner, but it was a Pyrrhic victory. She had succeeded in getting her way over certain passages that most people would have regarded as invasions of her privacy and which the publishers would certainly have agreed to anyway. But, as *Newsweek* pointed out, her crusade against sensationalism had already brought out enough of Manchester's history to make it the most sensational story of the year. Jackie herself was too intelligent not to realize the futility of her action, writing to Lyndon Johnson in response to a kindly letter from him telling her not to worry about the Manchester "slander" on his account, describing her victory as "hollow" with everything she objected to being printed anyway. Later, in a highly emotional state, she wrote from Antigua on January 9, 1967, again to Johnson, of her horror at reading in a magazine that she had objected to his calling her "Honey." "All the rage that I have been trying to forget down here boiled up again," she told him.

That New Year of 1967, as she swam with the children off Antigua under the protection of Bunny Mellon, Jackie reflected on the Manchester storm and its consequences, the bad publicity she was receiving, for the first time, which was damaging her image with the public, and not only hers but, equally importantly, Bobby's. What she saw as a courageous defense of her rights in the face of a betrayal of confidentiality, the American public perceived as an arrogant abuse of power and an attempt to stifle their cherished right of freedom of speech.

CHAPTER SEVENTEEN

Odysseus

⌒

> *Onassis's hero was the mighty Odysseus, whose fabled journey was an inspiration for his own life.*
>
> —Onassis's secretary, Kiki Feroudi Moutsatsos[1]

"Jackie comes off her pedestal," the social columnist Liz Smith declared, in a series of articles published early in the New Year of 1967 in the wake of the Manchester affair. On December 29, 1966 the Gallup Poll had announced that, for the fifth consecutive year, Jacqueline Kennedy had been chosen by the American people as the most admired woman in the world. After the Manchester settlement, however, a poll taken by Lou Harris, John Kennedy's favorite pollster, published on January 31, 1967, showed that Jackie's popularity with the public had dropped: 33 percent of those questioned said they "thought less" of her as a result of the row, and 20 percent thought less of Bobby. By two to one people rejected the idea that Jackie's right to privacy might be invaded by the publication of an account of the President's assassination.

As Liz Smith pointed out, Jackie was experiencing the rockiest days to date in the "long, idolatrous affair the public has insisted on conducting with her since 1961." A critical spotlight was turned on every aspect of her life: her cost to the taxpayer ($50,000 a year for her private office, free mailing privileges for life, Secret Service protection for herself and her children), her men friends, her miniskirts, her trips to exotic locations. Instead of remaining the pure white marble mourning figure the American public wanted her to be forever, Jackie had decided to join real life. She had, one female columnist sneered in a reference to Fellini's famous film of Roman decadence, "opted for *la dolce vita*." "From Mourner to Swinger" blared the headline of a long piece in the *National Enquirer* devoted to Jackie's life from 1963 to 1966.

Jackie was concerned enough about the bad press she had been receiving to give a rare interview to two sympathetic journalists, Frank Conniff, Kennedy friend, and editor of the *New York World Journal-Tribune*, and Bob Considine, its chief columnist. The interview was aimed at rekindling the public's admiration for "the beauty known as Jacqueline, the sprite called Jackie, widow of a slain president, loving mother of his daughter and son." It was frankly adulatory: the writers invited the public to share their sympathy with "the young woman who bears such assorted burdens as Gallup's pronouncement that she is the most admired person of her sex in the world . . . a woman who has been on the best-dressed lists most of her adult life . . . the smile that had launched a thousand magazine covers . . ." Tactfully, the journalists omitted Jackie's passionate endorsement of Bobby: "I'd jump out of the window for him." She had made her endorsement personally clear at the St. Patrick's Day parade that year. Standing on the street with John and Caroline, when Bobby drew level she had leaped out to give him an enthusiastic public embrace.

Yet in that same month of March a line was drawn beneath Jackie's Kennedy life when she returned to Washington for the reburial of Jack with Patrick and their stillborn daughter at the completed Arlington grave site. She had not been able to face the sight of the three coffins being lowered into their respective graves the previous evening, witnessed by Bobby and Teddy, both in tears. But she was there, clutching a bouquet of lily-of-the-valley, at seven the following morning with ten other Kennedys and Lyndon Johnson to hear Cardinal Cushing intone: "Be at peace, dear Jack, with your tiny infants by your side, until we all meet again above this hill and beyond the stars . . ."

The grave was the first of the Kennedy monuments to be completed; Jack Warnecke's work was over, as was his relationship with Jackie. To his dismay, Bunny Mellon had taken over the final landscape design of the site. Three years earlier he had had a major disappointment when architect I. M. Pei had been given the commission to design the Kennedy Library and School of Government. Warnecke said that he was told later by Jackie that Bill Walton and another had advised that he was "just too close to the family and it wouldn't look good."[2] Walton and Jackie worked closely together on the library project. Asked if their input was equal, I. M. Pei replied, "No, the judgment was hers and she shared her judgment with Bobby Kennedy. I mean Bobby Kennedy was important [but] Bobby was not a person who understood much about architecture so therefore he probably, but only probably, said, 'Jackie, you decide.' "[3]

That summer, there was a further diminution in the circle of friends Jackie had shared with Jack. On May 30 David Harlech's lovely and beloved wife, Sissie, was killed in an automobile accident. Jackie and Bobby flew to the funeral in England; it seemed that violent death was never far away from them. In June Jackie rented a large Georgian house in Ireland, Woodstown, near Waterford, with her Pleasant Valley neighbors, the Murray McDonnells. Jackie-mania seized the Irish—she was mobbed in Shannon Airport when they arrived and in the melee, Peggy McDonnell was knocked over a seat. The party of three adults and ten children took a chartered bus to Woodstown; the roads were lined with people craning for a glimpse of Jackie. "You stand up and wave," Jackie ordered Peggy. When they reached the house all the staff were lined up as if for a royal reception, and were taken aback when a crew of noisy children tumbled first out of the bus. Woodstown, Peggy said, was typically Irish: "49 bedrooms and one bathroom."[4] Jackie was a friend and client of Irish designer and Dublin grande dame, Sybil Connolly, who persuaded her to help the fledgling Irish Georgian Society founded by Desmond Guinness. "She [Sybil Connolly] realized that it would help the cause of the Irish Georgian Society and the opening of Castletown, this great house near Dublin," Desmond Guinness said, "which was the first house in the province of Leinster to be opened to the public, if Mrs. Kennedy visited it. Because we were very, very short of visitors because people in the Irish Republic were really almost frightened to go up the drive of a house like that. And so we leaked it to the press that she was coming and about seven hundred people came in order to see Mrs. Kennedy. We photographed her in every possible room being shown around . . ."[5]

Jackie also used her stay in Ireland as an opportunity to tour the Waterford glass factory and to order chandeliers for the Kennedy Center. She met President de Valera and took the children to the Kennedy ancestral village of Dunganstown, which Jack had visited four years before in the last summer of his life. Otherwise she relaxed, riding and swimming with the children. One afternoon her passion for swimming alone and far out to sea almost cost her her life: leaving the McDonnells and the children at a picnic, she walked half a mile up the beach behind the dunes to a channel she normally swam across at low tide. But it was high tide, and in midchannel she found herself struggling against a fierce current that carried her past a spit of land into the huge bay outside. She wrote afterward:

> The water was so cold that one could not hold one's fingers together. I am a very good swimmer and can swim for miles and hours, but the combination of current and cold were something I had never known. There was no one in sight to yell to.
>
> I was becoming exhausted, swallowing water and slipping past the spit of land, when I felt a great porpoise at my side. It was Mr. Walsh [of the Secret Service detail]. He set his shoulder against mine and together we made the spit. Then I sat on the beach coughing up sea water for half an hour while he found a poor itinerant and borrowed a blanket for me.[6]

It had been Mr. Walsh, she said, who had saved John Jr. from being badly burned when he fell into a campfire the previous year. Now he had saved her life. She recommended him for the highest honor at the FBI's disposal. Walsh was the children's favorite Secret Service man. Protection for Jackie and the children had been renewed in the summer of 1967 for a further two years since an incident in which a madwoman had leaped out at Caroline, screaming that her mother had killed three people, while children had followed John Jr. from school taunting him that his father was dead. The FBI files on Jackie were filled with investigations on obsessive lunatics making threats against her. The threats against her children, the combination of adulation and resentment that the public felt for her, was making Jackie's life in America increasingly difficult.

Unkind people noted that Jackie's trip abroad had meant that she had missed the entire four-week run of her sister's acting debut as Tracy Lord in *The Philadelphia Story*, which opened on June 20 at the Ivanhoe Theater in Chicago, where Lee was staying in the Ambassador East Hotel in a suite apparently arranged for her by Aristotle Onassis. Lee, forever casting around for fulfillment, had been encouraged to try her hand at acting by her new best friend, Truman Capote. After the publication the previous year of his sensational *In Cold Blood*—followed by his Black and White Ball, the highlight of the New York winter season—Capote was at the height of his social power and literary reputation. (Jackie had been invited to the ball and had even got as far as ordering an elaborate mask for it, but was advised not to go by Bobby on political grounds as the war in Vietnam escalated.) Lee, who seems to have had a penchant for homosexual men, and Truman, who loved beautiful, socially glittering women, had become soulmates.

Lee's principal qualifications for her role as Tracy Lord, flighty Main Line society girl—a role made famous by Katharine Hepburn on film—were her upper-class accent, stunning looks and ability to wear clothes (Yves Saint-Laurent in this case). The play was a sellout, although Lee's "wooden" acting was panned by the critics. According to a colleague, the women came to see Lee Radziwill, celebrity, not Lee Bouvier, actress. "They gave Lee a new costume every time she went onstage, and the women in the audience would start discussing it out loud each time . . ." Lee's second attempt at stardom came in a television adaptation of *Laura*, a role first played by Gene Tierney. Once again, Capote was her enthusiastic supporter and promoter; he wrote the adaptation for her and pressed her talents on the president of ABC-TV, Tom Moore, and producer David Susskind. *Laura* was broadcast on American television on January 24, 1968; again, it was widely watched and ferociously criticized. This time Jackie was at the Radziwills' apartment when they gave a party to watch it. Capote, defending Lee on David Susskind's talk show, blamed her failure to a large extent on the Jackie factor: "We had not foreseen the extent to which no matter what Lee did, the press was going to come down on her like hell . . . because they really wanted to say nasty things about Mrs. Kennedy and never could at that time because Jackie was still the widow lady, a little saint. There was underneath all that adulation a tremendous resentment and envy for this beautiful girl who had everything. And here was this other girl who wouldn't have got the part if she weren't Mrs. Kennedy's sister . . ."7

In the autumn of 1967 *Women's Wear Daily* predicted that Jackie would soon announce her engagement to David Harlech, prompted, perhaps, by Harlech's presence in Washington on a lecture tour during which he had dined with the Alsops and spent the weekend with Bobby at Hickory Hill, and by his admission that Jackie had invited him to join her forthcoming tour of Cambodia. Harlech, now forty-nine, was tall, poised, elegant, with a brilliant brain. "He was witty, charming, the most attractive man," a friend remembered. David Harlech was the son of the 4th Baron Harlech and Lady Beatrice Cecil, daughter of the 4th Marquess of

Salisbury, and therefore part of the large and influential Cecil clan. Kathleen Kennedy's husband, Billy Hartington, had been David's first cousin and Kathleen herself had been a great friend of his wife, Sissie. David Harlech was totally unstuffy (or he would never have been a friend of Jack); he had had a playboy reputation in his youth, and a passion for racing, jazz and fast cars. He was extremely indulgent toward his five children, who were noted for their hippie lifestyle and the commune they established in the grounds of the ancestral home in Shropshire.

David Harlech had adored his wife and was devastated by her death, as he wrote to Joe Alsop: "Of course it is hard to see much point or pleasure in life now but we had a glorious 27 years together and perhaps the happiest were in Washington . . ."[8] As one of Jack Kennedy's oldest and closest friends, there was a deep bond between him and Jackie. As a trustee of the Kennedy School of Government at Harvard, Harlech flew over for the annual meetings. He had been there in the month before his wife's death. They had seen each other when Jackie had flown over for Sissie's funeral early in June and he had visited her in Ireland. On October 22 he was at Hyannis Port, and it was probably then that Jackie asked him to join her on the projected, semiofficial trip in November to Cambodia and Thailand, with Mike Forrestal, now a lawyer in New York, and the Bartletts.

Although both denied any idea of an engagement, romance and marriage were in the air and, as Harlech admitted under pressure, they had slept together. In Boston for a meeting of the trustees of the Kennedy School of Government at Harvard, they shared adjoining rooms at the Ritz-Carlton.[9] Huge press speculation followed Jackie and Harlech on her semiofficial visit to Cambodia and Thailand; Jackie's job—as it had been in India and Pakistan in 1962—was to use her huge international popularity to temper anti-American feeling in the area raised by U.S. activity in Vietnam, and she captivated Prince Sihanouk of Cambodia just as she had entranced Nehru. The trip was carefully planned: Jackie had ordered a complete wardrobe from her new favorite couturier, Valentino, whom she had been patronizing since 1964. She even told Stanley Tetrick that she would like him to take a photograph of her at Angkor Wat and have it featured on the cover of Look. The press, of course, was more interested in the presence of Harlech at Jackie's side, than in Sihanouk, caparisoned elephants, temples, or even a visit by their unofficial queen to the King and Queen of Thailand.

Cambodia was the end, rather than the beginning, of the relationship, a moment when reality impinged on romance, although the press naturally was unaware of this. "I think what happened was [after Jack was killed, then Sissie] they [David and Jackie] just as it were fell on each other to commiserate together—they'd both been left and I think, what I could gather from David, it was kind of a nice idea," said Pamela Harlech, David's New York–born second wife. "Because they knew each other terribly well and they were friends and David and Sissie and Jack and Jackie had gone places together. It was all very comfortable. And I think they both thought that would be a very nice idea. When they went to Angkor Wat, you know, she was still flirting with Ros Gilpatric. I don't think she wanted to be pinned down to anything but she thought David was attractive, David was one of Jack's best friends, he was very presentable, she didn't have to put on anything with him. And he was devastated when Sissie died, absolutely devastated, and sort of wanted to get away . . . the children, he just couldn't cope. And I think when she said, 'Come on a trip,' he just said, 'Yes.' But I think he'd had enough. By the time he got back from Angkor Wat, I think he'd had it up to here . . . You know, she would do all this thing like arriving late and not being able to pull herself together—not because she was upset, she just was never on time—and all the kerfuffle that went with it . . . I think he was very fond of her but he realized she wasn't going to live in Oswestry, which is where he lived . . . [but] if Jackie'd wanted David, she could have had him . . ."[10]

Most friends of the couple think that although they might have come close to marriage it was never really on the cards on either side. "My view is, having known both of them quite well," said Lord Jenkins of Hillhead, "that if Jackie had asked him to marry her he probably wouldn't have been able to resist it but I doubt if he . . . He had a very good sense of self-preservation and he had a very good hedonistic calculus . . . My view is that he would have had the sense to see that life married to Jackie would have a lot of disadvantages and wouldn't really have suited him . . ."[11] Harlech himself once admitted to a close friend that there were two reasons why marriage to Jackie would not have worked out for either of them: "(A) I'm not rich enough for her and (B) it would have been like having a sixth child because she had to have the kind of adoration a child asks from you and the constant attention . . ."[12]

Harlech was talking after the event. Evidence from people close to Jackie indicates that he wanted to marry her, even after the Cambodian trip. "Of course she won't marry that fool David, although he goes on about it the whole time," Lee told Cecil Beaton in June, adding mysteriously, "but she may quit and start a new life."[13] He and Jackie remained lifelong friends, corresponding as she did with all her "fan club." "He was very fond of her," Pamela Harlech admitted. Harlech was attractive, good company and a convenient smoke screen that drew press attention away from her other romantic attachments—and a possibility that was forming at the back of her mind.

While the American press were still following the Harlech trail, even to the extent of traveling to his remote Shropshire estate, Woodhill, and interviewing his eccentric children[14] as late as June 1968—having just caught up with the possibility that Jackie might marry Jack Warnecke in April 1967, almost a year after their affair had ended—Jackie's principal beau was Roswell Gilpatric, formerly Deputy Secretary of Defense in the Kennedy administration. "Ros was a very nice, good-looking man," an old friend said. "He was rather glamorous but I never thought he was terribly interesting. He, as a man, wouldn't want to get his hair messed up. I don't think that urge was strong. I think that was why she was so happy with him because I don't think he was trying to get her into bed the whole time . . ."[15] Ros Gilpatric was not yet separated from his wife, Madelin, who later divorced him. (When asked if the two of them had gone to bed together, she apparently snapped, "Once.") "What Ros and Jackie really had," said Gilpatric's widow, Mimi, "apart from really caring for each other is they shared their intellect. They were both very intellectual. I've seen some of the letters they wrote and they were really charming letters."[16]

The press were alerted to Gilpatric's presence in Jackie's life when the two of them went on a trip to Mexico in March 1968 to see the Mayan ruins. Agnes Ash of *Women's Wear Daily* was less interested in the ancient civilization than she was in the sight of Jackie and Gilpatric holding hands and flirting openly together. As so often, the press were on to the romance when it was already over. The pattern of their relationship followed Jackie's experience with Harlech, as Gilpatric told Jackie's biographer, C. David Heymann: "The strange thing about the Yucatán trip is that by then I realized we weren't going to work out. While we were on the trip, Jackie alluded several times to Onassis, and told me her intentions. I found her very straightforward. She hadn't entirely decided [on Onassis] but seemed to be leaning that way."[17] Ros Gilpatric, like David Harlech, was not in the "big bucks" league. And, like Harlech, despite his charm and intelligence, he did not have the quality of danger that really attracted Jackie. Neither had the overwhelming self-confidence and animal physical attraction to appeal to her. One man, however, had all those qualities in abundance: Aristotle Onassis.

In the high summer of 1967 Taki Theodoracopoulos and Gianni Agnelli were sailing on Agnelli's yacht from Greece to Italy when they decided to drop in on Onassis on his private Ionian island of Skorpios. "We got off the boat," said Taki, "and Onassis seemed very inhospitable suddenly. He took us around the island in his car, a little buggy—he almost, I remember, fell over a cliff. He showed us around and then, as we were coming down to the tiny harbor, we saw a woman leaving. I didn't recognize her but Gianni said to me, 'You know who that was? It was Jackie.' I said, 'No, I didn't notice.' She took off waterskiing and she stayed away the whole hour that I and Gianni—a couple of hours—were there. And then we felt that's why Onassis wanted to get rid of us because he was ill at ease. I never understood why, if he was pissed off at us or at Jackie, because he obviously would like us to know that she was on the island—this was a year and a half before it happened. So she was already there . . ."[18]

Onassis had kept Jackie in mind ever since the famous cruise on the *Christina* in October 1963. He had flown to comfort her in the White House on the weekend after Jack's assassination and they had kept in touch on the telephone ever since. Onassis loved to capture beautiful and famous women: his mistress since his divorce from his first wife Tina, in 1959, had been the internationally celebrated Greek-born diva Maria Callas. "All his life my brother loved meeting and making love to famous women," his sister Artemis said. "The more important or well-known the woman, the more he loved to love her. Maria was the most famous Greek woman of our time. It was inevitable he would love her."[19] But Callas paled into insignificance beside Jackie, the most famous and admired woman in the world, and Onassis was prepared to sacrifice even his passion for Maria to possess her.

By 1967, he and Maria had been together for eight years, during which time he had not always been faithful. Piquantly, it was his affair with Lee that had most enraged Callas. When Onassis invited Lee on to the *Christina* Callas told him to ask her to leave, and when he refused, gathered up her belongings and flounced back to Paris, where she lived. Lee left and Callas returned, but months later Callas saw a newspaper photograph of the two of them in a nightclub and telephoned Onassis at his office, screaming hysterically and threatening to throw herself off the yacht. Onassis hastened to Skorpios bearing a million-dollar necklace to calm her down. By 1967, the year that Taki and Agnelli spied Jackie on Skorpios, things had begun to deteriorate between Onassis and Callas with blazing rows and frequent separations. By the spring of 1968 Callas seems to have been aware of her lover's interest in Jackie. Young George Loudon, whose parents were frequent guests on the *Christina*, in Monte Carlo and on Skorpios, remembered Maria Callas as normally being "great fun and very nice to the young," but the last time he saw her and Onassis together was having dinner in Monte Carlo in the spring of 1968 when "she seemed very down."[20]

She had good reason to be, for Onassis's pursuit of Jackie was heating up at last. As an astute businessman and a player of the long game, his sense of timing was impeccable, and in the spring of 1968, he sensed that Jackie was ready to change her life. Jackie's thoughts had been turning for some time toward the Mediterranean as a fantasy escape from America—she had written to Harold Macmillan of the appeal the Mediterranean held for her and the Greek way of life in particular—and as both she and Bobby devoured the Greek classics, this ancient culture and myth came to have increasing significance for her. Michael Cacoyannis's film *Zorba the Greek*, based on Nikos Kazantzakis's novel and starring Anthony Quinn, with its haunting bouzouki music by Theodorakis, had come out in 1964. Later Jackie saw it with Jack Warnecke: "I remember being at the movie, *Zorba the Greek*, with her near the end [of their affair] and she said, 'I know what I want to do,' so Onassis must have been pursuing her . . ."

Onassis fed Jackie's fantasy with his own, of himself as Odysseus, hero of Homer's epic poem, born a prince on the rocky island of Ithaca, within sight of Skorpios. As a young man Odysseus left Ithaca to fight in the siege of Troy, and endured many years of hardships and trials by gods and giants before returning home to slay his enemies and regain his wife and his throne. As captain of his ship, the *Christina*, Onassis ploughed the seas, confronting many enemies and defeating them, but always returning to his native Greece. Jackie was able to see him as a romantic figure, instead of the tough, squat, wily, ruthless businessman he appeared to others. Onassis was a pirate, a type that had always appealed to her— "There are no rules in business," he used to tell his associates. Like old Joe Kennedy, he was always looking forward to the next deal, accumulating and accumulating, winning at all costs. The Kennedys, however, did not see Onassis this way: they saw him as a threat, who might snatch away their Helen of Troy, removing their most valuable political asset and undermining their own Kennedy myth.

Onassis, with his piratical image and jet set baggage, was a politically undesirable connection for the Kennedys. Things were to get worse: in April 1967 the democratically elected Greek government was overthrown in a military coup; shortly afterward the young King Constantine was sent into exile. The Greek government was now a military dictatorship and consequently a political pariah. Politics meant nothing to Onassis, who was doing everything he could to please the junta, competing with Stavros Niarchos over plans for a huge oil refinery nicknamed Project Omega. Liberals in America were outraged by the government of the "colonels," and the political fallout of a family relationship with Onassis for Bobby, should he run as the liberal candidate in the 1968 election, could be disastrous.

Whatever direction her own private ambitions might have been taking, Jackie was still politically committed to Bobby and his agenda. When he had visited South Africa in 1966 and seen Ian Robertson, an anti-apartheid campaigner under house arrest by the regime, she sent Robertson via Bobby a signed copy of Jack's *Profiles in Courage*. Now she was on the side of the anti–Vietnam War campaigners; on one occasion she was seen to beat her fists on McNamara's chest, imploring him, "You've got to stop this war."

As 1968 opened, Bobby hovered on the sidelines, undecided whether to declare himself as a candidate against Johnson in the forthcoming presidential race. The Tet offensive in late January, when the Vietcong overwhelmed U.S.-held bases and territory, provided a huge impetus to the antiwar movement. Still Bobby hesitated. While Ethel and his sisters pushed him to declare his candidacy, Jackie wrote out excerpts from an anti-imperialist essay ridiculing the United States' stance in Vietnam as a "civilizing mission" against Communism, and sent them to him on February 29. "There is not a civilized nation in the world which does not talk about its civilizing mission as grandly as we do . . . They are all ridiculous . . . including ourselves," she told him.[21] She probably intended this as material for antiwar speeches; there is no reason to believe that she really wanted him to run, with all the physical risks that would involve. On March 16 Bobby announced that he was entering the race. On March 31 Lyndon Johnson, anguished by Vietnam, fears for his own health and a recurrent nightmare of a resurgent Bobby claiming the throne in the name of his dead brother, renounced his own candidacy: "I shall not seek, nor will I accept, the nomination of my party for another term as your President."

A few days later, at a New York dinner party on April 2, Jackie took Arthur Schlesinger aside and confided to him her fear for Bobby: "Do you know what I think will happen to Bobby?" she said. "The same thing that happened to Jack . . . There is so much hatred in this country, and more people hate Bobby than hated Jack. I've told Bobby this, but he isn't fatalistic like me."[22] Just two days later, as Bobby began his campaign for the nomination in the Indiana primary, Martin Luther King was shot dead in Memphis. When Bobby heard the news, he shrank back: "Oh God, when is this violence going to end?" he cried.[23] That night, as Schlesinger put it, fury raged in the ghettos of America. There were riots in 110 cities; 39 people were killed, mostly black, and more than 2,500 injured, echoing the violence in Watts the year before. Jackie flew to Atlanta for King's funeral on April 7. She returned in despair at the state of her country, telling Schlesinger, "Of course people feel guilty for a moment. But they hate feeling guilty. They can't stand it for very long. Then they turn."[24] For Jackie it all recalled Dallas, and she feared not only for Bobby but for herself and her children. America seemed an unsafe place to bring them up, a place from which, more and more, she felt she must escape.

Because of her dazzling celebrity, even New York was becoming claustrophobic for her. Going to the theater with her was an unnerving experience, as Joan Thring, Rudolf Nureyev's personal assistant and tour manager, recalled: "One night we were in the theater and we were about in the fifth front row and when the interval came up, I said, 'Let's go and have a drink,' and she said, 'I can't, I can't do that.' And suddenly—all the people had gone out—suddenly somebody said, 'There's Jackie Kennedy,' and there was this thunderous thing of feet running down either aisle, either side of us, and then they just filed in rows in front of us just staring. It was terrifying. I said to her, 'Jackie, does this . . . ?' and she said, 'This happens all the time, just pretend it's not happening.' "[25] But under the surface Jackie's nerves were raw. At a Balanchine ballet performance with Cecil Beaton, in February 1968, a couple of revolver shots were fired on stage: "Jackie nearly jumped out of her chair and over the rail of the mezzanine," Beaton noted. "I felt sorry for her in such a state of nerves . . ."[26]

And there were other considerations, as her friend and confidant Robin Douglas-Home put it in a series of articles that finished their friendship:

> If Robert Kennedy ever does recapture the White House, it will be Ethel Kennedy (with whom she [Jackie] has little affinity) and not she who will be in the center of the stage. Ethel Kennedy will make quite sure of that.
>
> Jacqueline Kennedy's support is needed to get Robert Kennedy there. Once there, he must discard her. He would have to be seen to be concentrating on his future, not cashing in on the past . . . The political usefulness of Jacqueline Kennedy will then be obsolescent— perhaps even an embarrassment. Any appearance of relying upon Jacqueline Kennedy as an emotional magnet or prop would surely undermine his position.[27]

The unpalatable facts of political life were brought home to her in a scene at Hyannis Port in the early spring of 1968 when Bobby was leading in the presidential polls. Jackie, according to a witness, was "more excited than I had seen her for years." "Won't it be wonderful when we get back in the White House?" she called out to the assembled clan. Ethel, who had gallantly closed her eyes to the relationship between her husband and her sister-in-law, cut her cold: "What do you mean, we?" Jackie fled the house. Bobby did not follow her.

By then Jackie was thinking seriously about Onassis as a prospective husband. The Kennedys were aghast. "Bobby at some point told her that over his dead body would this happen," a close friend of Onassis said.[28] The Kennedy family was extremely concerned at the effect her marriage would have on Bobby's campaign; according to Joan Kennedy, Teddy was dispatched to plead with her not to do anything until after the November election. On May 6, the eve of the

Indiana primary result, Rudolf Nureyev and Joan Thring gave a dinner party in the apartment Lee had lent them, for Jackie and Onassis, Bobby and Ethel, and Janet Auchincloss. "It was sort of brewing then," Joan Thring remembered. "It had been brought up, in front of the mother, with Bobby. It was sort of talked about and Bobby was in a fit about it and also Jackie had said to me at one point that . . . she was thinking about getting involved with Ari and Bobby was against it . . ." Asked what it was like when they were all sitting there, Joan Thring replied, "Like a family. That was all right, and they were alright with Ari in front of other people but Bobby . . . it was a little bit edgy about what could happen with him and Ari if somebody said something they didn't like. But she was very concerned that Bobby would agree, I mean she wanted badly for Bobby to agree to it, she didn't want to fall out with him but, I think, you know at the end of the day it was going to happen."[29]

Later that month, while Bobby was on the west coast of America campaigning in the Oregon primary, Jackie spent five crucial days with Onassis on the *Christina* cruising in the Virgin Islands. Joan Thring had been invited by him to accompany him back to Europe at the end of the ballet company's American tour: "It became very clear to me immediately that I was a front," she said, "to hide Jackie from Maria Callas who was going to murder him on the spot." Joan and Onassis embarked on the *Christina* at Miami on May 21 with Cary Grant, Kirk Kerkorian and his wife, and Onassis's friend and lawyer, Johnny Meyer, for a cruise around the Virgin Islands. On the twenty-fifth, when they reached St. Thomas, the rest of the party disembarked. "Suddenly all the slipcovers were taken off the drawing-room sofas and things," Joan said, "and a lot of photographs of Jackie and Jack Kennedy suddenly appeared from nowhere, and we all laughed with each other because Ari never told you anything, it was very secretive, and he just went about doing whatever he was doing. He never said, 'Well, Jackie's arriving tonight,' or anything like that. So I said to them, 'Guess who's coming to dinner—it must be Jackie.' They were all getting off that day so I went to see them off and then I came back and about an hour later I looked out of my window and there was Jackie arriving . . ."

Joan Thring was sure there was nothing sexual between Onassis and Jackie then. "She was with me all the time. And she certainly wasn't sleeping in his room because first thing in the morning she used to ring me—there were two kitchens on the yacht, one was French and the other Greek—and she'd say, 'Oh, you must try scrambled egg from the Greeks this morning—it's delicious!' . . . They never behaved as if anything was going on. There were no endearments or touching or anything like that . . . I was absolutely convinced that nothing had gone on while we were there . . . I think in the afternoons they spent an hour or two together, and they were working out some sort of agreement . . . It was just all business talks and there weren't that many . . . Most of the time we were there he didn't even have lunch with us."[30]

On May 28 Jackie disembarked at St. Thomas. On that same day Bobby lost the Oregon primary to the first Democratic candidate in the field, Eugene McCarthy. No Kennedy had ever before lost a political election. The next day he flew south to California for the most important primary. At 12:15 A.M. on the morning of June 5, as he walked through the kitchen of the Ambassador Hotel in Los Angeles after announcing his victory in the ballot, another lone gunman, Sirhan Sirhan, shot him through the head. At that moment Jackie was asleep in bed in her New York apartment, having attended a rally for Bobby the previous evening with Ros Gilpatric. She was woken at four o'clock by Stas Radziwill, calling from London. " 'Isn't it wonderful?' she said to Stas. 'He's won—he's got California!' 'But how is he?' asked Stas. 'Oh, he's fine, he's won!' 'But how is he?' 'What do you mean?' 'Why, he's been shot.' "[31]

Ros Gilpatric heard the news on the radio almost simultaneously. He called Jackie, who asked him to come over. Stas Radziwill was catching the first available flight to New York. Gilpatric telephoned Tom Watson of IBM and arranged for him to lend his private jet; the pair of them accompanied Jackie to the airport to wait for Stas. Jackie was muttering desperately, "No! It can't have happened. It can't have happened. Tell me it hasn't happened." At Los Angeles they were met by Chuck Spalding. "What's the story?" Jackie asked him. "I want it straight from the shoulder." "He's dying."[32]

Two of Bobby's inner circle, Richard Goodwin and Ted Sorensen, had been in a suite upstairs at the hotel when the shooting happened. "The night Bobby was killed we were both at the Ambassador Hotel in L.A.," Goodwin remembered. "I was going to go down with Bobby but I was on the telephone or something and then I heard all this screaming in the corridor, and I ran into a room to sit and watch it on the television as it unfolded downstairs and they were talking about the fact that the Senator might be . . . and I had the immediate sense that Bobby was dead. And I looked across the room and there sitting on the opposite side of the bed was Ted Sorensen. I thought that was the most eerie thing in the world because we both knew that Bobby was dead, we knew he had to be dead, even though it hadn't been said yet. And we had both been through the other one . . ."[33]

But Bobby's heart was still beating, although there was no hope that he could be revived as a human being. He remained technically alive on a life-support system until 1:44 A.M. the next day, June 6. "Jackie was the one who turned off the machines," Richard Goodwin said. "She flew in and nobody else had the nerve. The poor guy was lying there, his chest going up and down—you know they have those machines that keep your body going forever—and he was brain dead and the doctors didn't dare pull the plug. Ethel was in no shape to do anything, she was lying on the bed moaning. Teddy was kneeling in prayer at the foot of the bed and finally Jackie came in and told the doctors they had to do it. It was the final seal for her."[34]

On Air Force One, carrying Bobby's body across the country to New York, Jackie appeared composed, calmly discussing plans for the funeral with Ethel. The service was held at St. Patrick's Cathedral. Lady Bird Johnson remembered the streets of New York as "a strange sight," lined with people who stood silent, motionless. Inside the cathedral it was Jackie, in black and heavily veiled as she had been at Jack's funeral, who stood out as if she were the widow, walking solemnly up the aisle with her children to take her place in the front row on the right-hand side with the Kennedy family. President Johnson caught sight of her and rose, as did the entire congregation. In contrast, Lady Bird noted, Ethel and her children slipped in quietly. After the service, Lady Bird found herself standing in front of Jackie. "I called her name and put out my hand," she wrote. "She looked at me as if from a great distance as though I were an apparition. I murmured some word of sorrow and walked on . . . It was somewhat bewildering."[35] Later, reflecting on the incident, she said, "I had the feeling that she must have been given a sedative . . ."[36]

On the funeral train down to Arlington later, Jackie again appeared to be playing the marble-widow part, as she had at Jack's funeral in 1963; she was described by one journalist, Pete Hamill, as "looking sort of icy." His companion, Shirley MacLaine, remembered: "The two women, Mrs. Ethel Kennedy and Mrs. Jackie Kennedy, came through [the train], Jackie first, very regal, as only she can be, with this marvelous sense of sort of anticipatory dignity. She was always able, somehow, to anticipate when the train was going to lurch or when it would bump, and queenlike, take hold of something so that, when the bump came, she wasn't disturbed or dislodged."[37] It was past nine at night when the cortège reached the resting place, close to Jack's, on the hill at Arlington. Candles held by hundreds of mourners lit the dark as, first, Ethel and her children, then the Kennedy sisters and their children, then Jackie, alone, followed by John and Caroline, knelt and kissed the coffin. It was all terribly reminiscent of that other day at Arlington, only four and a half years earlier, except that the scene was illuminated by a huge midsummer moon.

No sedative, however, could erase Jackie's pain for long. While after Jack's death she had managed to hang on to her self-control during the four days that followed, this renewed horror overwhelmed her with panic and loss. Bobby had been there for her when Jack died, now he would never be there again. Ros Gilpatric saw her shortly after her return to New York and was horrified. "After Bobby's death Jackie became alarmingly distraught," he said. "[She] seemed highly agitated, even unbalanced. Among other things she kept referring to Bobby as her husband. She became very imperious, barking orders as if she were still First Lady. It was as if Jackie could take one such tragedy, but not two."[38] While Ethel, pregnant with Bobby's last child, comforted herself with the Catholic idea that the husband she had worshipped would be in Paradise with Jack, Joe Jr. and Kathleen, Jackie could only rage against the fates.

However, there was one powerful figure to whom she could turn in Aristotle Onassis. Bobby's death, as Richard Goodwin had observed, was the final seal for Jackie on her life in America. "There was a terrible vacuum caused by Bobby's death," said William vanden Heuvel, Bobby's close friend and political aide. "It was the finality that wasn't really there with Jack's death. After the President's death, Robert Kennedy was left to survive and to lead the generations, to be *pater familias*, and to be extraordinarily helpful to Jackie and the children. His death removed such a vitally important part of everybody's life, and I think the violence of America in 1968, the Martin Luther King assassination and then Bobby's assassination two months later, the street riots, all of that, it was that kind of violent year and I think she was very anxious to protect the children. Onassis was a powerful figure in the sense of a man with enormous wealth, who could give what almost no government could give, which was privacy. Whether it was a yacht or an island, it was privacy—and also out of the United States."[39] After Bobby's death in Los Angeles, Jackie's subconscious instinct for self-preservation was as strong as it had been when she reached out for Clint Hill in the moments after Jack had been shot in Dallas. She had already been considering, as she always had at key points in her life, moving on to another plane. Now, just as she had with the Bouviers (but not as definitively), she was preparing to abandon the Kennedys to their shattered dream and their dangerous legacy.

Onassis, of course, immediately seized the opportunity presented by the death of Bobby, the principal obstacle to his marriage to Jackie. He flew to the United States to be with her. She took him down to Hyannis Port in June; Rose, the matriarch, had already met him a number of times on her travels abroad, in Paris or the South of France. Although she had as yet no inkling of his intentions toward Jackie, she did not share Bobby's antagonism toward him. "I liked him," she wrote. "He was pleasant, interesting, and, to take a Greek term, charismatic." Just over three months later, when Jackie telephoned to tell her she was going to marry Onassis, Rose encouraged her: "I told her to make her plans as she chose to do, and to go ahead with them with my loving good wishes."[40] When her daughter Kathleen had married a Protestant, then wished to marry a divorced man, the deeply religious Rose had threatened to cut her off. Onassis was also a non-Catholic (he was Greek Orthodox), and divorced. Rose did not turn a hair.

In this she was almost alone. Jackie had taken Onassis up to Hammersmith to introduce him to the Auchinclosses. In refined Newport he stuck out like a sore thumb. Janet thought him vulgar, not least for the way he was reported to have treated her while he was having an affair with Lee. Janet had been told that Lee was in a certain suite in a Paris hotel, and had been ushered upstairs. She walked in to find Onassis in his dressing gown. "Where's my daughter?" she asked stiffly. "Madame, she has just left," Onassis replied.[41]

"I think she was heartbroken by [Jackie's] marriage to Onassis," a friend and fellow trustee of Stratford Hall recalled. "We were at Stratford listening to a lecture after dinner when they came from the office and told Janet she had a telephone call. She was gone quite a while and when she came back she was ashen, and it was a telephone call from Jackie, telling her that she was going to marry Onassis two days later and wanting her mother to come to the island of whatever it was for the wedding. And we said, 'Oh, Janet, what's the problem?' And Janet said, 'It's not critical but it is a tragedy.' She was heartbroken by the marriage to Onassis and I think any mother in her circumstances would have been, because it was obviously not a deep love affair."[42]

Another person who loved Jackie was equally upset: André Meyer. Janet's view of Onassis had almost certainly been colored by his affair with Lee and the ungentlemanly way in which he had brazened out their first meeting. But Meyer knew Onassis far better: "He had great charm, great intelligence. *Great* intelligence. But he was rough, yacht or no yacht. And there was his reputation—with Callas and all that." Onassis called on Meyer as Jackie's financial adviser. "You know she's in love with me," he boasted reportedly. Meyer, hurt and upset but still concerned about his "little girl's" welfare, tried to persuade Jackie to let him negotiate a financial settlement for her.[43] To his chagrin, she refused. Jackie herself told Truman Capote that talk of a prenuptial contract with Onassis was "a lie." "I didn't make any premarital agreement with Ari," she said. "I know it's an old Greek custom, but I couldn't do it. I didn't want to barter myself."[44]

The sad fact is that history was repeating itself. She was in love with Onassis, as she had been with Kennedy, and was desperate to marry him. As before, she was giving herself to a man who regarded her principally as an asset rather than as a woman. But money was important to Jackie; she could not envisage a future without "big bucks," which was more than the Kennedys, with their annual $200,000, plus clothes allowance, would provide. Yet, for her, materialism had to be clothed in passion, with Onassis as with Jack. Sex appeal was part of the package, and Onassis, although physically ugly where Jack had been handsome, certainly possessed that. Ugly men have to try harder to win women, and Onassis had an international reputation as a lover. Gina Lollobrigida said of him that he was "a great lay."[45] Jack, having no need to, never bothered to try—Angie Dickinson is alleged to have said that sex with him lasted "seven and a half minutes."

A year later Meyer told Dorothy Schiff that "he had spent two weeks trying to persuade Jackie not to marry Onassis. He had tried to get a settlement for her but had failed because she flew over and married him suddenly. He said she wanted to marry Onassis more than Onassis wanted to marry Jackie. I think she did it," Schiff added, "in reaction to Bobby's death. She was shocked and in despair; the kind of support she was looking for was not what some say—money."[46]

There was another factor in the equation: Jackie's desire for freedom—her dream of being a bird flying away where she wished. She wanted to be free, emotionally and financially, from the hard-core Kennedys, free (temporarily at least) from the burden of being the slain hero's widow, the high priestess of the cult, whose behavior must conform to her worshippers' demands. And she wanted her children free of them too; free of the financial bonds that tied the heirs to the Kennedy fortune, free of the political legacy stemming from old Joe's ambition, the presidency of the United States.

The Kennedys, however, were not prepared to alienate Onassis, whose generous contributions to Bobby's campaign had not gone unnoticed. In August Teddy, representing the family and presumably also acting as a media "chaperone" to Jackie, left New York with her to visit Skorpios and cruise on the *Christina*. Onassis had issued the invitation on a second visit to Hyannis Port that summer. He returned to Greece and Maria Callas, only to order her off the yacht. "I want you to go to Paris and wait for me there," he told her.

"Go to Paris in August? Are you mad?"

"I'm having company and you can't be aboard." Anguished, Maria announced she was leaving him, after nine years of passion.[47]

Although Onassis had told Maria nothing, continuing to fly from Jackie in the

United States to her in Paris, and was still promising to see her in September, Callas was deeply suspicious of what was going on between him and Jackie. She had been told of their many telephone calls; she knew that George and Eleni, the couple in Onassis's Paris apartment, had been forbidden to leave their quarters one night when Onassis had served dinner himself to a mystery guest. Had Jackie known of the often brutal way in which Onassis had treated Callas, she might have paused before committing herself to him. In the Athens office he was known as "Megalo," the big boss; Maria herself used to refer to him as "my boss." Although her singing had brought her the fame that had originally made her desirable in his eyes, he hated opera, and would humiliate her, saying, "What are you? Nothing. You just have a whistle in your throat that no longer works."[48] Joan Thring described how on their return journey across the Atlantic, when she and Onassis indulged in a casual affair, they would sit together beside the pool flinging Callas's records into the ocean. "He was never nice about Callas. He said she used to drive him mad with practicing on the piano and doing scales and everything. He said it was awful, he hated it."[49] In Onassis's world, as in the Kennedys', women occupied an inferior position. "Business first, family after," he used to say. Jackie may have discounted Maria as a discarded mistress, but she underestimated the attraction Callas still held for him. Onassis would not have married Maria, but he could not leave her either. From the beginning their relationship cast a shadow over Jackie's marriage.

Jackie had one important ally against Callas in Onassis's older sister, Artemis Garofalidis. Just as she had sensed the importance of winning over old Joe Kennedy where Jack was concerned, so she had taken trouble to exercise her charm on Artemis, whom she had first met on the *Christina* in 1963. Artemis had never thought Callas a suitable partner for her adored brother, and had always worried at the thought he might marry her. But she was enthusiastically in favor of Jackie, whose celebrity would endow Onassis with even greater glory. She was also enchanted by her: Jackie was to find Artemis and, to a lesser extent, Onassis's half sisters, Merope and Kalliroi, warm, welcoming and supportive. Early in August Jackie visited Artemis at her villa at Glyfada, near Athens Airport, where she was to dine and spend the night. Artemis's house, at Vassileo Georgiou 35, was connected by a garden to a similar villa occupied by Onassis. He and his two children, Alexander and Christina, always ate their meals there, and Christina had an upstairs apartment there. In effect, Artemis's house was the family home in Athens. The roar of airplanes landing and taking off reverberated around the house, but none of the family seemed to mind: Onassis owned Olympic Airways, and the appalling noise was merely a reminder of his power.

Artemis Garofalidis was a small, slight woman, obsessed with fashion; on this evening when she entertained Jackie to dinner, alone except for Onassis's young secretary, Kiki Feroudi, she wore a long evening dress, loads of expensive jewelry and a great deal of makeup. She was seventy years old, two years older than her brother, and took enormous pains to conceal it. Jackie herself wore a short sleeveless dress, a single string of pearls and simple gold earrings. On her finger she wore a "beautiful" ring, which, to Feroudi, looked like an expensive one Onassis had recently ordered in Spain. "My first impression was that she was childlike, innocent and gentle," Feroudi wrote. "Yet even in that first moment, I glimpsed a sense of wisdom, of cleverness that was barely hidden in her simplicity."[50]

Back in America, Jackie was still encountering Kennedy opposition to her plans, albeit behind the scenes. Pressure had been brought to bear on the "family" Cardinal to dissuade her from marrying Onassis. After all, Onassis was divorced, and it was unlikely that the marriage would be approved by the Vatican. Cushing, however, suffering badly from emphysema (he had had a severe attack on Bobby's funeral train) and approaching retirement, received her with humanity and understanding, and told her that he would publicly support her—a decision for which he was later roundly condemned.

It was not long before the rumors started. Truman Capote already knew—Lee had called him, distraught. "How could she do this to me?" was her theme. She felt utterly betrayed; it was she, after all, who had asked Jackie on the *Christina* cruise nearly five years earlier and, for all her other affairs, Onassis had remained a prospect on her horizon. Now her sister had deprived her even of that. "She's crying and weeping and sobbing," Capote told friends. "I can't tell you what she said, but it's going to be in the news. It's the biggest piece of gossip there is, and she's crying her eyes out because of it." Again, according to Truman, Onassis tried to placate Lee with a highly desirable piece of property near Athens.[51] It was no consolation and she sold it as soon as she could. On the surface, Lee was too proud to show anything of the despair she felt and issued a supportive statement, but in reality Jackie's marriage to Onassis marked the beginning of the end of their closeness.

Jackie had only got away with it for so long because to most people a marriage between the sainted widow and the Greek tycoon seemed unthinkable. When Doris Lilly, gossip columnist of the *New York Post*, predicted it on a New York chat show, she was booed and jostled by Jackie fans denouncing her "garbage." Christina's friend, Marina Dodero, had an uncle and aunt who lived in the same apartment block as Jackie. "Every day they would see that a present arrived for Jackie from Van Cleef or Cartier or bouquets of flowers, every day, every day, and they knew it was from Mr. Onassis. So I said, 'I think there is a story going on between Jackie and Ari,' and everybody laughed . . ."[52] It was not until October 15 that the *Boston Herald-Traveller* announced that John F. Kennedy's widow and Aristotle Onassis were planning to marry soon.

The Kennedys, their worst fears confirmed, moved to limit the damage. Pierre Salinger, who was in England, was told by Stas on the day he left that Jackie was going to marry Onassis but not to tell anybody yet. "And then I came back to the U.S.A.," Salinger recalled, "and about four days later I got a call from Steve Smith, the husband of Jean Kennedy Smith, and he says, 'You've got to come to New York right now to see me because we've just discovered that Jackie is going to marry Ari Onassis and it's a disaster for the Kennedys.' And anyway, when he got me there he said that the Kennedy family were very, very unhappy that she was going to marry Ari Onassis. They thought that she should have stayed as the widow of JFK and then he said to me, 'Maybe you can play a role for me, though. We don't want the marriage to take place in the United States, we want the marriage to take place in Greece.'

"So what I did was, I wrote a long letter to Jackie telling her that I totally agreed with her, that she had the right to do anything she wanted to do with her life, including marry Ari Onassis . . . but then I ended up saying, '. . .but, Jackie, I think it would be intelligent if you did the marriage in Greece.' Jackie wrote me a letter and said, 'I really appreciated your letter and you were right and we are going to get married in Greece.' "[53]

Plans were made swiftly by Onassis's aides for a ceremony on Skorpios. On October 17 Nancy Tuckerman made an official announcement: "Mrs. Hugh D. Auchincloss has asked me to tell you that her daughter, Mrs. John F. Kennedy, is planning to marry Aristotle Onassis sometime next week. No place or date has been set for the moment." Two hours later an Olympic Airways flight, from which the scheduled passengers had been ejected at a moment's notice, took off with a party of eleven for a Greek air force base. Aboard were Jackie and her children, her mother and stepfather, Little Janet and her husband, Lewis Rutherfurd, a nanny and Secret Service agents, Jean Smith and Pat Lawford, with her daughter Sydney.

Public reaction was uniformly hostile worldwide, from top to bottom of the social spectrum. Everyone felt that Jackie had betrayed her husband's memory, demeaning herself by marrying a vulgar, foreign tycoon. Even people who knew Onassis found it difficult to accept. The Queen had abdicated. The Princess was marrying a toad. The Vatican denounced her as a sinner, who would be banned from taking the sacraments. The words of General de Gaulle, who had once held her up as "an example to the world of how to behave," were repeated throughout the beau monde. Observing Jackie's jet setting activities in 1966, the prescient statesman had pronounced, "After all, she is a star [not meant kindly] who will end up on some millionaire's yacht."[54] The marriage drew a rare joke from Mao Tse-tung: "If Mr. Khrushchev had died," he commented, "I doubt if Mr. Onassis would have married Mrs. Khrushchev." Onassis's comment on this last was significant: "Can you imagine?" he told Marina Dodero, a friend of his daughter Christina. "I wasn't known in China until marrying Jackie. She was my last diamond on my crown."[55]

The feelings of most people were expressed in the headline of a Stockholm newspaper: "JACKIE HOW COULD YOU?" One man in particular was enraged, as Onassis had intended he should be: Stavros Niarchos. "It nearly killed Niarchos, whatever he said, when Onassis married Jackie because that was a winner," a friend of Niarchos remembered. "What could he do? This was a winning shot."[56]

Most appalled of all were Alexander and Christina Onassis, his children by Tina. They hated Maria Callas as the cause of the breakup of their parents' marriage and, like many children of divorced parents, they had harbored the dream that Ari and Tina would remarry. Onassis, after all, made it no secret that he still loved Tina, still thought of her in some ways as his wife. The announcement of their father's imminent marriage to Jackie struck them like a thunderbolt.

Neither Alexander nor Christina was close to their father, who had little time for them—"Business before family." His massive ego and formidable rages made him a figure to be feared as much as loved. He took an intense Greek pride in Alexander, aged twenty and the eldest, as his son, but never hesitated to take out his moods or displeasure on him, laughing and embracing him at one moment, throwing things at him or even striking him across the face at another. Perhaps worse, he would belittle him in front of other people. Tina, Alexander's mother, was not close to Alexander, much as he loved her. A child when she was first married, she was pretty, spoiled, selfish and pleasure-loving, too busy living her own fast life to devote much attention to her son. He grew up quiet, withdrawn and shy, with an air of sadness. He worked for his father at Olympic Airways but his real interest was Olympic Aviation, the air taxi and charter service that Onassis gave him. No intellectual, he loved fast cars, boats and small planes, which he piloted himself. But his great love was a woman sixteen years older than himself, Fiona Thyssen (née Campbell-Walter, daughter of a British admiral), one of the great beauties of her time, a former debutante and model, divorced from Baron Heinrich Thyssen by whom she had two teenage children. Onassis disapproved intensely of the relationship but Alexander paid no attention to him. Neither did he pay any attention to his father's pleas that he make friends with Jackie, to whom he referred as "the American woman."

Their mutual dislike of Jackie drew the Onassis children closer together. Christina, two years younger than Alexander, was a sad figure, longing only for the approbation of her father, who largely ignored her. When Tina was pregnant with her daughter, Onassis had beaten her so savagely that there was blood on the carpet. He had been hoping to cause Tina to lose her child. Christina was born unwanted. While Alexander was handsome in his way, and attractive to women, Christina resembled her father rather than her pretty, slim, youthful mother. She had beautiful dark eyes and looked attractive or not, according to her mood swings. She suffered from depressions and a deep sense of being unloved, which resulted in binges of chocolate and Diet Coke.

A few days before the wedding both Onassis and Artemis made great efforts to bring the children around, without success. Onassis told Alexander and Christina how important it was to him that they liked Jackie, that she resembled his late mother, Penelope, with her wide-spaced dark eyes, that she was "nice and polite and honest, and that they would like her if they gave her a chance." After he had retired from Artemis's house defeated, she talked to the pair all night long in an effort to convince them about Jackie. They refused to listen, saying rudely that Artemis only "cared about this foreign woman and her children . . . they said that if I truly loved them, I would not love this woman . . . I do not know what I can do to help my brother's children love his wife."[57]

So it was in many ways an ill-assorted group that gathered in the tiny chapel of Panayitsa on Skorpios for the marriage of Jackie to Aristotle Onassis on the evening of October 20. The weather was chilly and wet. Apparently rain is a sign of luck at a Greek wedding, but did not appear so to the foreign guests, almost none of whom was deliriously happy about the match. Alexander and Christina were remarked for their "unhappy, angry faces"; they stood close together, whispering to each other. Hughdie Auchincloss escorted Jackie into the church, just as he had for her marriage to Jack Kennedy. Jackie was radiant in an ivory lace dress by Valentino, with ribbons in her long dark hair. Her bridegroom, three inches shorter than she was, wore a dark blue suit, with a red rose in his buttonhole. Artemis acted as sponsor throughout the forty-five-minute Greek Orthodox service with its carefully choreographed ritual. John and Caroline stood on each side of the couple, holding tall white candles, their faces serious and nervous. Their new stepfather had gone to great lengths to make friends with them but it must have been an unnerving experience, so soon after the tragic death of their beloved uncle Bobby, to be in an unknown place and listening to an incomprehensible language as they watched their mother take a new husband.

CHAPTER EIGHTEEN

"One Foolish Dream"

~

This was a marriage that included many moments of love and affection. I will not say that this love was strong enough to overwhelm catastrophic obstacles later placed in its path by the sad fates that ruled their lives . . .

—Kiki Feroudi Moutsatsos[1]

Whatever the feelings of the group at their marriage may have been, the newly-wed couple showed every sign of being in love. At the end of their honeymoon cruise on the *Christina*, Artemis and Kiki had prepared a special surprise for them: they had arranged that the entire first-class seating should be taken out and replaced by an enormous bed for the flight to New York. Shortly after takeoff, a cabin steward accidentally opened the curtains shutting off the compartment. Behind him Jackie and Ari, oblivious to everything else, were making passionate love.

The couple made no attempt to hide their physical attraction. Michael Bentley, then manager of Claridge's Hotel in London where they used to stay, remembered in the early years how they looked very much in love, sitting at a corner table in the restaurant holding hands, then they would go for a walk around Grosvenor Square, returning to tell him how happy they were that "in London everyone leaves us alone."[2] At times, according to Feroudi, they behaved "like teenagers, unable to keep their hands or lips off each other's bodies. Artemis would smile at me when they did that in front of her . . ."[3] They would have sex in all sorts of unconventional places, airplanes, small boats, the beach, regardless of who might be watching—or photographing. The brother of one of Jackie's Washington friends was shocked by the way Onassis would drag Jackie suddenly into any one of the cabins on the *Christina* and make love to her without bothering to shut the door. This sort of exhibitionism satisfied his ego—he would boast embarrassingly to Jackie's friends, like Pierre Salinger, of her sexual appetite and his own prowess in bed with her. Jackie went along with this, installing an extra large bed in the bedroom at Glyfada. On the *Christina* she appears not to have minded sleeping in the bed he had shared with Maria Callas for the past nine years. She did, however, have the huge portrait of Tina moved from its dominant position on the staircase before the wedding. She later confessed to Artemis that she realized that in many ways Ari still loved his first wife and that it upset her to see "that beautiful face."

It was not Tina, however, but Maria who posed the threat. "Mr. Onassis went back to her directly," Marina Dodero said. "A few days after the wedding he was back in Paris whistling under Maria's window," Maria's friend Robert Sutherland wrote. "I've made a big mistake," he [Onassis] told her.[4] Maria never came again to Skorpios, but her apartment in Paris at 36 Avenue Georges Mandel was conveniently close to the Onassis apartment at 88 Avenue Foch. According to the staff of both apartments, Onassis and Maria appeared closer and happier together now than they had been before his marriage to Jackie, but Onassis, for once, did what he could to conceal his frequent rendezvous with Maria. He warned her to switch off the lights at the entrance to her apartment when he was due, so that no one could see him arriving, and he arranged to see her through his aide, Miltos Yiannacopoulos, and never, at least during these first years, called her directly. Artemis was sure that he was doing what he could not to embarrass or upset Jackie: "He may not be faithful," she said, "but he is considerate and discreet."[5]

But Jackie, Artemis suspected, was aware of her husband's continuing affair with Callas, and was hurt by it. Once again, she was not number one in her husband's life; once again she was unable to obtain from a man she loved the total devotion and love she had had from Black Jack. For all the satisfactory, frequent sex, the kissing and touching, the little endearments—"honey," "my darling"—the surprise presents and romantic notes, there was an element of unreality in their marriage. "Aristo," as she and the rest of his Greek family and friends called him, treated her like a princess, a beautiful, fragile porcelain doll. She was kept away from his business affairs, except for one occasion about a month after her marriage when she was present at a dinner to impress the dictator Papadopoulos, a key figure on Onassis's Project Omega. "It would bore you, honey," he said, just as Jack had not wanted to discuss the political issues of the day with her. With Maria, it was different. No one who saw them together at this time thought that Onassis went to her only for sex. "Their relationship went beyond sex," Feroudi said. "He needed her to discuss his problems, his innermost thoughts and feelings. Had Jackie been able to assume that role, perhaps he would not have craved Maria. I do not know why he went to Maria so often. All I know for certain is that he went."[6]

In reality Jackie was psychologically terribly wounded by the traumas of the past five years and the deaths of Jack and Bobby. The assassination at Dallas was a recurring ever-present nightmare for her, which she would recount to people as though by telling these terrible details she could somehow exorcise them. As the fifth anniversary of the assassination came around, not long after her wedding, she was alone on Skorpios with Artemis and noticeably sad. When Artemis asked her what was wrong, she burst into tears, explaining, "I'm having a very bad day. I know I should be happy now, but all I can think about is my first husband and what happened to him in Texas. Sometimes I think I will never be able to be truly happy again."[7]

"She was," said the daughter of a close friend of Onassis's, who met her for the first time shortly after the marriage, "truly a deeply shattered person. And I think that anyone who saw her and observed her closely beyond the witticisms, beyond the charm—because there was undoubtedly a charisma and a radiancy and all of that—there was somebody who had been absolutely shocked. How could it be any different? She spoke to me of the assassination, of how she felt during it, immediately afterward, what it was like coming back to the White House in that state. And I remember when I first saw her there were two things that struck me. Physically the image which one saw in photographs corresponded absolutely to what one saw. But what one doesn't see in photographs was that her face was entirely labored by these tiny crack marks everywhere. She was like a piece of glass that had been shattered and put together. Like crackle glaze on porcelain. I don't know whether she would in any case have become like that—I'm not a dermatologist—but it struck me because it was such a contrast to the wide-eyed, radiant, flawless look. And that, I don't know why, but to me it meant something. It was almost like the only sign, the outward sign of what she had gone through.

"The other thing was the extreme tenderness with which she—we were having dinner and my son was then a tiny little boy younger than her own son. And she said, 'Oh, shall we go and see him?' And I said, 'Well, you know he's in bed, he's asleep.' And she went down and I remember she knelt by the bed and sat there with her hand on this little sleeping body. And really she was a very true person at that moment. Not putting anything on."[8]

In Greece, and particularly on Skorpios, Jackie finally had the freedom to be herself—in so far as she ever could be. She could never really escape being "Jackie," the image and the persona: "She herself was aware of the public person, the public image, she had become," a Greek friend said. But she tried hard to immerse herself in her new Greek life and her new role as a Greek wife. She learned Greek and insisted that John and Caroline learn it also. She was taught how to dance the *syrtaki* by Athens antique dealer Costas Haritakis, and bought old Greek silver objects from him. She studied Greek history and art, and spent hours discussing Greek literature with one of Onassis's closest personal friends and associates, Professor Yiannis Georgakis, who would also search for books for her. She visited museums and ancient sites with her new friend, Niki Goulandris, director of the Natural History Museum, and shopped for antiques with her in Monastiraki in the old quarter of Athens. Her knowledge of Greek archaeological sites was profound enough to impress Robert Pounder, professor of Classics at Vassar. Meeting her at a party given by the Schlesingers some twenty years later, he was struck by "how much she knew about Greece, contemporary Greece and Greek archaeology. We discussed the excavations at Samothrace. She had all the landscape and excavations in her memory . . ."[9]

She enjoyed the presents Onassis lavished on her, the diamond bracelets wrapped in her breakfast napkin, the romantic notes inviting her to dinner, the nights they tangoed together on the dance floor above the swimming pool. She did not know—but Callas did—that many of the objects had once been given by Onassis to Maria and had been left in the Glyfada safe when Maria had stormed off the *Christina* for the last time. Gore Vidal remembers a conversation he had with Callas in Rome, soon after Jackie and Onassis were married: "She was getting ready to make *Medea*. And Pasolini was there [but] all she wanted to talk about was Jackie. Very funny about her. The jewelry that Jackie had got: 'I know those jewels, they're nothing, they're second-rate except the ruby earrings are quite good. I remember those and I almost took them but they really weren't right for me.' The rest of it, she said, was just trash. Then she said, 'But of course, she wouldn't know the difference, would she?' "[10]

Jackie's main preoccupation in the early months of her marriage was the decoration of the Pink House on Skorpios, in which Onassis encouraged her. "Skorpios is a beautiful island," a Greek friend, who helped her with the Pink House, said. "Very, very beautiful. Very lush, very green, very idyllic. It's really an Ionian island, very different from the Aegean. There was an old house from the beginning of the nineteenth century which was more or less abandoned, not derelict but abandoned. Ari had had his house built on the top of the hill for all the obvious reasons but in a way he didn't live there, his home was his boat, the *Christina* . . . So when he married Jackie she decided, quite rightly, to make the old house her house."[11] Jackie employed several decorators, her old acquaintance from New York, Billy Baldwin, whose work Onassis apparently considered too New York for a Greek island, the brilliant Milanese designer, Renzo Mongiardino, who had decorated Lee's country house, Turville Grange, and Bunny Mellon's interior designer, Paul J. Leonard, who, as he put it, helped her "fluff up" the island. Jackie was constantly changing the decoration and moving the furniture about, just as she had in Georgetown. She tackled the gardens around the house and the landscaping on Skorpios itself, driving around in her red jeep inspecting the work in progress.

Some of the workers on the island were resistant to Jackie's changes, accusing her of wanting to remove all traces of her husband's past. "Look at these stones," one gardener protested as he dug them out. "I remember the day when Winston Churchill's feet touched these stones. Should I take them and throw them into the ocean just because Mrs. Jackie doesn't think they're good enough to touch? Nothing is good enough for her. Soon not even Mr. Onassis will be good enough for her."[12] Other Onassis employees who resented her as the new wife were either dismissed or left of their own accord. On the whole, however, Jackie was loved by her Greek staff, whom she treated with a consideration to which they were unaccustomed.

Onassis was happy to indulge Jackie over the Pink House, and willingly paid large bills for imported furniture and local artifacts but he would not allow her to touch the *Christina*, which he regarded as his domain. He preferred to eat his meals and sleep on the yacht, rather than in the house.

Jackie really preferred the simplicity of the Pink House to the yacht's opulence, which she found a touch vulgar. She particularly disliked sitting on the bar stools, upholstered in a whale's scrotum (and Onassis's earthy joke: he asked women if they enjoyed sitting on the largest balls in the world) or resting her feet on the footstools made of polished whale's tooth. When, however, she suggested they might be reupholstered there was a storm, and Jackie, who always avoided a confrontation if possible, immediately backed down. Artemis warned her that Onassis loved every single thing on the *Christina*, which he had personally chosen, and that it would not be wise for her to criticize anything. So she learned to live with the ostentatious marble balustrades on the staircase, the huge living room with its lapis-lazuli fireplace, and Vertès mural of the four seasons, which depicted Tina, Alexander and Christina, the two El Grecos and valuable jade Buddha. The main bar, with the infamous whaleskin stools, was decorated with scenes from the *Odyssey*. There was a playroom hung with tapestries depicting fairy tales, a hospital, a movie theater, and a swimming pool decorated with mosaics, whose floor could be raised to form a dance floor—Jackie irreverently referred to it as "the bathtub." The nine guest suites were named after Greek Islands: Ithaki, Mykonos, Lesbos, Andros, Chios, Santorini, Crete, Rhodes and Corfu; each had marble bathrooms and gold fittings. The master suite consisted of four rooms on the bridge deck. Jackie and Onassis always slept together in the main bedroom; his bathroom had a sunken blue marble bath surrounded by a reproduction of a mosaic of fish in the Palace of Knossos and eighteenth-century Venetian mirrors. There were two chefs, one specializing in Greek food and one in French. The menus were always ordered by Onassis, never by Jackie. The *Christina* was his kingdom. Sitting by the pool, dressed in short-sleeved shirt and baggy pants, smoking a huge cigar, a glass of *ouzo* by his side, he ran his empire, linked to it by telephones operated by a special communications expert who could connect him to anywhere in the world.

It was a curiously rootless life for Jackie, who was often left alone in the Pink House on Skorpios when Onassis flew off on business to Monte Carlo or to Paris, where he combined business deals with trysts with Maria. Or she would spend a few days at Artemis's villa at Glyfada. Beyond Artemis, Niki Goulandris and Professor Georgakis and his daughter, Chloe, she had few Greek friends. According to one, "She had no real life in Greece and not a circle of friends so she naturally turned to things which were interesting, to looking at places, seeing places, to archaeology, to art, whatever anyone with any sense would do. She wasn't interested in Athenian 'social life' and who could blame her? Onassis' circle was strictly a business circle. He actually didn't have a Greek social life either, Aristo. He'd have his business things and he'd go out at night to unwind . . . That wedding came at a funny time for Aristo because he'd lived all those years in a long-lasting relationship with Maria Callas, and there they certainly had, Maria and he, a circle of friends, Costa Gratsos, old friends of Ari's, not particularly of Maria's, but whom she had met and befriended. There was that life on board. When he married Jackie I think this in a way had changed. There were no big parties, just Aristo and Jackie and I, it was very tranquil. Our days were very, very quiet. We read, we walked, we went swimming, we used to go across to Corfu to find things for the house. I thought the best thing one could do was to get her to see things which were disappearing. So I took her to places in Attica, which I felt were still unspoiled, or we used to go to various islands. We went to Rhodes, to Lindos, to see the various houses there and walk up to the old temple or into the country, or Patmos where there were friends like Teddy Millington-Drake."[13]

Teddy Millington-Drake, the artist, and his friend, the designer John Stefanidis, had a house on Patmos, which was often featured in smart design magazines. Jackie and Lee, who happened to be staying with her, were eager to see it and were invited to lunch. The visit was somewhat marred by the late arrival of Jackie's helicopter; there was a fierce head wind and by the time they arrived Teddy and his party, including Lulu de la Falaise and Bruce Chatwin, had "eaten all there was to eat and drunk all there was to drink. And we arrived in a house full of corpses," one of Jackie's party remembered.[14] In an effort to preserve Jackie's privacy, Teddy had confined all the maids to the house so they wouldn't tell the villagers. "They [Jackie and Lee] went up to the deserted monastery and as they were looking around a cruise ship had arrived full of American tourists who shouted, 'Is that her?' 'No, can't be her.' Then a shout went up, 'It's Jackie!' They ran into the church and chased her down the hill taking photographs and yelling, 'But we love you, Jackie!' "[15]

The Onassis compound at Glyfada was not exactly the sort of setting to which Jackie had been accustomed. The Glyfada villas were "typical of Athenian bourgeois taste," according to a friend. "There were two of them because there was a sort of family plot and Onassis's sister took care of him, his real sister, Artemis, the others are half sisters . . . He was very fond of all of them but, I mean, she was really his blood sister and older than Ari, and very protective toward him, and would have given her life for him. She was always there on call, whatever time of day or night, ready with that extraordinarily warm and hospitable side. But— apart from that—Artemis was not intellectual, she had no conversation, she was there as the great family woman and held things together and took care of his house, which was next door. To Jackie, Artemis was very warm, and very loving and very welcoming because basically she wanted her brother to be happy and, of course, Jackie's glamour again was something that impressed Artemis. And I think Jackie found it all a bit . . . not what she was used to . . ."[16]

Damaris, Lady Stewart, wife of the British ambassador in Athens, Sir Michael Stewart, described the Onassis Glyfada villas as "appalling, of no taste or interest whatsoever." Invited by Jackie to lunch there with Artemis, Lady Stewart had the impression that Jackie had nothing to do with the running of the houses. "When I went to lunch with her he [Onassis] was having a lunch in the next-door house, because the food was coming backward and forward across the lawn . . . When we got to the pudding stage—it was a sort of bought chocolate cake—we had half, the other half had presumably gone there . . . My superficial impression," Lady Stewart went on, "was that she was bored and didn't feel in any way at home. I don't think she was terribly happy in Athens. She never actually said that she wasn't—to anyone I knew or to me—I just thought that she was switched off. It was a mystery to me why she married him—they appeared to have nothing in common. He was a very powerful figure, not attractive in a sense that you and I would think attractive but nevertheless attractive in his magnetic personality. Michael [the ambassador] saw much more of him than I did, with Yiannis Gorgakis, his right-hand man. They'd come to dinner and then they'd say they were going to a nightclub and he'd go and break plates even though the colonels [the Greek junta] didn't allow it. He was allowed to, though . . . He'd stay up to three or four and then I'm told he'd be up again by half past six or seven working."[17]

On one occasion, Jackie and Onassis went to an informal dinner party at the British embassy. The writer Patrick Leigh Fermor was there and Yiannis Georgakis, whom Leigh Fermor described as Onassis's "rather brilliant and not so *grise* eminence":

> "I sat next to Jackie and was fascinated by her," he remembered. "Her face was somehow rather wildly put together, eyes very wide apart but captivating and unusual. Her voice was so quiet it was almost a coo: 'Oh, yaiss . . .' She reminded me faintly of a sort of quiet, intelligent and beautiful-mannered little girl, the sort that wants to please and wins all hearts . . . Onassis, opposite, seemed the acme of boisterous vigor and much nicer than I had imagined he would be . . . there was a great feeling of cheerful interruptions and laughter. Later, after coffee and more delicious drinks, I remember Onassis, Yanni and I singing some very out-of-date Athens music-hall songs, the older the better, and illustrating dance steps by demonstration and even joining hands on shoulders, proving proficiency and concord in the extraordinarily elaborate hesitating and suddenly speeding-up evolution said to have first seen the light in the penumbra of the hashish-smoking dens of Smyrna . . . Jackie later wrote to Damaris [Stewart] that she had never seen an embassy turned into a wild Albanian brigand's cave before . . ."[18]

Not all the Onassis circle, however, was warm and welcoming. Quite apart from Alexander and Christina, who remained bitterly hostile to Jackie, there was Costa Gratsos, one of Onassis's oldest friends and a devoted partisan of both Maria and Christina. Gratsos had been unequivocal in his denunciation of Ari's proposed marriage to Jackie. "He felt that Jackie was just an adventuress, that she'd got him for the money and therefore he disliked her and was quite open about it," said a member of the Onassis circle. "I think he didn't see that she could be anything but trouble for Ari. And she came between them in a way—not wittingly, but this was an old friendship, and whereas he used to see Ari a great deal, for a time they didn't speak. Costa himself came from an old shipping family."[19] As Jackie's spell over Onassis faded, so Costa's influence grew, as he worked on his friend's atavistically superstitious nature.

Alexander and Christina were irreconcilable and Jackie made little effort to win them over. "I will never sleep in the same house as that American woman," Alexander told his father's secretary, even before the wedding. The moment she had arrived, he had his things sent to the Hilton, where he subsequently maintained a suite. "Since my father married, I have no home," he said.[20] Usually when Jackie arrived in Glyfada or on Skorpios, Alexander left immediately. On the rare occasions that he did stay, he made his feelings plain. Once when Jackie was lunching at Glyfada with Onassis, Artemis and Kiki Feroudi, Alexander refused to join them. Onassis left the table several times to try to persuade him to come down and eat with them, returning without him and angrier than ever. Finally Alexander came down and sat at the table but picked at his food and said not a word. Jackie continued to behave normally, smiling and enjoying her lunch, appearing not to notice her stepson's hostile behavior.[21] Onassis's efforts to improve relations only seemed to make things worse: once when he was about to leave with Jackie for New York, he told her to wait while he went off to find Alexander to come and say good-bye to her. After fifteen minutes, Jackie, increasingly nervous, dispatched Kiki Feroudi to fetch him because they were going to miss their flight. Feroudi overheard Alexander flatly refusing to do what his father wanted. Jackie was furious and her usual self-control deserted her. "I was surprised when Mrs. Jackie said, 'I do not know why your children are so rude to me.' Usually she was so careful in the way she treated her husband. 'I have done nothing to deserve such rude treatment.'

" 'Worry only about your own children, not mine, my dear,' he told her nastily, as he walked so fast to the plane that there was no way she could keep up with his pace."[22]

Alexander even forbade his driver to let her use his car. Jackie was under no illusions about the depth of his hostility, and became angry and alarmed when she overheard her husband discussing with Miltos Yiannacopoulos who should manage his property in the event of his death. The suggestion was that Alexander should take charge of everything. "Jackie kept looking up at her husband and tried to get his attention, but he refused to look at her. It was obvious to anyone who saw her face that she was not pleased with what he was saying. However, her husband continued walking and talking as if she were not there . . . Finally Jackie got up from her seat looking quite angry now, and left the deck . . ."[23]

Alexander's reaction to Jackie was relatively calm compared with Christina's. "Christina resented her terribly because Christina herself had had an impossible childhood," a family friend said. "Because of that, her father meant a great deal to her . . . She was a completely neurotic girl, hanging on to everything which could give her some sort of security . . . She would have resented anyone because she was too insecure herself. She was much younger than me, Christina, but I remember Ari asking me once if I could try and take her out to lunch, get her to meet younger people so that she would have more of a life in Athens. Because she hadn't grown up in Greece . . . So I organized a small lunch party and she came to pick me up from home—she was in her car but I couldn't see her. And the driver opened the door and she was lying there absolutely terrified that anybody would see her. Now, for a young girl of eighteen this shows that she was constantly in a state of huge distress. I mean that girl was not all right. Ari was not a good father at all but she was doubly unfortunate because the tradition is that the father's the one who takes care of the business, takes care of the money, that provides and it's the mother that brings up the children, and in a way her mother was quite incapable of bringing up her children. Tina was never what Jackie was to her children."[24] Christina was terrified of her father at the same time as longing for his approbation. "He inspired so much fear," Marina Dodero said. "One day he said, 'Christina, come and sit down here.' And he shouted so much at her, and then he said, 'You can go.' And she was grown-up and she said, 'No. Daddy, I can't get up,' and he shouted, 'Go on, get up.' And she had peed on herself because she was so afraid."[25] When she was thin, Christina was a very pretty girl, with large dark eyes, delicate wrists and ankles, but when she became particularly depressed, her weight yo-yoed. Jackie, with her slim elegance, was a constant reproach to her, even had she not appeared as a threat to take her father away from her. And while, at the beginning, Onassis was hugely generous to Jackie, he had always been mean with Christina. Once when a telex arrived at the Athens office announcing the imminent arrival of a fur coat for Jackie from New York, Christina pounced on it, screaming and yelling about Jackie, and ripped the telex to shreds. She made no secret of her hatred for her stepmother, to whom she referred sarcastically as "Kyria" or "Madame," and would make fun of her behind her back.

As Kiki Feroudi Moutsatsos wrote,

> When Christina called to speak to Alexander or went into his office to speak to him, they always spoke about their father, discussing his moods and his plans. They liked to know exactly where he was and with whom and for how long. But when the two of them started to discuss Jackie, their voices changed. They were no longer concerned, loving children; they were scheming, unhappy stepchildren. If anything, their dislike for Jackie drew them closer together, as she was the common enemy they both wanted to defeat. So often, they spoke of the time when Jackie and their father would separate, always keeping hope alive in each other.[26]

Artemis was upset that Jackie seemed not to care about the situation or about either of her stepchildren. In contrast, Onassis made considerable efforts to get on with Caroline and John, and to see that they enjoyed themselves. He seemed delighted when they arrived to spend vacations on Skorpios, canceled business meetings so that he could spend time with them, took them for walks and for rides in his speedboat. He bought a white pony for Caroline, and took John with him to Athens so that he could go to the movies. Despite their dislike of Jackie, Alexander and Christina, too, were fond of her children, played with them and took them for speedboat rides. When Caroline and John were in Skorpios they would even break their rule and have dinner with the family, studiously ignoring Jackie. "Ari was very sweet to the children when they were young," Marina Dodero remembered. "Particularly to John. Caroline was more aloof, not liking him. I felt she would sulk a bit. To have had a very good-looking father who was

President of the United States and then to see this man short and Greek and loud . . ."27

Caroline and John remained Jackie's principal preoccupation. "She was always terribly mindful of the children," a Greek friend said. "I remember there was always this thing of looking at things that would be of interest, could be of interest to the children, editing them out, cutting things out, having them done for the children."28 Increasingly, Jackie's divided loyalties placed a strain on her marriage. She always put the children first.

Just before her marriage, Jackie had finally found someone who could be to the children what Maud Shaw had been in their lives, a rock, someone who would always be there with them and for them. The talent scout, as she had been for Maud Shaw, was Janet Auchincloss. In Washington Janet had encountered Marta Sgubin, a young Italian girl who looked after the children of a French diplomatic couple, named Gaussens, and spoke fluent French. Marta was also involved in helping with receptions given by the couple in their Washington diplomatic career. When the Gaussens had moved back to Paris, Marta received a letter asking if she would like to work with the Kennedy family. Later, a month before she married Onassis, Jackie wrote again, suggesting they meet. Marta was interviewed in Paris, first by Onassis and then, in July 1969, by Jackie. She agreed to join the children in late summer in Newport, where they were staying with their grandmother. As John F. Kennedy Jr. wrote:

> When I was eight years old and my sister was eleven, we were introduced to our new governess while staying at my grandmother's house during the summer. Her name was Marta, and I was told that she didn't speak English. That made me immediately suspicious because I'd heard this before about the other bilingual au pairs who had helped care for us. It was part of my mother's tireless effort to get my sister and me to learn French. But after a few weeks they'd break down and . . . we'd say a tearful good-bye (in English) and wait for the next one to appear. Marta broke down and started speaking English after about twenty-four hours, and thirty years later she is still part of our family . . .29

Marta progressed from being governess to the children, to companion and cook-housekeeper to Jackie, remaining with her until the end.

That first year, 1969, Jackie was so preoccupied with her life with her new husband that she left John and Caroline in the charge of Janet and Marta. It was Marta who had to take John on his first day to his new school, Collegiate, and both the children on their after-school activities like playing in Central Park. Weekends were spent with their grandmother back in Newport. It was only several weekends later that Jackie arrived. It was a jet set life for the children and Marta; the *Christina* was based at Puerto Rico and they would fly down for weekends to cruise around the Caribbean before returning to New York for school.

Easter vacations might be on the *Christina* at Palm Beach, or on Skorpios. They always spent a month and a half of the summer vacation on Skorpios, where the main event was Jackie's birthday on July 28. For her fortieth birthday, in the first year of her marriage, Onassis gave a party for her at his favorite *bouzoukia*, the Neraida, and loaded her with jewelry. There were the famous moon earrings, made and designed for her by the Athens jeweler Ilias Lalounis, commemorating the Apollo space landing on the moon, which cost him over $500,000; a huge forty-carat diamond ring from Cartier, $740,000 (with Onassis's usual 30 percent discount); and a gold belt with a lion's head as a clasp, for her astrological sign, Leo. The ring was hugely ostentatious and awkward to wear as it covered the knuckle, making it difficult for Jackie to bend her finger. She did not wear it often; her large hands were not her best feature, and this ring seemed designed to draw attention to them.

To please Jackie, Onassis frequently invited Rose to join them on the *Christina*—three times during the first year of their marriage. Jack's death had removed all cause for jealousy between Jackie and her former mother-in-law, and both women had come to appreciate the other through their shared experience of marriage to Kennedy men. "Jackie said to me at some point, much later," Doris Kearns Goodwin said, "and I'm sure that to some extent that was reflecting her own experience with Jack, that she came to have great respect for what Rose had endured. And not only with the deaths but with the whole way of life with Joe, and that she came to feel greater empathy toward Rose than Joe . . . She talked about that balance shifting over time."[30] Teddy Kennedy also came often, escorting his mother. The Kennedy sisters were never invited.

⌒

Meanwhile, back in the United States, the Kennedy legend was crumbling. Jackie's marriage to Onassis had been a serious blow, but what happened on the night of July 18, 1969, ten days before Jackie's fortieth birthday, was far, far worse. Earlier that year, after witnessing Teddy Kennedy's bizarre drunken performance on an overnight airplane flight, a journalist had described him as "an accident waiting to happen." On July 18 on the tiny island of Chappaquiddick off Martha's Vineyard, Teddy was returning from a party on the island and drove his 1967 Oldsmobile off the Dike Bridge, drowning his passenger, a Kennedy "boiler-room girl," Mary Jo Kopechne. The whole incident, bad as it was, was made worse by his inexplicable behavior. He stumbled back to the cottage where the party was being held but instead of calling the rescue services he enlisted his cousin Joe Gargan to dive with him to the submerged car. When they failed to rescue Miss Kopechne, he swam the narrow creek dividing Chappaquiddick from Martha's Vineyard, returned to his hotel, made a 2:30 A.M. appearance in the lobby, then retired to his room where he made seventeen telephone calls, none of which were to the police.

In the morning, after having made small talk with guests about the regatta due to start that day, he took the ferry back to Chappaquiddick where he learned that the body had been found. Only then did he make his report. At Hyannis Port he went into a huddle with the old Kennedy hands, McNamara, Burke Marshall, Richard Goodwin, Ted Sorensen and others. He drafted and delivered a statement to the police a week after the accident. Attempts to represent him as having made heroic efforts to rescue the girl by "diving into the strong and murky current," and speculations about "some awful curse" hanging over the Kennedys (later used as a frequent excuse for reckless family behavior), had the opposite effect. The circumstances surrounding the accident were never fully explained, but evidence showed that poor Mary Jo's head had been in an air bubble and she might have been rescued if prompt action had been taken. The words "panic," "cowardice" and "cover-up" were bandied about. In a hideous reversal of the PT-109 incident, Teddy Kennedy's actions, or lack of them, had cost the life of his friend instead of saving it. Shortly afterward his wife Joan had a miscarriage. At the Kennedy compound, the younger children were running wild in a gang known as the HPTs—the Hyannis Port Terrors—led by Bobby Jr.

In the senior Kennedy house, the patriarch, grandfather Joe, was dying. Once the head of the family, the ultimate authority symbol, he lay in bed wasting away, almost blind, his vocal cords no longer functioning. Just before the sixth anniversary of Jack's assassination, Jackie was alerted that the end could not be far away and flew in from Greece. She spent hours in the old man's room, soothing him with a soft monologue and kept vigil all night, sleeping fitfully in a chair, with Teddy in a sleeping bag on the floor. On the morning of November 18, he died. Had they been ancient Greeks, the Kennedys would have attributed his long, lingering death to hubris, the sin of overwhelming human pride that the gods would inevitably punish. His grandson Chris Lawford reflected, "It made me wonder what my grandfather could have done for God to do this to him."[31] In years soon to come, Jackie's new husband, Aristotle Onassis, would be punished for the same sin and in much the same manner.

CHAPTER NINETEEN

The Curse of the House of Onassis

∼

Where have you brought me—and to what a house! The house of Atreus . . .
a house God hates . . . !

—Aeschylus, *Agamemnon*

On February 10, 1970, Jackie's old Washington bugbear Maxine Cheshire reported that four of Jackie's letters to Ros Gilpatric, written between 1963 and 1968, had mysteriously surfaced and were to be sold at the Hamilton Galleries. Snippets of text were published. Two of the earlier letters were merely short thank-you notes, the others were long and affectionate. One, dated June 13, 1963, thanking Ros for a "slim volume," was couched in the intimate, flirtatious style that Jackie used in letters to her men friends. The last had been written while on her honeymoon with Onassis, again in the most affectionate terms:

> Dearest Ros, I would have told you before I left [about her forthcom-
> ing marriage to Onassis]—but everything happened so much more
> quickly than I'd planned.
> I saw somewhere what you had said [wishing her happiness] and I
> was very touched—dear Ros—I hope you know all you are and ever
> will be to me—with my love, Jackie.[1]

The way in which the news broke, and its timing, caused a sensation. The autograph dealer Charles Hamilton revealed that "Mr. Gilpatric sounded as if he were weeping when he called. His voice was shaking and he was concerned that the sale, if it went through, would ruin his friendship with Mrs. Onassis." Coincidentally, Gilpatric's estranged third wife, Madelin, chose that day to file for divorce but denied that the letters could have had anything to do with it. Nancy Tuckerman was forced to issue a press statement denying that Jackie was involved in the break up of Gilpatric's marriage but Mrs. Gilpatric undid the good work by being quoted as telling the *Chicago Daily News* that her husband and Jackie were "very, very close," adding, "I have my own feelings about that but I won't go into them. Just say it was a particularly warm, close, long-lasting relationship."[2]

Onassis could discount Jackie's friendship with Gilpatric, which was not exactly unknown to him (her Yucatán trip with him in March 1968 had been extensively reported in the press), but his Greek male pride was offended by his new wife having sat down on their honeymoon to write warm notes to another man. Nor did he like the publicity, which he saw as reflecting badly on him. He is said to have told Costa Gratsos, "My God, what a fool I have made of myself."[3]

In a deliberate show of tit-for-tat, he dropped his discretion where Callas was concerned. He spent four successive evenings with her in May and was seen leaving her apartment at one o'clock in the morning. On May 21 he was photographed dining with her, and her friend, Maggie van Zuylen, at Maxim's. Alerted by Artemis, Jackie flew to Paris to take Maria's place. Johnny Meyer, Onassis's fixer and trouble-shooter, was ordered to ensure that photographers caught the scene. From Maxim's, Jackie and Onassis went on to Régine's nightclub. The message from Jackie to Maria was clear: I'm his wife, I'm number one. Distraught at being used once again, Callas spent three sleepless nights and accidentally overdosed on sleeping tablets. She successfully sued a radio station and a Paris weekly for alleging that she had attempted suicide. It was now impossible for Jackie to pretend that her husband was not with his mistress whenever her back was turned or that he was using Callas to keep her in line. On August 15, Maria's name day, an important celebration in Greece, Onassis flew by helicopter to the Embiricos's private island of Tragonisi, where Maria was a guest, to present her with antique earrings and a lingering kiss on the mouth, which was caught by a paparazzo whom he had undoubtedly alerted beforehand. Once again Jackie's response was immediate and public, so much so that it made the pages of *Time*: "Responding like a Dalmatian to the firebell," the magazine reported, "Jackie flew to Greece, to Onassis, to the yacht *Christina*, and to squelch rumors."

Jackie's marriage to Onassis was not in trouble—yet—but the strains underlay it. Onassis was still beguiled by Jackie who, when in Greece, was prepared to act like a Greek wife. Some of her habits irritated him—her constant smoking of L & M's, her habitual lateness. However, unlike Jack Kennedy, he did not hang around: Onassis left when he was scheduled to leave—with or without Jackie, even if it meant she would have to stay on Skorpios until the following day and miss whatever engagement they had. She submitted to his tirades like an obedient child: "Yes, Ari," was all she would say.

"It was amazing the way she knew how to behave around her husband," Kiki Feroudi Moutsatsos said. "She treated him with so much respect and admiration when he was in charge. Yet when it was her turn to be in control, she fussed over him and cared about nothing except his pleasure . . ."[4] She attuned herself to his moods, letting his angry shouting pass, leaving him alone, never speaking to him when he was quiet and obviously didn't want to talk. It was a delicate balancing act that became less and less rewarding.

Onassis was proud of her, of her beauty and her taste, the impeccable way she ran her households, but he was not cut out for the delicate minuets he had to dance with Jackie. At heart he was a night owl, a drinker, a plate-breaker, happier on the banquettes of his favorite haunts, El Morocco or Régine's, happiest of all on an all-night carouse in a Piraeus *bouzoukia* with an old Greek friend. She was a rococo indulgence, like the Louis XV *boiserie* which she had picked out in a New York antique store for the Avenue Foch apartment but which was never installed. Onassis refused to let her change all but one small room of the gloomily grandiose Paris apartment. He became bored with her feyness and fantasy, her need for reassurance and admiration, contrasting it with Maria's wholehearted passion. "It wasn't that he didn't like Jackie," Marina Dodero said. "How can I put it? They were so different, there was nothing, there was nothing there . . . But with Maria Callas, he was in love with Maria Callas, they had this thing in common, this is what Christina told me, they were both self-made people . . . They would get into a room on a Friday and not come out until Monday because they had a little kitchenette. She would sing, cook, throw spaghetti at him, they used to fight like crazy, they were temperamental . . ."[5]

For the first two years at least, despite Maria, the Onassis marriage went well; but as things began to go wrong in his business and private life, darker shadows than his mistress fell across their happiness. From early 1969 Onassis was engaged in a deadly duel with his detested rival, Stavros Niarchos, who was threatening to scupper Project Omega by offering the Greek junta a larger investment package, provided he and not Onassis was awarded the contract to build a third oil refinery for the government. Since his marriage to Jackie, Onassis seemed to have lost his phenomenal skills in putting together a deal and single-mindedly pursuing an objective. He attempted to bring in the American aluminum company, Alcoa, to finance the refinery, carrying on the negotiations himself—badly. "After his marriage he just lost all his sense of proportion," an Alcoa executive told Onassis's biographer, Peter Evans. "His must-win mentality tipped over into pure megalomania. His terms were not terms, they were commandments. You couldn't reason with the guy. He seemed to think that we'd agree to just about anything for an invitation to dine with him and Jackie aboard the *Christina*."[6] In the end, the dictators divided the spoils between the two, but disillusionment with Onassis was beginning to set in, even with his patron, Papadopoulos. "It was kind of sad," an official involved with Project Omega said. "He was a dinosaur. It was all over for him. The conviction began to grow even on Papadopoulos that everything Ari now touched was going to be a mess, a disaster . . ."[7]

On May 3, 1970, the first in a series of family deaths, which were to darken the rest of Onassis's life, occurred when his former sister-in-law, Eugenie Niarchos, took her life on her husband's private island of Spetsopoula. The reason, ostensibly, was her despair on finding out that Stavros had invited his former wife, Charlotte Ford (they had been divorced in 1967), and their daughter Elena to come over that summer. (Another version is that Niarchos invited Henry Ford and Charlotte to lunch.) Eugenie, a gentle woman whom everyone loved, took an overdose. Mystery surrounded her death; her body was found covered with bruises, which Niarchos claimed were a result of his and his valet's unsuccessful attempts to revive her. "I'm certain he didn't kill her," said a Niarchos intimate. "He might have done if he'd been on his own, but as he was with the valet, he certainly didn't. I think he was trying to get her right . . ."[8] Onassis, probably for his own reasons, believed Niarchos had killed her; to his disappointment, the matter was dropped.

Onassis's business with the colonels went from bad to worse: failing to get Alcoa to invest in Omega, he attempted to woo the Russians, thus infuriating the U.S. government who got back at him the following year. At the same time he seemed to be losing control of his family. In July 1971 Christina, aged nineteen, for whom he had planned a suitable marriage with Greek shipping heir Peter Goulandris, married Joseph Bolker, a forty-eight-year-old California-based real estate dealer, without telling her father. Onassis was celebrating Jackie's forty-second birthday on Skorpios when the news came through of the Las Vegas marriage. Peter Beard, the rich, handsome explorer and wildlife photographer, whom Jackie had met in 1967, was staying on Skorpios when Onassis heard the news: "I can tell you the shite has hit the fan over Christina's brilliant job of attracting attention in Las Vegas (nuptials with a Liberace . . . ?), which has got Ari so volcanic & up tight it's not true—Lee Radziwill's guests fled, 2 others were canceled & it is strictly tensionsville—I hang about as the court jester & divert his maj with such pranks as (yesterday) winning $2000 bet staying underwater for over 4 minutes, breaking my ankle on an Olympic trampoline he has set into concrete & bagging stitches in my lip . . ."[9]

Christina's marriage to Bolker outraged Onassis because he saw it as an act of defiance against his rights over her as a father. (In February 1972, after months of pressure, Christina and Bolker were divorced amicably.) To him it was a symptom of his loss of control in other areas. In October, after a visit by Vice President, Spiro T. Agnew, who was of Greek descent, the colonels definitively dumped Onassis and Project Omega. That month he suffered a blow that hit him personally and left him reeling: eighteen months after Eugenie's death, Niarchos married his former wife, Tina, in Paris on October 22. Illogically, although the divorce from Tina had been the direct result of his open adultery with Maria Callas, the failure of his marriage had hurt. To him Tina was always his true wife and the mother of his children; he had been offended when she had married "Sunny," Marquess of Blandford, heir to the Duke of Marlborough, but he saw, probably correctly, Tina's marriage to Niarchos as her last act of revenge for his own marriage to Jackie.

The whole story was intricate, semi-incestuous and very Greek. Tina's mother, Arietta Livanos, adored Stavros Niarchos and actually applauded the wedding between Niarchos—who by his behavior had contributed to if not actually caused the death of her eldest daughter Eugenie—to her youngest daughter, Tina. More complicated still was the fact that Tina and Stavros had been having an affair before Eugenie died. "Everybody knows that they had a story when the sister was alive," Marina Dodero said. "Not openly. But when Eugenie died we [Christina and Marina] went to Blenheim [actually Lee Place nearby] and Tina was all dressed in black, black lace, and she was wearing a double necklace of rubies and diamonds, and she said, 'Look what Stavros gave me . . .'" If Onassis was shocked, Christina and Alexander were even more so. There was now no hope that their parents would remarry, and their mother had married their father's greatest enemy. According to Marina, Alexander told Tina when she married Niarchos, " 'You'll never see me again, only dead.' And she never saw him again, only dead . . ."[10]

Early the following year there were more deaths: the Kouris brothers, two of the Onassis family's favored pilots, lost their lives in a mysterious crash of Onassis's Lear jet off Nice. It was the maiden flight of the new private jet; the pilots were supposed to leave Athens for Nice where they were to pick up Alexander and fly him to Paris. Five minutes before they were due to land in Nice, the plane crashed into the sea. Neither of the pilots' bodies nor a single piece of the jet was ever recovered. The Onassis entourage believed that there had been an explosion on board the plane and that Alexander had been the intended victim. A search was to be organized with the help of Jacques Cousteau, the underwater expert; mysteriously it was called off on Onassis's orders. When Onassis's friend and lawyer Stelio Papadimitriou asked him whether he was worried by the potential cost, Onassis exploded, "Of course not! Are you crazy to think of such a thing? I will not risk my son's life for anything. Do not ask any further questions. This matter is closed."[11] Alexander and his friends became convinced that Onassis was afraid of something, that he had received threats against Alexander's life if he delved too far into the accident. He had made many enemies in his business career, most recently in his dealings with certain members of the Greek junta. In the jungle that lay beneath the surface of Onassis's millionaire trappings, there were no rules beyond kill or be killed. Just the previous year, Fiona von Thyssen had found evidence by accident that in his efforts to separate Christina from Bolker, Ari had been contemplating using thugs "to do a number" on Bolker and frighten him off. For Onassis, nothing and no one was off limits.

Jackie's marriage was gradually falling apart. Once she had finished decorating the Pink House there was less and less for her to do in Greece. For her, Skorpios was now not so much the fantasy isle where she lived out her dream with Onassis, more a place to which she went out of duty and to take her children on vacation. As the terrible events of the sixties faded, New York and real life began to take over.

In her early years with Onassis Jackie had seen little of her old friends. It seemed to them that she was slightly ashamed of her marriage. She saw more of the Radziwills and Lee in particular than anyone else, despite the background rivalry. Onassis, after all, was Stas's boss, despite or perhaps because of "Princess's" relationship with him. "He didn't mind," a friend said of Stas, "he was almost a professional brother-in-law."[12] Christmas with the Radziwills continued to be a family tradition, but now it was normally spent at their English country house,

Turville Grange. The children acted a nativity play just as they always had, the main difference being that instead of a playful, handsome Jack to watch them, they had their swarthy stepfather. To Harry Ashcombe, a fellow guest, Jackie appeared "slightly nervous with Onassis. At that particular time I think she was nervous . . . and I think there was one night when she wanted to unload her problems on me because I used to have a sympathetic face, but I didn't play the game because it would embarrass me . . ."

In the winter of 1970 Ashcombe saw them again. When the *Christina* arrived off Barbados in the winter of 1970, he had Jackie and the children stay. Stas, Lee and their children were there too. "He [Onassis] and Jackie arrived by the *Christina* and then went off on this damn boat. He hated being on land, he just wanted to be on the boat. Jackie, I think, liked to be on land." Ashcombe went by speedboat with Jackie and Onassis to visit the Club Méditerranée in Guadeloupe. "That was the only time I saw her not deliberately annoying Onassis but it did irritate him because she did like to be seen around and a lot of people came up to her and that sort of thing." Asked what the relationship was like then, Ashcombe replied, "A bit edgy . . . but I liked Ari—so much better than Niarchos, given a choice of the two. He was a peasant, really. He liked getting very, very drunk with the sailors. Sitting in bars drinking masses and masses of ouzo or something. From that point he was rather attractive but I do think he was probably an absolute shit." Jackie he said "was very good with the children."[13] The photographer Peter Beard had been invited to Skorpios primarily to amuse them. "She was a gutsy mother, very gutsy mother," Beard remembered. "That's the thing I admired in her most. Everything in life is priorities. They were her first major priority."[14] Caroline and John, he said, were "ideal little children, little rebels, imaginative, artistic, funny. We used to have a lot of good times." Jackie was never an overprotective mother; she encouraged Peter Beard to lead them in diving off the highest part of the *Christina*— "It's a long way down, I'm telling you that," he said. "But she thought they were in good enough hands. She allowed taking chances." She also let him take them off on adventure expeditions without her. "John was such a great mimic and such a good little actor, I couldn't believe it," Peter Beard recalled. "His speciality was Mick Jagger—singing, dancing, talking. The best I ever saw. One winter I took John and Caroline to the Everglades, where reporters would follow us around, practically into the swamp. Early one morning, as we were leaving the hotel to go on a snakehunt, we went right past this reporter who'd been on our trail for days without getting a single picture and had finally fallen asleep in frustration in the lobby, and John just spontaneously started doing 'Jumpin' Jack Flash.' The reporter woke up to this amazing act, and while he was reaching for his camera John turned around and did his Mick Jagger walk-off and that was that. The poor guy never got the shot."[15]

On Skorpios and the *Christina*, Beard observed, "Jackie did a lot for Ari and Ari was constantly complaining . . . I saw the biggest fights between them. He would blow up all the time—tantrums about everything. Yelling and screaming at her . . . what Ari hated most was any kind of mess. I remember once we had all gotten haircuts on the *Christina* from Marta, the very nice governess. And Ari was stomping around the deck, just exploding with anger at the fact that these little hairs were in the bathroom—John and I hid in the shower bath. When he was mad at Jackie he used to say how he'd given up 'an artistic cultural international background' for 'this American.' She [Jackie] was a rebel, quietly against Ari."[16] Jackie, Beard thought, was a "person hiding from in-depth experiences in life," and he, too, noticed that her face was heavily wrinkled. She would refuse to look beneath the surface of life because it was too painful to contemplate—the reality of her life in the past and the reality of the present. "She was on the surface of life, trying to remain there."[17]

One reality that Jackie appeared not to notice was that Lee and Peter were beginning an affair right there on Skorpios under Stas's nose. Asked about the Lee–Jackie relationship, Beard said, "All the older sister, younger sister cliché . . . Jackie the classic responsible older sister, Lee the rebellious younger one. Lots of loyalty, lots of bad things."[18] Peter Beard was sleeping with Lee, but he shared much in common with Jackie, an interest in art and photography. He was famous for his huge albums of collages, which Jackie enjoyed. Jackie herself was a keen photographer—"We took so many photographs on Skorpios that Onassis never stopped complaining about the 'photographic bills,'" Beard said. "She did fantastic scrapbooks too—huge ones."[19] They were also discussing a book Beard was to do, *Longing for Darkness*, based on tales from Karen Blixen's *Out of Africa*, retold by Kamante, Blixen's Kikuyu cook who, since her death, had been living on Beard's Hog Ranch in Kenya.

Beard hoped to publish *Longing for Darkness* with his old friend Steven M. L. Aronson, the co-publisher of Harcourt Brace Jovanovich. But Aronson was reluctant to proceed without the guarantee of a lengthy introduction by Jackie, which Beard was dangling. In order to "nail it," he prevailed upon Aronson to write him a rhapsodic letter about the project, which he could use for leverage with Jackie. "She lapped it all up," Beard reported back, to the point where she was extending an invitation to Aronson to join them on the *Christina* for further discussions—the visit was derailed by the Bolker explosion.

Eighteen months later, when Beard was living at Montauk, Long Island, in Andy Warhol's house with Lee, Jackie sat down to write the foreword she had promised: "What an extraordinary surprise and gift it was, when Peter Beard first showed me the fables and drawings of Isak Dinesen's beloved Kamante . . . To hold his drawings was like touching a talisman that took you back to a world you thought had disappeared forever . . ."[20] She wrote in a careful, beautiful, almost childlike hand, at Montauk, on June 1, 1972. With this she was beginning to take tentative steps toward a new, more realistic and satisfying future, toward America where her Greek life would fade like a fantastic dream.

⌒

For his part, Onassis's record with women was of getting bored with them and he was getting bored with Jackie, who increasingly was getting on his nerves. He resented her increasingly frequent and prolonged trips to America to see the children or to attend Kennedy functions, when as a Greek wife, his faithful Penelope, she should be sitting at home waiting for him. Even Artemis complained of her behavior: "I wish she would be more of a Greek wife," she said. "Jackie is not doing so well to leave Aristo and go to New York for weeks at a time. It is not good for the Greek family to be separated like that. One should not go to one place and the other to somewhere different. A Greek man and his wife should stay together as much as possible."[21]

Onassis himself began to complain about Jackie to his Greek friends and, naturally, to Maria Callas. She was never with him, she was cold, she spent too much money. Even sexually now he found her dull. "He called Callas and he told her, 'I'm just a babysitter for this woman. I have to sit and wait and wait for this woman.' He also said that going to bed with her was like going to bed with a corpse," Gore Vidal recalled, of a conversation with Callas about 'The Gold-digger,' as she always called Jackie.[22] Onassis complained about Jackie to old mutual friends, too, like Benno Graziani. "He complained about her very much," Graziani said. "He complained to me about the money and everything. And about her coldness to him . . . She was cold with him. At the beginning no, but after she understood that he was nothing to do with her . . ."[23]

They were the same complaints that Jackie had heard during the bad years with Jack, coldness and spending—above all, spending. "Both sisters were brought up like geishas," Gore Vidal said, "to get money out of men."[24]

Just as he had with Callas, Onassis began to humiliate Jackie publicly. Her capacity to "tune out" irritated him as much as it had Jack Kennedy. One rainy evening in Glyfada, Kiki Feroudi witnessed a typical scene. Onassis and his friends Miltos Yiannacopoulos and Yiannis Georgakis had been talking to each other all evening while Jackie sat opposite them, silent, reading a book about Socrates. Finally, she put down the book to ask Yiannis Georgakis whether he thought that Socrates had really existed or whether he had been an invention of Plato to represent the Athenian philosophers. As Georgakis began to answer seriously, Onassis jumped up from the sofa and began to scream at Jackie: " 'What is the matter with you? Why do you have to talk about such stupid things? Don't you ever stop to think before you open your mouth? Have you ever noticed the statue of a man with a mustache that is in the center of Athens? Are you too stupid to know that is a statue of Socrates?' "[25]

Jackie, in tears, whispering to herself in French to make sure that if she was overheard she would be understood, went upstairs, came down wearing a raincoat and walked out. Onassis even refused to bring Jackie in out of the rain himself but ordered Yiannacopoulos to do so. Without saying a word, Jackie came in, walked upstairs, expressionless, returned and sat down silently beside Gorgakis. Onassis did not say one word of apology but sat back muttering about "idiotic conversations" and closed his eyes. His form of apology was an expensive gold bracelet, from Athens jeweler Zolotas, that he gave her some days later. In Kiki's opinion, he had "acted like a true Greek man who liked to scream and say whatever he wanted. For her part, Mrs. Onassis acted like a true Greek wife . . ."[26] In fact, Jackie had won the battle without saying a word, with enormous self-control and an actress's sense of how to steal a scene. Silent withdrawal, as she had learned with Jack, was one of her most potent weapons. Far from being "a true Greek wife," she was a quiet rebel.

Onassis simply did not know how to deal with her, and the great publicity coup he thought he had achieved in marrying her had turned sour. Since everybody believed that she had only married him for his money, the reports of her spending—real and exaggerated—made him look like a sucker. Her devotion was to her children, her real life in America, and not in Greece, or even Paris, with him. "The little bird who requires her freedom," as he had once described her to the press, was, now that her broken wing had recovered, a strong-willed woman. He planned to reassert himself by divorcing her and by making sure that she would not get away with a large slice of the Onassis fortune. In October 1972, Jackie celebrated their fourth wedding anniversary with a lavish party in New York. Meanwhile her husband had already laid his plans and in November he sprang his first trap for Jackie. That month he presented her with a legal document for signature. It was entitled "Mutual Waiver and Release." It had been drawn up by his lawyer and taken to Jackie's apartment by the lawyer's notaries who witnessed her signature. Under the terms of the waiver, the document stated that in return for $2 million in bonds which Onassis had given her as a wedding present and other things with which he had hitherto presented her, she thereby waived and released every claim she might possibly have to inherit anything from his estate. The document also stated, "Each party declares that he or she had been represented by independent counsel in the negotiation and execution of this agreement," which was false. Only Onassis's lawyers were involved in this; Jackie had not consulted anybody. While she believed the document effectively waived any legal right she had to inherit, she also believed Onassis's representations that it was simply a matter of business and that he would make adequate provision for her. However, as it was, the document had no legal validity and could not affect Jackie's right to inherit a one-eighth share of Onassis's property under Greek law. As it turned out, this document was merely the first stage in the saga: her husband was planning to use his influence with the junta to have the law changed in order to legitimize the waiver and thus deprive her of her statutory rights. Just under three years later, when Jackie's lawyers were shown the document, which Onassis had tricked her into signing, they were appalled.[27]

Two months later, Ari contacted the infamous Roy Cohn, an unscrupulous lawyer who had every reason to hate the Kennedys, with a view to collecting evidence for a divorce from Jackie. Cohn told Onassis's biographer that "Onassis had definitely concluded that he wanted to break the marriage and had been consulting his Greek lawyers . . . and that there were a lot of complications over there, and he wanted to know whether I would be prepared to handle the American end, because he had assets over here, and to participate in the overall strategy . . ." He complained about her spending and that she was always where he didn't want her to be. The marriage, he said, had become "a monthly presentation of bills."[28]

Onassis had already thought of bugging 1040, and had ordered Johnny Meyer to arrange it, but the continued presence there of the children's Secret Service agents apparently made carrying out the monitoring of Jackie's telephone conversations too difficult. He also told Meyer to have round-the-clock surveillance by private detectives on his wife in an attempt to get evidence. It was pointless: despite his provocations and his visits to Maria, Jackie was not carrying on an affair.

The idea of divorcing Jackie, of showing her and the world who was boss, and depriving her of access to any of his fortune, became an obsession with Onassis. He was in his seventies and aging. To Jackie, Onassis appeared to be cracking up in front of her. His son, Alexander, with whom he was constantly at loggerheads, either over his ambitions for Olympic or his relationship with Fiona Thyssen, taped his telephone conversations with his father. One revealed Onassis, drunk, calling from New York croaking out "Singin' In The Rain" with a medley of oaths, inanities, orders and complaints. "It's two o'clock in the afternoon over there," Alexander commented, "and he's completely drunk out of his mind."[29] Sexually, he was no longer the man he had been. "He [Onassis] was horrid to all his women in the end. He was horrid to Tina. He was horrid to Callas," said Reinaldo Herrera, a friend of both Jackie and Onassis, who had been Tina's lover before her divorce. "I think it was a sign of impotence, you see. I know he was impotent with Tina. I'm sure she [Jackie] was very unhappy, just as Tina was very unhappy, just as that woman he had before [Ingeborg Dedichen] was unhappy, just like Callas was desperately unhappy. And I think it all happened because there was a sexual thing there that didn't work. For a man I understand that being very frustrating and wanting to blame somebody for it rather than himself."[30] Again, just as she had with Jack, Jackie began to taunt Onassis, saying biting things in her own inimitable way, although rarely in public.

By the New Year of 1973 Ari was prepared to tell Alexander the news his son longed to hear. He was planning to divorce Jackie. The two men dined together on January 3; later that month Onassis flew back to New York to rejoin Jackie. Jackie, as it was soon to be revealed, knew of the divorce discussions, although no figures had been put forward. Her experience with the "waiver" had no doubt unnerved her. Onassis kept her in the dark.

Alexander, however, did not tell his father of his plans to marry Fiona Thyssen, but returned to Athens delighted, as he told her about his father's plans to "divorce the Widow." On January 22 he was at the controls of the elderly Piaggio which, he had told his father, was a "deathtrap," on what was to be a training flight for the pilot, who was to take the plane to Miami to be sold. Seconds after takeoff, the plane hit the runway, leaving Alexander with irreversible brain damage. Jackie and Onassis were in New York when they heard the news. Onassis immediately summoned the two best neurosurgeons in the world, one from Boston and one from London, and flew to Athens with Jackie. Fiona had been in London for her brother's wedding, which Alexander had originally been expected to attend. Christina was in Brazil. Tina and Stavros Niarchos were in St. Moritz.

As family and friends gathered at the Athens hospital where Alexander lay in a deep coma, his face shattered and the right side of his brain a pulp, Jackie "did something so shocking that I can't talk to you about it," according to one of those present. "It showed Jackie's insensitivity, her hard side. She approached Fiona Thyssen, sitting waiting frozen with grief; Fiona Thyssen thought Jackie was about to offer her sympathy. Instead, knowing that Alexander told Fiona everything, she asked her if she knew what Ari was proposing to offer her as a divorce settlement."[31] Taken aback, Baroness Thyssen replied that that was a question she should ask her husband.[32]

Money alone had not been behind Jackie's marriage to Onassis, but the knowledge that he could give her and her children financial freedom and independence in general, and from the Kennedys in particular, had been an important factor. Now, as the spell had gone from their relationship and Jackie knew that Onassis planned to rid himself of her—no doubt, as cheaply as he could—she was desperate to know what he had in mind. Nothing else can explain her crude approach to Fiona Thyssen at a time of such anguish. Jackie, of course, could only experience the anguish by proxy: Alexander had detested her and had been consistently rude to her. But his death was a tragedy for her also: it destroyed Onassis as a man and all semblance of a relationship between them.

"He was a shattered, shattered man," the daughter of one of his friends said. "I went to see him at the airport after Alexander's funeral. I remember all we could do was sort of hug each other."[33] Onassis did not want to bury Alexander, as if that would be too final. It was almost a month after the accident before he could bring himself to do so. Alexander was buried on Skorpios beside the tiny church in which his father had married Jackie.

Onassis remained inconsolable. Shortly after Alexander's funeral, Christina and Marina Dodero went to Skorpios to be with Onassis. "He put us on the boat, the *Christina*," Marina remembered, "and I would see a light every night and I told Christina, 'There's a light, I'm sure it's your father.' And she said, 'No, you know my father.' And I said to her, 'Come with me,' and we went in one of those little cars, and in the light of the cars—you would come up three steps and go in the little church, and there he was, crying. So I told him that I believed very much in God and what happens afterward and I said to him, 'Don't cry and have peace. You will see him again, you will meet somewhere.' And he said, 'No, my son is here, he is dead, and I don't believe what you are saying . . .' "[34]

CHAPTER TWENTY

Greek Labyrinth

~

O what a tangled web we weave, when first we practice to deceive!
—Sir Walter Scott, *Marmion*

In the immediate aftermath of Alexander's death, Jackie and her husband were close again, as his anguish awakened her compassion. Forty-eight hours after the disaster, Jackie called Pierre Salinger in Paris where he had just joined the staff of *L'Express*. "She said, 'Boy, do I need help, Peter, right now,'" Salinger remembered. "I said, 'What is it?' and she said, 'Well, Ari's son just got killed in a plane crash and he's in a very bad mood. We're going to take a cruise across the Atlantic and I'd like you very much to come because I know you could talk to Ari and get him into a better mood.'"[1] The other old friend whom Jackie called was Solange de la Bruyère: "Ari was in a dreadful state, and Jackie called me and said, 'I think the only thing to do is to get him on a boat because he loves that, and he's drinking too much. Will you join us on a cruise? Go from Dakar to Guadeloupe?' And she really sounded as if she needed me, I was quite busy at that time, but I dropped everything and I went ... On board the Olympic Airways plane that had been made empty for us were the Salingers—Pierre and [his third wife] Nicole—and Felix Mirando who was a great friend of Bobby's."[2]

The eleven-day crossing was rough. While Jackie read from the mountain of books she had brought with her, Solange recalled, "Ari was in very bad shape. He was drinking a great, great deal. He had just lost his son, you know, and he paced the deck and mumbled to himself—it was terrible." On board all they could do to cheer him was play poker and talk. He spent the nights discussing American history and politics with Salinger, pacing up and down the deck arguing. "The point of the trip was to cheer him up, and I think we did that," Nicole Salinger said. "His mood improved. Of course he was a man who was very badly wounded. You could *feel* he was . . . The trip was a distraction for him, and it was good for him to have someone like Pierre along . . . They went on for hours and hours, pacing up and down the deck, talking and arguing. Jackie was very thoughtful and protective of Ari and her idea of inviting Pierre was perfect."[3] On one occasion the guests dined ashore because Jackie and Onassis had made it clear that they wanted to be alone together. "When we came back," Solange said, "it was wonderful to see the two of them dining downstairs in a very romantic setting. It was a touching scene. But afterward he turned . . ."

After the cruise, Jackie and Onassis returned to Skorpios, where they were joined by Christina and Marina. "On the island there were three days that Jackie was there when we were there," Marina remembered. "People can like her or not like her but she was a very impressive woman." Then Onassis took the girls to Paris to stay with him at the Avenue Foch apartment. "He took us to Maxim's every night, always the same table, always the same menu, and would dance with us one after another."

Immersed in his immediate grief, Onassis did not strike out at Jackie but the tensions between them had resurfaced by the time Jackie arranged another cruise in the Caribbean for Easter 1973, inviting Lee and her children, Alan Jay Lerner's wife, Karen, and Jay Mellon, a friend of Peter Beard and Lee. "There were all sorts of friction on board when I was there," Jay Mellon recalled. "One would want to do one thing and the other would want to do something else. And then one day we got down to Harbor Island down in the Bahamas. The girls wanted to go ashore and go shopping and look at the town and the boat was anchored about, I'd say, four hundred meters off the shore. It was the nearest we could get—that boat drew about twenty-five feet of water and the Bahamas are shallow—and Ari said, 'No, no, we're not going ashore, we're staying on the ship.' And Jackie said, 'Oh, come on, please let's go ashore.' And she got crankier and crankier and, I'm not kidding you, this is what happened. She got into her bathing suit and suddenly there was a splash and she just jumped overboard and just swam to the shore and that was that . . . And here he was in front of fifty Greek sailors with this woman who was the biggest catch in the world and he could not be talked down to in the presence of these people by this woman—you know it would have been a loss of face. He always gave the orders—he said, 'Now we're going to do this,' and she'd say something and he'd say, 'No, no, no, not now.' He always [tried to keep] the dominant position like this because he felt he had to do that or everybody on the ship would be talking and saying, 'This American woman is running Ari now.' He was used to being the boss of every single thing in his life. And here was this woman who was also used to being the boss of every single thing in her life, plus also she was an American woman with a much more liberated personality than a Greek woman . . . No, they didn't get along very well, there was chafing all the time . . ."[4]

"When he was being really awful she never complained about him," Karen

Lerner said. "He called her Mummy. She made this big scrapbook for him about Ulysses but it was Ari, a huge, huge thing. Someone on the ship said that when she gave that to him, this incredible work with her drawings and poetry that she'd written and Greek quotations, he said, 'Oh, that's very nice, Mummy,' and then put it right underneath the table . . ."

Despite her quiet acts of rebellion, Jackie continued to put on a brave face to the world. She could not publicly admit that her marriage was failing, so she was prepared to put up with a great deal from Onassis, pretending that nothing was wrong. On that Easter cruise of 1973 Jackie and Karen Lerner had lunched with the Wrightsmans before boarding the yacht. Jackie was questioning the Wrightsmans about the New York doctor whom Onassis was to consult. "Ari joined us the next days," Karen recalled. "He flew back to New York for a couple of day trips from the *Christina* but he was more or less with us for a week. He used to tell really obscene jokes at the dinner table, I mean filthy jokes, truck driver jokes . . . She would just say, 'Oh, Ari!' "[5]

At his worst Onassis would be publicly hostile toward Jackie. Aileen Mehle, the society columnist "Suzy," recounted the scene at Gemini, the Loel Guinnesses' house in Florida when Jackie and Ari and the children came to lunch from the *Christina*. Gloria Guinness, a permanent fixture on the list of the world's best-dressed women, was dressed as "a ravishing gypsy," while her husband Loel was impeccable in navy blazer and cravat. It was no surprise to see Onassis looking rumpled as usual but Jackie had obviously "been to hell and back": "She wore no makeup, an unbecoming cotton dress and an odd cotton scarf tied at four corners completely covering her hair. Assured of an audience, Onassis turned on her: 'Look at you,' he shouted. 'How can you be seen looking like that? You don't see Gloria and Aileen in that kind of get-up. What *is* your problem?' For a moment a look of hurt and sadness crossed Jackie's face, then she deflected the situation. She smiled brightly, 'Yes, don't they look great?' and calmly asked Loel if he would give John a ride in his helicopter that afternoon. After lunch, at which Ari had behaved boisterously, drinking a great deal of red wine, he stumbled onto the beach and slept, curled up in a fetal position."[6]

Meanwhile the Radziwill marriage, too, was breaking up. Lee had fallen in love with Peter Beard, and by early 1973 had decided to turn her back on Stas and England and return to the United States and a new life. In March 1973 Stas, anguished by Lee's abandonment and by what he saw as his friend Peter Beard's betrayal, began divorce proceedings. "Why did Princess leave?" he would ask plaintively. In the same year, his friend and business partner Felix Fenston died and the property market, in which Stas was heavily involved, crashed. This, combined with the Radziwills' extravagant way of life, left him balancing precariously on the edge of bankruptcy and facing an expensive divorce. The breakup of his family, which was to be made final in 1974, signaled the beginning of the end for him. Turville Grange, his beloved country house, decorated at the height of expensive taste by Lee and Mongiardino, had to be sold. The children were divided: Tina was sent to live with her mother in America while Stas kept custody of their son, Anthony. Jackie adored Stas and remained loyal to him. According to Lee's biographer, she did not mince her words as to her opinion of Lee's behavior.

Jackie's own position was becoming increasingly more untenable. Her husband, deeply superstitious, was beginning to believe the whispers circulating among his entourage, specifically from Christina and her principal ally Costa Gratsos, that Jackie was the bearer of bad luck. Even employees at Olympic Airways began to talk of Jackie as the cause of Alexander's death, *"atyhya,"* "the curse." Christina, if Onassis's secretary is to be believed, told her in dramatic terms: "I have always known that Jackie was a curse. Before she entered our family we were strong and well. Now the Kouris brothers are dead, my aunt Eugenie is dead, my brother is dead, Olympic Airways is slipping away and so is my father. Before she came to us, she was by her American husband's side when he died . . . Now the curse is a part of our family, and before long she will kill us all . . ."[7] She repeated this frequently to her father, who at first silenced her but eventually did not.

Gratsos, once again a close associate of Onassis and always Jackie's enemy, was bluntly obscene, using a horrible Greek phrase to describe her, of which "Black Widow" is the politest interpretation. Ari himself began to refer to her derisively as "the Widow"; when he sarcastically called her "Mummy," it was a reference to her affection for her children, which was intended to hurt. Nothing that Jackie or anyone else could do comforted him for the loss of Alexander, his grief compounded by guilt at his shortcomings as a father, or for the Greek sense of being punished by the fates, which was undermining his self-belief and his will to live. His behavior was increasingly morbid; night after night on Skorpios he would take a bottle of ouzo and two glasses up to Alexander's grave, pour one for himself and one for his son, and sit there crying and talking to Alexander. Or he would invite Jackie or Artemis and her husband to lunch beside the mausoleum, sitting at a table set with linen tablecloth, silver and glass, toasting his son.

At heart, Onassis did not hate Jackie. In his drunken states he would take out his frustration and rage on her, not just for what had happened but for what could never happen. He wanted her to be his Greek wife, at his beck and call as Callas had been. He resented her devotion to her children to the exclusion of his own wishes. He resented her Kennedy life, the constant reminders of her first husband, the anniversaries and the memorials; even, perhaps, while drinking pink champagne late at night with close women friends on the *Christina* that she would go over the assassination, again and again, making that arcing gesture to describe the trajectory of a piece of Jack's skull.

Although he and his clique liked to represent Jackie as "the Gold-digger" he had not, considering his wealth, been generous to her financially, apart from lavishing gifts upon her in the early days of their marriage. Jackie had refused Meyer's advice to draw up a prenuptial agreement. In marrying Onassis she had forfeited access to the Kennedy trusts and was, therefore, financially dependent on him, apart from the $2 million in bonds he had given her as a wedding present—hardly a fortune in his terms. Gifts of jewelry that she would wear were ostentatiously intended to enhance his reputation. She had no property of her own—apart from the Fifth Avenue apartment—and he refused to buy her a country house, which she had pressed him for. He retained checkbook power over her by paying her monthly bills for clothing and decoration, then complained of her extravagance, representing as "embezzlement" the fact that, as all rich and not so rich women do, she sold unwanted clothes to accumulate money to buy more without recourse to his financial control. For Onassis money, like Samson's hair, was the source of his power, which no one but he could touch. He liked to boast that he would die owning only the shirt on his back; nothing could be traced back to him through the complicated web of nominees, offshore funds and other tax dodges he had set up and whose details were in his head.

Intimations of mortality were all around him, even before Alexander's death had dealt him the ultimately fatal blow. His heavy drinking was limiting his capacity to function as a businessman, let alone as a husband. He was a sick man. He became more and more determined that Jackie, if she would not bend to his will in life, should not profit from his death. She should not have even what was hers under Greek law.

To further his aim Onassis took two definitive steps. He drafted a will in his own hand—to comply with Greek procedure. It was only the last of several that his lawyer, Stelio Papadimitriou, had been asked to draft over the previous year, and it was not a generous one, considering his wealth or that the marriage had already lasted five years, that Onassis had been unfaithful to his wife with Callas since the beginning and that Jackie had never paid him back in coin. Under its terms Jackie was to receive a lifetime income of $100,000 a year, with $25,000 each to John and Caroline until they reached the age of twenty-one, at which time the amounts were to be added to her income. In addition Jackie was to be given a 25 percent share in both the *Christina* and Skorpios in partnership with Christina, provided she bore the proportionate share of the not inconsiderable cost of upkeep. Should she choose to dispute the will, she would immediately forfeit her annuity, and Onassis's executors and his heirs were to fight her "through all possible legal means."[8] According to Papadimitriou, Onassis had been playing a game of asking him to draw up divorce writs again and again over the past two years, and Jackie was aware of this. She was not, however, aware of the existence or the terms of the will, which Onassis had not as yet signed, or, more important, of the further steps he was undertaking to nullify her rights to 12.5 percent of his total fortune under Greek law and validate the waiver she had so trustingly signed.

Onassis pocketed his will, unsigned, and left to join Jackie for New Year 1974 in Acapulco, the place where she and Jack had begun their honeymoon, just over twenty years before. If it had been planned by Jackie as a romantic trip, it turned out to be a disaster. On the return journey in their private jet, after a row over Jackie's plans to build a house in Acapulco, in which she told him a few unwelcome truths, he signed the will. Article 14 of the document specifically stated, "Any prior testament of mine is revoked by the present which I have written personally from beginning to end in New York, or rather on the private plane Lear, en route from Acapulco, Mexico to New York on the day of the week Thursday between the hours of 4 P.M. and 10 P.M. on the third of the month of January of the year 1974."

On January 14, 1974, he wrote Christina a letter telling her he had signed a will and asked her to try to carry out its provisions. Typically, he also advised her not to publish it as it might create tax problems, although if, after consultation with the Onassis advisers whom he named, saying they were aware of this, she might find it preferable to probate the will, then she could go ahead and publish it.[9]

In June that year he moved to stage two of excluding Jackie from her legal rights. At his behest his friends, the government of Greek "colonels," passed a special law. Dubbed by Jackie's legal advisers "Lex Onassis," it was entitled "Regulation of Certain Matters of Greek Nationals Domiciled Abroad." Onassis's purpose with "Lex Onassis" was to validate the waiver he had induced Jackie to sign in 1972, and which was of dubious validity. The waiver would entitle him to leave her what he wished and what he had now designated under his will. The law of June 1974 stated that agreements concluded abroad in private or notorial deed (i.e., the waiver of November 1972) between persons who intend to get married or who are already married, one of whom is of Greek nationality (i.e., Onassis) and the other of foreign nationality (i.e., Jackie), who are both domiciled abroad at the time of the agreement (both happened to be in New York), by which the foreign party waives any inheritance rights from the estate of the Greek party, will be valid. According to this law, Onassis hoped, Jackie would be unable to challenge the terms of his January will.

Inexorably, disaster seemed to follow upon disaster for him. The fourth Arab-Israeli war and the Arab oil-producers' decision in the autumn of 1973 to increase their oil prices had hit the tanker business, as the resulting severe recession was to destroy Stas's property business. Olympic Airways was similarly going downhill. On the personal side of the Onassis family, things went from bad to worse. In August, instead of going to Skorpios, Christina took an overdose of sleeping pills in London but was taken to the Middlesex Hospital in time. Tina flew in to be with her; Onassis was not told until she had recovered. Less than two months later Tina herself was found dead in her bedroom in the Niarchos' Paris house. No signs of violence were found on her body; after an autopsy demanded by a suspicious Christina, she was found to have died of "acute edema of the lung." But Tina's misery in her marriage may have contributed to her death: she had been smoking and drinking too much. "Her life with Mr. Niarchos at the end was a misery," said Christina's best friend. "She wasn't happy with Niarchos at the end."[10]

Several weeks after Tina's death, Onassis's own health deteriorated sharply and he was admitted to a New York hospital where he was diagnosed as suffering from myasthenia gravis, an incurable disease, apparently brought on by stress, alcohol and fatigue. Callas was touring in Japan when she heard the news. "He's scared to go into the hospital because he thinks he will never come out again," she told the accompanist, Robert Sutherland. "He needs to know I'm thinking of him, but I can't phone or even send a telegram because it would soon be all over the newspapers . . . We have a basic understanding," she went on. "He can talk to me about his business problems and he knows there's always his favorite champagne in my house." She reminisced for some time, Sutherland recorded, even mentioning "the Gold-digger": "She doesn't understand him, never was right for him. It's hard work keeping a man happy. She's away too much. She tried to change his whole way of life, tries to redecorate everything. It's like taking away his past. I never did that . . ."[11] Shortly afterward, on November 11, 1974, Callas gave her last public performance.

Onassis's career was also coming to an end. On the day he discharged himself from the hospital, his face swollen from cortisone treatment to counter his decreased adrenal function, his drooping eyelids held up with plaster behind his dark glasses, he received news that Olympic Airway's cash flow had reached a point where its scheduled flights could no longer be maintained at the same level. He had already heard the news that his plans for an oil refinery in New Hampshire had been turned down. In Greece, his junta friends had been replaced by a democratically elected government headed by an old acquaintance, Constantine Karamanlis. Against his doctor's advice, Onassis flew to Athens in December determined to negotiate government backing for Olympic. He seemed not to be aware that, as a close associate of the disgraced junta, he was out in the cold as far as the new government was concerned. "He'd lost his touch completely," an aide recalled. "He was played out. His name had once acted like a spell in Athens, now his world had turned upside down."[12] On January 15, 1975, after almost twenty years of Onassis' ownership, Olympic was sold back to the Greek government. The blow to his sense of his own prestige was immeasurable. It seemed to him that he did nothing but lose.

Jackie's relationship with her husband was also at an all-time low, so much so that she did not accompany him to Athens this time, but went skiing with John at Crans-sur-Sierre instead. She took the same attitude toward Onassis's business operations as she had to Jack's continual political campaigning, but at this crisis in his affairs her presence in Greece might have helped him both personally and from a public-relations point of view. She did not seem to care. She did not return to him until she received a message from Christina at Glyfada saying that he had collapsed with severe abdominal pains on February 3, 1975. Christina had also telephoned Professor Jean Caroli, a gastroenterologist in Paris, and Dr. Isadore Rosenfeld, the New York heart specialist, who flew to Athens with Jackie. At Glyfada the specialists differed sharply over how Onassis should be treated and where. Caroli wanted him to have his gallbladder removed at the American Hospital in Paris, Rosenfeld thought him too weak to undergo major surgery and recommended he be flown to New York for treatment. Christina, who seems to have been calling most of the shots over her father's treatment, and Artemis, decided it should be Caroli and Paris.

On February 6 Christina and Jackie flew with Onassis to Paris. He had been too feeble even to walk to the car to be taken to the airport. Instead he was carried downstairs by the loyal butler, Panagiotis, and placed in the waiting Cadillac. In Paris, flanked by Jackie and Christina, he made a supreme effort to walk into 88 Avenue Foch on his own, past the ranks of photographers, to spend what would be his last night there.

Although Jackie and Christina appeared in public together with Onassis, in private they were distant. While Jackie spent the night at Avenue Foch, Christina checked into the Hôtel Plaza Athenée. The following day, again surrounded by journalists and even television cameramen, they took Onassis to the American Hospital. The doctors there decided to remove his gallbladder.

After the operation, on February 10, he weakened dramatically and for the next five weeks lay there kept alive by a ventilator and fed intravenously, dying slowly. Jackie flew back and forth between New York and Paris to be with him. Artemis, whose husband was ill in Greece, flew between Paris and Athens. His two half sisters, Merope and Kalliroi, arrived to stay at the Avenue Foch. Christina, knowing it would please her father, had agreed to marry an old friend from a well-known Greek shipping family, Peter John Goulandris; in one of his moments of clarity, Onassis gave their engagement his blessing.

While Jackie was in Paris in February she was joined by Caroline, who was working for Karen Lerner on an NBC documentary about Adnan Kashoggi. "I was doing an interview with Kashoggi off camera in a place next to the Plaza Athenée," Karen recalled. "Jackie met Kashoggi and then the tabloids started reporting that she was involved with him . . . Christina took us out to dinner, Caroline, me, Jackie, at L'Orangerie. The crew came along—the sound man, the camera man, and Caroline was the electrician on our crew!" Karen sensed no hostility at the time from Christina toward Jackie: "She knew how to be a good hostess anyway."[13]

One woman was not allowed to be at Onassis's bedside: Maria Callas. Middle-class Greek morality forbade it: Artemis, never a friend to Callas, was afraid that if Callas visited it would be reported in the press and be seen as an affront to Jackie. Callas, however, received daily bulletins from a friend, Vasso Devetzi, whose mother was being treated on the same floor as Onassis. Only once did she manage to slip into the hospital unrecognized. On March 10 she could bear the situation no longer and fled to Palm Beach.

That same week Jackie, too, aware that Onassis would not recover, but advised by the doctors that his condition had stabilized and that he was unlikely to die in the near future, decided to leave for New York. The air date for Caroline's NBC program was to be March 16; Jackie was due to give a small dinner party at 1040 for the people concerned on the night the program was broadcast. On her arrival in New York she checked with Artemis, to be told that Ari's condition was unchanged.

Christina never left her father's bedside during all the time of his hospitalization. He was all hers at last, and she was not prepared to share him with Jackie. According to one source, she instructed the doctors not to tell anyone else that he was dying, so Jackie was still in New York when Artemis telephoned to urge her to return to Paris; the next morning as she was preparing to leave, she called again to tell her that he was dead. Aristotle Onassis died on March 15, 1975; of all his family only Christina was with him at the end. After he died, she made an attempt to slash her wrists but was saved by an alert doctor.

Karen Lerner was staying for a week at Jackie's apartment at 1040 and sleeping on Onassis's bed in the room adjoining Jackie's. "On the morning of March 15 she came in and said, 'Ari's died.' You know, she got a lot of criticism for being in New York and not at his bedside but she was in New York because she was giving a party on the day this little documentary aired for Caroline. And so she had invited the NBC producer of my show, the editor and my boss who was head of a documentary unit. There were just eight or nine people invited to this little dinner and she said, 'I am going to Paris, so you stay here and you be the hostess and I don't want anything to disturb this—it's for Caroline and I want it to go ahead.' "[14]

Jackie's absence from her husband's bedside when he died made the worst possible public impression, giving ammunition to her enemies in the Onassis camp. Contrary to most reports, this did not include Onassis's sisters, Artemis, Merope and Kalliroi. Artemis had always been Jackie's most loyal supporter and remained so. Stories that Jackie was ostracized by the Onassis women are simply untrue. But now, more than ever, she was seen as an outsider in Greece. Arriving at Aktion Airport near Skorpios she waited, dressed in a black turtleneck and leather skirt under a heavy leather trench coat, with Teddy Kennedy by her side, and with her three sisters-in-law for the arrival of her husband's body, accompanied by Christina, who was now head of the family and of the Onassis empire. As she stepped forward to greet Christina, photographers snapped. What was visible of her face beneath her trademark huge dark glasses was the wide frozen smile that had become an almost automatic reflex. That smile and the aggressively fashionable yet informal clothes immediately struck a wrong note to the watching world. She appeared fierce, icy, remote, uncaring, as far removed as it was possible to be from the image of the dignified, grieving widow she had presented at John F. Kennedy's funeral. Despite her celebrity, she was no longer the leading lady; that role belonged to Christina.

And it was at Onassis's funeral, just as at Alexander's deathbed, that Jackie's hard streak surfaced inappropriately. Escorted by Teddy Kennedy, she got into the lead car with the grief-stricken Christina for the drive to the fishing village of Nidri where Onassis's body was to be carried by boat to Skorpios. Suddenly the car stopped, Christina got out and ran back to her aunts' car immediately behind. The reason for this surprise move, Christina told Marina Dodero after the funeral, was that Teddy had leaned forward and said to her, "And now, what about the money?" Teddy had blurted it out but he would hardly have done so without Jackie's previous agreement.[15]

It was a gray and windy wintry day on Skorpios when Onassis's coffin was lowered into the vault beside Alexander's. Of the five Onassis women, Jackie was the only one who did not weep, as her husband of almost seven years was buried in the church where they had been married. There were mutterings of *"atyhya"* "the curse" among the congregation. Jackie's thoughts were bitter as she reflected on the way her marriage had turned out, standing there in the knowledge that his plans to divorce her had been complete. Her sense of sadness and failure were overwhelming.[16] Yet despite his treatment of her during their latter years together, she was never heard subsequently to criticize him and always expressed great fondness for him. On the day of the funeral she vowed to Christina that she would always keep the Onassis name. She returned twice to Skorpios that year, the first time for the memorial service to mark the end of forty days of mourning after Ari's death, but in effect her Greek life was over.

Just under a month after the funeral, on April 18, the *New York Times* broke the story that Onassis had been planning to divorce Jackie and that Christina was reportedly "bitterly hostile to Mrs. Onassis." Jackie was deeply upset and telephoned Christina to ask her to deny it publicly. For the sake of peace, Christina did so, but the story was true. A divorce settlement had been drawn up and she was indeed "bitterly hostile" to her former stepmother. "The divorce settlement was definitely there. Of that I can guarantee you," a source close to Christina said.[17] "It was in the process of settlement, almost done, but I don't think it was delivered and therefore came all the complexity of the negotiations afterward . . . Let's say it was divorce *de facto* but not completed *de jure* . . ." Christina's feelings toward Jackie had, if anything, grown more bitter. In her view her father had been "used, abused" and badly treated by Jackie, and nothing was going to convince her otherwise. Nonetheless a façade of togetherness was presented in July when Christina, pressured by Artemis, invited Jackie to attend her wedding on Skorpios to Alexander Andreadis (soon after Onassis's death Christina had decided against the marriage to Goulandris, whom she saw as an intimate friend rather than a husband). Jackie appeared with John Jr., amid expressions of affection for Christina, but behind the scenes negotiations were going on for a final financial settlement.

Christina was transformed by the death of her father. Some of her neuroses seem to have been buried with him. One of her husbands described her as "very nice, perceptive, businesslike with a good, warm, Greek personality. She was very much a daughter of her father but at the same time she had a feminine twist to her which was the most incredible combination of the gifts of her father combined with feminine intuition . . . It is almost impossible to understand what the life could be of a girl who had everything on her plate, having lost her brother, her father, her mother, being alone in charge. That's a little bit of a burden to put it mildly . . ."[18] Christina had inherited her father's flair, toughness and lack of sentimentality when it came to business. She had also inherited his wiliness and secretiveness, and his determination that Jackie should have as little as possible from his estate.

Christina and her lawyers denied the existence of a will and started the bidding with an offer of a mere two or three million dollars to Jackie. Tough negotiations led to a settlement in May, one provision of which declared "the daughter and wife each hereby confirm that to the best of her knowledge and belief that the father died intestate leaving no will or testament of any kind, granting rights or wishes to the wife or to her children." "I found it very strange that he had not left a will," said one of Jackie's legal advisers. "We negotiated quite heavily for a four- or five-week period and reached a settlement. She [Jackie] before the colonels got involved would have been entitled to one-eighth of something and the something would have taken three lifetimes to turn over every rock to find. He owned nothing, everything was in foundations, or twenty miles offshore or nominee names or whatever . . ."[19] The Onassis side alleged that Jackie had signed a waiver "which was valid," to which Jackie's side replied that it was "fraudulently produced and was invalid in its execution" under New York law, which required that when such an agreement was entered into "you must have independent counsel and knowledge of the facts—'both absent here.'" Jackie's lawyers threatened that they would allege fraud on this and have the waiver declared null and void. They scoured Europe for evidence of Onassis's assets and found, as he had predicted, no visible leads to his hidden fortune. Nonetheless they pressed on to come to a settlement.

Meetings took place at the Onassis headquarters in Monte Carlo between Alexander Forger and William Jackson of Millbank, Tweed, Hadley and McCloy representing Jackie, and Stelio Papadimitriou, assisted by Nicolas Cokkinis, managing director of the Onassis companies, for Christina. According to Papadimitriou, "Christina was angry as hell. She thought that Jackie was behaving badly by asking for a bigger share of the estate. Costa Gratsos was egging Christina on, urging her to resist Jackie's demands. But I thought Jackie was entitled to a piece of the cake. I had to fight very hard with Christina, who wanted to give Jackie nothing . . ."[20]

Feelings on the part of Christina's friends ran high—"Basically it was a matter of very greedy negotiations on Christina's father's tomb," said one. They urged her to stand up to Jackie. "We used to see quite a lot of Christina after she became an orphan," Taki Theodoracopoulos said. "She played her cards very close to her chest—she didn't exactly volunteer information—but we did say to her, 'Don't take any crap from that woman, this is your money, come on.' She [Jackie] was married seven years to Onassis, he had settled a lot of money on her. He was definitely at the end extremely bitter about her. Roy Cohn did fuck up completely and they weren't speaking, they were going to divorce. And of course when he was ill in the hospital she was flying back and forth to New York—she hardly went over, she just did it to look good in the eyes of the world. So we all said to her, 'Tell her to go screw herself.' I don't know what happened—she gave in like that. Christina didn't want a messy public fight."[21] According to Papadimitriou, what happened was that he fought to convince Christina that Jackie was being reasonable in the circumstances: "We finally settled on a reasonable cash figure, which was a fraction of what Jackie would have obtained by application of the forced heirship provisions of Greek law before the amendment of the law . . ."[22]

Under the terms of the settlement Jackie received over $20 million (there were estate taxes), $500,000 of which went to her lawyers. The agreement was signed on May 7, 1975. But where Onassis's affairs were concerned, nothing was that simple. Four weeks later Onassis's will, to the surprise of Jackie's side, surfaced and was probated. Some people suspected an intrigue or battle of wills involving

Christina and a member of the Onassis circle, which led to publication. Jackie's lawyers immediately telephoned Christina's side: "Well, fancy that, we all thought there was no will, where did this come from?" The Greek response was to tell them, in so many words, "You've got your settlement. Now go away."

But Jackie's lawyers did not go away. Armed with the opinion of Greek counsel that Lex Onassis could be attacked as "unconstitutional," and the belief that the earlier settlement was infected by blatant misrepresentation, they were in a strong position. The mysterious appearance of the will had given them even more leverage. "I said," one of her lawyers recalled, "that if I had known of this provision of the will that guaranteed her [Jackie] $200,000 per year for life, etc., then I would have been even more forceful in my efforts to attack this waiver and get a bigger share of the estate. So I have no embarrassment in claiming this, and if you guys want to resist we'll do it in the press . . ."[23]

It took an additional two years to negotiate a further settlement, which was finally reached on October 5, 1977. Jackie was to receive the income provided for her in the will for the rest of her life, notwithstanding her release of all claims in the 1975 agreement. Caroline and John were to receive their yearly payments of $25,000 each until the age of twenty-one when their payments went to Jackie. All payments were to be index-linked to the rate of inflation. In return, Jackie renounced her 25 percent share in Skorpios and the *Christina* and her position on the board of the Onassis foundation, which carried with it a percentage of the profits, pension and medical insurance policies. Christina told her intimates that the negotiations were "greedy, greedy, greedy. Bad publicity against cash on the table."[24]

Christina represented Jackie as "greedy"—but the lawyers on both sides involved in the negotiations did not. She had married Onassis without conditions, refusing to "barter" herself. His "wedding gift" of $2 million in bonds to compensate her for what she had lost in Kennedy funds by marrying him was a mere fleabite in terms of a fortune estimated, in so far as it could be, at more than $500 million. Thanks to him, she had had the privacy and ostensible freedom she craved for but this in no sense represented financial independence. His reasons for marrying her had been more cynical than hers for marrying him. To him she had been the ultimate trophy wife, the crowning victory in the Trojan War he fought against Niarchos. To her, he had appeared as not only a safe refuge from a violent America and an escape to a Mediterranean fantasy but also, more importantly, as the ideal father/lover who would protect her and physically satisfy her. In the end, both had been disillusioned. Onassis, looking for a little-girl wife like Tina, with the passionate but acquiescing characteristics of Maria Callas, had discovered a little-girl attitude that concealed a real independence of spirit. Jackie, while behaving well—even heroically so—in public, in private found herself increasingly alone, her sexuality and her intellectual ability denigrated or ignored. Her Kennedy children were her primary responsibility, but Onassis who had never regarded his own children in that light until it was too late, had not been able to accept her divided loyalty.

At Orly on her arrival from America after Ari's death, Jackie had read to the assembled press a sanitized but generous epitaph on her marriage: "Aristotle Onassis rescued me at a moment when my life was engulfed with shadows. He meant a lot to me. He brought me into a world where one could find both happiness and love. We lived through many beautiful experiences together which cannot be forgotten, and for which I will be eternally grateful."

Emotionally Jackie's second marriage had exacted a high cost, but psychologically and financially it had given her the strength—and the means—to return to her spiritual home, New York.

CHAPTER TWENTY-ONE

New York—New Life

~

She became a real New Yorker. She used to leave her building and take a yellow cab. She just wanted to be an ordinary person. She loved gossip, all the latest things that were going on, especially with a certain group of people . . .

—John Fairchild[1]

For all her European veneer, Jackie was a New Yorker through and through. To her it was home; she had lived most of her life there, and 1040 had been her base since 1964. She enjoyed the pace of life in the city, the relative anonymity it could provide and, contradictorily, the opportunities to play a leading role. It was her natural stage, the theater of her life. It was here that she could develop her personality, her own carefully wrought invention, no longer just Kennedy or Onassis but herself in her own right.

"She was an actress and she liked to act," Jay Mellon said. "Almost everything she did had a premeditated quality about it. Sort of dramatic, theatrical quality which she enjoyed enormously. The first time I saw her was in the Spanish Institute . . . There was about a hundred people who had paid I don't know how much, and there she was suddenly and I watched the end of the room. She appeared in the center of the archway that led into the room and just stood there motionless, beautifully dressed, standing just absolutely stock-still, standing there for a long time, looking like this and then—it was all choreographed, it was all so stylish— she took a few steps forward, and then she stopped again and looked like this and then she took a few more steps forward. She was enjoying every minute of it—she was watching herself as she did it . . . It made me a little bit curious about what made her tick."[2]

For the publicity conscious, New York is the center of the world and Jackie was the center of New York. Publicity can be an affirmation of self, like looking into a mirror and seeing the image you have of yourself, and with Jackie, as with all celebrities, it was a carefully cultivated image that she was determined to control—as the New York photographer, Ron Galella, had discovered to his cost. In nothing was she more contradictory than in her attitude to publicity, seemingly fleeing from it but actually courting it. She liked to pretend that she never read what was written about her but she would ask friends to buy tabloids about herself and flip through them to see what they were saying about her. "She really did like publicity," John Fairchild, editor of *Women's Wear Daily*, said. "And very calculated. I remember one time we took photographs of her outside the gym and Nancy Tuckerman, her secretary, called and said, 'Oh, John, please don't run those photographs—she's not looking her best. But, I tell you what, tomorrow she's going to be at such and such a place and you'll get your pictures." This is always the way it was with her. And then, if I'd done something wrong or written something she didn't like, she used to give me the iciest stare you've ever seen . . . I used to watch her a lot," he went on. "You noticed that her eyes, her face—the minute she saw a lens her eyes became like a lens of a camera . . . It was like a lens making love to a lens, the minute the camera was there. Her whole demeanor turned on when she saw a camera."[3]

If Jackie had really wanted to hide, she would not have lived on Central Park or gone out wearing her huge trademark sunglasses (a basket containing dozens of pairs was always kept in the hall of the apartment so she could pick up a pair as she left). Nor would she have gone out always looking stunning, even in sweater and tie-dye jeans as in Galella's favorite photograph of her. When Jackie was depressed or out of the public eye, she could be surprisingly scruffy, even unkempt. One of her admirers complained of how when they were traveling she would wear the same T-shirt and jeans for several days. The designer clothes were the Jackie her public expected to see. The image they wanted to see was, as Galella said, "beauty, wealth and glamour and Jackie symbolizes all three . . . Yet Jackie also has a quiet aesthetic beauty. She is sensitive, poetic and independent. Millions of people never get enough of her."[4]

Jackie, however, had quickly had enough of Galella and his dedicated stalking. From 1967 until 1973, when she obtained a court order forbidding him to approach her within photographic distance, Galella devoted his life to snatching pictures of her. He pored over gossip columns to find out where she would be, dated her maid, and used a range of disguises—sunglasses, pipe, hippie wig, salt and pepper wig, Afro wig and several mustaches—so that she would not immediately recognize him. He froze outside expensive restaurants, lurked on Capri, broiled in the sun in a boat off Skorpios, and bribed a Chinese restaurant to let him hide in the coat rack to take pictures of Jackie and Onassis. Like most Jackie-watchers he was in love with her—"I'll always remember wandering through Central Park on fall afternoons and all of a sudden finding her like a diamond in the grass . . . I wonder whether Jackie ever thinks about me any more . . ." he wrote after being ordered by the U.S. Court of Appeals to stay at least twenty-five feet away from Jackie and thirty feet away from her children.[5]

The order was the culmination of a three-year legal battle between Jackie and the photographer, originally initiated when Galella filed suit against her and the children's Secret Service agents for interfering with the pursuit of his lawful occupation, and for malicious prosecution, false imprisonment and harassment. Jackie had had the agents block Galella's view when he attempted to take pictures, and had once had him arrested. He demanded $1.3 million compensation. Jackie countersued, charging harassment and violation of her right to privacy, asking for $6 million in damages. The *New York Times* called the subsequent six-week trial "the best off-Broadway show in town."

Jackie claimed that Galella "terrified" her, but his flattering photographs hardly compared as harassment with those snatched by Mediterranean paparazzi stationed off Skorpios who caught her swimming nude ("The Billion Dollar Bush" as *Hustler* captioned the pictures) or even having sex on the beach with Onassis (later he apparently confessed to having paid Italian paparazzi to station themselves off the beach with snorkels). What *Life* called the staggering pettiness of the dispute was merely the backdrop for the Jackie O Show. During her days in the witness box the courtroom was jammed; as soon as she had finished testifying, most of the spectators left. Onassis had been furious with Jackie for bringing the suit, telling her that she was only giving Galella oceans of free publicity; he was even angrier when the resulting legal bills landed on the desk of his New York office. His own way with photographers whose pictures annoyed the Onassis family was simply to buy them off.

Jackie craved fame and celebrity from her earliest years but on her own terms. She liked to be recognized, an affirmation of her celebrity but at a distance. If a stranger came too close, addressed her or, worst of all, touched her, she froze or fled. Richard de Combray, the writer with whom she worked in the early eighties, compared her with Garbo, whom he also knew, and who, he said, "fascinated" Jackie. "Garbo, of course, wanted to have two lives, that of the anonymous unobserved woman who is also the great star, so that she required you to look at her when you saw her in the street, but as soon as you acknowledged her, she'd shy away as if you'd done something shocking. Jackie was similar. Like Garbo she'd like to have had both lives too. I remember taking her to a show at the Whitney before it opened properly and some construction workers noticed her, and she obviously liked that, but when someone she didn't know tapped her on the shoulder, she became almost crazed with fear and anger."[6]

Some things were beyond her control. As she returned to America, ghosts of the past began to surface from depths she had never cared to plumb, to intrude into the present over which she preferred to skim. In 1975 the myth of Camelot, which she had so unwisely propagated a decade earlier, began to crumble. She remained fiercely protective of Jack Kennedy's image, not only for her own sake but, above all, for the children's. She had taken endless trouble to fix their father in John and Caroline's memory. Although only a small photograph of JFK was visible in the living rooms of 1040, the children's rooms, especially Caroline's, were plastered with pictures from their life together. A large portrait dominated one room. After their cruise on the *Christina* in 1973, Jackie had invited Pierre Salinger to Skorpios specifically to talk to the children about their father. "I want you to spend an hour, an hour and a half every day with the kids and brief them totally on what their father did, because they don't really—they haven't really looked at what their father was doing . . ."[7] According to Salinger's printed memoir, he talked to the children about their father's love of history and his passion for reading. "They laughed when I mentioned that it wasn't safe to leave anything that looked interesting on one's desk in the White House for fear their father would stroll by and make off with it." He had tried, he said, to counteract what he dubbed the "Camelotization" of JFK and the Kennedy years, and commented, "Having seen Caroline and John . . . growing into interesting, responsible adults, I was always pleased to see that their view of their historically important father was kept in a healthy perspective, that of the loving children of a man they understood had been a human being not a myth."[8]

Pierre Salinger was a trusted friend in Jackie's life. Ben Bradlee, it turned out that year, was not. Jackie had always been nervous about her husband's friendship with a man whose trade was journalism and who was keeping a diary of the times they spent together. In a diary entry for March 21, Bradlee wrote that he thought the President knew he was keeping a record and did not object, but "I was not so sure about Jackie, who is much more nervous and easily distraught by this kind of thing . . ."[9] Bradlee agreed with Kennedy and Jackie not to publish anything without Kennedy's permission for at least five years after they left the White House. No one could have then envisaged that almost exactly eight months later he left it in a coffin.

Toward the end of 1974 Jackie got wind that Ben Bradlee had prepared a book, on the basis of his journal, about his friendship with Jack and her hackles rose. "I got a call from Jackie, the first time I had talked to her since the funeral train bearing Bobby Kennedy's body on the way back to Arlington Cemetery. She wanted to know when I was going to let her read the book, mentioning she had heard I had shown it to Joe Kraft and some others. I told her I was waiting to get it in shape to show it to her, and I did send it off a week later." Jackie's reaction to Bradlee's book was much the same as it had been to Red Fay's memoir, haughty, dismissive and wounding. "She didn't like it, it was obvious, when she called a week after that. 'It tells more about you than it does about the President,' she said. And she didn't like the bad language. She said she thought her children would be offended. I was not sure she was coming clean with why she didn't like it," Bradlee said.[10]

"Bad language" was, as Bradlee suspected, merely a cover. Everyone who had served in the armed forces in the Second World War in Jack's era had carried the same language on into civilian life almost as a badge of male pride, at the very least out of habit. What Jackie hated was exposure of the details of her private life with Jack even outside the bedroom; both Arthur Schlesinger and William Manchester had felt the force of her disgust on her personal level. She had an absolute, almost irrational aversion to people she knew making money out of her personal life. Beyond this, as far as she and the children were concerned, she disliked the raising of the Durie Malcolm affair and, more recently and possibly more important, Bradlee's revelations of Jack's reactions to her 1963 cruise on the *Christina* with Onassis, recording the Bradlee/Kennedy dinner discussions in which Jackie appears distinctly on the defensive.

That someone should have put into print that Jack knew her Onassis cruise had damaged him politically was unbearable to Jackie, as was the revelation that he had forbidden Onassis to set foot in the United States until after the 1964 election. Not only had Onassis been an honored guest in the White House one month and one day later, on the weekend after Jack's assassination, but he had continued to pursue Jackie despite the hostility of the Kennedy family, and of Bobby in particular, until after Bobby's assassination.

Her reaction was predictable. Bradlee, like others before and after him, was cast into the outer darkness. "I saw Jackie twice [afterward]," Bradlee recorded. "Once Sally [his present wife] and I were arriving at a party hosted by Arthur Schlesinger during the Democratic Convention in New York in 1976. Just as she was leaving, I . . . stuck out my hand, and said, 'Hi, Jackie.' She sailed by us without a word. Sometime later, Jackie and her two children had the cabana next to us at La Samanna in St. Maarten. For a week we seemed to be staring at each other on the beach, but never ran into each other until one night when we almost collided as we left our cabana to go up to the restaurant for dinner. From twelve inches away, she looked straight ahead, without a word, and I never saw her again."[11]

"Jackie thought Ben had been disloyal to Jack," a friend said. In Jackie's book disloyalty was the unforgivable sin.

Beginning in 1974 more and more allegations about John Kennedy began bubbling to the surface. Earl Wilson, the newspaper columnist, published a book claiming that, as Jackie suspected, he had had an affair with Marilyn Monroe. Far worse, from Jackie's point of view, were the leaks from the report of the Church Committee, originally set up to investigate the involvement of the Secret Service in assassination plots or attempts against foreign leaders. Judith Campbell Exner's simultaneous relationship with the President and Sam Giancana came to light, and with it the whole question of Kennedy-Mafia relationships for the first time. The first leak emerged in the *Washington Post* on November 16, 1975 when it was reported that investigators had found evidence of some seventy phone calls from Campbell during an eleven-month period in the log of former presidential secretary Evelyn Lincoln, on file in the Kennedy Library, beginning on March 29, 1961. Several of Campbell's calls had been made from the Oak Park, Illinois, residence of Sam Giancana.

On December 17 Judith Campbell, now married to professional golfer Dan Exner, surfaced with a press conference in San Diego to declare that she had enjoyed a "relationship of a close personal nature" with John Kennedy, to whom she had been introduced in February 1960 by a "close personal friend," generally assumed to be Frank Sinatra. The Kennedys immediately closed ranks against Exner. Dave Powers, now curator of the Kennedy Library and keeper of the secrets of Jack and the women, said, "The name doesn't ring a bell with me," and that Secret Service files at the library showed no record of any visits by "the woman" to the White House. Steve Smith, suffering from convenient memory loss, "could not recall any visits with the President to Las Vegas" at the time, and as for Exner, he had "no recollection of her name." Evelyn Lincoln repeated what she had told the commission, that Judy Campbell was a campaign volunteer and had telephoned the White House but she had never put the calls through to the President. Kennedy's political aide Hyman Raskin and his old Harvard friend, Blair Clark, then working for CBS, who were both with Kennedy and Sinatra at Las Vegas on February 8, 1960, could not recall seeing anyone of Campbell Exner's description.[12]

There was a brief respite over Christmas but, for Jackie, worse was still to come. On January 15, 1976, the *New York Times* announced that Judith Exner was to write a book about her relationship with Kennedy, giving dates and places and spicing it up with revelations about her sexual relationship with Sinatra, and Ted Kennedy's "childish" attempts to start an affair with her. Most hurtful from Jackie's point of view was the report that in mid-1961 Campbell Exner had met Kennedy twenty times in the White House and that he had told her "that his marriage had been in poor shape and that his wife Jacqueline had made known her intention to divorce him," and that "The Kennedy family managed to hold the marriage together by telling Mrs. Kennedy that 'a divorced Catholic from Boston stood small chance of gaining the Democratic Presidential nomination or winning the general election.'" Exner touched on her relationship with Giancana saying that they had "joked together" about her affair with the President. She also hinted that Giancana's influence had weighed in Kennedy's favor in Chicago in 1960. Her final unwelcome revelation was that she, Kennedy and Jackie had been treated by Max Jacobson, "a Manhattan practitioner who specialized in providing his patients with injections of amphetamines and whose relationship with the late President has been rumored but never established."

By the time Judith Exner "revealed" the Jacobson allegations, the Jacobson-Kennedy story was well and truly over. On April 25, 1975, after more than two years of hearings, the New York Board of Regents revoked Jacobson's medical license. Among other things, he was convicted of administering amphetamines without sound medical justification, and failure to keep adequate records of his use of controlled substances. He died two years later, leaving an unpublished autobiography, and a widow, Ruth, who felt that he had been let down by his prominent patients, including the Kennedys and Jackie in particular. According to Jacobson's autobiography and the testimony of his widow, two days before the first medical panel hearing in the investigation to be held on May 30, 1973, Jacobson had a two-hour meeting alone with Jackie, arranged over the telephone by Chuck Spalding, during which they discussed the recent media revelations about his treatment of the President, notably an article by Ben Reisenberger in the *New York Times*. "Jackie asked me what I would say if the White House came up during the hearings," Jacobson wrote. "I reassured her that there was no reason for concern . . ." He told her that he was in need of money to pay his legal expenses and was later assured by Chuck Spalding that "help was forthcoming." No contribution arrived.[13]

As if all this were not enough, in the March issue of the *National Enquirer*, released in the last week of February, Jack's affair with Mary Meyer came to light in the most sensational terms. "JFK had 2 Year White House Affair," which was followed up by newspaper headlines everywhere "JFK Had Affair with D.C. Artist, Smoked 'Grass' . . ." The revelations were based on an interview with James Truitt, former vice president of the *Washington Post*, who, with his wife, Ann, were friends of Mary Meyer's.

"Jackie put on such a wonderful face to the world," said Karen Lerner, Alan Jay Lerner's ex-wife and a close friend of Jackie's at the time. "But I do know she was in a depression the day that Judith Campbell Exner's name was first in the papers in New York. She showed up at my apartment which totally surprised me and she just slumped down on the sofa and she didn't seem to be seeing anything—she certainly didn't talk about that—she was just very kind of resigned and depressed."[14] In Utah for New Year's week with Teddy and assorted Kennedys as guests of Dick Bass at the Snowbird resort, Jackie "merely smiled at reporters' questions about President Kennedy's alleged love affairs."

The public questioning about Jack's infidelities hurt, however, and was still hurting almost two decades later, the year before her death. Karen Lerner remembers a dinner given for Pierre Salinger's retirement from ABC News on September 28, 1993, when she was vice president of the Museum of Television and Radio: "There was a question-and-answer session before this dinner and Richard Wald, a television executive, asked Pierre from the audience, 'How did you handle questions of President Kennedy's infidelities when you were in the White House?' And it was at this moment that Jackie walked in! . . . And she sat down right behind Dick Wald and Pierre waxed a bit more about the question. He didn't see her. He said, 'Well, even though we knew it was happening it was a different time and . . .' Well, on the way to dinner after the question-and-answer session, I walked with Jackie and she sort of leaned against the wall for support, she just looked exhausted. And I said, 'You know I feel so badly about . . . feeling responsible for inviting you to this evening which has got off to such a horrible start,' and she said, 'Oh, it's not your fault, it's not anything to do with you, it's not your fault.' And she was very upset, very upset . . . it was a ghastly scene."[15]

⌒

After her two experiences as the wife of rich men, Jackie was determined not to repeat it. Once, in these years, she said to her friend Aileen Mehle, "Suzy," " 'Why don't you write about all these very prominent social women who have married vast fortunes and who are envied high and low? How everything seems wonderful on the surface but underneath life is hell, hell, hell . . .' And I thought," Suzy said, "*Et tu*, Jackie?"[16] She had enough money—entrusted to André Meyer who knew how to increase it—to be independent. She had 1040, where she was looked after by Marta, now the cook-housekeeper, and a butler, Efgenio. On weekends she drove herself down to Far Hills to ride, hunt and exercise, where she was cherished by a Portuguese couple.

"Jackie changed more during the year after Ari died than at any other time I knew her," Karen Lerner said.[17] She was seeking a new life for herself and this time a new man was not a priority.

"I didn't think that her identity in the first instance totally rested on men," Gloria Steinem said. "She had a more European, what Americans think of as a much more European vision of marriage—that is, she did always have a separate life and I am sure she knew that they had separate lives, and women really didn't seem to care that much as long as they were discreet and so on."[18] Jackie had never been as passion driven or man obsessed as most other women. "She in the beginning was not as male identified as we were, or as addicted to men as the rest of us of a similar generation," Steinem said.

In the years immediately after Onassis's death Jackie's name had been linked as usual with a number of men, some of them lovers, some just friends, even the occasional one-night stand. Jackie moved with the times, doing exactly as she pleased in matters of sex. As an irrational aspect of human behavior it amused her, particularly the couplings of people she knew. "Sex is dirty sheets," she joked to a friend, describing the rather prim weekend a close friend of hers and her lover had spent together. It was not a subject that she discussed often with women friends,[19] but Truman Capote boasted to Cecil Beaton that at dinner with the Fosburghs, "Jackie *et moi* spent the whole evening talking about sex." The Fosburghs were mad at him, he said, "They thought it was *my* fault. Ha ha!"[20] She was amused by the description of the eminent but flabby lover of a friend, whose conviction of his own importance was such that he simply lay there like a pasha and let the woman do the work. "Jackie was fascinated with knowing what he was like in bed!" the friend recalled. "So, well, I said, 'He doesn't have one muscle in his body!' And she just laughed and laughed . . ."[21]

Curiously, for someone who was so suspicious of the media, Jackie was drawn to writers and artists, and Pete Hamill, "a gentlemanly Irishman," as his late friend Brendan Gill described him, was both: a working journalist, novelist and painter and, in the opinion of many New York women, "very juicy." Pete Hamill would not talk about his relationship with Jackie beyond once saying that going out with her was "like taking King Kong to the beach." Their friendship ended, Jackie apparently not so much taking offense at an old column attacking her "mercenary" marriage to Onassis, which Hamill's old newspaper, the *New York Post* resurrected and printed to embarrass him, but because she disapproved of his treatment of his two troubled daughters, whom he had dropped when he went to live with Shirley MacLaine. Subsequently Jackie had a relationship with another media man, television producer Peter Davis. "Jackie was very, very, romantic but not sexy," said Peter Duchin. Duchin, the top society bandleader and pianist, used to play at the Kennedys' White House parties and he and his first wife, Cheray, were close to Jackie after Jack's death, throughout her marriage to Onassis and after. Sometimes, however, Jackie would follow her impulses like any liberated woman. A woman whom Jackie knew and admired was surprised when a television producer, who was recently divorced and therefore enjoying the rare single-man status in New York, complained that he had been shocked to discover that "there were all these women who behaved about sex in a way that he had thought only he would behave. And he was complaining in particular about this woman who had asked him to lunch and then said, 'Perhaps you'd like to bathe . . .' And anyway they'd gone to bed and he'd never heard from her again. What always gave me pause, and I could be completely wrong about this, but he exactly described Jackie's apartment where he did not know I had ever been, and he never told me her name so it isn't as if he was bragging."[22]

Stories have appeared naming Frank Sinatra as having an affair with Jackie during the seventies. Peter Duchin, who reintroduced them on March 16, 1974, dismisses it as absolutely without foundation. Sinatra had been kept at arm's length by Jackie in the White House years as a dangerous element in Jack's other life but he still worshipped Jackie from afar. "Here's what happened," Peter Duchin said. "Sinatra, who was a friend of mine, said, 'God, I've got to meet Jackie.' So I said, 'Well, fine, I'm sure she'd love to meet you.' So he said, 'See if she's free on such and such a night because I'm giving a concert in Providence, Rhode Island, and I'll send the plane and pick up you and Cheray and Jackie, fly out to Providence, and then we'll fly down to New York together and have dinner after the concert.' So I said to Jackie, 'Would you like to see Sinatra next week? He's giving a concert in Providence, Rhode Island, he wants to send a plane, have dinner, that sort of stuff.' And she said, 'Well, that would be kind of fun, wouldn't it?' And so we got in this plane, she and my wife, Cheray, and I, and we flew up and we went to the concert and came back, and limos were whisking us around and we went to some place for dinner, and at the end of it, she said, 'Well, I don't really think he's my type.' And we laughed. Nothing happened that night, as far as I know, because I think she would have told me or Frank would have told me. Nothing happened. It really is amazing, you can write something that is totally wrong and people will believe it."[23]

Jackie liked the companionship of old friends, some of them divorcees with children, like Tom Guinzburg and William vanden Heuvel, with whom she would take family vacations in the Caribbean or Florida. Once vanden Heuvel had escorted her to a fund-raising benefit in Los Angeles organized by Norman Chandler of the *Los Angeles Times* in the aftermath of the Watts riots. "She was interested in helping in the racial problems of Los Angeles," he said. "She went out actually for that event . . . we toured Watts together—seeing what it had been like in the riots and how it had been reconstructed. Then there was a benefit concert by Ray Charles, and as the concert was going forward, some fellow got up from the audience—a big, strong black man—and walked on the stage and started choking Ray Charles."[24]

Jackie was levelheaded in her perception of men. "Men are like dogs sniffing each other in the park," she told Karen Lerner. "Women are much more trusting."[25]

"Jackie was not a feminist," Gloria Steinem said. "She was supportive. She was kind and generous with her women friends. I always had the impression that she did care and she did support all the issues but she disliked public life. So much as I used to try and get her to come out for the equal-rights movement or something, she wouldn't. She did contribute some small sums to the *Ms.* foundation for instance . . . She was cheering on, she was cheering everybody on. She thought it wonderful as far as I could tell. But she was on her own kind of life-track, which was not different but was unique to her. It wasn't anti, it wasn't traditional. She really didn't like public events. That wasn't who she was. She really didn't want to, and I admired that. But she remained faithful to the causes she started out with, all the architectural restoration kind of things."[26]

Yet the Ladies who Lunch life, as depicted by Truman Capote in *La Côte Basque*—which, when published in *Esquire* in May 1975, ended his social career—was not enough for her: she saw herself as a serious person. (Among Truman's deliberately placed insults and scandalous stories about his greatest friends, he wrote of Jackie, after seeing a drag queen contest in which by far the most popular impersonation was of Jackie, "And, in life, that is how she struck me—not as a bona fide woman, but as an artful female impersonator impersonating Mrs. Kennedy.")[27]

Part of Jackie's personal evolution was to take a job for the first time since her brief career as a journalist on the *Times-Herald*. According to Thomas Guinzburg, then the president and editor-in-chief of Viking, his family publishing firm, the idea that Jackie should work there as an editor came from Tish Baldrige, who suggested it to Jackie, then called him. "I immediately saw all the public-relations values of any kind of arrangement we would be able to make with Jackie," he recalled. Tom had known her and Lee since the Canfield days when he had been part of the literary band that included George Plimpton and John P. Marquand Jr. In terms of author appeal, Jackie's name would be irresistible. He hastened to lunch with Jackie at her apartment. Caroline appeared, replete with teenage cynicism. "Hey," she said to Tom, "is my mum really going to work for you?" When he confirmed that she might, Caroline's comment was "But what's she going to *do*?"[28]

That was the crucial question, and the first that Jackie put to Guinzburg at their meeting. She was worried that they would only use her as a lure for celebrity authors. Guinzburg wanted to allay this fear and to offer her enough for her to feel validated in her work. "You're really not equipped to be an editor," Guinzburg told her. "It's not that you don't have the talent for it, the ability for it, but you don't have the background and the training and you, I think, would suffer in a publishing house because that would set up some kind of competitive atmosphere with the other editors. But what you can do is to be a consulting editor . . .

"I explained that that could be just about anything one might want to define it as . . . somebody who didn't have what we call line responsibilities, they're not assigned books, they don't even have necessarily to work out of the office. Their primary job is to acquire books," Guinzburg said. "I then explained to her that as she became more familiar with publishing procedures, she could work on the books and with the writers to whatever extent appealed to her. She could create books and so on . . . She was in a unique position in the world. It didn't much matter who she was having dinner with—it was likely to be somebody who was of interest to other people and a certain number of these people wanted to write books." They agreed she should be paid $10,000 a year, not enough to arouse envy in the professionals yet enough not to seem a mere gesture.

The idea of Jackie Kennedy Onassis actually getting an office job made her arrival at the Madison Avenue building a freak show. To avoid trouble, Viking refused to specify a day, merely saying she would be starting during the last week of September. (She actually began work there on September 22.) "Maybe the vigil started the Friday before," Guinzburg said. "Monday there was a pack out there. I told her to stay home the first day of the week. The second day she came in the paparazzi were all there. It was a circus, of course, because of who she was, how she would accommodate herself to normal life. There were bomb threats, security people, press people dressed up as messengers. Suddenly, friends I didn't know I had in the broadcasting and television business, columnists who hadn't thought I was the most exciting boy in town up to then, were very friendly." One network TV reporter got in on the pretext of a job interview. Jackie's office was swept for bugs to ensure her privacy.

Given the hullabaloo, introducing Jackie to her Viking colleagues was, Guinzburg recalled, "awkward": "There was a certain scab feeling about this famous woman who was going to come in and who was just going to be an ornament. The first few days were very hard for her because the paparazzi in large numbers were out there, and we made it more difficult by not giving interviews. And the people inside Viking were remote. They were friendly, amicable . . . correct. They were not relaxed with her, they didn't know what to wear. The first few weeks everybody was wearing their best clothes . . . She would sit in her office, I think, waiting for something to happen."[29]

A publishing colleague at Viking, Alan Lang, was assigned to give Jackie two months of informal weekly tutorials in the publishing business. "She was thrown into the thick of it from day one," he recalled, "and very much handled herself in a very professional manner. She was very understated in her demeanor and very smart. We actually just had lunch in the restaurant over the street to save time so that most of our time was devoted toward discussion of the editorial process, copy editing, design, production, sales and marketing, just so that she understood what happened to her manuscript after it was acquired. [We discussed] where she could be valuable in going through the book, any contacts she might have, how she wanted to be treated in terms of being the editor of the book because in many cases books that she acquired didn't say 'Jackie Onassis, Editor' on the copyright page, but you know her contacts were invaluable in terms of publicizing books. I think Jackie's help in acquiring and dealing with authors, when she ultimately was not the acquiring editor, made her time at Viking invaluable . . . I didn't find her to be anyway anything other than a very good colleague. She made, I think, a very good effort, successfully, of not abusing her position . . ."[30] Over a chicken salad in the Edwardian Room of the Plaza Hotel, Tom and Jackie discussed possible catches: "We'd sit around and giggle and say—how do we get Sinatra?" he remembered. "I'd say, 'Frank Sinatra would kill for you,' and she'd joke, 'Yes, but it's that lawyer of his . . .' "[31]

Jackie was particularly involved in illustrated books during her time with Viking, a field in which Bryan Holme, the director of Studio Books, acted very much as a father figure to her. "He was really her mentor," said Tom Guinzburg. One of her most important titles was *In the Russian Style*, to be published in connection with the exhibition at the Metropolitan Museum of Art, and in the summer of 1976 she went to Russia with her friend, Diana Vreeland, and Thomas Hoving, the then director of the Metropolitan Museum.

In 1972 Jackie had been one of the contributors to a fund for the salary of Diana Vreeland as a special consultant to the Metropolitan Museum where she was to organize exhibitions. She became close to the museum, supporting it via Diana Vreeland and Ashton Hawkins, a new friend who was its legal counselor. "Her contributions were to help with Mrs. Vreeland's expense account, which was obviously larger than we were used to, and she wanted to support it rather than salaries," Hawkins said. "By then, of course, Mrs. Vreeland was very established here, but it was a great help to have that kind of money coming in, always without any acknowledgment other than from me to her, and she didn't want it known. She also at one point—I think it was in the middle seventies—chaired a Costume Institute Benefit, which was the first sort of public thing since she came back to New York." "What she did for the Met was, she made the Costume Institute projects that she worked on more serious than Diana could have done—that was by publishing those books and getting these things together."[32]

Jackie felt symbolically connected to the Metropolitan Museum by the Egyptian Temple of Dendur, which she could see from her apartment windows.[33] Initially, she had been far from supportive when its director, Thomas Hoving, had applied to have the Temple of Dendur set up at the museum instead of at a site on the Potomac as she had originally envisaged. When Hoving first approached her to enlist Bobby's help, as Senator for New York, in forwarding his proposal to the commission appointed by President Johnson to decide the matter, she was furious.

"I know the Senator has obligations and constituents in New York, but I don't care about them," she told Hoving firmly. "I won't let him write a letter to stick that temple in some dusty museum in New York. Jack got that temple for the United States. If Jack had not helped out Egypt at the critical moment, the temple would never have been awarded to us. I don't want it in some museum. I don't care if you are going to put a glass over it to protect it. I don't like the way Johnson is shopping it around the country. I don't care if the temple crumbles into sand, but I want it to be built in the center of Washington as a memorial to Jack. I don't care about the Met. I don't care about New York. Or Bobby's senatorial duties. Or his constituents. Or scholarship. Or this conservation business. Or President Johnson. It's going to be built in Washington."

Hoving sat there stunned, but within minutes Jackie had called back. This time her voice was soft and conciliatory: "I want to stress that I think President Johnson is doing a superb job in allowing various cities around the country to compete for the temple. I want to emphasize that I have no personal interest in where it goes. I feel Bobby should work on behalf of his constituents. I would never try to influence him to do anything else. I profoundly admire President Johnson's commission. I want Bobby to have the temple where he wants it."

In Hoving's view, the sudden turnabout on Jackie's part was caused by Bobby, who foresaw the political furor it might cause if the Kennedys were seen to be backing the interests of Washington against those of New York. In the end neither Jackie nor Bobby did anything to help Hoving bring the Temple of Dendur to the Metropolitan, but neither did they oppose it. Today it stands in its own glass wing of the museum, magically lit at night and in full view of Jackie's apartment. The lights were even specially turned on for her on one occasion when she had a dinner party.[34]

Jackie was entranced by working on *In the Russian Style*, which had to be ready to go to press by early September 1976. She wrote to Vreeland, enclosing a "superb" introduction by Audrey Kennett and describing the cover that Bryan Holme envisaged for the book, a piece of Russian brocade with arched windows cut through it with costumes or engravings of rulers in the windows, and asking if she could come to the museum for a particular piece of Russian brocade, which she had seen there.

In the Russian Style was published in the spring of 1977. It was to be the last of Jackie's big productions for Viking. That year, Guinzburg was in London and, alerted by his friend Deborah Owen, Jeffrey Archer's British literary agent, he looked over the manuscript of Archer's second book, *Shall We Tell the President?*, the successor to his bestseller *Not a Penny More Not a Penny Less*. The plot, on the lines of Frederick Forsyth's thriller *The Day of the Jackal*, about the attempted assassination of de Gaulle, was designed to appeal to the American market and was about the killing of a future President, clearly modeled on Teddy Kennedy, who had declined to run for the Democratic nomination in 1976. Both Guinzburg, Deborah Owen and the distinguished editor Cork Smith thought the book had real commercial possibilities. What they were all concerned about was how would it sit with Jackie Onassis? Guinzburg said he would take care of that. He told Jackie, " 'I've got a problem about a manuscript I want to talk about.' I then told her quite succinctly what the basic plot was and I remember seeing her wince—'Won't they ever stop?' Then she collected herself and said, 'Is this pretty commercial? Will I have to read it?' I said, 'You don't have to know anything more about it.' Jackie said, 'If we don't publish it, will somebody else?' 'Yep, Random House,' I told her. Jackie said, 'You think I don't know, Tom, the books you've turned down for my sake and for members of the family—As long as I don't have to read it and you can get rid of all that [Kennedy] stuff as best you can.' "[35] Deborah Owen said, "I know he had a conversation with her because we were very much waiting until he had . . . I'm very, very sure in so far as I'm sure of anything that Tom would not have proceeded without talking to her—he valued her too highly."[36]

As she had with the Manchester book, Jackie put it out of her mind. Guinzburg would perhaps have been better advised to ensure that she read the book. With hindsight it seems odd that no one foresaw the scandal that the Teddy Kennedy plot would cause. Guinzburg and Jackie had no further discussions about the book until what he describes as "the day of hysteria." A bad review by the influential John Leonard in the *New York Times* ended with a carefully directed barb: "There is a word for such a book. The word is trash. Anybody associated with its publication should be ashamed of herself."

"That was when the fan became loaded," Guinzburg reflected. "She simply panicked and calls began coming in from every member of the Kennedy tribe. She kept saying she didn't know anything about it." Tom Guinzburg told the *Boston Globe* that, yes, she had known about it but, no, she hadn't had anything to do with it. The newspaper omitted the last part of his statement. Jackie refused to see Guinzburg or to return any of his calls.[37]

Guinzburg was distraught; even today it is a painful subject for him (and, in the end, contributed to his being fired from the firm his family had founded by its new owners, Pearson). "The Kennedys stirred it up—they were the ones who were making the calls. John Leonard would never acknowledge the deliberate cruelty of his remark. It was not only gratuitous, it was an uncalled-for *ad hominem* statement."[38]

Even if the whole affair was a misjudgment on the part of those concerned with it, Guinzburg was probably right when he said that Jackie "panicked." The implications of a Kennedy assassination stirred up her emotions, which she was incapable of dealing with rationally. Jackie resigned and the incident ended the warm friendship she had had with Guinzburg. "The portcullis came down," he said mournfully. Only the previous year they had gone on vacation together at Round Hill in Jamaica. "The tabloids made it out as a romantic escapade because I had been separated a couple of months before," he recalled. The headlines were "Jackie to Marry Boss." "But my kids were there, and Jackie's kids. We did things together but it was not romantic. We celebrated my fiftieth birthday. She was so warm and genuine and cute. I just wish she could have had more of those innocent days . . ."[39]

⁓

Innocent days and Kennedy politics, however, were hardly compatible. Since Bobby's death there had been something of a diaspora of the clan. Only Rose and Ethel still made Hyannis Port their summer base. Pat Lawford, divorced from Peter, spent much of her time in France. Peter himself lived on the west coast in a haze of drugs, alcohol and voyeuristic sex. The Smiths, whose marriage was going through a rough patch, had withdrawn from Hyannis Port to Bridgehampton on Long Island. At least three of the younger generation were on heroin, in company with Jack's old friend Lem Billings. The Teddy Kennedys still had a house at Squaw Island, but Teddy's private life was a shambles, his womanizing notorious while his wife, Joan, struggled against alcoholism. For these reasons, and fearing the current revisionism where the Kennedy legacy was concerned, Teddy had decided not to run for the presidential nomination in 1976 but to concentrate on reelection to his Massachusetts Senate seat instead.

The Shrivers now provided the moral center of the family. Eunice, always the most religious and upright of the sisters, welcomed her disoriented nephews, ran summer camps for retarded children and brought Rosemary out from her nursing home for visits. Her particular interest was the Special Olympics, which she had helped to found. As the only senior member of the family with a blameless private life, Sargent Shriver, not recognizing that the glory had faded, stepped into the political breach left open by Teddy, invoking the spirit of Jack's administration and announcing, "I intend to claim that legacy."

Jackie had loyally contributed $25,000 to Sargent Shriver's campaign; and to shore up the Kennedy political presence she attended the Democratic Convention in New York in July at which Jimmy Carter won the nomination. (She was escorted to that event by her old friend Hugh Fraser, whose wife, Antonia, had left him for Harold Pinter in 1975; according to some sources, Fraser had hopes of marrying Jackie.) Lee, who had parted from Peter Beard in 1974, was there with her new lawyer boyfriend, Peter Tufo. Jackie did what she could to help Joan Kennedy, whom the rest of the family, except Eunice, tended to dismiss. It was Eunice who had persuaded Joan to enter treatment for her alcoholism.

Jackie did her best to bring Joan out of her loneliness and desperation. "I remember at one point I was just so depressed," Joan said, "and I called Jackie in New York. This was when I was living in Washington, D.C. And she said, 'Come right up.' So I got on the next plane and I left a note on the bathroom mirror for Ted . . . I stayed practically the whole week and Jackie was fabulous. She heard my story and then she told me *her* story, which absolutely bowled me over because I didn't have a clue. You have to remember that there was nothing in the United States press about Jack and the women until the mid-seventies. And nobody in the family was going to tell me. But the same thing was happening with my own husband.

"She shared everything with me. How she felt and what it did to her morale and her self-esteem. Then she said to me, 'Joan it has *nothing* to do with you. Teddy loves you . . . He loves you dearly and he's devoted to you, but it's like he can't help it, he does these other things.' She said, 'Don't let it get to you because don't take it personally . . .'

"So it went on and like another year later I called Jackie and I went up again to visit her. And that time she talked me out of divorcing Teddy. So she's very loyal to Teddy and the family—loyal to me too. She thought I should stay but then she encouraged me to do my own thing and to get more involved with my music and to see more of my women friends and lead my own life. And to be more independent. A lot of sisterly advice on how to survive . . .

"I think it was sort of like I was her sister, her younger sister, and she once said to me, which made me feel very sad, she said, 'You know, I envy you your women friends.' She said, 'I've no women friends except Bunny Mellon or women who are old enough to be my mother.' And then she said, 'And I don't even like my sister.' "[40]

⁓

In 1974 *One Special Summer*, the journal written by Jackie and Lee with illustrations by Jackie about their first trip to Europe together in 1951, had been published. Its appearance was the result of rummaging through Janet's attics when Jackie and Lee had been looking through letters, diaries and old photographs for a book of reminiscences that Lee planned but never completed. It represented a record of a happy sisterhood that no longer existed.

The germ of the Bouvier sisters' Proustian recall to Long Island had been the sudden emergence into the public eye of their aunt and cousin, Big Edie and Little

Edie Beale, who were threatened, in the summer of 1971, with eviction from their cat-haunted, dirt-encrusted, creeper-draped house, Grey Gardens, in East Hampton. Alerted by the headlines, Jackie, who had had no truck with the Bouviers since the "family" reception in the White House in 1961, asked her trusted friend, William vanden Heuvel, to deal with the situation. "I went down with Lee Radziwill the first time to see Mrs. Beale's house," he recalled. "You wouldn't have known there was a house there to begin with, the grass had grown up so wild. Here in the very manicured area of East Hampton were this couple of acres of jungle. The house, a twelve- to fifteen-room house, was practically beyond salvation . . . It was like Miss Havisham's house in *Great Expectations*. You'd come into the living room and there was at least a ten-foot pile of cat-food cans, and if you went into the dining room the spiderwebs were so thick and there were cats everywhere. The roof was practically nonexistent, the kitchen beyond use. There was a dead cat in Mrs. Beale's bedroom . . . And then I would come back," he said, "and describe to Jackie and Ari what I'd seen. And then Ari would get on the phone and he'd sing in response to the song that Big Edie was singing, and he said, 'Look, whatever has to be done, I'll pay for it . . .' "[41]

Two years later, Lee went to live with Peter Beard in Andy Warhol's house at Montauk on Long Island. Beard brought in filmmaker Jonas Mekas to make a film recalling Long Island in its heyday. They shot a number of sequences on Long Island, of Jackie and Lee swimming, Jackie and Caroline waterskiing, John Jr. and Anthony Radziwill riding on top of a station wagon. "We used a number of photographs from Jackie's childhood scrapbooks and a lot of background music. For example, there would be a still on screen of Black Jack Bouvier, and, as an accompaniment, a recording of 'My Heart Belongs to Daddy,' " Mekas recalled.[42]

The summer of 1974 seems to have been a watershed in the tortuous relationship between Jackie and Lee. The split had really begun with Lee's decision to leave Stas and go to live with Peter Beard. Jackie disapproved of Lee's behavior and said so. She loved Stas and the Radziwill children, and clearly took Stas's side. At Montauk, where Lee and Peter spent the summer, Truman Capote often came to visit, voicing complaints about Jackie's cavalier treatment of friends that were music to Lee's ears. According to Lee's biographer, Diana DuBois, Jackie reminded Truman "of a little girl who had a lot of toys in her room, and one day she's playing with this one red ball and it rolls under the bed, and then she doesn't notice or think about it again until a few years later when she happened to find it and starts playing with it again."[43] Jackie, for her part, told friends she was shocked by Lee's extravagance—"How can she need *twelve* sets of Porthault sheets?" she exclaimed.[44]

Jackie had forbidden Lee to attend Onassis's funeral, possibly because she did not want the press raking up the ashes of past relationships; of Lee's affair with him preceding her own marriage to him, the two sisters mourning the man they had shared. Lee's reaction was scornful and bitter. "Jackie finally has what she wanted," she told a mutual friend. "She's walking in black behind another coffin."[45]

Lee, understandably, was resentful. She began to feel left out of Jackie's new life, that her sister had dropped her now that she no longer needed her comfort as she had in the days of her marriages. As Lee drifted from one project to another, Jackie seemed to have her life worked out. Lee was furious when Jackie's Viking job was announced and attacked Tom Guinzburg about it when she found herself sitting next to him at dinner. The relationship had become a prickly one; there was anguish on Lee's side, irritation and even dislike on Jackie's. Some ten years later an Italian friend spent two weeks on a boat cruising up the Turkish coast to the Greek islands; there were only four on board, including Lee, who, she recalled, never stopped talking about her sister—and Onassis. "When we arrived in the Greek islands what she used to say was so shattering you understood that she suffered so much that I was horrified. It was really, really shattering . . ."[46] To Cecil Beaton one night, Lee had exploded with frustration against Jackie: "She goads me to such an extent that I yell back at her & say 'Thank heavens at last I've broken away from my parents & from you & everything of that former life . . .' "[47]

Family relationships were shifting. What had seemed the familiar pattern of life was now disrupted as one by one the older generation disappeared from the scene. Stas Radziwill died suddenly of a heart attack in his sleep on June 27, 1976. Jackie and Caroline flew over for the funeral in the chapel that Stas had built in memory of his mother near Turville. His coffin was draped with the Radziwill flag lent by a Warsaw museum. For Jackie, the death of Stas, whom she had always loved and appreciated, was another nail in the coffin of the Kennedy era. Hughdie Auchincloss died aged seventy-nine on November 20 that year in Georgetown. He was almost broke, having honorably taken on himself to pay off the debts of his firm. Janet loyally helped him with money from the legacy of her father James T. Lee, with whom she had become reconciled. (Lee's will had mentioned all his grandchildren, except Jackie and Lee, even the young Auchinclosses, who were well provided with trust funds.) Negotiations for the sale of Hammersmith Farm had been going on for at least eighteen months before Hughdie's death and were still not complete. There had been ideas of the state's buying it as a national park, even as a Kennedy memorial site, none of which had come to fruition. Hammersmith was eventually sold for $825,000 in August 1977 to a group of private investors who planned to make it a tourist attraction. Hughdie's funeral was held on November 26 at Trinity Church, Newport, at which, the local newspaper noted, Jackie and Lee arrived in separate cars and entered the church minutes apart.

Janet moved into the Castle, a charming yellow-painted eighteenth-century brick and shingle house on the Hammersmith grounds. Her care for Hughdie, who had suffered from emphysema for some years, impressed all her friends, said Mary Tyler McClenahan: "As he became more and more ill, she was one of those infinitely caring people, she did everything to make life easier for him. She found sheets that were so soft that you didn't feel them and she was just wonderfully imaginative and loving to this man. There was one of our directors [of Stratford Hall] who was a lung specialist and he was so impressed with the care that she had for her husband that he asked her to come and speak to their Annual Lung Association Meeting in Atlanta. And he said that she was the best speaker in her own quiet way that they had ever had, that she had a standing ovation, just talking in her own natural way about the care she had given him."[48]

Janet did not remain a widow for long: on November 25, 1979, she married widower J. Bingham Morris, a retired investment banker from Southampton, whom she had known since childhood and whose late wife had been a bridesmaid at her wedding to Black Jack. Jackie had flown up in August to Newport for lunch at Bailey's Beach, to meet her new stepfather and tour Hammersmith's Farm for the first time since its sale in 1977. She and Lee had tried to dissuade their mother from this marriage but, with John and Caroline and the rest of the close Auchincloss family, they attended the wedding at the Castle, described by Lee as "a happy family party."

Earlier that year Lee had almost preceded her mother to the altar. Her intended bridegroom was Newton Cope, owner of the prestigious Huntington Hotel in San Francisco, a friend of Jack Warnecke. Lee had begun a decorating business using space afforded to her by Warnecke in his New York office at Fifth Avenue and 58th Street, and one of her commissions was the redecoration of suites at Cope's Huntington Hotel. Lee and Newton Cope had been carrying on a transcontinental romance since the breakup of her relationship with Peter Tufo, a New York lawyer and, later, U.S. ambassador in Prague. Her engagement to Cope was announced in late April, the wedding to take place in San Francisco on May 3. Just two hours before the ceremony, however, the couple called it off. It was termed a postponement rather than a cancellation, and they went on their Hawaii honeymoon as planned.

Cope thought he saw the hand of Jackie in the background. Not long before the wedding she had given a small dinner party to meet him, to which she had asked mutual friends, the decorator Mark Hampton and his wife. Cope found it difficult to get anywhere with Jackie: "It was rather hard work, definitely not my cup of tea," he said. "I think the voice would have driven me crazy after a week! It was sort of like a baby talk, like she was putting it on, but evidently she did talk that way but for somebody from the Wild West out here, it didn't appeal." On that one occasion when he saw them together, he thought Lee was "intimidated" by Jackie—"The intimidation was just overpowering as far as I could tell," he said. "It's hard to put in words but every time she [Jackie] talked to her she would just stiffen up and look like—well, it's hard to explain but a physical thing was there, you could just see like a little girl talking to her mother or something . . ."[49]

The sticking point was to be Jackie's insistence that her extravagant, always-in-debt sister would be finally taken care of. "Lee was always sort of broke," Cope said. "She was always just one step ahead of the sheriff! That's why she sold that beautiful apartment she had on Park Avenue, which was a pity because right after that the market went crazy. It was on two floors and it was a beautiful place. But she got very low and then she had to keep renting places—I think at the time she was rather desperate because when we made our prenuptial agreements she was sort of broke."[50]

Jackie got her lawyer, Alexander Forger, to call Cope and discuss a prenuptial agreement. No more was heard of the matter until just two hours before the wedding when Lee called her prospective bridegroom from the hairdresser's and said, "I just got this call from Alexander Forger and he said that you didn't sign anything. What's this all about?" She put last minute pressure on him to sign. "Why won't you sign? Why don't you sign for the fifteen thousand a month?" Cope became suspicious: was this now Lee as well as Jackie or was it an agreed ploy by both? "I'm not going to do a damn thing," he told Lee. "The whole thing is upsetting, this is not for a wedding day." And he said, Cope recalled, " 'What do you want to do about it?' I said. 'Do you want to call it off until the fall, with our families, do it properly? And get all these things behind us and straightened out?' And she said, 'It's too late.' And I said, 'Let me handle it.' So I called the judge and I called all the people involved and I got it postponed. And I called her back and said, 'It's finished.' And she said, 'You're a miracle worker. We'll do it in the fall when we can get it organized with our families and children . . .' "[51]

The couple never married and their friendship was shaken by Truman Capote's vengeful revelations about Lee on *The Stanley Siegel Show* live on television on June 5, 1979. Enraged by Lee's comments to Liz Smith about her refusal to testify for Capote in his long-running dispute with Gore Vidal—"I am tired of Truman riding on my coattails to fame. What difference does it make? They are just a couple of fags"[52]—Truman quoted unpleasant comments from Lee's past: how she had said that both Peter Tufo and Newton Cope were publicity-crazy nobodies riding on her coattails. He also revealed publicly how jealous she was of Jackie. Lee's outbursts, such as those reported by Truman, may have been alcohol fueled, but Cope was puzzled by her comments as he had never seen her drunk or sneaking a drink. Nevertheless, their friendship survived and the last time she came out to stay with him, in 1981, she told him, "I just want to apologize for all the strange things I've said over the last year or so . . . It was very wrong of me."

To Lee, Jackie was still Big Sister and now, as a multimillionairess, had even more of the upper hand. Jackie did not abdicate what she saw as her responsibility for Lee, helping her financially, but the emotional rapport was no longer there. Jackie's successful life was a reproach to Lee. Also, relations between Lee and her daughter Christina were strained. "She [Lee] was very strict with the two children, Anthony didn't seem to mind but Tina was rebellious," Cope said.[53] After a bitter row, Christina ran to Aunt Jackie, and stayed away a long time, which caused an embarrassing rift between the sisters.

On October 21, 1979, the John F. Kennedy Library was formally opened after more than a decade of costly changes of site and plan. "It took every bit out of me," the architect I. M. Pei recalled, "and eventually she [Jackie] gave up on it before I did . . . the negotiating with Harvard University was very complicated." Harvard was interested in housing the Kennedy School of Government and its endowment but not the Kennedy Library. "Harvard are always coming out on top and they got the School of Government and they got rid of . . . the Kennedy Library . . . I was quite unhappy with the outcome because my choice for that site was very definitely in Harvard Square, and that was the site which President Kennedy had himself wanted . . . We were given many other sites and I spent I don't know how many years just looking at sites—and one time we were even looking over at Springfield, Massachusetts . . . So we, the architects, exhausted ourselves trying to find a design for each one of those sites. The Kennedy Library Foundation exhausted the financial resources in the process so from 1964 to 1970, those years were extremely costly to them . . . So by the time we were offered Dorchester we all breathed a sigh of relief. This one would not be contentious because, after all, that's where he came from. He was the congressman from Dorchester and that was the coping stone of his career . . .

"By then there was very little money left. We started with $27 million dollars . . . probably one third was left, clearly not enough to do a library, and to raise money was out of the question because the Kennedy name had faded, the Vietnam War had come and gone—there was one blow after another, with Bobby's assassination, Jackie's remarriage and then Chappaquiddick . . . So the family came up with a piece of money to make a go of it at least. It was a great letdown. When the end came and we could do something we had very little to work with. We tried to make the best of the site offered, which was then a tip. And we fought hard, with Jackie's help, to put the building at the tip [of Columbus Point]."[54]

The library is a beautiful glittering glass tower alone on a somewhat desolate site but right on the edge of the water, blown by winds and salt, just as Jack Kennedy would have wanted. Ironically, the Harvard establishment had rejected the Kennedy Library just as it had rejected old Joe and—almost—young Jack. Far from the WASP stronghold, Jack's library stands fittingly on Irish immigrant territory. Its first librarian was Dave Powers, guarding the Kennedy secrets within its walls as he had guarded the secrets of Jack's private life.

At the dedication ceremony Caroline spoke first, then John Jr. read Stephen Spender's poem "I Think Continually of Those Who Were Truly Great," followed by Bobby's son, Joseph P. Kennedy II, as he now grandly entitled himself, with a speech, "The Unfinished Business of Robert Kennedy." It was almost a denunciation of the unfortunate President Carter, against whom Teddy Kennedy would imminently declare himself for the Democratic nomination and who irritated Jackie by presuming to kiss her ("as if he had *droit de seigneur*," she complained to Arthur Schlesinger). There was a certain amount of resentment among Bobby's more politically minded heirs at the primacy accorded to their uncle Jack and his more relaxed children, Caroline and John, and the length of the film about Jack—forty minutes—as against the ten minutes dedicated to Bobby. Young Joe's passionate speech about moral courage had the grandchildren on their feet, shouting and applauding; as one observer commented later, "It's Robert, not Jack, who is the once and future Kennedy in this family."[55] The whole occasion and its timing announced to the world that in the autumn of 1979 the Kennedys were on the march again. In November, two weeks after the JFK Library dedication, Teddy declared his candidacy in Fanueil Hall, Boston.

But it was a different kind of march in different times. Although polls showing Carter as virtually unelectable in 1980 panicked Democrats into urging Teddy to run, old Kennedy hands, like Ted Sorensen and Richard Goodwin, argued against it. "I was involved more on the fringes once he got into it," Ted Sorensen recalled.

"I was very involved in the discussions that led up to him getting involved in it—in fact, I was opposed to his getting into it . . . But if Jackie was, as you say, 're-luctantly for,' that certainly sounds right . . . Of course, Chappaquiddick was an unsolved problem that cast a pall over the campaign, but I also felt that to run against an incumbent Democratic President was not his best shot, and he only had one shot."[56]

"I was involved but that was a hopeless campaign—hopeless, mismanaged, mis-conceived," Richard Goodwin said, "I was with Teddy at the beginning, living down at his house when he was getting ready to run, but from the beginning it was doomed . . . Teddy was in such deep trouble from day one that it was over."[57] By the end, Teddy had lost primary after primary and, with few exceptions, been humiliated on television and in the press. His speech at Georgetown University and rousing conclusion at the Democratic National Convention in August, at which President Carter won the nomination, were, however, outstanding pieces of oratory and kept the Democratic liberal banner aloft. But the presidency, which the Kennedys had come to regard almost as theirs of right, had finally slipped from the grasp of the generation of Jack and Bobby.

Jackie had played her part, a powerful symbol of the Kennedys' right to be considered America's royal family. She had stood uncomfortably on the platform at Teddy's declaration as the Kennedys trooped on to be introduced one by one, almost as if in conclusion to a vaudeville show. She and her children stood mainly aloof from the campaigning in which the other Kennedy women and children took part, until Teddy reached New York, apparently on the eve of disaster, in March 1980. Polls predicted a devastating loss for him in New York, hitherto considered the family's "home state" after Massachusetts. Jackie held a council of war of old Kennedy hands at 1040 to discuss ways of persuading him to withdraw and avoid final humiliation. In the end luck saved him. Carter's U.N. ambassador offended the Jewish community by condemning Israeli settlement policy and denying Israel's sovereignty over Jerusalem. Inflation and interest rates went up and the stock market down, contributing to discontent with Carter. Encouraged, the Kennedy camp made last-minute efforts; Jackie appeared in Spanish Harlem and at a large Greek-American meeting in Queens, where she was greeted with rapture, and Teddy won the New York primary. On June 21 the Kennedys cele-brated the matriarch Rose's ninetieth birthday with a huge family fund-raiser and "Rose" parades in Boston. But it was all to no avail: Teddy won a few battles but, at huge political and financial cost, he lost the war. "For me, a few hours ago," he concluded, "this campaign came to an end. For all those whose cares have been our concern, the work goes on, the cause endures, the hope still lives and the dream shall never die."

Jackie, however, wanted no part of it for herself or for her children. She did not want to see them burdened by the weight of the Kennedy dream, the dreaded "legacy." Jackie's acute instinct of self-preservation and her ability to move on-ward and upward from a losing situation was to preserve her and, above all, her children from the Kennedy family disasters still to come.

CHAPTER TWENTY-TWO

Private Lives

⁓

*. . . the real Jackie, she was real with her kids, everything was for the kids. She
lived for her kids, she would have done anything for them.*

—Peter Beard[1]

Jackie always remained loyal to the Kennedys but by 1979 she had succeeded in
establishing a life of independence from them, both for herself and for her children. Her primary objective, as she had told Pierre Salinger in the days immediately after Jack's assassination, had always been to bring up Caroline and John as
capable, successful human beings. As an old Kennedy friend had said in 1968,
Jackie had been determined from the first that her children should not be subsumed into the Kennedy embrace: "Jackie intends to raise the children herself.
She has no intention of letting Caroline and John become the eleventh and
twelfth children of Bobby and Ethel. She wants her children to realize that, even
though the family is now reduced to three, it is still a unit, and they still belong to
the President and to her."[2] She had seen to it that they kept that identity through
the years of her marriage to Onassis, at considerable cost to her own relationship
with her Greek husband.

Caroline was twenty-one years old when she stood up as the first of the
younger generation to celebrate the dedication of her father's library. She had
been approaching her sixth birthday when her father had been killed nearly sixteen years before, old enough to remember him and the shock of his death, the
all-encompassing grief and the solemnity of his funeral obsequies, the days of her
mother's weeping, the change of circumstance between the White House and its
aftermath. She had been seven when she had flown with her family to England to
visit the Queen and have tea at Windsor Castle, then to be separated from her
nanny, Maud Shaw, the one person who had always been with her since she was a

baby. She had been ten years old when her adored uncle and father figure, Bobby, was killed in Los Angeles, occasioning another unbelievable, tear-filled funeral and aching sense of loss. Three months later, she had been a solemn, confused witness as her mother had married a Greek old enough to be her grandfather, surrounded by strangers in a strange land. She had been brought up in a world of butlers, maids, chauffeurs and Secret Service agents, designed to keep at bay a gawking world of people and photographers who leaped out from behind bushes in Central Park. Through her teenage years she had become used to a world of private jets and yachts, to a sense of apartness from the common herd. For all her mother's efforts to shield Caroline's privacy and to enable her to lead a normal life, her life experience so far had not been normal and never could be.

Jackie had been determined that Caroline should remember her father with pride, despite the distasteful revelations about him that erupted around her from 1975 onward. One wall of Caroline's room was plastered with photographs of him and of Caroline with her father; she kept albums of stamps bearing his portrait. It had been she who had proudly dedicated the new aircraft carrier, the *John F. Kennedy*. Yet while Caroline and John Jr. were always conscious of being their father's children, Jackie was anxious that they should not become involved in the more dangerous aspects of the Kennedy culture, as practiced by their cousins. "You know, it was a pretty wild scene down at Hyannis after Bobby died," Richard Goodwin said, "with drugs and drinking. She [Jackie] wanted the kids to keep their distance so she was never close to that generation, really. She did stay at Hyannis itself for a few years before she moved to the Vineyard. I just think they were different kind of people . . . Half the stuff became totally destructive," Goodwin went on. "They had a troubled childhood, those kids. Ethel was a difficult mother. Yelling things and then withdrawing, the worst possible combination. But you can understand why she had problems."[3]

Jackie's marriage to Onassis had removed John and Caroline from the scene just as the younger generation began to descend into wildness after Bobby's death. Summers were largely spent on Skorpios, with brief visits to Hyannis Port and to Janet at Newport, Easter vacations often cruising on the *Christina*, Christmas and New Year's usually with the Radziwills at Turville or in the Caribbean. On the whole they saw more of Anthony and Christina Radziwill, described by a friend of Lee as "really nice, well-brought-up classy kids,"[4] than of their Kennedy cousins. Caroline, in particular, loved riding and foxhunting at Far Hills in winter and spring. They did not, therefore, have to share the claustrophobic, competitive, troubled atmosphere surrounding the Bobby Kennedy and Peter Lawford sons in which drugs played a large part, and the sense of the Kennedy legacy weighed down on them.

Then there was Marta, their "governess" and constant companion since 1969 and before Caroline went to boarding school. According to Marta, they were never in New York in the summer after school closed; while Onassis was alive they went to Skorpios and would come back to Hyannis Port in August until September. There was swimming, sailing, waterskiing, running on the beach and, at Hyannis Port, touch football and baseball. On winter weekends they went to

New Jersey or skiing at Hunter Mountain in upstate New York; the *Christina* would be moored in the United States and the children would join Onassis on her for some exciting warm-weather cruises. After Jackie's last summer on Skorpios in 1975, when her settlement was being thrashed out, she took the children to Hyannis Port but she was already planning an escape for herself and for them, a house on Martha's Vineyard which was completed in 1980.

After school Marta would take the children to play in Central Park, and once a week, until it got cold, for tennis lessons watched by the Secret Service and occasionally stalked by Ron Galella. At home they would have tea—hot chocolate with whipped cream and marshmallows, and cinnamon toast. Jackie liked what John called her "diet food" but "Madam," as Marta always referred to her, would have what the children liked—creamed chicken or beef Stroganoff—at mealtimes when they all ate together. Taking a leaf out of Grandfather Joe Kennedy's book, Jackie had a world map pinned to the wall of the dining room so that she could show them where she and their father had traveled. John's birthday was on November 25, and Caroline's on the twenty-seventh. They always celebrated them separately and always over Thanksgiving weekend in New Jersey. They would drive down on Wednesday and Jackie would immediately go riding.

Their childhood in New York and New Jersey, insulated by wealth and privilege, was very much like that of any rich east coast family, but for one thing: the American public's perception of them as America's own royalty. "Things happen to them that do not necessarily happen to other children," Jackie said. "Caroline was knocked down by a charge of photographers when I took her out to try to teach her to ski. How do you explain that to a child? And the stares and the pointing . . ."

Caroline's first school was the Convent of the Sacred Heart at 91st Street and Fifth Avenue, run by an order of nuns that was originally French; the order had been founded in 1800 for the specific purpose of educating the daughters of the upper classes. John attended St. David's, a school for boys established for "the scholastic and moral preparation of young men as Christian gentlemen" run on the same principles by Catholic laymen. At ten, Caroline looked like a Kennedy, with a mane of thick dark blond hair, bright blue eyes, the prominent Kennedy nose and flashing teeth. She had the Kennedy athleticism but in temperament she was more like her mother, shy but with a wickedly observant eye and an inquiring, quick intelligence. At school, the other children were all too aware of who she was and particularly who her mother was. She stuck close to her two Lawford cousins, who were at the same school, and for a time found it difficult to make friends because other mothers felt shy about asking her over. Her Christmas treat, hardly the normal ten-year-old's experience, was to take six friends to lunch at La Caravelle, one of Manhattan's smartest restaurants.

John, an exuberant, extroverted little boy with his mother's thick dark hair, brown eyes and well-shaped features, had the capacity to make friends easily and communicate with anyone he met; he encountered fewer problems than his sister had at school. He was only four when he entered St. David's, where his classmates had not the faintest idea who he was, and not yet five when his absence from roll call was explained, "John's gone to London to see the Queen," at the time of the Runnymede dedication. In September 1968 Jackie transferred him to Collegiate School. Caroline was later moved from the Sacred Heart Convent to Brearley, the smartest of New York's girls' schools. In the autumn of 1972 Caroline began her first year of boarding school at Concord Academy, in Massachusetts. Jackie tried to make Caroline's New York upbringing mirror her own. Remembering how much she had loved ballet, she tried to instill her enthusiasm into Caroline. Never one to do things by halves, she had Caroline given private lessons by the prima ballerina Maria Tallchief and enrollled her in the School of American Ballet but Caroline dropped out halfway through the course. "I love ballet and she doesn't," Jackie said. "She just wasn't interested. She loves horses."[5]

To protect the children's privacy and allow them the maximum chance of leading a normal life, Jackie imposed the no-publicity regime even more strictly than she had during the White House years when occasionally, to please Jack, she had allowed carefully vetted beautifully photographed pictures of happy-family scenes. To keep away photographers and reporters, Secret Service men escorted Caroline to Brearley and stationed themselves outside her classroom door. Although the Collegiate School bus stopped for a neighbor, John never took it, but left 1040 by a side entrance accompanied by Marta, Muggsy O'Leary, and the spaniel, Shannon, and climbed into a battered cream and tan Oldsmobile to be driven across town by a Secret Service man to the school at 241 West 77th Street, on the then unfashionable Upper West Side.

The Secret Service agents were a necessity: the FBI files report several kidnap threats against the children, but Jackie was anxious that they were exposed to life as much as possible and not cocooned in cotton. As Peter Beard said, she was a "gutsy" mother, determined that the children should face life without fear. In 1968 she pleaded with the Secret Service director James Rowley, asking him to order his men to "back off" in the closeness of their surveillance: "Agents tramp outside the children's windows all night, talking into their walkie-talkies," she wrote. "Cars pile up in the driveway so that our little country house looks like a used-car lot." When John, aged thirteen, was mugged in Central Park she apparently told her bodyguards that it would be a good experience for him, and that he "must be allowed to experience life . . . and that unless he is allowed freedom, he'll be a vegetable."

If Caroline didn't share her mother's enthusiasm for ballet, she was interested, like Jackie, in photography, and encouraged by Peter Beard. In the summer of 1973 she spent four weeks living with a local family and helping make a government-sponsored documentary on the daily life of coal miners' families in the small Appalachian town of Clairfield in eastern Tennessee. The following summer, aged sixteen, she worked as an unpaid intern in her uncle Teddy's Senate office on Capitol Hill, and stayed with her aunt Ethel at Hickory Hill. At the beginning of 1975 she and Karen Lerner worked on the Kashoggi project for NBC and later went to Sweden.

After graduating from Concord in the summer of 1975, Caroline was due to enroll at Radcliffe College, Harvard, carrying on the Kennedy tradition. In the autumn Jackie, always keen to involve Caroline in her own interests and, above all, enable her to make her own way in life, sent her to London to take a fine arts course at Sotheby's, where she was to stay in Campden Hill Square, Notting Hill, with Hugh Fraser. The Frasers' daughters, Flora and Rebecca, were around Caroline's age, and able to introduce her to a wide circle of friends. The idea of Caroline's taking the Sotheby's course apparently stemmed from the family's friendship with Mark Shand, the dashing blond nephew of the Kennedys' friend Harry Ashcombe (and brother of Camilla Parker Bowles) whom Jackie and Caroline had met in the Bahamas in 1972. Shand had been on the first of the art courses and was now an art dealer. His circle included the smart or amusing people of his age—Lord Hesketh and his brother Bobby, Nicholas Soames, Adam Carr.

Escorted principally by Mark Shand, Caroline quickly became popular and had a lively social life, nightclubbing at Annabel's and Tramp, eating in her group's favorite restaurants, Morton's and the Meridiana, going to deb dances and weekends in the country, notably at the Heskeths' superb house in Northamptonshire, Easton Neston, designed by Nicholas Hawksmoor. In London she attended a launch party for Andy Warhol, crowded with celebrities dressed in outrageous London clothes ("Freaks—all freaks," a delighted Warhol exclaimed). Patrick Lichfield, the celebrated photographer and cousin of the Queen, met Caroline there for the first time: "She's much better-looking than her pictures suggest," he said. "A strong, interesting face. A face that reveals personality."[6]

In London, Caroline enjoyed a freedom she could never have had in New York or in Cambridge, Massachusetts, where the Kennedy name meant that she was never left alone. For the first time, she was away from her mother so could do more or less as she pleased and live the life of her contemporaries—dancing, having a drink, smoking the occasional joint. The paparazzi were still a pest, however, and Caroline resented it: "Why should I be a public figure?" she asked a friend.[7] She dressed simply and unfashionably, even in the evenings, wearing very little makeup, as if she wanted not to be noticed. In the boisterous company of her friends, she was easily the quietest person at the table.

Inevitably, however much Jackie might try, Caroline suffered from having a famous, glamorous mother. At the age of almost eighteen, she rebelled against her mother's constant solicitude and attempts to guide her. At the Royal Geographical Society where Jackie had taken her in the hope of awakening an interest in geography, the director noticed with some amusement that while Jackie asked all the interesting questions, Caroline just stood there "looking absolutely spaced out." Despite her popularity, life was not easy for her, she could never feel sure that people liked her for herself rather than for her unwanted celebrity. She was going through a difficult time and Jackie was having difficulties with her. At Claridge's, where Jackie always stayed when she was in London, the manager found a touching message to her daughter scrawled in lipstick on the mirror over the basin: "Darling, Always remember that Mummy loves you."[8]

While in London, Caroline almost became yet another Kennedy fatality. Just before nine o'clock on the morning of October 23, Hugh Fraser was about to leave the house with her, giving her a lift to Sotheby's before going on to the

House of Commons where he was a Member of Parliament, when he was called back to the telephone. Minutes later a huge explosion rocked the house. Fraser's green Jaguar, parked outside, was wrecked. A distinguished cancer specialist, Gordon Hamilton Fairley, walking past with his dogs at the time, was killed, his body hurled into the Frasers' garden. The bomb had been placed by the IRA and designed to go off when the car moved. Fraser and Caroline had been saved by a telephone call.

Fraser immediately telephoned Pamela Harlech, and asked, "Can you come and get her? Can she stay with you? Because we're surrounded by the press. Also, in case there's another one . . ." The Harlechs lived within a few hundred yards of the Frasers. "So I said yes," Pamela Harlech recalled, "and I brought her back with me and she stayed with us for about a week because we were then, in fact, going to New York. I spoke to Jackie every single day twice a day because she wanted to know how it was . . ."

Not for the last time, Pamela Harlech was to find her husband's old friend less than warm. Arriving in New York, where David Harlech was due to give some lectures, she received the "Regal Jackie" treatment. "Jean Smith gave a drinks party for us. And we were standing around and Jackie walked in and I was going to do the usual kissing on both cheeks and she said, 'Hello,' sticking out a regal hand. I'm not the only person she did this to because Betsy Whitney, who loves the world—she's wonderful—once said to me, 'There are very few people I dislike in this world and Jackie's one of them.' Because she'd do exactly the same. She'd go and stay with Jock and Betsy and then the next time she saw them she'd say, 'Hello,' like that, like the Queen . . ."9

Jackie's capriciousness, her ability to withdraw and turn cold were curious aspects of her character to which many people who knew her, but not those closest to her, were exposed. She could deliberately tease people, sometimes light-heartedly, sometimes protractedly like a cat playing with a mouse. One friend remembers being asked to lunch at 1040 to help entertain Rose Kennedy and the Duchess of Windsor: "Both quite old and a little bit gaga. So it was clothes, clothes, admiring clothes, looking at clothes, and I had met the Duchess in her prime and she was definitely over the edge and Mrs. Kennedy wasn't really a very interesting woman, I don't think. I remember we went into the dining room and there was a beautiful sort of gold belt with beautiful turquoise in it and studded with precious stones. 'Oh,' Mrs. Kennedy said, 'that's the most beautiful belt, Jackie—you should wear it—it would make any dress.' 'Oh,' Jackie said, 'a *petit rien de tout.*' It was from the King of Persia, I guess. And then the same thing happened again. On the table there was a great big gold handbag with a jeweled clasp on it. Mrs. Kennedy and the Duchess were just absorbed in those details. And I could see that Jackie was a little embarrassed about it but she was also having quite a bit of fun . . ."10 In the days when she was married to Onassis, Jackie liked to tease women whom she saw making up to her husband by mischievously sending them flowers the next day "from Ari."

Sometimes she seemed to enjoy elaborate charades of game-playing, usually with ex-admirers and their wives. On one occasion she invited a couple staying with friends on Cape Cod over for lunch at her house on Martha's Vineyard. "You're not going to like this," the husband told his wife. "Jackie wants us to come for the day to Martha's Vineyard . . . We've got to." Jackie offered to send a private plane over to fetch them, and when they demurred, said, "Just think of it instead of a rich dessert . . ." They arrived and there was no Jackie: "It was so hot outside you wouldn't believe. There was no real airport, just a sort of hangar, no place to sit. So we were sitting on the curb in this boiling sun. About half an hour later a Range Rover type thing rolls up with Jackie at the wheel and we all pile in. I remember I had my daughter on my lap and Jackie drove barefoot like a maniac. We arrived at the house and she said, 'What do you all want to do?' This was about half past twelve and I said, 'Well, a Bloody Mary would be quite nice,' and she said, 'Well, we're going to the beach first.' "

The party sat boiling on the beach, watching Jackie do her prescribed laps up and down and then go swimming. "My husband—because he has better manners than the rest of us—went and joined her swimming . . . OK, we went back and we said, 'Now we can have a Bloody Mary?' And this is the hostess of the White House, you understand. And she said, in her little-girl voice, 'But I don't know what goes into a Bloody Mary.' So I said, 'OK, Jackie, I'll tell you exactly what goes into a Bloody Mary and I'll make it.' I couldn't stand this, and I asked for Worcestershire sauce and lemon, you know—'Oh, really?' And then she said to my husband, 'I don't know how to load the camera, it's so complicated.' So he put the film in, moved it along, shut it and off it went. And she said, 'Oh, that was so clever. I can never do anything with the sprockets.' And I thought, Sprockets? And he said, 'Well, Jackie, actually all you have to do is read the instructions'—I mean, even he was getting a bit fed up. It was so tiring because the whole thing was a performance and not taking care of the guests but sort of 'Here I am, folks, aren't you lucky?' So we went through this charade."[11]

"She was full of complexities and contradictions," a woman who had known Jackie since she was a teenager said. "There was a great sense of competition and hostility. Taking people up, making much of them, then a drop and no one ever knew why. In the time after Onassis died we were having a dinner party. There was a man she was going out with and I arranged for him to pick her up. She was outraged and canceled at twenty minutes to eight. You could count on her where children and animals were concerned, it was only people there were difficulties with . . ."[12]

Canceling a dinner party because she had taken umbrage at what was meant to be a helpful gesture was petty, designed to punish her erstwhile friend for having presumed to make such an arrangement without consulting her. Another victim of "Regal Jackie" was Andy Warhol, who had the temerity to turn up for one of her parties not only inexcusably late but bringing with him an uninvited friend, Bob Colacello. While this might be considered a more serious social offense, Jackie's retaliation was excessive and vindictive. Her friend, Marietta Tree, former U.S. ambassador for human rights to the United Nations, an American aristocrat and social queen of New York, refused to allow Warhol's friend and patron, Henry Gillespie, to include Warhol in a party he proposed bringing to Marietta's

Sutton Place apartment.[13] She later confessed to him that her reason was a ukase issued by Jackie. "Jackie had asked Marietta and her other friends to punish Warhol for this rudeness by not inviting him to their parties."[14]

At times even her admirers found it difficult to penetrate the public persona. Asked to describe Jackie, a cousin said, "It's very, very hard because the enormous warmth and outgivingness had a quality of the stage. It was certainly not all sincere but you were very grateful for having it put on. It was kind of a compliment to you that she put it on at all. She was constantly acting, there's no question about that. But she wasn't a total actress, there were some parts that were true." He compared Jackie with the most celebrated of American geishas, Pamela Harriman: "Mrs. Harriman had that marvelous quality of making you feel you were the only man in the room, in the world. Jackie had some of that quality too, but on the other hand, Mrs. Harriman heard everything you said and Jackie half the time wasn't listening . . . She also had a quick way of assuming that because of the enormous power of her personality people were going to do as she said. And I remember once when I was turning her down on a proposition . . . she wasn't listening to me at all. And finally she said, 'You mean you won't do it?' She thought she had me all buttoned up and then . . ."[15]

The actor Anthony Quinn, formerly on friendly terms, was frozen out in 1975 for agreeing to star in The Greek Tycoon, a film obviously based on the Onassis-Jackie story. Immediately after the project was announced, he received a telephone call from Nancy Tuckerman. She said she was calling on behalf of Mrs. Onassis who had "a high regard" for him but would be most appreciative if he did not do the picture. Quinn called back, "Please tell Mrs. Onassis that the picture is only an idea . . . But in any case, my involvement is the best insurance that she will be treated with respect and affection." Quinn could hear Nancy conferring with Jackie, who did not come to the telephone herself; the message was that "Mrs. Onassis would appreciate it very much if you would deny that you are going to appear in the picture." What Quinn did, however, was to appear at the Cannes film festival in a publicity stunt for the picture (which as yet had not even a script) that involved a party on a yacht (actually a tourist sightseeing boat) and photographs of him wearing a pair of Onassis-style sunglasses. Later that week he was lunching at the Colombe d'Or in St. Paul de Vence when Jackie walked in. Quinn started to get up to greet her, ". . . and she walked right by me as if we had never met," he recalled. "I tried to catch her eye, and I even waved. But there was nothing. No acknowledgment."[16] What, one might wonder, had Quinn expected?

Even those who knew her well, like Louis Auchincloss, could be surprised by her capriciousness. They had worked together on Maverick in Mauve, the diary of Auchincloss's wife's grandmother, Florence Adele Sloane. Auchincloss was puzzled and a little annoyed by Jackie's sudden refusal to attend the publishing party for the book in 1983, showing what he described as "a curious quirk in her nature . . . stemming from her ambivalent attitude toward the press, which had brought her both fame and pain." She had suggested that it might be a good idea to give the party at the Museum of the City of New York, combining it with photographs of New York in the 1860s as a background to Florence Sloane's diary. "As I was president of that institution and willing to pay for the show, it was easily arranged but, at the last minute, I was informed that Jackie might not attend the party because there would be reporters there!" Auchincloss said. Nancy Tuckerman conveyed the message. Usually, he said, Nancy was an independent, rather vital source, but when he told her, " 'Well, Nancy, you must talk to her. I mean this is nonsense, you know it's nonsense,' Nancy collapsed on me, completely collapsed on me. She was her [Jackie's] slave. She wouldn't do a damn thing. I said, 'Well, you tell her I'm going to write a letter to her.' And Jackie instantly saw the point. She came early, stayed late, charmed everybody and made the party," Auchincloss recorded.[17]

Back in 1978, Jackie had taken two major steps toward independence and self-fulfillment. The first was the creation of her own private kingdom on Martha's Vineyard, distinct from the Kennedy compound at Hyannis Port. The island was a short plane hop away but it was a different world, more select, and difficult of access. "I think she was very proud of that property," her friend Ashton Hawkins said, "she loved it and I think it made her very happy, sort of reminded her of a lot of good things, but it wasn't connected with the Kennedy family in any way. So similar to what they had there but a different place. I remember feeling that she was extremely proud of that, that was sort of like maybe the first place she built on her own . . ."[18] As Jackie had once written, "I think that one of the finest things one can do in life is to create a loved house that shelters generations and gives them memories to build on."[19]

She had bought some four hundred acres of Martha's Vineyard wetlands near Gay Head on the old Hornblower estate farm for just under a million dollars. On a site overlooking the freshwater Squibnocket Pond toward the ocean she loved, she built her favorite house. Jackie's land had once belonged to the Wampanoag Indians, descendants of whom still live on the island. It is the part of the island known as Upisland, a landscape of woods and ponds, with traces of stone walls built by the farmer-settlers. An area of larger estates, with dirt roads to discourage adventurous tourists ("These are privacy people," said the guide—the approach to Jackie's house was guarded by a menacing-looking warden), her property stretched down from the road between Chilmark and Menemsha, in an expanse of grass and native shrubs, to the ocean.

The architect was Hugh Newell Jacobsen, a fashionable and successful Washington-based architect recommended to her by I. M. Pei and Bunny Mellon. "I had met the lady, danced with her once," Jacobsen remembered, "but she wouldn't remember me at all . . . And I got a call and, my God, there was that name and that voice and she asked me whether I'd be interested in doing it. I said, 'Of course,' and I flew up to Hyannis Port."

Asked what Jackie was like to work for, he said, "She was great to work *with*, because she really got into it, and really didn't know how to read drawings—very few people do and most people lie about it. It's like admitting that they've got something terribly wrong with them if they can't read a blueprint—and she didn't play any games like that. She laid the whole house out in string on the beach in Hyannis so that she could walk from room to room."[20] Sometimes they went over to Osterville to meet the Mellons for lunch and go over the plans again with Bunny, whose vision for the house and gardens was the paramount influence on Jackie.

For all the forethought and carefully placed strings, when it came to the site on the Vineyard, things occasionally went awry. Bunny and Jackie arrived one day with Jacobsen to find that the string had been strung and the site staked out with the orientation facing the wrong direction. "Jackie was not at all pleased by her architect," Jacobsen said. "She said, 'If you'd been like Alex [Forger, her attorney] you would have been up here the day before and checked that—I'm always having to come up here and check things.' And I said, 'That's why we always do it in string,' but it didn't work, and I was abandoned on the island. They left in the plane without me as I restrung the place!"

Jacobsen designed the house as a series of connected pavilions, one wing of which was specifically designated "Bunny's room," built of the local white cedar shingles with white-painted windows and doors. There was a separate barn—guesthouse with a big living room and three bedrooms and a "grain silo," which was John's—a bedroom, a bath and a huge room eighteen feet in diameter.

Although Jackie loved the house, Jacobsen unwittingly offended her; in typical Jackie fashion she cut off relations with him without saying why. Jacobsen was puzzled, and when he went to Alex Forger for his final payment, said to him, " 'All of my clients are my friends, and this is the first client I've ever lost. I haven't talked to her for nearly two months.' And he said, 'Well, I'll tell you exactly what happened, Architect'—which is what he always called me. 'It was on October 23 at four o'clock in the afternoon when you had driven up to Derry End for her to see a new house that you had just completed up there to show her the lighting you wanted to use. You said something to her that no one has ever said to her—you implied that she had no taste.' "[21]

As with everything Jackie did, her house on Martha's Vineyard, Red Gate Farm, aroused enormous curiosity. Invisible from the road and guarded, the only approach was from the air. *Women's Wear Daily* organized an aerial photographic raid; the maid told her story and the plumber sold copies of the plans. The Kennedy sisters were particularly curious—and were not invited to inspect it. Joan, however, was. "The first summer she was there, I remember her calling me in Hyannis Port and she invited me to come over for the weekend. So I said, 'Well, thanks, I'd love to go,' because everyone in the world was dying to find out about the house because nobody could get close enough to photograph it. Jackie had said to me when I was leaving, 'You know what's going to happen when you get back? They're all going to be on top of you asking questions.' She thought it was funny, she enjoyed the fact that they were all dying to come over but didn't quite get why she'd invited me and not them. She was never unkind or malicious to them but she had this delightful tease aspect . . ."

Jackie also enjoyed teasing Teddy, of whom—apart from at certain moments in their lives—she was very fond. "The other tease aspect," Joan said, "was when I would be visiting her after I'd found out about one of Teddy's women. I'd call her up and run up and stay a few days. Especially the first time—Teddy called the next night to see how we were doing. She spoke to him very politely and then when she hung up the phone, she said to me, 'He is *dying* . . . He is absolutely because he knows I'm going to tell you everything. He wants to know what we're talking about. He knows he can't ask you and he can't ask me.' She got a kick out of the fact that she was making him extremely uncomfortable."[22]

In March 1979 Gloria Steinem wrote a piece in *Ms.* reflecting on Jackie's life, past and present, her Kennedy and Onassis marriages and her experience in those cases of "being treated like a totally different person even though the only change is the identity of the man standing next to her." Even when she was alone again after Onassis's death, the speculation about her future could base itself on only two possible patterns resulting from her previous marriages. "Would she become a Kennedy again (that is, more politically influential and serious) or remain an Onassis (more supposedly social and simply rich)? No one was predicting that she might go back to work in the publishing world she had entered briefly after college—and to the kind of job she could have had years ago, completely on her own." For the Most Famous Woman in the World to take a job and enter the ordinary world required courage and resolve: "Given the real options of using Kennedy power or of living an Onassis-style life, how many of us would have the strength to return to our own careers—to choose personal work over derived influence?" Steinem asked.[23]

In February 1978 Jackie had returned to work in publishing with Doubleday, where Nancy Tuckerman had once worked in the publicity department and whose president was an old friend, John Sargent. She had cut her teeth and learned her trade in her time at Viking; the years she spent at Doubleday, from 1978 until her death, were increasingly to become the most successful and satisfying of her publishing career. As a writer *manquée* she was the perfect editor, treating other people's texts with the precision and intelligence with which she edited her own life—shaping, cutting, deploying the *mot juste*, the precise image.

Being an editor appealed to her sense of adventure. "What I like about being an editor," she said, "is that it expands your knowledge and heightens your discrimination. Each book takes you down another path . . ." *In the Russian Style* had taken her to Moscow and St. Petersburg with Diana Vreeland and Tom Hoving; *Atget's Gardens*, photographs by the French photographer of royal parks and gardens, recalled her youthful experiences of Versailles and her passion for French history, as did Deborah Turbeville's *Unseen Versailles* and Olivier Bernier's lives of Louis XIV and Marie Antoinette. *Paris After the Liberation: 1944–1949*, by Artemis Cooper and Antony Beevor, described a world Jackie had encountered when she first visited Paris; Jonathan Cott's *The Search for Omm Sety*, the story of a twentieth-century English priestess of Osiris, recalled her fascination with ancient Egypt (she had met Dorothy Eady, alias Omm Sety, living in a mud hut at Abydos, when she was on a trip down the Nile with Onassis). She had loved Indian art since her first visit to India in 1962; Naveen Patnaik's *A Second Paradise: Indian Courtly Life, 1590–1947* was an opportunity for further exploration, touring India with her friends Cary and Edith Welch and Patnaik himself, brother of Gita Mehta, and visiting old friends like the Jaipurs. She enjoyed working with friends like George Plimpton on a collection of Toni Frissell's photographs and his own book on fireworks, Mark Hampton on twentieth-century decorators, John Pope-Hennessy and André Previn on their autobiographies, and on Diana Vreeland's *Allure*. She persuaded Rudolf Nureyev to write a foreword to a book of Pushkin's fairy tales, and ballerina Gelsey Kirkland to write the controversial story of her life. "When Jackie gave me the opportunity to write my autobiography, she helped me recover my life and my career," Kirkland recalled.[24] With an old friend, Marc Riboud, she worked on *The Capital of Heaven*. She joined him in China while he was photographing at the University of Beijing, acting as his assistant. For an entire day at the university she went unrecognized, an unusual pleasure.

Even old friends found that working with Jackie as an editor revealed a side of her that they had not been aware existed. "I knew Jackie for many years," Marc Riboud recalled. "But it was only when we worked together that I started really to know her. We were now accomplices, with one goal: the success of a book. Then, beyond the surface brilliance, I discovered an intense seriousness and an astonishing strength of will. With intelligence and passion, she demanded the highest quality."[25]

Although she never worked a full week in the office, she gave of herself hugely to her authors even when she wasn't there. Working with Louis Auchincloss on *False Dawn* (1984), a series of biographical essays on women of the seventeenth century, she took the manuscript with her to Martha's Vineyard and worked on it without stopping for a day and a night. She sent him seven pages of critical factual details, then launched into her general impressions of the book, revealing her feeling for its subjects:

> I have always thought Henriette d'Angleterre must have been one of the most enchanting women who ever walked on this planet. Could we have more about her? . . . Maybe Elizabeth of Bohemia wasn't that beautiful, but the poem Henry Wootton wrote about her is one of the loveliest things ever written about a woman . . . The Grande Mademoiselle is my favorite chapter . . . I can see and hear everyone as I write this, feel the cold when she is by the fire with Lauzun, sense the excitement on the ramparts, see her big red nose and ungainly walk . . . I want every chapter to be a novel so that I can know more about these people, and imagine them in their settings . . .[26]

As Louis Auchincloss wrote, "Doesn't that show why she was a writer's dream as an editor? Where would you find her today in a world of megapublishers?"[27] Even shortly before her death she was putting her all into the books she was working on. "She was brilliant in the way that she saw what was needed in the final chapter," Antony Beevor recalled, of the book he wrote jointly with his wife, Artemis Cooper, on Paris after the Liberation. "She said, 'What you've got to do is bring your three themes together in a crescendo where they come together naturally.' She was absolutely right—and that was what brought together and sorted out the whole book in the end, the right advice at just the right moment."[28]

Stephen Rubin, who as president and publisher at Doubleday worked with Jackie from 1990 to 1994, remembered that she would work on some projects as a good team player but "When the project was hers and hers alone and something that she was quite passionate about, every *i* and every *t* was dotted and crossed, and she got involved in the acquisition including negotiating with agents. She was smart enough to know what she didn't know so if someone came at her with something that was slightly—where her antenna went up, she would come straight to me and say, 'Can I do that?' She didn't say, 'That's OK,' and then suddenly we found ourselves involved in a stupid contractual dispute. When the manuscript was finished she got involved in the scheduling of the book, in the designing of the book, in the flap copy of the book, clearly in the jacket of the book, and if it was hers, something she was genuinely involved with, she would also, if there was a publication party, go. Now, she hated those things. However, trouper that she was, she would be the first one there and the last one to leave. She did evolve really good relationships, as any good editor should, with all her authors, and she was quite the mother hen who clucked quite a bit, when it was necessary, to protect her authors."[29]

Jackie, however, was quite practical when it came to the financial viability of a project. Steve Rubin described himself as being "in a state of terror when I first had to deal with her, because I thought, 'Oh, God, here I am, taking over this company at a time when it really wasn't very healthy, and do I have to let her do books which are going to lose us money?' I think we evolved a very good working relationship pretty quickly . . . If she brought in something that I didn't quite get, that made financial sense, sure. If it didn't make financial sense I would have a conversation with her and she did pull away from those things . . ."

The important thing with Jackie in the office, Rubin said, was to behave normally. "The deal was that the only way you were going to evolve any kind of relationship with Jackie was to treat her like anyone else. The minute you treated her like Jacqueline Onassis, this guard would come up and an invisible shield would slam down and you wouldn't get through. She would close down in a way that was absolutely chilling and terrifying. So that essentially you had to learn that this woman was indeed at the Xerox machine by herself, that all those stories were true, that she was getting her own coffee, that she was going to boring meetings . . . You had to get beyond that point and once you got beyond that point it was great. Because she always had something interesting to say and it was always slightly left or right of center, not banal, it was absolutely fresh . . ."

Rubin was amused to see how Jackie dealt with the electric reaction to her presence. "It was just amazing to get into an elevator with her and to watch everyone go—and Jackie, of course, in small spaces was just like a horse with blinders on and she just wasn't paying any attention . . . I saw her walking out of the building one day and I decided to just walk behind her to see what happened, and I saw her make herself invisible. She knew how to do it, she sort of folded into herself just walking along the street and she had a kerchief and shades on . . ."

As a colleague, he said, Jackie was "fantastic": "She would often go to them [the other editors] for help, for second readings on things. She was very insecure in some ways. She would say, 'Oh, this came in, I don't know what to do, do you think I could ask so and so?' And they would love it. And they would go to her and say, 'Jackie, could you read this?' And then she was always fantastic, anything that people asked her to do, and she was always available on the phone when she wasn't in the office."

In return, the staff at Doubleday was protective of her. "The key with Jackie was to get her out of the way," Rubin said, "so she had the dumpiest little office as far away as you could possibly imagine with a rinky-dink disgusting metal desk . . . We had a terrible problem with security because people could come up on the elevators and just walk in and say, 'I want to see Jacqueline Onassis.' You have no idea about the crazies who would come in. And we had this divine woman receptionist who could just deal with everything, a wonderful black lady called Emma Bolton, who loved Jackie—and Jackie loved her—who would protect her."[30] Beyond protecting Jackie's physical privacy, the unwritten law at Doubleday was not to talk about her.

And at Doubleday, as at 1040, the essential ingredient in making Jackie's life run smoothly, in protecting her from the unwanted aspects of the outside world, was Nancy Tuckerman. During Onassis's lifetime, Nancy had had a job in public relations for Olympic Airways. (While she was there she had hired Pierre Cardin to design the stewardesses' uniforms but neither he nor she had envisaged what the Greek girls would look like in the chic sleeveless numbers he created. When they leaned upward to check the overhead lockers, it was all too obvious to the passengers that the girls had hairy armpits. Nancy's efforts to drill them in the finer points of etiquette were equally unrewarding.) Calls to 1040 for Jackie or the children would be put through to Nancy at the Olympic office for screening.

Now she worked for Doubleday in the mornings and for Jackie in the afternoons, an arrangement that suited all parties. "She helped us on all the PR fronts with Jackie, and she could handle Jackie better than anyone," a colleague said. At Doubleday, Nancy's office was next door to Jackie's. "Jackie always used to duck her head into Nancy's office, or call her in," said Scott Moyers, Jackie's editorial assistant, who occupied the office next to Nancy's. "It was very warm, it was just wonderful . . . because you were working around two good friends who had grown up together, who were comfortable with each other, and there was just a lot of laughter and it was a hoot, it was a lot of fun."[31]

For outsiders, there was no getting around Nancy Tuckerman. "There were people who tried to take Nancy out," a colleague said, "along the lines of 'Let's give her a couple of rounds of bourbon and see what we can get out of her,' and they didn't get anything out of her. You would get whatever Nancy wanted you to know and that's it. You couldn't get beyond Tuckerman if she didn't want you to. Very polite, tough as nails. I suppose if you've been protecting a Jacqueline Onassis all your life, there's nothing left, there's absolutely nothing else that's going to throw you . . ."[32]

Within four years of joining the firm Jackie was beginning to get a team of her own in place. She had a senior editor, Shaye Erhart, who had worked with her for years. Shaye did some of the "dirty work," one of the team said, "negotiating the fine points of contracts, presenting books in marketing and sales meetings, writing the facts sheets the sales reps used, so that she [Jackie] was really only doing the interesting stuff, acquiring and editing."[33] Later she worked with another assistant editor, Bruce Tracy, and Scott Moyers worked almost exclusively for her. This was his first job. "I started right out of school," Moyers said, "handling her submissions, opening her mail, answering her phone, general editorial-assistance stuff. And I stayed with her three years and it was a pretty magical three years. She was just an incredible positive life force, a fascinating woman with incredibly catholic taste and I was exposed to her areas of interest because those were the sort of books she worked on—her French history, her Russian history, dance, architecture, the fine arts in general, you know she had a pretty broad range."

Jackie, Scott said, was very anxious not to be seen as a figurehead and consequently put pressure on herself. "She wanted to contribute and she was very loyal to the firm, which was why when Steve [Rubin] and others before him would prevail upon her to write to a celebrity, she'd do it in the spirit of things but it wasn't her first instinct usually." People liked to exaggerate the extent of Jackie's relationship with her major celebrity authors. Moyers, who answered the telephone and noted all the calls, is indignant at such claims: "Michael Jackson's calling her when he was in trouble—it didn't happen. Shaye Erhart spent much more time with Michael Jackson than Jackie did." Jackson's first book, done under Jackie's supervision, *Moonwalk*, was a huge commercial success. On his second book, *Dancing the Dream*, Jackie "didn't want to have anything to do with him and Shaye handled that entirely. At that point his weirdness had manifested itself." And again: "All that stuff that Jackie called Camilla Parker Bowles and offered her two million dollars for a book, that's hogwash, just a fiction. I was there when that ostensibly happened and it didn't happen."

One of Jackie's biggest coups was to secure the rights for Doubleday to publish the Egyptian writer and Nobel Prize winner Mahfouz Naguib in America. She had already read him in French. She also rediscovered the black American writer Dorothy West on Martha's Vineyard. In her nineties when Jackie met her, West was the oldest surviving member of the Harlem Renaissance. She had moved to Oak Bluffs, a resort on Martha's Vineyard built by rich black Bostonians, and wrote a column in the *Vineyard Gazette*, religiously read by Jackie when she was on the Vineyard. West had been contracted in the fifties to write a novel, which she had never completed; in the early nineties a New York lawyer friend urged her to finish it and thought she could get her a contract. "So, simply because Jackie was famous and lived on Martha's Vineyard and was the only editor she's ever heard of," Scott Moyers said, "she sent her the first sixty pages of this novel with the outline and a copy of the Virago edition of her previous book. Stuck it in the mail and sent it to Doubleday. I opened it up and there it was, clearly a classic by this historic figure, a second novel after forty years . . . But . . . Dorothy was having problems writing it, so in the summer when Jackie was in Chilmark, she would drive over to Oak Bluffs every week to see how she was doing. If Jackie hadn't paid those weekly visits the book would never have been finished, and that book, *The Wedding*, is hailed as a real classic."

Jackie's routine rarely varied: she came in on Tuesday, Wednesday and Thursday mornings, lunching at her desk on the sandwiches, carrots and celery she brought with her from 1040. "I would always hear from her, Monday and Friday, I would messenger stuff to her at home and she would work from home," Moyers said. "She didn't fuss very much what she wore. If she had a meeting or something she had a work outfit that she wore repeatedly. A pants suit, black with a white pinstripe silk top.

"What I most remember about Jackie," he went on, "is her incredible enthusiasm. Her compassionate rejection letters and her elation at the hunt, at getting books she was after, and holding a finished book for the first time, seeing a book come out. When things were going well she had a great girlish giggle and she'd rub her hands together. She was absolutely without affectation and was just completely unselfconscious. She would get down on her knees and spread out the photographs to have a look at them, just very comfortable with herself."[34]

Bruce Tracy, the senior editor on what Steve Rubin called "the Onassis SWAT Team,"[35] who worked particularly with Jackie on the illustrated books, stressed: "The important thing is that she was really good at what she did . . . I think people always assumed it was this made-up job to legitimize her, and nothing could have been further from the truth. Every book that she edited and published was her right through. There was an extraordinary range of content and subject matter and . . . she really loved the process of working on the books, and had a very parental attitude to those of us who worked with her, in that it seemed very important to her when we were working on a book whose subject matter we didn't know anything about, that we learned. And that was something for which I'll be eternally grateful because I got exposed to people and things and ideas, and I'm not just talking about notable figures she happened to be able to attract, but the subject matter, because she really, really cared about it."

The other thing that Tracy remembered about Jackie was that she always made her own telephone calls, always greeted her own guests, never sent an assistant to greet a guest in the reception area, ever. "I don't know if it's the same in the U.K.," Tracy said, "but here you sort of send the message that you're a big shot by having your assistant make the calls, greet the guests."[36]

⌒

Jackie was criticized because she did not use her huge political and social influence for charitable causes. The endless committees and charity functions that were the high-profile territory of rich New York society women were not for her. However, she was well aware that her influence was all the more effective for being used sparingly. She did not have a "social conscience"; the cares of the world were for others to sort out. She made her contribution to the causes that interested her and these were exclusively centered on New York. The only community-welfare institution with which she was associated over a long period was the Bedford-Stuyvesant Corporation in Brooklyn, originally initiated by Bobby Kennedy and for that reason cherished by her. Bedford-Stuyvesant, across the East River in central Brooklyn where 450,000 people lived cheek by jowl, 84 percent black, 12 percent Puerto Rican, was the largest nonwhite ghetto outside Chicago's South Side, and described by a contemporary survey as "more depressed and more impaired than Harlem." On February 4, 1966, Bobby had met the black community leaders and felt their anger. The solution was to be a partnership between the community, who would put forward the programs, and business leaders, who would provide outside investment and managerial assistance. The idea was self-help, not federal welfare (although it was originally funded primarily by the government), to combine housing and physical renovation with jobs and social services. By 1978 an expert dubbed it "a modest success—which in the context of so many failures, is to say a remarkable success." It is still in existence today as the Bedford-Stuyvesant Restoration Corporation. Ethel Kennedy and her son Robert Jr. are on the board and regularly attend meetings.

Jackie's role was in the arts department, where she was particularly interested in the Design Works, producing handmade textiles, established in 1969 and described as "the brainchild of Jackie Onassis."[37] It became part of the total project when Jackie saw the possibilities of capitalizing on the creative talents of artists in the area. The inspiration was African, with strong colors and bold designs. Jackie used the materials in her living rooms at 1040 and invited *House Beautiful* to photograph them in November 1971 with an accompanying article "Art Power at Work—The Fabrics of Bedford-Stuyvesant."

In 1974 an "Exhibition of African-Inspired Textiles from Bedford-Stuyvesant" opened with a gala preview of fashion using the Design Works materials by New York designers like Pauline Trigère at the Brooklyn Museum. Jackie also arranged an exhibition on November 29 at the Metropolitan Museum. She was careful not to tread on Ethel's toes where the affairs of the corporation were concerned, as she wrote to designer Leslie Tillett: Ethel was to arrive at the museum before her with the most fanfare they could contrive. It was to be Ethel's day, Jackie underlined, and not hers, "because after all Bedford-Stuyvesant was Bobby's idea." Jackie would be waiting at home for the call to come over to the museum only after Ethel had made her triumphant appearance. It was a complicated plan, but, as Jackie said, there were nuances and it was important they work out well.

"If you cut people off from what nourishes them spiritually, something in them dies," Jackie said in 1984. "The future of New York City is bleak if the landmarks which mean so much to everyone who lives there, and their children, and their children's children, are taken away." Jackie was a doughty fighter for "her city," the central Manhattan she had known and loved all her life. People accused her of elitism and they were right. She was focused on the few square miles that formed her world. Perhaps her greatest achievement was her campaign to stop developers from erecting a fifty-nine-story development on top of Grand Central Terminal. The old Pennsylvania Station had already been torn down.

In 1975, when she read that Grand Central was under attack, she joined the board of the Municipal Art Society, a civic group that had unsuccessfully opposed the destruction of Penn Station in the 1960s and had helped set up the city Planning Commission and the Landmarks Preservation Commission. The great preservation battle of the seventies was fought over Grand Central and, in the opinion of everyone connected with MAS, Jackie's intervention was crucial. That February she wrote a passionately eloquent letter to Mayor Abraham Beame, asking him to change his mind and appeal an adverse lower court ruling.

"Is it not cruel to let our city die by degrees," she pleaded, "stripped of all our proud monuments, until there will be nothing left of all her history and beauty to inspire our children? If they are not inspired by the past of our city, where will they find the strength to fight for her future?"[38]

In 1978, three years after Jackie joined, the society won the twelve-year fight when the Supreme Court upheld the building's landmark status. "There would have been no victory at the Supreme Court, no landmarks law, and no Grand Central without her generalship and carefully doled-out celebrity," Frederick Papert, Jackie's mentor on municipal preservation affairs, said.[39]

For Jackie it was the continuation of the battle she and Jack had waged over Lafayette Square and the preservation of historic Washington in the 1960s. With Philip Johnson, the celebrated architect, Jackie led a campaign to save Lever House, a thirty-one-year-old twenty-four-story blue-glass building on Park Avenue from developers who wanted to replace it with a massive forty-story tower. She enlisted the powerful support of Mayor Koch and personally lobbied city comptroller Harrison J. Goldin, whose two votes could swing the decision to confirm landmark status for the building. A photograph shows Jackie giving Goldin the full benefit of her "lighthouse" look; afterward he let it be known that he was "leaning" toward upholding landmark status.

One of the bitterest preservation fights of the decade in which Jackie was immersed with her friends Frederic Papert and Brendan Gill, on behalf of the Municipal Art Society, was over the prestigious St. Bartholomew's Church and Community House at Park Avenue and 50th Street. The church proposed to ruin the architectural harmony of the church, Community House and garden by tearing down Community House and replacing it with a forty-seven-story glass and steel skyscraper. As usual money was at the heart of the battle. The church enlisted Catholic, Protestant and Jewish leaders to endorse the plan, which they claimed was to generate revenue to help the poor. It was dismayed when Jackie, "who chooses her issues carefully and has obvious influence over public opinion," entered the fray on the opposing side. The rector invited her and Frederic Papert to tea in an effort to win her over. "She didn't budge," said Papert. He then took the opportunity to attack Jackie in his sermon the following Sunday—"What did she know about the people the church had to serve etc.?"[40] The case went to the courts and the Municipal Art Society won. In 1987 Jackie won another battle on behalf of the New York skyline, this time to make the developer Mort Zuckerman lower the height of the towering high-rise he planned to build on the Coliseum site at Columbus Circle. "They're stealing our sky," she said.

"There's a direct connection between the Municipal Art Society and the fight to save Grand Central and the not-for-profit 42nd Street Development Corporation," said Frederic Papert. "In the middle of 1975 she and I walked west on 42nd Street to what we all remembered as one of the great places in New York. The

soul of New York was seventeen blocks starting at 42nd with all those great theaters from the 1920s. Although we were none of us old enough to have seen it in
its great heyday, we knew very well that it was one of the city's memories, and
that it was living like a bum. We started a company to see if we could halt its fall
from grace, and failed roundly in many ways, but occasionally succeeded." Today
the section between Ninth and Tenth Avenues is a thriving Theater Row. "Anyhow she was a marvelous board member. As an organization we didn't have very
many board meetings but she came to every board meeting she was asked to, and
there wasn't an opening either, a ribbon cutting or a symbolic hard hat with a
shovel in your hand that she wouldn't put the hard hat on and grab the shovel and
do whatever she had to do. She was quite wonderful about that and when we had
to go and lobby for things she would come. I remember once we went to see a
very highly placed city official, and at the end of the meeting he said, 'Would you
mind if some reporters who know you're going to be here, would you mind if they
came in'—and she was very on to that and said, 'No.' And he opened the door and
six photographers came in to shoot him with her—he was about to run for office.
She understood all of that very, very well."[41]

"I think she was really an amazing New Yorker," Ashton Hawkins, who worked
with her at the Municipal Art Society from the mid-1980s, said. "I think that she
felt that New York was really her home, that was where she was most complete.
Even though she liked to go away on the weekends and go foxhunting and do all
the other things that she did, the center of her life was New York and she liked
that, she relished it, she used it very well and she was not afraid of it, and she
really mastered it at a certain point . . . So I always felt that Jackie's priorities were
pretty well organized from her point of view. She liked the American Ballet Theater, she liked the MAS, she liked 42nd Street and she liked the Costume Institute, and she pretty much kept out of other areas unless they were absolutely
telling for one reason or another such as some Kennedy event that she would
have to do."[42]

Jackie enjoyed her independent professional life, the more so because there was
now a central stabilizing presence for her, the "third man," Maurice Tempelsman.

CHAPTER TWENTY-THREE

Matriarch

⁓

She did evolve as a human being in a wonderful way and she became herself more and more. And human, very human. I think she certainly, as she grew older as a person, she was probably a little bit ashamed that she was not nice to people.

—Edith Welch[1]

On September 9, 1979, Jackie's old friend André Meyer died in Lausanne; even on his death bed he was still concerned for her. "The last thing he said to Gianni Agnelli was to take care of Jackie—'Make sure Jackie's all right,' " a friend of Agnelli's said. "He went to his death worrying about a woman who had millions . . . André Meyer, who was really a tough cut-throat, head of Lazard Frères, all he cared about was talking about Jackie on his deathbed."[2] Jackie attended his memorial service and afterward walked a few blocks with Ros Gilpatric. "She was very sad," Gilpatric recalled. "She felt that in her life there was nobody else to take his place."[3] But Maurice Tempelsman would be able to take care of her, not only financially by transmuting the capital from the Onassis settlement into a far larger fortune but also by providing an emotional security she had never before experienced.

Maurice Tempelsman was just under a month younger than Jackie. He had been born in Antwerp, Belgium, on August 26, 1929, son of Leon and Helene Tempelsman, both Orthodox Jews. Maurice and his younger sister Rachel spent their early years in the Jewish quarter of the port city where their father was in the import business. Like their neighbors, the family spoke Yiddish at home. After the outbreak of the Second World War, the Tempelsmans fled the Nazis to Manhattan's Upper West Side, where they lived in a close-knit refugee community. Maurice married a woman from this community, Lilly Bucholz, two years older than himself; they subsequently had three children, Rena, Leon and Marcy. Maurice, who never graduated from college, joined his father in a new business, Leon Tempelsman and Son, Inc., diamond merchants, and proved to be a visionary diamond trader. In 1950 he created a new marketing niche by persuading the U.S. government to stockpile African diamonds for industrial and military purposes, with himself as middleman. In 1957, aged twenty-seven, he and his lawyer, Adlai Stevenson, traveled to Africa where he made many contacts, eventually ranging from the ANC leader Oliver Tambo, to Mobutu Sese Seko, the notorious dictator of Zaïre. He owns an interest in a diamond mine in Ghana and a diamond-polishing factory in Botswana. According to sources, Tempelsman is a "major, major player" in Africa, the kind of person who "jets in for a barbecue with the President of Namibia."[4]

Now a general partner in the family business (his father died in 1955) and chief executive of Lazare Kaplan International, one of the U.S.'s oldest diamond firms, Tempelsman is also one of only 160 "sightholders" in the world, which means that ten times a year he is permitted to buy diamonds directly from the powerful de Beers cartel. A former chairman of the New York City-based African-American Institute, and a consistently generous contributor to Democratic causes, he also brings his influence to bear in Washington and was especially active in 1988 when a proposed embargo of South African diamonds threatened his business.

It was Africa that brought the couple together. In the late 1950s, the then Senator Jack Kennedy wanted to meet representatives of the South African diamond business, and it was Tempelsman who arranged the meeting. He had attended functions during the White House Kennedy years, but it was not until after Aristotle Onassis's death that he and Jackie became close.

By the late 1970s they were regularly seen attending the opera or charity events together, but it was not until the mid-eighties that the romance became known. Tempelsman, after all, was a married man—not that that had ever worried Jackie. He looked older than he was, and his low public profile and lack of physical glamour helped to keep the affair secret. When it did become public, there was none of the scandal that might have been expected in the press, such was Jackie's status with her fellow New Yorkers.

In 1982, Tempelsman finally left his wife, moving first into the Stanhope Hotel near Jackie's apartment, and then into 1040. Although Maurice and Lilly never formally divorced, Lilly, a marriage counselor with the Jewish Board of Family and Child Services in New York, subsequently granted her husband a "*get*," an Orthodox Jewish divorce. To this day, according to an intimate of Maurice, he and Lilly have stayed in touch, and he is reportedly close to his children and six grandchildren. The name of his yacht, the *Relemar*, comes from his children's initials. Leon, a graduate of the Harvard Business School, works with his father as president of the company, and Marcy designs jewelry for the firm. Tempelsman's children also became close to Jackie and her family, visiting them in the summer at Martha's Vineyard. His daughter Rena once told a friend that Jackie was "like a grandmother to my children."

Some of Jackie's New York social circle were also taken by surprise. Marietta Tree was not impressed initially, writing in her diary for April 28, 1986: "Had a fairly interesting lunch with Maurice Tempelsman. He is currently Jackie Onassis's best friend. He is v. dependable, which is a quality she obviously likes in a man, having seen it so seldom . . ."[5]

"He's a very nice man," said one of Jackie's English friends. "He's a sort of soft-spoken rather heavy diamond merchant. The attraction I would say is that he's very comforting. Easy. Very civilized. Quite unlike Onassis . . . Gentle and civilized. Not boring but not scintillating . . ."[6]

"He was the nicest man she ever had, far and away," said Aileen Mehle.[7]

Asked what common denominator there could possibly have been for Jackie between Jack Kennedy, Onassis and Tempelsman, Lee said succinctly: "Success . . ."[8]

Not everyone agreed with Mehle. An old friend of Jack's took a different view. "I think the guy's perfectly horrible," he said. "I know there's a New York Tempelsman fan club but you talk to some of the people in South Africa and you get a little bit of a feeling of where I'm coming from. I just couldn't understand it. To me he's not the most physically attractive man in the world. I could understand Onassis as a sort of sex symbol but this guy doesn't seem to me to have that. He's good at diamonds, I guess. Seemed to make Jackie very happy, that's the only thing I feel gratitude to him for." Bill Walton was another non-fan: "Bill Walton hated Maurice Tempelsman, hated him and he would say, 'I'm going to see Jackie this week because *he's* going to be away!' He never referred to him by name. I think partly because he loved being with Jackie, and Maurice was just there and he just thought Maurice was very jealous and pushy. Maybe just because he'd moved into Jackie's life . . . I think he had nothing in common with him and wasn't interested in the things Maurice talked about."[9]

"I don't think it was primarily a sexual relationship," a woman friend of Jackie's said. "But I think they were very close. They spoke French together and they read poetry together. I think it was very strange, that relationship, because it wasn't earthy or even worldly. It was all sort of high culture. I think they were very, very fond of each other and I think he gave her good advice. He is a wise man, he will make philosophical comments about everything and anything, and so he instantly has a way of putting things in perspective. He really is a political animal and if I wanted to talk to him about the events in the country today he would put it in a long-term way. But he likes to be sort of jolly. I say he likes to be because I'm not sure he really is, but he's always smiling and, you know, slightly wicked and giggly, but I don't think he comes like that naturally. He acts that way. I think maybe he learned that to please her, because she likes being wicked and naughty and funny and giggling at people, and I think he adopted that."[10]

At first, Tempelsman had displayed signs of insecurity in Jackie's intimate circle. "When I first met Maurice it was the first Christmas party that Jackie had where Maurice was. And after the Christmas party, I think about twelve or fifteen of us stayed for supper and sat around the floor, around the coffee table in her library, and I was asking a couple of questions about the house on the Vineyard . . . and every time I asked Jackie a question Maurice would answer, and it was on that occasion that Caroline said, in a terrible sort of way, 'That's the date of the year. That's the couple of the year.' But I think it was Maurice's insecurity at being on display there as Jackie's live-in, that made him do that. He would talk all the time and answer every question, and just had to get his two cents in about how they were doing the house on the Vineyard, and he talked a lot about the birds and the swans, and it seemed to me that it was all Maurice talking. He didn't seem to be that way as time progressed.

"And then he evidently felt very secure. I remember asking him once, 'Why don't you marry Jackie? Why don't you get divorced and marry her?' And he said, 'I'm not the marrying type.'" Asked whether Jackie would have liked to marry him, the woman replied, "No, probably not. I think he enabled her to be completely independent and yet have a man around the house. And a businessman, which was very good for her, she liked that . . ."[11]

"Maurice, he was the *grand seigneur*. It was her apartment, he took it over and he really loved her," said a friend. "And, like a lot of Jewish guys—they make great husbands—he was there for her when she was sick. Nancy told me, 'Can you imagine Aristotle Onassis or Jack Kennedy saying, 'It's time to take your pills, dear'? Well, that's the kind of attention Maurice gave her, and they had a great relationship. He was so protective in a wonderful way. It was very, very touching to see them together."[12]

Antonia Fraser remained friends with Jackie after her marriage to Harold Pinter and the Pinters enjoyed dining with the couple at 1040: "I think Maurice with his extreme reliability, no infidelity, making lots of money for her, was ideal for her. When we went to supper there—her beautiful apartment—I must say it was absolutely wonderful, everything went incredibly smoothly, cars purred more or less into the drawing room. You know, even having supper there I felt rather taken care of. Perhaps that's what she wanted."[13]

Jackie bolstered Tempelsman's confidence by seeming to defer to him in public. "What she did was to make sure he was central," Edna O'Brien recalled. "I remember one dinner we had with quite a lot of people—some very important diplomat—and with Maurice she did, it's true, defer or make sure that Maurice was the host even though it was her house."[14] Other friends noticed that at times she liked to play the little-girl card with him, telling jokes and looking to him for approval "as if she were performing for Daddy."[15] This time, for the first time in her life, she had a man upon whom she knew she could rely, a man for whom she was absolutely and forever number one. "She adored Maurice," her friend Vivi Stokes Crespi said. "I think he brought her peace of mind."[16]

Despite their earlier reservations, Tempelsman developed a "close relationship" with Caroline and John Jr., according to Ted Sorensen.[17] As Tempelsman arrived in Jackie's life, her children were making lives of their own. "I would say personally that she wanted independence for the children," said Reinaldo Herrera. "She wanted the children to be totally independent and not to have to rely on any family, be it the Kennedys, or the Auchinclosses or anybody. She wanted her children to be independent and she wanted to give them the freedom—and this she always talked about—she wanted to give them the freedom that she felt she hadn't had, freedom of choice."[18]

"I think she [Jackie] really had a feeling of letting them fly—she even used that expression about Caroline, 'let her grow her own wings,' " Karen Lerner said. " 'She has to lead her own life, she has to learn to fly . . .' "[19]

"My family is extremely close," John Kennedy Jr. said. "My mother has never had an agenda for me or my sister. That's probably why we're all so close and have had a relatively normal life. Not being a Kennedy, she could recognize the perils and the positive aspects. One thing she has done is kept the memory and the character of our father very vivid for us. She has not made us look to our father's life to worship it at the expense of our own. Whatever Caroline or I choose to do, provided we were serious and committed about it, she would have supported."[20]

"You know people think that she [Jackie] disliked the Kennedys," Herrera said. "It's not true. She did not. Not only did she stick with them, she was extremely loyal to them. What she did not like was the way they were raising their children. That she did not like. At all. She thought it was absolutely bad. She thought they were abandoned and they were treated with money and privileges in a way that she never treated hers, and they had more money and more privileges and more position than the others. Never. Caroline was treated like a normal child and John was treated equally. John was the passion of her life, you know . . . so good-looking. But, of course, the most interesting and similar to her is Caroline. Caroline's exactly like she is in personality and brains. He's much more of a Kennedy in person and Caroline is totally her mother's daughter, mentally. I once asked her, 'Why don't you run for office? You should run for office.' Oh, no, she was terrified. Terrified."[21]

Jackie had good reason to be proud of both her children. Caroline had graduated from Radcliffe College, Harvard, with a fine arts degree in 1980 and had joined the Office of Film and Television at the Metropolitan Museum, of which she later became manager and coordinating producer. While at Harvard she had had a two-and-a-half-year romance with a young writer, Tom Carney, but in 1980 they split and Carney married someone else. Since 1981 she had been seeing Edwin Arthur Schlossberg, a tall, graying intellectual thirteen years her senior. Schlossberg has been variously described by his friends as "a Renaissance man, an artist, poet, designer, scientist and freelance thinker, an intellectual jack-of-all-trades and friend to New York's cultural nobility."[22] Among that "cultural nobility" could be included George Plimpton, who had known Caroline since her childhood when he helped organize "pirate parties" on the beach to amuse her and was a favorite guest at her birthday parties. Plimpton called Caroline "a marvelous creature": "When she was seven or eight," he recalled, "we'd lie on the floor and have the most amazing adult conversations. It was enchanting to talk to someone that young with that sort of fancy."

"Caroline is hilarious," said a friend of pre-Schlossberg days. "I mean, she has a great sense of humor and a way with words. She is a very funny, ironic girl and has the same black humor Jackie had. She was just really funny and fun."[23]

Like Jackie, Caroline was shy and also like Jackie she had the burden of celebrity to bear while trying to live her own life and maintain her own privacy.

Again like her mother, she was searching for a father figure as a refuge from her state of fatherlessness. The age gap between her and Schlossberg was almost exactly the same as that between Jackie and Jack Kennedy. And, like Jackie too, she was attracted by Schlossberg's brilliance and self-confidence. Like Jack, it might be said, he did not have "a steady job," nor did he have to worry too much about money. He came from a wealthy textile family with a home on Park Avenue and he himself was equipped with the regulation loft and a converted barn in the Berkshires. The only difference that might have come between them was their religion; she was from an Irish Catholic family while the Schlossbergs were practicing Jews.

In the end neither family stood in their way and on July 19, 1986 Caroline became Mrs. Edwin Schlossberg at a Catholic service at the simple clapboard church of Our Lady of Victory in Centerville, Massachusetts, although there was no nuptial mass. This was "America's Royal Wedding," to be compared with the wedding later that month of the Queen's second son, Prince Andrew, to Sarah Ferguson. As *Newsweek* pointed out, there had been half a dozen First Daughters since Caroline's father had occupied the White House but "she remains America's princess." Some two hundred reporters and photographers and a thousand spectators crowded outside the church, making such a noise that the bride, arriving with her uncle Teddy, had to shush them with a finger to her lips. Caroline's close friend and cousin, Maria Shriver, who had married Arnold Schwarzenegger in April, was matron of honor; John Jr. was best man.

Caroline's wedding dress had been designed by Carolina Herrera, Jackie's favorite designer since 1982. "It was a great experience," Carolina said, "because she [Jackie] trusted me totally. She said, 'I am going to let Caroline decide with you what she wants. I am not going to be interfering because I had a very bad experience with my wedding. It was the dress that my mother wanted me to wear and I hated it. I am not going to do the same with Caroline—she has to decide what she wants to wear.' And, do you know, she only saw the finished dress when it arrived in Hyannis Port two days before the wedding.

"We used to talk on the phone all the time and I'd say, 'I did the fittings and it's looking wonderful.' 'Is she happy?' she used to say. 'Yes. She's very happy.' 'Does she like it?' 'Yes, she loves it.' 'Perfect, that's the most important thing.' She was like that. And, you know, Caroline wanted to do her own wedding her own way, the way she wanted to do it, with the French invitations, not the classic way, and Jackie was very happy about that. And the boys wanted to wear not morning suits but white pants and blazers and she was quite happy about that. She said, 'If they're happy, it's perfect. Let's do it.' "[24]

The boys' dress for the wedding was indeed unconventional, designed by Ed Schlossberg's friend, the black designer Willi Smith, in collaboration with Schlossberg to achieve a "sophisticated yet breezy" effect. The bridegroom wore a "non-conventional navy blue linen suit with a fashionably oversized look," while the ushers were outfitted in violet linen blazers, white linen trousers and pink linen ties.

The arrangements for Caroline's wedding were masterfully planned by Jackie's friend George Trescher, the number-one fund-raiser and charity-ball organizer. Robert Isabell did the flowers and on the lawn outside Rose Kennedy's house Robert Stan had created a dazzling white tent over a circular dance floor, suspending above it a giant puffball filled with hundreds of thousands of flowers. Sean Driscoll, owner of the chic New York catering firm Glorious Food (transcribed in the *Hyannis Gazette* as "Gloria's Food"), provided the food, planning the menu in consultation with Jackie, who commented, "I don't know how this is going to go down with those meat and potato, vanilla ice cream Kennedys."[25]

The wedding was an emotional moment for Jackie: as they left the church after the ceremony she leaned tearfully on Teddy's shoulder. Teddy appeared miraculously recovered from early hours frolicking in the sea with local waitresses (watching the scene, a witness said, "You know what was creepy? It was the eve of Chappaquiddick . . .").[26] At the reception he brought tears to everyone's eyes when he toasted Jackie as "that extraordinary gallant woman, Jack's only love." Carly Simon, a new friend of Jackie's, and her neighbor on Martha's Vineyard, sang "Chapel of Love," and George Plimpton rounded off the occasion with a fireworks display featuring tokens for fifteen family members and friends—a rose for Rose Kennedy, a sailboat for Teddy, a bow tie for Arthur Schlesinger. "I wanted the fireworks to suggest the essence of each individual," Plimpton said. "And then there was the main body of the show which I called 'What Ed Schlossberg Does.'[27] There was a problem here because by the time this part of the show took place, a fog bank had rolled in off the ocean. I tried to get the show moved up to beat these clouds that were coming in off the sea, but Carly Simon's manager wouldn't let her sing earlier than scheduled. So she sang, and then the fog rolled in. And that's the one thing that kills fireworks. When fireworks go off in a cloud, they sort of fizzle. It's like summer lightning. You just see the colors and they are usually diffused by the fog. I was very disappointed but as it turned out everyone loved it because they felt it typified the theme. It faithfully represented 'What Ed Schlossberg Does.' " Plimpton opened the show by saying, " 'And this is Ed Schlossberg and nobody is quite sure what he does . . .' "[28] What Ed Schlossberg did for a living remained a mystery but the couple were devoted to each other and Schlossberg was to guard and protect his wife from the outside world.

At the rehearsal dinner the night before, John Jr. had given the prospective bridegroom a welcoming toast: "The three of us have been alone for such a long time," he said. "We welcome a fourth person." When Jackie looked at John Jr., she saw Black Jack's dark looks and handsome physique, his devil-may-care attitude to life. Like his father and Black Jack, John was proud of his body and liked to show it off, ambling round Hyannis Port with a towel draped around his hips, or bicycling round Central Park in tattered T-shirt and sweatpants held together with safety pins. Like his father he was tall, six foot one, with broad shoulders, narrow hips, long legs; his torso was as powerful as his father's but still showed signs of what Jack Kennedy had crossly called "Fitzgerald breasts." He had inherited his mother's acting ability and capacity for mimicry—he could imitate any accent and showed ability in his acting debut in the Irish play *Winners* in 1985. His mother did not encourage his penchant for acting, but her friend Rudolf Nureyev once told him to go ahead and do what he wanted: "Go on, have some balls."[29] He lacked his father's intellectual brainpower so instead of Harvard he went to Brown University in Providence, Rhode Island, where he had graduated in 1983, majoring in American history. Afterward he attended law school at New York University, and then famously failed the bar exam twice (earning the unkind headline "The Hunk Flunks") before finally passing it in 1989 and taking a job in the Manhattan District Attorney's office. John had inherited the Kennedy passion for risky physical undertakings, parachuting and diving off the Cape Cod and Martha's Vineyard coasts. On one occasion in a faint echo of PT-109, he saved the life of a colleague in a dangerous underwater rescue.

John Jr. was turning out to be what Jackie secretly wanted him to be, a heartbreaker with a huge zest for life. In 1988 the year that Caroline gave birth to her first child, Rose, *People* dubbed twenty-eight-year-old John F. Kennedy Jr. "The Sexiest Man Alive": "The pecs, the pedigree, the charm, the torso—who else but JFK Jr. could be the Hunk of the Year?" the magazine asked. "Is this the Handsomest Man in the World?" ran another headline. Unlike his father, he had long-term relationships with women. Alice Munro and Christina Haag were both Brown graduates; his relationship with Alice lasted for four years, and he was with Christina, with whom he fell in love during *Winners*, for six.

He had his father's ease with photographers and journalists. He was poised, articulate, funny, and handled himself well in public on such occasions as introducing his uncle Teddy at the 1988 Democratic Convention. When asked the inevitable question as to whether he would run for office, he revealed his ambivalence. Obviously it was something that he thought about but, he said, "I frankly feel there are many opportunities and avenues outside of elected office to become involved in issues that have the same broad scope that government or elected office provides you. Once you run for office, you're in it. Sort of like going into the military—you'd better be damn sure that it is what you want to do and that the rest of your life is set up to accommodate that. It takes a certain toll on your personality, and on your family life. I've seen it personally. So if I were to do it, I would want to make sure that was what I wanted to do, and that I didn't do it because people thought I should . . . I want to make sure I have some life experiences before I think about it."[30] Joseph Nye, dean of the Kennedy School of Government, remembered asking him, as they stood together in a White House reception line, "Do you remember this place?" The answer came, "Only vaguely." Nye asked, "Do you want to come back?" John Kennedy Jr. smiled and repeated, "Only vaguely . . ."[31]

"Jackie, oh, Jackie just loved John," Karen Lerner said. "When you mentioned John's name to Jackie, her voice became a gentle laugh. She used to say, 'Oh, John . . .' She just loved him so much but she didn't know quite what to make of him because he was so, he was a sprite when he was little, he was just so darling and unpredictable and, you know, as he grew up she was able to give him his freedom."[32] Edna O'Brien agreed: "I would say her son was her greatest luminous thing in life, and Caroline she loved too, but I think probably sons and mothers, the old story . . ."[33]

"Sybil [d'Origny] told me that at the end of her life, Jackie had become very much the head of the clan, the person to whom everyone turned for advice and healing," said Antony Beevor. "Rose was in her dotage and the frankly dysfunctional Kennedy family, with a few exceptions, was going to pieces."[34] Jackie's extended family included not only Kennedys, but Lee's children, Yusha Auchincloss's two children, Little Janet and her children—particularly Little Janet's children. In the summer of 1985, while on a family vacation on Fisher's Island with her husband and children, Sybil, a family friend from Newport days, and her husband Henri, Vicomte d'Origny, and her children, Little Janet was diagnosed with lung cancer and died within a few months. Little Janet, pretty, lively, with a terrific sense of humor, had been a favorite of Jackie's. Friends described her as "beguiling" and her handsome, athletic husband as "dazzling": "She was the most lovely, most adorable girl, the best of the bunch," Oatsie Leiter Charles, a close friend of the family, said. After her marriage to Lewis Rutherfurd she had moved with him to Hong Kong and had two sons and a much younger daughter. She had never smoked and, after the diagnosis, was operated on, but the cancer had already spread. While Lewis Rutherfurd commuted between Massachusetts and Hong Kong, Jackie flew to Boston to give blood for Janet's transfusions. "She was terribly, terribly good with Janet and very loving," said Sylvia Whitehouse Blake.[35]

Jackie took a protective interest in her beloved Yusha's two children, Cecil and Maya, by his Russian wife from whom he was divorced. Maya said: "I think she was protective of everybody—she'd never let anyone she liked be hurt. Aunt Janet [Jackie's mother] could be awful to everybody." One day Jackie found Maya crying because "Aunt Janet had been horrible. Jackie said, 'Don't worry, Mother can be as cold as ice—it's not meant personally.'" Jackie, Maya said, was "so good to her nieces and nephews. Little Janet stayed with Jackie, and Alexandra [Janet's two-year-old daughter] was picking things up and throwing them out of the window. Jackie would say, 'Oh, for God's sake, they're just things.' She loved children. She was the opposite to her mother in that she didn't have things you couldn't touch. She just wanted you to be comfortable."[36]

Christina Onassis and Jackie remained on superficially polite terms. After she divorced Andreadis, Christina married and divorced a Russian, Sergei Kauzov, with whom she remained the best of friends. On February 25, 1984, she announced her engagement to a Frenchman, Thierry Roussel, with whom she was besotted; on March 17 she married him in Paris. Probably in the hope of impressing Thierry, Christina took him to meet her famous stepmother in New York.

Some ghosts of the past were also slipping away. Jack's great friend Lem Billings, who had transferred all his love and pride in Jack and Bobby to Bobby's children, particularly Bobby Jr., died in May 1981. Jackie had not allowed Lem near her children as they were growing up: he took drugs with his favorite Kennedy and Lawford "honorary nephews" at his New York apartment and in that regard she did not consider him a good influence. But toward the end Caroline had grown close to him: he had been, after all, her father's oldest and closest friend.

Peter Lawford died on the morning of Christmas Eve 1984, of a massive hemorrhage, his organs destroyed by drink and drugs. "There was a telephone call from Jackie Onassis after I returned home," his last wife, Patricia Seaton Lawford, recalled. "She was gentle, kind, understanding of the horror that I had witnessed. She had undoubtedly arranged with the hospital to be called at the moment of Peter's death, for she apparently knew about the nightmare of blood passing from his body. She mentioned the fact that when her husband was assassinated she had held bits of his brain in her hand. And for a moment we were two women, united in grief, who shared the experience of the disintegration of the men we loved . . ."[37]

Jackie had last seen Peter at the wedding of his daughter, Sydney, in September the year before when he had almost played the part of Black Jack at her wedding to Jack. Although he had tried to keep sober and trim to take his daughter down the aisle, the thought of confronting the family who had ostracized him had caused him to down straight vodkas on the morning of the wedding. Unlike Black Jack, however, he managed to give his daughter away. Jackie, perhaps reminded of her father's behavior and conscious that Jack had always liked Peter, switched place cards at the postwedding dinner so that she could sit next to him.

It was not Jackie, but Caroline who had been in Palm Beach in April 1984 when Bobby and Ethel's tragic son David, a family outcast, had died of a drug overdose at the age of twenty-eight. Caroline had flown in to say good-bye to grandmother Rose, who had suffered such a severe stroke on Easter Sunday that it appeared certain she would die (she did not, but was left severely incapacitated). David had just come out of a treatment program in St. Paul, Minnesota, after attempting everything from psychiatrists to group therapy, methadone to "neuro-electric therapy." He had tried to exorcise the family demons by talking to a journalist, David Horowitz, who was coauthoring a book on the Kennedys that had just been serialized in the April edition of *Playboy*.[38] In so doing David had transgressed the ultimate Kennedy taboo. Shocked by the infantile helplessness of his once-powerful grandmother, he had taken to the bottle and found a local source of drugs. When he tried to visit the Kennedy house at Palm Beach he was drunk and abusive, and was turned away by a security guard. At dinner that night the Kennedy women worried about David and what he might do, not only to himself but to the family name. The following morning Caroline drove to the hotel where he was staying and called his room. There was no answer. Later, a "Mrs. Kennedy from Boston" called, and asked the receptionist to check the room; when Caroline and Sydney returned they were told that David was dead. Although the police found evidence of drugs flushed down the toilet bowl, there was no serious investigation beyond the arrest of two bellhops who had supplied David with cocaine.

The Kennedys quickly removed the body to Hickory Hill for a memorial mass before burial in the family plot at Brookline. It was less than a year since Bobby Jr. had been arrested for possession of heroin in Rapid City, South Dakota, in August 1983. That, for the time being, was the last of the Kennedy family disasters. Jackie's achievement in bringing up her children to love and revere their father but to express their loyalty to his family at a distance seemed all the more remarkable set against this background.

On January 26, 1985, another man who had been an important figure in Jackie's past—and Jack's—David Harlech, died as a result of a car crash the previous day in England. "Practically the first telephone call I got was from Jackie," said Pamela Harlech, "saying 'We want to fly over for the funeral.' Well the church where he is buried is minute, it takes sixty at a push. And I said, 'Jackie, it's very sweet of you, do come, but I can tell you it's going to be a bit of a bunfight because the family will take up most of it.' She said, 'No. We have to be there.' So she and Teddy and Jean Smith and one of the Shriver boys, who's sweet, came over. I didn't have them staying. I put them in a hotel just above the property because I—there were no bedrooms left anyway, they were all occupied and also I wouldn't have been able to stand it. Of course, the entire press corps arrived and the entire Welsh police force. There were about twenty-seven for dinner, which I cooked for them, and Teddy behaved appallingly. He got drunk as usual and was behaving really badly. And I said to Jackie, 'Could you please do something about it because you know my husband's going to be buried tomorrow and I'm not up to this?' And she said, 'Oh, I couldn't do anything.' And Jean Smith said, 'No, I can't do anything.' So the Shriver boy, bless his heart, said, 'You want me to do it?' And I said, 'Yes. Would you get your uncle out of here because I'm going to kill him otherwise. You know, this is not playtime.' And so they did.

"And then Jackie appeared at the funeral like the widow—a lot of that went on—she appeared very much the widow," said Pamela Harlech. During drinks after the funeral, Jackie said to Lord Jenkins of Hillhead, an old friend of hers and David's, and Pamela, "You know, I think we ought to do something in memory of David, a scholarship or something in memory of David. I'll start raising funds in America." Anyway, she went back to America and we started soon after, writing to people and saying, 'We want to do this Harlech scholarship.' Betsy Whitney, bless her heart, gave something like twenty thousand dollars. Jackie gave two thousand, which her dresses didn't even cost. I mean, this is the woman who's gotten all of this money from Onassis and is meant to be David's great friend . . ."[39]

The Kennedy presence—and Jackie in particular—had attracted such press attention that, in Pamela Harlech's opinion, it turned the occasion into a "three-ring circus." When Jackie asked the date of the memorial service in London, Pamela wrote back to say, " 'Quite honestly, Jackie, I don't want to see *a* Kennedy at this memorial service. Because I've gone to great trouble to do this for David and I don't want this to turn into the three-ring circus that you all made at his funeral.' To give her her due, she wrote back and said, 'I do understand.' "[40]

To Jackie's relief, Lee, after all her romantic and other troubles, married for the third time. The bridegroom was a well-known Hollywood director, Herbert Ross, with films such as *Funny Girl*, *The Turning Point* and *Steel Magnolias* to his credit. They were married on September 23, 1988, in Lee's apartment, with Rudolf Nureyev as one of the witnesses. Afterward Jackie gave a dinner party for the couple at 1040. She was not on close terms with Lee at the time and did not know Herbert Ross but, as she told a friend, "I'm happy, whatever he is or whoever he is, I'm happy for Lee, because between you and me Lee has stared into the jaws of hell."[41] At last Jackie could feel that her responsibility for Lee was over. She remained close to Lee's children, Christina and Anthony. Anthony, in particular, was a close friend of her own son, John.

⌒

"Newport society bids farewell to a lady," the *Providence Journal Bulletin* reported as prominent Newporters turned out for Janet Bouvier Auchincloss Morris's funeral on June 27, 1989—among the honorary pallbearers were some of the great names of Newport: Senator Claiborne Pell, John J. Slocum and John R. Drexel, and celebrated later arrivals like Alan Pryce-Jones. For the past seven years Janet had been suffering from Alzheimer's, which she had fought with characteristic courage. "Jackie was beyond extraordinary the last seven years of our mother's life," Lee Radziwill said. "She really focused on her. She called her every single day. It was very difficult to deal with her a lot of the time and then, of course, it became most of the time. I don't know too many children who would have behaved better and been more certain of her comfort, attention and care."

As the disease took hold, Janet's mind wandered back into the past, in which Black Jack featured large. At the time she never acknowledged that he had died. "It was really extraordinary," Lee remembered. "So I think her self was incredibly wounded. But it was so strange to me because of the last eight, ten years of her life she referred to him all the time. I mean, she was sick and as you do when you're getting older, she reminisced more, not about the last twenty years or ten years but way back and so she was suddenly—we had never been allowed to mention his name in her house or her name in his house, though he mentioned it plenty— she was always referring to Jack Bouvier and I and the horses we had and the things we did and I really thought that I was hearing things. That was very strange."[42] Sally Ewalt, who helped care for Janet with the Auchincloss house-keeper, Lisa Sullivan, confirmed this: "Mrs. Auchincloss said every night that her father hadn't wanted her to marry Mr. Bouvier 'so perhaps that's why I went ahead and did it . . . ' "[43]

Jackie behaved with great tenderness and care toward her mother in her final illness, but her inner feelings toward her remained complex, a mixture of guilt and gratitude, dislike and appreciation, heavily tinged with exasperation. In some ways she was grateful to her for pushing her toward her place in the sun, enabling her to reach the higher planes she yearned for; in others, she resented the distortion this had imposed on her own character. She never spoke about her mother to her own friends. "There was some darkness there," Edna O'Brien divined. At Janet's funeral Oatsie Leiter Charles was surprised by Jackie's distance: "The very last time I ever saw Jackie was at her mother's funeral," she said. "It was almost as though she'd never seen me before. I was rather surprised by Jackie's attitude toward me. I don't know if she felt that with her mother's death it was the end of, you know . . . We were friends to a degree and I couldn't really understand it and I still don't. I don't think it was a deep-seated reason against me. I think there was something emotional, or shock, or something that didn't include me . . ."[44]

Janet's death had drawn a line under the past, which now seemed distant. Jackie had not attended the joint eightieth birthday party of her twin Bouvier aunts, Maude Davis and Michelle Putnam. When Michelle Putnam had died in September 1987, she was at the funeral service in New York but "barely spoke" to Maude Davis, and not at all to Maude's son, John, who had incurred her displeasure by writing two books, one about the Bouviers, the other about his clan by marriage, the Kennedys. But when Steve Smith died in 1990, Jackie went to the funeral service and to the interment in East Hampton, once so much the center of Bouvier life. William vanden Heuvel accompanied her: "She and I walked over to the Bouvier plot and she identified each one," he said, "but I don't think she had much time for them . . ." The following year when Steve's son, Willie Smith, stood trial for rape, Jackie was noticeably absent from the lineup of senior Kennedy women—Eunice, Pat and Jean—who attended court every day, but on the whole, as vanden Heuvel said, "She showed a remarkable tolerance toward the peccadilloes of her nephews."[45]

⌒

With Maurice, a loving support at the center, Jackie felt free to lead an independent life, to travel, to see old friends and to make new ones. In 1984 she returned to Middleburg to ride and hunt. Down in Virginia, among old friends like Charlie Whitehouse, Bunny Mellon and Eve Fout, she enjoyed a freedom that she found nowhere else. "She decided first of all that she found New Jersey unexciting," Charlie Whitehouse said, "and she loved the open spaces and the big fields of Virginia, and the galloping down here. One of her charms was this extraordinary girlish quality. I often felt that down here she saw herself a little bit in the spirit of books about sixteen-year-old girls and horses."

"She was a many-faceted person with this very romantic streak," he reminisced, "and to a degree the excitement and beauty of a sport like foxhunting or even riding through these woodlands on a spring day with an old chum brought out her romantic spirit. It came out also in her willingness to stay out in the rain and in the cold, because that was sort of romantic, to be uncomfortable, with snow on the ground, us coming back from hunting, all the coat collars turned up, miserable rain falling. When I got home I was soaked through right to my underwear and so was she. She lived in the intense enjoyment of the moment, the crackling fire, the jolly friends, the good dessert. I think that worry and sorrow bring out that quality of appreciating the glory of the moment in some people. I think it had in her . . ."[46]

Jackie went down in November and March, at first staying with the Whitehouses but mainly at Bunny Mellon's Oak Spring where she kept her horses. For a good many years she had her own house at the Mellons', a cottage in the garden next door to the main house, so that she could feel independent. When she felt she was imposing, she rented a tiny two-story verandaed stone and clapboard cottage. "I remember how much she enjoyed being alone," Charlie said. "She had her books. I used to tease her that she was probably going to starve to death because I didn't think she knew how to boil water, so she would get these precooked meals that you could pop into the oven." Instead of being surrounded by maids, she had a cleaner "who came in daily to toss the dust around"; but her riding clothes and boots were looked after at the Mellons'. "She would come to us maybe once a week for supper. She would hunt with us Monday and Wednesday and with the Piedmont Foxhounds Tuesday and Friday and then she alternated some Saturdays with us, some with the others. Sometimes she'd dine at Willow Oak with Pam Harriman who hunted here a lot." Maurice came very occasionally, sometimes for the "team chase" organized by Eve Fout, or when she took one of her falls. Otherwise Jackie would fly back up to New York once a week from time to time. "She had two bad falls," Charlie recalled, "both at the very end of November. One was the year before she died, the other about two years before that."[47]

At this stage in her life Jackie traveled a great deal, going to China in October 1979 with I. M. Pei and his wife, Eileen, in a party that included New York grandes dames like Marietta Tree, Evangeline Bruce and Bunny Mellon, for the opening of Pei's Fragrant Hill Hotel, near Beijing. With new friends Cary and Edith Welch, she made two extensive trips to India, the first to the north in January 1984, the second to the south in January 1989. She and Cary, one of the world's foremost experts on Indian art, worked on two projects together: *A Second Paradise* by Naveen Patnaik, for which Cary wrote the foreword, published by Doubleday in 1985, and the catalog for a huge exhibition at the Metropolitan Museum, "India, Art and Culture, 1300 to 1900."

"One realizes that she had a kind of genius for friendship," said Cary Welch. "I guess you must have found out that she had more really close friends than you'd ever heard about . . . I also think," he went on, "that she was very much drawn to men who were father figures rather than lover figures. I always thought that, although I was barely a minute older than she, maybe because I was *hors de combat* as someone who was married and had a whole bunch of children and was from a different world, that I was some kind of father figure . . . She would telephone me just out of the blue from time to time, and she would say all kinds of interesting— the word human keeps coming up—very personal things that had touched her or amused her or she thought I would be intrigued to hear."

The Welches saw Jackie as a person who had been through the fire and somehow survived. "Knowing her well only in the last decade of her life, our view of her therefore is based on the person who had already suffered terribly. So the person we knew was someone who had been through all that and who had enormously wisened and who had gained in breadth and depth because of those miseries and who had become much more herself. Cleansed by the fire, but terrible fire," he went on. "I remember once I was having a conversation with her in southern India and I had had a sort of jolly time myself in the 1960s meeting people like Mick Jagger and that sort of thing, and I asked her what she thought of the period and, whoops, I had asked the wrong thing. Because, of course, this was the time of great pain; and she wasn't thinking of it as rock and roll and everybody having a delightful time, she was thinking of a hail of bullets . . . It was as though we had been sailing along and suddenly, wham, we hit an iceberg."[48]

Jackie's circle of friends was remarkably diverse. It included the grandes dames of New York, headed by Brooke Astor, with whom she lunched regularly at the Knickerbocker Club, where the tables were widely spaced enough so that other diners could not hear them gossiping and giggling together over the inanities of their friends and acquaintances.[49] It was no longer the raffish social whirl of the 1970s, the years of Warhol and Studio 54: Jackie now concentrated on dinners for six or eight people at 1040. She reached out to people who interested her, most of them writers and talented people younger than herself who became close friends—Jane Hitchcock, Edna O'Brien, Carly Simon, Joe Armstrong.

With all of them it was Jackie who took the initiative. Joe Armstrong, a young Texan from Abilene, had rescued *Rolling Stone* magazine from obscurity in the early 1970s. He raised staff morale by putting on a song called "Dropkick Me Jesus (Through the Goalposts of Life)" and directing the speaker out of the window on to Park Avenue. "Jackie heard about this from a friend of mine and she broke into laughter so hard that she cried and said, 'Get me Joe Armstrong's telephone number,'" said Armstrong. "She just called me for lunch. She wanted the record and the only place I could find it was an antique-record shop in Dallas. And Jackie memorized all the words to that song."[50]

Jackie's friendship with singer-songwriter Carly Simon, whom she met on Martha's Vineyard, also began around that time, in the mid-1980s. To Joe Armstrong and Carly, Jackie was "like a big sister." She edited Carly Simon's children's books. "I know that on her children's books, Carly was completely dependent on her. I mean Carly and Jackie were very interesting," said a friend. "Mother-daughter might be stretching it too far—maybe sister-older sister, [it was a] strange, interesting relationship . . ." "Jackie was so proud of Carly," Joe Armstrong said. "She took me to her opera, *Romulus Grant.*"[51]

"They were very, very close. And it was sweet to watch them together. There was a real something going on there. It was a complicated relationship," said a fellow publisher.[52]

"Jackie confided in Carly," said a mutual friend. She even told Carly how deeply hurt she had been by Jack Kennedy's infidelities: "After a while," she said, using the third person about herself, as she was accustomed to do when discussing something deeply personal, "one does switch off . . ." Carly turned to Jackie for advice on her disintegrating marriage to singer James Taylor. Jackie would try to boost her self-confidence, calling her up after she had heard a song by Taylor on the radio or had seen him on TV. "She [Jackie] would say, 'You know he doesn't look happy. And you are blossoming!' She was always being the mother hen."[53]

Suffering over men and problems with mothers were themes in Jackie's friendships with younger women. Carly Simon had a notoriously difficult relationship with her mother, Andrea, as did another of Jackie's friends, the writer Jane Hitchcock. Jackie particularly liked Jane's book *Trick of the Eye*, about a difficult mother-daughter relationship. Their friendship had begun in 1985 after Jackie found a copy of a book by Jane at Bunny Mellon's house at Upperville. They met at a dinner at the Morgan Library where Jackie leaned across the table and started a conversation with her: "'I was just reading the book you gave Bunny . . .'" Jane Hitchcock recalled. "She took me under her wing. I wrote two of my books at her house on the Vineyard." Jane, too, was suffering in an unhappy marriage and leaned on Jackie for support. She thought that Jackie saw her as herself when young, insecure, highly strung. "She became like a surrogate mother to me and certainly taught me how to behave. She was the standard by which I measured myself . . . I think she had several friendships like this with women, that she guided. She was very generous with her friendship and her time. She was very much a woman who understood about being a woman alone and the courage that they needed, and having felt alone a great deal of her own life and having made something of herself within those boundaries . . ."[54]

Jackie reached out to Edna O'Brien in much the same way: "I had a play in rehearsal at the Public Theater in New York," she recalled, "a play about Virginia Woolf, and one day during rehearsal a stagehand came over to me and said, 'It's probably a hoax call but it's Jackie Onassis asking for you.' So I go to the phone and, of course, it is Jackie and I recognize the voice and she said, 'Edna, would you have any time for me?' and she asked me to dinner. She had a great feeling for friendship. There was a book of mine called *Time and Tide*, which many a critic savaged, and she wrote to me and said, 'I read your heart-wrenching book and I could not look up from it. I have been hit in the solar plexus. It is not a book that you could ever put out of your mind.' And then she said that it's the greatest book she ever read about the pain and love for one's children and she did love her own children. I mean she truly did and she knew I did. She was capable—she could retreat and withdraw and I had seen her very cold to people—but she was capable of very childlike intense sort of affection . . . In that sense she was a very, very magnetic person."[55]

"So many of her qualities—that breathless enthusiasm, a certain giddiness late at night, a passionate love of clothes—revealed the perennial child," Edna wrote later of her friend. "But the barriers which she built around herself betray a woman who had espoused self preservation from the start." Episodes in the past that had hurt her, old jealousies and slights, the ancient agonies of her parents' divorce and her relationships with them, were confined to "the ice zones." She thought that revelation was tantamount to "showing a wound." Psychologically she had taught herself not to crack. "Distance and distancing were central to her," O'Brien wrote, "not only from others but from huge parts of herself. It was what gave her that inexplicable aura. Her mystery was that she was a mystery to herself. She was caught in the gap between *ingénue* and empress, between innocence and worldliness."[56]

Worldliness was Jackie's shield and her disguise. In June 1988 she became a grandmother with the birth of Rose Schlossberg who, with wide-spaced eyes and dark hair, looked exactly like her. Her response to her new status and to her own sixtieth birthday was to have a face-lift. She had already changed her look from the sexy opulence of Valentino to the more ladylike restraint of Carolina Herrera, and had left Kenneth, her hairdresser of many years who had done so much to build the "Jackie" image, and his assistant, Mary Farr, for the younger Thomas Morrissey, who had opened his own salon with her colorist, Joseph Spadaro, in an upheaval that occasioned a piece in the *New York Times* entitled "Salon Wars." She dieted, jogged, did yoga and acupuncture like all other New Yorkers who could afford it. She apparently went to a psychoanalyst. But, as a friend said, "There is an inner life and an outer life and they don't always coincide." It would be comforting but too glib to say that Jackie, for all the outward contentedness of her life, had solved all her inner tensions. They were an unresolved part of her, her own heart of darkness. "I'd see her life like one sees fairy tales with a lot of jeweled beauty and a dark tragic shadow within," O'Brien said. "But it is a fairy tale and like all fairy tales it has a tragedy in it . . ."[57]

"A few years ago," Reinaldo Herrera said, "we were having one of those heart to hearts that one has from time to time and I committed a grave error, saying, 'Jackie, you know you are such a great mother.' And that got her so wound up. She said, 'Even the worst criminal's a good mother, or should be. I take that nearly as an insult,' she said, 'to be called a good mother. I have great children.' "[58]

In May 1988, a month before she gave birth to Rose, Caroline had graduated from Columbia Law School; she took the bar exam, passing at her first try in February 1989. As she turned thirty she was becoming a beauty, with looks that were distinctly Kennedy, not Bouvier. Caroline seemed not to want to be a social star in her mother's footsteps; there were no expensive decorators working on the Schlossbergs' apartment on Park Avenue, and her husband took responsibility for that as he did for almost everything else. The family took their vacations on Long Island, away from the Kennedy compound, and rarely visited Martha's Vineyard. Caroline was working on a coauthored book with Ellen Alderman, a classmate at Columbia Law School, on the Bill of Rights, which was to be published early in 1991,[59] by which time she had given birth to a second daughter, Tatiana. She was president of the John F. Kennedy Library Foundation, a commitment she took seriously. To Jackie's delight Caroline was turning out to be the intellectual she had hoped.

To publicize her book, Caroline emerged from her strictly private life to do a tour with her coauthor, which entailed giving interviews, which she intensely disliked. On June 1, 1992, she wrote a passionate piece for *Newsweek* entitled "My Father's Legacy":

> May 29 would have been my father's 75th birthday. Maybe because he's not with us, I've thought a lot recently about what was important to him, and how we can make up for how much we miss him still. For years I've been reluctant to discuss this publicly. I still am. But I worry sometimes that the larger message of his life is still being obscured . . .
> . . . Lately it has seemed to me that what I remember, have learned, and know to be true about my father are being pushed aside. His name is being exploited in a way that is an insult to him and his presidency, and a disservice to all the people today who are working, in and out of public life, to make this country better . . . Young people in particular have no recollection of my father and of the idealism and enthusiasm for public service that he inspired. And it is this larger idea—the shin-

ing message of his life—that is being threatened . . . My father believed that politics was not only a noble profession, but the best way to solve our common problems.

That is why, she said, the family had instituted the John F. Kennedy Profile in Courage Award, to reward politicians who, like the men in his book, had shown outstanding examples of political courage. Caroline wanted passionately to remind people that her father had represented public service as an ideal: "They joined the Peace Corps because of him; they worked in the inner cities because of him; they ran for office because he asked them to give something back to their country . . ."

It was Caroline now, rather than Jackie, who was the keeper of the Eternal Flame, who had held up her head through all the stories of scandal, all the denigration of her father, to preserve the memory of the Kennedy legacy. Caroline, along with her favorite aunt Eunice and her older cousin Kathleen Kennedy Townsend, was showing the best, the idealistic side of the Kennedys, and the strength of the Kennedy women. Jackie was proud of her. Caroline's son, John Bouvier Kennedy Schlossberg, was born on January 19, 1993.

John Kennedy Jr. had enjoyed the experience of the District Attorney's office in some ways, meeting and talking to people he would not otherwise have met at the cliff face of underprivileged New York. But he was John Kennedy's son, not Bobby's, and thanks to his mother, he had not emulated his cousins in their often tortured drive to live up to their father. Neither serious law nor serious politics attracted him. In 1993 an idea was slowly maturing in his mind, to go into journalism and the media, which had always attracted his father. "When John knew he was ready to leave the DA's office," Joe Armstrong recalled, "Jackie asked me to meet with him, to talk to him about what he might do next. Jackie admired the fact that he was so open to things, so curious, that he loved adventures. She identified with John—he was full of life and good humor, a constant spark—but she worried about him, too. She knew he had leadership potential, but he was so charmingly casual all the time. He needed to go out and do things on his own, but she was always working behind the scenes, totally vigilant, trying to subtly make things happen, come up with options and ideas."[60] However, she was not absolutely convinced by John's advocacy of what was to become his political-celebrity magazine, George, which was finally unveiled in September 1995.

CHAPTER TWENTY-FOUR

Pilgrim's End

⌒

Give me my scallop-shell of quiet,
My staff of faith to walk upon,
My scrip of joy, immortal diet,
My bottle of salvation,
My gown of glory, hope's true gage,
And thus I'll take my pilgrimage.

—Sir Walter Ralegh

In June 1993, Jackie, with Maurice, retraced some of the places and experiences of her student life in France. They went on a barge trip down the Rhône through Provence and the Camargue, which was, as Maurice said, "Jackie's France." The wild white horses appealed to her romantic nature. At the helm of the barge was a descendant of the great French writer Victor Hugo. Only a hovering concern about Jackie's health lingered like a shadow over the trip. She was very thin. "We knew something wasn't right but we didn't know what," Maurice told a friend later.

A few other people suspected something "wasn't right," among them Valentino, Jackie's former designer and friend of nearly thirty years. "I remember," he said, "every time when I used to arrive in New York, in May, in September, in November, I always used to call her and say, 'Jackie, so we have a date, we'll have tea or lunch or something?' And I . . . remember almost one year before she died, she said, 'I am very, very busy. Maybe we'll speak on the phone next week.' She tried to avoid any agitation and I knew from my boutique because she passed vibes to my boutique, she was already not feeling so well . . . She wrote me a beautiful letter but maybe she didn't want to show herself to somebody who might notice these things . . ."[1]

Among those who came to stay at Jackie's Red Gate Farm on Martha's Vineyard that August were Solange Herter and her husband, Dr. Frederick Herter. Jackie and she had been friends now for more than forty years, from their Paris days through the ups and downs of Solange's first marriage, through the tragedies and triumphs of Jackie's life as a senator's wife in Georgetown, the White House years, the terrible days of her year of mourning in New York and through her marriage to Onassis. As always, Jackie had been a true friend in Solange's illnesses: "I became sick and had a cancer scare about twenty years ago," Solange recalled. "She was so wonderful. The first time around, many people had given me up but she came to see me every day. And then the second time, a year later, I had a totally unrelated cancer scare and it had to be operated on and she did the same thing. Then eight or ten years ago, something like that . . . I had a very bad back problem . . . And she came to lunch here and I told her, 'Oh, Jackie, I can hardly stand up,' and she called up Dr. James Nicholas, who had treated her and had helped her a lot with falls and all those injuries from riding. Of course, he's very difficult to get an appointment with—I'd have had to wait weeks normally but he came to see me immediately."[2]

The Herters stayed in "Bunny's Room," simply decorated with painted wooden shutters and no curtains, with plain furniture made by local carpenters, blue-gray chintz wallpaper and a tiled fireplace. The view looked straight out to sea. Outside Jackie had a hammock suspended from a tree. They took sea trips on Maurice's *Relemar* or on Jackie's little motorboat. A photograph taken by Frederick Herter on the boat shows Jackie, upright and alert, wearing white duck trousers and a striped sailor's *maillot*, navy baseball cap and trademark sunglasses. They went swimming; on Dr. Nicholas's orders Jackie now wore a snorkel and mask because the injuries to her back from her riding falls caused her problems in turning her head left and right.

There were lunches and dinners with old Vineyard friends, like Rose and William Styron, Art Buchwald and Carly Simon. Lady Bird Johnson, staying with Kay Graham, came to Sunday lunch. "We ate out under an arbor of vines, with the sea, across the sand dunes and grasses, murmuring out beyond," she recalled. "We did not reminisce about the past . . ."[3] New friends, the Clintons, came in August to celebrate the President's birthday. Jackie felt an affinity with him and his wife. Of course she knew of the photograph of the young William Jefferson Clinton in the Rose Garden with Jack, and there were many things about him that reminded her of Jack, his famous charm and intellectual curiosity, as well, no doubt, as the rumors of sexual peccadilloes. With the arrival of the President on Maurice's boat, old political instincts stirred in Jackie. She turned to Teddy, who was standing beside her as Maurice went down to meet Clinton. "Teddy, you go down and meet the President," she said.

"But Maurice has gone."

"Maurice isn't running for reelection."

Over dinner at an inn run by singer James Taylor's family, Jackie talked at length to Clinton, unusually about her life with Jack in the White House. She empathized with Hillary, who was going through a period of unpopularity after her husband's election. Jackie and Hillary were "great pals," according to Arthur Schlesinger. When Schlesinger tentatively suggested that Hillary was "humorless," Jackie told him, "You couldn't be more wrong. She's great fun and entertaining." To Vivi Stokes Crespi she said of her, "Finally, a woman who is just not going to cut ribbons and open bazaars . . ."

Jackie's interest in the Clintons went back to 1991 when, according to Hillary, Clinton was told that Jackie and John Jr. had been talking about him as a possible presidential prospect. They were among the earliest contributors to his campaign. In June 1992 she had invited Hillary to lunch at 1040: "When I met her in that marvelous apartment with books everywhere, she made me feel like we were old friends. What could have been a short, courtesy lunch turned into a several-hour conversation. She had out a lot of her latest projects and the books that she had edited, and other books she was interested in. We talked a lot about our mutual interest in writing and kicked around ideas for other books she might do in the future. Mostly, we talked about our children, what it's like to live in the White House. She was convinced my husband was going to win, and she wanted to give me advice . . ." Jackie spoke to Hillary in Washington on the telephone and invited her to another long lunch. "She gave me good pieces of advice on trying to get the White House to be a home," Hillary Clinton said. "She was conscious of how, in her own time, it was a real challenge to fulfill her roles and responsibilities in a way that not only bore her own stamp, but also fit who she was. 'You've got to do things that are right for you. Don't model yourself on anybody else. There are certain things other people may have done that are of interest to you, that you should learn about, but you have to be yourself.' "[4]

At the traditional Labor Day picnic Jackie gave at Red Gate Farm, she and Carly Simon sang silly songs to Jackie's grandson, Jack, aged seven months. Then Jackie, like thousands of other Americans, headed back to the city. In October she was in Boston for the rededication of the John F. Kennedy Library, attended by President Clinton. It was noticeable that she did not flinch from Clinton's kiss as she had from that of his Democrat predecessor Jimmy Carter. In November she was in Virginia, riding her favorite big gray horse, Frank. Around the time of the thirtieth anniversary of Jack's death, she had a bad fall, was knocked unconscious for thirty minutes, and was kept in the hospital. She returned to New York, and for the first time in years did not appear at the Thanksgiving meet of the Essex Hunt in Bernardsville. Curiously, at around that time the local *Courier News* reported that Jackie had sold her Far Hills property to John and Caroline for a token sum. She must have been contemplating the move, in the interest of tax avoidance, for some time—intimations of mortality, perhaps.

While she was in the Virginia hospital a doctor had noticed a swelling in Jackie's groin that he attributed to an infection and had given her antibiotics. "When she came out of the hospital she called me," Carolina Herrera said, "and she said she had a terrific cold that she couldn't get rid of . . . And then she said— she didn't talk about what she had—she needed a blouse or a jacket that was straight and I said, 'Why?' and she said to me, 'I don't know what's happened to me but since the accident [my waist] is very big and I have to go out.' So, I think that was the beginning, she knew already."[5]

Jackie and Maurice were cruising in the Caribbean after Christmas in 1993 when she began to feel very unwell. She had an agonizing pain in her groin, which refused to disappear. She returned to New York with painful swellings in her neck.

> There she consulted Dr. Carolyn Agresti, a head and neck surgeon at the New York Hospital Cornell Medical Center, who found enlarged lymph nodes in her neck and armpit. A computerized axial tomography examination, or CAT scan, showed that there were swollen lymph nodes in her chest and deep in her abdomen, an area known as the retroperitoneal area. Dr. Agresti ordered a biopsy of one of the neck nodes, which revealed that Jackie had non-Hodgkin's lymphoma. A pathologist told Lawrence Altman, a medical expert who wrote for the *New York Times*, that the cells were anaplastic—that is, they were undeveloped, what doctors call "embryonic" or "primitive," indicating that the disease was highly malignant and could spread to other parts of her body.[6]

"She was secretive about her life and she was secretive about her death," Edna O'Brien said.[7] Her trips to the clinic for chemotherapy and for periodic CAT scans were conducted in cloak-and-dagger fashion. She would arrive wearing a hooded cape and only go in after Maurice had ensured that no one was in the waiting room. To her friends she was persistently upbeat, joking with Arthur Schlesinger that she wished now she hadn't wasted time "on all those push-ups." It was as if, she said, that the gods had wanted to punish her hubris—her pride in her fitness and the efforts she had made to maintain it, the yoga sessions, the jogging around the reservoir, the marathon swims. She made light of the trials of chemotherapy—"It gives me a chance to read a book," she told Schlesinger.[8] Survival rates for her type of cancer after five years were published as being 50–52 percent. Whether or not Jackie believed it, she remained outwardly confident. John, who had given up his job in the DA's office, left his downtown apartment and moved to a nearby hotel so that he could see his mother and walk with her every day, which suggests that he did not share her confidence.

Meanwhile, on February 11, Nancy Tuckerman issued a press statement confirming that Jackie had non-Hodgkin's lymphoma but that "She's doing very well. She's maintaining her schedule. There is an excellent prognosis. The doctors are very optimistic." The statement shocked everyone outside her immediate family; no one had been aware that anything was wrong. Her "SWAT team" at Doubleday subconsciously refused to accept that she was dangerously ill. "We were so sure she was going to be there," said Scott Moyers, "because she was so brave, so indomitable, never complained. She always said she wouldn't talk about it but you got the sense of her talking about it to Nancy Tuckerman, and she put on a brave face, long after she clearly knew probably that it was irreversible . . ."[9]

On March 2 Jackie wrote to Solange Herter what her friend describes as "just a remarkable letter," in which she made light of her illness. "I think she wrote to a lot of her friends as though things weren't as bad as they were," Solange said. In

March, she began to experience spells of mental confusion. She went to see an eminent neurologist at the New York hospital, who gave her an MRI scan. This revealed that the lymphoma had disappeared from her neck, chest and abdomen but that the cerebellum, the membrane covering her brain, had been affected, as had her spinal cord. Her neurologist told her that her best hope of survival lay in a new procedure that involved opening the skull and inserting a tube to feed an anticancer drug directly into the brain. Jackie submitted to this intervention, virtually a last hope.

On January 31 she had drawn up in her own hand a list of personal bequests of objects: "to my friend Rachel Lambert Mellon . . . in memory of . . . designing the Rose Garden in the White House," two Indian miniatures, one entitled *Gardens of the Palace of the Rajh*; "to my friend, Alexander D. Forger," the copy of JFK's Inaugural address signed by Robert Frost "for JBK"; and "to my friend, Maurice Tempelsman, a Greek alabaster head of a woman." Two months later on March 22, she signed her final will and testament. The main beneficiaries were, of course, Caroline and John; Lee "whom I hold in great affection," was left nothing because "I have already done so during my lifetime" but Lee's children were left a trust fund of half a million dollars each. Other beneficiaries included Nancy Tuckerman, Marta Sgubin, Provi Paredes and Jackie's butler, Efgenio Pinheiro. The only Bouviers to benefit were the descendants of the one member of the family with whom Jackie had remained friends, her cousin and godfather, Miche. Yusha was left the interest in Hammersmith Farm, which Jackie had inherited from her mother; provision was made for Little Janet's children. Jamie Auchincloss, outlawed for having spoken to Kitty Kelley for her 1979 biography of Jackie, was left nothing. She made careful arrangements to enable her children to sell any of her property that they did not want. Jackie had not lost her sense of mischief and irony, even when she was dying. Looking around her apartment "at the very end," she told her children, "Sell everything. You'll make a lot of money."[10] It was as if she foresaw the three days of hysteria as her belongings were sold at Sotheby's two years later—the lines around the block, people fighting to pay vastly inflated prices for even the smallest part of her, as if they were the relics of a medieval saint. Jackie knew the price of icon status.

On April 14 Joe Armstrong and Carly Simon, whose mother had died just four months before, gave Jackie lunch "to cheer her up." "She kept saying to us," Joe Armstrong recalled, " 'Just four more weeks and I'll be myself again . . . ' " As Jackie was leaving, Carly handed her the sheet of music for a song she had just written, "Touched by the Sun." "This is for you," she told her. "You inspired it."[11] The following day, Jackie collapsed. The steroid treatment she had been receiving had caused a perforated ulcer; she was taken to the hospital for surgery. After she came out she made every effort to continue her normal life, lunching with friends like John Loring and Carolina Herrera. She and Carolina usually went to Mortimer's, where Jackie always had the corner table—"Shall we go to Mortimer's?" Carolina suggested, when Jackie called her after she came home. But Jackie, thoughtful as always, knew that Carolina was busy on her April show and that Mortimer's would be too far uptown for her to come. "She was so incredible because she knew that I was very busy because I had a show coming on and she knew that I liked 44, the Royalton, where everybody goes during fashion week, and I said, 'Are you sure you want to go there?' And she said, 'Yes, yes, yes,' and so she arrived. She was sick that day, very, very sick. She couldn't eat so she brought her own soup in a Thermos."

Gallantly, Jackie never admitted to friends, perhaps not even to herself, that she might die. She thought of all the friends she loved and would not see, and wrote to them, yet always as if this were not her last spring. To William vanden Heuvel, she sent a note—"just a paragraph, when we knew what was close, just to say what our friendship had meant to her. She was one of the most beautiful letter writers I had ever encountered in my life."[12]

There were suggestions of radical treatments, such as a bone-marrow transplant. The doctors were uncertain as to what to advise: the treatment is not normally given to patients over fifty but Jackie's physical fitness might have counteracted that. "Doctors have a very odd ambivalence about someone as celebrated as that," said a friend. "I mean, obviously they were unsure whether to really get into it and try something radical, or treat her with kid gloves . . ."[13] But Jackie felt that further hospital treatment would be pointless. "She felt that the children had left the nest, like she's done her job with her children and she wasn't going to fight for life. She wasn't going to take extraordinary measures to prolong her life."[14] She felt, too, that she would not be able to do those life-enhancing things that had been so important to her, like riding free in Virginia. It was of Virginia and her friends there that she was thinking when she wrote what Eve Fout described as "my favorite letter from Jackie, I carry it around,"[15] on April 19. Eve and Charlie had been leading a great fight to prevent Disney from creating a huge theme park near Middleburg, which Jackie had backed enthusiastically. Jackie thanked Eve for keeping her in touch with Middleburg, the place where she had been so happy. "I pray against Disney ever night . . ." "She died just before we won," Charlie Whitehouse commented. "She allowed us to use her name and she sent us significant contributions and loved talking about the horror of it to friends . . ."[16]

Cary and Edith Welch were due to drop in to see Jackie before leaving for Europe—it was to have been on Thursday, May 11, but Jackie telephoned and said, "Come Wednesday . . ." They had a perfectly normal conversation. "One of the things I find difficult to understand," Cary Welch said, "when we came back from Europe following her death, I was handed by our son Thomas a heap of newspaper accounts of her last days, and according to those, on the day when we saw her she would have been so absolutely undone with disease that it would have been impossible to have the kind of conversation that we had—and I find that quite at odds with our experience." As they were leaving Cary said, " 'Jackie, we look forward to . . .' I didn't know how serious it was but what do you say? And we embraced, and Maurice was shaking his head. He made a comment—'We're pretty much stuck in port these days,' or something of that sort." [17]

That was Wednesday, May 10. On Sunday, May 15, Jackie took a walk in Central Park with Maurice and her grandchildren. On Monday she was taken to the hospital suffering from chills and incipient pneumonia. The cancer had invaded her liver. On Wednesday she discharged herself and went home to 1040 to die. Among the few men admitted to see her then was Yusha Auchincloss, who had loved her since they first met in Washington in 1941. As he wrote,

> I should have felt sad, but she made me feel very happy and proud to realize how privileged I was to have shared her friendship at the close. She could still show that same impatient move ahead motion in her soft breathing and firm touch that she had exhibited as a champion equestrienne. I knew that she knew when it was time to go on, and she would not like to keep her maker waiting. She left without self-pity . . .[18]

She died at 10:15 P.M. on the evening of Thursday, May 19. The next day John Jr. made a simple announcement to the waiting press: "She did it her own way and on her own terms and we all feel lucky for that." In private, Maurice Tempelsman, who had been with her every moment, said, "She went out with her usual courage and style."

Courage and style but also with the sense of ritual and of theater that had always attended her. TV lights lit up the night and hundreds of people crowded at a respectful distance outside the building. Inside 1040 Fifth Avenue, America's Queen had met death serenely, lying in her elegant bed, surrounded by her family and staff, attended by a few chosen friends. It was a scene that, over the ages, had attended the passing of kings, emperors, queens. Outside, commentators were struggling to explain why this was happening in democratic America, why so many people mourned the disappearance of a rich, sixty-four-year-old woman.

To the mourners Jackie was inextricably bound up with the history of their country and their time, an image of a better America that perhaps had existed only in their minds. She had been part of their lives for more than thirty years. The drawn face they saw in photographs taken in her last days had been real, no longer a beautiful mask. As her friend Edna O'Brien said, it was "the face of a woman who had indeed lived life and was about to live death . . ." The nymph of Central Park, whose essence they had never really captured, had vanished before their eyes.

And So Farewell . . .

On Sunday, May 22, Jackie's coffin lay, covered with her antique bedspread, in front of the fireplace in her drawing room. Earlier that morning Maurice had sat beside it, reading the Sunday newspapers as they had always done together. He and the children had invited friends and family to an informal wake, Jackie's last party before the funeral. Caroline was distraught and sobbing, quite unlike her usual composed self; John Jr., on the other hand, perhaps in a state of shock, kept his emotions under control. At one point he even waved to the crowds below, with his current girlfriend, actress Daryl Hannah. Bunny Mellon was there and, of course, Nancy Tuckerman, who had had the strength to make the arrangements for the funeral of her oldest and closest friend. Mike Nichols and his wife, Diane Sawyer, Richard and Doris Goodwin, Jane Hitchcock, Karen Lerner, Joe Armstrong and Carly Simon were there. There was a slight commotion when Carly Simon tried to place a note she had written to Jackie on the coffin and was ordered by Ed Schlossberg to remove it: that was a privilege reserved for children and grandchildren. In the garage below the apartment, Bunny Mellon had been organizing the heaps of flowers that had been pouring in—among them two dozen red roses from Frank Sinatra, with the message "You are America's Queen," and, brought by Lisa Sullivan, a basket of cornflowers, Jackie's favorite flower, as much her symbol as the pilgrim's shell on her writing paper.

The funeral service, on Monday, May 23, was held in the church of St. Ignatius Loyola, where she had been christened and confirmed. Jackie's pallbearers were headed by the family's much-loved Secret Service man, John F. M. Walsh, and included Anthony Radziwill, Timothy Shriver, William Smith, Robert Kennedy Jr., Christopher Lawford, Edward Kennedy Jr., and Little Janet's husband, Lewis Rutherfurd. Provi's son, Gustavo Paredes, was among the ushers. In a poignant opening, John F. Kennedy Jr. told the congregation how they had struggled to find readings for the service "that captured my mother's essence. Three things came to mind over and over again . . . They were her love of words, the bonds of home and family, and her spirit of adventure."

The Bible readings were given by John Jr., Jane Hitchcock and Mike Nichols, with prayers by Nancy Tuckerman, Sydney Lawford McKelvy, Anna Christina Radziwill and Edwin Schlossberg. Teddy Kennedy delivered a moving and eloquent eulogy: "No one else looked like her, spoke like her, wrote like her, or was so original in the way she did things. No one we knew ever had a better sense of self . . ." Most moving of all were the readings by Maurice Tempelsman and Caroline of two of Jackie's favorite poems, "Ithaka" by C. P. Cavafy, and "Memory of Cape Cod," by Edna St. Vincent Millay, the latter from the prize book that Jackie had won at Miss Porter's in 1946. It evoked past summers on the Cape, the long beaches and the ocean that Jackie and Jack had loved:

> The wind in the ash-tree sounds like surf on the shore at Truro.
> I will shut my eyes . . .
> They said: Leave your pebbles on the sand, and your shells,
>   too, and come along,
> we'll find you another beach like the beach at Truro.
>
> Let me listen to the wind in the ash . . . it sounds
> Like surf on the shore.

Cavafy's "Ithaka" invokes the adventures of Ulysses, which had played such a strong part in Jackie's life during her marriage to Onassis, and which symbolized her spirit of adventure, as well as the sense of having reached her journey's end.

> As you set out for Ithaka
> hope your road is a long one,
> full of adventure, full of discovery.
> Laistrygonians, Cyclops,
> Angry Poseidon—don't be afraid of them:
> You'll never find things like that on your way
> As long as you keep your thoughts raised high,
> As long as a rare excitement
> Stirs your spirit and your body . . .
>
> Hope your road is a long one,
> May there be summer mornings when,
> with what pleasure, what joy,
> you enter harbors you're seeing for the first time . . .

Keep Ithaka always in your mind.
Arriving there is what you're destined for.
But don't hurry the journey at all.
Better if it lasts for years, so you're old by the time you
    reach the island,
wealthy with all you've gained along the way . . .

Wise as you will have become, so full of
Experience, you'll have understood by then
what these Ithakas mean . . .

And to this Maurice added his own sad farewell:

And now the journey is over,
too short, alas, too short.
It was filled with
adventure and wisdom
laughter and love
gallantry and grace . . .

For the purpose of the service, Caroline dropped her married name and re-
verted to "Caroline Kennedy" and, although Jackie's gravestone was to bear the
name Jacqueline Kennedy Onassis, the name Onassis was otherwise not mentioned, either at the church service or during the burial at Arlington. Afterward
Jackie's body was flown to Washington to be buried beside Jack's at Arlington.
Her grave lies between the stones marking those of her stillborn baby daughter
and Jack; Bobby's grave is not far away. In death she remains part of the Kennedys
and Queen of Camelot.

Epilogue

～

Born of the sun, they traveled a short while towards the sun, And left the vivid air . . .

    —Lines from the poem by Stephen Spender recited by
    John F. Kennedy Jr., aged nineteen, at the opening of the
    John Fitzgerald Kennedy Library

Jackie was spared what would have been for her an unbearable tragedy. On the evening of July 16, 1999, her adored son, John F. Kennedy Jr., with his wife, Carolyn Bessette Kennedy and sister-in-law Lauren, plunged in his small plane through the darkening sky into the ocean some four miles off Martha's Vineyard. Wreckage washed up on the beach at Gay Head, within a mile of Jackie's much-loved haven, Red Gate Farm. In the line of myth and tragedy that had epitomized Jackie's life, John's death might be seen as the modern fulfillment of the myth of Icarus, which his stepfather, Aristotle Onassis, had told him long ago on Skorpios, of the boy with waxen wings who flew too close to the sun and fell to earth.

ACKNOWLEDGMENTS

I owe a huge debt of gratitude to all those who have helped me in the course of four years' work on this book, by giving interviews, information and guidance, photographs, correspondence, often hospitality. I am equally grateful to those who have preferred to remain anonymous. If I have unwittingly omitted anyone whom I should have thanked, I beg their forgiveness.

Henriette, Lady Abel Smith, Howard W. Adams, Jonathan Aitken, Susan Mary Alsop, Jean Paul Ansellem, Robert Sam Anson, Joe Armstrong, Steven M. L. Aronson, Lord Ashcombe, Brooke Astor, Hugh D. Auchincloss III, Jamie Auchincloss, Louis Auchincloss, Maya Auchincloss, Sylvie Avizou, Letitia Baldrige, Louise Baring, Louis M. S. Beal, Charles Bartlett, Najma Beard, Peter Beard, Antony Beevor, Michael Bentley, James Biddle, Deeda McCormick Blair, Joan and Clay Blair, Sylvia Whitehouse Blake, Bill Blass, Maggie Boellart, Jean Bothorel, James Bowman, John Bradlee, the late Hon. Dinah Bridge, Mary L. Bundy, James McGregor Burns, Grace Mirabella Cahan, Ariadne and Mario Calvo-Platero, R. Campbell James, Cape Cod Chamber of Commerce, Teresa Cárcano, Elizabeth Carpenter, Oleg Cassini, Edward Lee Cave, Alexander Chancellor, Marion Oates Leiter Charles, Blair Clark, Nancy Tenney Coleman, Amy Fine Collins, Artemis Cooper, Janet Felton Cooper, Richmond J. Cooper, Newton Cope, the Committee and staff of the Cosmopolitan Club, New York, Jan Cowles, Geoffrey Crawford, Countess Vivi Crespi, Robert Dallek, John H. Davis, the late Maude Davis, Richard de Combray, Elizabeth de Cuevas, Comte Paul de Ganay, Hubert de Givenchy, Vicomtesse de Ribes, Michael Deeley, the Duke and Duchess of Devonshire, Douglas Dillon, Betty di Robilant, Ellen Gates D'Oench, Vicomtesse d'Origny, Marina Dodero de Tchomlekdjoglou, Sholto Douglas-Home, Tiffany Dubin, Peter Duchin, Claude du Granrut, Grace, Countess of Dudley, Robin Biddle Duke, Domenick Dunne, Senator Mario D'Urso, William Voss Elder III, Marina Emo di Capolista, Sally J. Ewalt, John B. Fairchild, James Fallon, Hubert Faure, Paul B. "Red" Fay Jr., Frances Daly Fergusson and the staff of Vassar College, Alastair Forbes, Sir Edward Ford, M. Burch Tracy Ford and the staff of Miss Porter's School, Eve Fout, Lady Antonia Fraser, Lady Fraser, Professor and Mrs. J. K. Galbraith, Princess Irene Galitzine, Valentino Garavani, John "Demi" Gates, Brigitte Gerney, Philip and Cecilia Geyelin, Joan Gardner, Alxis Gregory, Geordie Greig, the late Brendan Gill, Benno Graziani, Mrs. Roswell Gilpatric, Viscountess Gormanston, Deborah and Loyd Grossman, Richard N. Goodwin, Doris Kearns Goodwin, Professor Lewis L. Gould, Louis Carron Greig, Lilian Grueff, Thomas H. Guinzburg, William Guthrie, Hon. Desmond Guinness, Viscount Hambleden, Nigel Hamilton, Benjamin E. Hammond, Lord Harlech, Pamela, Lady Harlech, the late Elizabeth Forsling Harris, Cholmondeley Harrison, Kitty Carlisle Hart, Nicholas Haslam, Lady Selina Hastings, Eugenie Havemeyer, Ashton Hawkins, Professor Peter Hennesey, Carolina Herrera, Reinaldo Herrera, Solange Herter, C. David Heymann, Minnie Cassatt Hickman, the late Derek Hill, Barry Hillenbrand, Jane Stanton Hitchcock and Jim Hoagland, Lord Holderness, Nancy Holmes, Alistair Horne, Tony Howard, Heywood Isham, John Isham, Hugh N. Jacobsen, Ruth Jacobson, HH The Rajmata of Jaipur, Lord Jenkins of Hillhead, Peter Jennings, Mrs. Lyndon B. Johnson, Mark Jones, Peter Keating, Joan B. Kennedy, James Roe Ketchum, David Koch, Suzanne P. Kloman, Lord Lambton, Kenneth Lane, Alan Lang, Laurence Leamer, Walter Lees, Patrick Leigh Fermor, Karen Lerner, Frances Lewine, Marguerite Littman, George Loudon, Principessa Letizia Buoncompagni Ludovisi, Diana MacArthur, Colin Mackay, Catherine Maclean, Priscilla Johnson Macmillan, Bronwen Maddox, Professor William Manchester, Professor Burke Marshall, Martha's Vineyard Chamber of Commerce, the Master and Fellows of St. John's College, Cambridge, Christopher Mason, Mac McGarry, Mary Tyler McClenahan, Camilla McGrath, Stryker McGuire, Kay Meehan, Aileen Mehle, Jay Mellon, David Metcalfe, Pauline C. Metcalf, Mrs. Cord Meyer, Melody Miller, Roderick B. Mitchell and staff of the Bedford Stuyvesant

Corporation, Wendy Morgan, Thomas Morrissey, Scott Moyers, Edna Harrison Murray, Richard A. Nelson, Bruce M. Newman, Viscount Norwich, Edna O'Brien, Columbus O'Donnell, Deborah Owen, Stelio A. Papadimitriou, Frederic S. Papert, Naveen Patnaik, the late Endicott Peabody, Sam and Judy Peabody, John Pearson, Contessa Viviana Pecci Blunt, I. M. Pei, Senator and Mrs. Claiborne Pell, Princess Luciana Pignatelli, John Pierrepont, George Plimpton, L. Frank Plugge, Professor Robert L. Pounder, the late Alan Pryce-Jones, Eben Pyne, Lee Radziwill, Maree Rambo, Coates Redmon, Professor Richard Reeves, Tom Rhodes, John Richardson, Marie Ridder, Ian and Jenny Roberts, Professor and Mrs. Walt M. Rostow, Stephen Rubin, Pierre Salinger, John Sargent, John Saumarez Smith, Gloria Schiff, Professor Arthur M. Schlesinger Jr., Marian Cannon Schlesinger, Caroline Seebohm, Jeff Seroy, Everett Sevier, John Schute, James Sherwin, Dawn Langley Simmons, Senator George Smathers, Theodore C. Sorensen, Joseph Spadaro, Elizabeth Coxe Spalding, Thomas F. Staley, Francesca Stanfill, John Stefanidis, Gloria Steinem, Damaris, Lady Stewart, Viscountess Stuart of Findhorn, Julien Stock, the Earl of Stockton MEP, Dr. Thomas Stuttaford, Lisa Sullivan, David Sulzberger, John A. H. Sweeney, Milbrey Rennie Taylor (Missie Rennie), Noreen Taylor, Taki Theodoracopoulos, Franklin A. Thomas, Michael Thomas, Susan Norton Thomas, Joan Thring, Helen Thomas, D. D. Tillett, Robert Tracy, Bruce Tracy, Aileen Bowdoin Train, the late Michael Tree, Baroness Trumpington, Jack Valenti, William vanden Heuvel, Hugo Vickers, Gore Vidal, Claus von Bulow, Peggy McDonnell Walsh, Hon. Claire Ward, John Carl Warnecke, Washington Chamber of Commerce, Lord Weidenfeld, Edith and Cary Welch, Robert White, Philip Whitehead MEP, Hon. Charles S. Whitehouse, Tom Wicker, Nia Mai Williams, David Williamson, Susan Neuberger Wilson, Helen and John Winslow, Philip Ziegler.

I have been fortunate in having the skilled assistance of researchers in the various archives in the United States and the United Kingdom and it would be no exaggeration to say that without them this book could not have been written. The principal burden has been borne by Christopher Carberry of the Massachusetts Historical Society, who has combed the archives of the John Fitzgerald Kennedy Library, Boston University, the Massachusetts Historical Society and the New Hampshire Historical Society. In Washington D.C. Martin Morse Wooster has not only brought the weight of his erudition to bear at the archives of the Library of Congress and the FBI, but has hunted down essential source material in the form of books and articles, and greatly assisted with the picture research. In New York Ann Chisholm has been invaluable in tracking down cuttings at the New York Public Library, and oral history interviews at the University of Columbia. Bill Pugsley of the Texas Information Network has been indefatigable in mining the extensive resources of the Lyndon Baines Johnson Library at Austin. In the United States I should also like to thank Allison Bozniak, T. Mike Griffin, Carole-Anne Elliott, Laura E. Beardsley of the Historical Society of Pennsylvania, Lynn Roundtree for his work at Duke University, Julia Soyer for hers at the Arthur and Elizabeth Schlesinger Library on the History of Women in America, and Suzanne Steele for her informative tour of East Hampton and help with Long Island sources.

In the United Kingdom Dr. Saul Kelly has kindly interrupted his own work to help me in the Public Record Office at Kew and the Cecil Beaton Papers at St. John's College, Cambridge. Guy Penman of the London Library has been indefatigable in rounding up books from all over Britain. Eileen Penman of the American School in London has kindly provided me with essential works.

I would like to thank the following archivists, curators and librarians who have given generously of their time to help me with the research for this book.

Eileen Penman, Senior Class Dean, the American School in London
Dr. Vincent Giroud, Curator of Modern Books and Manuscripts, the Beinecke Rare Book and Manuscript Library, Yale University Library
Mary Clapinson, Keeper of Special Collections, Helen Langley, Senior Assistant Librarian, Department of Western Manuscripts, Bodleian Library, University of Oxford
Patrick T. Lawlor, Rare Book and Manuscript Library, Anne M. Gefell, Oral History Research Office, Columbia University in the City of New York
Danielle Haase-Dubosc, Director Reid Hall and Associate Provost, Columbia Univierity
Frederick Bauman Jr., Ernest Emrich, Jeff Flannery, Henry Heiss, Library of Congress Manuscript Reading Room
William R. Erwin Jr., Senior Reference Librarian, Dr. Linda M. McCurdy, Director of Reference Services, Special Collections Library, Duke University
John Wickman, Director, Linda K. Smith, Archives Specialist, Dwight D. Eisenhower Library
Merle Thomason, Delano Knox, Fairchild Fashion Library
The Clerks at the FBI Reading Room
Harry Middleton, Director, Claudia Anderson, Senior Archivist, Lyndon Baines Johnson Library
William Johnson, Supervisory Archivist, Megan Desnoyers, Archivist, Allan Goodrich, Audiovisual Archivist, John Fitzgerald Kennedy Library
Jeffrey Suchanek, Coordinator, Modern Political Archives, Margaret I. King Library, University of Kentucky
Richard Williams, Librarian, Anna A. Malicka, Library Services Assistant, the Lewis Walpole Library
Dr. Alan Bell and the staff of the London Library

Shirley Langhauser, Archivist, Miss Porter's School
Cathy O'Callaghan, Municipal Art Society
Kevin Scott, The Museum of Television and Radio
The Librarian, *The News*, Portsmouth
Susan Naulty, Archivist, the Richard Nixon Library and Birthplace
Philadelphia City Archives
Philadelphia Historical Society
William Joyce, Director, Princeton University Library
Anne Engelhart, Associate Curator of Manuscripts, Ellen M. Shea, Reference Assistant, The Arthur and
    Elizabeth Schlesinger Library on the History of Women in America, Radcliffe College
Raymond Teichman, Supervisory Archivist, Franklin D. Roosevelt Library
Amanda Saville, Librarian, Elizabeth Quarmby Lawrence, Special Collections Librarian, St. John's College,
    Cambridge
Susan Scott, Archivist, the Savoy Group, London
Michael Brunton, Time Magazine Library
Dennis E. Bilger, Archivist, Harry S. Truman Library
Elizabeth Monkman, Curator, the White House
Judith Ann Schiff, Chief Research Archivist, William R. Massa Jr., Public Services Archivist, Manuscripts
    and Archives, Yale University Library

The work put into the production of this book by the staff of Viking Penguin in London and New York has
been monumental and of the highest quality. In London I would like particularly to thank Helen Fraser,
Juliet Annan, Kate Barker, Keith Taylor, Antonia Till and Hazel Orme, and in New York Wendy Wolf and
Clifford J. Corcoran. Lynda Marshall has been a brilliant picture researcher on this as on my previous books
and I am grateful to her for her vision and hard work.

Gillon Aitken, my agent, has been a tower of strength throughout, as has his assistant Lesley Shaw, and
I would like to thank also Clare Alexander and Sally Riley of Gillon Aitken Associates for their help and
support.

Lastly I would like to thank my assistant, Camilla Eadie, who knows far better than I could express the
depth of my gratitude to her for her technical expertise, her efficiency, dedication and kindness through
moments good and bad. I honestly could not have done it without her. Similarly my husband, William Bangor, has been utterly selfless in his help and encouragement through these long four years when I have
leaned on him for support which he has always given.

NOTES

INTRODUCTION: FOUR DAYS IN AMERICA: NOVEMBER 22–25, 1963

1. Ambassador William J. vanden Heuvel, interview with the author, April 1, 1998.

CHAPTER 1: GOLDEN GATSBY YEARS

1. Lee Radziwill, interview with the author, November 2, 1997, and quote from Lee Radziwill, "Opening Chapters," *Ladies' Home Journal*, January 1973.
2. Interview with the author, December 3, 1997.
3. Radziwill interview.
4. See John Vernou Bouvier Jr., *Our Forebears*, p. 39.
5. John Vernou, petition for citizenship of the United States, annotated "Sworn & admitted Oct. 25 1808" Philadelphia City Archives.
6. Francis J. Dallett, see John H. Davis, *The Bouviers*, 1993, p. 180.
7. See *New York*, January 10, 1972.
8. Gore Vidal, interview with the author, September 30, 1996.
9. See *Our Forebears*, p. 39.
10. John "Demi" Gates, interview with the author, May 11, 1997.
11. Carl Sferrazza Anthony, *As We Remember Her, Jacqueline Kennedy Onassis, in the Words of Her Family and Friends*, 1997, p. 12.
12. Flora Rheta Schreiber, "What Jackie Kennedy has learned from her Mother," *Good Housekeeping*, October 1962.
13. Demi Gates interview.
14. See Mary Van Rensselaer Thayer, *Jacqueline Bouvier Kennedy*, 1961, p. 22.
15. Radziwill interview, November 2, 1997.
16. Vidal interview.
17. Radziwill interview.
18. *Ibid.*
19. See John H. Davis, *The Bouviers*, 1993, p. 268.
20. Radziwill interview.
21. Interview with the author, October 28, 1997.
22. Interview with the author, December 3, 1997.
23. Radziwill interview.
24. Quoted in C. David Heymann, *A Woman Named Jackie*, 1994, p. 43.
25. *Ibid.*
26. *Ibid.*
27. Radziwill interview.
28. In Mary Van Rensselaer Thayer, *Jacqueline Bouvier Kennedy*, 1961, p. 26.

1. Peter Duchin with Charles Michener, *Ghost of a Chance, a Memoir*, 1996, p. 334.
2. Written information kindly provided by Minnie Cassatt Hickman, July 14, 1997.
3. Radziwill interview.
4. Minnie Hickman, July 14, 1997.
5. Van Rensselaer Thayer, p. 36.
6. Janet Felton Cooper, interview with the author, April 27, 1997.
7. Sally Smith Cross, July 1, 1994, in response to appeal for reminiscences of Jackie by Vassar classmates.
8. See Carl Sferrazza Anthony, *As We Remember Her, Jacqueline Kennedy Onassis in the Words of Her Family and Friends*, 1997, p. 18.
9. Lee Radziwill interview.
10. Hugh D. Auchincloss III, "Growing up with Jackie, my memories 1941–1953," in *Groton School Quarterly*, May 1998, vol. lx, no. 2, kindly provided to the author by Hugh D. Auchincloss III, p. 13.
11. *Ibid.*, p. 14.
12. Gore Vidal, *Palimpsest*, 1995, p. 15.
13. Jacqueline Bouvier to Hugh D. Auchincloss III, January 14, 1946, Hugh D. Auchincloss III Collection.
14. Hugh D. Auchincloss III to Jacqueline Bouvier, April 1946, Hugh D. Auchincloss III Collection.
15. Auchincloss, "Growing up with Jackie," p. 15.
16. Radziwill interview.
17. James Auchincloss, interview with the author, May 1997.
18. Solange Batsell Herter, interview with the author, May 11, 1998.
19. Gore Vidal, *Palimpsest*, p. 373.
20. Interview with the author, December 3, 1997.
21. Vidal, *Palimpsest*, p. 373.
22. James Auchincloss interview.
23. Mrs. Robert Oates "Oatsie" Leiter Charles, interview with the author, May 5, 1997.
24. Interview with the author, December 3, 1997.
25. Vidal interview.
26. Baroness Trumpington, interview with the author, June 24, 1997.
27. See Heymann, p. 59.
28. Aileen Bowdoin Train, interview with the author, May 6, 1997.
29. Coates Redmon, interview with the author, April 28, 1998.
30. *Palimpsest*, p. 373.
31. Radziwill interview.
32. Vidal interview.
33. Charles interview, April 2, 1998.
34. Radziwill interview.
35. See Anthony, p. 28.
36. Jacqueline Bouvier to Hugh D. Auchincloss III, Auchincloss Collection.
37. Radziwill interview.
38. L. Frank Plugge, interview with the author, September 16, 1996.
39. Kathleen Bouvier, *To Jack with Love, Black Jack Bouvier, A Remembrance*, 1979, p. 205.
40. Mrs. Cord Meyer, telephone interview with the author, May 1, 1998.
41. Mrs. Ellen "Puffin" Gates D'Oench, interview with the author, May 7, 1998.
42. Nancy Davis and Barbara Donohue, *Miss Porter's School, A History*, 1992, p. 52.
43. Puffin D'Oench interview.
44. Cited in Mary Van Rensselaer Thayer, *Jacqueline Bouvier Kennedy*, 1961, p. 29.
45. Puffin D'Oench interview.
46. "A Remembrance of Jackie by Ellen Gates D'Oench, class of 1947," dated 7/5/94 and kindly given by Mrs. D'Oench to the author.
47. Puffin D'Oench interview.
48. Isabel Eberstadt interview with the author.
49. Radziwill interview.
50. Interview with the author, October 28, 1997.
51. Jacqueline Bouvier to Hugh D. Auchincloss III, Auchincloss Collection.
52. [Jacqueline Bouvier] "Spring Fever," *Miss Porter's Salmagundy*, February 13 and March 17, 1947.

CHAPTER 3: THE EDUCATION OF A NYMPH

1. Cited in Mary Van Rensselaer Thayer, *Jacqueline Bouvier Kennedy*, 1961, pp. 64–65.
2. Cited in Carl Sferrazza Anthony, *As We Remember Her, Jacqueline Kennedy Onassis in the Words of Her Family and Friends*, 1997, p. 22.
3. *Ibid.*
4. Priscilla Johnson Macmillan, interview with the author, May 9, 1998.
5. Interview with the author, May 9, 1998.
6. Susan Neuberger Wilson, interview with the author, April 29, 1998.
7. Columbus O'Donnell, telephone interview with the author, June 25, 1998.
8. R. Campbell James, interview with the author, April 27, 1997.
9. Hugh D. Auchincloss III to Jacqueline Bouvier, Auchincloss Collection.
10. Hugh D. Auchincloss III, "Growing up with Jackie," *Groton School Quarterly*, p. 17.
11. Mrs. Susan Mary Alsop, interview with the author, May 5, 1997.
12. The Honorable C. S. Whitehouse, interview with the author, May 1, 1998.
13. Edna Harrison Murray, telephone interview with the author, May 11, 1998.
14. *Ibid.*
15. Quoted in Heymann, p. 73.
16. Kathleen Bouvier, *To Jack with Love, Black Jack Bouvier, A Remembrance*, 1979, p. 232.
17. Radziwill interview.
18. Pamela, Lady Harlech, interview with the author, January 28, 1997.
19. Lord Jenkins of Hillhead, interview with the author, November 6, 1996.
20. George Plimpton, interview with the author, April 25, 1997.
21. Shirley Langhauser, interview with the author, October 30, 1997.
22. R. Campbell Jones, interview.
23. Interview with the author, January 28, 1998.
24. John Richardson, interview with the author, April 9, 1997.
25. Richard de Combray, interview with the author, October 31, 1997.
26. Samuel Peabody, interview with the author, March 1, 1997.
27. Gore Vidal, *Palimpsest*, 1995, p. 310.
28. Interview with the author, May 11, 1997.
29. Interview with the author, October 28, 1997.
30. Quoted in C. David Heymann, *A Woman Named Jackie*, revised edition 1994, p. 83.
31. *Ibid.*, p. 69.
32. Letter from Joan Kupfer Ross to Charlotte Look, in response to appeal in the *Vassar Quarterly*, June 1994.
33. Shirley Oakes was the daughter of Harry Oakes, the Nassau-based Canadian gold millionaire and friend of the Duke of Windsor, who was brutally murdered in 1943. His son-in-law, Alfred de Marigny, was tried for the crime but acquitted; the murderer was never convicted. Shirley herself was to die in controversial circumstances in 1986.
34. Eugenie Aiguier Havemeyer, memoir kindly provided by Mrs. Havemeyer to the author.
35. Poem by Jacqueline Bouvier partly printed in Edward Klein, *All Too Human, The Love Story of Jack and Jackie Kennedy*, 1996, p. 27. From a copy of a poem kindly provided to the author by Ellen Gates D'Oench.
36. Wilmarth Sheldon Lewis to Mrs. Lesley Kinney, January 19, 1949, courtesy of the Lewis Walpole Library.
37. *Social Spectator*, August 15, 1949.
38. Jacqueline Bouvier to Hugh D. Auchincloss III, Auchincloss Collection.
39. Black Jack Bouvier to Jacqueline Bouvier, courtesy of L. Frank Plugge.
40. Jacqueline Bouvier Kennedy to Ann Plugge, c. March 10, 1955, courtesy of L. Frank Plugge.
41. I am indebted to L. Frank Plugge for providing the documentation concerning the date of his mother's arrival back in England in June 1943 and the twins' birth certificates dated November 4, 1944, which conclusively prove, contrary to allegations in previous biographies of Jackie, that the Plugge twins could not have been fathered by Black Jack. The twins, Gale and Greville, both died violently in the same year, aged twenty-eight. Gale, after a society wedding and subsequent divorce, became involved with black-power revolutionaries and was murdered by the followers of Michael X in Trinidad in 1972. Her brother Greville was killed in a motor accident on the hippie trail in southern Morocco.
42. Black Jack Bouvier to Jacqueline Bouvier, January 10, 1950, courtesy of L. Frank Plugge.
43. Jacqueline Bouvier to Hugh D. Auchincloss III, Auchincloss Collection.
44. See Anthony. p. 42.
45. Comte Paul de Ganay, interview with the author, June 27, 1997.
46. Jean Bothorel, *Louise, ou la vie de Louise de Vilmorin*, 1993, pp. 224–26.
47. Antony Beevor and Artemis Cooper, *Paris after the Liberation, 1944–1949*, 1994, p. 447.

48. John "Demi" Gates interview with the author, May 11, 1997.
49. Jacqueline Bouvier to Hugh D. Auchincloss III, Auchincloss Collection.
50. Frances Daly Fergusson, interview with the author, April 21, 1998.
51. Jacqueline Bouvier, *Vogue*, Prix de Paris Material, JFKL.
52. The basis for this account of the 1951 European trip is *One Special Summer*, written and illustrated by Jacqueline and Lee Bouvier, Delacorte Press, 1974.
53. Baroness Trumpington, interview with the author, June 24, 1997.
54. Interview with the author, October 28, 1997.
55. *One Special Summer.*
56. Contessa Viviana Pecci Blunt, Principessa Letizia Buoncompagni Ludovisi, Donna Marina Emo Capolista and Senator Mario d'Urso, interview with the author, March 5, 1997.
57. Typed memoir provided to the author, source confidential.

CHAPTER 4: THE DARING YOUNG MAN ON THE FLYING TRAPEZE

1. Quoted in Mary Van Rensselaer Thayer, *Jacqueline Bouvier Kennedy*, 1961, p. 36.
2. *Ibid.*, pp. 83–84.
3. Typescript memoir. See note 57, chapter 3.
4. *Ibid.*
5. "Girl Reporter" by Chuck Conconi in *The Washingtonian*, July 1994.
6. *Washington Times-Herald*, September 9, 1952, May 30, 1952, May 15, 1952, March 19, 1952.
7. Mac McGarry and Everett Sevier, telephone interviews with the author, April 28, 1998.
8. Charles Bartlett, interview with the author, May 6, 1997.
9. John White, interviewed by C. David Heymann in *A Woman Named Jackie*, 1994 edition, pp. 101–3.
10. Mrs. Mary Bundy, interview with the author, October 28, 1997.
11. William Walton, interview with Joan and Clay Blair.
12. Charles Bartlett interview.
13. Lee Radziwill interview.
14. Interview with the author, December 3, 1997.
15. Cecilia and Philip Geyelin, interview with the author, April 27, 1998.
16. R. Campbell James, interview with the author, April 27, 1997.
17. *Quest*, May 1997.
18. See Heymann, p. 108.
19. Interview with the author, January 28, 1997.
20. Mary Van Rensselaer Thayer, *Jacqueline Bouvier Kennedy*, 1961.
21. Rose Fitzgerald Kennedy, *Times to Remember, An Autobiography*, 1974, pp. 321–22.
22. Thayer, p. 95.
23. See Carl Sferrazza Anthony, *op. cit.*, p. 71.
24. See Nigel Hamilton, *J.F.K., Reckless Youth*, 1992, p. 422.
25. See Seymour M. Hersh, *The Dark Side of Camelot*, 1997, p. 22.
26. Cecilia Geyelin interview.
27. Aileen Bowdoin Train, interview with the author, May 6, 1997.
28. Hersh, p. 13.
29. *Ibid.*, p. 24.
30. Richard Reeves, *President Kennedy, Profile of Power*, 1993, pp. 18–19.
31. It was later discovered that Kennedy had been born with one leg shorter than the other, causing scoliosis and acute pain.
32. Hersh, p. 24.
33. The Kennedy press release of 1960 denied that the candidate had Addison's because he did not have the symptoms of the disease as described by Addison in 1855: low blood pressure, tuberculosis or pigmentation. This may well have been partly true, although not all of Addison's patients had tuberculous adrenals and if he had once had low blood pressure this would have been counteracted by the steroid treatment. Although no pigmentation showed (for the same reason) in 1960, in 1947 when the London diagnosis was made he was pigmented around the lips and mouth (Dr. Hugh L'Etang, *Fit to Lead*, pp. 27–28). Friends during the late forties and early fifties in Washington remembered his "liver-colored complexion." Shortly before polling day in November 1960, Walter H. Judd, a Republican congressman and medical missionary, demanded that Kennedy confirm or deny whether he had Addison's disease, as he had been identified as the patient, with Addison's disease and spinal trouble, whose case history had appeared in a surgical journal in 1955. Painstaking research work in 1967 indeed identified Kennedy as this patient, and the article clearly defines the state of his adrenals and his need for steroids such as cortisone.
34. Symptoms of Addison's do not appear before 90 percent of the adrenal cortex is destroyed—the time

lag between the shipwreck in 1944 and his first diagnosis in London in 1947 would suggest this is the case. Information provided by Dr. Thomas Stuttaford in an interview with the author, May 7, 1999.

35. John Buchan, *Memory Hold-the-Door*, 1940, p. 59.
36. *Washington Times-Herald*, September 12, 1952, September 23, 1952, April 30, 1952.
37. Jacqueline Bouvier to Bess Furman Armstrong, quoted in Thayer, *Jacqueline Kennedy, The White House Years*, 1967, p. 293.
38. Countess Vivian Stokes Crespi, telephone interview with the author, May 12, 1998.
39. Interview with the author, April 24, 1997.
40. Jay Mellon, interview with the author, October 23, 1997.
41. Interview with the author, May 11, 1998.
42. See Diana DuBois, *In Her Sister's Shadow, An Intimate Biography of Lee Radziwill*, 1995, p. 61.
43. Interview with the author, December 3, 1997.
44. Charles Bartlett interview.
45. Typescript memoir.
46. See Heymann, p. 118.
47. See Heymann, p. 117.
48. See Hamilton, p. 357.
49. Aileen Bowdoin Train interview.
50. Lady Abel Smith, interview with the author, March 25, 1997.
51. Aileen Bowdoin Train, interview.
52. John "Demi" Gates interview with the author, May 11, 1998.
53. Aileen Bowdoin Train interview.
54. Gore Vidal, *Palimpsest*, 1995, pp. 309–10.
55. See Hamilton, p. 206.
56. Interview with the author, December 3, 1997.
57. John "Demi" Gates interview.
58. Alexis Gregory to the author, May 3, 1997.
59. Arthur M. Schlesinger Jr., interview with the author, October 31, 1997.
60. Recalled by Mrs. Marian Cannon Schlesinger, interview with the author, November 4, 1997.
61. Frederick S. Papert, interview with the author, April 23, 1998.
62. Elizabeth Coxe Spalding, interview with the author, April 29, 1998.
63. Heymann, p. 122.
64. See Heymann, p. 113.
65. Alastair Forbes, telephone interview with the author, November 27, 1996.
66. Gunilla von Post with Carl Johnes, *Love, Jack*, 1997, p. 32.
67. Laurence Leamer, *The Kennedy Women, The Triumph and Tragedy of America's First Family*, 1995, p. 521.
68. Charles Bartlett interview.
69. Author telephone interview with a friend of JFK who did not wish to be identified, May 1, 1998.
70. Aileen Bowdoin Train interview.
71. *Ibid.*
72. Author telephone interview with a friend of JFK who did not wish to be identified, June 30, 1998.
73. Gore Vidal, interview with the author, September 30, 1996.
74. Lee Radziwill, interview with the author, November 2, 1997.
75. *Newport Daily News*, September 12 and 13, 1953.
76. Mrs. Robert Oates "Oatsie" Charles, interview with the author, May 5, 1997.
77. Alan Pryce-Jones, interview with the author, April 29, 1997.
78. *Ibid.*
79. Interview with Philip and Cecilia Geyelin.
80. See Heymann, p. 132.
81. *Ibid.*
82. *Ibid.*
83. *Providence Sunday Journal*, September 13, 1953.

CHAPTER 5: CLAN INITIATION

1. Paul B. Fay Jr., *The Pleasure of His Company*, 1966, p. 141.
2. *Ibid.*, p. 143.
3. *Ibid.*, p. 148.
4. *Ibid.*, p. 141.
5. Arthur Schlesinger Jr., interview with the author, October 31, 1997.
6. See Nigel Hamilton, *J.F.K., Reckless Youth*, 1992, p. 59.
7. Stephen Birmingham, *Real Lace*, 1973, p. 42.

8. Doris Kearns Goodwin, interviewed by Phillip Whitehead for *The Kennedys*, TV series, WGBH Boston and Thames TV, 1992.
9. Rose Kennedy, *Times to Remember, An Autobiography*, 1974, p. 72.
10. *Ibid.*, p. 78.
11. See Ronald Kessler, *The Sins of the Father, Joseph P. Kennedy and the Dynasty He Founded*, 1996, p. 41.
12. See Hamilton, p. 47.
13. *Ibid.*, p. 214.
14. Gore Vidal, interview with the author, September 30, 1996.
15. Hamilton, p. 485.
16. Eben Pyne, interview with the author, October 22, 1997.
17. Joseph W. Alsop, oral history interview with Elspeth Rostow for the John F. Kennedy Library, June 18, 1964. (MS Division, Library of Congress)
18. See Hamilton, p. 420.
19. William Walton, interview for CBS ("We lived in cubicles in a row . . . dim figure in his life").
20. Doris Kearns Goodwin, interviewed by Phillip Whitehead for *The Kennedys*, TV series.
21. See Kessler, p. 264.
22. William Walton, interviewed by Phillip Whitehead for *The Kennedys*, TV series.
23. See Hamilton, p. 510.
24. *Ibid.*, p. 478.
25. Charles Bartlett, interviewed by Phillip Whitehead for *The Kennedys*, TV series.
26. See Hamilton, p. 766.
27. Heymann, p. 103.
28. Alastair Forbes, telephone interview with the author, November 27, 1996.
29. Elizabeth Coxe Spalding and Nancy Tenney Coleman, interview with the author, April 19, 1998.
30. Gore Vidal, *Palimpsest*, 1995, p. 285.
31. Doris Kearns Goodwin, interview with the author, May 9, 1998.
32. Interview with the author.
33. Laurence Leamer, *The Kennedy Women, The Triumph and Tragedy of America's First Family*, 1995, p. 305.
34. *Ibid.*, p. 506. In 1956 Eunice persuaded her father to devote the funds of the Joseph P. Kennedy Foundation to helping research into mental retardation and devoted her time to the promotion of the Special Olympics.
35. See Leamer, pp. 388–89.
36. Kennedy, *Times to Remember*, p. 48.
37. Leamer, p. 290.
38. Arthur Schlesinger Jr. interview.
39. Richard Naradof Goodwin, interview with the author, May 9, 1998.
40. Doris Kearns Goodwin, interview with the author, May 9, 1998.
41. Viscountess Stuart of Findhorn, interview with the author, June 5, 1997.

CHAPTER 6: TWIN ICEBERGS

1. Mrs. Wendy Morgan, interview with the author, April 30, 1998.
2. Mrs. Robin Biddle Duke, interview with the author, May 6, 1998.
3. See Rose Kennedy, *Times to Remember, An Autobiography*, 1974, pp. 326–27.
4. Janet Lee Bouvier Auchincloss, Oral History with Joan Braden, September 5, 1964, John F. Kennedy Library.
5. Robin Biddle Duke interview.
6. JFK Personal Papers, Box 11A, Herbst Medical File, JFKL.
7. According to a recent study, chlamydial infection has rendered one in four Ugandan women sterile. Information provided by Dr. Thomas Stuttaford.
8. Evelyn Lincoln, *My Twelve Years with John F. Kennedy*, 1965, p. 50.
9. Senator Edward M. Kennedy and Letitia Baldrige, cited in Carl Sferrazza Anthony, *As We Remember Her, Jacqueline Kennedy Onassis in the Words of Her Family and Friends*, 1997, pp. 87, 88.
10. Theodore C. Sorensen, *Kennedy*, 1965, p. 37.
11. Gunilla von Post with Carl Johnes, *Love, Jack*, 1997, pp. 37 and ff.
12. Lincoln, p. 53.
13. See Heymann, *A Woman Named Jackie*, 1994 edition, pp. 170–71.
14. Interview with the author, October 29, 1997.
15. Robin Biddle Duke interview.
16. Grace's best friend and bridesmaid, Maree Frisbee Rambo of Philadelphia, testifies to Jackie's dislike of Grace and Grace's awareness of it. There is no question of Grace and Jack ever having had an affair.
17. Gore Vidal, *Palimpsest*, 1995, p. 374.

18. Priscilla Johnson Macmillan, interview with the author, May 9, 1998.
19. Interview with the author, October 29, 1997.
20. Priscilla Johnson Macmillan interview.
21. *Ibid.*
22. Paul B. Fay Jr., *The Pleasure of His Company*, 1966, pp. 149–50.
23. Heymann, p. 172.
24. Elizabeth Coxe Spalding, interview with the author, April 29, 1998.
25. Lincoln, p. 68.
26. Janet Auchincloss Oral History, JFKL.
27. Interview with the author, November 22, 1996.
28. Interview with the author, January 13, 1997.
29. Michael Canfield MS Engagement Diaries, 1955, courtesy of Hugo Vickers.
30. Gunilla von Post with Carl Johnes, *Love, Jack*, 1997, p. 103.
31. Interview with the author, July 24, 1997.
32. The Hon. Claire Ward, telephone interview with the author, June 1997.
33. Diana DuBois, *In Her Sister's Shadow, An Intimate Biography of Lee Radziwill*, 1995, p. 82.
34. William Douglas-Home, *Old Men Remember*, 1991, pp. 93–94.
35. Interview with the author, September 30, 1997.
36. *Ibid.*
37. *Ibid.*
38. *Ibid.*
39. Peter Evans, *Ari, the Life and Times of Aristotle Socrates Onassis*, 1986, p. 164.
40. von Post and Johnes, p. 103.
41. Sorensen, *Kennedy*, p. 81.
42. *Ibid.*
43. See Heymann, pp. 185–86.
44. Senator George Smathers, interview with the author, April 30, 1998.
45. See Heymann, p. 192.
46. Gore Vidal, interview with the author, September 30, 1996.
47. Lady Antonia Fraser, interview with the author, November 22, 1996.
48. Michael Tree, interview with the author, February 19, 1998.
49. *Ibid.*
50. Alastair Forbes, *The Spectator*, September 28, 1996, p. 45.
51. Michael Tree, interview with the author, February 28, 1998.
52. Sorensen, *Kennedy*, pp. 99–100.
53. Heymann, p. 118.
54. Lee Radziwill, interview with the author, November 2, 1997.

CHAPTER 7: SEEKING THE GOLDEN FLEECE

1. Rose Kennedy, *Times to Remember, An Autobiography*, 1974, pp. 326–27.
2. Janet Auchincloss Oral History, JFKL.
3. Maud Shaw, *White House Nannie, My Years with Caroline and John Kennedy, Jr.*, 1966, p. 60.
4. Janet Auchincloss Oral History, JFKL.
5. Elizabeth Coxe Spalding, interview with the author, April 29, 1998.
6. William Walton, CBS interview.
7. Lord Harlech, Oral History, JFKL.
8. Katharine Graham, *A Personal History*, 1997, p. 259.
9. Joseph W. Alsop to Jacqueline Kennedy, December 12, 1956, Joseph Alsop Papers, Box 13, MS Division Library of Congress.
10. Joseph Alsop to Mrs. William Patten, April 30, 1958, Alsop Papers, Box 14.
11. Joseph Alsop to Mrs. David Bruce, March 5, 1959, Alsop Papers Box 15.
12. Interview with Jacqueline Kennedy Onassis for the University of Kentucky "John Sherman Cooper" Oral History Project, May 13, 1981.
13. Seymour M. Hersh, *The Dark Side of Camelot*, 1997, p. 340.
14. Kenneth P. O'Donnell and David F. Powers with Joe McCarthy, *"Johnny We Hardly Knew Ye," Memories of John Fitzgerald Kennedy*, 1972, p. 145.
15. *Ibid.*, p. 160.
16. Mary Barelli Gallagher, edited by Frances Spatz Leighton, *My Life with Jacqueline Kennedy*, 1970, pp. 54–55.
17. Mr. and Mrs. Ian Roberts, interview with the author, February 19, 1998.
18. Richard Goodwin, interview with the author, May 9, 1998.
19. Edmund M. Reggie, Oral History, JFKL.

20. Jacqueline Kennedy to Joseph Alsop, [August 1960], Alsop Papers, Box 130.
21. James McGregor Burns telephone interview with the author, June 25, 1998.
22. Nigel Hamilton, draft, "The Rise and Fall of Camelot," made available to the author courtesy of Nigel Hamilton.
23. Laura Bergquist Knebel, Oral History, December 8, 1965, John F. Kennedy Library.
24. *Ibid.*
25. *Time*, December 2, 1957.
26. James McGregor Burns, interview with the author,
27. Laura Bergquist Knebel, Oral History.
28. Benjamin C. Bradlee, *Conversations with Kennedy*, 1976, p. 23.
29. *Ibid.*, p. 26n.
30. Joseph W. Alsop with Adam Platt, *"I've Seen the Best of It," Memoirs*, 1992, p. 420.
31. Senator and Mrs. Claiborne Pell, interview with the author, May 2, 1998.
32. Gore Vidal, interview with the author, September 30, 1996.
33. See Laurence Leamer, *The Kennedy Women, The Triumph and Tragedy of America's First Family*, 1995.
34. *Ibid.*, p. 582.
35. Richard Goodwin, interview with the author, November 4, 1997.
36. Joan Bennett Kennedy, interview with the author, November 4, 1997.
37. *Ibid.*
38. Bradlee, *Conversations*, p. 28.
39. *Ibid.*
40. Laura Bergquist Knebel, Oral History.
41. Professor John Kenneth Galbraith and Mrs. Kitty Galbraith, interview with the author, November 4, 1997.
42. Leo Damore, *The Cape Cod Years of John Fitzgerald Kennedy*, p. 176.
43. Mailer had conducted his own defense in front of an exotic crowd in the Provincetown courtroom, men in flowered bathing trunks and glamorous society ladies surprising the more staid locals. The presiding judge found Mailer guilty of the drunk charge but condemned the police for overreaction. Mailer left the court in triumph.
44. Norman Mailer, *The Presidential Papers*, 1964.
45. *Ibid.*, p. 86.
46. *Ibid.*, p. 47.
47. Robert Dallek, *Flawed Giant, Lyndon Johnson and his Times, 1961–1975*, 1998, pp. ix–x.
48. Mrs. Lyndon B. Johnson, interview with the author, May 4, 1998.
49. Cited in Jan Jarboe Russell, *Lady Bird, A Biography of Mrs. Johnson*, 1999, pp. 186–7.
50. Conway Oral History, JFKL, cited in Arthur M. Schlesinger Jr., *Robert Kennedy and his Times*, 1978, pp. 220–21.
51. Joseph Alsop to JBK, August 4, 1960, Alsop Papers, Box 130.
52. See Heymann, *A Woman Named Jackie*, 1994 edition, p. 240.
53. Joseph Alsop to JBK, August 4, 1960, Alsop Papers, Box 130.
54. *Time*, September 26, 1960.
55. JBK to Ted Sorensen, n.d., [September ?, 1960].
56. Roy Jenkins, "Why We Mourn Jacqueline Kennedy," *The Times* (London), May 21, 1994.
57. Joan Braden, *Just Enough Rope, An Intimate Memoir*, 1989, p. 110.
58. Janet Felton Cooper, interview with the author, April 27, 1998.
59. See Hersh, *The Dark Side of Camelot*, p. 138.
60. Blair Clark, interview with the author, April 24, 1997.
61. Hersh, p. 300.
62. T. H. White, *The Making of the President, 1960*, 1962, pp. 288–89.
63. Alsop with Platt, *"I've Seen the Best of It,"* p. 427.
64. White, p. 291.
65. Leo Damore, *Cape Cod Years*, pp. 213, 216.
66. *Ibid.*, pp. 220, 222.
67. See Arthur M. Schlesinger Jr., *Robert Kennedy and His Times*, 1978, p. 220.
68. Damore, *Cape Cod Years*, p. 226.
69. *Ibid.*, p. 227.

CHAPTER 8: QUEEN OF THE CIRCUS

1. Elizabeth Coxe Spalding, interview with the author, April 29, 1998.
2. J. B. West, *Upstairs at the White House, My Life with the First Ladies*, 1974, p. 192.
3. *Ibid.*, p. 194.

4. Mrs. Henry Parish II to JBK, undated draft letter shown to the author courtesy of Richard Nelson.
5. Mary Van Rensselaer Thayer, *Jacqueline Kennedy, The White House Years*, [1967], pp. 18–19.
6. Igor Cassini with Jeanne Molli, *I'd Do It All Over Again, The Life and Times of Igor Cassini*, 1977, p. 173.
7. Oleg Cassini, *In My Own Fashion, An Autobiography*, 1990, p. 329.
8. John Fairchild, interview with the author, March 27, 1998.
9. Letter from M. de Givenchy to the author, September 17, 1999.
10. Mary Barelli Gallagher, edited by Frances Spatz Leighton, *My Life with Jacqueline Kennedy*, 1969, p. 52.
11. JBK to Marita O'Connor, see Sotheby's Catalog, April 8, 1998.
12. JBK to Oleg Cassini, December 13, 1960, see Oleg Cassini, *A Thousand Days of Magic, Dressing Jacqueline Kennedy for the White House*, 1995, p. 30.
13. JBK memo to Pamela Turnure, see Mary Van Rensselaer Thayer, *Jacqueline Kennedy, The White House Years*, pp. 33–34.
14. Laura Bergquist Knebel, Oral History, JFKL.
15. Helen Thomas, *Front Row at the White House, My Life and Times*, 1999, p. 244.
16. Mary Bass Gibson, Columbia Oral History.
17. Eleanor Roosevelt to JBK, December 1, 1960, JFKL.
18. JBK to Eve Fout, [1960]. Mrs. Paul Fout Collection.
19. West, *Upstairs at the White House*, pp. 236–37.
20. Hon. C. S. Whitehouse, interview.
21. Mrs. Marie Ridder, interview with the author, May 1, 1998.
22. William Walton, interview with Joan and Clay Blair.
23. Interview with the author, October 29, 1997.
24. *Ibid.*
25. Robin Biddle Duke, interview with the author, May 6, 1998.
26. Mrs. Kater's story first appeared in full in May 1963 when it was published in the *Thunderbolt*, the organ of the extremist, antiblack National States Rights Party based in Birmingham, Alabama.
27. William Guthrie, interview with the author, November 4, 1997.
28. See Cartha "Deke" DeLoach, *Hoover's FBI, The Inside Story by Hoover's Trusted Lieutenant*, 1995, p. 29. These files, known as "Official-and-Confidential," were open only to authorized personnel for obvious reasons.
29. See Richard Gid Powers, *Secrecy and Power, the Life of J. Edgar Hoover*, 1987, p. 357.
30. FBI, J. Edgar Hoover O & C Files #17 (Kennedy, Joseph Patrick), Federal Bureau of Investigation Reading Room, Washington, D.C.
31. FBI, J. Edgar Hoover O & C Files #96 (Kennedy, John Fitzgerald), Memorandum 7.13.60.
32. Confidential Airtel to J. Edgar Hoover from SAC Los Angeles, April 1, 1960, FBI.
33. Interview with the author, October 28, 1997.
34. Gore Vidal, *Palimpsest*, 1996, p. 19.
35. Diana DuBois, *In Her Sister's Shadow, an Ultimate Biography of Lee Radziwill*, 1995, pp. 107–8.
36. Michael Tree, interview with the author, February 19, 1998.
37. Lord Ashcombe, interview with the author, March 4, 1998.
38. Viscountess Stewart of Findhorn, interview with the author, June 5, 1997.
39. *Ibid.*
40. Unpublished autobiographical manuscript by Dr. Max Jacobson, kindly provided to the author courtesy of Mrs. Ruth Jacobson.
41. Gallagher, pp. 76–77.
42. Evelyn, Lincoln, *My Twelve Years with John F. Kennedy*, 1965, p. 220.
43. Janet Travell, Oral History, JFKL.
44. See Robert E. Gilbert, *The Mortal Presidency, Illness and Anguish in the White House*, 1992, p. 157.
45. Gallagher, p. 75.

CHAPTER 9: CORONATION

1. Paul B. Fay Jr., *The Pleasure of His Company*, 1966, p. 79.
2. Mary Van Rensselaer Thayer, *Jacqueline Kennedy, The White House Years*, 1971, p. 64.
3. *Ibid.*, p. 66.
4. *Ibid.*, p. 69.
5. Fay, p. 81.
6. See John H. Davis, *The Kennedy Clan, Dynasty and Disaster 1848–1894*, 1985, p. 266.
7. Thayer, *White House Years*, p. 90.
8. Fay, p. 84.
9. Peter Duchin, interview with the author, October 24, 1997.
10. Joseph W. Alsop with Adam Platt, *"I've Seen the Best of It,"* pp. 431–32.

1. J. B. West, p. 240.
2. William V. Elder III, interview with the author, April 27, 1998.
3. Alsop, typed, pp. 637–40, partly published in Alsop with Platt pp. 434–35.
4. Richard Nelson, interview with the author, May 18, 2000.
5. Mary Van Rensselaer Thayer, *Jacqueline Kennedy, The White House Years*, 1971, p. 108.
6. J. B. West, *Upstairs at the White House, My Life with the First Ladies*, 1974, p. 235.
7. Doris Kearns Goodwin, interview with the author, May 9, 1998.
8. West, pp. 235–36.
9. *Ibid.*, p. 234.
10. Lee Radziwill interview.
11. Alastair Forbes, Oral History, JFKL.
12. During the Second World War IG Farben put all its U.S. holdings including Agfa, Bayer-Leverkusen, etc., into a Swiss trust, Interhandel. During the war the U.S. Government blocked "all German proper-ties." Arkady Gerney and Stas Radziwill, on Interhandel's behalf, persuaded JFK and RFK to unblock it and made a great deal of money. Information from Alexis Gregory, May 3, 1997.
13. West, *Upstairs at the White House*, pp. 195–96.
14. *Ibid.*, p. 198.
15. *Ibid.*, p. 200.
16. Clark Clifford with Richard Holbrooke, *Counsel to the President, A Memoir*, 1991, p. 362. Among other vital assistance Clifford had provided, apart from easing the transition between the Eisenhower and Kennedy administrations, he had negotiated the sale of the Kennedys' Georgetown house and their leasing of Glen Ora.
17. Actually the date was February 21—see report of Henry F. du Pont, David Finley Papers, Library of Congress.
18. Thayer, *The White House Years*, p. 283.
19. Janet Felton Cooper, interview with the author, April 27, 1998.
20. William Elder III, interview with the author, April 27, 1998.
21. James Roe Ketchum, interview with the author, April 27, 1998.
22. James A. Abbott and Elaine M. Rice, *Designing Camelot, The Kennedy White House Restoration*, 1998, p. 21.
23. *Ibid.*, p. 24.
24. *Ibid.*, p. 25.
25. *Ibid.*, p. 29.
26. Interview with the author.
27. Mrs. Susan Mary Alsop, interview with the author, May 5, 1997.
28. Lorraine Waxman Pearce to Henry du Pont, December 13, 1961, Winterthur Archives, see Abbott and Rice, p. 37.
29. William Elder III interview.
30. Abbott and Rice, p. 41.
31. JBK to Henry du Pont, September 20, 1962, described in Abbott and Rice, p. 232, *n.* 31.
32. See Abbott and Rice, p. 83.
33. *Ibid.*, p. 161.
34. *Ibid.*, pp. 203–4.
35. HMS *Resolute*, part of the expedition sent to search for Sir John Franklin in 1852 in northern latitudes, was rescued by a U.S. whaler three years later.
36. See Abbott and Rice, p. 114.
37. Arthur M. Schlesinger Jr. to JBK, January 9, 1963, AMS Papers, Box WH24, White House Files, JFKL.
38. JBK to James T. Babb, April 30, 1963, AMS Papers, Box WH24, White House Files, JFKL.
39. See Christopher Ogden, *Legacy: A Biography of Moses and Walter Annenberg*, 1999, p. 375.
40. David E. Finley to Mrs. John N. Pearce, December 1, 1961, David Finley Papers, Box 6, MS Division, Library of Congress.
41. Mario E. Campioli to Senator Carl Hayden, January 8, 1962, copy in the LBJL.
42. JBK to LBJ, May 5, 1962, White House Famous Names File, LBJL.
43. JBK to LBJ, June 5, 1962, *ibid.*
44. James Biddle, interview with the author, February 15, 1997.
45. Janet Felton Cooper interview.
46. James Roe Ketchum interview.
47. William Elder III interview.
48. West, *Upstairs at the White House*, p. 209.
49. *Ibid.*, p. 211.
50. *Ibid.*, p. 215.
51. *Ibid.*, p. 216.

52. Nancy Tuckerman and Pamela Turnure, Oral History, JFKL.
53. Susan Neuberger Wilson, interview with the author, April 29, 1998.
54. *Ibid.*
55. Maud Shaw, Oral History, JFKL.
56. *Ibid.*
57. Letitia Baldrige, *In the Kennedy Style, Menus and Recipes by White House Chef, Rene Verdon*, 1998, p. 50.
58. *Ibid.*, p. 50.
59. *Ibid.*, p. 69.
60. Cited Baldrige, *In the Kennedy Style*, p. 90.
61. Blair Clark, interview with the author, April 24, 1997.
62. Norman Mailer, *The Presidential Papers*, 1964, p. 87.
63. *Ibid.*, p. 97.
64. Richard Goodwin, interview with the author, May 9, 1998.

CHAPTER 11: AMERICA'S QUEEN

1. Robin Biddle Duke, interview with the author, May 6, 1998.
2. Letitia Baldrige, *In the Kennedy Style*, 1998, p. 36.
3. Aleksandr Fursenko and Timothy Naftali, *"One Hell of a Gamble," Khrushchev, Castro and Kennedy 1958–1964*, p. 97.
4. AMS Papers and Writings, Box W-7, JFKL.
5. Robin Douglas-Home, in *Now*, March 1967.
6. *Ibid.*
7. Marie Brenner, "Carly Simon's Mother Load," *Vanity Fair*, August 1995.
8. Dr. Max Jacobson unpublished memoir.
9. Mode Givenchy, letter to the author, September 27, 1999.
10. Sir Piers Dixon to the Earl of Home, June 1, 1961, tel. 191, PRO, PREM, 11/3319, Public Record Office, Kew.
11. Anthony Rumbold to the Earl of Home, June 7, 1961, PRO, FO 371/160444, Public Record Office, Kew.
12. *Time*, June 9, 1961.
13. Fursenko and Naftali, p. 130.
14. *Ibid.*
15. Richard Reeves, *President Kennedy, Profile of Power*, 1993, p. 172.
16. Harold Macmillan to Queen Elizabeth II, Alistair Horne, *Macmillan 1957–1986*, 1991, pp. 303–4.
17. Joseph Alsop, interview with Elspeth Rostow, June 18, 1964, JFKL.
18. *Ibid.*
19. Susan Mary Alsop, interview with the author, May 5, 1997.
20. Harold Macmillan diary entry for June 11, 1961. Mss Macmillan dep. 42, Bodleian Library, Oxford.
21. See Gore Vidal, *Palimpsest*, 1995, pp. 371–2.
22. Robin Biddle Duke, interview with the author, May 6, 1998.
23. Gore Vidal, interview with the author, September 30, 1996.
24. Vidal, *Palimpsest*, p. 312.
25. Cecil Beaton MS Diaries, Beaton Collection, St. John's College, Cambridge.
26. United States Secret Service Appointment Logs, Boxes 2–12, JFKL.
27. Vidal, *Palimpsest*, p. 371.
28. Pamela, Lady Harlech, interview with the author, January 28, 1997.
29. John "Demi" Gates, interview with the author, May 11, 1997.
30. Robin Biddle Duke interview.
31. William Guthrie, interview with the author, November 4, 1997.
32. Robin Biddle Duke interview.
33. Ellen d'Oench interview and letter to the author, May 29, 2000.
34. See Reeves, p. 290.
35. Hersh, p. 389.
36. Interview with the author.
37. Letter from Adlai Stevenson to Marietta Tree, March 10, 1963, Tree Papers, The Arthur and Elizabeth Schlesinger Library on the History of Women in America, Radcliffe College.
38. Vidal, *Palimpsest*, p. 311.
39. Ellen Gates d'Oench interview.
40. Benno Graziani, interview with the author, June 27, 1997. C. David Heymann quotes reporter Francis Lara as telling him that Jackie, when showing him [Graziani] around the White House, opened the door of the office where Fiddle and Faddle worked, and said, "Those two are my husband's lovers." "The

story is not true at all," Graziani told the author. "This man called Francis Lara who was a French news-paperman, the AFP in Washington, I don't know why he said that, it's absolutely false. I told Jackie, she says, "I know, I know you didn't say that . . ." He repeated, "Jackie would never do that."

41. Interview with the author.
42. Marian Cannon Schlesinger interview with the author, November 4, 1998.
43. Pierre Salinger interview with the author, May 2, 1998.
44. Richard Goodwin, interview with the author, May 9, 1998.
45. Robin Douglas-Home, *Now*, March 1967.
46. Vidal, *Palimpsest*, p. 380.
47. Gallagher, p. 195.
48. *Ibid.*, pp. 220–1.
49. *Ibid.*, p. 203.
50. Bradlee, *Conversations with Kennedy*, 1976, p. 118.
51. *Ibid.*, p. 122.
52. Bradlee, *A Good Life*, 1995, pp. 229–30.
53. Blair Clark, interview with the author, April 24, 1997.
54. Truman Capote, as part of his long-running feud with Vidal, later alleged in an interview with *Playgirl* in 1975 that Vidal was physically thrown out of the White House, and that Lee had told him so. This led to a lawsuit, settled out of court in 1983 when Capote apologized and withdrew his allegation.
55. Vidal, *Palimpsest*, p. 380.
56. *Ibid.*, p. 364.
57. Richard Goodwin interview.
58. Jeffrey Potter, *Men, Money & Magic, The Story of Dorothy Schiff*, 1976, p. 292.
59. Vidal, *Palimpsest*, p. 365.

CHAPTER 12: SALAD DAYS

1. Edna O'Brien, *Independent on Sunday*, May 22, 1994.
2. Helen Thomas, *Front Row at the White House*, 1999, p. 247.
3. John Kenneth Galbraith, *Ambassador's Journal, A Personal Account of the Kennedy Years*, 1969, pp. 246–7.
4. *Ibid.*, p. 247.
5. *Ibid.*, p. 249.
6. Arthur M. Schlesinger, *A Thousand Days*, p. 188.
7. Galbraith, p. 251.
8. *Ibid.*, p. 270.
9. *Ibid.*, p. 326.
10. *Ibid.*
11. HH the Rajmata of Jaipur, interview with the author, July 23, 1997.
12. Galbraith, p. 300.
13. J. K. Galbraith and Kitty Galbraith, interview with the author, November 24, 1997.
14. Mrs. Kitty Galbraith, interview with the author, November 4, 1997.
15. J. K. Galbraith interview.
16. Truman Capote to Cecil Beaton, February 9, 1962. Cecil Beaton Collection, St. John's College, Cambridge.
17. Benno Graziani, interview with the author, June 27, 1997.
18. J. K. and Kitty Galbraith interview.
19. Diana DuBois, *In Her Sister's Shadow*, 1995, p. 139.
20. That the Vatican would have preferred these not very creditable proceedings to remain secret was evident when on November 12, 1967, the Italian police confiscated all copies of a magazine named *ABC*, which contained a detailed account—see Diana DuBois, *In Her Sister's Shadow*, 1995, pp. 112–20.
21. Marie Ridder, interview with the author, May 1, 1998.
22. Nancy Dickerson, *Among Those Present, A Reporter's View of Twenty-five Years in Washington*, 1976, pp. 110–11.
23. Patricia Seaton Lawford with Ted Schwartz, *The Peter Lawford Story, Life with the Kennedys, Monroe and the Rat Pack*, 1988, pp. 159–60.
24. FBI, J. Edgar Hoover O & C Files #9 Robert F. Kennedy, 6/14/65, FBI.
25. See Seymour M. Hersh, *The Dark Side of Camelot*, 1997, interview with Exner, p. 314.
26. Rumors that the Kennedys were in some way responsible for her death are ignored by Monroe's latest, authoritative biographer, Barbara Leaming, as not worthy of mention.
27. John "Demi" Gates, interview with the author, May 11, 1997.
28. Nina Burleigh, *A Very Private Woman, the Life and Unsolved Murder of Presidential Mistress Mary Meyer*, 1998, p. 170.

29. Philip and Cecilia Geyelin, interview with the author, April 27, 1998.
30. Burleigh, *A Very Private Woman*, p. 213.
31. *Ibid.*, p. 216.
32. Arthur Schlesinger, pp. 650–1.
33. *Ibid.*, pp. 643–4.
34. *Ibid.*, pp. 644 and 646–7.
35. *Ibid.*, p. 646.
36. Fay, p. 163.
37. Reeves, p. 347.
38. Viscount Hambleden, interview with the author, December 4, 1996.
39. Irene Galitzine, *Dalla Russia Alla Russia, Memorie di Irene Galitzine raccolte da Cinzia Tani*, 1996, p. 158.
40. Drew Pearson Papers, LBJL.
41. Leamer, pp. 670–1.
42. FBI, J. Edgar Hoover, O & C Files, Hoover Memorandum for Personal Files, November 22, 1961, FBI.
43. Mrs. Marion Oates "Oatsie" Charles, interview with the author, May 5, 1997.
44. See Clark Clifford with Richard Holbrooke, *Council to the President, A Memoir*, 1991, p. 365.
45. Benjamin C. Bradlee, *Conversations with Kennedy*, 1975, p. 49.
46. Letter from Mrs. Elizabeth Coxe Spalding to the author, dated July 7, 1999, following telephone interview, July 3, 1999.
47. Oatsie Charles interview.
48. Drew Pearson Papers, File 22, LBJL.
49. Mary B. Gallagher, *My Life with Jacqueline Kennedy*, 1970, p. 218.
50. Mrs. Lyndon B. Johnson, interview with the author, May 4, 1998.
51. Mrs. Elizabeth Carpenter, interview with the author, May 4, 1998.
52. August Heckscher, Oral History, JFKL.
53. William Walton, interview for CBS.
54. John Carl Warnecke, interview with the author, May 16, 1998.
55. William Walton interview.
56. J. C. Warnecke interview.
57. JBK to Bernard L. Boutin, June 1962, Bernard Boutin Papers, New Hampshire Historical Society.
58. For the Kennedy tapes of the October 1962 Missile Crisis see Ernest R. May and Philip D. Zelikow (eds.), *The Kennedy Tales, Inside the White House during the Cuban Missile Crisis*, 1997; also Fursenko and Naftali, *"One Hell of a Gamble," Khrushchev, Castro and Kennedy, 1958–1964*, 1997.
59. David Harlech, Oral History, JFKL.
60. Robin Douglas-Home in *Now*, March 1967.
61. Susan Mary Alsop, interview with the author, May 5, 1997.
62. Benno Graziani, interview with the author, June 27, 1997.
63. Harlech Oral History, JFKL. Ormsby-Gore's judgment on Kennedy's handling of the Cuban Missile Crisis is borne out by the two most recent publications: Ernest R. May and Philip D. Zelikow (eds.), *The Kennedy Tapes*, and Aleksandr Fursenko and Timothy Naftali, *"One Hell of a Gamble,"* based on both U.S. and Russian archives.
64. Fursenko and Naftali, p. 284.
65. Robin Douglas-Home, *Now*, March 1967.
66. Interview with Senator and Mrs. Claiborne Pell, interview with the author, May 2, 1998.

CHAPTER 13: RENDEZVOUS WITH DEATH

1. Alan Seeger, "I Have a Rendezvous with Death."
2. Mary B. Gallagher, *My Life with Jacqueline Kennedy*, 1969, p. 234.
3. Letitia Baldrige to Clare Boothe Luce, January 8, 1963, Clare Boothe Luce Papers, Box 39, Manuscript Division, Library of Congress.
4. Letitia Baldrige, telephone interview with the author, May 2, 1997.
5. J. B. West, *Upstairs at the White House*, 1974, p. 265.
6. John Fairchild, interview with the author, March 27, 1998.
7. Mary Van Rensselear Thayer, "First Lady Will Be 'Found Laughing with Tucky,'" *Washington Post*, February 23, 1963.
8. Benno Graziani, interview with the author, June 27, 1997.
9. Bernard L. Boutin to JBK, January 25, 1963, Boutin Papers, New Hampshire Historical Society.
10. JBK to Boutin, January 30 and April 7, 1963, *loc. cit.*
11. Richard Goodwin, interview with the author, May 9, 1998.
12. Letter by Burke Marshall to the author, February 19, 1998.

13. See memo by Letitia Baldrige to Ralph Dungan, May 17, 1963—"We have made it a firm policy to invite at least three Negro couples to all official dinners and luncheons . . . ," White House Social Files, 946, JFKL.
14. Benjamin C. Bradlee, *Conversations with Kennedy*, 1975, pp. 167–9.
15. *Ibid.*
16. Benjamin C. Bradlee, *A Good Life*, 1995, p. 240.
17. Bradlee, *Conversations*, p. 191.
18. *Ibid.*, p. 160.
19. Maud Shaw, Oral History, JFKL.
20. Bradlee, *Conversations*, p. 161.
21. Maud Shaw, Oral History, JFKL.
22. Basil Rathbone Papers, Box 8, Boston University.
23. JBK to Rathbone, *loc. cit.*
24. Bradlee, *Conversations*, p. 195.
25. *Ibid.*, p. 197.
26. *Ibid.*, pp. 201–2.
27. Katharine Graham, *Personal History*, 1997, p. 337.
28. Bradlee, *Conversations*, p. 170.
29. On January 9, 1964, Cassini and his partner were fined $10,000 each and placed on six months' probation.
30. Elspeth Rostow, interview with the author, May 4, 1998.
31. Nancy Tuckerman and Pamela Turnure, Oral History, JFKL.
32. Paul Fay Jr., interview with the author, June 30, 1998.
33. Mary B. Gallagher, *My Life with Jacqueline Kennedy*, 1970, p. 262.
34. Evelyn Lincoln, *My Twelve Years with John F. Kennedy*, 1965, p. 355.
35. Bradlee, *Conversations*, p. 206.
36. *Ibid.*, p. 208.
37. Pamela Turnure, Oral History, JFKL.
38. Irene Galitzine, *Dalla Russia Alla Russia*, 1996, p. 167.
39. Mrs. Suzanne Kloman, interview with the author, April 8, 1998.
40. Interview with the author, April 6, 1998.
41. Peter Evans, *Ari, The Life and Times of Aristotle Socrates Onassis*, 1986, p. 26.
42. *Ibid.*, p. 102.
43. *Ibid.*, p. 195.
44. Bradlee, *Conversations*, p. 219.
45. *Ibid.*
46. Taki Theodoracopoulos, interview with the author, March 20, 1997.
47. Galitzine, *Dalla Russia*, p. 169.
48. Robert White, telephone interview with the author, June 22, 1998. Robert White became a collector of Kennedy memorabilia through his friendship with Evelyn Lincoln who gave him the letter in question (probably the one which Jackie herself showed to authorized biographer William Manchester, author of *Death of a President*). According to Mr. White, after Evelyn Lincoln's death, her husband told him that Jackie had given it to Mrs. Lincoln, saying, "If anyone ever questions the love that we had, this letter will prove differently." Despite having been offered a very large sum for the letter, White returned it to the Kennedy family.
49. JBK to JFK, October 1963. See *Stern*, March 1968.
50. Coates Redmon, interview with the author, April 28, 1998.
51. Reeves, *Profile of Power*, p. 565.
52. *Ibid.*
53. Nelson D. Lankford, *The Last American Aristocrat, The Biography of David K. E. Bruce 1898–1977*, 1996, p. 321.
54. JBK to Harold Macmillan, cited Alistair Horne, *Macmillan, 1957–1986*, vol. II, 1989, p. 514.
55. *Ibid.*
56. J. Edgar Hoover O & C Files, memo of meeting, dated July 2, 1963, forwarded to Hoover by C. A. Evans, July 3, 1963. FBI.
57. J. Edgar Hoover O & C Files. The Keeler-Profumo case was known appropriately as "Bowtie." Hoover's aides appear to have made diligent attempts to investigate links between JFK and call girls run by Harry Alan Towers. FBI.
58. In an echo of the Profumo case, "Gloria" "got one of the Russian diplomats in the sack and was willing to give him up with pictures, the whole bit." Cartha "Deke" DeLoach, *Hoover's FBI, The Inside Story by Hoover's Trusted Lieutenant*, 1995, p. 38.
59. Bradlee, *Conversations*, p. 230.
60. William Manchester, *Death of a President*, 1967, p. 9.
61. Galitzine, *Dalla Russia*, p. 170.
62. *Ibid.*, p. 173.

63. Robin Douglas-Home, "The Private Thoughts of Jacqueline Kennedy," *Now*, March 1967.
64. Charles Bartlett, Oral History, JFKL.
65. Laura Bergquist Knobel, Oral History, August 1, 1977, JFKL.
66. Manchester, *Death of a President*, pp. 11, 18–19.
67. Interview with the author, October 29, 1997.
68. Elizabeth Forsling Harris, interview with the author, April 20, 1998.
69. Manchester, *Death of a President*, p. 10.
70. Lincoln, *My Twelve Years*, pp. 365–6.
71. Galitzine, *Dalla Russia*, p. 173.
72. *Ibid.*, p. 282.
73. Gallagher, *My Life*, p. 282.
74. Manchester, *Death of a President*, p. 82.
75. *Ibid.*, p. 84.
76. *Ibid.*, p. 87.
77. *Ibid.*, p. 114.
78. Gallagher, *My Life*, p. 286.
79. Manchester, *Death of a President*, pp. 116, 117, 119–20.
80. *Ibid.*, p. 121.
81. *Ibid.*, p. 130.
82. John Connally, Governor of Texas, "Why Kennedy Went to Texas," *Life*, November 17, 1967, p. 104.
83. Manchester, *Death of a President*, p. 158.
84. Testimony of Mrs. John F. Kennedy, Friday, June 5 1964, *Hearings Before the President's Commission on the Assassination of President Kennedy*, vol. V, 1964.
85. Manchester, *Death of a President*, p. 158.
86. *Ibid.*, p. 159.
87. *Ibid.*, p. 161.

CHAPTER 14: PROFILE IN COURAGE

1. Lady Bird Johnson, *A White House Diary*, 1970, p. 4.
2. William Manchester, *Death of a President*, 1967, p. 171.
3. Elizabeth Forsling Harris, interview with the author, April 20, 1998.
4. *Ibid.*
5. Manchester, *Death of a President*, p. 185.
6. Vice Admiral George Gregory Burkley (MC), U.S.N, Oral History, April 8, 1969, JFKL.
7. Johnson. *A White House Diary*, p. 5.
8. Jack Valenti, interview with the author, May 12, 1998.
9. Elizabeth Forsling Harris, fax to the author, June 3, 1998.
10. Vernon Oneal, the Dallas undertaker who provided the "Britannia" model coffin, was concerned that its pale green satin lining might be stained. One layer of plastic sheeting lined the coffin, another wrapped the body. Seven layers of rubber material enveloped Kennedy's damaged head. The coffin, damaged in transit, was not used for the funeral and February 18, 1966, on Bobby Kennedy's orders, it was dropped from a Navy plane into 9,000 feet of water off the Maryland-Delaware coast.
11. Valenti interview.
12. William Manchester's account of the journey back from Dallas emphasizes the estrangement and hostility between the Kennedyites and the Johnsonites. Both Powers, in his memoir of Kennedy, and Valenti, in an interview with the author, deny that this was so, with the exception of Godfrey McHugh, who swiftly curtailed his career by shouting out, "My President's back there in that box!" in Johnson's hearing.
13. Kenneth P. O'Donnell and David F. Powers with Joe McCarthy, *"Johnny, We Hardly Knew Ye," Memories of John Fitzgerald Kennedy*, 1970, pp. 42–3.
14. Manchester, *Death of a President*, p. 387.
15. See C. David Heymann, *RFF, A Candid Biography of Robert F. Kennedy*, 1998, p. 350.
16. Manchester, *Death of a President*, p. 406.
17. *Ibid.*, p. 507.
18. *Ibid.*, p. 416.
19. Janet Auchincloss, Oral History, JFKL.
20. Maud Shaw, *White House Nannie, My Years with Caroline and John Kennedy, Jr.*, 1966, p. 20.
21. Manchester, *Death of a President*, p. 409.
22. *Ibid.*, p. 418.
23. *Ibid.*, p. 435.
24. *Ibid.*, pp. 443–4.

25. Janet Auchincloss, Oral History, JFKL.
26. Manchester, *Death of a President*, p. 491.
27. *Ibid.*, pp. 503–4.
28. *Ibid.*, p. 517.
29. *Ibid.*, p. 518.
30. *Ibid.*, p. 534.
31. *Ibid.*, p. 542.
32. *Ibid.*, p. 546.
33. *Ibid.*, p. 590.
34. *Ibid.*, p. 603.

CHAPTER 15: THE KNIGHTS OF CAMELOT

1. Nigel Hamilton, interview with the author.
2. JBK to LBJ, November 26 [1963], LBJL, see Merle Miller, *Lyndon, An Oral Biography*, 1980, p. 335.
3. See Jeff Shesol, *Mutual Contempt, Lyndon Johnson, Robert Kennedy and the Feud That Defined a Decade*, 1997, p. 104.
4. See Jan Jarboe Russell, *Lady Bird, A Biography of Mrs. Johnson*, 1999, p. 231.
5. LBJ to JBK, December 1, 1963, LBJL.
6. Charles Bartlett, interview with the author, May 6, 1997.
7. Jacqueline Kennedy Onassis, Oral History, LBJL.
8. Jarboe Russell, *Lady Bird*, pp. 230–1, citing a tape recorded by a Johnson secretary.
9. LBJ telephone conversation with JBK, Tape K6312.14 (no. 9), December 21, 1963, 6.55 pm, LBJL.
10. LBJ telephone conversation with Pierre Salinger, Tape K6312.6 (no. 5), December 23, 1963, [pm], LBJL.
11. JBK telephone conversation with LBJ, Tape K64.01 (no. 4), January 9, 1964, LBJL.
12. Handwritten notes and typescript of Theodore White's "Camelot" interview with JBK, Theodore White Papers, Box 40, JFKL.
13. *Ibid.*
14. *Ibid.*
15. Theodore White interview with C. David Heymann, *A Woman Named Jackie*, 1994 edition, p. 419.
16. Karen Lerner, telephone interview with the author, December 4, 1998.
17. Pierre Salinger, interview with the author, May 2, 1998.
18. Maud Shaw, *White House Nannie, My Years with Caroline and John Kennedy, Jr.*, 1966, pp. 167–8.
19. Theodore White Papers, JFKL.
20. Shaw, *White House Nannie*, p. 31.
21. Mary B. Gallagher, *My Life with Jacqueline Kennedy*, 1970, p. 303.
22. Shaw, *White House Nannie*, p. 165.
23. *Ibid.*, pp. 165–6.
24. Theodore White Papers. Box 40, JFKL.
25. Cited Heymann, p. 426.
26. Gallagher, *My Life*, p. 312.
27. *Ibid.*, p. 312.
28. *Ibid.*, p. 327.
29. *Ibid.*, pp. 328–9.
30. Cecil Beaton, unpublished section of Diary, June 1968, Cecil Beaton Collection, St. John's College, Cambridge.
31. Diana Vreeland to Cecil Beaton, n.d., Cecil Beaton Collection, St. John's College, Cambridge.
32. Ben Bradlee, *A Good Life, Newspapering and Other Adventures*, Touchstone Edition, 1996, p. 262.
33. *Ibid.*, p. 263.
34. Bartlett, see Heymann, *A Woman Named Jackie*, p. 448.
35. William vanden Heuvel, interview with the author, April 1, 1998.
36. Charles Bartlett, interview with the author, May 6, 1997.
37. See Heymann, p. 448.
38. Robin Biddle Duke, interview with the author, May 6, 1998.
39. Elizabeth Coxe Spalding, interview with the author, April 29, 1998.
40. Robin Biddle Duke interview.
41. Interview with the author, December 4, 1998.
42. Interview with the author, October 28, 1997.
43. Interview with the author, December 4, 1998.
44. Joseph W. Alsop with Adam Platt, *"I've Seen the Best of It,"* 1992, p. 464.
45. Joseph Alsop transcript memoir.

46. Interview with the author, May 11, 1998.
47. Arthur M. Schlesinger, Jr., *Robert Kennedy and His Times*, 1978, p. 611.
48. For Walton's Moscow mission and the KGB analysis of the right-wing conspiracy theory, see Aleksandr Fursenko and Timothy Naftali, *"One Hell of a Gamble," Khrushchev, Castro and Kennedy, 1958–1964*, 1997, an account based principally on Soviet sources, pp. 344–9.
49. Goodwin interview.
50. See Schlesinger, *Robert Kennedy*, p. 612.
51. *Ibid.*, p. 613.
52. See C. David Heymann, *R.F.K., A Candid Biography*, 1998, p. 354.
53. J. C. Warnecke, interview with the author, May 16, 1998.
54. Schlesinger, *Robert Kennedy*, p. 618.
55. See Edith Hamilton, *The Great Age of Greek Literature*, 1942, including material previously published in 1930 as *The Greek Way*.
56. Gore Vidal, *Palimpsest*, 1995, p. 311.
57. Schlesinger, *Robert Kennedy*, p. 654.
58. Charles Bartlett interview.
59. For these two conversations, see Michael R. Beschloss, *Taking Charge, The Johnson White House Tapes, 1963–1964*, 1997, pp. 125, 128.
60. *Ibid.*, p. 451.
61. Robert McNamara telephone conversations with LBJ: August 1, 1964, 9:00A, Tape WH6408.01 (4601); August 3, 1964, 10:20A, Tape WH6408.03 (4633); August 9, 1964, 7:25A, Tape WH6408.14 (4832), LBJL.
62. Edward Kennedy telephone conversation with LBJ, August 13, 1964, in Beschloss, *Taking Charge*, p. 514.
63. William vanden Heuvel interview.
64. The day after she left N Street for good, Jackie sent Muggsy O'Leary to present Mary Gallagher with a gold and turqoise brooch with which she professed to be delighted. Yet a vein of resentment was to run through the memoir which Gallagher wrote with Frances Spatz Leighton and published five years later.
65. JBK to Harold Macmillan, January 31, 1964, Ms. Macmillan dep.c.553, Bodleian Library, Oxford.
66. Kitty Carlisle Hart, interview with the author, March 11, 1997.
67. William Manchester, *Controversy and Other Essays in Journalism*, 1976, p. 6.
68. *Ibid.*, p. 11.
69. Harlech to Macmillan, June 2, 1964, Ms. Macmillan dep.c.553, Bodleian Library, Oxford.
70. Laura Bergquist Knebel, Oral History, December 8, 1965, JFKL.
71. Laura Bergquist, subject files on Kennedy, Box 1–2, Boston University Library.
72. *Ibid.*
73. Solange Herter, interview with the author, May 11, 1998.
74. Jeffrey Potter, *Men, Money & Magic, The Story of Dorothy Schiff*, 1976, pp. 291–5.

CHAPTER 16: LA DOLCE VITA

1. Theodore C. Sorensen, interview with the author, May 6, 1998.
2. Confidential interview with the author.
3. Richard Goodwin interview with the author.
4. Taki Theodoracopolous, interview with the author, March 20, 1997.
5. A reference to Fisher's leaving Debbie Reynolds for Elizabeth Taylor.
6. Doris Kearns Goodwin, interview with the author, May 9, 1998.
7. J. C. Warnecke, interview with the author, May 16, 1998.
8. Lady Antonia Fraser, interview with the author, November 22, 1996.
9. *Ibid.*
10. JBK to Macmillan, May 17, 1965, Macmillan Papers, Ms. Macmillan dep.c.553, Bodleian Library, Oxford.
11. Maud Shaw, *White House Nannie, My Years with Caroline and John Kennedy, Jr.*, 1966, pp. 201–3.
12. Paul Fay Jr., telephone interview with the author, June 30, 1998.
13. Theodore Sorensen interview.
14. Schlesinger to Robert F. Kennedy, September 4, 1965, AMS Papers, Writings, Box W-7, JFKL.
15. Arthur M. Schlesinger, Jr., *Robert Kennedy and His Times*, 1978, p. 817.
16. *Ibid.*, p. 808.
17. J. K. and Kitty Galbraith, interview with the author, November 4, 1997.
18. John Pierrepont, interview with the author, November 1, 1997.
19. See Cary Reich, *Financier, the Biography of André Meyer, A Story of Money, Power, and the Reshaping of American Business*, 1997, p. 81.
20. *Ibid.*, p. 250.

21. *Ibid.*, p. 252.
22. *Ibid.*
23. Senora Teresa Cárcano, telephone interview with the author.
24. J. C. Warnecke interview.
25. *Ibid.*
26. William Manchester, *Controversy and Other Essays in Journalism*, 1976, footnote p. 60.
27. William Atwood, Oral History, Columbia University Library.
28. Manchester, *Controversy*, footnote p. 60.
29. Richard Goodwin, interview with the author, May 9, 1998.
30. On June 17, 1968, shortly after Bobby's death, Jackie wrote Manchester an emotional letter over five handwritten pages addressed to "Dear Bill," telling him how much his actions had been appreciated and how "my adored brother-in-law" had prevented her writing to tell him so because he had wanted to write himself to thank Manchester for "wiping off the blackboard of the past" and "a generosity of such magnitude and sacrifice." A copy of the letter was kindly made available to the author by Professor Manchester.

CHAPTER 17: ODYSSEUS

1. See Kiki Feroudi Moutsatsos with Phyllis Karas, *The Onassis Women, An Eyewitness Account*, 1998, p. 3.
2. The decision was made before Warnecke's involvement with Jackie. Warnecke's involvement with JFK's Washington projects, his work for Teddy and Bobby and the Arlington commission, would have been enough to justify Walton's opinion.
3. I. M. Pei, interview with the author, April 23, 1998.
4. Mrs. Peggy McDonnell Walsh, interview with the author, May 12, 1998.
5. The Hon. Desmond Guinness, interview with the author, August 1998. A footnote to this story occurred the following January 1968 when Guinness proposed showing the photographs taken at Castletown at the Society's stall at the New York Antiques Fair with Jackie's permission. "And then the people who ran the Antiques Fair said, 'Oh, no, we can't have a picture of Mrs. Kennedy on display because this is Election Year and that's a political gesture . . .' "
6. See C. David Heymann, *A Woman Named Jackie*, 1994 edition, pp. 471–2.
7. See Diana DuBois, *In Her Sister's Shadow, An Intimate Biography of Lee Radziwill*, p. 184.
8. Harlech to Alsop, June 18 [1967], Joseph Alsop Papers, Box 130, Manuscript Division, Library of Congress.
9. Coates Redmon, interview with the author, April 28, 1998.
10. Pamela Harlech, interview with the author, January 28, 1999.
11. Lord Jenkins of Hillhead, interview with the author, November 6, 1996.
12. Interview with the author, January 28, 1997.
13. See Cecil Beaton, Diary, June 6, 1968, Cecil Beaton Collection, St. John's College, Cambridge.
14. *Ladies' Home Journal*, June 1968.
15. Pamela, Lady Harlech, interview.
16. Mrs. Roswell Gilpatric, interview with the author, November 7, 1999.
17. See Heymann, p. 477.
18. Taki Theodoracopolous, interview with the author, March 20, 1997.
19. Moutsatsos, *The Onassis Women*, p. 69.
20. George Loudon, interview with the author, July 18, 1998.
21. JBK to RFK, cited in Schlesinger, footnote p. 845.
22. See Arthur M. Schlesinger Jr., *RFK*, 1978, p. 857.
23. *Ibid.*, p. 874.
24. *Ibid.*, p. 878.
25. Joan Thring, interview with the author, February 11, 1998.
26. Cecil Beaton, Diary, February 19, 1968.
27. Robin Douglas-Home, "The Private Thoughts of Jacqueline Kennedy," *Now*, March 1967.
28. Joan Thring interview.
29. *Ibid.*
30. *Ibid.*
31. Cecil Beaton's account of a conversation with Lee after dinner on June 6, Diary.
32. Heymann, p. 484.
33. Richard Goodwin interview.
34. *Ibid.*
35. Lady Bird Johnson, *A White House Diary*, 1970, p. 684.
36. Mrs. Lyndon B. Johnson, interview with the author, May 4, 1998.

37. See Heymann, p. 485.
38. See C. David Heymann, *RFK, A Candid Biography*, 1998, p. 511.
39. William vanden Heuvel, interview with the author, April 1, 1998.
40. Rose Kennedy, *Times to Remember, An Autobiography*, 1974, pp. 446–7.
41. Peter Evans, *Ari, the Life and Times of Aristotle Socrates Onassis*, 1986, p. 218.
42. Mary Tyler McClenahan, interview with the author, November 7, 1997.
43. Carl Reich, *Financier, The Biography of André Meyer*, 1997, p. 254.
44. See Gerald Clarke, *Capote, A Biography*, 1988, p. 384.
45. Princess Luciana Pignatelli, interview with the author, June 23, 1998.
46. Jeffrey Potter, *Men, Money and Magic, The Story of Dorothy Schiff*, 1976, p. 313.
47. See Arianna Stassinopoulos, *Maria, Beyond the Callas Legend*, 1980, p. 249.
48. *Ibid.*, p. 234.
49. Joan Thring interview.
50. Kiki Feroudi Moutsatsos with Phyllis Karas, *The Onassis Women, An Eyewitness Account*, 1998, p. 5.
51. Clarke, *Capote*, p. 384.
52. Marina Tchomleyjoklu Dodero, interview with the author, June 18, 1998.
53. Pierre Salinger interview.
54. Nancy Mitford to Cecil Beaton, October 24, 1968: "When the General saw widow Kennedy two years ago he said to Gaston [Palewski] '*au fond c'est une vedette—tout ca finira dans le yacht d'un millionaire,*'" Cecil Beaton Collection, St. John's College, Cambridge.
55. Marina Tchomleyjoklu Dodero interview.
56. Michael Tree interview.
57. Moutsatsos, *The Onassis Women*, p. 121.

CHAPTER 18: "ONE FOOLISH DREAM"

1. Kiki Feroudi Moutsatsos with Phyllis Karas, *The Onassis Women, An Eyewitness Account*, 1998.
2. Michael Bentley, interview with the author, March 10, 1997.
3. Moutsatsos, *The Onassis Women*, p. 186.
4. Robert Sutherland, *Maria Callas, Diaries of a Friendship*, 1999, p. 121.
5. Moutsatsos, *The Onassis Women*, p. 145.
6. *Ibid.*, p. 145.
7. *Ibid.*, p. 225.
8. Interview with the author, June 26, 1997.
9. Professor Robert Pounder, interview with the author, April 21, 1998.
10. Gore Vidal, interview with the author, September 30, 1996.
11. Interview, June 26, 1997.
12. Moutsatsos, *The Onassis Women*, p. 156.
13. Interview with a member of the Onassis circle who wishes to remain anonymous.
14. Interview with the author, June 26, 1997.
15. Alexis Gregory, interview with the author, May 3, 1997.
16. Interview with the author, June 26, 1997.
17. Damaris, Lady Stewart, interview with the author, June 2, 1997.
18. Letter to the author from Patrick Leigh Fermor, September 2, 1997.
19. Interview with the author, June 26, 1997.
20. Moutsatsos, *The Onassis Women*, pp. 91, 107.
21. *Ibid.*, p. 117.
22. *Ibid.*, pp. 176–7.
23. *Ibid.*, p. 177.
24. Interview with the author, June 26, 1997.
25. Marina Tchomleyjoklu Dodero, interview with the author, June 18, 1998.
26. Moutsatsos, *The Onassis Women*, p. 138.
27. Marina Tchomleyjoklu Dodero interview.
28. Interview with the author, June 26, 1997.
29. Foreword by John F. Kennedy, Jr., to Marta Sgubin and Nancy Nicholas, *Cooking for Madam, Recipes and Reminiscences from the Home of Jacqueline Kennedy Onassis*, 1998.
30. Doris Kearns Goodwin, interview with the author, May 9, 1998.
31. See Peter Collier and David Horowitz, *The Kennedys, An American Drama*, 1984, p. 478.

Chapter 19: The Curse of the House of Onassis

1. JBK to Ros Gilpatric, [October 1968], *Time*, February 23, 1970, and *passim*.
2. Peter Evans, *Ari: The Life and Times of Aristotle Onassis*, 1986, p. 261.
3. Kiki Feroudi Moutsatsos, *The Onassis Women: An Eyewitness Account*, 1998, p. 211.
4. *Ibid.*
5. Marina Dodero, interview with the author.
6. Evans, *Ari*, p. 232.
7. *Ibid.*, p. 238.
8. Michael Tree, interview with the author, February 19, 1998.
9. Peter Beard to Steven M. L. Aronson, August 1, 1971.
10. Marina Dodero interview.
11. Moutsatsos, *The Onassis Women*, p. 125.
12. Michael Tree interview.
13. Lord Ashcombe, interview with the author, March 4, 1998.
14. Peter Beard, telephone interview with the author, October 31, 1997.
15. Interview with Peter Beard by Steven M. L. Aronson, kindly provided by Steven Aronson to the author.
16. Peter Beard telephone interview.
17. Peter Beard interview with Steven M. L. Aronson.
18. Aronson and Peter Beard interviews.
19. Peter Beard interview.
20. JBK "afterword" to Peter Beard's *Longing for Darkness*. In 1975 when the book was going to press, Jackie attempted through her lawyers to withdraw her introduction, having fallen out meanwhile with Beard over what she saw as his taking advantage of her by sponsoring a show of Caroline's photography at his Manhattan photo-developers, Lexington Labs. The publishers resisted and this became her first published work since "Spring Fever" and the first for general publication.
21. Moutsatsos, *The Onassis Women*, p. 248.
22. Gore Vidal, interview with the author, September 30, 1996.
23. Benno Graziani, interview with the author, June 27, 1997.
24. Gore Vidal interview.
25. Moutsatsos, *The Onassis Women*, pp. 239–40.
26. *Ibid.*, p. 240.
27. Information relating to the legal matters between Jackie and Onassis and later Christina has been obtained from a confidential source unless otherwise stated.
28. Evans, *Ari*, p. 268.
29. *Ibid.*, pp. 266–7.
30. Reinaldo Herrera, interview with the author, April 24, 1997.
31. Interview with the author, June 26, 1997.
32. See Evans, *Ari*, p. 272. In reply to the author's request for an interview, Baroness Thyssen wrote that she was unwilling to talk about Jacqueline Kennedy Onassis "as we only met once, and believe me when I say you would not wish to know what was discussed." Letter to the author, July 12, 1998.
33. Interview with the author, June 26, 1997.
34. Marina Dodero interview.

Chapter 20: Greek Labyrinth

1. Pierre Salinger, interview with the author, May 2, 1998.
2. Solange Batsell Herter, interview with the author, May 11, 1998.
3. See Pierre Salinger, *PS: A Memoir*, 1995, p. 211.
4. Jay Mellon, interview with the author, October 23, 1997.
5. Karen Lerner, interview with the author, December 4, 1998.
6. Aileen Mehle, "The Jackie I Knew," *Good Housekeeping*, September 1994.
7. Kiki Feroudi Moutsatsos, *The Onassis Women: An Eyewitness Account*, 1998, p. 279.
8. See Edward Klein, *Just Jackie: Her Private Years*, 1998, p. 261, confirmed to the author by Mr. Stelio Papadimitriou.
9. Details concerning Onassis's will on this page and the following pages from a confidential source unless otherwise stated.
10. Marina Dodero, interview with the author, June 18, 1998.
11. Robert Sutherland, *Maria Callas: Diaries of a Friendship*, 1999, pp. 263–4.
12. Peter Evans, *Ari: The Life and Times of Aristotle Onassis*, 1986, p. 298.
13. Karen Lerner interview.
14. *Ibid.*

15. Marina Dodero interview. Jackie's biographer, Edward Klein, *Just Jackie*, 1998, p. 285, claims that the story was "false" and attributes it to the malice of Costa Gratsos. "I wasn't there, but she [Christina] called me immediately on the phone," Marina Dodero told the author, "and there are people who were in front. Teddy said to her, 'And now what about the money?' "
16. Moutsatsos, *The Onassis Women*, p. 301.
17. Confidential interview with the author, April 6, 1998.
18. *Ibid.*, April 6, 1998.
19. Confidential legal source.
20. See Klein, *Just Jackie*, p. 288, subsequently confirmed to the author as "substantially correct" by Mr. Papadimitriou.
21. Taki Theodoracopoulos, interview with the author, March 20, 1997.
22. Klein, *Just Jackie*, pp. 288–9.
23. Confidential legal source.
24. Interview, April 6, 1998.

CHAPTER 21: NEW YORK—NEW LIFE

1. John Fairchild, interview with the author, March 27, 1998.
2. Jay Mellon, interview with the author, October 22, 1997.
3. John Fairchild interview.
4. Ron Galella, *Jacqueline*, 1974, excerpt from *Good Housekeeping*, August 1974.
5. *Ibid.*
6. Richard de Combray, interview with the author, October 31, 1997.
7. Pierre Salinger, interview with the author, May 2, 1998.
8. Pierre Salinger, *PS: A Memoir*, 1995, p. 212.
9. Benjamin C. Bradlee, *Conversations with Kennedy*, 1975, p. 152.
10. Benjamin C. Bradlee, *A Good Life*, 1995, pp. 399–400.
11. *Ibid.*, p. 400.
12. See *The Washington Post*, November 18 and 19, 1975.
13. Chuck Spalding denied that he had ever spoken to Mrs. Jacobson to make the appointment. She, however, affirms that she kept a record of the call and made an entry in the appointments book. She showed her husband's typed account of the incident to C. David Heymann and Professor Richard Reeves, and kindly allowed the present author access to it.
14. Karen Lerner, telephone interview with the author, December 4, 1998.
15. Karen Lerner interview.
16. Aileen Mehle, "Suzy," telephone interview with the author, May 8, 1998.
17. Karen Lerner interview.
18. Gloria Steinem, interview with the author, November 5, 1997.
19. Private interviews with the author.
20. Truman Capote to Cecil Beaton, [Bridgehampton], June 11, 1964. Cecil Beaton Collection, St. John's College, Cambridge.
21. Interview with the author, November 5, 1997.
22. Confidential interview.
23. Peter Duchin, interview with the author, October 24, 1997.
24. William vanden Heuvel, interview with the author, April 1, 1998.
25. Karen Lerner interview.
26. Gloria Steinem interview.
27. Truman Capote, *Answered Prayers: The Unfinished Novel*, 1986, p. 153.
28. Thomas Guinzburg, interview with the author, April 23, 1997.
29. Thomas Guinzburg, Oral History, Columbia University.
30. Alan Lang, interview with the author, June 24, 1998.
31. Thomas Guinzburg interview.
32. Ashton Hawkins, interview with the author, April 22, 1998.
33. According to Dick Goodwin, one of the reasons Dendur was chosen was that its situation on the Nile could be mirrored on the Potomac in Washington. Kennedy was dead by the time the temple arrived in the U.S. and, according to Goodwin, the Smithsonian was outmaneuvered by Hoving and the Met, so the Temple went to New York instead.
34. See Thomas Hoving, *Making the Mummies Dance: Inside the Metropolitan Museum of Art*, 1963, pp. 60–1.
35. Thomas Guinzburg interview.
36. Deborah Owen, telephone interview with the author, July 2, 1998.
37. Thomas Guinzburg interview.
38. *Ibid.*

39. *Ibid.*
40. Joan Kennedy, interview with the author, November 4, 1997.
41. William vanden Heuvel interview.
42. Heymann, *A Woman Named Jackie*, 1994 edition, p. 550. The film eventually made was *Gray Gardens*, focused on the Beales, produced and directed by the Maysle brothers.
43. See Diana DuBois, *In Her Sister's Shadow*, 1995, p. 234.
44. Interview, December 4, 1998.
45. *Ibid.*
46. Donna Marina Emo Capodilista, interview with the author, March 5, 1997.
47. Cecil Beaton Diary, June 6, 1968, Cecil Beaton Collection. St. John's College, Cambridge.
48. Mary Tyler McClenahan, interview with the author, November 7, 1997.
49. Newton Cope, telephone interview with the author, May 27, 1998.
50. *Ibid.*
51. *Ibid.*
52. This referred to a forthcoming lawsuit in which Gore Vidal was suing Truman Capote for a million dollars for libel over an interview Capote had given in 1975 in which he had described the famous incident at the White House in 1961 but had said that Vidal had been bodily thrown out which was untrue.
53. Newton Cope interview.
54. I. M. Pei, interview with the author, May 12, 1998.
55. Peter Collier and David Horowitz, *The Kennedys: An American Drama*, p. 547.
56. Theodore Sorensen, interview with the author, May 6, 1998.
57. Richard Goodwin, interview with the author, May 9, 1998.

CHAPTER 22: PRIVATE LIVES

1. Peter Beard, interview with Steven M. L. Aronson, May 1994.
2. *Ladies' Home Journal*, June 1968.
3. Richard Goodwin, interview with the author, May 9, 1998.
4. Jay Mellon, interview with the author, October 23, 1997.
5. See Steven Birmingham, "How Jacqueline Onassis Is Shaping Her Children," *McCall's*, January 1973, p. 16.
6. See Willi Frischauer, "Caroline Kennedy: Adventures of an Innocent Abroad," *Ladies' Home Journal*, February 1976.
7. See Peter Benson, "Caroline Kennedy—On Her Own in London," *Good Housekeeping*, April 1976.
8. Michael Bentley, interview with the author, March 10, 1997.
9. Pamela, Lady Harlech, interview.
10. John Pierrepont, interview with the author, November 1, 1997.
11. Interview, January 28, 1997.
12. Interview, October 28, 1997.
13. See Pat Hackett (ed.), *The Andy Warhol Diaries*, 1989, December 20, 1978.
14. Caroline Seebohm, *No Regrets: The Life of Marietta Tree*, 1997, p. 368.
15. Interview, December 3, 1997.
16. Anthony Quinn, "Ari Onassis & Me," *Ladies' Home Journal*, June 1978.
17. See *Quest*, May 1997.
18. Ashton Hawkins, interview with the author, April 22, 1998.
19. See obituary by Antony Beevor and Artemis Cooper in the *Independent*, May 21, 1994.
20. Hugh Newell Jacobsen, interview with the author, May 3, 1998.
21. *Ibid.* Jacobsen was later forgiven this faux pas by Jackie. Meeting with mutual friends some years later, she greeted him with a kiss on the cheek.
22. Joan Kennedy, interview with the author, November 4, 1997.
23. Gloria Steinem on Jacqueline Kennedy Onassis, "Why Women Work," *Ms.*, March 1979.
24. See Doubleday: *A Tribute to Jacqueline Kennedy Onassis*, 1995, p. 12.
25. *Ibid.*, p. 26.
26. *Quest*, May 1997.
27. Auchincloss, *ibid.*
28. Antony Beevor, interview with the author, May 21, 1997.
29. Stephen Rubin, interview with the author, January 28, 1998.
30. Rubin interview.
31. Scott Moyers, interview with the author, April 23, 1998.
32. Private interview.
33. Scott Moyers interview.
34. *Ibid.*

35. SWAT, i.e., "Special Weapons and Tactics" teams, special police units attached to every U.S. city police force to deal with riots, terrorism, etc.
36. Bruce Tracy, telephone interview with the author, June 23, 1998.
37. See *New York Amsterdam News*, May 4, 1974.
38. See John Belle and Maxine R. Leighton, *Grand Central: Gateway to a Million Lives*, 1999, p. 18.
39. Frederic S. Papert, interview with the author, April 23, 1998.
40. Papert interview.
41. Frederick Papert interview.
42. Ashton Hawkins interview.

CHAPTER 23: MATRIARCH

1. Edith and Stuart Cary Welch, interview with the author, May 9, 1998.
2. Taki Theodoracopolous, interview with the author, March 20, 1997.
3. Cary Reich, *Andre Meyer*, p. 348
4. Anonymous source quoted in *People*, "The Man Who Loved Jackie," July 11, 1994, p. 76.
5. See Caroline Seebohm, *No Regrets: The Life of Marietta Tree*, 1997, p. 373.
6. Lord Jenkins of Hillhead, interview with the author, November 6, 1996.
7. Aileen Mehle telephone interview with the author, May 8, 1998.
8. Interview with the author.
9. Interview with the author, January 21, 1999.
10. Interview with the author, December 20, 1998.
11. *Ibid.*
12. Interview with the author, January 12, 1998.
13. Lady Antonia Fraser, interview with the author, November 22, 1996.
14. Edna O'Brien, interview with the author, November 2, 1999.
15. John Richardson, telephone interview with the author, April 9, 1997.
16. Countess Vivi Crespi, telephone interview with the author, May 12, 1998.
17. Theodore C. Sorensen, interview with the author, May 6, 1998.
18. Reinaldo Herrera, interview with the author, April 24, 1997.
19. Karen Lerner, interview with the author, December 4, 1998.
20. Interview with William Norwich in *Vogue*, June 1993.
21. Reinaldo Herrera interview.
22. *People*, March 17, 1986.
23. Karen Lerner interview.
24. Carolina Herrera, interview with the author, May 6, 1998.
25. Interview with the author, October 26, 1997.
26. *Ibid.*
27. C. David Heymann, *A Woman Named Jackie*, 1994 edition, p. 620.
28. *Ibid.*
29. Robert Tracy, telephone interview with the author, November 7, 1997.
30. Interview with William Norwich, *Vogue*, June 1993.
31. John Updike, "Comment," *The New Yorker*, August 2, 1999.
32. Karen Lerner interview.
33. Edna O'Brien telephone interview with the author, May 8, 1998.
34. Antony Beevor, interview with the author, May 21, 1997.
35. Sylvia Whitehouse Blake, telephone interview with the author, April 28, 1998.
36. Maya Auchincloss, interview with the author, April 28, 1997.
37. Patricia Seaton Lawford with Ted Schwarz, *The Peter Lawford Story*, p. 240.
38. Peter Collier and David Horowitz, *The Kennedys: An American Dream*, 1984, and see Lawrence Leamer, *The Kennedy Women: The Triumph and Tragedy of America's First Family*, 1994, pp. 874–7.
39. Pamela, Lady Harlech, interview with the author, January 28, 1997.
40. *Ibid.*
41. Interview, December 1994.
42. Lee Radziwill, interview with the author, November 2, 1997.
43. Lisa Sullivan and Sally Ewalt, interview with the author, April 28, 1997.
44. Mrs. Robert Oates "Oatsie" Charles, interview with the author, April 2, 1998.
45. William vanden Heuvel.
46. Charles Whitehouse, interview with the author, May 8, 1997 and May 1, 1998.
47. *Ibid.*
48. Stuart Cary Welch, interview with the author, May 9, 1998.
49. Mrs. Vincent Astor, interview with the author, April 22, 1998.

50. Meghan Daum, "Urban Cowboy," *Texas Monthly*, March 1999.
51. Joe Armstrong, conversation with the author, May 6, 1998.
52. Interview with the author, January 28, 1998.
53. See Marie Brenner, "Carly Simon's Mother Load," in *Vanity Fair*, August 1995.
54. Jane Stanton Hitchcock, interviews with the author, April 30, 1998.
55. Edna O'Brien interview.
56. Edna O'Brien in *Independent on Sunday*, May 22, 1994.
57. Edna O'Brien interview.
58. Reinaldo Herrera interview.
59. *In Our Defense: The Bill of Rights in Action* (New York: William Morrow, 1991).
60. Joe Armstrong in *New York*, August 2, 1999.

CHAPTER 24: PILGRIM'S END

1. Valentino Garavani, telephone interview with the author, November 4, 1999.
2. Solange Batsell Herter interview.
3. See Anthony, *As We Remember Her: Jacqueline Kennedy Onassis in the Words of Her Family and Friends*, 1997, p. 345.
4. *Ibid.*, p. 328.
5. Carolina Herrera interview.
6. See Klein, pp. 352–3 and C. David Heymann, p. 654, *A Woman Named Jackie*, 1994 edition.
7. Edna O'Brien, interview with the author, November 2, 1999.
8. Arthur Schlesinger, "Why We Mourn Jacqueline," *The Times*, May 21, 1994.
9. Scott Moyers, interview with the author, April 23, 1998.
10. Frederic Papert, interview with the author, April 23, 1998.
11. Marie Brenner, "Carly Simon's Mother Load," *Vanity Fair*, August 1995.
12. William vanden Heuvel, interview with the author, April 1, 1998.
13. Interview, December 4, 1998.
14. *Ibid.*
15. Eve Fout, interview with the author, April 1, 1998.
16. Charles Whitehouse, interview with the author, September 1, 1998.
17. Stuart Cary Welch, interview with the author, May 9, 1998.
18. Hugh D. Auchincloss III, "Growing Up with Jackie," *Groton School Quarterly*, May 1998, vol. lx, no. 2, p. 20.

SOURCES

SELECT BIBLIOGRAPHY AND ARCHIVES

SELECT BIBLIOGRAPHY

The books listed below are those used in the research for this book and which are mentioned in the end-notes. These editions are from various publishers and printing locations and the page numbers in the endnotes refer directly to the editions as listed.

Abbott, James A., and Rice, Elaine M., *Designing Camelot: The Kennedy White House Restoration*, Van Nostrand Reinhold, New York (1998)

Abramson, Rudy, *Spanning the Century: The Life of W. Averell Harriman*, William Morrow, New York (1992)

Adams, William Howard, *Atget's Gardens*, Doubleday, New York (1979)

Alphand, Hervé, *L'étonnement d'être, Journal 1939–1973*, Fayard, Paris (1977)

Alsop, Joseph W., with Platt, Adam, *"I've Seen the Best of It": Memoirs*, W. W. Norton, New York (1992)

Alsop, Susan Mary, *To Marietta from Paris 1945–1960*, Weidenfeld and Nicolson, London (1976)

Andersen, Christopher, *Jackie after Jack: Portrait of the Lady*, William Morrow, New York (1998)

Anderson, Jack, *The Anderson Papers*, London (1974)

Anthony, Carl Sferrazza, *As We Remember Her: Jacqueline Kennedy Onassis in the Words of Her Family and Friends*, HarperCollins, New York (1997)

Anthony, Carl Sferrazza, *First Ladies, Volume II: The Saga of the Presidents' Wives and Their Power 1961–1990*, William Morrow, First Quill Edition, New York (1991)

Aronson, Steven M. L., *Hype*, William Morrow, New York (1983)

Baldrige, Letitia, *In the Kennedy Style: Magical Evenings in the Kennedy White House*, with recipes by White House chef René Verdon, Doubleday, New York (1998)

Baldwin, Billy, *Billy Baldwin Remembers*, Harcourt Brace Jovanovich, New York (1974)

Ball, George, *The Past Has Another Pattern: Memoirs*, W. W. Norton (1982)

Beale, Betty, *Power at Play: A Memoir of Parties, Politicians, and the Presidents in My Bedroom*, Regnery Gateway, Washington D.C. (1993)

Beard, Peter, *Longing for Darkness: Kamante's Tales from Out of Africa*, Harcourt Brace Jovanovich, New York (1975)

Beevor, Antony, and Cooper, Artemis, *Paris after the Liberation, 1944–1949*, Hamish Hamilton, London (1994)

Belle, John, and Maxine R. Leighton, *Grand Central: Gateway to a Million Lives*, W. W. Norton, New York (1999)

Bergquist, Laura and Tretick, Stanley, *A Very Special President* (1965)

Beschloss, Michael, *Taking Charge: The Johnson White House Tapes 1963–1964*, Simon and Schuster, New York (1997)

Birmingham, Stephen, *Jacqueline Bouvier Kennedy Onassis*, Victor Gollancz, London (1979)

Birmingham, Stephen, *Real Lace: America's Irish Rich*, Hamish Hamilton, London (1973)

Birmingham, Stephen, *The Right People: A Portrait of the American Social Establishment*, Little Brown, Boston (1984)

Bothorel, Jean, *Louise, ou la vie de Louise de Vilmorin*, Bernard Grasset, Paris (1993)

Bouvier, Jacqueline and Lee, *One Special Summer*, Delacorte Press, New York (1974)

Bouvier, John Vernon, Jr., *Our Forebears*, privately printed (1931, 1942, 1944, 1947)

Bouvier, Kathleen, *To Jack with Love: Black Jack Bouvier: A Remembrance*, Kensington, New York (1979)

Braden, Joan, *Just Enough Rope: An Intimate Memoir*, Villard, New York (1989)

Bradlee, Benjamin C., *A Good Life: Newspapering and Other Adventures*, Touchstone, New York (1995)

Bradlee, Benjamin C., *Conversations with Kennedy*, Quartet, London (1975)

Bryant, Traphes, and Spatz Leighton, Frances, *Dog Days at the White House: The Outrageous Memoirs of the Presidential Kennel Keeper*, Macmillan Inc., New York (1975)

Buchan, John, *Memory Hold the Door [The Pilgrim's Way]*, Hodder and Stoughton, London (1940)

Burleigh, Nina, *A Very Private Woman: The Life and Unsolved Murder of Presidential Mistress Mary Meyer*, Bantam, New York (1998)

Burns, James MacGregor, *John Kennedy: A Political Profile*, Harcourt, Brace and World, New York (1961)

Cafarakis, Christian, *The Fabulous Onassis, His Life and Loves*, William Morrow, New York (1972)

Canfield, Cass, *Up and Down and Around*, Collins, London (1972)

Capote, Truman, *Answered Prayers: The Unfinished Novel*, Hamish Hamilton, London (1986)

Carpenter, Liz, *Ruffles and Flourishes*, Texas A & M University Press, College Station (1993)

Cassini, Igor, with Molli, Jeanne, *I'd Do It All Over Again: The Life and Times of Igor Cassini*, G. P. Putnam's Sons, New York (1977)

Cassini, Oleg, *In My Own Fashion: An Autobiography*, Picket, New York (1987)

Cassini, Oleg, *A Thousand Days of Magic: Dressing Jacqueline Kennedy for the White House*, Rizzoli, New York (1995)

Cerf, Bennett, *At Random: The Reminiscences of Bennett Cerf*, Random House, New York (1977)

Chellis, Marcia, *The Joan Kennedy Story: One Woman's Victory over Infidelity, Politics and Privilege*, Sidgwick and Jackson, London (1985)

Cheshire, Maxine, *Maxine Cheshire, Reporter*, Houghton Mifflin, Boston (1978)

Churchill, Sarah, *Keep on Dancing: An Autobiography*, Coward, McCann and Geoghegan, New York (1981)

Clarke, Gerald, *Capote: A Biography*, Hamish Hamilton, London (1988)

Clifford, Clark with Holbrooke, Richard, *Counsel to the President: A Memoir*, Random House, New York (1991)

Collier, Peter, and Horowitz, David, *The Kennedys: An American Drama*, Pan, London (1985)

Cooper, Diana, *The Rainbow Comes and Goes*, Rupert Hart-Davis, London (1958)

Crick, Michael, *Jeffrey Archer: Stranger than Fiction*, Hamish Hamilton, London (1995)

Curtis, Charlotte, *First Lady*, Pyramid, New York (1962)

Dallek, Robert, *Flawed Giant: Lyndon Johnson and His Times, 1961–1973*, OUP, New York (1998)

Damore, Leo, *The Cape Cod Years of John Fitzgerald Kennedy*, Prentice Hall Inc., Englewood Cliffs, New Jersey (1962)

Davis, John H., *Jacqueline Bouvier: An Intimate Memoir*, John Wiley and Sons Inc., New York (1996)

Davis, John H., *The Bouviers: From Waterloo to the Kennedys and Beyond*, National Press, Washington D.C. (1993)

Davis, John H., *The Kennedys: Dynasty and Disaster*, Sidgwick and Jackson, London (1985)

Davis, Kenneth S., *The Politics of Honor: A Biography of Adlai E. Stevenson*, G. P. Putnam's Sons, New York (1967)

Davis, Nancy, and Donohue, Barbara, *Miss Porter's School: A History*, Miss Porter's School, Farmington, Connecticut (1992)

De Gaulle, Charles, *Mémoirs d'espoir: Memoirs of Hope: Renewal 1958–62* and *Endeavor: 1962*, Weidenfeld and Nicolson, London (1971)

DeLoach, Cartha "Deke," *Hoover's FBI: The Inside Story by Hoover's Trusted Lieutenant*, Regnery Publishing Inc., Washington D.C. (1995)

Dempster, Nigel, *Heiress: The Story of Christina Onassis*, Weidenfeld and Nicolson, London (1989)

Dickerson, Nancy, *Among Those Present: A Reporter's View of Twenty-five Years in Washington*, Random House, New York (1976)

Doubleday, *A Tribute to Jacqueline Kennedy Onassis*, Doubleday, New York (1995)

Doubleday, *In Memoriam Jacqueline Bouvier Kennedy Onassis 1929–1994*, Doubleday, New York (1995)

Douglas Home, William, *Old Men Remember*, Collins and Brown, London (1991)

DuBois, Diana, *In Her Sister's Shadow: An Intimate Biography of Lee Radziwill*, Little Brown, London (1995)

Duchin, Peter, with Charles Michener, *Ghost of a Chance: A Memoir*, Random House, New York (1996)

Evans, Peter, *Ari: The Life and Times of Aristotle Onassis*, Jonathan Cape, London (1986)

Exner, Judith, as told to Ovid Demaris, *My Story*, Grove Press, New York (1977)

Fay, Paul B., Jr., *The Pleasure of His Company*, Author's Edition, U.S.A. (November 1982)

Fursenko, Aleksandr, and Naftali, Timothy, *"One Hell of a Gamble": Khrushchev, Castro and Kennedy 1958–1964*, W. W. Norton, New York (1997)

Galbraith, John Kenneth, *Ambassador's Journal: A Personal Account of the Kennedy Years*, Hamish Hamilton, London (1969)

Galella, Ron, *Jacqueline*, Sheed and Ward, New York (1974)

Galitzine, Irene, *Dalla Russia Alla Russia, Memorie . . . Raccolte da Cinzia Tani*, Longanesi and C., Milan (1996)

Gallagher, Mary Barelli, (ed. Frances Spatz Leighton), *My Life with Jacqueline Kennedy*, Michael Joseph, London (1970)

Goodwin, Doris Kearns, *The Fitzgeralds and the Kennedys: An American Saga*, Weidenfeld and Nicolson, London (1987)

Goodwin, Richard N., *Remembering America: A Voice from the Sixties*, Little Brown, Boston (1988)

Graham, Katharine, *Personal History*, Alfred A. Knopf, New York (1997)

Guthman, Edwin, *We Band of Brothers: A Memoir of Robert F. Kennedy*, Harper and Row, New York (1971)

Hackett, Pat (ed.), *The Andy Warhol Diaries*, Simon and Schuster, London (1989)

Halberstam, David, *The Best and the Brightest*, Barrie and Jenkins, London (1972)

Halberstam, David, *The Fifties*, Villard Books, New York (1993)

Hamilton, Edith, *The Great Age of Greek Literature*, W. W. Norton, London (1942)

Hamilton, Nigel, *Life and Death of an American President, Volume One: Reckless Youth*, Random House, London (1992)

Harrison, Rainie and Quinn, John, *Growing Up Kennedy: The Third Wave Comes of Age* (1983)

Hersh, Seymour M., *The Dark Side of Camelot*, Little Brown, Boston and New York (1997)

Heymann, C. David, *A Woman Named Jackie*, complete updated edition, Birch Lane Press, New York (1995)

Heymann, C. David, *RFK: A Candid Biography of Robert F. Kennedy*, Heinemann, London (1998)

Horne, Alistair, *Macmillan 1957–1986*, Macmillan, London (1989)

Horwitz, Helen Lefkowitz, *Alma Mater: Design and Experience in the Women's Colleges from Their Nineteenth-Century Beginnings to the 1930s*, Alfred A. Knopf, New York (1984)

Hoving, Thomas, *Making the Mummies Dance: Inside the Metropolitan Museum of Art*, Simon and Schuster, New York (1993)

Isaacson, Walter, and Evan Thomas, *The Wise Men, Six Friends and the World They Made: Acheson, Bohlen, Harriman, Kennan, Lovett, McCloy*, Simon and Schuster, New York (1986)

Johnson, Lady Bird, *A White House Diary*, Holt, Rinehart and Winston, New York (1970)

Kelley, Kitty, *Jackie Oh!*, Hart-Davis MacGibbon, Granada Publishing, New York and London (1978)

Kennedy, John F. (ed.), *As We Remember Joe*, privately printed (1945)

Kennedy, Rose Fitzgerald, *Times to Remember: An Autobiography*, Collins, London (1974)

Kessler, Ronald, *The Sins of the Father: Joseph P. Kennedy and the Dynasty He Founded*, Warner Books, New York (1996)

Klein, Edward, *All Too Human: The Love Story of Jack and Jackie Kennedy*, Pocket Books, New York (1996)

Klein, Edward, *Just Jackie: Her Private Years*, Ballantine, New York (1998)

Koestenbaum, Wayne, *Jackie under My Skin: Interpreting an Icon*, Fourth Estate, London (1996)

Krock, Arthur, *Memoirs: Sixty Years on the Firing Line*, Funk and Wagnalls, New York (1968)

Kunhardt, Philip B., Jr., (ed.), *Life in Camelot: The Kennedy Years*, Little Brown, Boston (1988)

Kuntz, Tom and Phil (eds.), *The Sinatra Files: The Secret FBI Dossier*, Three Rivers Press, New York (2000).

Lacouture, Jean, (tr. Alan Sheridan), *De Gaulle, The Ruler (1945–1970)*, Harvill, London (1991)

Landon, Angela, *"We Meet in Grief": The Relationship between Jacqueline Kennedy and Lyndon Johnson*, unpublished thesis

Langley Hall, Gordon and Pinchot, Ann, *Jacqueline Kennedy: A Biography*, Signet, New York (1966)

Lankford, Nelson D., *The Last American Aristocrat: The Biography of David K. E. Bruce, 1899–1977*, Little Brown and Company, Boston and New York (1996)

Lash, Joseph P., *Eleanor: The Years Alone*, Andre Deutsch, London (1973)

Lawford, Patricia Seaton, with Schwarz, Ted, *The Peter Lawford Story: Life with the Kennedys, Monroe and the Rat Pack*, Carroll and Graf, New York (1988)

Leamer, Laurence, *The Kennedy Women: The Triumph and Tragedy of America's First Family*, Bantam, London (1995)

Leaming, Barbara, *Marilyn Monroe*, Weidenfeld and Nicolson, London (1998)

Lilly, Doris, *Those Fabulous Greeks: Onassis Niarchos and Livanos: Three of the World's Richest Men*, Cowles Book Company, Inc., New York (1970)

Lincoln, Anne H., *The Kennedy White House Parties*, The Viking Press, New York (1967)

Lincoln, Evelyn, *My Twelve Years with John F. Kennedy*, David McKay, New York (1965)

Lowe, Jacques, *Jacqueline Kennedy Onassis: A Tribute*, Jacques Lowe Visual Arts Project, New York (1995)

Macmillan, Harold, *At the End of the Day*, Macmillan, London (1973)

Macmillan, Harold, *Pointing the Way*, Macmillan, London (1972)

McTaggart, Lynne, *Kathleen Kennedy: Her Life and Times*, Dial Press, Doubleday, New York (1983)

Mailer, Norman, *The Presidential Papers*, Andre Deutsch, London (1964)

Malraux, André, *Antimémoires 1*, Gallimard, Paris (1967, 1972)

Malraux, André, *La Corde et les Souris*, Gallimard, Paris (1976)

Malraux, André, (tr. Irene Clephane), *Fallen Oaks: Conversation with de Gaulle*, Hamish Hamilton, London (1972)

Manchester, William, *Controversy and Other Essays in Journalism*, Little Brown, Boston (1976)

Manchester, William, *The Death of a President: November 20–November 25, 1963*, Harper and Row, New York (1967)

Manchester, William, *The Glory and the Dream: A Narrative History of America 1932–1972*, Bantam, New York (1980)

Martin, John Bartlow, *Adlai Stevenson and the World: The Life of Adlai Stevenson*, Doubleday, New York (1977)

Martin, Ralph G., *A Hero for Our Time: An Intimate Story of the Kennedy Years*, Ballantine Books, New York (1983)

Martin, Ralph G., *Seeds of Destruction: Joe Kennedy and His Sons*, G. P. Putnam's Sons, New York (1995)

May, Ernest R., and Zelikow, Philip D. (eds.), *The Kennedy Tapes: Inside the White House During the Cuban Missile Crisis*, Harvard University Press, Cambridge, Massachussetts (1997)

Morris, Sylvia Jukes, *Rage for Fame: The Ascent of Clare Boothe Luce*, Random House, New York (1997)

Mosley, Charlotte (ed.), *The Letters of Nancy Mitford: Love from Nancy*, Hodder and Stoughton, London (1993)

Moutsatsos, Kiki Feroudi, with Karas, Phyllis, *The Onassis Women: An Eyewitness Account*, G. P. Putnam's Sons, New York (1998)

O'Donnell, Kenneth P., and Powers, David F., with McCarthy, Joe, *Johnny, We Hardly Knew Ye*, Little Brown, Boston (1970)

Oppenheimer, Jerry, *The Other Mrs. Kennedy, Ethel Skakel Kennedy: An American Drama of Power, Privilege, and Politics*, St. Martin's Press, New York (1994)

Paglia, Camille, *Sexual Personae: Art and Decadence from Nefertiti to Emily Dickinson*, Penguin Books, London (1992)

Peyser, Joan, *Bernstein: A Biography*, William Morrow, New York (1987)

Plimpton, George, *Truman Capote*, Picador, London (1998)

Potter, Jeffrey, *Men, Money and Magic: The Story of Dorothy Schiff*, Coward, McCann and Geoghegan Inc., New York (1976)

Powers, Richard Gid, *Secrecy and Power: The Life of J. Edgar Hoover*, The Free Press, New York (1987)

Reeves, Richard, *President Kennedy, Profile of Power*, Simon and Schuster, New York (1993)

Reeves, Thomas C., *A Question of Character: A Life of John F. Kennedy*, Forum, Prima Publishing, Rocklin, CA (1997)

Reich, Cary, *Financier: The Biography of André Meyer: A Story of Money, Power and the Shaping of American Business*, John Wiley and Sons, Inc., New York (1997)

Rhea, Mini, *I Was Jacqueline Kennedy's Dressmaker*, Fleet, New York (1962)

Rostow, Walt W., *The Diffusion of Power: An Essay in Recent History*, Macmillan, New York (1972)

Rusk, Dean, *As I Saw It: A Secretary of State's Memoirs*, I. B. Tauris (1991)

Russell, Jan Jarboe, *Lady Bird: A Biography of Mrs. Johnson*, Lisa Drew/Scribner, New York (1999)

Salinger, Pierre, *P.S.: A Memoir*, St. Martin's Press, New York (1995)

Salinger, Pierre, *With Kennedy*, Doubleday, New York (1966)

Schlesinger, Arthur, *A Thousand Days: John F. Kennedy in the White House*, Andre Deutsch, London (1965)

Schlesinger, Arthur, *Robert Kennedy and His Times*, Andre Deutsch, London (1978)

Seebohm, Caroline, *No Regrets: The Life of Marietta Tree*, Simon and Schuster, New York (1997)

Sgubin, Marta, and Nicholas, Nancy, *Cooking for Madam: Recipes and Reminiscences from the Home of Jacqueline Kennedy Onassis*, Lisa Drew/Scribner, New York (1998)

Shapley, Deborah, *Promise and Power: The Life and Times of Robert McNamara*, Little Brown, Boston (1993)

Shaw, Mark, *The John F. Kennedys: A Family Album*, Noonday Press, New York (1964)

Shaw, Maud, *White House Nannie: My Years with Caroline and John Kennedy, Jr.*, New American Library, New York (1966)

Shesol, Jeff, *Mutual Contempt: Lyndon Johnson, Robert Kennedy, and the Feud That Defined a Decade*, W. W. Norton, New York (1997)

Sidey, Hugh, Clifton, Chester V., and Stoughton, Cecil, *JFK: The Memories*, W. W. Norton, New York (1973)

Smith, Sally Bedell, *Reflected Glory: The Life of Pamela Churchill Harriman*, Simon and Schuster, New York (1996)

Solway, Diane, *Nureyev: His Life*, Phoenix, London (1998)

Sorensen, Theodore C., *Kennedy*, Hodder and Stoughton, London (1965)

Stassinopoulos, Arianna, *Maria: Beyond the Callas Legend*, Weidenfeld and Nicolson, London (1980)

Stein, Jean, and George Plimpton (eds.), *American Journey: The Times of Robert Kennedy*, Harcourt Brace Jovanovich, New York (1970)

Sulzberger, C. L., *The Last of the Giants*, Weidenfeld and Nicolson, London (1972)

Sutherland, Robert, *Maria Callas: Diaries of a Friendship*, Constable, London (1999)

Taki, *Princes, Playboys and High-class Tarts*, Karz-Cohl, New York (1984)

Tapert, Annette, and Edkins, Diana, *The Power of Style: The Women Who Defined the Art of Living Well*, Crown Publishers, New York (1994)

Thayer, Mary Van Rensselaer, *Jacqueline Bouvier Kennedy*, Doubleday, New York (1961)

Thayer, Mary Van Rensselaer, *Jacqueline Kennedy: The White House Years*, Little Brown, Boston (1967)

Thomas, Helen, *Front Row at the White House: My Life and Times*, Lisa Drew/Scribner, New York (1999)

Thompson, Lawrence, and Winnick, R. H., *Robert Frost: The Later Years, 1938–1963*, Holt, Rinehart and Winston, New York (1976)

Truman, Margaret, *First Ladies: An Intimate Group Portrait of White House Wives*, Random House, New York (1995)

vanden Heuvel, William, and Gwirtzman, Milton, *On His Own: Robert F. Kennedy 1964–1968*, Doubleday, New York (1970)

Vidal, Gore, *Palimpsest: A Memoir*, Andre Deutsch, London (1995)

von Post, Gunilla, with Carl Johnes, *Love Jack*, Crown Publishers (1997)

Vreeland, Diana, (ed. by George Plimpton and Christopher Hemphill), *D.V.*, Da Capo Press, New York (1997)

West, J. B., with Mary Lynn Kotz, *Upstairs at the White House: My Life with the First Ladies*, W. H. Allen, London and New York (1974)

White House Historical Association, *The White House: An Historic Guide*, Washington D.C. (1967, 1995)

White, Theodore H., *In Search of History: A Personal Adventure*, Warner Books, New York (1978)

White, Theodore H., *The Making of the President, 1960*, Jonathan Cape, London (1962)

Wills, Gary, *The Kennedy Imprisonment: A Meditation on Power*, Little Brown, Boston (1981)

Wofford, Harris, *Of Kennedys and Kings*, Farrar, Straus and Giroux, New York (1980)

Youngblood, Rufus W., *20 Years in the Secret Service: My Life with Five Presidents*, Simon and Schuster, New York (1973)

Ziegler, Philip, *Diana Cooper*, Hamish Hamilton, London (1981)

ARCHIVES

U.S.A.

John Fitzgerald Kennedy Library (JFKL): The major repository of documents, photographs, cuttings and memorabilia of the Kennedy family and Presidency. Papers consulted include Oral Histories, White House Social Files, Secret Service Gate Logs for the White House, Arthur M. Schlesinger Papers, August A. Heckscher Papers, Kay Murphy Halle Papers, JFK Personal Papers, Medical Records, Dr. William P. Herbst Medical File. JBK's private papers are closed, although her correspondence with William Walton, 1960–1964, has recently been released

New Hampshire Historical Society: Bernard Boutin Papers, including JBK's correspondence with Boutin about restoration and conservation matters concerning the White House and Lafayette Square

Massachusetts Historical Society: Lyman Butterfield Papers, including Correspondence about the White House Library and furnishings between Butterfield, JBK, H du Pont and others; Correspondence between JBK and distinguished Massachusetts figures

Dwight D. Eisenhower Library: President's Personal File (PPF), White House Social Office Records, Mamie Doud Eisenhower correspondence, and DDE Post Presidential File contain correspondence between the Eisenhowers and JBK, 1954–1964

Lyndon Baines Johnson Library: A vast collection which contains much of interest to students of JBK. Lyndon B. Johnson Daily Diary (Worksheet) November 22 to December 6, 1963; Appointments Diaries and records; Secret Service Logs for the same period; White House Famous Names File; JBK's correspondence with LBJ and Mrs. Johnson 1954–1968; Tapes of Telephone Conversations between LBJ and JBK and between LBJ and others concerning JBK; White House Central Files relating to JBK; Drew Pearson Collection, principally cuttings concerning JBK during and after the presidential years, Pearson's autograph jottings

Federal Bureau of Investigation Reading Room: Available material on JBK herself relates principally to threats to her security, letters about her by lunatics, and, more significantly, her use of the Bureau to investigate unauthorized sales of her letters. Other Files from J. Edgar Hoover Official and Confidential Files "O and C" include #26 Joseph Alsop; #13 and #96 JFK: associations with women, Sinatra and Lawford, gangsters, etc.; #17 Joseph Kennedy, relations with Hoover and the Bureau; #9 RFK allegations of sex activities; #150-40018-1 Marilyn Monroe; #100-125834-1 Aristotle Socrates Onassis; Frank Sinatra #92=3171

Franklin D. Roosevelt Library: JBK's correspondence with Eleanor Roosevelt

Herbert Hoover Library: letters from JBK to Hoover 1956-1964

University of Kentucky Library: John Sherman Cooper Collection includes JBK Oral History concerning the Coopers

University of Notre Dame Archives: Rev. John J. Cavanaugh CSC Oral History

Lewis Walpole Library: Wilmarth Sheldon Lewis Papers, JBK's correspondence with Lewis

Miss Porter's School: Printed material, photographs and memorabilia relating to JBK's time at the school

The Museum of Television and Radio Library, New York City

The Richard Nixon Library and Birthplace Foundation, Yorba Linda, California: Original Letters of Jacqueline Kennedy Onassis in the Nixon Library Collections, 1954–1975

The Philadelphia City Archives: John Vernou application for citizenship

Philadelphia Historical Society: documents relating to the Bouvier and Vernou families

The Arthur and Elizabeth Schlesinger Library on the History of Women in America: Lorraine Rowan Cooper Papers, Gloria Emerson Papers, Edith Spurlock Sampson Papers, Dorothy Feiner Rodgers Papers, Helen Hill Miller Papers, Marietta Tree Papers (closed)

Harry S. Truman Library: Papers of Harry S. Truman, Post-Presidential Files, 1961–1963; Papers of Clifton and Margaret Truman Daniel; Papers of James P. Hendrick, correspondence between JBK and Hendrick relating to security matters, 1967–1969

The Beinecke Rare Book and Manuscript Library: Nina Berberova Papers
Yale University Library, Department of Manuscript Archives: JBK correspondence with Dean Acheson, Chester Bowles and Walter Lippmann; Miscellaneous MSS including some correspondence between JBK and James T. Babb concerning the White House Library
Library of Congress, Manuscript Division: Joseph Alsop Papers, Clare Boothe Luce Papers, David Finley Papers, Mies van der Rohe Papers, NAACP Papers, Agnes Meyer Papers, Bess Furman papers
Boston University Library: Laura Bergquist Papers include correspondence with JBK and others on Kennedy-related subjects; Basil Rathbone papers include a brief but interesting correspondence with JBK
Princeton University Archives, Seeley G. Mudd Manuscript Library: JBK correspondence with Arthur Krock 1960–1965, Adlai E. Stevenson 1960–1965, Bernard Baruch 1954–1962, David A. Morse, 1988–1992
Municipal Art Society Archives, New York City
Columbia University in the City of New York: Oral Histories
Duke University Special Collections Library: Angier Biddle Duke Papers, containing correspondence between Angier Biddle Duke and JBK and papers relating to the Kennedy White House
Friends and connections of Jacqueline Kennedy Onassis have allowed me access to their private correspondence with her which has provided insights not available through the public collections. Her letter-writing style was very much her own, with a unique turn of phrase and an imaginative use of words. Her private correspondence reveals an independence of mind and spirit, a keen grasp of politics and a shrewd perception of the realities beneath the veneer of public and social life. For these privileged insights I am extremely grateful.

U.K.

Bodleian Library, Department of Western Manuscripts: Harold Macmillan Archive. Harold Macmillan Diaries and his correspondence with JBK (not yet available for general research)
The Library, St. John's College, Cambridge: Cecil Beaton Collection, Cecil Beaton Diaries and Correspondence with JBK and others
Public Record Office, Kew: PRO, PREM 11/3319; PRO FO 371/160444
Michael Canfield MS Diaries, courtesy of Hugo Vickers
Hugo Vickers Diary, 1989, 1990
Archives of Brook-Lapping Productions: Oral interviews by Philip Whitehead and Marilyn Mellowes with important figures in the Kennedy circle for *The Kennedys* TV series (WGBH Boston and Thames TV 1992). Not available for general research

PERMISSIONS

Material by Jacqueline Kennedy Onassis is reprinted by kind permission of Caroline Kennedy.

From *I've Seen the Best of It: Memoirs* by Joseph W. Alsop and Adam Platt. Copyright © 1992 by Joseph W. Alsop and Adam Platt, reprinted by permission of W. W. Norton & Company, Inc.

From "Growing Up with Jackie, My Memories" in the Groton School *Quarterly*, May 1998, Copyright © 1998 Hugh D. Auchincloss III, reprinted by kind permission of the author.

From the *In the Kennedy Style* by Letitia Baldrige, Copyright © 1998 Letitia Baldrige, reprinted by kind permission of the author.

From Cecil Beaton Papers © The Literary Executors of the late Sir Cecil Beaton, reprinted by kind permission of Hugo Vickers Literary Executor to Sir Cecil Beaton.

From *Paris After the Liberation 1944–1949* by Antony Beevor and Artemis Cooper, Copyright © 1994 by Antony Beevor and Artemis Cooper, reprinted by kind permission of the authors.

From an Obituary of Jacqueline Bouvier Kennedy Onassis by Antony Beevor and Artemis Cooper in *The Independent*, May 21, 1994, reprinted by kind permission of the authors.

From *Louise ou la vie de Louise de Vilmorin* by M. Jean Bothorel, Copyright © 1993 M. Jean Bothorel, reprinted by kind permission of the author.

From *A Good Life: Newspapering and Other Adventures* by Benjamin Bradlee, copyright © 1995 by Benjamin Bradlee. Reprinted by permission of Simon & Schuster Inc. and Benjamin Bradlee.

From *Conversations With Kennedy* by Ben Bradlee. Copyright © 1975 by Benjamin C. Bradlee. Used by permission of W. W. Norton & Company, Inc.

From Cavafy, C. P.; *Collected Poems*. Copyright © 1992 by Princeton University Press. Reprinted by permission of Princeton University Press.

Copyright © 1967 by Leo Damore. From *The Cape Cod Years of John Fitzgerald Kennedy* published by Prentice Hall. Reprinted by permission of McIntosh & Otis, Inc.

"The Private Thoughts of Jacqueline Kennedy," *Now*, March 1967, Copyright © 1967 Robin Douglas-Home, reprinted by kind permission of Sholto Douglas-Home.

From *Ari: The Life and Times of Aristotle Socrates Onassis* by Peter Evans, Copyright © 1986 Peter Evans, reprinted by kind permission of the author.

From *Ambassador's Journal: A Personal Account of the Kennedy Years* by John Kenneth Galbraith, Copyright © 1988 by John Kenneth Galbraith, reprinted by kind permission of the author.

From *My Life With Jacqueline Kennedy* by Mary Barelli Gallagher, edited by Frances Spatz Leighton, Copyright © 1970 Mary Barelli Gallagher, reprinted by kind permission of the author and editor.

From *A Woman Named Jackie: An Intimate Portrait of Jacqueline Bouvier Kennedy Onassis* by C. David Heymann, Copyright © 1989 by C. David Heymann, reprinted by permission of William Morris Agency, Inc. on behalf of the author.

PHOTO CREDITS

INDEX

FOR THE BEST IN PAPERBACKS, LOOK FOR THE

In every corner of the world, on every subject under the sun, Penguin represents quality and variety—the very best in publishing today.

For complete information about books available from Penguin—including Puffins, Penguin Classics, and Arkana—and how to order them, write to us at the appropriate address below. Please note that for copyright reasons the selection of books varies from country to country.

In the United Kingdom: Please write to *Dept. EP, Penguin Books Ltd, Bath Road, Harmondsworth, West Drayton, Middlesex UB7 0DA.*

In the United States: Please write to *Penguin Putnam Inc., P.O. Box 12289 Dept. B, Newark, New Jersey 07101-5289* or call 1-800-788-6262.

In Canada: Please write to *Penguin Books Canada Ltd, 10 Alcorn Avenue, Suite 300, Toronto, Ontario M4V 3B2.*

In Australia: Please write to *Penguin Books Australia Ltd, P.O. Box 257, Ringwood, Victoria 3134.*

In New Zealand: Please write to *Penguin Books (NZ) Ltd, Private Bag 102902, North Shore Mail Centre, Auckland 10.*

In India: Please write to *Penguin Books India Pvt Ltd, 11 Panchsheel Shopping Centre, Panchsheel Park, New Delhi 110 017.*

In the Netherlands: Please write to *Penguin Books Netherlands bv, Postbus 3507, NL-1001 AH Amsterdam.*

In Germany: Please write to *Penguin Books Deutschland GmbH, Metzlerstrasse 26, 60594 Frankfurt am Main.*

In Spain: Please write to *Penguin Books S. A., Bravo Murillo 19, 1° B, 28015 Madrid.*

In Italy: Please write to *Penguin Italia s.r.l., Via Benedetto Croce 2, 20094 Corsico, Milano.*

In France: Please write to *Penguin France, Le Carré Wilson, 62 rue Benjamin Baillaud, 31500 Toulouse.*

In Japan: Please write to *Penguin Books Japan Ltd, Kaneko Building, 2-3-25 Koraku, Bunkyo-Ku, Tokyo 112.*

In South Africa: Please write to *Penguin Books South Africa (Pty) Ltd, Private Bag X14, Parkview, 2122 Johannesburg.*